MW00583996

New Church Handbook

Nuts & Bolts for Planting New Churches in the Wesleyan Tradition

by Bob Crossman

Copyright © 2018 by Bob Crossman
All Rights Reserved

Published by Crossman Printing, Inc. of Conway, Arkansas
www.crossmanprinting.com

No part of this work may be reproduced or transmitted in any form or by any means, electronic or mechanical, including photocopying and recording, or by any information storage or retrieval system, except as may be expressly permitted by the 1976 Copyright Act or in writing from the author. Request for permission should be addressed in writing to Bob Crossman, 8 Sternwheel Drive, Conway, Arkansas 72034-9391 or emailed to bcrossman@arumc.org

ISBN 978-0-9996578-0-5

You are about to embark on a ministry that will require more than the strength of your hands and the sweat of your brow.

Church Planting will require
your mind to be a mind in harmony with the mind of Christ,
your mouth to be a mouth through whom Christ speaks, and
your hands to be hands through whom Christ touches your mission field.

You will need to be in touch with the one who said,
"I am the vine and you are the branches." (John 15:5)

Your personal prayer life and spiritual disciplines will be an essential part in preparing you and sustaining your ministry as a new church planter.

Bob Crossman

Part of Path 1's Wesleyan Church Planting Resources

A Missionary Mindset: What Church Leaders Need to Know to Reach Their Community - Lessons from E. Stanley Jones, by Douglas Ruffle (2016)

Descubriendo Tus Dones Espirituales: Una guía teorética y práctica, by César Durán (Scheduled for publication, 2018)

Don't Look Down (working title), by Rosario Picardo (Scheduled for publication, 2018)

Failing Boldly: How Falling Down in Ministry Can be the start of Rising Up, by Christian Coon, Foreword by Bishop Robert Schnase (2017)

Flipping Church: How Successful Church Planters Are Turning Conventional Wisdom Upside-Down, by Michael Baughman (2016)

New Church Handbook: Nuts & Bolts for Planting New Churches In The Wesleyan Tradition, by Bob Crossman (2018)

Small Church Checkup, by Kay Kotan and Phil Schroeder, (2018)

Viral Multiplication in Hispanic Churches: How to Plant and Multiply Disciple-Making Churches in the Twenty-first Century America, by Iosmar A'lvarez (2016)

Vital Merger: A New Church Start Approach That Joins Church Families Together, by Dirk Elliott, published by Fun and Done Press (2013)

© 2018 Robert O. Crossman, www.UMNewChurch.org

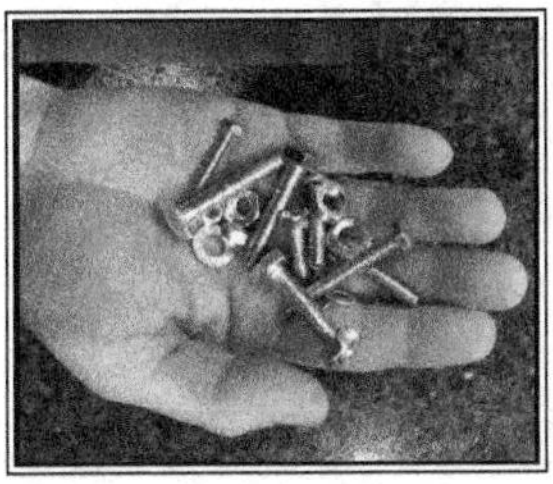

New Church Handbook

Nuts & Bolts for Planting New Churches In The Wesleyan Tradition

Table of Contents

by Bob Crossman

© 2018 Robert O. Crossman, www.UMNewChurch.org

 © 2018 Robert O. Crossman, www.UMNewChurch.org

© 2018 Robert O. Crossman, www.UMNewChurch.org

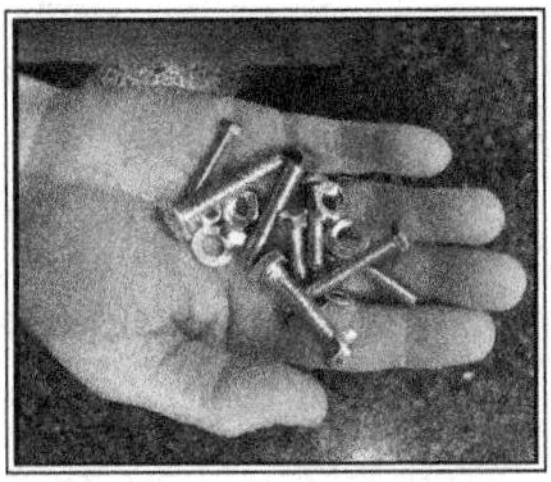

New Church Handbook
Nuts & Bolts for Planting New Churches In The Wesleyan Tradition

"Introduction"

by Bob Crossman

Welcome to the New Church Handbook.
This handbook attempts to answer 110 of the frequently asked questions about church planting. Scan the table of contents for articles that respond to your burning questions. You may also enjoy reading this handbook "cover to cover" to increase your knowledge of best practices in church planting across the country.

You are about to embark on a ministry that will require more than the strength of your hands and the sweat of your brow.

Church Planting will require your mind to be a mind
in harmony with the mind of Christ,
your mouth to be a mouth through whom Christ speaks, and
your hands to be hands through whom Christ touches your mission field.

You will need to be in touch with the one who said,
"I am the vine and you are the branches." (John 15:5)
Bob Crossman

I took the photo on the front cover of this book in October of 2017, when I had the honor of joining Bishop Gary Mueller and about 140 congregants in an open field north of Old Washington, Arkansas to celebrate the planting of Henry's Chapel, the first congregation in the Arkansas Territory. That day we broke bread together in that holy place under the hot fall sun, remembering the 1817 new church planter, William Stevenson. Brother Stevenson had a passion to reach the people of southwest Arkansas. He also felt called by God to reach the French citizens across the state line to the southwest, the Native American citizens to the west in Oklahoma, and the residents of Louisiana to the south. Out of this congregation, Methodist laity were the first Protestants to carry the Gospel to the French (in territory now called Texas). Following the heart of Francis Asbury, William Stevenson influenced the next generation of Arkansas' Methodist circuit riders to spread the Gospel of Christ across the territory.

During the past five years I have had the privilege to serve as a New Church Strategist for Path 1, Discipleship Ministries *(General Board of Discipleship)*. I wasn't aware at the time, but the Lord began to prepare me for my current responsibilities more than twenty years ago.

In 1994, to my surprise one Saturday morning, Bishop Richard Wilkie invited me to his office to "inform" me that I was going to join Dr. Joel Cooper in starting a new church in west, Arkansas. The wisdom, patient instruction, and friendship of Craig Miller and Steve Compton at those early Schools of Congregational Development helped me over the next ten years to witness 200 baptisms, worship attendance of 500+, 700 full members and 1,000 people in the new church's family.

In 2004, after serving ten years with Joel Cooper as a church planter of Grace UMC in Conway Arkansas, Bishop Janice Riggle Huie invited me to join her Arkansas Conference staff. My new title became Arkansas Conference Congregational Minister for New Church Starts. My responsibilities, concerning the planting of new churches, was expressed in three sentences:

- *Develop and oversee a model for selecting, training, and supporting pastors to work new church plants.*
- *Develop a strong cadre of clergy and laity who have missionary hearts totally filled with evangelistic fervor.*
- *By the grace of God, be able to lead people to do what they might think is impossible.*

While Bishop Huie had great confidence in my abilities, the truth is that I was totally relying upon the power of God, not my own limited abilities, to guide the Annual Conference toward a fruitful strategy of starting new churches.

The Arkansas Conference adopted a new emphasis to start more new churches. I immediately began to be the recipient of questions. There were lots of questions. There were questions that I did not have quick answers for.

Fortunately, I was able to make connections with a National Network of United Methodist Congregational Developers — a group of about 30 conference staff from 30 different annual conferences scattered across the nation. *{The network has now grown to about 60 conference staff as more Conferences join the church planting movement.}* These wonderful New Congregational Developers became my encyclopedia, my dictionary, my tutors, my mentors, my source for answers, my colleagues and my friends.

To help the cabinet, clergy, laity and local churches of the Annual Conference begin to know and support the new initiative of planting new churches, I wrote a series of policy papers for the cabinet to review, amend and hopefully adopt. These policy statements helped to form a series of articles I wrote for our conference newspaper. They also became the initial documents in my growing three ring binder with the title of "*New Church Handbook*" written across the front.

That first year the Arkansas cabinet identified twenty-five pastors they perceived had the gifts and graces to plant new churches. Upon the wise advice of George Howard and Dirk Elliott, I developed a New Church Leadership Institute to encourage, train, and empower these potential planters — giving them an environment for self-discernment of their calling to be a planter. We met six times that first year, at each of

 © 2018 Robert O. Crossman, www.UMNewChurch.org

the six newest churches in Arkansas, with Steve Compton, George Howard and Dirk Elliott as visiting faculty that first year.

The following year, the South Central Jurisdiction College of Bishops began to send their potential planters to Arkansas. Very quickly I was training 75 to 150 pastors each year in the New Church Leadership Institute.

The New Church Leadership Institute was held at Mount Sequoyah, the South Central Jurisdiction retreat center, from 1995 to 2012. I was blessed to be able to recruit some of the finest faculty in the country for the Institute.

For example, the 2008-2009 faculty for the New Church Leadership Institute, included Jim Griffith, Bishop Scott Jones, Junius Dotson, Don Smith, Ruben Saenz, Bob Farr, Jacob Tsotigh, Karen Doris, Olu Brown, Mike Roberts, Elaine Heath, Steve Compton, Tom Butcher, Clif Christopher, Karen Horan, Candace Lewis, and Brad Kalajainen. New church planters on the faculty included: Mark Foster, Rob Williams, Robert Johnson, Arturo Reyna, Javier Rios, Aaron Saenz, Mike Felder, Ramiro Lizcano, Blake Lasater, Steven Blair, and Tammy Garrison.

I served as the Director and Registrar, while my wife, Marcia, served as host of the event. While these amazing faculty and practitioners were speaking, I was on the back row taking notes!

Those notes were gathered in my three ring binder, with the title *"New Church Handbook."* It grew to some 700 pages, and was given to each registrant at the New Church Leadership Institutes. The content changed and grew each year as I learned from more and more of the best and brightest church planters in the country.

As the hundreds of graduates of the New Church Leadership Institute were deployed by their bishops to start new congregations, they continued to stay in touch. **More than 100 of their more frequent questions, along with the content of my *"New Church Handbook,"* have formed the content of this collection of articles.**

Over the past five years I have been fortunate to be a part of the Church Planting Leadership Forum led by Ed Stetzer. This forum meets twice a year, with directors of church planting from 64 different denominations. The knowledge I share in this handbook reflects my personal experience and best practices from these denominations.

Rick Warren and Bob Crossman attending the Church Planting Leadership Forum in Nashville.

It is my prayer that these articles will help the next generation of planters to be more faithful and fruitful in planting new churches that make new disciples who make more new disciples of Jesus Christ for the transformation of the world.

†††

© 2018 Robert O. Crossman, www.UMNewChurch.org

I. Why Start New Churches?

New Church Handbook
Nuts & Bolts for Planting New Churches In The Wesleyan Tradition

"What Is A New Church?"

Path 1, at Discipleship Ministries, often hears the question by email, Facebook or telephone, *"What is a new church start?"*

As United Methodists, Path 1's passion and commitment to discipleship is one of their distinguishing characteristics. Path 1 seeks *"to witness to Jesus Christ in the world, and to follow his teachings through acts of compassion, justice, worship, devotion, under the guidance of the Holy Spirit."* (The Book of Discipline, ¶118 2a).

The mission of Path 1 is to make disciples of Jesus Christ for the transformation of the world. Path 1 lives out this mission by creating new places for new people within and beyond the bounds of existing churches. Path 1 has discovered that when creating new places for new people one size does not fit all. Established congregations, districts, and annual conferences have discovered that they can plant in a variety of ways. Some of these ways include new missional communities, second campuses, newly charted congregations, and a wide variety of what Paul Nixon calls "weird churches." *(Weird Church: Welcome to the Twenty-First Century by Paul Nixon and Beth Ann Estock.)*

Rather than describing planting strategies or quoting paragraphs from The Book of Discipline of The United Methodist Church, Path 1 leaves flexibility for the Holy Spirit to move. Path 1 prefers to describe characteristics of new congregations as organized places for new people that are committed to making disciples of Jesus Christ and seeks to do the following:

- Gather frequently to worship;
- Celebrate the sacraments of baptism and Holy Communion;
- Make disciples through small-group covenant, spiritual formation, and mission;
- Teach and practice biblical stewardship of money and time;
- Engage in mission and works of peace and justice aimed toward community transformation;
- Welcome and encourage new disciples;
- Celebrate lay and clergy involvement;
- Foster a culture of ministry multiplication and commit to planting other new congregations within three to five years, and;
- Remain connected and accountable to The United Methodist Church. Path 1 understands that each planting opportunity and method will vary by the context of the mission field in which it is located.

Source: *The State of United Methodist Church Planting In The United States*, edited by Candace Lewis, Douglas Ruffle, and Phillip Brooks, published by Discipleship Ministries, 2016, page 6.

 © 2018 Robert O. Crossman, www.UMNewChurch.org

New Church Handbook
Tools for Planting New Churches In The Wesleyan Tradition

"Why Start New Things for New People?"

by Bob Crossman

Some of you may be asking, *"Why? Why start new things and new churches for new people? Don't we have plenty of churches now? Shouldn't we take care of supporting the strong churches we have; revitalizing the churches that are struggling; and offering compassion for churches that are dwindling — before we start new ministries or any new churches?"*

Good questions. Very sincere questions.

The truth is that across the entire church we have been, and will continue, spending the vast majority of our resources caring for and working to revitalize the churches we already have.

- The bulk of our denomination's strategic initiatives primarily focus on helping our existing churches to discover new life and mission.
- The primary passion of most of our pastors is to revitalize the church they are now serving.
- The primary passion of most of the United Methodists sitting in worship every Sunday is to care for the church they are now attending.
- The primary responsibility of most of the conference staff is to revitalize our existing congregations.
- The primary passion of most of us United Methodists, is to teach, baptize, inspire, and build up those who are already sitting in our pews every Sunday.

Thank God, that revitalization is a priority in our churches, districts and conferences. **However, there is more expected of us.**

The teachings of the New Testament call for us to care for our own. However, the New Testament also teaches us to reach out to new communities with the saving Gospel of Jesus Christ.

"...Go and make disciples of all nations, baptizing them in the name of the Father and of the Son and of the Holy Spirit, and teaching them to obey everything I have commanded you." Matthew 28

You and I are faithful to this Biblical calling each week as we invite our friends, relatives, neighbors, and associates to worship with us on Sunday. We are also faithful to this calling when we start a new church designed to reach a new mission field in an "underserved" or growing part of the mission fields around us.

I do not believe we have to choose between strengthening our existing churches, or starting new churches. I believe we must accomplish both of these missions. We must accomplish all six of the Vision Pathways of the Council of Bishops - all four of the Provocative Proposals of the Connectional Table - all four foci of the General Conference.

Bob Crossman

For example, over the past few decades in Arkansas, the population has been growing, shifting within the state, and changing ethnically. We have started forty-eight new United Methodist Churches in Arkansas in the past thirty-nine years, eleven of them in non-anglo contexts, but that pace has not kept up with the faster pace of the changing demographics within our state.

When **Steve Compton** was the Executive Director of the Office of Congregational Development for the North Carolina Conference, offered these six reasons to plant new churches:

- New people are more likely to join new churches than old churches;
- Old churches are moved toward renewal by the presence of new churches in their communities;
- Old denominations are renewed as the percentage of new churches in their total number of churches increases;
- New churches are more likely than old churches to be open to all kinds of people (inclusive of race, ethnicity, socio-economic, nationality, gender, etc.);
- New churches are more likely than old churches to call or receive pastors who are women or whose cultural background, race, ethnicity, or nationality differs from that of the majority membership; and,
- New churches find it easier than old churches to live out new paradigms of mission and ministry (overnight hospitality for the poor and homeless, contemporary worship, etc.)

© 2018 Robert O. Crossman, www.UMNewChurch.org

Lyle Schaller, suggest twelve reasons to start new churches: (Source: *Forty-four Questions for Church Planters,* by Lyle Schaller, page 27-36.)

- The Great Commission given by Jesus (Matthew 28: 18-20);

- We cannot rely on long-established congregations to reach all the new generations of people;

- Historically new congregations have turned out to be the most effective approach to reaching new generations of people;

- A different style of worship and ministry can be more effective in reaching people outside the church than the style that attracts already committed Christians;

- New churches reach those venturesome personalities who enjoy helping pioneer the new;

- New churches are focused on evangelism and mission, while long established congregations are often overly concerned with institutional survival goals;

- The presence of two or more congregations with the same denominational affiliation usually results in a higher level of congregational health and vitality than if one congregation has a denominational monopoly in that community;

- No one congregation possesses the skills and can muster the resources necessary to reach, attract, serve, and be responsive to the needs of every resident;

- No one congregation has the resources to reach both young religious pilgrims, mature adults, parents of young children, and also those who are focused on social justice;

- To reach people who have moved out to suburbs on the edge of town;

- Starting new churches can be an effective means of changing the denominational mix, experimenting with changing the racial/economic/theological mixture of people, ideas, approaches to ministry, models of congregational life, and style of corporate worship; and,

- If we don't do it, someone else will.

Not convinced yet?
Still wondering why we are attempting to start new churches and multi-site congregations?

Let me share some of my personal motivations.

One of the most compelling reasons for me, comes from Jesus' invitation found in Luke 15. The crowd was wondering why Jesus was spending so much time with sinners and outcasts. Jesus turned to his objectors and told them a parable. He said,

> *"Suppose one of you has a hundred sheep and loses one of them. Do you not leave the ninety-nine in the open country and go after the one lost sheep until you find it? And when you find it, you joyfully put it on your shoulders and carry it home. You call your friends and neighbors together and say, 'Rejoice with me; I have found my lost sheep.' I tell you, that in the same way, there will be more rejoicing in heaven over one sinner who repents than over ninety-nine righteous people who do not need to repent."* *Luke 15: 4-7*

That parable compelled me to join Dr. Joel Cooper in starting the new Grace UMC in Conway two dozen years ago, and compels me now to be part of working toward the goal of starting one new United Methodist church a day in the USA. I believe that there will be rejoicing in heaven as these new churches search and find the 'lost sheep.'

A second compelling reason for me comes from Jesus' command found in Matthew 28. In Jesus' parting words before He returned to heaven, Jesus said,

> *"...Go and make disciples of all nations, baptizing them in the name of the Father and of the Son and of the Holy Spirit, and teaching them to obey everything I have commanded you."*

Those words are called "The Great Commission." We start new churches because we have a great commitment to that great commission. Our local churches are invited not only to make disciples at home in 'Jerusalem' but also to start new churches in 'Judea and Samaria' (Acts 1:8). We are also faithful when we follow the pattern of the Antioch church (Acts 13), sending our pastors to start new churches in new mission fields across town and around the world.

 © 2018 Robert O. Crossman, www.UMNewChurch.org

There is a third compelling reason for me: it is faithful to our DNA as United Methodists.

The founders of the United Methodist church: John Wesley, Francis Asbury, Philip William Otterbein, Martin Boehm, and Thomas Coke all had a passion to disciple those who were already active in church. But their passion didn't stop there. They also had a passion for those outside of the church walls; for the downtrodden; and for the lost who needed a Savior. That passion drove them to give their time and energy to preach outside in the city parks; to preach by the exit doors when the factory shift changed; to preach at the coal mine entrance as miners walked home; and to send circuit riders out into the wilderness of America looking for settlements that did not yet have a church.

It is faithful to our DNA as United Methodist Christians to start new churches with a passion for those in our pews, AND a passion for those who are not yet in any pew.

Bob Crossman

A fourth compelling reason for me, evidenced in the national survey of new churches completed by Ed Stetzer and Lifeway in 2016, is the fruit we are already witnessing in the early stages of the United Methodist Church's goal of moving toward starting one new church a day in the USA.

There is a fifth, and practical reason to be starting the things for new people. When a GROUP *(Bible Study, Sunday School Class, UMW Circle, UMMen, or congregation)* "decides" NOT to reach out to involve new people, that GROUP has also decided to DIE within the next ten years. When a group says, *"We don't want new people. We like our group just the way it is today, with the people we have today. ..."* that group has also decided to DIE within the next ten years. A GROUP must receive NEW PARTICIPANTS, if it wants to exist more than ten years. How can I say that with such certainty?

© 2018 Robert O. Crossman, www.UMNewChurch.org

Well, for example, lets look at another group - a typical college. The University of Missouri, with 33,000 students — is going to close in the next 48 to 60 months. All the faculty and staff will be fired, the buildings will be closed up and perhaps sold. **The college WILL indeed close in 48 to 60 months IF the recruiting office does not bring in a new class of freshmen each year.** Without new freshmen, in 48 to 60 months all of the student body will either graduate, run out of student loans, transfer, or drop out. We all know that. It makes sense. Colleges are on a 48 to 60 month clock. They must replace their constituents every 48 to 60 months.

Another example: Small businesses, (i.e. bakeries, dry cleaners, furniture stores, kitchen stores, pet shops, printing shops) lose about 15% of their customer base each year. If the owners do not bring in new customers, their customer base will eventually shrink and the business will fail.

In a similar way local churches loose, on average, 10% of their active participants each year. Why? Because each year the typical church will have members die or drop out of active participation. This will happen because of health changes, moves to other towns, transfers to other churches, or members who become disenchanted with the church or denomination.

So... if your local church does not bring in new people (about 10% new faces each year) in about 120 months you will loose 'critical mass' and 'viability.' In ten years you will be saying, *"We used to have a full time pastor; we used to have a choir; we used to have a nursery; we used to have Vacation Bible School; we used to have two women's groups, and we used to have a youth group..."*

Survival Goal: each year bring in new members at a rate of about 10% of your average worship attendance — this should keep your worship attendance stable.

Kingdom Goal: find every 'lost sheep' and welcome every 'prodigal son and daughter' in town... open doors... open hearts... open minds... making new disciples who then make more new disciples.

If we are called by this variety of sources
to have a missionary heart for the unchurched,
how do we best reach the unchurched?
We reach them every way we can, and every time we can!

Bob Crossman

There is an interesting fact about new churches. We may wish it were not this way, but it seems to be true. Steve Compton, for the United Methodist Church, and Kirk Hadaway, for the Southern Baptist Church, have studied the effect of establishing new churches in both of our denominations. They discovered that in

 © 2018 Robert O. Crossman, www.UMNewChurch.org

the first thirty years of existence, a new church grows faster and witnesses more professions of faith than an established congregation. Lyle Schaller also proposes a dozen reasons why a central component of any evangelistic strategy should be to plant new churches (*44 Questions For Church Planters*, pp. 13 - 36) These studies propose to us, that if we want to accept Jesus' invitation to find the lost sheep, to be about the business of welcoming the prodigal sons & daughters back home, or to obey Jesus' command to make new disciples — one of the best ways to do that is to start new churches.

Rick Warren writes,
"The single most effective method for fulfilling the Great Commission that Jesus gave us is to plant new churches! Two thousand years of Christian history have proven that new churches grow faster, and reach more people, than established churches."
(Viral Churches, by Ed Stetzer
forward by Rick Warren, 2010, page xi)

HOW MANY NEW CHURCHES SHOULD WE START?

Lyle Schaller proposes that a "survival goal" for an Annual Conference of 700 existing churches is to start 7 new churches each year (that is 1%) to offset those churches that disband or "move into the terminally ill stage of their institutional life."

Schaller also proposes that if the goal was for substantial growth, an Annual Conference of 700 existing churches needs to start between 14 and 21 (that is 2% to 3%) new churches each year.

I am thankful that revitalization of our existing churches is a priority in our churches, districts and conference. I am also thankful, that we have a new strategic initiative to re-evangelize the United States and reach more people, more young people, and more diverse people by creating new places for new people.

†††

NOTE: This article reflects the personal opinions of the author and does not necessarily reflect an official position of Discipleship Ministries or Path 1..

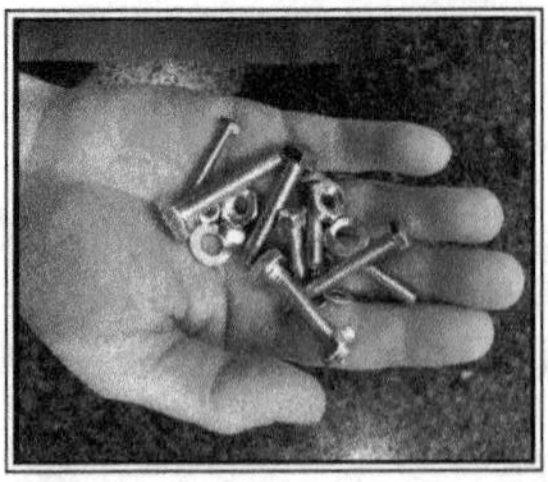

New Church Handbook
Nuts & Bolts for Planting New Churches In The Wesleyan Tradition

"Why Are Wesleyans Starting New Churches?"

by Bob Crossman

(Note: This article, an abbreviated version of the previous longer article, "Why Start New Things for New People" is designed as a discussion starter for small groups.)

As Christians with a Wesleyan heritage, we are not starting new faith communities and churches to compete with the Baptist, Assembly of God, or Latter Day Saints. Nor are we starting new churches to ensure the survival of a denomination. Rather, Wesleyans are starting new faith communities and new churches across the land because it is the Wesleyan thing to do.

New church planting is faithful to our DNA as Wesleyans. John Wesley and his early associates (Francis Asbury, Philip William Otterbein, Martin Boehm, and Thomas Coke) all had a passion to disciple those who were already active in church. But their passion didn't stop at the church doors. They also had a passion to disciple those outside of the church walls; for the downtrodden; and, for the lost who needed a Savior. That passion drove them to give their time and energy to preach outside in the city parks; to preach by the exit doors when the factory shift changed; to preach at the coal mine entrance in the very early hours as miners walked to work; and to send circuit riders out into the wilderness of the American colonies looking for settlements that did not yet have a church.

It is faithful to our DNA as Wesleyans to start new churches and new faith communities with a passion for those in our pews, and a passion for those who are not yet in any pew.

For me, a second compelling reason comes from Jesus' invitation found in Luke 15. In Luke 15, a crowd was wondering why Jesus was spending so much time with sinners and outcasts. Jesus turned to his objectors and told them a parable. He said,

---

> [4] *"Suppose someone among you had one hundred sheep and lost one of them. Wouldn't he leave the other ninety-nine in the pasture and search for the lost one until he finds it?* [5] *And when he finds it, he is thrilled and places it on his shoulders.* [6] *When he arrives home, he calls together his friends and neighbors, saying to them, 'Celebrate with me because I've found my lost sheep.'* [7] *In the*

 © 2018 Robert O. Crossman, www.UMNewChurch.org

same way, I tell you, there will be more joy in heaven over one sinner who changes both heart and life than over ninety-nine righteous people who have no need to change their hearts and lives." (Luke 4-7 CEB)

That parable compelled me to join Joel Cooper in starting a new church in Conway, Arkansas. Today, Luke 15 compels me to be part of a movement to start 1,000 new Wesleyan churches across American by 2020. I believe that there will be rejoicing in heaven as these new churches search and find the 'lost sheep.'

A third compelling reason for me comes from Jesus' command found in Matthew 28. In Jesus' parting words before He returned to heaven, Jesus said,

---

"...go and make disciples of all nations, baptizing them in the name of the Father and of the Son and of the Holy Spirit, teaching them to obey everything that I've commanded you."

(Matthew 28: 19-20 CEB)

Those words are called "The Great Commission." I believe we should start new churches and new faith communities because we have a great commitment to the great commission. Our local churches are invited not only to make disciples at home in 'Jerusalem' but also to start new churches in 'Judea and Samaria' (Acts 1:8). We are also faithful when we follow the pattern of the Antioch church (Acts 13), sending our pastors to start new churches in new mission fields across town and across the state.

A fourth compelling reason for me is the fruit we are already witnessing in the early stages of this recently revived Wesleyan church planting movement. There is an interesting fact about new churches. We may wish it were not this way, but it seems to be true. Steve Compton for the United Methodist Church and Kirk Hadaway for the Southern Baptist Church have studied the effect of establishing new churches in both denominations. They discovered that in the first thirty years of existence, a new church grows faster and witnesses more professions of faith than established congregations.

Rick Warren writes,
*"The single most effective method for fulfilling the Great Commission that Jesus gave us is to plant new churches!
Two thousand years of Christian history have proven that new churches grow faster, and reach more people, than established churches."*
(Viral Churches, by Ed Stetzer forward by Rick Warren, 2010, page xi)

If we want to accept Jesus' invitation to find the lost sheep, to be about the business of welcoming the prodigal sons and daughters back home, or to obey Jesus' command to make new disciples, then one of the best ways to do that is to start new churches.

I am thankful that revitalization of our existing churches is a priority in our Wesleyan conferences. I am also thankful that so many Wesleyan conferences and local churches are catching the vision to support the planting of NEW faith communities to spread Scriptural Holiness across the land.

Reflection Questions:

- If you are a Wesleyan, how important is the fact that church planting is part of your heritage?
- What are you currently doing to reach lost people with Jesus, and make new disciples who then make more new disciples?
- If you are not personally active in evangelism now, how could you begin to support evangelistic efforts in your local church?
- If you are part of the leadership of an established church, what are several ways you could support the planting of a new church?
- How could you find out if starting a second campus of your church would be an effective and fruitful way to make new disciples?

†††

(See also the longer article on this subject: "Why Start New Things for New People.")

NOTE: This article reflects the personal opinions of the author and does not necessarily reflect an official position of Discipleship Ministries or Path 1..

 © 2018 Robert O. Crossman, www.UMNewChurch.org

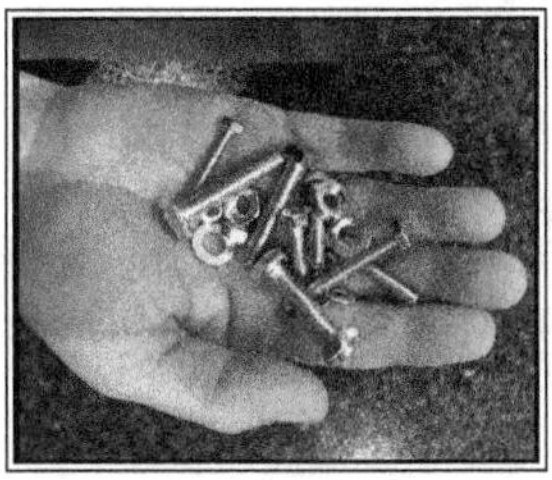

New Church Handbook
Nuts & Bolts for Planting New Churches In The Wesleyan Tradition

"8 Great Reasons to Start New Churches"

by Dirk Elliott

One million new disciples! That is the goal for the next four years set by the 2016 General Conference. To accomplish this goal, the General Conference challenged us to start 1,000 new churches by the end of 2020! So, why start new churches?

1. Jesus Commissioned Us.

"Therefore, go and make disciples of all the nations . . ." (Matt 28:19 NLT) Making disciples is our commission and our responsibility.

Approximately twenty percent of people in the United States are actively involved in a church. If this is true, then over 259,600,000 people are not. As Jesus said, *"The harvest is plentiful . . .."* (Luke 10:2 NIV) John Wesley said, "The world is my parish," yet we can meet many people in our own neighborhoods who are searching for God and a caring faith community. Potential disciples are young and old, new and long-time residents, as well as diverse ethnically and culturally. We encounter potential new disciples on the streets we walk and in the stores we shop. Jesus calls us to reach out to them, to *"go out and train everyone you meet, far and near, in this way of life . . .."* (Matt 28:19 MSG)

2. New churches are most effective in making disciples.

Donald McGavran and George Hunter, in Church Growth: Strategies that Work quote Lyle Schaller, saying, *"Numerous studies have shown that 60-80% of the new adult members of new congregations are persons who were not actively involved in the life of any worshiping community. — By contrast, most long established churches draw the majority of their new adult members from persons who transfer in from other congregations."*

Tim Keller, founding pastor of Redeemer Presbyterian Church in New York City, a large congregation with over 5,000 in attendance, agrees, saying that *"the average new congregation will bring six to eight times more new people into the life of the body of Christ than any older congregation of the same size."*

3. Starting a new church helps the parent church grow.

If an existing healthy church starts a new church, it becomes a much stronger, healthier church. By starting a new church, the existing church extends its reach into new communities to make new disciples.

Sycamore Creek Church in Lansing, Michigan, is a 17-year-old church that five years ago was a one-campus church averaging 107 in attendance. Now Sycamore Creek has four campuses with six worship services, and last year (2016) attendance averaged 229 in worship. By opening their minds, hearts, and doors, going into their neighborhoods, connecting with people, and making new disciples, Sycamore Creek Church is a vibrant, growing congregation.

4. **Changing and new communities need new churches.**

The population of the United States continues to grow, while the number of churches continues to decline. Some ask, *"Why start a new church when we have so many struggling churches? Wouldn't it be better stewardship to invest in existing churches?"* Many struggling churches do need help. Many of these churches are land-locked, are in need of repair, or are in facilities that are inefficient and costly to maintain. Some existing churches struggle to reach out and make new disciples in their changing neighborhoods.

Some churches make the painful decision to close even though new people are moving into their communities. At the same time, new subdivisions are springing up as the population spreads from cities into surrounding farmland. Because new churches are more effective in making new disciples, the ministries of new churches are needed especially in both urban and suburban locations.

5. **New churches are more effective in reaching unreached people groups.**

Many communities are becoming more diverse. While we strive for multi-ethnic or multi-cultural churches, many people prefer to worship God in their native language using their native customs. They prefer to worship with others of similar background. As Chad Hall, founder of Coach Approach Ministries, states, *"While we all long for a church of all nations, the reality is that most lost people are best reached by a community that is similar to the lost person."*

Recently a group of Korean pastors were meeting to discuss how best to reach their community. As they studied the demographics, it became apparent that the largest ethnic group in that community was from India. They immediately discussed how they could start a new church to reach these Indian people in their own language and culture.

6. **A new church start creates a new life cycle.**

Churches, like people, have a life cycle. They are born and started, grow and mature, age, and die. Many United Methodist churches are aging. Some congregations are at the end of their life cycle. Quite simply, new churches start a new life cycle and attract more people, more young people, more diverse people.

7. **New churches are innovative centers for outreach and evangelism.**

Junius Dotson, General Secretary of Discipleship Ministries, says that new churches are the "R & D" of the church world. Because they are creating new local

 © 2018 Robert O. Crossman, www.UMNewChurch.org

traditions and because they have more disciples new to the Christian faith, they are quicker to try new ideas that often appeal to new and more diverse people. They are also more likely to take church into their neighborhoods. New churches are started in pubs and parks, in pizza shops and laundry mats, in theaters and schools, anywhere unchurched people gather. Faith communities begin with people who share hobbies and activities such as rock climbing, running, cycling, health and wellness, recovery, justice concerns, or various types of service. New disciples are made in these relational settings.

8. **New disciples have a new place to grow.**

New small groups, faith communities, and churches are easier entry points into the community of faith than are long-established ones. New disciples are looking for a place to grow in their faith and to be on the discipleship journey with others. Starting new churches provides a new place for new disciples to grow.

The ultimate goal is not to plant churches; the ultimate goal is to make disciples. By starting 1000 new churches in the next four years, the United Methodist Church will be better able to welcome one million new disciples of Jesus Christ, including "more people, more young people, more diverse people."

†††

This article by Dirk Elliott is reprinted here by permission of the author granted August 24, 2017.

Dirk Elliott is Director of New Faith Communities and Congregational Development for the Detroit Annual Conference. Dirk comes to the Detroit Annual Conference after serving in East Ohio Conference as the Director of Congregational Development for ten years. Prior to his ministry as part of Conference Staff, Dirk served for 18 years in pastoral ministry in three appointments. He is a graduate of the West Ohio New Church Start Academy. Much of his continuing education has been in the areas of church growth, evangelism and faith sharing. He has taken part in the General Board of Discipleship Faith Sharing and Offering Christ Today. He has taken Herb Miller's workshops on Effective Worship, Visionary Leadership, and Evangelism. He is also a trained consultant in Natural Church Development. He has served as Spiritual Director on many Emmaus Walks and has served as Community Spiritual Director for the Central Ohio Emmaus Community. Dirk is on the Board of Directors for the Bishop Rueben Job Leadership Development Center. He is the North Central Jurisdiction representative to the Path 1 Team, the United Methodist's church planting initiative through the General Board of Discipleship.

NOTE: This article reflects the personal opinions of the author and does not necessarily reflect an official position of Discipleship Ministries or Path 1..

New Church Handbook

Nuts & Bolts for Planting New Churches In The Wesleyan Tradition

"What Does The 2016 UMC Book of Discipline Say About Planting New Churches?"

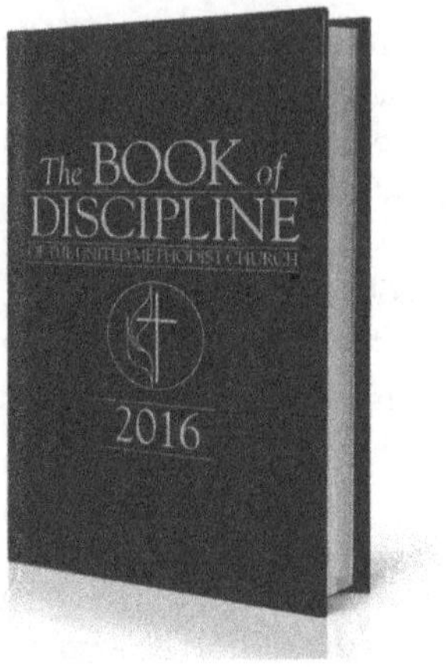

What Is the Method for Organizing a New Local Church in the United Methodist Church?

Section VII,
The Method of Organizing a New Local Church *¶259*

1. A new local church or mission congregation shall be established **only with the consent of the bishop** in charge **and the cabinet** and with due consideration of the **conference entity assigned the responsibility for congregational development.** The bishop shall designate the district within whose bounds the church or mission congregation shall be organized. The district superintendent of that district, or his or her designee, shall be the agent in charge of the project and shall recommend to **the district board of church location and building** *(¶2519)* the method of organization, and whether a specific site shall be selected or an area of organization be designated. The district superintendent shall avail him/herself of existing demographic, lifestyle and ethnographic information in the process of establishing a new congregation and its location, or shall recommend to the board of trustees of a selected local church that they share their facility with the proposed congregation. **If there is a city or district missionary organization, or if funds for the project are anticipated from a conference organization, those bodies shall also be asked to approve the method of organization and location for a new congregation.**

a)A **mission congregation** may be designated when any of the following conditions exist: 1) Membership opportunities and resources are limited and not likely to result in a chartered congregation for an extended period of time. 2) A strategic demographic, cultural or language opportunity for serving a limited population is present. 3) It is expected that long-term sustaining funding from sources outside the congregation will be necessary to enable the congregation to exist, and the assumption of full connectional support items by the congregation is unlikely. 4) It is probable that the annual conference will need to provide long-term administrative guidance, including attention to the distinctive property needs of the congregation. When any of these conditions exist, the cabinet, in consultation with the congregational development area of the annual conference, may designate an entity a mission congregation.

© 2018 Robert O. Crossman, www.UMNewChurch.org

The mission congregation may be organized in the same manner and have the same rights and powers as any local church.

2. The bishop may appoint a pastor to launch a **new local church**, or with the bishop's approval the district superintendent may authorize a local church or group of local churches to launch a new church by gathering interested people in small groups for Bible study, outreach, community building, and worship at a site in an area approved by the district board of church location and building.
3. A pastor of The United Methodist Church, while serving as the pastor of a new church prior to the convening of a constituting conference *(¶259.7)*, may receive a person into the membership of The United Methodist Church under the conditions of *¶217*. When a person is received as either a baptized or a professing member, the pastor shall send the name, address, and related facts to the annual conference secretary for recording on a general membership roll. These names shall be transferred as soon as possible to the roll of the new church, when constituted, or to another church upon the member's request. If the new church is being sponsored by an existing church, membership may be recorded on the roll of that church.
4. Each annual conference or its equivalent may determine the minimum number of members and other criteria required for the organization of a local United Methodist church.
5. When the number of people interested in being charter members of the new church reaches the number necessary as set by the conference to charter a new church, the district superintendent shall call the interested people to meet at an appointed time for the purpose of organizing them into a chartered (organized) local church, or may by written authorization designate an elder in the district to call such a meeting. The district superintendent or the designated elder shall preside and shall appoint a secretary to keep a record of the meeting. Following a time of worship, opportunity shall be given to those in attendance to present themselves for membership.
6. People desiring to become professing members by transfer or on profession of their faith in Christ shall also be given opportunity to present themselves for membership. Any who have not been baptized shall receive the sacrament of baptism, profess their faith and be received as members. Other baptized people are to be received as baptized members.
7. Those who will be members of the constituting church conference shall be those received into the professing membership.
8. The constituting church conference shall then be called to order by the district superintendent or by an elder whom the superintendent designates *(see ¶ 246.5)*. A committee on nominations, elected on nominations from the floor as the conference may determine, shall nominate members of the proposed church council. The chairperson of the committee on nominations shall be the appointed pastor *(see ¶258.1c)*. When the members have been chosen, the district superintendent or the designated elder shall declare the church properly constituted.
9. The district superintendent or an elder whom the superintendent designates

shall then adjourn the constituting church conference and call to order the charge conference of the pastoral charge. The membership of the charge conference shall be those newly elected, and any others entitled to membership. The charge conference shall then elect such officers of the church as the Discipline requires, including trustees of church property, and shall organize its structure as provided in the Discipline. When such officers have been duly elected and such structure put in place, the church is duly organized, and from this point its work shall proceed as described in the Discipline, provided that when a newly organized church is attached to a circuit, the charge conference shall not be held until such time as representatives from all the churches of the charge can be properly assembled for that purpose.

10. The charge conference may take action, at its discretion, authorizing and directing the newly elected trustees to incorporate the newly organized church in accordance with local laws and the provisions of the Discipline.

In the UMC, whose approval must be obtained before an area is selected for a new church to start?

(¶259.1 selected phrases) **A new local church or mission congregation shall be established only with the consent of the bishop... the cabinet ..the conference entity assigned the responsibility for congregational development... and the district board of church location and building.**

... If there is a city or district missionary organization, or if funds for the project are anticipated from a conference organization, those bodies shall also be asked to approve the method of organization and location for a new congregation.

¶259.2. The bishop may appoint a pastor to launch a new local church, or with the bishop's approval the district superintendent may authorize a local church or group of local churches **to launch a new church** by gathering interested people in small groups for Bible study, outreach, community building, and worship at a site **in an area approved by the district board of church location and building.**

At the local church level, who approves the idea of starting a multi-site or satellite?

¶247.22 When authorized by the district superintendent and the district board of church location and building, the charge conference may provide for the **sponsoring of satellite congregations.**

In the UMC, who must approve the potential location for starting a new church?

¶259.2. ... **in an area approved by the district board of church location and building.**

¶2520. Duties and Responsibilities of the District Boards of Church Location and Building-1. *Local Church Building Sites and Plans* — The Board of church location and building **shall investigate all proposed local church building sites,** ascertaining that such sites are properly located for the community to be served and adequate in size to provide space for future expansion and parking facilities. *(See ¶¶259.1,2544.2)*

 © 2018 Robert O. Crossman, www.UMNewChurch.org

The Annual Conference shall give recognition to any new churches...

¶604.10 The annual conference shall **give recognition to any new churches** that have been organized during the year and shall, through the presiding bishop and the secretary, send to each new church a certificate of organization, which the district superintendent shall, on behalf of the conference, present to the new church in an appropriate ceremony.

Conference Board of Global Ministries shall support, research and assist...

¶633. Conference Board of Global Ministries ...*¶633.5* ...shall establish a committee on Parish and Community Development.. *¶633.5.e...* encouraging and supporting the **development of new... congregations**; conducting research studies and community surveys that plan for and assist with developing innovative strategies for mission; and reviewing, evaluating, and making recommendations for loans, donations, and grants from the General Board of Global Ministries.

The Annual Conference shall plan the establishment of new churches...

¶642 Each Annual Conference shall... *¶642.4.b* recommend to the conference ... in cooperation with the bishop and the cabinet... planning for mission with other judicatories, particularly in the **establishment of new churches**, yoked congregations, and in the process of local church union efforts.

GBOD and GBGM support of new church development...

¶1101.1. There shall be a General Board of Discipleship... *¶1112. Evangelism Responsibilities:* In response to God's love in Jesus Christ... *¶1112.13* Work with the General Board of Global Ministries for the extension of the Church. To this end there shall be a Joint Committee on Congregational Development with equal representation of members from the General Board of Discipleship and the General Board of Global Ministries, which shall meet regularly for mutual learning, developing strategies for Church extension, and providing resources and assistance to conferences and districts **in the field of new congregational development** and congregational revitalization.

GBGM mission programming around establishing new congregations...

¶1314 The program responsibilities within the General Board of Global Ministries... shall engage in mission programming around the following areas: ...*¶1314.1.b.* Strategic new mission initiatives and **establishing new congregations** where United Methodism and / or cooperative church relationships do not exist.

†††

New Church Handbook
Nuts & Bolts for Planting New Churches In The Wesleyan Tradition

"Biblical Foundations for New Church Development"

By Wesley S.K. Daniel

This article by Dr. Wesley S. K. Daniel first appeared in the United Methodist Manual for New Church Development, editors Scott Ray and Clay Jacobs.

Striving to grow and revitalize the Church of Jesus Christ encourages faithfulness to the Great Commission of our Lord to make disciples and be His witnesses. Further, by equipping and nurturing disciples to grow in Christian discipleship, the kingdom of God is thereby built, expanded and extended throughout the world.

It is imperative to fully comprehend and understand the teaching of the Scripture as the subject of growth, revitalization and new church development is considered. In Matthew 16.18, Jesus declared, *"Upon this rock I will build my church…."* In this article, an attempt will be made to explore how God began the "building program," the program of building God's church from the very beginning of time, and the program that continues to challenge the Church today to be about the task of proclaiming the Good News and expanding the kingdom of God.

Old Testament Understanding of Growing the Church

God's plan for the growth of the Body of Christ begins in Genesis 1.28 when God says to Adam, *"Be fruitful and multiply and replenish the earth, and subdue it; and have dominion."* This is simply more than an attempt to promote biological growth. What God also meant is that the earth is to be filled with" "knowers of God." Adam was called to extend the "garden of God" to the uttermost boundaries of the entire earth (Ezekiel 28.13; 31.8-9). It was God's expressive desire to fill the earth with priests, kings and prophets so that the covenant purposes of the grace of God can be fulfilled throughout the earth.

In Genesis 3.15, the loving heart of God can be seen reaching out to Adam and Eve. Even though they had sinned, God gives them *"the promise of the One who will bruise the serpent's head, lifting the curse."* By faith, the son of Adam and Eve, Abel, offered the blood of the lamb as his offering (Hebrews 11.4; Genesis 4.4), and that faith came by hearing God's Word (Romans 10.17). Cain heard the Word of God, but he rejected it; and yet God pled with him for his repentance (Genesis 4.7). Seth, the next son born to Adam and Eve, promulgated God's Word in a way that the future generations included Enoch and Noah. Enoch prophesied of the Lord's coming, *"With ten thousand of his saints, to execute judgment…"* (Jude 14-15). Noah, says the

 © 2018 Robert O. Crossman, www.UMNewChurch.org

Scripture, is justified by faith (Genesis 6.8-9; Hebrews 11.7), and thus became the progenitor of all humankind.

Further, in Genesis 12, God revealed Himself to Abraham and called Abraham to usher into being "a nation of priests" who would proclaim the Jehovah to the world. Through Abraham's descendents, Isaac, Jacob, Judah and Joseph, God's continued redemptive work to save and reach out in love to draw people into His fellowship is observed.

In the book of Exodus, it is further perceived how the redemptive God remembers to keep God's side of the covenant promise of blessing to the nations of Abraham, Isaac and Jacob (Exodus 2.24). Over and over again, God gives Pharaoh many opportunities to "repent" as He sends Moses to deliver His people. Even in the awesome history-making division between Egypt and Israel (Exodus 8.23; 9.4; 11.7), through plagues and the dividing of the sea, the nations bear witness to the salvation of God (Exodus 7.5). And God rightfully declares, *"And the Egyptians will know that I am the Jehovah, when I have gotten my honor upon Pharaoh, upon his chariots and upon his housemen,"* (14.18). The song of deliverance sung at the shores of the Red Sea clearly acknowledges the redemptive work of God: *"The people have heard, they tremble; pagans have taken hold on the inhabitants of Philitia. Then were the chiefs of the Edom dismayed; the mighty men of Moab trembling taken hold of them; all the inhabitants of Canaan are melted away"* (Exodus 15.15).

Other examples of what God had in store for the pagans are Rehab the Canaanite (Joshua 2; 6.17; Hebrews 11.31), and Ruth the Moabites (Ruth 1.16-17; Matthew 1.5). God made it clear to the Israelites that He did not love them more than the pagans around them, but that they, the Israelites, were special to God because He had chosen them so that through their witness the whole earth would be made aware of God's redeeming love, redemption, and provision for the salvation of all persons.

This intention of God was well understood by the Psalmists, especially David, who had the clearest revelation of all. The Psalmists encouraged God's people to sing praise to the God of salvation: "to the ends of the earth" and to the "uttermost parts" (2.8; 65.8). Approximately fifteen times it is proclaimed that nations will worship the living God: *"All the nations: will call him blessed (72,17), and this salvation is to be received by the nations (67.2). God is the king of all the earth (47.8), and kings and rulers will bow before him (2.10-11). Prophetically speaking of Messiah, the Father promises," "I will give you the heathen for your inheritance"* (2.8). As Israel reveals God as Savior and Judge (67.3-7), other nations will be enlightened and forsake idols (96.1-13). Israel was, in her worship, something very akin to the New Testament Church shown in the Psalmists encouragement of prayer, praise, and testimony in the community of faith (22.22-25; 35.18; 107.32). It is no wonder that the book of Psalms is filled with exhortations to praise Jehovah, whose love, mercy, and grace are revealed to all who need deliverance from sin, hopelessness and loneliness.

In the ministry of the prophets, furthermore, Isaiah talks about the Messiah as the Light unto the Gentile world (Isaiah 42.6; 60.3). Isaiah speaks of Israel as the vineyard planted by God (Isaiah 5.1ff) who carried the fruits of her sin, briars and thorns (Isaiah 7.23-25; 9.18; 10.17; 27.4; 32.13; 33.12). Jeremiah speaks of the day when "all the nations" will be gathered to Jerusalem, "to speak of the name of the Lord." Prophet Haggai proclaims the Lord to be" "the desire of all nations" (2.7), and Habakkuk realizes that it is God's yearning that all the earth *"is filled with knowledge of the glory of the Lord..."* (2.4). Finally, in the book of Jonah, the missionary nature and heart of God can perhaps best be seen.

God is also discerned in the Old Testament as the: 1) God of Abraham, Isaac and Jacob is a God who SEEKS OUT; 2) God of the Old Testament is a God who desires to RECONCILE AND RESTORE broken relationships; 3) God of the Old Testament is a God who TRANSFORMS human nature and makes all things new; 4) God of the Old Testament is a God who REDEEMS, RESTORES, AND DEVELOPS individuals and nations to grow and blossom; and, 5) God of the Old Testament is also a God who brings SALVATION, PEACE AND LIFE ETERNAL to all those who seek Him.

The Old Testament is not simply a collection of historical writings, but it is the history of the faith-formation and building of God's people... and, it is filled with acts of God's saving grace within history. These acts of God in history provide the very foundation of Israel's faith; being unique because it is essentially works of salvation - - acts of God's saving power of God's people. Such salvation history of the Old Testament becomes a background by which God's unconditional love, saving action and the growth and expansion of God's church is fully discerned.

Throughout the Old Testament, it is revealed how God extended God's grace and love to people and nations so that ALL may be redeemed, restored, saved and brought into the loving embrace of God. Although terms such as "church growth, evangelism, new church development, revitalization" do not appear in the Old Testament, it is clearly evident that the concepts of God's love, divine grace, salvation, spiritual and numerical growth, church development and discipleship are clearly present.

New Testament Understanding of Growing the Church

God's divine will to save all people and bring them to redemption, as seen in the Old Testament times, is stated even more explicitly in the New Testament writings. The coming of the Holy Spirit marks the beginning of the God's harvest to build, extend and expand the Church of God.

More than any other book in the New Testament, in the book of Acts people are seen responding in large numbers to the salvation message offered through the power of the Gospel. As mentioned in Acts, the early church grew at a rapid rate. In Acts 1.15, it is explained that the church was begun with 120 people. At Pentecost, however, the congregation grew to 3,000 (2.41). Later, the growth continues to five thousand believers. Luke writes, *"The Lord added to their number daily"* (Acts 2.47), and Acts 5.14 indicates there were even more believers in multitudes added to the Body of Christ.

 © 2018 Robert O. Crossman, www.UMNewChurch.org

In Acts 6.7, the number of disciples increased in Jerusalem daily. A great awakening in Samaria takes place (8.5-25). Further, the churches in Judea, Galilee and Samaria multiplied and grew (9.31), and all who were living in Lydia and Sharon and Joppa also believed (9.35,42). Acts 11.21, 24 and 26 tells of a movement in Antioch, and it says that many believed and turned to Christ. The first part of Acts concludes with this statement: "But the Word of the Lord continued to grow and was multiplied" (12.24). In 21.20, James, summarizing the results of the growth of the church says that there were tens and thousands of Jewish believers in Jerusalem and the community. Paul's report given to the Jerusalem church, recorded in 21.20, acknowledges that thousands of Jews were added to faith in Christ. The book of Acts unequivocally provides a clear picture of the numerical, as well as the spiritual expansion of the early church. Similar accounts of the growth of the church are recorded in Acts 13.48-49.

There are other references to growth in the development of the church as well: Acts 13.43-44, 48-49; 14.20-21; 16.5; 17.2,4; 18.8-11; 28.24,30-31; Ephesians 19.10; Romans 28.31; 15.19,23. Luke further elaborates on the maturity and breadth of the growth and expansion of the church in Acts. In addition to the numerical and geographical growth of the early church, Luke also gives attention to growth in moral, ethical and spiritual dimensions as well.

As one studies the growth dimension of the early church in the New Testament, one will discover that there were basically four dimensions of growth: growth in spiritual life; growth in Christian fellowship and prayer, growth out in Christian service, and finally, growth in numbers.

God's plan for the growth and expansion of the Church cannot be ignored in the New Testament; it is clearly seen throughout the writings of the New Testament and especially, in the Book of Acts. In fact, carefully reading the entire Scripture with "growth eyes," it is difficult to conclude anything other than the Old and New Testaments were written by missionaries to missionaries. In this respect, they are the greatest manuals for growing and expanding the Church of Jesus Christ!

God Wills and Wants the Church to Grow

Why should the church be engaged in the ministry of seeking the lost? Why should the church be engaged in the ministry of proclaiming the Good News and building new faith communities? Why must Christian believers be concerned about the growth and revitalization of the Body of Christ? Why must the task of saving the lost and the proclamation of the Good News be the top priority in the life and the mission of the church? I believe the answers to these questions are simple: God demands it! God wills and wants the Church of Jesus Christ to multiply, grow and expand.

When we talk about the growth of the church and new church development, it needs to be understood as a theological stance. It rises out of unshakable theological conviction that God desires and wants the kingdom of God to expand, spread and grow. In fact, God requires it.

Growing the Body of Christ, making new disciples for Jesus Christ (the process of faith development), and building new faith communities are definitely the will of God, and therefore, it must become the primary task of the Church today. John Wesley argued that growth was definitely a sign of God's grace, and decline was a sign of decrease in God's grace. The central or the primary task of God's people then, is to make known the essential facts of the Good News, that Jesus Christ died for all persons, and that there is salvation and new life in Christ Jesus, and intentionally disciple and grow persons within the context of faith communities — the Body of Christ.

The theological base on which revitalization and new church development can take place is to perceive the church as an agent of outreach and reconciliation, and also, to perceive the church as faithful to our Lord's command to go and make new disciples and build new faith communities. In Matthew 28.18-19 Jesus' own words commands:' *"All authority in heaven and on earth has been given to me. Therefore, go and make disciples of all nations, baptizing them in the name of the Father and of the Son and of the Holy Spirit, and teaching them to obey everything I have commanded you. And surely I am with you always, even to the very end of the age."* Growing the church and creating new faith communities is truly being faithful to the Great Commission. Ultimately, it is faithfulness to God.

It is important to keep in mind that churches exist not only to help and nurture Christians, but also to give believers a "center" of operation from which to consistently launch intentional ministries of reaching the lost and to invite persons into the fellowship of the Body of Christ. The primary purpose for the existence and mission of the church is to boldly spread the power of the Gospel, to make new disciples, and to engage in the expansion of the kingdom of God by building new faith communities throughout the world.

There are basically three reasons why growth and expansion of the church of God is a necessity:

1. The church of God is a living organism. It is alive and full of life from God. Every living thing grows and expands.... The only thing that can cause that which was once growing to abruptly stop growing is a process of death. God dislikes death; God overcame death. God is the giver of life and life more abundant. There is no sadder sight than that of a dying church or denomination. Renewal and expansion of the church in and through the power of the Holy Spirit is its only hope.

2. The church itself definitely needs to grow, expand and spread. There is nothing more joyous to see and experience than growth itself, both spiritual and numerical. To see men, women and children being brought to the saving knowledge of Christ and incorporated into new faith communities sustains much excitement.

3. The world has no hope for hearing the Gospel except through God's divinely

 © 2018 Robert O. Crossman, www.UMNewChurch.org

ordered medium, which is the Body of Christ, the faith community of believers. The responsibility of spreading the Good News to every person on earth and expanding the Body of Christ has been clearly given to the Church — to every disciple of Christ.

Conclusion

The Scripture, of course, has ample examples and illustrations from Genesis to Revelation of a God who 1) seeks; 2) saves; 3) finds; 4) restores; 5) enables growth; and 6) builds. Therefore, God calls for the faithful people of His church to follow Him in this task of seeking, saving, finding, restoring, growing, and building God's kingdom. God's objective is to not only proclaim, but also to gather together the results of the proclamation; to build, expand and grow the church of God through the formation of new faith communities. God is well pleased when the church grows, expands, multiplies and prospers; this brings glory and honor to God. The power and strength for this all-important divine task comes from God the Holy Spirit. Without His empowerment, we can do nothing!

This article first appeared in the
United Methodist Manual for New Church Development,
editors Scott Ray and Clay Jacobs.

†††

NOTE: This article reflects the personal opinions of the author
and does not necessarily reflect an official position of Discipleship Ministries or Path 1..

This article by Dr. Wesley S.K. Daniel
is reprinted here by permission of the author
granted June 21, 2017.

 © 2018 Robert O. Crossman, www.UMNewChurch.org

II. Do I Have the Gifts & Graces for Church Planting?

New Church Handbook
Nuts & Bolts for Planting New Churches In The Wesleyan Tradition

"13 Characteristics of a New Church Leader"

There is no single inventory that clearly measures the gifts and graces for church planting. In this articles, and in the half dozen that follow it, you will find several inventories that might inform your thoughts and conversations with family, colleagues and supervisors about the possibility of requesting an appointment to plant a new church.

THIRTEEN CHARACTERISTICS OF A NEW CHURCH LEADER

by Charles Ridley

Charles Ridley is professor of counseling psychology at Texas A & M University. Previously, he has taught at Indiana University and the Graduate School of Psychology at Fuller Theological Seminary. A licensed psychologist and Fellow of the American Psychological Association, he earned his Ph.D. from the University of Minnesota. Dr. Ridley conducted a study of church planters in the United States and Canada. His subjects in the study represented 13 Protestant denominations. Based on his research and subsequent field-testing, he developed a list of 13 prominent performance characteristics. For over a decade, these characteristics have been used to identify potential church planters. These criteria are heavily weighted toward an entrepreneurial, apostolic start from scratch/parachute/pioneer/zero-based style of planting. Here are his 13 criteria:

1. ***Visionary Capacity***: Ability to project a vision into the future, persuasively motivate people toward that vision, and bring it into reality. Ability to Develop a plan for the future that is different and preferable to the present, and helping other people to see that plan as something to be grasped. The ability to build something from nothing.
2. ***Personal Motivation***: Approaches ministry with a commitment to excellence through long hard work, persistence, being a self-starter, demonstrating energy and vitality. Accomplishing goals based upon inner passion. working without external support.
3. ***Creates Ownership of Ministry***: Instills in people a sense of personal responsibility for the growth and success of ministry so well that people "receive and carry the baton." Trains these new leaders to reproduce leaders.
4. ***Relates to the Unchurched***: Understands the mentality of the unchurched. Ability to develop rapport, break through barriers, and encourage unchurched people to examine themselves and commit to a relationship with God and lead people to a saving knowledge of Jesus Christ.

© 2018 Robert O. Crossman, www.UMNewChurch.org

5. ***Spousal Cooperation***: Creating a workable partnership that agrees on ministry priorities, each partner's roles and involvement in ministry, and the integration of ministry with family life. This is a partnership in ministry and marriage: problem solving, negotiating, and resolving conflict, modeling healthy family decision making.

6. ***Effectively Builds Relationships***: Takes the initiative in getting to know people and deepening relationships as a basis for more effective ministry. Ability to take relationships beyond superficiality to intimacy, working through relationship struggles.

{NOTE: Ridley calls the first six criteria on the previous page "knock out areas." If there is significant lack of competency if any of these first six criteria, there is no need to go further.

7. ***Committed to Church Growth***: Values church growth as a method for building more and better disciples; strives to achieve numerical growth within the context of spiritual and relational growth. The ability to grow a church numerically and spiritually (qualitatively and quantitatively). The ability to assess new church develop resources, and to resist the temptation to move into the 'maintenance' mode of ministry.

8. ***Responsive to the Community***: Adapts the ministry to the culture and needs of local residents while seeking to engage community issues and concerns. Ability to adapt to the local culture and needs, identifying and assessing community needs, setting a priority on which needs will be addressed... changing when the local community changes.

9. ***Utilizes Giftedness of Others***: Ability to discern, develop, and deploy people to do ministry according to their unique gifts and graces.

10. ***Flexible and Adaptable***: Ability to adjust to change and ambiguity, shift priorities when necessary, and handle multiple tasks at once.

11. ***Build Group Cohesiveness***: Enables the group to work cooperatively toward a common goal and skillfully handles divisiveness and disunifying elements to positive resolutions. Getting people on the same page and keeping them on the same page. Managing conflict, and helping them work through differences in perspective and priorities.

12. ***Demonstrates Resilience***: Ability to sustain oneself emotionally and physically through setbacks, losses, disappointments, and failures. "Bounce back" ability. Resilience is when you come roaring back after disappointment, loss or set backs.

13. ***Exercises Faith***: Demonstrates how one's convictions are translated into personal and ministry decisions and possesses a vital spirituality.

†††

NOTE: This article reflects the personal opinions of the author and does not necessarily reflect an official position of Discipleship Ministries or Path 1..

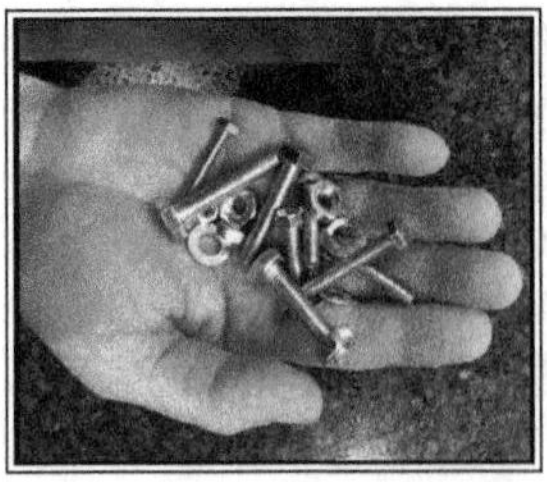

New Church Handbook
Nuts & Bolts for Planting New Churches In The Wesleyan Tradition

"8 Great Essentials for Spiritual Pioneers"

"Roehl's Great Eight"
by Tim Roehl

Tim Roehl has condensed Charles Ridley's 13 core competencies (see previous article) into eight essentials for spiritual pioneers.

Both Roehl's and Ridley's most important truth is when it comes to evaluating the essentials: **'The best indicator of future performance is past behavior."**

1. *CHARACTER*
   - Strong consistent walk with God. Deep prayer life.
   - Sticks to commitments even under tough circumstances. Perseveres Bounces back after setbacks.
   - Strong sense of call.
   - Spiritual gifts 'package' that includes leadership, faith, discernment, evangelism.

2. *CASTS VISION*
   - Communicates vision in an inspiring and practical manner.
   - Can 'see' into the future with faith.
   - Creates and initiates projects from the ground up.

3. *CAPACITY FOR EFFECTIVENESS* ***(some would say excellence)***
   - Self-starter and self-managed - strong need to achieve.
   - Strong work ethic.
   - Strives for excellence.

4. *CREATES OWNERSHIP OF MINISTRY*
   - Recruits, coaches and delegates effectively.
   - Reproduction mindset - develops an ever widening circle of reproducing leaders and groups
   - Releases others into ministry - assesses gifts, equips wisely.
   - Receptive to other's ideas - flexible, yet builds group cohesion and agenda harmony around the vision.

 © 2018 Robert O. Crossman, www.UMNewChurch.org

5. *COOPERATION OF SPOUSE AND FAMILY*
   - 'Heart agreement' about roles and expectations in ministry.
   - Healthy family life.
   - Helped by strong support system of family and friends.

6. *CONSTRUCTIVE, COMPASSIONATE PEOPLE SKILLS*
   - Appreciates and accepts a wide variety of people, able to respond with compassion with needs arise.
   - Approachable and active in developing relationships.
   - Able to handle conflict constructively and deal with difficult people.

7. *CONSISTENT FRUITFULNESS*
   - Consistently develops relationships with unchurched people.
   - Continual evidence of people coming to Christ.
   - Church planting and church growth mindset - sees evangelism as essential.

8. *COMMUNITY RESPONSIVE, CULTURALLY RELEVANT MINISTRY MINDSET*
   - Studies local community - understands the needs and opportunities.
   - Starts ministries that meet needs in the community.
   - 'Seen' in the community as a positive influence.
   - Strategic intercession practiced intentionally.

NOTE: This article reflects the personal opinions of the author and does not necessarily reflect an official position of Discipleship Ministries or Path 1..

Tim Roehl grew up in Sleepy Eye, Minnesota. His pastoral ministry has included planting Christ Life Evangelical Church in suburban Minneapolis; a "restart" in urban Milwaukee, Wisconsin; Lead Coach for the Church Multiplication Training Center; Director of Harvest Ministries for The Evangelical Church; Director of Church Health and Multiplication for The Wesleyan Church; and currently Director of Training and Development for One Mission Society.
He is the author of "Surprised by Grace: Twelve Stories of Lives Changed," TransforMissional Coaching: Empowering Leaders in a Changing Ministry World," "The Day that Changed Forever: Twenty One Life Changing Experiences at the Cross," "Fit and Flourish: Discover How God Created You to Make a Difference," and "Game Plan: Developing Intentional Missional Ministry,"

http://timroehl.net/home/
TimRoehl@usfamily.net

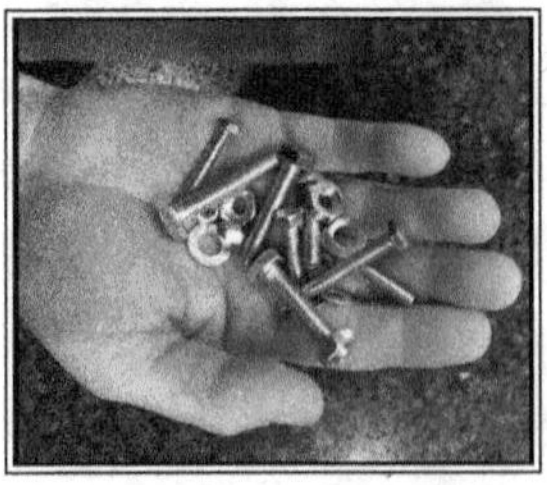

New Church Handbook
Nuts & Bolts for Planting New Churches In The Wesleyan Tradition

"17 Questions to Ask Yourself Before Requesting an Appointment to Plant a New Church"

1. Is my primary motivation for considering planting a new church a positive one *(such as the Glory of God and the salvation of people)* and not dissatisfaction with my present situation? __ Yes __No __Not Sure

2. Is there objective evidence that I am comfortable relating well with pre-Christians and effectively inviting them to make a public profession of faith and to begin the journey toward Christian Discipleship? __ Yes __No __Not Sure

3. Can I identify numerous people who have made professions of faith and are still growing as Disciples of Christ as a result of my witness?

   __ Yes __No __Not Sure

4. Have I *(and spouse, if married)* had enough exposure to church planting events *(such as New Church Leadership Institute, Boot Camp, Launch Pad, Exponential, and Conference Co-hort),* and by meeting with new church pastors in the field, so that I know what the new church planter's life is like?

   __ Yes __No __Not Sure

5. Is my spouse (if married) and family supportive, and even enthusiastic, about starting a new church? __ Yes __No __Not Sure

6. Am I assured of God's call on my life to plant a new church planting, instead serving an existing church? __ Yes __No __Not Sure

7. Do I have the necessary training needed to do church planting effectively?

   __ Yes __No __Not Sure

8. Can I clearly list my gifts and personal characteristics that would make me effective in planting a church in the type of mission field I'm considering?

   __ Yes __No __Not Sure

9. Do I have the personal spiritual disciplines and integrity necessary for being a spiritual leader above reproach? __ Yes __No __Not Sure

 © 2018 Robert O. Crossman, www.UMNewChurch.org

10. Is there objective evidence that I have the self-management disciplines *(work ethic, consistency, honesty, keeping appointments, etc.)* that will encourage followers to trust my leadership? __ Yes __No __Not Sure

11. Have I developed a relatively comprehensive vision *(values, mission, core beliefs, philosophy of ministries, gathering strategies, etc.)* of the kind of church I feel God is calling me to plant? __ Yes __No __Not Sure

12. Have I developed a relatively comprehensive discipleship system for leading inquirers into the faith and to begin a lifelong journey toward mature Christian Discipleship? __ Yes __No __Not Sure

13. Am I considered a "people person," and someone who is a good listener, teachable, coachable, patient and winsome? __ Yes __No __Not Sure

14. Do I have a track record of increasing worship attendance during my appointment - people tend to sit-up, listen and come back when I preach - giving evidence that my preaching and communication gifts are above average?

__ Yes __No __Not Sure

15. Do spiritually wise, influential people in my life tell me that church planting is right for me? __ Yes __No __Not Sure

16. Do I have a positive track record, giving strong evidence of my ability both to lead people and to raise up leaders? __ Yes __No __Not Sure

17. Do I have a positive track record of personally giving 10% of my income to the church offering (the tithe)? __ Yes __No __Not Sure

18. Is church planting compatible with my personal career goals, or is it merely a 'stepping stone' to some other ministry in the future?

__ Yes __No __Not Sure

AM I A CHURCH PLANTER?

__ If you answered 14 or more with a 'yes' - probably so.
__ If you answered 8 to 13 with a 'yes' - think, pray and talk to your spiritual leaders before deciding.
__ If you answered less than 8 with a 'yes' - possibly not.

†††

NOTE: This article reflects the personal opinions of the author and does not necessarily reflect an official position of Discipleship Ministries or Path 1.

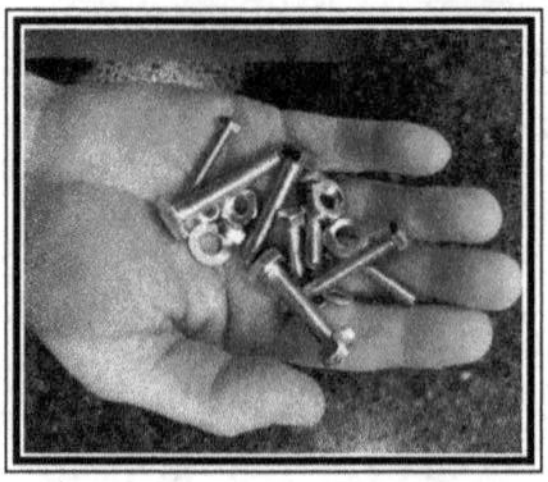

New Church Handbook
Nuts & Bolts for Planting New Churches In The Wesleyan Tradition

Personal Inventory:

Am I A Church Planter?
Do I have the Gifts & Graces to Be A Planter?

by George Howard

**Rate yourself on a scale of 1 to 5
with 1 meaning that particular trait is not descriptive of you,
and 5 meaning it is highly descriptive of you.
Please circle the appropriate number.**

*You might be interested to know if
your family, friends, colleagues, or church members would 'rate' you the same?*

1 2 3 4 5 Committed to the mission and the ministry of the United Methodist Church.

1 2 3 4 5 Understand the Primary Task of the church as "Making Disciples of Jesus Christ."

1 2 3 4 5 Good communicator with a willingness to talk about Jesus.

1 2 3 4 5 Articulate the Gospel in ways his/her constituents can connect with life's experience.

1 2 3 4 5 Able to move comfortably in the cultural setting where the new church start is to be located.

1 2 3 4 5 Highly energetic and confident.

1 2 3 4 5 Entrepreneur - innovative and self-starter.

1 2 3 4 5 Understanding and commitment to small group ministry.

1 2 3 4 5 Demonstrated ability to develop and implement a plan.

1 2 3 4 5 Adapts herself/himself well institutions which require constant change.

1 2 3 4 5 Visionary - envisions the direction and goals for the church.

 © 2018 Robert O. Crossman, www.UMNewChurch.org

1 2 3 4 5 Spouse *(if married)*, primary friends, and family have understanding and support for the unique challenges facing a new church start.

1 2 3 4 5 Physical appearance and style appropriate to the particular setting where the new church will be located.

1 2 3 4 5 Spiritually centered and respected as a person with integrity.

1 2 3 4 5 Personal history of giving at least a tithe (10%) of income to the church offering.

1 2 3 4 5 Ability to think in business terms:
i.e. banking, architecture, organization, finance.

1 2 3 4 5 Strategic thinker.

1 2 3 4 5 Friendly, outgoing and a sense of humor.

1 2 3 4 5 Optimistic and persistent.

1 2 3 4 5 Demonstrated ability to develop ministry qualitatively and quantitatively.

1 2 3 4 5 Committed to leadership development and to team ministry.

Reflect on the group of items you marked with a '1' or a '2' and contrast with the group of items you marked with a '4' or '5.' What might these groupings reveal about your potential to be a fruitful new church planter?

If you asked family, friends, colleagues and church members to 'rate' you, what did you learn from their marks on this inventory.

To what degree do you believe this inventory might be an accurate indicator of your gifts and graces for fruitful church planting?

†††

This Personal Inventory was designed by George Howard when he was the Congregational Developer for the West Ohio Conference of the United Methodist Church.

NOTE: This article reflects the personal opinions of the author and does not necessarily reflect an official position of Discipleship Ministries or Path 1.

© 2018 Robert O. Crossman, www.UMNewChurch.org

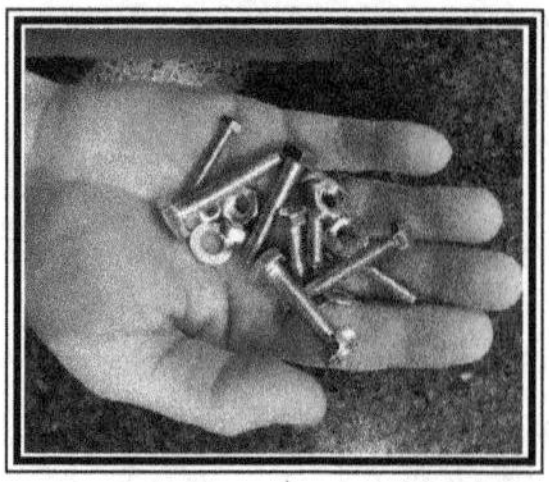

New Church Handbook
Nuts & Bolts for Planting New Churches In The Wesleyan Tradition

Do I Have the Characteristics, Competencies, Gifts and Graces for New Church Planting?

by Kevin Kloster

Reprinted with permission of the author on April 2, 2017.

We're embarking on a new yet familiar path. A path that leads to starting new United Methodist churches throughout the United States. Starting new churches is part of our biblical and United Methodist heritage. At our healthiest, we used to start one new church a day. We are seeking to do that again. We've made some great strides along the way and have successfully started many new churches who are now walking with people in their discipleship journey.

You may wonder why we need new churches when we have so many existing churches that have plenty of room. Some of those existing churches are no longer in the places where the people are. Some of those existing churches no longer resemble the communities in which they are located. Still others are at the end of their natural life cycle. As the United States population grows and shifts we need to start new churches just to be where the people are. Every day people are moving into the United States, people of various ethnicities and cultures. There are 195 million unchurched or dechurched people making the U.S. the third largest mission field in the English-speaking world and the fifth largest globally. These people need to know Jesus and the message of his grace and love. Romans 10:15 says, *"How beautiful are the feet of those who bring good news!"* The United Methodist Church is on a path to bring the good news to more people, more diverse people, more young people. We are creating new places for new generations through starting new congregations.

God is raising up new leaders who will join us on this journey of starting new United Methodist Churches across the United States. **It may be that God is calling you to step onto the path and join the journey.** God is already calling some people to be church planters, to go where the people are, and to lead them to Christ. God is calling some people to pray for church planters and new church starts as they emerge. Others are being called to support this incredible mission of starting new churches by giving generously. God is calling others to become members of a new church start and to use their gifts and resources to help make disciples for Jesus Christ whose new found faith will transform the world. God is also calling churches to multiply themselves. Wouldn't it be incredible if every healthy church started a new congregation that reached new people? Think of how many people we could reach. This is our mission. This is the path we are on.

This brief quiz will help you learn more about how you can step onto the path and join the journey already in progress.

 © 2018 Robert O. Crossman, www.UMNewChurch.org

This brief quiz is designed to help you discover if you possess the most common characteristics of successful church planters.

Instructions: Respond to the following statements according to the scale below marking the number that best describes you.

1=Strongly Disagree 2=Disagree 3=Undecided 4=Agree 5=Strongly Agree

1. I am passionate about starting business, projects and ministries from scratch
   1 2 3 4 5

2. I effectively communicate a vision in a manner so that people follow my lead
   1 2 3 4 5

3. I am a person of high energy and vitality.
   1 2 3 4 5

4. I effectively handle a demanding schedule with significant responsibility.
   1 2 3 4 5

5. I consistently give away responsibility to others.
   1 2 3 4 5

6. I coach others to develop their greatest potential.
   1 2 3 4 5

7. I lead persons to Christ and have helped them assimilate into a church.
   1 2 3 4 5

8. I consistently build relationships with unchurched people and can often be found on their turf.
   1 2 3 4 5

I have a fiance or spouse? (if no, skip next 2 questions)

9. My partner understands the toll church planting takes on a relationship
   1 2 3 4 5

10. My partner and I have a solid, trusting relationship.
    1 2 3 4 5

11. People tell me I have excellent people skills: great communicator, good listener, warm, friendly, and engaging.
    1 2 3 4 5

12. I develop strong social networks and start new relationships.
    1 2 3 4 5

13. I read extensively and attend training in the area of church planting.
1 2 3 4 5

14. I have a track record that demonstrates growth in the ministries, businesses and/or programs that I have started.
1 2 3 4 5

15. I can effectively design programs and ministries that successfully meet the needs of their targeted community.
1 2 3 4 5

16. I have repeatedly demonstrated the ability to assess and understand a community.
1 2 3 4 5

17. I recruit people to serve in areas that they are gifted instead of just finding people to fill ministry positions.
1 2 3 4 5

18. I help people discover their own spiritual gifts.
1 2 3 4 5

19. I successfully manage multiple tasks and responsibilities at the same time.
1 2 3 4 5

20. I refocus to make mid-course corrections during times of change and ambiguity.
1 2 3 4 5

21. I use small groups that multiply themselves to provide care and discipleship.
1 2 3 4 5

22. I consistently and assertively deal with conflict to resolve issues quickly.
1 2 3 4 5

23. I seek out help from others during times of crisis.
1 2 3 4 5

24. I quickly bounce back after facing times of discouragement.
1 2 3 4 5

25. I take significant risks believing that God will work things for the good.
1 2 3 4 5

26. I practice the spiritual disciplines to remain spiritually healthy.
1 2 3 4 5

 © 2018 Robert O. Crossman, www.UMNewChurch.org

So, am I a Church Planter?
Scoring: Add the score for each question, then divide by 2.

A score of 50-65:

Yes, you may indeed have the characteristics of a church planter. We would encourage you to continue your training to learn more about church planting. Talk and pray with members of your cabinet, board of congregational development, and spiritual advisors.

A score of 35-49:

You may *or may not* have the characteristics of a church planter. We would encourage you to continue your training to learn more about church planting. Talk and pray with members of your cabinet, board of congregational development, and spiritual advisors.

A score of under 34:

More than likely you do not possess the common characteristics of a church planter. This doesn't mean you aren't a good pastor or that you can't continue to learn more about church planting or even be involved in some role of a new church start. In fact, we would encourage you to continue to learn and grow in your knowledge of church planting because you can become a needed ally and person of support for creating new places for new generations.

This article is reprinted here with permission of the author, Kevin Kloster, granted on April 2, 2017.

Kevin's pastoral ministry has included appointments to plant two new churches. He is currently District Superintendent of the Prairie Hills District in the Dakotas Annual Conference.

†††

NOTE: This article reflects the personal opinions of the author and does not necessarily reflect an official position of Discipleship Ministries or Path 1.

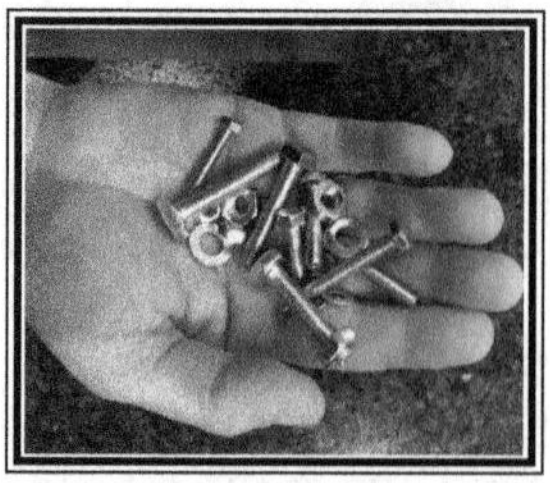

New Church Handbook
Nuts & Bolts for Planting New Churches In The Wesleyan Tradition

"Themes Present In Effective New Church Pastors"

**By the Reformed Church in America
The Gallup Organization**

Purpose

*The following traits **ARE** present in effective new church pastors.*

- Have an empowering mission to serve God and humanity.
- Dream of great accomplishment and express their dreams with significant goals and aspirations.
- Are able to block out distractions and stick with tasks and behaviors that lead to fulfillment of the dream.
- Have an awareness of others who have already accomplished great things in similar missions, and consciously use those persons as models.

*The following 'low' traits are **NOT** present in effective new church pastors.*

- *Tend to see work as an accumulation of tasks.*
- *Work hard to do a good job of unnecessary things.*
- *Limited ability to provide a sense of direction for own life or life of organization.*

Ego Drive

*The following traits **ARE** present in effective new church pastors.*

- Comfortable with the personal significance derived from a visible leadership role.
- High level of self-knowledge.
- Comfortable with a desire to be recognized as a significant contributor to the mission (average clergy is ambivalent/negative toward ego drive).
- Require a large amount of space and freedom to achieve significant things for the mission.

*The following 'low' traits are **NOT** present in effective new church pastors.*

- May strive to be the best they can, but will be limited in ability to reach for a standard of excellence as understood by experts or "consumers" in the field.
- Will need more direct supervision, are less able to claim significant goals, more difficult to motivate.
- Ability to motivate others may be affected by lack of confidence.

© 2018 Robert O. Crossman, www.UMNewChurch.org

Achiever

*The following traits **ARE** present in effective new church pastors.*

- Continually challenges themselves to set and meet goals.
- A strong sense of competitive urge, and enjoys the energy it provides.
- Want to be known as the best in their profession and compare their work to the performance of others.
- Get more done.
- Competition, excellence in execution and high levels of performance are distinguishing marks (qualities not often found in pastoral profession).

*The following 'low' traits are **NOT** present in effective new church pastors.*

- May find if difficult to do work in significant quality or quantity.
- May have trouble "self-starting," difficult to motivate.

Relator

*The following traits **ARE** present in effective new church pastors.*

- Believes in having close relationships with staff/members.
- Understand the importance of close relationships to success of mission.
- Demonstrate a very accepting, non-judgmental attitude.
- Ability to empathize can bring tears of joy or pain.
- Honor people's feelings and internationalize efforts to get to know them personally.

*The following 'low' traits are **NOT** present in effective new church pastors.*

- Will have limited success in using own talents to get people excited about ministry.
- Can be experienced as "stand-offish."

People Management

*The following traits **ARE** present in effective new church pastors.*

- Outstanding people managers because of their ability to see and respond to persons as unique individuals.
- Likes to recognize the gifts of others and develop them to benefit mission.
- Set others up for success, and provide lots of recognition.
- Know what motivates people and how best to give them recognition.
- Described as fair, encouraging, and supportive.

*The following 'low' traits are **NOT** present in effective new church pastors.*

- Limited success in setting people up for success.
- Limited in ability to manage persons as individuals.
- Restricts ability to match talent to task in delegation and reward/recognition to motivation in attempts to encourage and reward others.

Activator

*The following traits **ARE** present in effective new church pastors.*

- Always ready to make things happen in a variety of ways.
- Disciplined people who "plan their work and work their plan."
- Able to seize unexpected opportunity.
- Look for bright/energetic people as partners.
- Encourage others through a demonstration of faith in them.
- Demonstrate the capacity to act, even against accepted norms.
- Show a positive attitude toward the acquisition of wealth, seeing it as a way to increase action.

*The following 'low' traits are **NOT** present in effective new church pastors.*

- Limited in ability to behave in ways that model "faith in action" and in ways that stimulate others to act.
- Serendipity is "short suit."

Command

*The following traits **ARE** present in effective new church pastors.*

- Enjoy the ability to change others to their point of view.
- Does not play the role of a meek and mild person within their family.
- Beginning in childhood, experiences the need to take charge in various situations.
- Steps forward to direct people to action.
- Courage to do and say things many others would find intimidating.

*The following 'low' trait is **NOT** present in effective new church pastors.*

- Limited in capacity to be persuasive or to assert a course of action and see it through resistance and difficulty.

Business Thinking

*The following traits **ARE** present in effective new church pastors.*

- Measures progress with specific scores and goals.
- Exhibits good business judgement in work and personal life.
- Experience in starting a new organization, having served in a leadership role.
- Disciplined in time management, decision making, financial decisions and understand how this discipline supports effectiveness.
- Entrepreneurial and astute in organizational issues.

*The following 'low' traits are **NOT** present in effective new church pastors.*

- Believes great achievements are being made, but actually they are not.
- Limited ability to accomplish the financial and business sides of church development.

© 2018 Robert O. Crossman, www.UMNewChurch.org

Concept

*The following traits **ARE** present in effective new church pastors.*

- Ability to conceptualize the steps necessary to reach goals, and understands the relationship of personal discipline to the effectiveness of their effort.
- Ability to articulate an organized view of church planting process.
- Ability to tolerate ambiguity and view learning as an on-going process.
- Have a positive view of unchurched people.
- Enjoy expressing theories that make both themselves and others better practitioners.

*The following 'low' traits are **NOT** present in effective new church pastors.*

- Limited in ability to manage the sequenced process of organizational development.
- Limited ability to prioritize and manage time in personal and professional life.

†††

NOTE: This article reflects the personal opinions of the author and does not necessarily reflect an official position of Discipleship Ministries or Path 1.

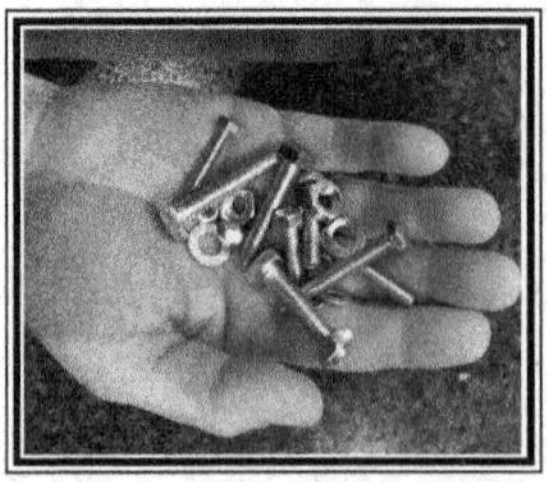

New Church Handbook
Nuts & Bolts for Planting New Churches In The Wesleyan Tradition

"Pastoral Leadership for New Churches"

Adapted from *Growing New Churches*, by Steve Compton

The selection of the right pastor for a new congregation is perhaps the single most important factor in the success or failure of a new church start. Each new church start is unique; therefore, it is critical that the pastor's particular gifts and graces be well matched to the new churches unique situation. The following are a few of the characteristics needed in every new church start.

While not intended to be exhaustive, the list marks the direction and pattern of growth for the pastor and, thus, serves as a guideline for those charged with the responsibility of pastor selection.

1. A new church pastor is ***VISIONARY.***
   The pastor must be able to clearly articulate:
   - A personal vision for life.
   - A personal vision for ministry.
   - A shared vision with the congregation.

   Seeing the vision and keeping it before the people and the community is critical. The ability to dream and envision what God would have a group of people do to transform the lives of individuals and to transform the community into a closer resemblance of the kingdom of God is critical for a new church pastor.

2. A new church pastor must be ***SPIRITUALLY CENTERED***.
   A new church pastor must believe that she/he is called to start a new church. New church pastors face some unique pressures:
   - Lack of adequate resources.
   - Peer jealousy.
   - No traditional accommodations (church and home).
   - Confused denominational expectations.
   - Threat to existing congregations in the area.
   - No core leadership group.
   - Little contact with others in the same type of ministry.

   In addition to the normal pressures of ministry, these particular concerns make it imperative that new church pastors practice the spiritual disciplines that will keep them centered and focused.

 © 2018 Robert O. Crossman, www.UMNewChurch.org

3. A new church pastor is ***ENTREPRENEURIAL.***
   This word literally means to undertake or to find another way when all other solutions seem to be blocked! The entrepreneurial pastor is one who is constantly looking for ways to make things work and never accepts "no" as a final answer.

4. A new church pastor needs to be ***FRIENDLY, OUTGOING***, and ***SHOULD HAVE A SENSE OF HUMOR***.
   The new church pastor must feel comfortable knocking on the doors of strangers, getting involved in the community, and have an outlook on life that can laugh them through the difficult times.

5. A new church pastor is ***ENERGETIC.***
   A high level of commitment and energy is required. Persons who are unwilling to give an extra measure of time to this work will probably be in regular conflict with themselves and others over the job at hand. The new church pastor must be a self-starter, able to set his or her own performance goals, objectives, and standards.

6. A new church pastor must be a ***STRONG ADMINISTRATOR***.
   A new church pastor must be competent and capable or handling the regular administrative duties of a growing congregation, while not confusing administration with leadership. New church pastors must be well read and informed.

7. A new church pastor is ***OPTIMISTIC*** and ***PERSISTENT.***
   There are many obstacles involved in starting a new church (reaching new people, finding a place to meet, securing financial resources, purchasing land, building facilities, recruiting volunteers and staff, etc.), and congregations will take their cue from the pastor. If the pastor is easily discouraged, the congregation will be easily discouraged. Likewise, if the pastor remains optimistic, hope and confidence will be conveyed to the congregation. The pastor may need help and encouragement. Modeling patience and hope is an important element of successful new church pastorates.

8. A new church pastor is a ***GOOD COMMUNICATOR***.
   A new church pastor must be an excellent preacher, innovative as well as captivating. Sermons need to be relevant, interesting, and challenging. Sermons must capture and maintain people's attention. Competent communication skills are also important for written materials.

9. A new church pastor is ***SELF-CONFIDENT.***
   Positive self-esteem is a must. A new church start can be a very lonely and demanding ministry. It takes a person who feels very positive about to make it through the long haul of leading a congregation through change.

10. A new church pastor is ***HEALTHY*** and ***WELL-MATCHED TO THE COMMUNITY***.

11. A new church pastor is committed to a ***LONG PASTORATE***.
A long pastoral tenure is almost always associated with congregations that are showing growth and vitality in their ministries. A long pastorate enables a congregation to follow through on long-range plans and goals. To stay at a growing new church start, the pastor must be willing to learn different leadership styles and change as the situation changes.

Summary

While no one person embodies all of these traits, a person who is deeply committed to being the pastor of a new church start can develop varying levels of competence in these characteristics with effort and determination.

On the other hand, persons who display only a few of these characteristics, or who are unwilling to work on areas where noticeable deficits are apparent, can avoid grief and unhappiness by focusing on another area of ministry.

A new church start is not for every pastor!

The secret of any successful ministry is finding the right person for the right job.

This article is reprinted here with the permission of the author, Steve Compton, given on August 21, 2017.

†††

NOTE: This article reflects the personal opinions of the author and does not necessarily reflect an official position of Discipleship Ministries or Path 1.

 © 2018 Robert O. Crossman, www.UMNewChurch.org

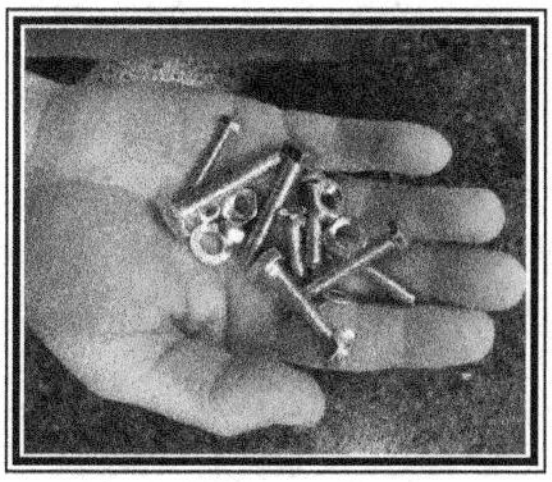

New Church Handbook
Nuts & Bolts for Planting New Churches In The Wesleyan Tradition

"Affirmation of Good Moral Character"

"Pastors must also have a good reputation with outsiders, so that they will not fall into disgrace..." I Timothy 3:7

Are there any of the following actions in your past that, if they came to light, would have a negative impact on your new church plant? If so, you may decide that pursuing planting a new church may not be appropriate at this time. If you have questions or concerns about any item below, please contact your conference director of new church starts to discuss the situation.

Crimes against the person
- Assault
- Battery
- Bigamy
- Child abuse
- Child Pornography
- Criminal negligence
- False imprisonment
- Felony sexual offences
- Home invasion
- Homicide
- Kidnapping
- Manslaughter, Murder
- Negligent homicide
- Neglect or exploitation (*of child, aged persons or disabled adults)*
- Public indecency
- Rape
- Robbery
- Sexual assault
- Vehicular homicide

Crimes against property
- Arson
- Blackmail
- Bribery
- Burglary
- Embezzlement
- Extortion
- False pretenses
- Fraud *(financial, medical, corporate)*
- Larceny
- Pick pocketing
- Possessing stolen property
- Robbery
- Scams or confidence tricks
- Smuggling
- Tax evasion
- Theft

Criminal Acts
- Adultery
- Creation of Obscenity
- Creation of Pornography
- Felony drug abuse
- Felony sale controlled substances
- Inappropriate internet texting
- Indecent exposure
- Lewd and lascivious behavior
- Perpetrator Incest
- Prostitution
- Perpetrator of domestic violence

Or, any other actions in your past that, if they came to light, would have a negative impact on your new church plant.

__**I HAVE** questions or concerns about one or more items above.

__**I DO NOT HAVE** questions or concerns about any of the items above.

Signed ________________________________ Date ________________

NOTE: This article reflects the personal opinions of the author and does not necessarily reflect an official position of Discipleship Ministries or Path 1.

© 2018 Robert O. Crossman, www.UMNewChurch.org

New Church Handbook
Nuts & Bolts for Planting New Churches In The Wesleyan Tradition

"What Are Some Traits of High Potential Planters?"

by Path 1

Few people will possess all of the traits listed below. People who possess seven or more of these traits may have the gifts and graces to be a high potential planters.

Traits marked below with an * can be nurtured by The United Methodist Church through our intentional investment, mentoring and grooming in the years, prior to a planting appointment.

1. **Something in their experience of God drives them to the edge of settled church life to want to reach new people for the kingdom.**
   This trait may get them labeled as non-conformists or problem children in a connectional appointive system, even if they are loyal United Methodists. They may be unusually impatient with business as usual in UMC life. They have apostolic zeal. They have led unchurched persons to Christ.

2. **They have history in at least one vibrant, growing church, possibly in a previous healthy new church start.***
   To know intuitively what a great church feels like and to know what is normal for growing ministries that are evangelizing people are invaluable experiences for a new church planter.

3. **They are self aware.**
   They understand their gifts and talents, personality traits, strengths and weaknesses. They are comfortable in their own skin. They strive for balance in their personal lives and in their relationships with family and friends.

4. **They have a coachable spirit.***
   Often, a successful planter or pastor has mentored them on her/his staff. When such a mentor endorses their readiness, they will very seldom fail. They continually strive for personal and professional growth and development.

5. **They have affinity for the mission field.***
   They know the territory where they are planting and really love it. They have often lived in the community or in very similar communities or have had previous experiences in getting to know the community, so they begin with good instincts. If not, they team with such people.

© 2018 Robert O. Crossman, www.UMNewChurch.org

6. **They already have a network of relationships in the community where they will be planting.***

    These relationships may be largely within the context of a sponsoring or partnering church where they have served on staff for a time before leaving to plant. They may have gone to school in the community.

7. **They and their spouse are at peace and unified about the ministry of new church development and they have embraced the sacrifices entailed.**

    New church projects are hard on marriages. Marriages that break early in the plant jeopardize the future of the new church.

8. **Their age at time of appointment is no more than ten years above the median age for the new population being targeted.**

    People can plant churches at any age, but good statistical evidence suggests that the age window from 25 to 45 is ideal for a planter on the front end of a project, especially if we want them to attract young adults with children. Older planters assigned to projects may have more difficulty understanding and relating to young adult culture and they may sometimes come with prohibitively high salary price tags.

9. **They demonstrate a vibrant faith.***

    The landmark study of successful mainline planters detailed in the book Extraordinary Leaders for Extraordinary Times revealed that effective planters have a strong sense of calling, deeply established prayer habits, and keen understanding that church planting is a God thing.

10. **They have demonstrated history of building relationships in the community and leading these friends into church life.**

    The best test in assessing high-potential planters is past behavior. No behavior has more relevance than past experience leading unchurched people to Christ and/or to church.

11. **They are catalytic innovators.**

    They have a history of leading successful start-ups. This relates to the "entrepreneurial gene" typically found in good planters. It almost always has evidenced itself prior to the church plant. In earlier life they may have started a small business, grown a youth ministry, led a major initiative in their college sorority or a guided a social justice project, mobilizing diverse parties from across the community. They may have started a church before and be ready to do it again.

12. **They are competent vision-casters.***

    Though styles and cultural norms vary across racial-ethnic groups, high-potential prospects are good communicators, often able to deliver compelling talks without notes. Good planters typically look you in the eye, talk to you in plain language about real life and how Christ makes a difference and why this new church is the best thing since sliced bread. They come across to unchurched people as down to earth and relevant.

13. **They are deeply committed to The United Methodist Church.***
    They are willing to support The United Methodist Church and to plant a church which they eventually will give over to another pastor whom the bishop appoints.

Traits marked above with an * can be nurtured by The United Methodist Church through our intentional investment, mentoring and grooming in the years, prior to a planting appointment.

†††

Reprinted here by permission of Bener Agtarap granted on January 26, 2018.
Source: www.Path1.org

PATH1

This pdf file can be found on the Path 1 web site at:

www.umcdiscipleship.org/new-church-starts/planting

 © 2018 Robert O. Crossman, www.UMNewChurch.org

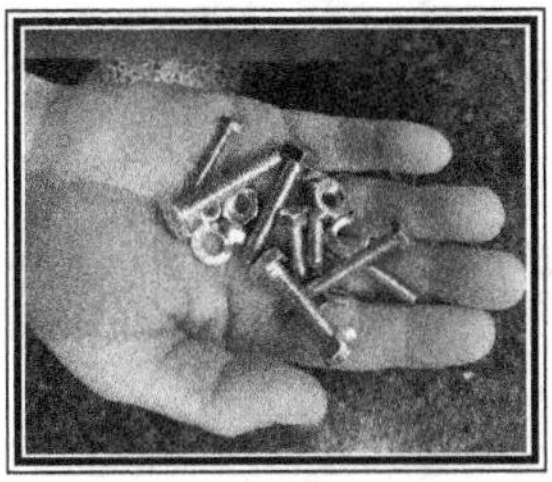

New Church Handbook
Nuts & Bolts for Planting New Churches In The Wesleyan Tradition

"Are There Any On-Line Assessments I Can Take?"

by Bob Crossman

Path 1 has a brief 26 question on-line assessment tool designed to help you determine if you possess the most essential characteristics typically found in high-potential church planters. Because no assessment tool of this type is definitive Path 1 recommends you participate in a more formal discernment process that includes an assessment interview.

Where to start:

1. Go to: www.umcdiscipleship.org/new-church-starts/assessment
2. Take the brief 26 question survey.
3. Click, "Get Your Results."

Path 1 has also partnered with Lifeway Research to offer The Church Planter Candidate Assessment. CPCA is a statistically validated online assessment instrument which helps potential church planters and their respective organizations identify areas of established strength and other areas needing development as they prepare to plant a church.

What traits should a church planter have? Are there discernible personal qualities evident among those who have planted successfully? LifeWay Research endeavored to discover the skills and mindsets common among the most proven church planters. What resulted were specific, measurable characteristics which were consistent among those who have had success in planting churches.

Where to start:

1. Go to **http://churchplanter.lifeway.com**
2. Listen to the two minute video clip of Ed Stetzer introducing the Church Planter Candidate Assessment (CPCA)

Church Planters

1. Determine if you are taking the CPCA as an individual or at the request of your annual conference.
2. Purchase survey.
   At the present time the survey only cost $29 when you select that you are United Methodist, and then select your annual conference from the list.
3. Register, log in and take survey.
4. Results are shared with the individual and with their organization when applicable.

Your Annual Conference may also ask you to take the Profile XT, DISC, and Strength Finders in their assessment process.

†††

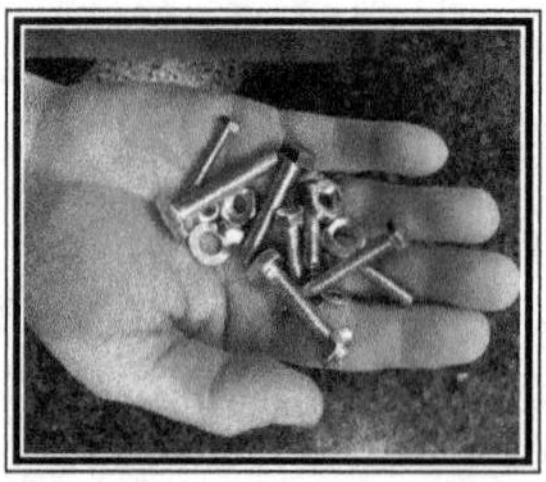

New Church Handbook
Nuts & Bolts for Planting New Churches In The Wesleyan Tradition

"What's All The Talk About Affinity?"

by Bob Crossman

"Affinity" refers to the spontaneous or natural liking for someone. In a church planting perspective, it's not who the planter likes, but rather who naturally and spontaneously likes the planter.

In church planting, we use the word "affinity" as part of a fundamental assumption that every prospective planter can NOT start a church in every context with equal effectiveness.

Your annual conference has the responsibility to know both the prospective planter and the context of the church plant in sufficient detail to determine the probable degree of affinity between the two.

The first 40 to 100 people who decide to be part of a new church, are frequently attracted to that church because of a natural affinity to the planting pastor. If they don't "like" the pastor, they will not even visit once, much less become active there. After the church has reached 100 or more active adults, the focus is not so much on the planting pastor. At that point people will become involved because their best friend is active, or they enter through the youth or music or sports or mission aspects of the church - perhaps before they have even met the pastor.

If my annual conference discovered a mission field in Arkansas where a significant portion of the population has a natural spontaneous attraction to things "Cowboy" such as horses, cattle, trail rides, barrel racing, Cattlemen's Association, boots & cowboy hats. In looking for a potential planter to start a new church in that mission field – I would NOT be the one the Bishop should deploy to plant that church.

While I have an admiration for horsemanship, I have no experience, history, or interest in the lifestyle and activities. Arriving in that mission field, the residents could tell from a mile away that I was an "alien" in that environment.

You, on the other hand may have grown up on a ranch, your parents were members of the cattlemen's association, and as a youth you enjoyed trail rides, barrel racing, or roping. It might be that you would have a natural affinity to this particular mission field, and would have a greater chance of being accepted by the residents, and welcomed into their homes and lives.

 © 2018 Robert O. Crossman, www.UMNewChurch.org

In his article, *"Recruitment, Assessment, Training and Deployment of New Church Pastors"* Jim Griffith (www.griffithcoaching.com) offers another example that will illustrate what happens all-to-frequently in the assignment of church planters.

> *A 25-year-old planter from a small farming community in the mid-west who was raised in a lower-income blue-collar traditional family is appointed to a planting project designed to reach affluent professionals working in the downtown business district or a major city in the northeast.*

Jim concludes that it is *"unlikely that this planter will have a high degree of affinity for either the context or the target population for the new church. In fact, the degree of discomfort could be so great as to cause the planter to quickly become discouraged or even quit. Deployment issues are critical decisions, not minor details."*

Affinities that influence a church planter's effectiveness might include:

economic affinities
educational level
recreational interest
occupation
geographic preferences
social standing
religious background
age
life-stage
language
political views

There are exceptions. There are rare planters that are cross-cultural, and have a natural spontaneous affinity with people from diverse backgrounds from their own. There are also planters with diverse affinities - in whose early life experienced a government housing project and food stamps, but as a youth lived in a gated country club community with their grandparents.

Affinity isn't "everything" but it can have a major influence on a planter's fruitfulness in a particular mission field.

†††

NOTE: This article reflects the personal opinions of the author and does not necessarily reflect an official position of Discipleship Ministries or Path 1.

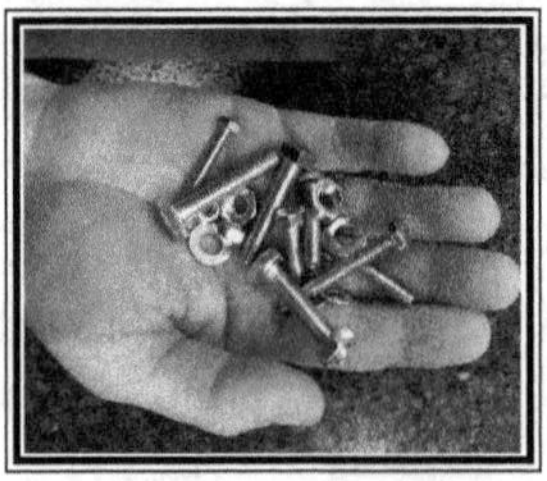

New Church Handbook
Nuts & Bolts for Planting New Churches In The Wesleyan Tradition

"What is a Self-Reflective Essay?"

by Bob Crossman

Some annual conferences ask potential new church planters to write a "Self-Reflective Essay" as part of the cabinet's discernment process to help decide who to deploy, and what mission field is most appropriate for that deployment.

Typically, this one page reflective essay should include these topics:

- Your Vision.
- Your Mission.
- Your Core Beliefs.
- Your Core Values.
- Summary of your affinity group.
- New church planting strategy that suits your profile. Why?
- Your optimal new church planting scenario. Why?
- Concerning your possible appointment to plant a new church:
  - what other conclusions have you made?
  - what questions remain for you?

If you have attended a "Launch Pad" event or the "Basic Training Boot Camp for Church Planters," the self-reflective essay may also address these additional subjects:

- Prepare a tentative budget for the first 24 months, including possible sources of income.
- Describe the critical benchmarks & priorities that need to be reached during the first 24 months.
- Describe the leadership characteristics needed to serve the targeted audience.
- Describe in detail your ministry plan for the first 6 months.
- Briefly describe your ministry plan for the second 6 months.
- (if married) List two measurable steps you are going to take to safeguard your relationship with your spouse and (if applicable) with your children.
- Describe the worship style most likely to appeal to the targeted audience.
- Describe the ministries most likely to appeal to the targeted audience.
- Any other information relevant to this particular situation.

 © 2018 Robert O. Crossman, www.UMNewChurch.org

In the appointment making process for a new church, it would be appropriate for this Reflective Essay to be reviewed by:

- The new church assessment team.
- The receiving district superintendent.
- The conference staff person who relates to new church starts or congregational advancement.
- The bishop and cabinet of your annual conference.
- If this is a multi-site, or the planting strategy includes a mother church, then the senior pastor of that mother church and perhaps its SPPR committee.
- It may also be appropriate for your ministry plan to be reviewed by the conference director of ethnic / multicultural ministries.

In a post-appointment / pre-moving day strategy session, you will work with the conference minister of new church starts and the district superintendent *(and mother church's senior pastor, if applicable)* to revise your ministry plan. **You will be held accountable to your ministry plan and the agreed upon benchmarks it contains.**

The following pages contain samples of Self Reflective Essays. Be sure and confirm with your District Superintendent or conference director of new church starts on the exact content and format they are requesting.

SAMPLE #1

Self Reflective Essay - New Church Leadership Institute

I don't remember having any "spoken" questions at our initial introductory meeting, but I know that the internal question that rolled through my mind was something like, "Is there a place for someone with my gifts and graces, and with my personality type in the life of the Baltimore Conference?" Being a driven person, and having experienced times of disappointment in my ministry journey, I have found a growing level of dissatisfaction with ministry in established churches that restrict creativity and leadership in its pastor, and seek only a maintenance engineer to keep what makes them comfortable afloat. I think this process has only intensified my understanding of my own discontent with "status quo ministry" while my personality type pushes me to be an innovator.

And speaking of personality types, my DiSC profile was that of a **Result-Oriented Pattern.** According to the classical profile, this means I am a person who is a quick thinker with self-confidence. I am determined, persistent and find my tolerance with the status quo to be very low. I am extremely competitive, and crave opportunities to be in first place, or to be the champion of the day, which is aided by the fact that I am not usually intimidated easily. Because I speak my mind clearly and directly, I have no trouble asserting my authority or ego strength. I know this also has some potential drawbacks, such as being impulsive at times, or acting too quickly before plans are thoroughly vetted. Because I am confident, this can sometimes come across as impatient or haughty. And I have experienced times when I have come across as blunt and uncaring, even though that wasn't my intended purpose. Fortunately, my ministry situations that have turned into "opportunities to grow" have been

Sample

greatly instructional in my character development, and by God's grace I have been working toward overcoming those flaws, or minimizing them as best as I am able.

As I assessed my strengths for church planting, I considered the four C's of Call, Character, Chemistry and Competencies.

In relation to my sense of Call, I am called to be a Pastor / Leader who leads the Church into the world to make disciples where others are afraid to go, and with those who have rejected the church. My calling is very focused in the direction of evangelism and disciple making, something I have excelled at in each of my appointments.

My Character attributes that fit me for church planting have been described above, but in addition, I would say that any character issues that might be a hindrance in this work I am seeking to engage, I have learned to compensate for. I have learned the importance of good team building, and my need to have people of other strengths work with me to overcome any areas I lack proficiency in.

In relation to my Chemistry (DNA): my core values are 1) to model Christian witness and discipleship in my personal and family life, 2) be relevant, 3) lead the Church as a servant, 4) model good financial stewardship, as well as stewardship of my time and talents, 5) give fully of myself to Christ. My personal vision for my future in ministry is to grow a church deeper into Christ, and wider in expansive ministry that reaches an ever broader part of the population, especially those who have been "de-churched;" all the while remaining relevant in communicating the truth of the Gospel and guiding the Church in living a missional and growth oriented life. My personal mission can be summarized, therefore, in this way: *Through my connection with God and the world, I will be relevant and real in my relationship with all God's people as I lead in faithful witness and life as disciples.*

My Competencies for doing the work of planting a new church include my driven, confident, competitive and task-oriented personality that is enhanced by my leadership style. It focuses on team building, discernment and system organization while constantly keeping the vision in front of everyone. I would consider my "world-view" to be that of a Post-Modern Christian who believes that God has given us abundant life through Christ – and we ought to be living out of that abundance, instead of living out of what we lack.

I think I would function best in an environment of middle to upper-middle class people with advanced educational degrees, who are eclectic in the spiritual dimension of their life. I like to lead God's people in experiencing a variety of traditions within the context of a single service of worship. I think a suburban setting is where my gifts are best utilized, but I am not opposed to exploring options in urban areas. My optimal new church start scenario is in a fast growing suburb where rapid growth and spiritual formation are valued instead of feared. I consider myself, as stated previously, to be a Post-Modern. As such, I don't believe the church is best served by a single style of worship or faith expression. This means I function best in a blended or "edgy-blended" environment (defined as one where the music and format of worship are more cutting edge, and the facility and dress more formal).

The church planting role, that I would fit in best, would be either as a modified "parachute drop" (give me some kind of team to start with please, even if it is from multiple churches), or a modified "mother-daughter" plant. Really these two could be seen as nearly the same, but the modified mother-daughter plant would mean all of my launch team comes from a single church. I think I could also work within a large local church that is wanting to start a "new kind" of worship service with a plan to birth that church after an extended period of

Sample

 © 2018 Robert O. Crossman, www.UMNewChurch.org

growth.

I would say the key word for me is "flexible." This is because I think I could plant a church in a multitude of circumstances, among a variety of different population groups, in varying manners; all depending on the needs of the mission field. My preferences would be to have a wide degree of leadership authority (modified "mother-daughter" or modified "parachute drop"), with the goal of creating a blended or edgy-blended community of believers with a vision for solid growth in numbers and relationship with Jesus Christ. I think my optimal church plant will use my gift for visionary leadership to start a church among a population of people who are proven to be unafraid of change, desiring unique spiritual expressions of the Christian faith to be practiced, and long to be engaged with the world in mission as we reach those who have been "de-churched," as well as those who have never been reached before.

Sample

In addition, I will add that my spouse has been very supportive of my ministry for the past 8 years. We have served as a true partnership in each of my ministry settings. My spouse is one of my greatest assets in planning and discovering new ministry ideas that will flourish. In fact, some of the ministries we started together in each of the places we have served still flourish to this day. Even more importantly, I think the idea of planting a church has been something God has been calling me to do since experiencing my initial call to ministry at age 11. I wasn't able to give voice to, or discern it well enough to understand that, but through time, discernment and experience I can see now how God has led me to a place where I am as prepared as I can be walk this next journey.

SAMPLE #2
Self – Reflective Essay

1. **Describe Your Affinity Group**
   - I feel the greatest affinity for the middle to upper middle class professional and blue-collar person(s) who live within corporate city limits.
   - I feel the greatest affinity for Northwest part of the state or the River Valley; however, the Southwest would be a possibility as well.
   - I do not relate well to rural, farming or factory only groups.
   - I desire to reach people within all groups with the gospel of Christ.
   - I also desire an ethnically diverse group where each group brings their heritage into the worship environment.
2. **What Questions Have Been Answered For You?**
   - I discovered what models the conference is going to endorse in starting a new church.
   - I am interested in the mother-daughter model of church planting but wish to have multiple mothers. I would like to pull resources from more than one church in a given area to start a new church.
   - The conversation with the whole district is important so each church feels some ownership or connection with the new church, which will help keep down an attitude of competition or surprise that could cause negative conversations or hostile attitudes from impacting a new start before it can begin to take off.
   - I have determined that starting a new church is more of a marathon than a sprint; however, I believe the first eighteen to twenty-four months are critical

for determining the success or failure of a new church.
- The person who is starting the new church must be focused and determined to accomplish the mission. This means the person must have a great passion for all people whom God created, and must have an equal passion for proclaiming the Gospel of Jesus Christ.
- The new church start pastor must also have a strong spiritual life to consist of prayer, devotion, and bible study. This person must also be surrounded with people who will encourage as well as keep accountable.

3. **What Questions Has This Process Raised For You?**
    - The major questions that I still have are: What is the financial commitment being made by the churches or the annual conference? How are those finances being distributed? How is the salary level determined for each pastor and positions as the need arises? Who determines staffing priorities and at what pace or level?
    - What impact can I expect a new church start to have on my family? I realize each family situation is different; however, I would like to meet or have testimonials from pastors who have done new church starts with similar family situations (two working professionals) and who have a successful track record, so my spouse and I can have some idea of what to expect for our family.
    - I presume I would be assigned a mentor or coach to work through some of these areas. I also presume we have an accountability method setup for financial accounting for new church start pastors.
    - I would need to see a proposed budget to insure I could hire someone like a music minister, as well as purchase the proper equipment necessary to begin a worship service, regardless of where that service might be held.
4. **What Conclusions Have You Drawn?**
    - I believe I have the gifts and graces for a new church start; however, there are some challenges and concerns, all of which can be addressed and overcome with careful attention.
    - I realize that I do not have to do a new church start and may not be the type of person the conference is looking for at this time.
    - Before I would be willing to do a new church start, I would have to see a budget and work with a group and coach to see what the conference vision for a particular area is.
    - I am aware I have weaknesses in some administrative areas, and for a while I can compensate by giving great attention to those areas; however, there are some gifts I do not possess, (i.e. music), which will require that I surround myself with persons who are strong in those areas.
    - Also, I have a family that I am not willing to sacrifice to start a new church, so I will need some idea on the time commitments during evening and weekend hours, which I know will be different than with an existing church.
5. **Describe your Best Case Church Planting Scenario**
    - Being able to work with an existing church (or multiple churches) in identifying

Sample

© 2018 Robert O. Crossman, www.UMNewChurch.org

individuals who have an entrepreneurial spirit, who have a passion for trying something new and who will invest their life into seeing an idea become a reality.

- I also, would want in this mix those who have been strong Methodist and committed to the tradition it brings to the community.
- Furthermore, I would want to identify a few people to serve on the focus design team who have not been churched.
- That community can meet in a school, home, storefront, in a park, or etc. The meeting place is not of great significance, it is the bringing of individuals together as a community to grow in faith and to be in a faithful journey that is critical.
- Providing a mixture of churched and un-churched alike will provide the eyes and ears needed to reach a diverse people with the gospel of Jesus Christ.

Sample

SAMPLE #3
Self – Reflective Essay

1. **Describe Your Affinity Group**
   - I believe my affinity group or mission field should be high school and college graduates in the middle class to upper middle class range.
   - In my former jobs and in working within the church, I find that I am able to get along with most people and have worked with people from different economic backgrounds. I also have worked well with people of color.
   - My best new start scenario would probably be somewhere between a daughter church and a parachute drop.
   - My steps would probably be: 1) start meeting the people in the target area, 2) establish a real presence in the target area, 3) start small groups meeting in the target area, 4) from the first day, be working with the launch team in planning for all of this, and 5) aim for worship beginning after 6 months.
2. **What Questions Have Been Answered For You?**
   - Through the New Church Leadership Institute I have leaned about the different methods of starting new churches and how these succeed or fail in different settings.
   - I have also learned that success depends on the new start pastor being spiritually sound, having a close personal relationship with Jesus Christ.
   - I know this is a lot of work.
   - I am one who thrives on challenges.
   - I have prayed about this and have turned it over to God. Either way, I will still be serving my Lord and Savior.
   - There are different methods of starting new churches, each good in the right place with the right person.
   - I have seen what others have done and had success at.
3. **What Questions Has This Process Raised For You?**
   - One thing I am still not sure of is exactly what role the conference will play, that is beyond the financial part.
4. **What Conclusions Have You Drawn?**

- I believe this is exciting and I have the gifts and graces to do it.
- Although there will be lots of work and long days, the new start pastor is not out there all alone. There will be support through a coach and the conference office.

5. **Describe your Best Case Church Planting Scenario**
   - My best new start scenario would probably be somewhere between a daughter church and a parachute drop.
   - The mission field would consist of people mainly from blue collar working families with high school and college educations.

SAMPLE #4
Self – Reflective Essay

1. **Describe Your Affinity Group**
   - The affinity group I relate to best is comprised of professionals and educators, young people, middle adult and retired people in Milwaukee, Wisconsin
   - My mission field is to non-Christians who have had some exposure to Christianity and a organized church. These are people who have not made a genuine profession of faith yet they are ripe for the harvest of the Kingdom!
   - I prefer a partnership model of church planting. The launch team could be comprised of a few folks from each the strong churches in the area. The common vision that God wants to start a new church should empower those local churches to come together and say We started a new church. Of course the number of committed launch team members would be proportional to the current strength of each church.'
2. **What Questions Have Been Answered For You?**
   - Geographic placement is very important.
   - The time line for beginning and implementation of new church start
   - I assume that something has to be in place for regular accountability.
3. **What Questions Has This Process Raised For You?**
   - What interactions will there be with the other churches in the area?
4. **What Conclusions Have You Drawn?**
   - I have determined that starting a new church is more of a marathon than a sprint; however, I believe the first eighteen to twenty-four months are critical for determining the success or failure of a new church.
   - I have a passion for reaching people for Jesus Christ but I don't know that I am being called to start a new church. I do have the gifts and graces to start a new church. I want to be open to the possibility.
5. **Describe your Best Case Church Planting Scenario**
   - My best case church planting scenario is utilizing a partnership model of church planting among the other established United Methodist Churches in Milwaukee, Wisconsin.
   - The launch team would consist of some members from these churches as well as some people we already have relationships with from the time we lived in that community before entering the ministry.

Sample

 © 2018 Robert O. Crossman, www.UMNewChurch.org

SAMPLE #5

Self – Reflective Essay

VISION: To be a fully devoted disciple of the Lord Jesus Christ.

MISSION: To start a new church filled with disciples, who are also committed to grow more new disciples of the Lord.

CORE BELIEFS:

The Bible	Albert Outler said, *"The Bible is the story of what God has been doing, and will always be doing on earth for his people. It is the story of what He has designed us for, and what He rightfully expects from us. It is the story of what we can count on from God: covenant making and covenant keeping on God's part, and covenant making and covenant breaking on our side. It is a book that helps us become truly human." {Interview with Bishop Wilkie, Disciple I Video}*
Genesis 1-2	We are not here on earth by accident, we are here by the very hand and word of God.
Exodus 20	God cares about how we live, and commands us to live by these ten basic Commandments.
Matthew 18:10-14	God is not willing for any one to stay lost, and calls us to search for that one lost sheep.
Luke 15: 11-31	God stands on the porch and waits for us to come to our senses, and return to His home.
Acts 9:1-19	No matter how far we have wandered, by God we can receive new life, a second chance.
Galatians 5:16-26	As we grow toward faithful discipleship, the fruits of the spirit grow as evidence.
James 1:27	True religion is caring for fatherless children and widows in their need.
Matthew 25:31-46	God calls and expects us to relieve suffering in Jesus' name.
Revelation 21:1-8	Our eternal hope is a heavenly home, in the presence of God.

CORE VALUES:

Grace -	No matter how far we stray, God's prevenient love reaches out to invite us to turn back home.
Transformation -	By God, the sinner can turn to the light, the weak can be come strong, those who doubt can discover faith, and broken marriages can be healed. By God, we can be transformed, even born again.
Missions -	Relieving suffering in Jesus' name is not an option for the faithful disciple (Matthew 25)
Diversity -	The Church, as the body of Christ, is made of many parts, with each function vital to the whole.

Sample

AFFINITY GROUP:

I can probably best relate to people from backgrounds similar to my own.

Geographic affinity: I would relate best in a small city (population of 30,000 +) or suburban community.

Economic affinity: middle-upper middle class, although I also have experience living in government housing/food stamps.

Religious affinity: I would relate best to persons with a modest church background, but perhaps have not yet had an adult conversion experience. I've worked with people who have a passive view of the church, but have never related to people who seem to hate the church or have a very negative view of the church. Also, I've never worked well with the 'super religious' or 'holier than thou' or 'pray without ceasing' church folks.

Recreational affinity: family, children, and history. No background in football, basketball, country clubs, or golf.

Social affinity: small business environment, Chamber of Commerce, Rotary Club, married with young children

Ethnic affinity: anglo

Sample

DISC INVENTORY:

My highest areas on this DiSC are: C,D. This means my strengths are attention to details and entrepreneurial type ventures. I am more task oriented and so I may need to pay attention to relationship issues more.

My lowest are(s) on the DiSC is (are): I,S This means my opportunities for growth or where I may need to utilize the strengths of others are in people-gathering, particularly in social settings, and networking.

CHURCH PLANTING STRATEGY THAT SUITS MY PROFILE:

I work well with my colleagues in ministry, and have always sought out relationships with fellow pastors. Based on that experience, I believe I would thrive in a "mother-daughter" strategy.

I have started a successful small downtown business from scratch that is still in operation. Based on that experience, I believe I would be successful in a parachute drop setting.

OPTIMAL CHURCH PLANTING SCENARIO:

Mother-daughter start in the suburbs of a large city, or in mid-size town, designed to reach middle income new residents and young families that have not yet found a church home.

CONCERNING MY POSSIBLE APPOINTMENT TO START A NEW CHURCH, CONCLUSIONS I HAVE MADE:

I believe that God has called me to start a new church. My spouse said (and I agree), "God has been preparing you for new start church ministry for a long time."

CONCERNING MY POSSIBLE APPOINTMENT TO START A NEW CHURCH, QUESTIONS THAT REMAIN:

I need to visit a few more of our newest churches. I am still not clear on exactly how to gather the first 40 people - I need to see and experience the "networking"

 © 2018 Robert O. Crossman, www.UMNewChurch.org

model to feel more comfortable with it. I would like to put some of those network strategies to the test in my current appointment so that I would better understand how that works.

I heard several of our speakers say, "You must have a discipleship system in place." I am still not clear on exactly what that might look like in a new church setting.

Also, I am not clear on the structure, if any, in a new church. Do I have a church council or finance committee? How are decisions made or approved?

**Before writing your self reflective essay
be sure and confirm with your district superintendent or
conference director of new church starts
the exact content and format they are requesting.**

†††

*NOTE: This article reflects the personal opinions of the author
and does not necessarily reflect an official position of Discipleship Ministries or Path 1.*

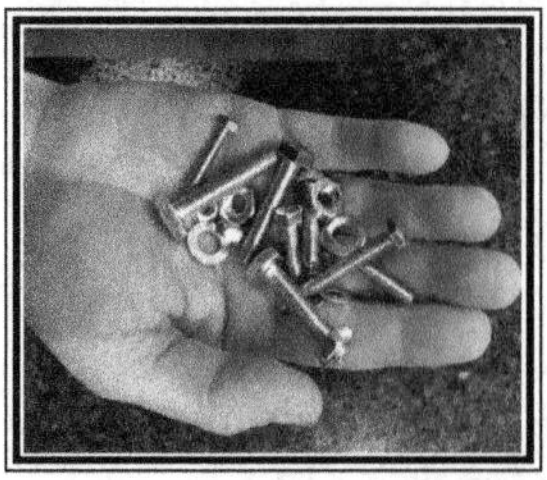

New Church Handbook
Nuts & Bolts for Planting New Churches In The Wesleyan Tradition

"Application For A Formal Interview"

After reading your self reflective essay,
your conference director of new church starts
MAY ask you to complete an application something like this one.

Application to Enter a Formal Debriefing and Assessment Process

Name: ______________________________ Date: ______________

Mailing Address: ____

Children living at home? (names and ages) ______________________

Health Status:

Your health:	__ excellent	__ good	__ fair	__ poor
Spouse's health:	__ excellent	__ good	__ fair	__ poor
Children's health:	__ excellent	__ good	__ fair	__ poor

Describe any limiting factors:

Yourself: ____

Spouse: ____

Children: ____

Education:

License to Preach School _____ Year Completed _____

Course of Study ______ Number of Years Completed ______

College ____________________ Major ___________ Year Graduated ____

Graduate School _____________ Major ___________ Year Graduated ____

Seminary ____________________Major ___________ Year Graduated ____

What workshops/conferences or books have given you the most clarity about the church planting process?

© 2018 Robert O. Crossman, www.UMNewChurch.org

Other experiences (professional, business or other):

Previous Pastoral Experience:

Charge & District ______________________________ Years _______to_______

Charge & District ______________________________ Years _______to_______

Charge & District ______________________________ Years _______to_______

Charge & District ______________________________ Years _______to_______

Charge & District ______________________________ Years _______to_______

If currently serving as a pastor, provide the following:

Present base salary $ ________________
Allowances/other $ ________________
Total Compensation $ ________________
Housing? $ ________________

Using statistics from the various churches you served during the past six years:

	2018	2017	2016	2015	2014	2013	2012
Professions of Faith:	____	____	____	____	____	____	____
Confirmation Class:	____	____	____	____	____	____	____
Baptisms:	____	____	____	____	____	____	____
Worship Attendance:	____	____	____	____	____	____	____
Membership:	____	____	____	____	____	____	____
Apportionments paid in full ?	____	____	____	____	____	____	____

Describe your past experiences in growing a church, a business, a small group, or a youth group?

What are your spiritual gifts?

Administration
Apostleship
Craftsmanship
Creative Communication
Discernment
Encouragement
Evangelism
Faith
Giving
Healing
Helps
Hospitality
Intercession
Interpretation
Knowledge
Miracles
Mercy
Prophecy
Shepherding
Teaching
Tongues
Wisdom

How have you used these spiritual gifts?

Do you currently financially tithe (give 10%) to the church you serve? __Yes __No

How many years have your tithed 10%?_______

Have you ever been part of a new church start? ___Yes ___No

If yes, please explain to what extent and where:

How does your spouse feel about you potentially being the pastor of a new church start?

List the top 5 to 10 values you live by - values that are absolutely non-negotiable.

In which model/strategy of planting would you be the most comfortable? (parachute, multi-site, etc.)

Describe the "ideal mission field" in which you prefer to plant:

In this mission field you list above, describe the demographic group you will strive reach:

When would you be ready to plant? ________________________________

Have you attached your:

- Self reflective essay? __ Yes __ No
- Two page paper stating your core theological beliefs? __ Yes __ No
- Church planter self-assessment? __ Yes __ No
- Signed covenant with the UMC? __ Yes __ No
- Spiritual gifts inventory? __ Yes __ No
- Affirmation of good moral character? __ Yes __ No

 © 2018 Robert O. Crossman, www.UMNewChurch.org

Have you enclosed a DVD of:

- Two recent sermons? __ Yes __ No
  (preferably sermons you might preach in the first few months of a new church start)

- An entire worship service you have conducted? __Yes __No

If not a US citizen, have you attached documentation of eligibility to be employed as a religious worker in US. __Yes __No

I grant permission for the annual conference to do a background check: __Yes __No

I grant permission for the annual conference to do a credit check: __Yes __No

List the name of three LAY references who know you well:

Name______________________________ Relationship _________________________

Address ____________________________________ Phone _________________

Name______________________________ Relationship _________________________

Address ____________________________________ Phone _________________

Name______________________________ Relationship _________________________

Address ____________________________________ Phone _________________

List three CLERGY references (your district superintendent and 2 additional clergy) who know you well:

Name______________________________ Relationship _________________________

Address ____________________________________ Phone _________________

Name______________________________ Relationship _________________________

Address ____________________________________ Phone _________________

Name______________________________ Relationship _________________________

Address ____________________________________ Phone _________________

By signing this enrollment form, I authorize my Annual Conference or its authorized agents to conduct a criminal background check and/or credit history, and to contact the lay & clergy references I have listed above, as part of the application process.

Signed: _____________________________________ Date: _____________

Print name: ____

NOTE: This article reflects the personal opinions of the author and does not necessarily reflect an official position of Discipleship Ministries or Path 1.

New Church Handbook
Nuts & Bolts for Planting New Churches In The Wesleyan Tradition

"Application To Start A New Church"

Each annual conference designs its own system for starting new churches. Check with your conference congregational developer, or district superintendent to find out the process in your annual conference.
The following application for launching a new United Methodist Church is adapted from an original designed by Anna Workman, when she was Director of Congregational Development for the Virginia Annual Conference.

The initial 'idea' of exploring a particular community as a potential site for a new United Methodist Church may come from the discernment of a variety of sources:

- Bishop
- District superintendent and appointive cabinet
- Conference minister of new church starts
- A nearby local church
- District Committee on Church Building and Location
- Committee on Parish & Community Development
- Board of Global Ministries
- Hispanic Ministries Committee
- Ethnic Local Church Committee
- Small Membership Church Committee; or
- any pastor or laity (active or retired)

Suggested Process For Seeking Approval to Start A New Church

1. Any of the above can initiate a conversation and file the following "Application for Approval to Launch a New United Methodist Church."
   a. The application includes a survey to be conducted in the targeted population to determine the number of potential members, and the needs of the targeted community (actually physically walking the neighborhood, door to door contact with residents, and using all available information from county/city planning departments, chamber of commerce, civic organizations, and MissionInsite.com).
   b. If the targeted population is a language/cultural group, the conference commission on ethnic local church concerns or the conference committee on hispanic ministries and the leaders of that population need to be consulted and assistance sought in planning the new mission congregation.

 © 2018 Robert O. Crossman, www.UMNewChurch.org

2. The bishop, the district superintendent, conference minister of new church starts, and cabinet will determine if a new church or mission church will be started in the area brought to their attention.

3. Upon recommendation of the district superintendent and conference minister of new church starts, the bishop and the cabinet determines when a new congregation is to be launched to serve an unchurched population, and the MODEL or STRATEGY to be used in the new church start.

4. The bishop and cabinet (in consultation with the conference minister of new church starts) will determine the appointment of pastoral leadership to the new church start.

5. In the appointive process, the bishop, conference minister of new church starts, and cabinet will determine the initial level of pastoral compensation required.

6. The host district superintendent and conference minister of new church starts will determine the initial level of financial support needed from all sources for the new church project. If this is a multi-site launch, the main campus will primarily make these compensation and budget decisions.

7. If this is a multi-site launch, the main campus will provide administrative over site.

8. In most other strategies, after the appointment is made, the district superintendent, conference minister of new church starts and the coach assigned to the new church pastor, will work with the new church pastor to fulfill the traditional functions of a church council, pastor parish relations committee, finance committee, and trustees until the church has grown large enough to complete the 'charter' process and thereby elect these committees. These committees/councils do not exist in a new church prior to the constituting church conference outlined in ¶ 259 of the *Book of Discipline.*

9. In most annual conferences, new church starts are not allowed to enter the 'charter' process (¶259.4 to ¶259.10) until they have at least 125 active adult members, have been financially self sustaining for at least twelve months, and have been holding public worship at least three years.

APPLICATION APPROVAL TO START A NEW UNITED METHODIST CHURCH

Notes: Typically this application is completed by a strong, health, growing congregation that is preparing to "give birth" to a new congregation. The district superintendent and the conference minister for new church starts shall have responsibility for reviewing plans for launching a new congregation and for providing recommendations to the bishop and cabinet. *(see ¶ 259.1)*

Time line: Typically for a pastor to be appointed to a new church start on July 1st, this completed application needs to be in the hands of your district superintendent and the conference minister for new church starts and congregational advancement **no later than October 15.**

District ________________City/Town ____________________________________

City/town for proposed church plant _____________________________________

Name of person submitting information ___________________________________

Signed ________________________________ Date ___________________
Senior Pastor of sponsoring church, if applicable

Signed ________________________________ Date ___________________
District Superintendent

Signed ________________________________ Date ___________________
District Board of Church Building and Location

Signed ________________________________ Date ___________________
Conference Minister for New Church Starts

The United Methodist Book of Discipline, Section VII, ¶259.1

"A new local church or mission congregation shall be established only with the consent of the bishop in charge and the cabinet and with due consideration of the conference entity assigned the responsibility for congregational development. The bishop shall designate the district within whose bounds the church or mission congregation shall be organized. The district superintendent of that district, or his or her designee, shall be the agent in charge of the project and shall recommend to the district board of church location and building (¶2518) the method of organization, and whether a specific site shall be selected or an area of organization be designated. The district superintendent shall avail him/herself of existing demographic, lifestyle and ethnographic information in the process of establishing a new congregation and its location, or shall recommend to the board of trustees of a selected local church

© 2018 Robert O. Crossman, www.UMNewChurch.org

that they share their facility with the proposed congregation. If there is a city or district missionary organization, or if funds for the project are anticipated from a conference organization, those bodies shall also be asked to approve the method of organization and location for a new congregation." *(see also ¶259. 2 through 259.9)*

I. General Information

What date is set to start this launch? ________________________________

A. Launch Options

Please check the Launch Option to be used:

1. _____ Mother/Daughter Launch
2. _____ Parachute" Launch
3. _____ Mission Launch
4. _____ Reclaim Discontinued Church Facility
5. _____ Satellite
6. _____ Other (please describe)

Do you believe that this church will have an average attendance of 350 or more within ten years? ___Yes ___No

We believe that this new church will have an average worship attendance of __________ within ten years.

Do you believe that this new church will be financially self-supporting within 3 to 5 years? ___Yes ___No

If no, please give more information:

B. Targeted Mission Field

Attach reports from MissionInsite.com

Describe briefly the community in which the congregation will be launched (such as people, environment, economy, etc.)

How many churches of other denominations are in the prime mission field?

To what degree have they saturated the mission field?

What percentage of the population is unchurched in the mission field?

What percentage of the population favors The United Methodist Church?

What is the predominant income level in the mission field?

What is the current population within the mission field?

How much has the population increased in the last year?

What will the projected population be within the mission field in:
5 years?
10 years?
20 Years

What percentage are in single family homes within the mission field?

What is the predominant age of the population in the mission field?

What is the predominant ethnic group in the mission field?

C. Target Audience

What methods will be used NETWORK with potential disciples?

Does the sponsoring church (and/or District Board) believe that:

- 125 adults will make up the attendance within 24 months of the appointment of a pastor? _____ Yes _____ No
- there will be sufficient members to financially support the congregation within 3 – 5 years? _____ Yes _____ No
- that the targeted area will sustain growth for the next ten years? _____ Yes _____ No

 © 2018 Robert O. Crossman, www.UMNewChurch.org

If you answered NO to any of the above, please give additional information:

D. Meeting Location

Has the district board of church location and building approved the site for a temporary location? _____ Yes _____ No

Is the site capable of accommodating 200 worshipers? _____ Yes _____ No

Is the site capable of accommodating 100 cars? _____ Yes _____ No

Please describe the worship facility (are you in a school, storefront, theater, existing church facilities, funeral home chapel, etc.)

Has a commitment for worship space use been secured? _____ Yes _____ No

What days and hours will you have access?

Is the location handicapped accessible? _____Yes _____ No

Is the meeting location within the area of the targeted population? _____Yes _____ No

Is there reasonable expectation that the congregation can remain at this location at least three to five years? _____ Yes _____ No

Please describe where small groups will meet.

Please describe the office space. *(if any)*

Has liability insurance been secured? _____ Yes _____ No

E. Site Information

What is the distance to the nearest United Methodist Church?

If it is less than 2 miles distant, why is this congregation being launched? (Note: If needed, please use an additional sheet of paper to answer)

IF LAND IS INVOLVED, ANSWER THE FOLLOWING QUESTIONS. IF NOT, SKIP TO SECTION G.

Does the District own the land? _____ Yes _____ No

Is it clear of debt? _____ Yes _____ No

If a debt is owed, how much? $__________________
What are the dimensions of the site? ______ ft. x ______ ft.

Does the site drain well? _____ Yes _____ No

How many buildable acres does the site contain? _________Acres
(Note: at least 7 buildable acres are recommended)

Are public utilities available to the site? _____ Yes _____ No

Is city water available? _____ Yes _____ No

Is city sewer available? _____ Yes _____ No

If not, is the site approved for septic tank? _____ Yes _____ No

Does this site have immediate access to a major thoroughfare with excellent visibility and accessibility to residents of the primary area as they conduct daily activities? _____ Yes _____ No

How is the land zoned?

Is the site near the center of the community the congregation will ultimately serve? _____ Yes _____ No

Does the project of building a church on this site meet with the district comprehensive plan? _____ Yes _____ No

G. Purpose Statement

Has the sponsoring church or agency developed a preliminary statement of purpose and vision for this new church? *(Please attach copy)* _____ Yes _____ No

H. Pastor Selection

Does the district superintendent believe capable pastoral leadership can be secured? _____Yes _____ No

If this is a multi-site, does the main campus have a staff member who will be the campus pastor? _____Yes _____ No

 © 2018 Robert O. Crossman, www.UMNewChurch.org

If yes, what is their name?

I. Housing for Planting Pastor

If a housing allowance is being provided, can adequate housing be found for the amount provided? _____Yes _____No

If a parsonage is being provided instead of a housing allowance, answer the following five questions:

Has a parsonage been secured? _____Yes _____No

If not, will one be ready before the new pastor arrives? _____Yes _____No

Will the parsonage meet conference parsonage standards? _____Yes _____No

If an existing parsonage is to be reclaimed for use, will it be refurbished? _____Yes _____No

If a house is to be rented/leased, will it be adequately furnished? _____Yes _____No

J. Office

Will an office be provided outside of the parsonage? _____ Yes _____ No

Will at least part-time secretarial help be available? _____ Yes _____ No

Will there be a budget for a computer, copier, internet, etc.? ____ Yes ____ No

K. Adjoining United Methodist Churches

Have all nearby United Methodist Churches been involved in the planning of this new church? _____Yes _____No

Describe the extent of their involvement and support:

II. FINANCING

Financial Plans:

Is there a projected a preliminary financial plan for this new church? _____Yes _____No

If "yes," please attach a copy of the plan to this application.

Summary of Anticipated Expenses:

© 2018 Robert O. Crossman, www.UMNewChurch.org

Cost of the worship site $___________/month

Terms of lease or rental agreement (please attached)
Cost of pastor's housing $____________

Pastor's total compensation package for one year $____________
Salary $____________
Utilities, Travel, Education $____________
Other $____________

Cost of sound, keyboard, projector, etc for worship $____________

Cost of office equipment, software, monthly fees $____________

Cost of promotions and other start-up costs $____________

Total Estimated Expenses for first 12 months $____________

Please describe expectations for pastor's work hours, days off, continuing education, health insurance, vacation, etc.

Summary of Anticipated Funding
What level of financial support do you anticipate receiving from the following funding sources during the first twelve months? *(Give projected amount)*

Contributions from the members of the new congregation $____________
Pledged support from pastor's family, friends, supporters $____________
Pledged support from "Mother" church $____________
Pledged support from the local district $____________
District board of church building and location $____________
Annual conference parish and community fund grant $____________
Other grants $____________
Source of these other grants:
Annual conference equitable compensation grant $____________
Annual conference new church apportionment funds $____________

TOTAL anticipated cash income for first 12 months $____________

Anticipated "in kind" gifts such as free housing, land, office space or worship space? (list)

NOTE: If in the process of completing this application, it is determined that a population is in need of ministry but cannot reach the benchmark of 125 average

© 2018 Robert O. Crossman, www.UMNewChurch.org

attendance within 24 months, and 125 adult members quickly thereafter, and have the financial resources to become financially self-sufficient within 3-5 years after the initial worship service, then proceed with the following "Application for Approval to Start a New Mission Congregation."

The sponsoring church may wish to ask the district board of church building and location and district superintendent to assist in finding a place for the mission congregation to meet. Limited funding for rental space may be available from the annual conference and district boards and agencies. The bishop and cabinet will assign a lay person or appoint pastor who may be less than full time. Also, limited pastoral compensation may be available from the commission on equitable compensation. Typically, housing arrangements (if any) for a mission congregation pastor shall be the responsibility of the local sponsoring church or the district.

¶259.1.a. A mission congregation may be designated when any of the following conditions exist: 1) Membership opportunities and resources are limited and not likely to result in a chartered congregation for an extended period of time. 2) A strategic demographic, cultural or language opportunity for serving a limited population is present. 3) It is expected that long-term sustaining funding from sources outside the congregation will be necessary to enable the congregation to exist, and the assumption of full connectional support items by the congregation is unlikely. 4) It is probable that the annual conference will need to provide long-term administrative guidance, including attention to the distinctive property needs of the congregation. When any of these conditions exist, the cabinet, in consultation with the congregational development area of the annual conference, may designate an entity a mission congregation. The mission congregation may be organized in the same manner and have the same rights and powers as any local church.

APPLICATION FOR APPROVAL TO START A NEW MISSION CONGREGATION

Time line: Typically for a layperson to be assigned or pastor to be appointed this completed mission application along with the "Application for Approval to Start a New United Methodist Church" needs to be in the hands of your district superintendent and the conference minister for new church starts **by October 15.**

In which district is the mission congregation to be located?

When did the district board of church location and building approve the launching of the mission?

What will be the name of the mission congregation?

Mailing address

What is the targeted population to be served?

© 2018 Robert O. Crossman, www.UMNewChurch.org

A. Has a survey been done to determine the potential number of persons to be served? _____ Yes _____ No

B. How many people live in the target area?

C. Does this mission congregation have the potential of at least 25 adults worshipping weekly? _____ Yes _____ No

Please identify the sponsoring agency (local church, or district agency) to which the mission congregation will be in a covenant relationship and will make regular reports.

Is qualified pastoral leadership available for the cabinet to appoint to serve this mission? _____ Yes _____ No

Projected Time line:

A. Date this application submitted
B. Date cabinet will be asked for approval
C. Date and / or Conference year pastor to be appointed
D. Date mission congregation services are to begin

Please share additional information that will help in the decision-making process concerning this mission congregation. ***(use additional pages)***

Signed: ______________________________ Date ___________
Approved Representative of Sponsoring Church

Signed: ______________________________ Date ___________
District Superintendent

Signed: ______________________________ Date ___________
Chairperson, District Board of Church Location and Building

Signed: ______________________________ Date ___________
Conference Minister of New Church Starts

Signed: ______________________________ Date ___________
Conference Hispanic Ministries Committee or
Conference Ethnic Local Church Committee, if Appropriate

 © 2018 Robert O. Crossman, www.UMNewChurch.org

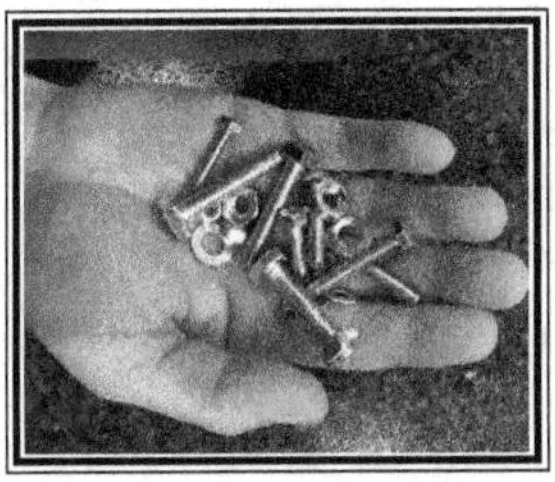

New Church Handbook
Nuts & Bolts for Planting New Churches In The Wesleyan Tradition

"Covenant Between New Church Planter & Their Annual Conference"

by Bob Crossman

While this covenant is NOT an official document of the United Methodist Church, your particular annual conference MAY have a church planting contact or covenant for you to sign. You might want to ask your conference director of new church starts or district superintendent, *"Is there some sort of contract or covenant that church planters are asked to sign?"*

Covenant Between New Church Planter and The ________________ Annual Conference

I________________________________, a pastor in the United Methodist Church, and a member of the ___________________ Annual Conference confirm that we are in agreement on the following:

1. I understand that the United Methodist Church will undertake to see that as a New Church Planter my family and I will have appropriate spiritual, emotional and professional support in place for our well-being and to promote the success of the project of starting a new United Methodist congregation. This support may include salary, housing, benefits, pension, covenant/accountability groups, spiritual directors, coaches, peer groups, training events, continuing education events, seminary tuition grants, counseling, paid days off, paid vacation, etc.

2. I have studied the doctrines of the United Methodist Church, and after full examination I believe that its doctrines are in harmony with the Holy Scriptures. I have studied the United Methodist form of Church discipline and polity, and I approve, support and will maintain our Church government and polity. *(From the Historic Questions, ¶330.d, asked of all candidates for full connection or ordination as Deacon)*

3. I understand the need for a Ministry Coach and will work constructively with the coach agreed upon between myself and the director of new church development in my annual conference.

4. I will adhere to the policies, procedures, and guidelines expected of me by my annual conference and any future amendments or modifications made in my annual conference policies, procedures, and guidelines.

© 2018 Robert O. Crossman, www.UMNewChurch.org

5. In recognition of the investment made in me as a United Methodist new church planter including specialized training, financial and other conference resources made available to me and confidential information provided to me by my annual conference *(and in the New Church Leadership Institute, Cohort, Incubator, LMPN, Boot Camp, School of Congregational Development, and/or Launch Pad events)* in connection or with respect to starting a new church, I agree that if for any reason I should leave the United Methodist Church, I will not attempt to create or plant any other new church or worshipping entity within 60 miles of the new church start location to which I may be appointed, for a period of at least 36 months from the date of ending my appointment as the United Methodist New Church Start Pastor.

   I understand that, in this event, the last paycheck or any form of severance from my annual conference of the United Methodist Church will be delivered to me upon the return of all items related to the new church start *(paid for by the conference, district and/or the new church such as electronics, sound equipment, projectors, computers, cell phones, furniture, trailers, etc)*, records *(including bank accounts, check books, financial statements, baptisms, member's contact information, contracts, deeds and titles)*, as well as all access codes and passwords *(including computers, websites, facebook pages, social media, bank accounts, etc.)*, as well as keys *(including storage units, properties, meeting locations, etc.)*, and that all other items have been returned as may be directed by my annual conference.

Signed: ____ Date ___________
Signature of New Church Planter

Signed: ____ Date ___________
Signature of District Superintendent

Signed: ____ Date ___________
Signature of Conference Director of New Church Development

†††

NOTE: This article reflects the personal opinions of the author and does not necessarily reflect an official position of Discipleship Ministries or Path 1.

 © 2018 Robert O. Crossman, www.UMNewChurch.org

III. What Are Some of the Ways New Churches are Planted?

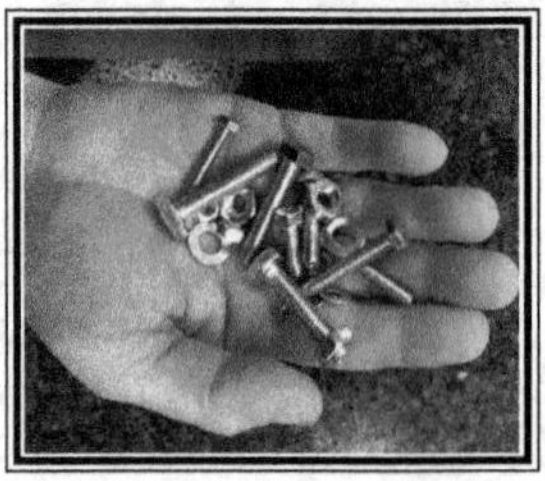

New Church Handbook
Nuts & Bolts for Planting New Churches In The Wesleyan Tradition

"What Are The 7 Seasons of Church Planting?"

PATH1

Seven Seasons of Planting a New Church

Season of Discerning

Do not be conformed to this world, but be transformed by the renewing of your minds, so that you may discern what is the will of God — what is good and acceptable and perfect. – Romans 12:2 (NRSV)

The discernment process begins when a prospective planter (or potential partner congregation) senses God's calling to plant a new church. Such a divine calling is greater than simply a desire to start a new community of faith. This calling gets affirmed by others who assess and affirm the necessary gifts for this ministry. Ongoing discernment could occur in regional training events, personal or corporate study, prayer, and conversations with experienced church planters or partnering congregations.

Are you called to be a church planter?
Are you called to be a partner church?
Is there confirmation from God?
Is there confirmation from others?

Season of Visioning

Then the Lord answered me and said, write the vision; make it plain on tablets, so that a runner may read it. For there is still a vision for the appointed time; it speaks of the end, and does not lie. If it seems to tarry, wait for it; it will surely come, it will not delay. – Habakkuk 2:2-3 (NRSV)

The soil in which God sows the seed of a new church is in the planter or planting church's heart. Vision offers a shared picture of a preferred future, inspired by God and often first articulated by leaders and then affirmed by God's people. A vision for starting a new church may arise from a need to reach a geographical area, cultural group or specific community of people. Energized by this vision, leaders motivate others to develop strategic plans and begin to enlist teams of persons to help that vision become reality. Visioning happens early in the planting process, often during the season of discerning or just beyond.

© 2018 Robert O. Crossman, www.UMNewChurch.org

What is God's dream for you?
For the people of your church?
For your community?
How will you begin to share that vision with others?

Season of Gathering

After this the Lord appointed seventy others and sent them on ahead of him in pairs to every town and place where he himself intended to go. He said to them, "The harvest is plentiful, but the laborers are few; therefore ask the Lord of the harvest to send out laborers into his harvest." – Luke 10:1-2 (NRSV)

Attracting and engaging a large number of people to help plant and nurture a new church (including members from a partnering church, friends, family and inquirers in the community) requires a great deal of invitation, networking and relationship-building. Church planting is never solo work. The planting team's first and most important task is to connect people to Christ, to the planter, to the vision, to each other, and to opportunities to make disciples of Jesus Christ for the transformation of the world. Gatherings of small groups, fellowship events, and preview worship services can ensure a critical mass of people necessary to plant and firmly establish the new church.

How do we attract and engage
a critical mass of people?
What are we doing to connect people to the planting team, vision, Christ,
and the mission of the church?

Season of Discipling

And Jesus came and said to them, "All authority in heaven and on earth has been given to me. Go therefore and make disciples of all nations, baptizing them in the name of the Father and of the Son and of the Holy Spirit, and teaching them to obey everything that I have commanded you. And remember, I am with you always, to the end of the age." – Matthew 28:18-20 (NRSV)

This season requires the planter to focus on leading, teaching, guiding, and growing the planting team both in size and spiritual depth. No new church needs to be encumbered with heavy systems and structures. However, SIMPLE organization needs to be in place to enable others to multiply themselves and mentor others in the faith. A Wesleyan model of church planting intentionally incorporates small groups for mentoring and multiplication. Spiritual growth and leadership development are the building blocks of a healthy faith community.

What process do we have to help people discover and release
their God-given gifts for ministry?
How do we encourage people to grow and
multiply themselves and their small groups?

Season of Worshiping

But the hour is coming, and is now here, when the true worshipers will worship the Father in spirit and truth, for the Father seeks such as these to worship him. God is spirit and those who worship him must worship in spirit and truth. – John 4:23-25 (NRSV)

We were created to be in relationship with God and one another. As human beings we have worship embedded in our very nature. One of God's great commandments to Israel set the tone for how we express that deep-seated love and worship of God: "You shall love the LORD your God with all your heart, and with all your soul, and with all your might" (Deuteronomy 6:5, NRSV). How we begin a church's public expression of worship requires careful planning and timing (not too soon and not too late). Worship styles vary greatly among cultural contexts, areas of the country, and age groups. Let the mission field guide your decision-making. Seek to meet their needs and interests. Experiment to see what will work in your setting. Worship is central to the church's launch, and to life itself!

What does worship mean to us?
When and how do we start worshipping
together as a new church?
When does it become
a public weekly experience?

Season of Maturing

He handed out gifts of apostle, prophet, evangelist, and pastor-teacher to train Christ's followers in skilled servant work, working within Christ's body, the church, until we're all moving rhythmically and easily with each other, efficient and graceful in response to God's Son, fully mature adults, fully developed within and without, fully alive like Christ. – Ephesians 4:11-13 (The Message)

As a congregation continues to develop and grow it becomes viable, sustainable and poised for multiplication. Growing people and developing healthy systems (leadership development, financial, structure, and discipleship) will help the church grow spiritually, multiply its mission and ministries and prepare itself for inevitable leadership transitions. Building a fruitful and multiplying church requires recognizing and honoring each person's God-given gifts, especially those that complement the planter's gifts. Recognizing your dependence on God, maintaining a consistent corporate life of spiritual discipline, and faithfully exercising the gifts of the Holy Spirit mean you will take big risks for Christ and experience personal and corporate growth and maturity.

What needs to happen next to grow people as
servants and systems for sustainability?

 © 2018 Robert O. Crossman, www.UMNewChurch.org

Season of Multiplying

He who supplies seed to the sower and bread for food will supply and multiply your seed for sowing and increase the harvest of your righteousness. – 2 Corinthians 9:10-11 (NRSV)

Healthy organisms reproduce and multiply and so do healthy churches! Healthy churches multiply disciples, leaders, ministries and congregations. Reproduction begins from day one and manifests itself throughout the various aspects and stages of church life. With multiplication in the DNA of a new church, reproduction happens more naturally. The gospel of Christ mandates churches to be healthy, grow in ministry and mission, reach new people for Christ, and reproduce. Through multiplication we build new bridges to the culture around us, introduce more people to Christ, and continue in ministry in fresh and vital ways.

How do we reproduce to build God's reign in vision-replicating, resource-honoring ways?
What can we do to ensure that multiplication remains in our church's DNA?

Scriptural Teachings on the Seasons of Planting a New Church

When a planting team is in a particular season of development they might find it valuable to study, reflect on and learn from these scriptures.

Discerning

Matthew 3:13-17 (John baptizes Jesus)
Luke 7:18-28 (John's disciples ask Jesus if he's "the one;" Jesus tells them to report what they see)
Matthew 16:13-28 (Peter declares Jesus is Christ; Jesus tells Peter he is going to build a church)
1 Samuel 1-3 (God answers Hannah's prayers for a child, Samuel; she devotes his life to the Lord and he begins to discern his calling as a prophet, through Eli's teaching)

Visioning

Luke 4:14-30 (Jesus declares his fulfillment of a prophet's vision) Matthew 9/Luke 10 (send laborers to the harvest)
Acts 10 (Peter/Cornelius – Peter is open to God's leading and vision; converts an entire household because of a new definition of "clean/unclean")
Nehemiah 1-2 (lay person following God's calling and vision to rebuild Jerusalem)

Gathering

Matthew 4:18-22 (Also Mark 1:16-20; John 1:35-51; Jesus calls the disciples)
Luke 6:12-16 (Jesus chooses the 12)
Acts 3 (Peter heals and preaches)

Exodus 3-5 (God calls Moses and Moses brings along Aaron for the job of addressing Pharaoh)

Discipling

John 3 (Jesus and Nicodemus; teaching about eternal life and new birth; life-long learning)

Mark 9:14-50 (healing/prayer – little one with the spirit disciples could not cast out; teachable moments about greatness in kingdom of God; sanctification)

Deuteronomy 4:5-14; also 11:18-25 (teach God's word to all of Israel)

Acts 13:13-53 (Saul and Barnabas teach in Antioch of Pisidia)

Matthew 5-7 (Sermon on the Mount on the Plain (Luke 6) – principles for living)

Worshiping

John 4 ("Worship in spirit and in truth" - woman at the well)

Acts 2 (temple courts and house to house – both public and private worship)

Acts 17 (Paul notices all the worship options and "unknown god" and uses that as an entry to preaching) 2 Chronicles 34 (Josiah consults the Law and prophets and restores Covenant)

Luke 2:41-52 (Jesus at age twelve – compelled to be in worship and study)

Maturing

Acts 5:17-42 (Gamaliel urges Jerusalem Council to leave the believers alone and see what happens) Acts 6:1-7 (Stephen and others distribute food to widows so apostles can keep preaching the gospel) Acts 15:1-35 (Jerusalem Council offers guidelines for Gentile believers)

Exodus 18 (Jethro observes Moses and advises him)

Romans 12 (be transformed by the Spirit and grow in faith together) Corinthians 2:6 (maturing breeds wisdom)

Ephesians 4:13 (our goal is becoming like Christ in all ways) Colossians 4:12 (prayer is crucial for maturing faith)

Hebrews 5:14 (training oneself and others to distinguish between good and evil) James 1:4 (the place of perseverance in the journey of faith and maturity)

Multiplying

John 6:1-14 (Jesus feeds five thousand)

Matthew 25:14-30 (Parable of Talents)

Matthew 13; Mark 4:1-9; Luke 8:4-8 (Parable of the Sower) Deuteronomy 6:1-3 (faithfully observe the law and you will multiply)

Reprinted here by permission of Bener Agtarap granted on January 26, 2018.
Source: www.Path1.org

†††

 © 2018 Robert O. Crossman, www.UMNewChurch.org

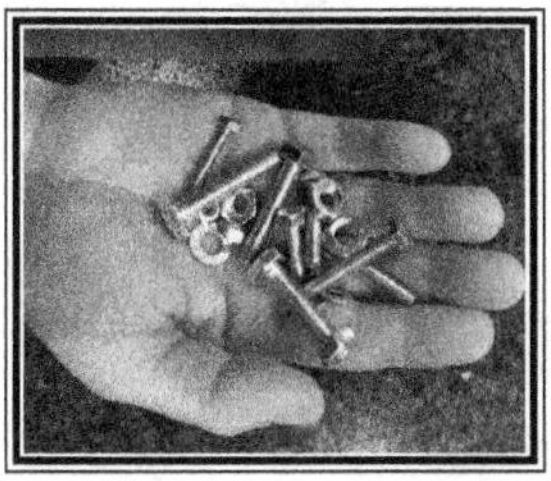

New Church Handbook
Nuts & Bolts for Planting New Churches In The Wesleyan Tradition

"Pre-Moving Day Strategy Session & Quarterly Follow-up"

by Bob Crossman

Much of this material is based on the process Don Smith began in the North Texas Conference and that Bob Farr implemented in the Missouri Conference.

WHAT IS THE STRATEGY SESSION?

The strategy session is a formal benchmark setting time prior to moving day, designed to clarify expectations and support between all the key involved parties.

At this strategy session the planting pastor, spouse if married, coach, district superintendent, (if there is a mother church, their *senior pastor, lay leader, council chair and treasurer from the mother church* and conference new church staff person all meet together to hear and 'sign off' on the planting pastor's plan, strategy, and financial projections.

After attending "Basic Training Boot Camp for Church Planters," it is suggested that a strategy meeting take place **BEFORE** moving day. Prior to the meeting time, the new church planting pastor would complete the following document, responding to as many of the topics/questions as applicable.

The new church pastor (or campus pastor) would forward the responses in advance of the meeting time to the participants which would probably include: the district superintendent, the new church development conference staff person, and the new church coach. If there are sponsoring churches or a mother church, this gathering also includes the senior pastor, council chair, treasurer, lay leader and SPPR chair from the mother church(es).

At the time set, the meeting would be called to order probably by the conference staff person, or the coach. The agenda for this gathering might look like this:

- Opening prayer

- Introductions

- Framework for the meeting
  - What is one hope that you have for this ministry to be formed?
  - What is one question that you would like to have addressed in this meeting?

- Review of the submitted materials
  - Launch initiative type
  - Demographic summary of target population
  - Financial projections
  - Participation benchmarks

- Review of funding from district and conference sources

- Next steps for this group

- Other issues to address

- Dismissal with blessing and signing the agreed upon strategy document

The United Methodist Book of Discipline,
Section VII, ¶259.1

> ¶ 259.1 A new local church or mission congregation shall be established **only with the consent of the bishop** in charge **and the cabinet** and with due consideration of the **conference entity assigned the responsibility for congregational development.** The bishop shall designate the district within whose bounds the church or mission congregation shall be organized. The district superintendent of that district, or his or her designee, shall be the agent in charge of the project and shall recommend to **the district board of church location and building** (¶ 2519) the method of organization, and whether a specific site shall be selected or an area of organization be designated. The district superintendent shall avail him/herself of existing demographic, lifestyle and ethnographic information in the process of establishing a new congregation and its location, or shall recommend to the board of trustees of a selected local church that they share their facility with the proposed congregation. **If there is a city or district missionary organization, or if funds for the project are anticipated from a conference organization, those bodies shall also be asked to approve the method of organization and location for a new congregation.**
> (see also ¶259. 2 through 259.9)

The form that will make up the content for this strategy session is printed on the following four pages.

Following those four pages
you will find information
about the follow up quarterly
strategy review sessions.

 © 2018 Robert O. Crossman, www.UMNewChurch.org

Pre-appointment Strategies and Benchmarks for Launching a New United Methodist Church

PART 1 - - TO BE COMPLETED BY THE PLANTING PASTOR

Timeline: This form is to be completed by the Planting Pastor after she/he has attended "Basic Training" (aka "Boot Camp") but prior to the Pre-appointment Strategy Meeting in late May. Therefore, unless otherwise specified, this form will be due to the Conference Office no later than May 15. Where narrative answers are requested, please feel free to use the additional pages as needed.

Geographic Description of Area to be Planted ______________________________

Municipality of Church to be Planted ______________________________ Today's Date ______________

I. Launch Initiative/Mission Field Information

A. Launch Initiative(s)

Please check **all** Launch Initiative(s) that apply:

1. _____ "Mother-Daughter" Launch
2. _____ "Parachute Drop" Launch
3. _____ Reclaim Discontinued Church Facility
4. _____ Extension Campus
5. _____ Multi-site
6. _____ Other - - please describe

____

I anticipate that this new church will launch weekly worship with __________ adults and ___________ children.

I anticipate that this new church will average weekly worship with ___________ adults and __________ children one year post-launch.

I anticipate that this new church will have an average worship attendance of __________ within three years.

If worship attendance is not an appropriate benchmark for your particular model/strategy, please describe: ______________________________

Do you believe that this new church will be financially self-supporting within 3 to 5 years? ___Yes ___No

B. Targeted Population Data

1. Based on what you have discovered thus far, describe briefly the community in which the congregation will be launched and the mission field into which the new church will be planted (such as people, environment, economy, etc.).
2. In addition to your observations, please submit the Mission Insite demographic data for the primary mission field .
3. How much has the community grown in the last year? ______________________________
4. What is the predominant age of the population in the area? ______________________________
5. What is the predominant economic class in the area? ______________________________
6. What is the predominant ethnic group in the area? ______________________________
8. What United Methodist congregations and churches of other denominations are in the mission field? ______________________________

9. Given the above considerations, describe in detail the piece(s) of the "mission field" that you envision targeting through the creation of this new congregation. Create a profile (such as a "Saddleback Sam" or an "Unchurched Harry and Mary") that represents the persons you believe God is calling this new church to reach.

10. Describe the plan for your first sixty days as a means of ascertaining the needs of the people living in the mission field and your plan for connecting with them.

II. Ministry Funding and Stewardship

A. <u>**Summary of Anticipated Ministry Expenses (NOT INCLUDING PASTORAL COMPENSATION)**</u>

1. Projected cost of the worship site? _____ rent? _____ lease? Terms: ______________________ $______________
2. Cost of sound, keyboard, projector, etc for worship? $______________
3. Cost of office equipment, promotions and other start-up costs? $______________
4. Compensation for any staff (please provide details) $______________
5. Other (please provide details) $______________
6. Total Estimated Expenses for first 12 months? $______________

B. <u>**Summary of Anticipated Income (BEYOND DISTRICT AND CONFERENCE SUPPORT)**</u>

1. What level of financial support do you anticipate receiving from the following funding sources during the first twelve months? (Give projected amounts)

- Contributions from the active participants of the new congregation? $______________
- Pledged support (virtue capital) from pastor's family, friends, supporters? $______________
- Pledged support from "mother" or partner church (if applicable)? $______________

TOTAL anticipated cash income for first 12 months (total of above amounts)? $______________

2. Are you commited to tithing? __Yes __No Are you committed to conveying tithing as an expectation for your Launch Team? __Yes __No

III. Participation Benchmarks

What is the effective date of your appointment?______________________________

What date is projected for the launch of the weekly worship ministry? ______________________________

© 2018 Robert O. Crossman, www.UMNewChurch.org

Please complete the chart below and include in it the benchmark dates and participation milestones for your pre-launch strategy and beyond. This will help in measuring the projected growth of the new church.

Milestone Event/Ministry	Projected Implementation Date	Number of adults present	Explanatory Comments
First Launch Team Meeting			
First "Taste and See" Event			
Final "Taste and See" Event			
Relational Groups Formed (Task **and** Small Groups) Prior to Preview Season		(number of RG's)	(List Groups Here)
First "Preview" Service			
Final "Preview" Service			
Relational Groups Formed Prior to Launch		(number of RG's)	(List Groups Here)
Launch Day			
Average Attendance of the four Sundays following Launch Day			
Average Attendance Six Months after Launch			
Average Attendance One Year after Launch			

Do you understand that continued funding is tied to the church's ability to "bear fruit" in the mission field through reaching the above goals? ___Yes ___No

Part 2 - - To be Completed by the Director of Congregational Excellence in Consultation with the District Superintendent

Timeline: This portion of the form is to be completed in preparation for the Pre-appointment Strategy Meeting in late May - - by May 15 or as otherwise requested.

© 2018 Robert O. Crossman, www.UMNewChurch.org

1. Scheduled funding for the coming years for this project. Please note amount and source:

Funding Source	**2017**	**2018**	**2019**	**2020**
Annual Conference				
District				
Other				

2. Schedule for pastor's housing? ___ parsonage? ___ allowance? $__________
3. Pastor's total compensation package for one year? $__________
   a. Salary $__________
   b. Utilities, Travel, Education $__________
   c. Insurance $__________
   d. Other $__________
4. Will the Annual Conference be assisting in the purchase of property? _____ Yes ______No
5. If so, what will the nature of the land funding be?__________
6. What benchmarks must be met for funding to be continued eighteen months past appointment date?__________

Part 3 - - Signatures to be Secured at the Conclusion of the Pre-Appointment Strategy Meeting

Signed __________ Date __________
Planting Pastor that has been Named to Start the New Church

Signed __________ Date __________
Senior Pastor of Sponsoring Church (where a Mother Church is involved in the planting of this congregation)

Signed __________ Date __________
Lay Leader or Lay Representative of the Sponsoring Church (where a Mother Church is involved)

Signed __________ Date __________
District Superintendent

Signed __________ Date __________
Conference Director of New Church Starts

© 2018 Robert O. Crossman, www.UMNewChurch.org

Quarterly Strategy Review Meetings for New Church Starts

by Don Smith and Bob Crossman

To insure clear lines of communication, a "Quarterly Connection" is held quarterly (or more frequently as needed) at the new church site.

Having been sent into a high stress ministry environment where the best laid plans often need to be modified, church planters need periodic "face time" with their respective support teams to celebrate victories, share disappointments and modify benchmarks and ministry strategies along the way.

The strategy review meeting provides a forum where this vital communication and collaboration can happen.

In the first year, I recommend these gatherings be quarterly. As the church matures, they should take place at least every six months.

Many new churches also have an annual unofficial "Charge Conference," to help the congregation begin to understand the connectional nature of the United Methodist Church and for the laity to begin the relationship with their district superintendent.

Who Participates:

While there is a larger group for the initial "Pre-Moving Day Strategy Session," often the quarterly follow-up meetings are only attended by:

- Planter and the growing launch team
- Planter's spouse *(if married)*
- Conference new church start director
- District superintendent
- Coach *(if available, they can join remotely)*

Other Details:

- Allow for one hour
- Meet in the planter's mission field, if possible

Sample Agenda

- Welcome and opening prayer
- Review purpose of this meeting

"Having been sent into a high stress ministry environment where the best laid plans often need to be modified, church planters need periodic 'face time' with their respective support teams to celebrate victories, share disappointments and modify benchmarks and ministry strategies along the way. The strategy review meeting provides a forum where this vital communication and collaboration can happen."

Report from the Planter

- What ministry milestone most accurately captures the essence of the new church that God is birthing through your leadership?
- What are two things that we can celebrate with you?
- What two pieces of this ministry best measure fruitfulness in this new church start?
- What two things are presenting the greatest challenges to your ministry?
- What two ways can this team be of support to you in the next six months?

Review of Benchmarks Presented by Planter Three Months Ago

- Launch team size projected for this month _______ (adults)
- Actual launch team size this month ________ (adults)
- Projected contributions $_________
- Actual contributions received $_______
- Number of relational groups projected to be formed by this month _____
- Actual number of relational groups presently in existence _________
- Number of adults presently involved in relational groups ________
- Has the income from your launch team met your benchmarks?
- Has the income from your family, friends and relatives network met your benchmarks?
- Have you received any special offerings or gifts for connectional ministries? (apportionments)?

Review of your Financial Report by Planter

- Walk us through your year-to date financial report
- Are there any larger purchases coming up that we need to approve today?

(In many annual conferences, the non-chartered new church start pastors have authority to request reimbursement for items up to $500 from their financial secretary. Each check beyond $500 must be approved by district superintendent or conference new church staff.)

Agenda for the January Strategy Review Session

- Walk us through your detailed end of year report
- Walk us through your detailed budget for the new year
- Walk us through your end of year Tables I, II, and III *(answers to 69 questions you will prepare for the conference treasurer's office)* -
- Are there any council, SPPR, finance committee or trustee decisions that need to be made today?

(NOTE: Second campus or multi-site starts relate to the main campus, but in all other new church starts, the district superintendent and conference staff person fulfill these functions until the new church has its constituting charge conference in year three or four.)

- What are your benchmarks for the next six months?
  Launch team size ______
  Contributions $_____

© 2018 Robert O. Crossman, www.UMNewChurch.org

Number of relational groups _______
Events ______
Attendance ______
Professions of faith _______

- What two ways have you most felt the support of the annual conference since the commencement of this appointment?
- What are two ways that the annual conference can be of greater support in the next six months?
- Based on your experience thus far, what benchmark modifications (dates, numbers, events, strategies) do you recommend, if any, for the next six months and beyond?

Group Discussion

- What specific ways can the planter and launch team be affirmed?
- What specific areas of concern can be identified?
- What benchmark modifications are to be affirmed and which will need further discussion?
- Is a follow-up meeting needed in three months? If so, when and where will it take place?

Other Issues to be Addressed

____

____

Date for Next Meeting

____

Closing Prayer (by district superintendent)

Much of this material is based on the process Don Smith began in the North Texas Conference and Bob Farr implemented in the Missouri Conference.

†††

NOTE: This article reflects the personal opinions of the author and does not necessarily reflect an official position of Discipleship Ministries or Path 1.

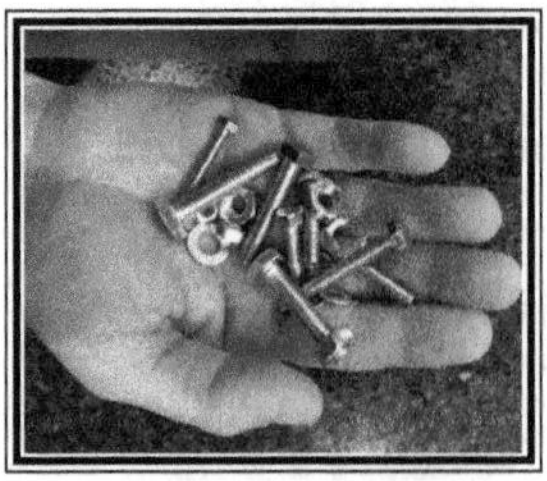

New Church Handbook
Nuts & Bolts for Planting New Churches In The Wesleyan Tradition

"What Are Some of The Strategies or Models for Starting a New Church"

by Path 1
With a few editorial notes by Bob Crossman

Introductory Note

The strategies for starting new churches are many and varied.

Across the United Methodist Conferences the New Church strategies/models used are as varied as the spirit leads and imagination will allow.

Any of these strategies can result in a new church that will be

- committed to growth and risk taking mission and ministry in the name of Jesus Christ.
- committed to giving birth to a daughter new congregation.

The Path 1 Team offers this "operational definition" of a new church:

A new congregation is a newly organized faith community that is committed to making disciples of Jesus Christ and

- **includes regular community worship**
- **is theologically Wesleyan**
- **is willing to plant a new congregation in its first decade**
- **has an effective–discipling system**
- **demonstrates faithful stewardship**
- **is deeply involved in community outreach;**
- **receives new members; and**
- **it is more than a mission project, a new worship service, or the construction of a new building.**

Annual Conferences across the country do not agree on the exact definition of a new church. Strategies, such as the "extension campus" or "second campus" are recognized a new church starts in some conferences, but not all. Most Annual Conferences have a working definition of a new church start that includes the following: newly chartered congregations, mission congregations, multi-site congregations (if geographically distinct), shared facilities (if not tied administratively to the host church), major restarts, major relocations to reach a new population.

New Church Development Strategies

In the early decades of the 21st century, United Methodists will use a variety of strategies and tactics for planting new congregations in the United States. Below you will find several of the most common strategies used within our denomination. We have ordered these from most to least pervasive along with some benefits,

 © 2018 Robert O. Crossman, www.UMNewChurch.org

challenges and tempting shortcuts associated with each. Please note that this is not intended to be an exhaustive list and that United Methodists will likely plant hundreds of new churches by intentionally blending two or more of the strategies. Lay or clergy planters serving full-time or in bi-vocational assignments could lead each of the following strategies. Depending on the planting context any strategy could be right for almost any people group.

Important Funding Note:

($ denotes costs associated with these strategies; fewer $ = lower conference investment; more $$$$ = greater conference commitment of resources).

Most new congregations will become financially self-sustaining. However, some churches – especially those who minister to low-income populations, may require long-term subsidy – which may be justified if they continue to bear good fruit. We caution against the use of the conference budget as a major funding source for long-term subsidy. We encourage the conference to develop streams of funding beyond the conference budget (from local churches, from individual donors, foundations, etc.), when long-term subsidy seems necessary. If we expect that a church will require many years of development before attaining financial self-sufficiency, it makes sense to plant such a church with the support of strong and committed connectional partners.

---

1. Partner Church/Multiple "Parent" Strategy ($$)

An existing United Methodist congregation – or, perhaps, several churches come together – as an anchoring, sponsoring or parenting force in launching a new church. This could be a cluster of partner churches or a combination of partner church(es) and another entity: a United Methodist campus ministry, retirement home or church agency. Each partner must have clarity about its role. In some cases, potential partner churches will need a year or more of preparatory time to be ready for the role. Also, each partner needs to be included in benchmarking updates. The planter often will serve briefly as associate pastor at a partner church or will come from the staff or lay membership of a partner church. The partner churches typically will provide some funding and launch team members. Exceptions to this member-sharing practice would arise when launching a church with a different racial- ethnic audience. In these cases, significant cross-cultural awareness and training will be important for all involved.

- **Benefits** – These types of plants have a higher than average incidence of success. The more credibility the planter has with the partner congregation(s) and the more the planting congregation(s) are willing to invest in the project, the stronger the new plant will be from the start. The planting project will be well connected to the United Methodist community, helping to facilitate various kinds of support from the partners, without sole reliance on any. Launch team members can be cultivated from each partner, in addition to the general community.
- **Challenges** – The planter may end up with too many chefs in the kitchen,

essentially navigating competing visions among the partners. Partner church leadership may seek to limit how many members go to the new church or to backtrack on promises made. It is important for the district superintendent or conference staff to review with the partner churches all agreements being made prior to commencement of the planting project. Covenants should be carefully discussed and preserved in writing. In the instance of multiple "parents" the partners may shrink back from total commitment, counting (mistakenly) on another partner – with the result that the new church's leader ends up feeling and functioning more like a "parachute drop" (see 2. "Classic Missionary Strategy" below) than a partnered plant.

- **Tempting Shortcuts** – The cabinet may rush a planter appointment forward based simply on the casual interest of potential partners. It is essential that a detailed planting plan be developed, with special attention to assessment, funding, conference expectations, and the relationship of the planter to the partners. If several United Methodist entities are embracing the idea of the plant, the district superintendent or conference staff may not insist on bringing all partners to the table to discuss roles, responsibilities and specific commitments regarding the plant. Also the cabinet may fail to consult with partner church leadership about characteristics they believe are essential for the planter's success. These kinds of plants work best when the planter aligns with the culture of the partner churches in key ways (although we also want her/him to fit the culture of the target mission population).

2. Classic Missionary Strategy ($$$$)

This strategy (sometimes known as "Parachute Drop") reaches all the way back to Paul's planting adventures in the first century. Any version of this approach, by our United Methodist polity, will be connectional in nature, unlike what may be experienced in other denominations. This type of plant happens when a cabinet sends a planter into a territory to plant a church and (1) that planter is not from that territory plus (2) there are no active partnerships in place with other United Methodist churches or institutions in the area. Many of the famous examples in United Methodist history that have worked in fact were not pure parachute drops – if, for example, the planter had some relationships already established in the community or grew up nearby. Or perhaps the planter discovered a very rich local source of prospective members that would not exist in just every community. When the planter has an informal network of relationships and support within the community, but proceeds without an official partner church, we could call this a modified missionary strategy.

- **Benefits** – in communities where no United Methodist congregations are ready or able to provide healthy partnership, this strategy offers a way to move forward. If the church we are planting will differ markedly in its congregational culture from any other United Methodist churches nearby,

 © 2018 Robert O. Crossman, www.UMNewChurch.org

this approach can offer the necessary space and freedom to color outside the lines of local convention. Some leaders have strong and magnetic personalities and this strategy enables them to collect people (what they do best), without having to negotiate constantly with partner churches (negotiation possibly being something the planter doesn't do well). Many of our largest and fastest growing new churches began in this way.

- **Challenges** – this is a risky strategy, with a high rate of project failure in the first three years. For this reason, some conferences with limited resources may choose not to employ this strategy. If the project involves an elder in full-time appointment, it is also a very expensive strategy – since there are no people to share the planter's salary expense for quite some time. Assessment of the planter is of paramount importance, as well as assessment of community readiness and of the match between the planter and the community. Clergy families that survive this type of plant will almost universally testify that this is stressful business – and not recommended for any but the heartiest marriages. Planters and their families may become isolated from others in the United Methodist connection and need to make a special effort to maintain supportive relationships.
- **Tempting Shortcuts** – When these projects succeed, they often succeed big – and it is tempting to model other projects after a very big and splashy success, assuming that we have discovered the eternal secrets of church planting. In reality, however, the highly successful parachute drops are rare. Most church plants will not grow as fast as the churches on the "planting legend" grapevine. Many church plants with excellent leaders will not take root at all, even when the leaders appear to be doing all the right things. A few among us truly have the gifts to pull off such an endeavor, and then only in the right circumstances. Diligent assessment and discernment by the appointive cabinet is critical.

3. Multi-site Expansion Strategy ($)

This strategy may look (at first glance) much like a Partner Church strategy where the partner church is simply very engaged. The difference here is that the new faith community meeting at the new site remains part of the original church, even as they may develop a distinct staff and ministry team system. Multi-sites may open up in other United Methodist buildings, in facilities purchased, leased or constructed by the congregation or in space that is essentially borrowed for a couple hours a week (e.g., movie theater, civic auditorium, school, etc.). Multi-sites vary in pastoral and staffing strategies. They typically have a site pastor – who may or may not be the lead preacher at the site. Some multi-sites utilize large video projection of sermons recorded by the senior pastor of the church at another campus. In some cases, cabinets appoint pastors to the site directly. In other cases, cabinets appoint simply to the church, which then deploys its staff and pastoral resources among its various sites.

- **Benefits** – This strategy enables healthy congregations to multiply their ministries and rapidly plant new congregations. Since the people of the original campus will remain organizationally connected to the ministry of the new site, it is often easier to raise local funds for the multi-site than for projects that will not carry the name of the original congregation. It may also be easier to share administrative resources, staffing expertise, etc., with the new campus when there is a perception that "we are all one church."

- **Challenges** – The relationship between the pastors of the campuses is critical. Most multi-sites (beyond The United Methodist Church) attempt to utilize staff members from the original campus, who already have loyalty to the senior pastor and know how to team with her/him. Whenever the cabinet appoints a planter to a multi-site project, that planter is typically an associate pastor. It is absolutely critical that the senior pastor of the church be consulted in the appointment. If there is a plan for the multi-site possibly to become a chartered congregation at some point in the future, this must be documented clearly from the outset. Otherwise, all parties (and pastors) should proceed with the expectation that the sites will remain bound together as one congregation permanently. These projects simply do not work when the pastors get caught in power struggles.
- **Tempting Shortcuts** – Because the funding and leadership may emerge mostly from within the congregational system, the district superintendent and conference staff may assume that no external help is needed. In fact, coaching is as critical with multi-site projects as in any other strategy – and the coaching relationship should involve both the senior pastor and site planter. Also, we should not assume that the local church is able to fund every expense needed for an optimal launch. The conference may need to make an investment alongside the local church. Finally, the local church should not try to stretch the staff from the original campus to cover ministry on two or more campuses. New staff must be added.

4. Church-Within-a-Church Strategy ($ - $$)

In a world of very expensive real estate, many new churches will share space with other churches (both partner churches and other collegial congregations). Existing congregations choosing to share property may find that new churches may better serve their immediate neighbors, especially when the new church specializes in a certain racial- ethnic culture and/or a certain generation or social group.

- **Benefits** – This strategy enables us to re-establish or renew United Methodist ministry within established neighborhoods and to utilize church property that may have become under-utilized in recent years as neighborhood populations changed. This strategy enables us to plant urban churches much more economically than if we had to buy or secure ministry space. Churches that serve economically challenged populations may discover the shared facility strategy as a pathway to financial sustainability.
- **Challenges** – Sometimes the mission field will best be reached in a setting outside the church building. If the new church is a United Methodist congregation,

© 2018 Robert O. Crossman, www.UMNewChurch.org

the host congregation should treat them as family, not renters. This means that negotiation of a reasonable building impact fee (sharing specific costs) makes more sense than a rental agreement. The new church does not exist to help the older church pay its bills, but rather to assist the older church in making disciples of Christ for the transformation of the neighborhood. Where the relationships fall into "us/them" and paternalistic patterns, trouble follows. It is critical that effective cross-cultural training be done before the start of the project.

- **Tempting Shortcuts** – In the early days we may not work intentionally to build a positive relationship with our partners. Prayer for one another and regular communication are essential. The district superintendent might check in early and often to see how it's going in the first months. Where strong, collegial relationships are formed, this strategy can work well.

5. The "Elijah/Elisha" Strategy ($ - $$)

This strategy involves congregations who haven't borne much fruit for past several years and/or who may be at the end of their natural life cycle. It requires a proactive discernment process with the district superintendent or conference staff. The congregation may either discover a new vision and recommit to fruit-bearing ministry or respond to God's call to become an "Elijah" new church start (2 Kings 2:1-14 tells how Elijah passed on the legacy of his ministry to Elisha). Elijah churches intentionally choose either to (a) join another church and give their physical assets to the conference to reach a new group of people or (b) open their doors to a planter and launch team that takes over management of the facility to start a new congregation.

- **Benefits** – United Methodist ministry continues for another generation in a community where otherwise it would end. The Elijah church chooses to offer a way forward in God's mission rather than a dead end. With thousands of churches teetering in survival-mode with just a handful of members left, this strategy offers a way to leverage untold millions of dollars in United Methodist resources for new church development.
- **Challenges** – If this becomes a well-known strategy in the conference, the prospective Elijah church may come to view their district superintendent as the "grim reaper." Some congregations may not be ready to face the reality that they need to let go of the past to enable something new to grow in their changed communities. Some districts and conferences do not have a system in place to recoup the assets of church closures for new church development.
- **Tempting Shortcuts** – In some cases, the temptation is to delay rather than to rush this process, allowing buildings to decay and cash assets to be depleted, with little ministry to show for all the lost years.

6. Vital Merger Strategy ($)

Most of the time, mergers do not truly create new churches. Two declining churches typically agree to share one facility and decline together rather than alone. However, East Ohio Conference, for example, has a strategy that requires both of the merging churches to sell their buildings, pool the funds, move to a temporary location, find a new name, receive a trained planter and proceed as if they were a new church. Leadership of the planter is key.

- **Benefits** – This strategy may solve several problems and give us a fresh new congregation as well. The problems could be decaying buildings, buildings too large or too small or problematic locations. The problem could be existing congregations with inadequate resources to do the quality of ministry they long to do. In a situation where transformational leaders are in short supply, the merger also creates a prime place to send such a leader.
- **Challenges** – Ghosts can abound. Old patterns, old prejudices, old attitudes – even old office-holders – these realities can really slow any possible momentum from the outset. Also if the merging congregations remain significantly older or culturally different from the mission field, there must be a plan to infuse some younger, more indigenous community people into the mix.
- **Tempting Shortcuts** – Just because it is not a typical merger does not mean we can ignore the careful weaving of traditions and people that are essential to pulling off mergers. We also must not back down, once into the project, about selling all existing properties and utilizing a trained church planter.

NOTE FROM BOB CROSSMAN

Dirk Elliott, author of **"Vital Merger: A New Church Start Approach That Joins Church Families Together"** *is the most knowledgeable person I know when it comes to mergers. Dirk recommends that to be considered a vital merger, the following must be part of the merger plan:*

- *The pastor must be enrolled, or have completed, the New Church Leadership Institute.*
- *The church must sell all property and relocate into a new location.*
- *There must be a focus on new mission and ministry. What will this new, vital church offer that neither of the former churches could?*
- *The new church needs a new name. The new name can not be a combination or variation of the old names.*

For more information about Vital Mergers, purchase "Vital Merger" at www.vitalmerger.com

7. Closed/Reopened Facility Strategy ($ - $$$)

Similar to the above strategies, except that there is no church left to share its facility, turn over its ministry, or merge with another congregation to create something new. The new church begins to address the needs and culture of the community population.

- **Benefits** – There is an existing building, often strategically located with respect to a population currently underserved by The United Methodist Church.

 © 2018 Robert O. Crossman, www.UMNewChurch.org

- **Challenges** – There is an existing building, often with enormous structural issues and liabilities. Also, the community may still associate the facility with the former congregation; so the story of the new church's birth must be carefully shared to engage and serve the community.
- **Tempting Shortcuts** – We may choose to re-open the building prematurely without engaging the community first. Or we may be stuck on re-opening a building, when the wiser path would be to sell the building and find another facility within the neighborhood.

NOTE FROM BOB CROSSMAN

The Elijah/Elisha Strategy has recently been called The Adoption or Friendly Take-Over Model or Repurposing Model.

Basics:

The adoption model starts with a declining church, great location, great facilities, within a promising missionfield. There must be a healthy growing UMC nearby with heart to reach the missionfield. After a 'reality check' with the small church, the church goes through a 3 to 9 month discernment time. The small church willingly OFFICIALLY CLOSES and gives their church keys and checkbook to the large church. They are saying, in effect, "We have forgotten how to reach the lost, please come and do that in this mission field. We will pray for you, and join with you, and support you any way we can."

Laity, musicians, and pastors from mother church TAKE OVER THE EMPTY BUILDING.

Benefits:

- *Reaches mission field that small existing church has been unable or unwilling to reach.*
- *Makes new disciples.*
- *Reaches the lost, least, and broken.*
- *Low cost (often all cost is carried by Mother Church).*

Disadvantages:

- *Hard to find small church willing to "give" their church away (the church must have a great location, great facilities, within a promising missionfield).*
- *Hard to find a mother church with a passion to reach the lost, and desire to become multi-site.*

CAUTION:

In most closed/reopened cases it is prudent to amend the incorporation documents (i.e. Wesley UMC doing business as Living Water UMC), replacing the names of the old board members. If you officially notify the state/city that the "old church" is closed, the city planning commission may require the "new" occupant to bring the building up to the new codes: (i.e. sprinkler systems, handicapped bathrooms, parking spaces, green spaces, signage, etc.) Although GCFA understands "Wesley" is closed, the state understands Wesley is 'DBA' Living Water.

8. House Church Strategy ($)

This may well be the oldest strategy for church planting that exists, certainly reaching back to Asia Minor in the first century, and also to frontier America when population was very thin. House churches are typically small, limited to the number that can fit in a home or a small meeting space. These churches may begin with as few as 6 or 7 folks, and grow to 12, or given the right space and leadership, they may grow to 50 or 60 folks. In some parts of the world, they multiply rapidly. Multiple house churches may gather monthly in a large worship venue. They are often lay-led, with clergy sometimes riding a circuit to bring the sacraments.

- **Benefits** – these projects can be extremely low budget, and they do not depend upon a large clergy supply (think early American Methodism). New leaders can be trained and deployed, so that where there is one house church, there may soon be six or more. Some conferences may yoke the house churches with a station church, and appoint a pastor to the station church who can also offer leadership to the house church leaders.
- **Challenges** – it is easy for a house church to forget its connection. In Methodism, we do not do "disconnected church." Some who feel led to a simple house church experience may resist United Methodist connection and accountability. Also, some house churches will quickly settle in and become closed groups with tight fellowship and few new participants. Those who lead such churches must help the participants keep an eye on multiplication, evangelism and missional service in the community.
- **Tempting Shortcuts** – The easy shortcut is to send persons to lead who are simply unprepared in terms of spiritual maturity, theology or group-leading skills. Just because the group is small does not mean that this is easy ministry. When leaders or potential leaders are unwilling to remain connected to the mission of the larger United Methodist church, or to share in the discipline of accountability to the pastor assigned to supervise them, we must remove them and deploy those who are willing to play for the team.

9. Intentional Communities ($)

While there is no singular micro-strategy for creating intentional communities they are, most basically, groups of people living together (in one residence or in several residences in close proximity) in a specific missional area who are bound by a covenant with common goals and vision. Often referred to as new monastic or neo-monastic communities these intentional communities gather together with the purpose of growing spiritually, following Christ and aligning around a particular focus on social justice and acts of love, mercy and hospitality toward others. The strategy is often traced back to the early church movement described in Acts 2. There have been intentional communities throughout most of Christian history, tracing their roots back to Franciscan, Benedictine and early Celtic orders. More contemporary examples of this strategy, still in existence, were founded in the early 1950s. Typically, intentional communities remain small in size (3-12 people) and have no plan to "formalize" as chartered churches with land and a church structure. These missional movements align and mesh with a particular community to develop intense relationships that seek to transform that community

 © 2018 Robert O. Crossman, www.UMNewChurch.org

in kingdom-building ways.

- **Benefits** – Practically no cost to congregations and conferences to implement this strategy. Mutual support and accountability. Intentional spiritual formation. Healthy inter-dependence among participants. Opportunity to connect with other congregations and Intentional Communities.
- **Challenges** – Creating and abiding by a shared covenant. Learning to share resources (space, finances, possessions). Respecting privacy. Building peace with other residents (conflict management).
- **Tempting Shortcuts** – Failure to develop a covenant and the basic rules of life for the group. Taking on more mission/ministry than the community can handle at the start. Inviting persons to become residents before they are ready.

10. The Surprise Birth ($)

Sometimes, churches are born unexpectedly – just as children may come along in a season when we did not expect them. Causes of surprise births would include church splits, a group that decides to affiliate with The United Methodist Church, a group of laity who envision a new church and proceed without asking permission, or a campus ministry that develops to the point that they desire to become a congregation in the fullest sense of the Book of Discipline. Whenever these new churches or new ideas pop up on the radar, it is easy for church officials to view them with skepticism, especially when "we did not think of it." However, some of our best United Methodist congregations have emerged in this way, as a work of the Holy Spirit and faithful laity. With wise pastoral care and negotiation, these projects often can be brought into the United Methodist fold as official new church projects.

- **Benefits** – Church planting does not get easier than this. When your region has a goal of five new churches and you only have money for three, what a blessing to discover another congregation coming to life without any conference investment!
- **Challenges** – The district may have had no input in deciding where they would meet. Such churches may choose to worship in close proximity to other area churches. In most cases, their style is such that they draw very different people from those at other nearby churches. Also, if the church has existed independently for a while, it needs to weigh carefully the commitments of moving into the United Methodist fold.
- **Tempting Shortcuts** – Be careful that financial incentives for groups to join The United Methodist Church are minimal, or at least that they are balanced by other connectional obligations. In this economy, people and groups are going to be drawn to money and subsidy wherever they smell it – this could distract the church from the most important questions of what it really means to become United Methodist.

11. Integrated Multi-Ethnic Projects ($$ - $$$)

This strategy results in an intentionally multi-ethnic church plant that worships as one integrated body to create a unique cultural expression and reflect all groups involved. This is what heaven looks like, so why not intentionally plant churches that are integrated? This strategy reflects the work of the Holy Spirit to bring together as one in Christ a multitude of cultural, racial and ethnic groups. We recognize that The United Methodist Church is just learning how to implement this strategy effectively.

- **Benefits** – Great cities were established because of the gathering of diverse people groups; a diverse church grows through the diverse talents and gifts found therein. The U.S. is becoming more and more diverse and church plants will begin to reflect this shift. This is a great opportunity to reach younger people, who often have more diverse natural networks of friends and colleagues than older generations. Often, they will bring their friends and families and may reflect a more economically diverse people. Ideally, this strategy brings authenticity, in that the church reflects our increasingly diverse communities and the unity that Christ prayed we would have (see John 17).
- **Challenges** – This is not an easy strategy to implement. Everything depends on the planter's ability to relate to, recruit leaders from, and be empathetic toward diverse ethnic-racial groups in building a multi-ethnic team. Creating a "third culture" (a space where all people are respected and participate in leadership roles) is a constant challenge. Learning to find leaders in new places requires the planter and key leaders to make an effort to connect with an ever-expanding network of diverse people. There may be slower growth in numbers of participants than in predominantly homogeneous congregations.
- **Tempting Shortcuts** – The ultimate goal in this strategy is transformation of the mission field, not simply gathering diverse multi-ethnic/racial people. Diversity of the plant is a by-product of the lead team and the mission field, its diversity, and the desire to be in mission with all people in the community. Hiring ethnic/racial staff (either lay or clergy) only because of their particular ethnic/racial background is not a good idea. Great chemistry, competence, character and commitment to shared values should be considered above all else.

NOTE FROM BOB CROSSMAN

12. New Expressions or Fresh Expressions

See the article:

"A Planter's Check List For Starting a New Expression of the Church."

**For additional information or support
exploring or implementing these strategies,
please contact any of the new church strategists on the Path1 staff.**

Reprinted here by permission of Bener Agtarap granted on January 26, 2018.

 © 2018 Robert O. Crossman, www.UMNewChurch.org

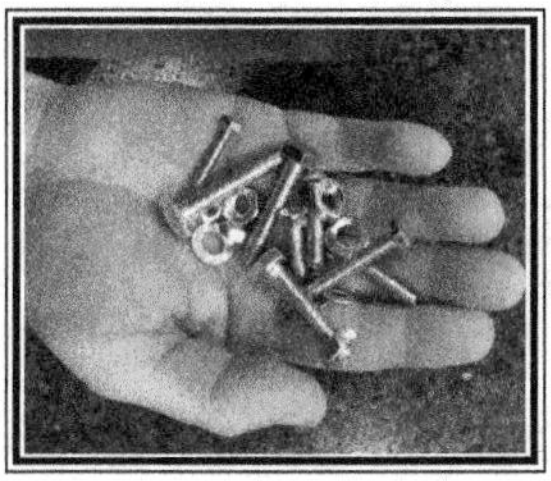

New Church Handbook
Nuts & Bolts for Planting New Churches In The Wesleyan Tradition

"Finding Support From Neighboring Congregations"

by Bob Crossman

If neighboring sister congregations only learn about the work to plant a new church after you arrive in town - that is a surprise. Surprised congregations often react badly. It's probably not a good idea to surprise the other congregations of your tribe that may already exist in mission fields near your assigned area or town.

With advanced notification of the possibility of a new church coming to town, support from sister congregations have been a contributing factor to the fruitfulness and success of a new church.

It is a great blessing when the other United Methodist Churches in neighboring towns are praying from the pulpit: *"Lord, bless our new mission to start a new congregation in New Hampton. Help them to reach new people for Christ, and to make new disciples for your glory."* Such a positive level of support has a real ripple effect through a community that yields great results.

While visiting a neighboring UMC, I was pleasantly surprised when the senior pastor, from the pulpit said, *"We are helping to launch a new church here in town. Rob Williams is going to be the pastor of the new church. I invite all of you to be praying, asking God if you should be a part of the launch team or a part of the launch pad as we help launch this new congregation. If you think you might like to help this new mission, just mark the attendance pad. I will call and make an appointment for you to meet the new pastor, and to discuss ways you might support this great work of Christ."*

On the other hand, I have heard planters report of "surprised" neighboring churches who not only felt threatened, but were almost "praying for the new church to fail" and speaking "evil" against the planting of the new church.

One planter, looking for a site to rent for planting, heard from several realtors, *"I'm sorry I can't help you. I've been told you were coming, and actually warned that if I assist you I will never sell another house in this town."*

In that same community, an early participant in the new church explained why he had to stop attending, *"I've had major clients threaten to pull their business if I continue to attend New Life UM Church. I'm sorry, but I just can't afford to lose any clients."*

A best practice would be this: a year or two before the new planter is appointed, for the **district superintendent** *(NOT THE CHURCH PLANTER)* to meet with the clergy and later with the lay leaders from UMC's within 5 to 10 miles to inform them that this mission field is being considered for the planting of a new church, and that they are being asked to support this new work for Christ.

A few months later, at a second or third gathering of these clergy and laity, it is often helpful to bring laity from other sponsoring churches from across the state to honestly tell their story and the impact or lack of negative impact giving birth to a new church had on their mother church.

The questionnaire of "Motions to Consider" below might be helpful to help the clergy and laity focus on the levels of support they might offer to the new ministry.

SIX MOTIONS FOR OUR CONSIDERATION:

1. _______UMC of _______, understands that a new UMC may start in _______, some time in the next three years. We **WILL NOT SUPPORT** that new United Methodist Church.

2. _______UMC of _______, understands that a new UMC may start in _______, some time in the next three years. We **WILL SUPPORT** that new church, **AS A SISTER CHURCH** with:
   a. our prayers.

3. _______UMC of _______, understands that a new UMC may start in _______, some time in the next three years. We **WILL SUPPORT** that new church, **AS A SISTER CHURCH** with:
   a. our prayers, and
   b. we hope to also support that new church with 'baby showers' to help provide some of the physical items the new church may need in preparation for her first worship services: (portable nursery equipment, coffee pots, chairs, sound / video components, signage, Bible study materials, etc.)

4. _______UMC of _______, understands that a new UMC may start in _______, some time in the next three years. We **WILL SUPPORT** that new church, **AS A SISTER CHURCH** with:
   a. our prayers, and
   b. we hope to also support that new church with 'baby showers' to help provide some of the physical items the new church may need in preparation for her first worship services: (portable nursery equipment, coffee pots, chairs, sound / video components, signage, Bible study materials, etc.), and
   c. we also hope to support that new church with volunteers in the early months (to make phone calls, distribute door hangers, worship greeters, nursery helpers, providing refreshments, etc.).

© 2018 Robert O. Crossman, www.UMNewChurch.org

5. ______UMC of _______, understands that a new UMC may start in _______, some time in the next three years. We **WILL SUPPORT** that new church, **AS A MOTHER CHURCH**, with:
   a. our prayers, and
   b. we hope to also support that new church with 'baby showers' to help provide some of the physical items the new church may need in preparation for her first worship services: (portable nursery equipment, coffee pots, chairs, sound / video components, signage, Bible study materials, etc.), and
   c. we also hope to support that new church with volunteers in the early months (to make phone calls, distribute door hangers, worship greeters, nursery helpers, providing refreshments, etc.)., and
   d. we also hope that _____ to _____ *(10 to 15) (15 to 25) (25 to 40) (40 to 50) (50 to 75) (75 to 100)* adults in our church family will want to be missionaries in the new church. Some of them may choose to stay, some may choose to be missionaries for two years and then return home to us.

6. ______UMC of _______, understands that a new UMC may start in _______, some time in the next three years. We **WILL SUPPORT** that new church, **AS A MOTHER CHURCH**, with:
   a. our prayers, and
   b. we hope to also support that new church with 'baby showers' to help provide some of the physical items the new church may need in preparation for her first worship services: (portable nursery equipment, coffee pots, chairs, sound / video components, signage, Bible study materials, etc.), and
   c. we also hope to support that new church with volunteers in the early months (to make phone calls, distribute door hangers, worship greeters, nursery helpers, providing refreshments, etc.)., and
   d. we also hope that _____ to _____ *(10 to 15) (15 to 25) (25 to 40) (40 to 50) (50 to 75) (75 to 100)* adults in our church family will want to be missionaries in the new church. Some of them may choose to stay, some may choose to be missionaries for two years and then return home to us, and
   e. we also intend to support the new church financially, providing a **partial housing allowance** of up to $______ ($100) ($250) ($500) ($750) ($1,000) per month for the first 36 to 48 months, and/or $______ ($250) ($500) ($750) ($1,000) ($1,500) per month in **partial salary support** each month, beginning as soon as ___________, and continuing for at least ______ months.

STRATEGY ANTICIPATED: __ Extension Campus/Satellite/Second Campus
___ Mother-Daughter New Church __ Partnership between two or more UMC
__ Other: ____

The above motion # ____was adopted on ___________, 20__ by the charge conference of the _________________ United Methodist Church.

Signed: Chair of the Council ______________________; Pastor ______________;
Lay Leader __________________; District Superintendent_________________;
Finance Chair __________________; Trustee Chair _______________________;
Conference Director of New Churches ____________________________.

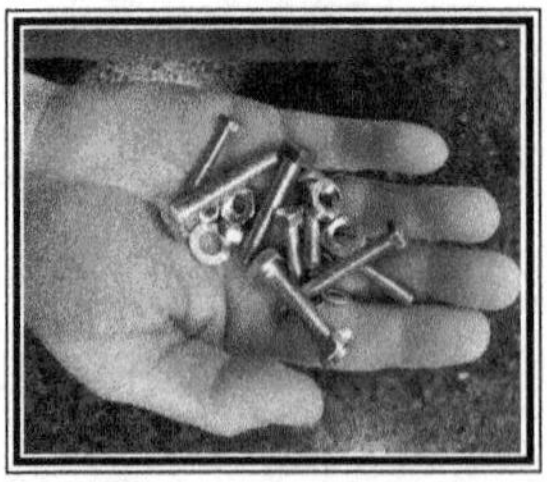

New Church Handbook
Nuts & Bolts for Planting New Churches In The Wesleyan Tradition

"One New Church Planter's First Year Checklist"

by Bob Crossman and Dirk Elliott

Because of the differing gifts and graces of pastors, and the wide diversity of mission fields - church planting is NO simple *"cookie cutter"* or *"one size fits all"* process. There is NO simple check list for all planters in all mission fields.

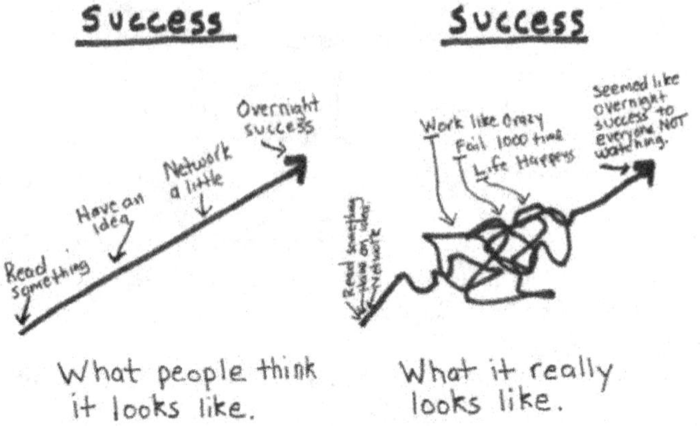

This napkin sketch has been attributed to Demetri Martin, the author of *This Is A Book.*

As you begin to develop your ministry plan, a review of this list might help you prioritize and plan for the ministry of starting a new church for the purpose of making new disciples of Jesus Christ.

The following check list assumes the appointment of a full-time pastor who will be living in a mission field with the potential of 350 to 500 in worship within the first five years. In other words, this check list is designed for planters who have been appointed to **"Launch Large."** If you have been appointed to use one of the strategies that intentionally **"Launch Small"** such as many of the new / fresh expressions and some of the "Weird Church" models, then major adaptations will be needed to this check list.

Of course, you will have to adapt this check list to fit your unique setting. In particular, if you are being appointed to start a second campus, a micro community, or serving as a part-time or volunteer or lay planter - adaptations will be necessary.

The United Methodist Church is attempting new church starts in a wide variety of geographic, ethnic, economic, and cultural environments. **While each of these environments are unique in particular ways, there are basic time-tested church planting principles that prove effective in every situation:**

© 2018 Robert O. Crossman, www.UMNewChurch.org

- The natural affinity of the planting pastor matching the mission field.
- The planter's ongoing, regularly scheduled relationship with a coach.
- The planter's "work ethic" and ability to keep their heart and hands engaged in the project.
- The planter's ability to stay in love with God.
- A strong intercessory prayer team praying for the planter to have the guidance, wisdom and grace to lead.
- The planters ability to adapt a personal "dream" church to the realities of the mission field.
- Holding off the launch of public worship until gathering enough people to have critical mass.
- Keeping focused on evangelism *(continuing to gather additional new people)* after launch.
- Keeping focused on financial tithing before and after launch.
- Keeping focused on "essential" ministries and postponing other non-essential ministries.
- Working through task forces or advisory boards, but not formalizing leadership too soon.

These basic principles are scattered throughout the check list below. As you adapt this check list to better fit your personal style and mission field, do not neglect to pay due attention to the eleven basic time-tested principles listed above.

The Year Before You Are Appointed

Personal

- Pray.
- Conversations with spouse (if married).
- Conversations with family, friends and colleagues directly asking for them to pray for you to have the behaviors, gifts and graces to be a fruitful new church planter.
- Take several discernment inventories. *(See article on the subject in chapter 2)*
- Take the spiritual gifts inventory. *(See article on the subject in chapter 2)*
- Invite friends, family colleagues or church members to "rate you" using the recommended inventory from article referenced above.
- Make an appointment to visit several new church pastors and their spouses in your area. *(with your spouse, if married)*
- Select three or more personal prayer intercessors - keep them informed of your prayer needs throughout this season of your life.
- Read Jim Griffith's book, *Ten Most Common Mistakes New Church Planters Make.*
- Take a nice, long, relaxing vacation with your family.
- The decision to request a church planting appointment is a family decision.
- Pray.

Is your Congregation Also in a Discernment Process - Should They Give Birth to A New Church?

- Path 1's "Readiness to Plant 360" process is an excellent assessment tool designed to help potential partner (mother) churches determine their readiness AND strengthen their capacity to plant a new church.
  For more information regarding this: www.readiness360.org

United Methodist

- Consult with your district superintendent, asking if they might nominate you to attend your conference's new church cohort, or discernment event. Many conferences use the ***New Church Leadership Institute,*** **or** ***Church Planter Discernment Workshop.***
  See www.UMNewChurch.org for event registration.
- At the ***New Church Leadership Institute****, and most conference discernment events,* you will be invited to write a self-reflective essay which will include your affinity group and your preferred church planting strategy (model).
- After attending the discernment event, make an appointment for a formal consultation with your district superintendent and conference director of new church starts.
- If invited, complete the formal assessment process designed by your annual conference. This normally includes one or more formal interviews. (These will include your spouse, if married).

If Appointed, then in the two to four months before moving day

- Pray.
- Take a nice, long, relaxing vacation with your family. Your next opportunity for another long uninterrupted vacation may be twelve to eighteen months away.
- With permission of your district superintendent do the following six things:
  - Take your family to visit the new mission field.
  - Take a long walk through the neighborhood where your new apartment/ parsonage will be located.
  - Take your children/youth to visit the school to walk around and discover the enrollment process.
  - Take a long walk/drive through the nearby business district.
  - As a family, begin to think about choosing a grocery store, pharmacy, gas station, auto mechanic, physician, dentist, etc.
  - Listen to your family. Pray together. Share your hopes and dreams for your family in this new place.
- Receive formal confirmation from your district superintendent of your new appointment, and the mission field you are being appointed to start the new church.
- Receive formal clarification of the strategy (model) that your conference director of new church starts and district superintendent are expecting

 © 2018 Robert O. Crossman, www.UMNewChurch.org

you to use. (i.e. satellite, connectional/parachute drop, mother-daughter, partnership, restart, fresh expressions, weird church, coffee house, etc).
- Working through your conference minister of new church starts, secure a coach.
- Re-read Jim Griffith's book, *Ten Most Common Mistakes New Church Planters Make*. Decide not to make those mistakes in planting your new church!
- Attend *"Basic Training Boot Camp" led by Jim Griffith and Griffith Coaching.* (Event registration at www.UMNewChurch.org)
- Following Jim Griffith's process - recruit 3 to 5 prayer partners, and keep in contact with them by email on a regular basis.
- Secure three to five colleagues who will hold you accountable for your spiritual growth. Keep in contact with them on a regular basis.

Mother-Daughter / Extension Campus / Second Sites
- If this is a mother-daughter or second campus strategy (model) the planter and senior pastor are encouraged to attend together the senior pastor day at boot camp for mother-daughter/extension campus/second sites.
- Schedule the first of many face to face meetings with the senior pastor to begin the relationship; hear each other's vision/hopes/dreams/plans for this new ministry.
- Clarify, and continue to clarify, mutual expectations of each other; level of financial support from main campus; decision making process; financial process; and "fishing rules" for planter within the main campus.
- In Extension Campus and Second Sites, clarify the planters role in the following list of administrative items.

Administrative
- With approval of your district superintendent, begin to search for housing to rent as your parsonage - must be located inside your mission field. Remember that your "office" will most likely be inside your home. *(i.e. in a spare bedroom?).* Most annual conferences will encourage you to rent instead of purchasing a home in these early years of your new church appointment.
- With permission of your district superintendent begin to identify potential worship sites:
  - generate a list of promising meeting locations in your mission field.
  - develop a checklist for ranking their suitability.
  - rank facilities using your checklist.
  - establish contact at each possible location.
  - get on waiting lists at each possible location.
- Write out the vision, core beliefs, and mission statements for your new church.
- Clarify your 30 second winsome and compelling answer to, *"Tell me about the new church you are starting?"*
- Clarify your 5 minute and 20 minute winsome and compelling answers to, *"Tell me about the new church you are starting?"*
- Propose a name for your new church, and seek formal approval of your district superintendent and conference director of new church starts. Before

making this decision, check in your county and state to see if other churches are already using the same or similar name.

- Receive in writing, clarification of the amount of financial grants (or in-kind gifts) that are coming from district, conference, and sponsoring church sources that are already committed for each of your first three to five years.
- Clarify with your conference director of new church starts and district superintendent the process for actually receiving the grants, and obtaining reimbursement for expenses in your new church.
- Develop a preliminary proposed budget.
- Obtain demographic reports on your mission field. Check with your Conference office - they may have already arranged for discount rates with MissionInsite for comprehensive demographic reports.
- With permission of district superintendent, test those demographics by driving/walking through your mission field. As a result of "walking around" obtain demographic reports that are not broad radius, but a more detailed shape that more accurately reflects your mission field and where your target audience lives.
- Develop a preliminary strategy for networking and obtaining your launch team. *(See the articles on networking, part 1 & 2 in chapter four)*
- Develop alternate strategies for networking.
  (i.e. "Plan B" in case your "Plan A" doesn't bear much fruit)
- Design the process for counting and depositing any funds given to your new church. *(See the articles on this subject)*
- Design your preliminary schedule for use of your time in the pre-launch season. *(i.e. what will a typical week look like)*
- Develop your initial benchmarks, such as:
  - projected date of your first launch team meeting, and number of adults who will be present.
  - projected date of your first "Taste & See" event, and number of adults who will be present.
  - projected number of relational groups (task and small groups) and number of adults.
  - projected date of your first "preview" worship service, and number of adults who will be present.
  - projected date of your final "preview" worship service, and number of adults who will be present.
  - projected number of adults you will need in worship to achieve "critical mass" in your particular mission field.
  - projected date of your public launch and **number of adults** who will be present.
    (Jim Griffith writes, *"We are seeing more and more that "volume" is what should determine launch, NOT just the calendar."*)
  - projected average attendance of the four Sundays following launch day.
  - projected average attendance six months after launch.

 © 2018 Robert O. Crossman, www.UMNewChurch.org

- projected average attendance one year after launch.

Connect

- Ask for a formal "Pre-Moving Day Strategy Session" *(following Don Smith's pattern)* to take place BEFORE moving day. *(See the article on this subject in chapter three.)*
  At this session, they will want you to bring most of the 12 to 15 items listed in this administrative section.
  In mother-daughter or second campus strategies - the "Pre-Moving Day Strategy Session" mentioned above should also include the attendance of the lay leader, treasurer, council chair, and SPR chair of the mother church.
- Secure a financial secretary - most annual conferences will require this to be the Financial Secretary of a nearby healthy United Methodist Church or the district Administrative Assistant.

Fundraising

- Following Jim Griffith's process - with approval of your district superintendent and conference minister of new church starts begin to ask for "virtue capital" financial gifts from family, relatives, and personal friends. *Many annual conferences expect the planter to raise $50,000 to $100,000 in three year pledges from this source. Clarify the amount with your conference minister of new church starts.*
- Is your district office willing to actively invite the established churches in that district to support this new ministry with a "baby shower" responding to your detailed list of equipment needed? You will have that list and be ready for the shower about three months prior to launch.
  (See article on Finding Support From Neighboring Congregations in chapter three.)

Moving Day

- Spend the rest of this week with your family to unpack, settle in, pray together, family worship in your new home, and begin to develop a routine for your family. Make sure your spouse and children have your attention without distraction.

In the First Two Weeks After Moving Day

Personal

- Pray and fast weekly.
- Continue to develop your prayer life and spiritual focus.
- Keep your intercessory team informed and updated.
- Keep your prayer team updated.
- Remember (and practice) the Sabbath.
- Maintain good exercise and discipline.
- Ask yourself, *"What will I do **today** to let people know we are planting a new church?"*

Administrative

- Contact other NEW churches in your conference to discover if they have any supplies/equipment they can donate to your new church start. *(i.e. Now that they are in their new building, do they have a trailer, portable sound, portable nursery, etc that they could donate.)*
- Check with your district superintendent and conference minister of new church starts - all your purchases and accounts may need to be in the name of your district since you will not be a chartered congregation for two or three years.
- Establish office *(probably in your home at first).*
- Rent post office box.
- Secure church phone number or cell phone number.
- Set up internet and email address for church.
- Subscribe to *Constant Contact* www.constantcontact.com (recommended by Dirk Elliott, Detroit Conference).
- Secure a EIN number from the federal government *(See article on this subject in chapter eleven)*
- Secure a "Group Ruling 501(c)(3)" letter for your church, and a copy of the 1974 IRS ruling from the general commission on finance and administration. *(See article on GCFA letter in chapter eleven)*
- With your district superintendent's approval, secure a church ID# from GCFA. *(See article on this subject in chapter eleven)*
- If your annual conference requires, begin the process to incorporate the new church. *(See article on this subject in chapter eleven)*
- Your state may require that you file for non-profit status or register with the state department of revenue.
- Check on state sales tax exemption/refund laws.
- If you have decided to use direct mail marketing, apply for nonprofit status with your local post office and get bulk permit number. Check with your district and conference office first to see if you can share their number.
- Check with conference before opening a checking account. *(See the article on "Financial Systems" in chapter eleven)*
- Give your financial secretary your personal tithe check (10%) for deposit into the church account.
- Obtain liability insurance, including corporate and personal *(See the article on this subject).*

Gathering

- Network in your mission field. *(See the article on "Networking" part 1 & 2 in chapter four)*
- Meet people and invite them into your home or meet for coffee.
- Revise and sharpen your networking strategy.
- Determine your mission field/target audience.
- Plan and hold first gathering of "first contacts."
- Begin to build your initial launch team of at least 35 adults.
- Every ten to fifteen days, make person eye-to-eye contact with these early

 © 2018 Robert O. Crossman, www.UMNewChurch.org

launch team adults.

- Develop a written ministry plan with strategy for all ministry areas.
- Discern the roles and kinds of people you need on the launch team.
- Begin to discern potential workers in all ministry areas: nursery, children, teens, small groups, set-up, tear down, electronics, music, hospitality, and follow-up.

In Month One and Two After "Moving Day"

Personal

- Pray and fast weekly.
- Continue to develop your prayer life and spiritual focus.
- Keep your intercessory team informed and updated.
- Keep your prayer team updated.
- Remember (and practice) the Sabbath.
- Maintain good exercise and discipline.
- Review and revise your initial benchmarks you proposed at your "pre-moving day strategy session" in cooperation with your coach and conference minister of new church starts.
- Ask yourself, "What will I do **TODAY** to let people know we are planting a church?"

Connect

- In mother/daughter, extension campus, or satellite strategies - maintain regular contact with mother church *(senior pastor and staff)* for support, prayers, and encouragement.
- Stay in regular contact with your coach. (either weekly or month as pre-arranged).
- Stay in regular contact (email bullet list every two weeks) with your conference minister of new church starts and your district superintendent - it is never a good idea to surprise your district superintendent!
- If you are a multi-site or second campus, your sponsoring church systems will fulfill the role of your church council, trustees, finance committee and staff-pastor parish relations committees.
- In traditional new church starts, until your church is ready for its constituting conference (¶259), your district superintendent and conference minister of new church starts will fulfill the role of your church council, trustees, finance committee and staff-pastor parish relations committees. Set up regular strategy review sessions with them *(perhaps quarterly at first)* for reporting and approval of major issues.

Naming

- Hire graphic designer to develop church logo. Your friend "Bubba" might be free but believe me he is not a graphic designer and neither are you. However, you may have a professional graphic designer in your new church already.
- Create branding identity.

Website

- Purchase domain name (and names that are similar to your domain name for protection) www.godaddy.com is one of the sources where you can see which names are already taken.
- Create and develop content for website. *(See the article on this subject in chapter four)*
  Start with home, about, new to us, ministries, get involved, what to expect, give now button, and FAQ sections.
- Finalize web site and get someone (other than you) to maintain the site.
- Post weekly blog.
- Develop facebook page for your church.
- Utilize all social networks: facebook, twitter, youtube, linkedIn, etc.
- Make sure you and your growing Team are inviting friends through all social networks.

Gathering

- Begin weekly gatherings of launch team for fellowship, planning, and leadership training. Begin building a team of at least 35 adults before launch.
- Revisit your earlier projection of the number of adults you will need in worship to achieve "critical mass" in your particular mission field. Ask yourself, *"What will I do **TODAY** to move closer to this critical mass number?"*

Networking

- Develop an invitation card to pass out to people.
- Personally contact local United Methodist pastors to build relationships and create ministry partners.
- Meet local pastors from other denominations.
- Meet/interview civic and governmental leaders.
- Meet funeral home directors.
- Meet police and fire chiefs; volunteer as chaplain.
- Meet school administrators.
- Hold neighborhood parties.
- Conduct information meetings.
- Join a gym for networking and for personal health.
- Join civic organizations for networking *(but do not take any leadership positions!!)*.
- Hold at least two people gathering events each month *(be sure you have a 'handoff' for participants)* to share the church vision with anyone interested in joining the launch team.
- Encourage launch team members to hold people gathering events for their sphere of influence.
- Take pictures and video to record these early days of the church, and to post on your new church's Facebook and website.
- Preach at area churches to share your vision.
- Begin developing content for your future discipling, leadership, and membership classes.

 © 2018 Robert O. Crossman, www.UMNewChurch.org

Small Group Plan

- Determine small group model to use, and write out the plan.
- Select study material.
- Select and train initial small group leaders.
- Start small relational groups.
- Start more small relational groups.

Servant Evangelism Plan

Perhaps it may be true that twenty years ago, a church only needed to offer heart warming worship and music to spark a word of mouth process that would bring new people causing the church to grow and prosper.

However, today in an increasing number of mission fields, people are seeking more than inspiring worship with great music. In an increasing number of mission fields in the USA, even the "nones," lost sheep, prodigals, and prospects somehow understand the heart of Matthew 25 and John Wesley's "Works of Mercy." Out of this intuition, they are only inclined to be a part of a church that is authentically "doing something," getting blisters in Jesus' name.

How can our churches continue to be faithful to Matthew 28 *(go make disciples, teaching and baptizing)* while experiencing an increasing faithfulness to Matthew 25 *(feed the hungry, cloth the naked, welcome the stranger, and visit the prisoner)*? *(see the article on Engaging Missionally in chapter four)*

- **www.servantevangelism.com**
  - Plan and conduct first servant evangelism project that fits your mission field and target audience. Be sure and have a 'handoff' for participants announcing and inviting them an upcoming gathering.
  - Evaluate project.
  - Plan second servant evangelism project.
  - Plan at least one servant evangelism project each month *(be sure you have a 'handoff' for participants)*.
  - Encourage small groups to conduct servant evangelism projects.

Administration

- Introduce tithing to team members, with the expectation that launch team will set the example for tithing with the new congregation. Invite team members to tithe or to set a date by which team members will step up to become tithers.
- Have offering envelopes printed and begin to use with your growing launch team.
- Obtain an on-line or electronic method for your launch team to give, and post on your web site.

Ministry Teams

- Identify list of desired ministries and ministry teams
- Identify basic processes for each ministry team.
- Choose team leaders *(after much prayer and discernment)*.

Staff

- Rank potential staff positions based on your church planting strategy.

- determine likely number of part-time staff needed.
- determine if interns are available.
- identify initial positions to fill.
- determine hiring time line.

• Discover process for getting criminal background checks for volunteers to work with children and teens. Your conference office may be able to assist with this.

Marketing

• Determine the distinctive ministry of the new church.

• Determine marketing strategy that fits your mission field and primary target audience.
It may include: (*order small quantities of these below because things will change)*
- Order marketing giveaways (T-shirts, cups, window stickers, etc.).
- Order business cards, note cards, envelopes, letterhead.
- Order yard signs, yard banners, etc.
- Order flyers for high visibility / foot traffic areas.
- Order door flyers.

• Is your mission field filled with "neighborhoods" or "subdivisions"?
In neighborhoods and subdivisions you can obtain a list of local home owner associations. Obtain their schedule of their events and purchase ads in their newsletter *(print or electronic)* or website. Hold multiple launch team prayer walks through these neighborhoods.

• Design a "survey monkey" for follow up after outreach events.

Information Meetings

• Continue to hold regular information meetings and sharing the vision of this new church.

Worship

• Begin to clarify the worship style (and dress code) needed to fruitfully reach your unique mission field. *(test this in your preview worship and elbow events)*

• Define music style, leadership style, format, preaching style *(test this in your preview worship and elbow events).*

• Secure worship leader.

• Develop music team, and begin practicing regularly. *(Purchase "Starting a Praise Band" by Abingdon Press.)*

• Identify location for public worship. **Do not sign any rental or lease agreement until it is reviewed by your district superintendent.** With that permission, sign the lease. In many conferences, the district superintendent will actually have to sign the lease *(and any other legal documents the first few years)* because your new church has not yet held it's constituting conference.

• Confirm / obtain liability insurance limits, including corporate and personal. Send copies of such confirmation to the district office. *(See the article on Insurance in chapter ten.)*

• If you plan to project words of music on a screen, obtain a church copyright

 © 2018 Robert O. Crossman, www.UMNewChurch.org

license from CCLI www.ccli.com *(See the article on Insurance in chapter ten.)*

- If you plan to project video clips of movies in worship, obtain a license from Christian Video Licensing International (CVLI). *(See the article on Insurance in chapter ten.)*
- Begin to decide on your first sermon series. Get a theme and start brainstorming ideas. Also think about the series you would like to do for the first few months.
- Set launch date when you see objective evidence that you will have the necessary critical mass of people not only on launch day, but four weeks after launch. Jim Griffith writes, *"We are seeing more and more that "volume" is what should determine launch, NOT just the calendar."*

Equipment

- Assess equipment needs such as instruments, projection screen, computer, sound system, trailer, platform decorations, chairs etc.
- Check with other planters for sources of equipment, and lists of equipment they needed.
- Ask your sponsoring church, district office, and your conference new church director to discover any source *(from a recently closed new church, for example)* for the equipment you need, and if they are willing to donate items to you.
- After obtaining approval of bids and written permission from your conference new church director, order needed equipment.
- Research and order needed chairs, banners, tables, directional signs, ministry signs, hospitality signs, etc.
- Determine storage system (trailer, used U-Haul truck, or on site?).
- Prepare shelves and tubs for organization.
- Research and order needed equipment for nursery.

Discipleship Process

- Firm up discipleship process.
- Develop new member orientation process.

Three Months Prior to Launch

Personal

- Pray and fast weekly.
- Continue to develop your personal prayer life and Bible study.
- Keep your intercessory team informed and updated.
- Keep your prayer team updated.
- Remember (and practice) the Sabbath.
- Maintain good exercise discipline.
- Review and revise your initial benchmarks you proposed at your "pre-moving day strategy session" in cooperation with your coach and conference minister of new church starts.
- Ask yourself, "What will I do **TODAY** to let people know we are planting a church?"

Connect

- In mother/daughter, extension campus, or satellite strategies -

maintain regular contact with mother church for support, prayers, and encouragement.

- Stay in regular contact with your coach. *(either weekly or month as pre-arranged).*
- Stay in regular contact by email with your conference minister of new church starts and your district superintendent. It is never a good idea to surprise your district superintendent!
- In most 'Launching Large' new church starts, until your church is ready for its constituting conference (¶259), your district superintendent and conference minister of new church starts will fulfill the role of your church council, trustees, finance committee and staff-pastor parish relations committees. Continue regular strategy review sessions with them (perhaps quarterly at first) for reporting and approval of major issues.

Networking

- Review your networking strategy and its level of fruitfulness. Revise and improve your networking strategy.
- If using direct mail piece, have it designed and approved.

Marketing

- Review marketing strategy based on what your have learned about the mission field and your target audience.
- Develop a final marketing push.
  - Determine what printed or electronic resources you need to put in the hands of your launch team for their final push to invite family, friends, neighbors, co-workers to the launch worship.
  - Determine which marketing strategies will be most effective in your mission field: facebook targeted ads, social media, billboard, flyers, window stickers, yard signs, mass saturation mailings, newspaper, or radio.
  - Implement marketing pieces on a timely basis.
- If using a direct mail piece, have it designed and approved by the post office before printing copies.
  Work with post office to determine timing of how bulk mail is delivered, and to discover which postal routes are within your mission field boundaries.
  Chart a time frame for design, printing and mailing so that direct mail reaches the households 10-14 days prior to launch.
- Order giveaways.
- Press releases to local newspapers and radio.
- Posters in windows of area businesses, community bulletin boards, etc.
- Approach athletic teams, restaurants, coffee houses, etc.
- Facebook targeted ads.

Signage

- Determine, design for indoor and outdoor signage/banners.
  Remember that only two things are needed on the signs: name of church and website address. The print must be large enough that someone driving

 © 2018 Robert O. Crossman, www.UMNewChurch.org

past at 35 miles an hour will be able to read the sign easily.

- Order large outdoor banner for front of building.
- Information flyer to include inside the launch worship bulletin.
- Develop welcome, hospitality or guest services center.
  - Order banner for booth six weeks in advance.
  - Invitation to a newcomers reception, 3 to 4 weeks after the launch.
  - Invitation to a membership class, 6 to 10 weeks after the launch.
  - Guests brochure and connect card.
  - Giveaways to pass out during launch worship.
  - Name tags for workers.
  - Facility map.

Preview Services

- Hold monthly preview worship services (in almost every case this will be at your future launch site).
- Train each team on excellence.
- Videotape each team at work.
- Evaluate preview services.
- Encourage launch team to invite their family and friends.
- Finalize launch date.
- Prepare for launch and launch season.

Children's Ministry

- Children's ministry forms such as application, accident report, activity consent, medical authorization, etc.
- Registration system, name tags for staff.
- Purchase children's curriculum.
- Design informational flyer for parents.
- Prepare registration tables.
- Order department banners six weeks in advance.
- Prepare display with connect cards, letter introducing the curriculum, visitor brochures, registration lists, name tags, etc.

Ministry Teams

- Develop and train hospitality team.
- Develop and train children's workers.
- Develop and train nursery workers.
- Conduct background checks on all children's and nursery workers.
- Develop and train set-up and tear-down teams.

Finances

- Continue to introduce tithing to team members, with the expectation that launch team will set the example for tithing with the new congregation. Invite team members to tithe or to set a date by which they will become tithers.
- Follow through on initial contacts with family and friends for "virtue" capital. *(see article on this subject in chapter eleven)*
- Follow through with earlier invitations for the district to ask congregations to have a "baby shower" for the new church, in response to the detailed

supply and equipment lists you have developed.

Worship

- Prepare for the first public worship service *(launch Sunday).*
- Prepare first sermon series.
  -bulletin covers, power point slides, video, platform decorations on theme, music, countdown clock.
- Prepare a message that explains the vision and mission of the church in a winsome and invitational way.
- Either start first series, or announce first series to begin next week.
- Be prepared to announce second sermon series during the last week or two of the first series.

Discipleship Process

- Develop new Christian class.
- Develop basic membership class.
- Develop basic spiritual growth class.

Final Preparation

- Hold two practice services setting up everything and going through the entire service.
- Plan a pre-launch party for volunteers the day before launch.

Launch Meal

- Provide a catered meal for all who attend the launch worship service.
- Have sign-up sheets and displays for small groups and other opportunities for people to get involved.
- Plan fun activities for the children during the meal (inflatable slides, carnival games, snow cones, etc.).

Follow-up

- Evaluate the launch Sunday.
- Implement follow-up strategy.
- Plan for repeated launch seasons during the first year.

Sources:

I appreciate the assistance of Dirk Elliott, Michigan Area Director of New Church Development, in preparing this check list.

Planter Check List, by Kevin Kloster, Lead Pastor, Faith United Methodist Church M: (701) 566-2163 O: (701) 232-6844

The Year Leading Up To Your Launch, by ARC (Association of Related Churches) www.arcchurches.com

†††

NOTE: This article reflects the personal opinions of the author and does not necessarily reflect an official position of Discipleship Ministries or Path 1.

© 2018 Robert O. Crossman, www.UMNewChurch.org

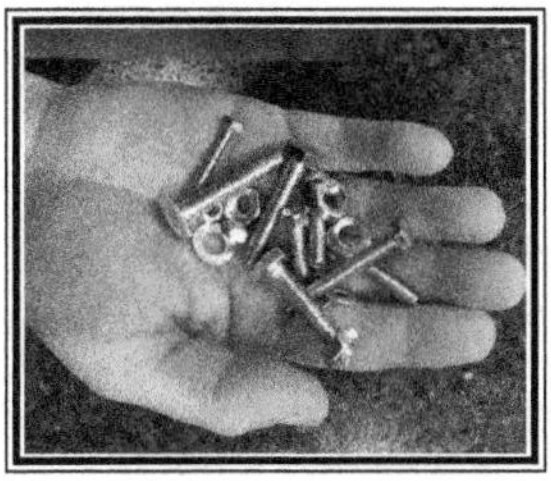

New Church Handbook
Nuts & Bolts for Planting New Churches In The Wesleyan Tradition

"A Planter's Check List For Starting a New Expression of the Church"

by Bob Crossman

1. Among Wesleyan churches, a "New Expression" or "Fresh Expression of Church" is designed primarily to engage people who have never been to church, using a wide variety of models that are each context appropriate. These expressions are *"a form of church for our changing culture, established primarily for the benefit of people who are not yet members of any church. It will come into being through principles of listening, service, incarnational mission and making disciples; It will have the potential to become a mature expression of church shaped by the gospel and the enduring marks of the church and for its cultural context."* [1]
2. One of the ways to start a new expression of the church is to re-discover one of the older ways laity started new faith communities or churches.
3. One of those older ways that might be worth re-discovering occurred across the American frontier in the 1800's.

American Frontier New Expressions

4. In the 1800's, as American laity moved west to seek their fortune, receive land grants, have a new beginning, or escape trouble - they carried their faith with them.
5. Methodist laity moving into the frontier would naturally build new relationships with their new neighbors as the interacted with their neighbors at the mercantile, one-room school house, livery stable, taverns, train station, telegraph / post office, bank, feed store, land office, rail depot or saloon in their new community.
6. Occasionally the subject of faith would enter the conversation. It was not unusual for the new neighbor to say, *"Let's continue this conversation next time your in town."*
7. Some of these casual, relationship based conversations would naturally result is a cluster of neighbors gathering on a regular basis to form what today we might call the beginnings of a lay-led small group, fresh expression, new expression, faith community, or weird church.
8. Some of these new expressions were short lived. Some of these lasted a few months. A few continued on longer.
9. Most of these regular gatherings had a lay person who served as the informal or formal convener of the group.

10. A few of these regular gatherings made connections with a circuit riding clergy who would stop by every 3 to 12 weeks to preach, baptize, serve the Lord's Supper, and conduct weddings. The local lay convener became the "Local Pastor" of the group in the months between the circuit rider's appearance.
11. A small number of these "preaching posts" on the circuit rider's route, through a series of twist and turns, gave birth to congregations that are still in existence 200 years later.

Be Clear What Your New Expression Vision Is

12. So, you are thinking and praying about starting a new expression of the church. Let's be clear, exactly what do you believe God is calling you to begin?
13. Who do you believe God is calling you to reach?
14. In the initial phases of this new expression, rather than attempting to appeal to or reach everyone in your community, spend time clearly discerning which particular group of people within your mission field God that is calling you to reach with this new ministry.
15. The opportunity scan feature of MissionInsight can highlight mosaic groups that your church is not currently reaching.
16. In your discernment process, you might ask several key questions, such as, *"Who is in my natural affinity group?" "What subgroup or culture might God be calling me to establish a new expression among?" "Who are my friends and acquaintances who never attend any church, temple or synagogue?"*; and, *"Is there a particular group already connected with one of the ministries I'm involved with?"*
17. Remember that ministries that truly bless a community often arise out of conversations where you listen for the hopes and dreams of people in your community.
18. Your discernment process might involve interviewing residents of the community, or sitting in a park, diner, or coffee house, simply asking yourself, *"What are challenges, hopes, longings and dreams God is putting in front of me?"* and, *"Who are the people God is continually introducing me to?"*
19. Discover ways to spend time with individuals in your mission field. You might even visit the volunteer fire department, diner, coffee shop, or sit in a park. Hannah Estock sat at Venice Beach, California with a sign that read, *"Tell me your story and I will give you a dollar."* Hannah was busy all afternoon, and a line of people formed to tell their story to Hannah. Engage with the people who accept your invitation, and slowly listen to their stories.
20. As you listen, don't let your pre-set ideas or pre-conceived notions shape the conversation. Rather, simply ask, "What are the challenges, hopes, longings and dreams of your neighbors?" Be willing to actively listen.

 © 2018 Robert O. Crossman, www.UMNewChurch.org

Build authentic relationships with People

21. Strive for meaningful engagement with others, not superficial gestures.
22. Make sure you are reaching out to people for the right reasons. If your motive is simply to get them to come to church, people will see right through to it.
23. Maintain appropriate boundaries, and respect all with whom you engage.
24. As you connect with people, discern those who want to connect with persons outside of the church to create a faith community with scriptural content.

    Those who have a different vision will need to be referred to another church or ministry effort.

    Also, begin the process of discerning those who have the gifts and graces to be part of your leadership team.
25. Be open to the guidance of the Holy Spirit as you connect with people and discern what kind of new expression God is calling you to begin.
26. New expressions that fruitfully bless communities in Jesus' name often arise out of unorganized, crazy and chaotic conversations where we listen for the hopes and dreams of people within a mission field.
27. Discern among two or three possible sub-groups (micro-cultures), outside of the church, where God is calling you to begin this new expression. It could be among:
    - The neighborhood youth who play basketball in the church parking lot. *{In Kentucky, the Upton congregation is reaching 100 youth every Thursday evening, witnessing 30 baptisms. At Dawson Springs Kentucky a church of 35 is reaching 85 youth each week.}*
    - The parents who bring their children to your annual easter egg hunt;
    - The participants at the local Wesley Foundation or campus ministry;
    - The participants in your English as a Second Language program;
    - The households who utilize your food pantry and clothing bank;
    - The regular Thursday night patrons at the local bar;
    - The neighbors who participate in your community garden project;
    - People without a church connection who have experienced a recent death of a loved one;
    - Residents of the local battered women's shelter, retirement village, nursing home, group home for challenged persons, independent living homes or half-way houses.
    - The men who sleep under the broadway bridge each evening;
    - The church custodian and lawn care workers;
    - The men who drink coffee at Bob's Grill early every weekday;
    - Single mothers in your neighborhood;
    - Ministry with specific groups in a biker church, cowboy church, trail riders, refugee groups, migrant workers, or ethnic groups.
    - Residents of the county jail; *{In Oldham County, Kentucky, they hold weekly*

worship, including family members, and pairing prisoners with trained mentors who continue contact after they are released.}

- The current patrons of the local 12 step residential facility or Celebrate Recovery programs;
- With volleyball leagues, jogging / running groups, or little league teams that travel on Sundays; or at
- Boating or camping sites at the state park.
- And unique to your mission field:______________________________.

28. The use of the dinner church model may prove fruitful in reaching many of the mission fields above: inviting people to quality dinners where trained volunteers are prepared to have "significant conversations" around the tables – and all the principles of a church, including worship, discipleship, and outreach) grow out of those "church meals". The principle is to do this "with" those who come, not just "for." *{In Kentucky, the Monticello congregation has 100 meeting in an abandoned restaurant, with similar results in Hopkinsville.}*
29. All of these new expressions should always be tethered to an existing church for help and accountability.
30. Collaborate with others who are also passionate about beginning a new expression of the church. Don't reinvent the wheel if you can partner with someone else serving the community.

Seek to Gain Support From your Sponsoring Church

31. Within your sponsoring church, encourage interest and excitement about the possibility of experimentation and connecting with people your church is not currently connecting with.
32. Tell stories of the people you are meeting, and the hopes and dreams you are discovering in the mission field.
33. Share how your heart breaks for the hundreds of households within 5 miles of your church whose children have never heard the story of Jesus; the adults who have never experienced the forgiveness of their sins; the families in grief without the loving support of Christian friends; the parents who do not have the increasing hope of an eternity in God's presence; and the youth who are making lifetime decisions about what kind of adult they will be and what kind of citizen they will become - all without the influence of solid Christian parents or grandparents.
34. Invite church members to think of their estranged family members who might find faith in a new expression.
35. Tell stories about the range of possibilities where a new expression might form and why that could matter.
36. Be prepared to give a short, 30 second, clear, brief statement *(elevator speech)*

 © 2018 Robert O. Crossman, www.UMNewChurch.org

about the possibilities of this new ministry.

37. Rehearse a 5 minute and 20 minute version of your "elevator speech" for those who ask to know more.
38. Build a lay group within your sponsoring congregation who will commit to pray for you daily, receive additional prayer request from you, and meet with you monthly to hold you accountable to the vision God has give to you.
39. If you happen to be a clergy person, be sure you have the support of your administrative body, and clarity about how many hours each week you will spend on this new ministry.
40. While most new expressions do not involve a financial investment from the sponsoring church, be clear in writing with your administrative body about any financial support expectations.
41. Within your sponsoring church, be clear that you are forming a new contextual church, but a different kind of church for those, who for a variety of reasons, would have a difficult time entering the doors of a traditional church building on Sunday.
42. Remind your sponsoring church that this New Expression is not a replacement of your church's wonderful ministries, but is an addition to the variety of your church's current outreach of love into the community.
43. Be looking for 3 to 8 people within the sponsoring church who might join you in birthing this new expression, or who might be the right people to start the second and third new expression. Ideally these are people with many friends who are outside of the church.
44. Travis Collins recommends establishing a **"tether"** between your new expression and the sponsoring church: so the traditional church can: a) encourage the pioneers; b) cooperate on ventures; c) provide opportunities the small group cannot provide (counseling to families in crises, i.e.), and d) to offer theological/biblical direction.

    The **tether** connectional element is found in: 1) regular meetings between leaders of the fresh expression and the leadership of the original congregation; 2) cooperative ventures like joint baptisms; 3) stories form the fresh expressions of church told in the original church, and; 4) direction without control.

Leaders Role and Expectations in the Early Stages

45. In the early stages the lay or clergy leader of this new expression will be spending a lot of time building relationships with people outside of the church.
46. The leader will be experimenting with several attempts to gather people to possible form a new expression. Some experiments will fail. Some experiments will be short lived. With God's Grace, some will be fruitful.
47. The goal is to build relationships, follow-up with connections, and build an initial new expressions.

48. Most new expressions do not attempt to launch large like other new church strategies such as multi-sites, mother-daughter, or parachute drops.
49. In many mission fields the goal is to have a network of new expressions - each with 10 to 50 people actively involved and regularly gathering... starting small and letting word of mouth and personal invitations driving growth.
50. Shannon Kiser, of Fresh Expressions USA, said, *"This is going to take some time. Don't expect to have something to brag about right away. A fresh expression of church is a new form of church that is meant to connect with people who are not currently engaging with a church. It is a way of loving and serving people in the beginning, developing community together, and ultimately growing in Christian discipleship together, and beginning the rhythms of holy living and church life. This takes a long time.*

    The Leader should hold their plans loosely, keeping your vision and intentionality yet learn to dance with the Spirit, pray a lot, and be attentive to what God is doing."

VIDEO: https://www.freshexpressionsfl.org

For more information you may contact:

Bob Crossman
bcrossman@arumc.org
The Path 1 staff at:
www.umcdiscipleship.org/new-church-starts/staff
Luke Edwards, King Street UMC at luke@kscboone.org
Paul Brunstetter, UM Kentucky Conference, at
paul.brunstetter@gmail.com

NOTES:

1 www.freshexpressions.org.uk/about/whatis

2 I appreciate the editorial assistance of Path 1 staff of Discipleship Resources - www.path1.org, Luke Edwards, pastor of King Street UMC (a network of fresh expressions in Boone, North Carolina); and Paul Brunstetter, Kentucky Conference.

NOTE: This article reflects the personal opinions of the author and does not necessarily reflect an official position of Discipleship Ministries or Path 1.

 © 2018 Robert O. Crossman, www.UMNewChurch.org

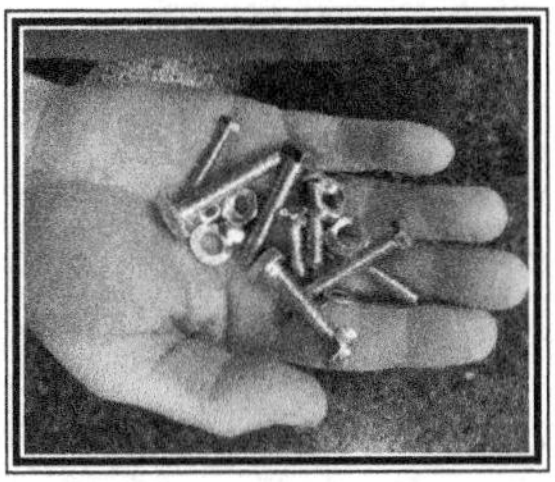

New Church Handbook
Nuts & Bolts for Planting New Churches In The Wesleyan Tradition

"Planter Check List For Mother-Daughter Plants"

by Bob Crossman and Tammy Garrison

The time line from appointment to launch of weekly worship may vary from 6 to 16 months based on the natural affinity the new church pastor has in the community; how soon a healthy launch team can be gathered; and how soon confidence is reached that a "critical mass" of people will attend the launch of weekly worship. Typically, launch worship would be in month six, or possibly as late as month fifteen. Jim Griffith, in *"Ten Common Mistakes New Churches Make"* has found that starting public worship too soon to be a factor in almost all church plants that fail.

6 MONTH CHECK LIST

In the time from receiving the appointment until moving day:

- Begin working on vision, mission, and core values.
- Begin assessing demographics.
- Set public launch date.

MONTH ONE:

- Begin networking in the community through Rotary, fire and police department, city council, public school, etc.
- Network through mother church, preaching and teaching Sunday school classes.
- Begin informational meetings about new church. Follow up with those who attend.

MONTH TWO:

- Continue networking.
- Continue to preach and teach in the mother church.
- Seek other opportunities to speak in the community.
- In consultation with mother church pastor, seek members from the mother church to become a part of the launch team.
- Begin meeting with launch team members weekly, bi-weekly or monthly. Use this time for Bible study and vision casting.
- Put musicians in place.
- Begin search for place to meet for weekly worship.
- Plan elbow/outreach events for the community. These are determined by the mission field. They include such things as concerts, carnivals, special worship experiences, and other events that are important to the mission field. Encourage the launch team to bring friends, family, co-workers and neighbors to these events.

MONTH THREE:

- Continue networking.
- Continue seeking opportunities to speak to various community groups/churches about the new church.
- Continue launch team meetings/Bible study.
- Begin small groups/discipleship system.
- Begin visiting other new churches with launch team.
- Hold first preview service. This may or may not be in the place you will be meeting at weekly. Launch team sign up for places of service - set up, break down, hospitality, etc.
- Hold first elbow/outreach event. An elbow event is one in which launch team members are expected to bring someone "on their elbow." Encourage launch team members to invite friends, family, co-workers and neighbors to elbow events and worship.

MONTH FOUR:

- Continue networking.
- Continue seeking opportunities to speak to various community groups/churches about the new church.
- Continue launch team meetings/Bible study.
- Visit other new churches with launch team.
- Hold second preview service. This may or may not be in the place you will be meeting at weekly.
- Hold second "elbow" or outreach event.

MONTH FIVE:

- Continue networking.
- Continue seeking opportunities to speak to various community groups/churches about the new church.
- Continue launch team meetings/Bible study.
- Visit other new churches with launch team.
- Hold third preview service. This may or may not be in the place you will be meeting at weekly. In a six -month launch that begins July 1, this preview service/elbow event may be Christmas candlelight services.
- Hold third elbow/outreach event. Launch team continue to invite friends, family, co-workers and neighbors to services and elbow events.
- At the end of this month, move to exhibition services. Preview services are held at other times than the time planned for weekly services. Exhibition services are weekly service 4 to 6 weeks prior to launch at the time weekly services will be held.
- If doing mass mailing/advertising, do so at this time.

MONTH SIX:

- Continue networking.
- Hold fourth elbow/outreach event.
- Continue to hold exhibition services. Launch team continue to invite friends, family, co-workers and neighbors to services and elbow events.
- LAUNCH every Sunday worship! If the appointment begins July 1, the launch

 © 2018 Robert O. Crossman, www.UMNewChurch.org

date for worship will be in January.

Post-launch:

- Continue networking.
- Continue to hold elbow/outreach events at regular intervals.
- Make sure discipleship system is in place.
- Discover which marketing brought in the most guest.
- Continue to follow up with worship guests.

†††

In settings where for a variety of reasons, the launch team is harder to gather, a 15 month model would typically look like this:

15 MONTH CHECK LIST

In the time from receiving the appointment until moving day:

- Begin working on vision, mission, and core values.
- Begin assessing demographics.
- Set public launch date.

MONTH ONE:

- Begin networking in community through Rotary, fire & police department, city council, public school, etc.
- Network through mother church, preaching and teaching Sunday school.
- Begin informational meetings about new church. Follow up with those who attend.

MONTH TWO:

- Continue networking.
- Continue to preach and teach in the mother church.
- Seek other opportunities to speak in the community.
- In consultation with mother church pastor, seek members from the mother church to become a part of the launch team.
- Begin meeting with launch team members weekly, bi-weekly or monthly. Use this time for Bible study and vision casting.
- Begin search for musicians.
- Begin search for place to meet for weekly worship.
- Plan elbow/outreach events for the community. These are determined by the mission field. They include such things as concerts, carnivals, vacation Bible school, special worship experiences, and other events that are important to the mission field. Encourage the launch team to bring friends, family, co-workers and neighbors to these events.

MONTH THREE TO FOURTEEN:

- Repeat this monthly pattern until there is evidence that the launch team is large enough to insure that critical mass will be present at the launch of weekly worship.
- Continue networking.
- Continue to preach and teach in the mother church.
- Continue seeking opportunities to speak to various community groups/churches about the new church.
- Continue launch team meetings/Bible study. This may now shift to reading a

book together about planting a new church. There are several that are good. *"Ten Common Mistakes New Churches Make"* by Jim Griffith is a good example. Order copies of Griffith's book from www.cokesbury.com

- Begin visiting other new churches with launch team.
- In month two, begin organizing teams to hold the elbow events.
- In month three, hold first elbow or outreach event where launch team brings friends, family, co-workers and neighbors "on their elbow." Repeat similar elbow event every month.
- In month four, form ministry teams for next month's preview worship experience (set-up, break down, hospitality, child care, music, tear-down, etc.)
- In month five, hold first preview service. This may or may not be in the place you will be meeting at weekly. In an appointment that begins July 1, this may be a Christmas candlelight service. Relevant targeted ads on Facebook, google pop-up ads, or mass mailing may be appropriate at this time.
- In month six, begin monthly prayer walks through the mission field to help your team begin to pray for those with no church home.
- In month nine, hold second preview service. In an appointment that begins July 1, this may be an Easter or sunrise service. Relevant targeted ads on Facebook, Google pop-up ads, or mass mailing may be appropriate.
- In months ten, continue monthly preview services. These are not typically at the time designated as your weekly worship time.
- In month fourteen, begin holding weekly pre-view services. These are typically at the time your weekly services will be held. Pre-view services are typically 4 - 6 weeks prior to launch Sunday. Relevant targeted ads on Facebook, google pop-up ads, or mass mailing/advertising is appropriate at this time.
- Through the above, develop list of contacts and make as many face-to-face appointments as possible in homes, over a cup of coffee, or over dinner. Tell your story and share the vision for the new church. Invite the people you meet to help with future elbow/outreach events.

MONTH FIFTEEN:

- Continue networking.
- Hold thirteenth elbow/outreach event.
- Continue to hold pre-view services. Launch team continue to invite friends, family, co-workers and neighbors to worship and elbow events.
- LAUNCH weekly Sunday worship! If the appointment begins July 1, the launch date will be in September or October.

Post-launch:

- Continue networking.
- Continue to hold elbow/outreach events at regular intervals.
- Make sure discipleship system is in place.
- Continue to follow up with worship guests.

†††

NOTE: This article reflects the personal opinions of the author and does not necessarily reflect an official position of Discipleship Ministries or Path 1.

 © 2018 Robert O. Crossman, www.UMNewChurch.org

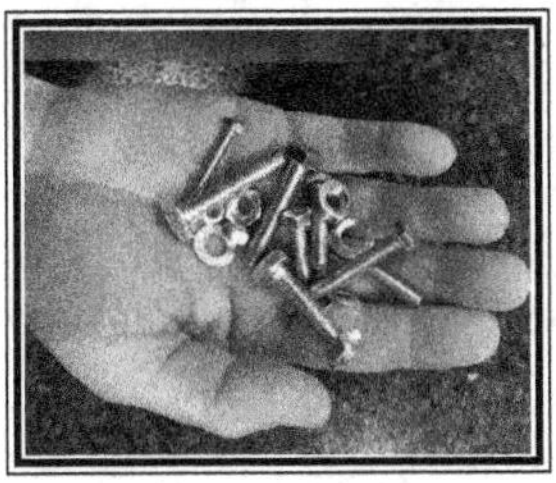

New Church Handbook
Nuts & Bolts for Planting New Churches In The Wesleyan Tradition

"Planter Check List For a Restart or Lazarus Strategy"

by Bob Crossman and Steven Murray

RESTART OR LAZARUS MODEL FOR STARTING A NEW CHURCH

This particular strategy starts with the death of a current congregation.

The "Restart" or "Lazarus" model can indeed result in the birth of a new congregation.

In Arkansas, the closest we have had to this model would be when the old Wiggins UMC in south Fayetteville intentionally closed. The largest congregation in the state, Central UMC in Fayetteville, remodeled that building and began Genesis UMC as a satellite of Central in the old Wiggins facilities about six months later. Within a year attendance had grown to over 300 in worship.

Also in Arkansas, the old Huntington Avenue UMC in downtown Jonesboro intentionally closed. Most of that congregation decided to be part of starting the Cornerstone UMC in northeast Jonesboro.

In Searcy, Arkansas the old Grace UMC intentionally closed. Most of that congregation decided to be part of starting the new St. Paul UMC.

The Arkansas Parish and Community Development Committee defines it this way: *"It shall be defined as an existing group becoming part a new church, with a new name, in a new area, having participated in training about what it means to be a new church."*

The Lazarus strategy is NOT simply changing the name of the church from Huntington to Cornerstone so that the congregation can get a $100,000 grant from the conference.

CAUTION: *In most cases it is prudent to amend the incorporation documents (i.e. Wesley UMC doing business as Living Water UMC), replacing the names of the old board members. If you officially notify the state/city that the "old church" is closed, the city Planning Commission may require the "new" occupant to bring the building up to the new codes: (i.e. sprinkler systems, handicapped bathrooms, parking spaces, green spaces, signage, etc.) Although GCFA understands "Wesley" is closed, the State understands Wesley is DBA Living Water.*

The following Guidebook was prepared by the New England Conference.

© 2018 Robert O. Crossman, www.UMNewChurch.org

LAZARUS CHURCH GUIDEBOOK

Prepared by Steve Murray, when he was chair of the New Church Development Committee of the New England Conference of the United Methodist Church

The Lazarus Church program is a plan for facilitating new church development within the New England Conference. It was developed out of the need to provide an alternative to the costly model used throughout much of our denomination. A traditional model for NCD would generally require an investment of approximately $250,000 to $500,000 spread over several years. In this traditional model, a church planter would be sent into a community or area which had no Methodist presence and start a new church "from scratch".

In contrast, a Lazarus church start would take place in a community which already has a United Methodist Church. Under this model, that church would make the conscious decision to allow itself to die, that it may be a seed for a new church start.

As we enter the new millennium, the reasons for wanting to do this are manifold. The church may be in a location that has no hope of expansion of facility or parking to allow for growth. It may be located in a geographic area which is no longer growing, or there may be other internal factors which keep the church from reaching its potential for ministry.

What ever the reasons may be for taking this step, it needs to be clearly understood that this is not simply a relocation, it is a new start.

The role of the committee on New Church Development would be:

- to assist in the selection of potential Lazarus church projects
- to provide grant money
- and to act as a consultant team, working closely with the church as it goes through the process.
- The committee will also help fund, when possible, the training of potential NCD pastors.

What follows is a detailed guide to the process. While there may be some latitude necessary from situation to situation, it is generally expected that these steps will be followed, and the NCD committee will hold the Lazarus church accountable to the process. This, we feel, will discourage the new church from cutting corners, as this often has serious negative consequences in the long run.

PROJECT SELECTION

One important step in this process is selecting a feasible site for a potential Lazarus Church. Projects to receive grant funding would be chosen (with considerable prayer) by the NCD committee in close consultation with the district

 © 2018 Robert O. Crossman, www.UMNewChurch.org

superintendent. In choosing a project (especially in years when there are more potential projects than grants available) the following lowing criteria would be considered:

- Percentage of the community which is un-churched
- Openness to change within the congregation
- Assets available to the church (value & marketability of church building, invested funds, etc.)
- Level of current indebtedness
- Availability and quality of interim meeting space
- Community growth potential
- Current average worship attendance
- Degree of support from the cluster and district
- Other demographic/ethnographic information

Note from Bob Crossman

In an increasing number of annual conferences the Lazarus model always intends to use the 'old' building for a new church start.

Additional criteria for using the 'old' building includes:

- *Is the building the right size? (not too small, and not too large)*
- *Is the building still in good repair?*
- *Is the building located in a mission field that we know how to reach?*
- *Do we have a potential planter who has an affinity with this particular mission field?*
- *Are financial resources available from the district, conference, or nearby church to help launch this new church?*

And if this is going to be a multi-site new church start:

- *Do we have a healthy, vital UMC within ten miles who has the heart/DNA/Vision/finances/personnel to start a multi-site in this location?*

PASTORAL LEADERSHIP

As with any new church start, the selection of the NCD (Natural Church Development) pastor can make or break the project. The pastor for the proposed Lazarus Church may already be in place, or it may be necessary for a transition in leadership. A NCD pastor does not need to have previous training in New Church Development. However, it is expected that he or she will attend training. Traits to look for in a potentially successful NCD pastor include:

- Entrepreneurial & visionary leader
- High level of energy
- Heart for evangelism & church growth
- Risk taker
- Stable family situation

The pastor taking on this challenge needs to realize that this is no ordinary calling. They will be required to make considerable sacrifice of time and energy, especially in the early stages. When potential pastors are identified by the cabinet, it is suggested that they be recommended to the NCD committee for training, even if there are no potential Lazarus churches open at the time. We have some money available to help with the cost of this training.

PREPARATORY STEPS

When a district superintendent identifies a project that he or she feels may be a potential Lazarus Church, it will be necessary to do some initial research. This information will be crucial in determining whether or not this location is likely to be a successful Lazarus Church. Once this process is started there quickly comes a point of no return. What's more, once this program catches on, it is likely that there will be more applicants than grants. At that point, the NCD Committee will need to allocate money on the basis of each project's potential for success and future growth. Timing will also be considered in choosing the projects. This information will also be important when he time comes to begin to introduce the idea to the church as a whole. People are most fearful of the unknown. The more information we can provide up front, the better. Also, if the initial research shows this community to be an unlikely project site, you have not raised false hopes. For these reasons, some of this preparatory research should be done by the pastor, the district superintendent, and a few key laity.

This initial research should include:

- **Demographic Research -** This is likely to cost a couple of hundred dollars. Before doing this, you will want to talk to the NCD to see if any demographics have already been done in this area.
- **Investigate land availability -** The place to start is obviously with a Realtor. However, some of the best sites are often not on the market. You will also want to look through the tax maps for suitable lots (see later section on lot selection). It may be necessary to make an offer on a lot that is not currently listed.
- **Seek potential buyers -** While you are talking with Realtors, ask them to evaluate the value and marketability of your current facility. Most church buildings are not highly marketable. However, on occasion they do sit on some highly marketable land. You may even be able to meet with potential buyers.
- **Talk with other churches in the community -** Find out what percentage of the community is actually attending worship, Sunday School, etc. at any church. Find out what ministry needs are being well met in your area, and which are going unmet. Find out which churches are growing, and try to discern why.
- **Locate potential interim meeting sites -** Is there a school, theater, or other accessible, modern, attractive facility that you could meet in during the interim time? Find out what it would cost to rent it. *(Don't let anyone tell you that you can not rent a public school. Under the laws of equal access, we have as much right to rent the building as any other group.)*
- **Compare the cost of moving to the cost of staying -** Take an honest look at what it costs the church to continue worshipping where it is. Include the cost

 © 2018 Robert O. Crossman, www.UMNewChurch.org

of heat, upkeep, electricity, repairs, cleaning, etc. Many churches are surprised to discover that they can move to rented space for a modest increase over what it is currently costing them to stay in their antiquated buildings.

- **Evaluate the mood of the church regarding change -** How has the church dealt with change and growth in the recent past. Does it seem content with it's current situation?

Once this information is obtained, the NCD committee should be contacted for time at the next meeting to hear and evaluate the results. Assuming the report shows reasonable potential and there are funds available, first stage approval can be given, allowing the church to begin to consider the idea as a whole.

TRANSITIONAL STEPS

Once the church has been approved as a potential Lazarus Church site, it can now begin to take the steps that can lead it to this transition.

Step One - Introduce the idea for exploration and establish an exploration and visioning committee. This committee should receive the preparatory information and draft a vision of what the church could be if it were to begin anew as a Lazarus Church.

For this to be a true new church start, this vision must be community need driven. The thing that keeps many of our churches from growing is that they have become internally focused. They exist to meet the needs, interests, and priorities of those who are already members, regardless of the ministry needs of the community around them *(i.e. Why should we start a Senior High Youth ministry? We don't have any Senior Highs!)* To determine the needs of the community, speak with people outside the church. Take time to talk with community leaders (selectmen, city council, mayor), school administrators, teachers, guidance counselors, local police, YMCA, and other active community groups.

It is important that the pastor be a part of the visioning process. It is also important that prayer be an ongoing part of the process. When we get caught up in the details of this process we run the risk of leaving out the Holy Spirit. We are seeking to meet the needs of the community, but we are not a social service agency, we are the church of Jesus Christ !

Step Two - Hold informational hearings. Once the visioning committee has drafted a working proposal, informational hearings should be held. It is suggested that they be held at least two different times. One possible model would be to hold a luncheon meeting to present the information to the older members who perhaps do not get out in the evening. Then hold an evening meeting for those not available during the day. The report should include feasibility information with as much detail as possible, and a vision report. Following the presentation, open the meeting for questions and comments. At the end of the hearing, ask, by a show of hands, how many people feel they could support this if their questions and concerns were addressed.

Step Three - Visioning committee comes back together to process input from the hearings, and to attempt to find answers to any questions that were raised. Also make it clear that the committee is open to hear any questions or concerns that have come to mind following the hearing. Be sure the congregation knows who is on the committee so people know who to pass their questions along to.

Step Four - Hold a second round of hearings. Present the refined report and allow for additional discussion. At the end of the hearing, ask, by a show of hands, how may people feel that their questions have be en answered and they are ready to support it at a charge conference.

Step Five - Evaluate Readiness. By the end of the second hearing , several months should have passed since the idea was originally presented. This has given people some time to process the idea. During this time, (especially between the first and second hearing) the pastor should make a priority of visiting home to home to talk with people, answer questions, and hear concerns. Between the pastoral visits, and the straw votes at the hearings, the vision committee should have a good idea of the level of support for the new start. If it appears that there is overwhelming support for this transition, the church is ready to call a charge conference. If there is not, the committee needs to determine what it is that the church is resistant to, and decide whether the planning process ought to continue, or be ended. If the process is ended (or put on hold indefinitely) the NCD should be alerted of that as soon as possible.

Step Six - Charge Conference. If it is clear that the overwhelming majority of the church (90% to 95%) is ready to take this step, you are ready to call a charge conference. This should be a brief and perfunctory meeting. This is not the time to debate or discuss the idea. All of that should take place at the hearings. If there are still considerable questions or resistance, then the church needs to be given more time to process that, and a charge conference is premature. It should not be necessary to count the vote at this meeting. If the vote is close enough to be counted, the church is not ready. Nor should it be necessary to have a paper ballot. A paper ballot implies unspoken resistance. This should be more of a consensus, with the voting being a formality. You may also want to hold the charge conference immediately following worship. This lessens the likelihood that long inactive members, who did not participate in the hearings, will come out to the charge conference to sabotage the process.

The motion that is being presented at this charge conference should include the following action only:

- Vote to close the building

 © 2018 Robert O. Crossman, www.UMNewChurch.org

- Vote to enter into a contract for temporary meeting space
- Set a date for the final worship service to be held within a month

Note from Bob Crossman

In many annual conferences the Lazarus model works best the the 'old' church officially closes and ceases to exist, with the keys and check book turned over to the district office. The former board, trustees, Sunday school and UMW cease to exist. The former members are encouraged to join nearby United Methodist Churches. The district gives the keys to a new church planting pastor, or a nearby UMC to use as a multi-site. The building is kept 'dark' for six months while remodeling takes place.

This motion should not include authorization to sell the building. Knowing that the building is still there helps people to make the transition. On the other hand, the pastor should not say to the people "Look at it this way. The building is still ours, we can always come back if we feel like it." It is simply easier (emotionally) to take the step of selling the building after you have been worshipping in temporary space for a little while. What's more, you may find that the old building has a place in your future ministry as a satellite station for some of your program ministries.

Step Seven - Hold final service. This should be a celebration, not a funeral! Celebrate the ministry that the church has provided through h it's history. Invite previous pastors to bring words of greeting (or send letters). Put up displays, news clippings, etc. that celebrate the church's history. Hold a dinner after worship. Special music, joyful preaching, testimonies, etc. should all be a part of this final celebration. Make it as upbeat as possible.

Note from Bob Crossman

This model from the New England Conference suggests that step eight last eight weeks. However, Jim Griffith's experience indicates this closed season needs to last closer to ***12 to 18 months****. The congregation needs time grieve for their loss, and to commit their hearts to this new mission field.*

Step Eight - Prepare for new start kick off. These next eight weeks will be absolutely critical. To prepare for the new start kick off Sunday you will need to do the following things:

- Begin worshipping in a temporary facility. This should not be your former place of worship, nor should it be the place you will worship as a new church. For these next eight weeks your faithful remnant should worship together anywhere you can find inexpensive space. You should not advertise this meeting place, nor should you invite anyone to worship with you who was not previously involved with the congregation The reasons for doing this are manifold. First of all, this will be a time of grieving, and working through the pain of leaving the familiar. This is not something you want to invite potential new members to participate in. You may want to focus on the theme of the Exodus as you wander in the wilderness. Secondly, it will be a time of confusion and of limited ministries. You will not be prepared to greet the visitors, nor offer them much in terms of ministry. This will be a time of internal focus, and of preparation for the Kick Off Sunday. You simply will not be ready to welcome guests.

Note from Bob Crossman

In many annual conferences the Lazarus model almost always intends to use the 'old' building for the new church. However, it is important that the old building be 'dark' for six months to help the community understand that the old church closed. During these six months, any interior remodeling takes place and work is done on the exterior. While some mother churches have spent $4,000,000 remodeling the facilities of the closed church, others are able to spend only $30,000 to remodel. The remodeling at a minimum should include a new entryway, landscaping, and new signage to help the community understand that something new is happening.

Another point of the remodeling is to help the facilities more closely match the quality of construction and household interiors in the mission field so the new comer feels at home.

These preview worship services in #8 above are then held in the remodeled building.

- Conduct an intense marketing campaign. This marketing campaign will use a variety of media, all aimed at inviting people to your opening kick off service. You will want to take advantage of press releases, public service announcements on radio and television, posters, signs, etc.

The marketing campaign is one of the steps for which the committee will provide considerable funding, and offer extensive consultation. The time frame is such that there is little room for experimentation with the marketing campaign. This is not the place to cut corners in term of time, effort, or spending.

- Make preparations for opening service. This will include designing your worship area. Since you are in rented space, you will need to design some type of set up that allows you to create a worship space which can be easily set up and broken down. Banners, artificial potted plants, etc. can be used to create an atmosphere that inspires worship. You will want to design a welcome center where people can be greeted when they come in, be given a name tag, and be shown the way to the worship space, nursery, etc. Speaking of nursery care, you will need to arrange range for space for the nursery and find someone to staff it (In the early weeks, you may want to hire nursery care from outside the congregation to allow everyone to participate in worship. This is also an area where the cluster could be helpful by donating volunteers for a few weeks). You will also want to make arrangements for the coffee hour to follow worship. You may well want to make it a light brunch; coffee, muffins, pastries, finger sandwiches, chips, etc.

 © 2018 Robert O. Crossman, www.UMNewChurch.org

KICK OFF SUNDAY

You have been through your transitional steps, you have closed your building, you have wandered in the wilderness, you've launched your marketing campaign, you have prepared to start anew. Now you are ready to hold your first service as a new congregation! Here are a few things to keep in mind for that first Sunday.

This should be a new start for everyone. The reason you worshipped in a temporary space during these past eight weeks is because this first Sunday needs to be new to everyone! You have invited a lot of new people to be a part of a new congregation. If they come that first Sunday and find that they were lost and confused, but you were not, they are already going to feel like outsiders in a church that is suppose to be brand new.

- **Welcome people.** The first thing people receive when they come in should be a warm welcome. The welcome center should be highly visible, cheerful, and (of course) welcoming. Everyone should receive a name tag, and guides should be there to help people find their way.
- **Choose an appropriate worship style.** Remember this is a new start, you are not tied to anything you have done in the past. You have demographic information that tells you something about the people you are expecting. You have researched the churches around you to see which ones are growing. Design a worship service that you feel will meet the needs of the community you are trying to reach, yet still speaks to the faithful remnant. This may well be some what of a blended service. What ever you choose, it needs to be guided by your vision statement of what you see this new church being, and whom you hope to reach.
- **When you are putting this service together, build the best service you can.** But also remember that you are setting a precedent. Don't bring in a 50 voice choir if every week after that you are going to have 6 to 8 in the choir. This service should be special, but not substantially different from what you will have to offer in the weeks to come.
- **Don't stack the service.** Well meaning neighboring churches may offer to send folks to your opening service. This will feel wonderful on the opening day, but will leave people extremely disappointed on the second week. As it is, you can expect as much as a 30% drop from the first week to the second week. Many people will come to the kick off service out of curiosity. Some will find exactly what they are looking for, and some will not. Your faithful remnant needs to be aware that this will happen.

A typical attendance track may be as follows: Before voting to close you were averaging 60 to 70 in worship. On Kick Off Sunday, you could easily have 200 in worship *(if you have followed your marketing campaign).* Second Sunday, that could be down to 150. In five to six weeks you may have settled in around 125, and will begin to grow from there. To head off the grumbling that might lead them back to Egypt, the pastor needs to help the remnant focus on the fact that they have doubled their worship attendance over this time last year, not that they have dropped from 200 to 125 in the past two months. This is something that can be addressed during the 8 weeks in the wilderness.

- **Prepare an inclusive, user-friendly bulletin.** Remember that you are not tied to the past. Your bulletin does not need to be a traditional folded 8 1/2 by 11 bulletin. Do not assume anything.

As for words to the music, use a projector and screen. Either way, remember your Christian Copyright License.

- **Schedule.** Again, this is a new start. Set a schedule you feel will work best for the church you are becoming. One time schedule that seems to work well is 9:00 AM Sunday School, 10:30 Worship followed by coffee fellowship. More people seem to stay for the fellowship time if the service ends before noon. If you are planning a service that will run significantly more than an hour, you may want less time between Sunday School and worship. For example, if you plan to use a contemporary style with 30 to 40 minutes of praise music at the beginning, you may want to start at 10:00 or 10:15.
- **Coffee Hour.** The fellowship time that follows the service is very important in these early weeks. Many of the people who come will not know one another. This is the place where relationships begin to be developed. It is very important that those from the "faithful remnant" do not bunch up. They need to be very intentional about visiting with people they do not know! This should also be talked about during the 8 weeks in the wilderness.

THE WEEKS FOLLOWING KICK OFF

There has been a tremendous amount of time and energy invested in making the transition and holding the opening service. At this point, many churches feel as though they have made it, and they are ready to rest. Unfortunately, this is not the time to rest. This is not the end of the process, but the very beginning of a new thing. We need to be prepared for the emotional let down that will take place at this time, and be prepared to re-energize ourselves for the work that now needs to be done. That work will include:

- **Visitor follow up.** Anyone attending this first service who was not part of the original congregation (and perhaps even those who were) need to be followed up on. They should receive a note of welcome from the pastor, and a call later in the week inviting them to next Sunday 's service. You may also have some kind of information packet that you will want to mail or hand deliver to them. There are several ways to approach this follow up, but it needs to be done.
- **Prepare to start ministries.** The first few weeks, don't plan on offering much more than worship. However, you should be announcing from the opening service what ministries will be starting soon. In most situations, this should at least include Sunday School and some kind of youth ministry. (If you could use guidance in this area, contact the conference office for information on people who could assist you with preparing these ministries). Make it clear that you are not only looking for people to participate in the classes, but for leaders as well. Do not assume that all of your teachers will (or should) be drawn from the remnant of your former congregation. Seek out volunteers from your new congregation, set up a training time, and prepare to start the new program in a few weeks.

 © 2018 Robert O. Crossman, www.UMNewChurch.org

You may want to take a similar approach to music. Whether you intend to use a traditional choir or some kind of praise team, you might want to start with soloists, or a borrowed choir/praise team, and announce that rehearsals for the church's own music ministry will begin within a week or two. This gives anyone in the new congregation the opportunity to participate without feeling as though they need to break into an existing program.

- **Continue your marketing campaign.** Promoting the ministries and programs of the church is something every church ought to be doing in an ongoing way. This will be especially important for this new church. Take every conceivable opportunity you can to publicize your new church. The most effective way to do this over the long haul is the use of social media. Every week you should be posting a blog or photograph about something that happened, or is about to happen in this new church. This is a percentage game. The more things you post, the more coverage you will get. And it's all free!
  If you have money left, you may also want to do some paid newspaper advertising, and some targeted direct mail marketing (our committee can help you learn how to do this).
- **Community Building Opportunities.** In these early weeks, it would be very helpful to sponsor activities or programs (beyond coffee hour) that allow people to get to know one another. Plan activities that fit the profile of the people you are reaching. For some communities a pot luck dinner would be ideal, for others you may want to have it catered. You get the idea!
- These steps will take a church from where they are, to a new beginning. Where you go from here will vary considerably according to the vision of ministry that you have adopted.

SUGGESTED TIMETABLE

The initial research leading up to a presentation to the NCD for Lazarus Church funding could easily be 18 months or more before the church reaches the point of a Kick Off Sunday. Once the NCD has given first stage approval, the time table might look something like this:

- Late Winter (February or March) -**Step One.**
  Introduce idea, establish exploration/visioning committee.
- Spring (April or May) - **Step Two**. Hold first hearing.
- Summer (June or July) - Refine proposal, Hold second hearing, evaluate readiness.
  Assuming church is ready, call a charge conference.
- August - Charge Conference **(Step Six)**
  Vote to close building and set date for final worship service.
- Mid-September - Hold final Service **(Step Seven).**
- Approximately next 8 weeks -
  Worship in temporary facility, undergo marketing campaign, prepare for Kick Off Sunday.
- First Sunday in Advent - Kick Off Sunday.
- Prepare Music Ministry to do one piece on Christmas eve.

- Early January - Begin Sunday School and Youth Ministry.
- February - Begin a process for choosing a name for the new congregation.
- Near Easter - Hold a chartering service. All present become charter members of the new church. *(You may want to hold that open for a few weeks).*

FINANCES

It is the New Church Development committee's hope to offer grants in the amount of $15,000 to the churches which have been selected for this project. The money would roughly break down in this way:

Marketing $1,000
Worship space rental $4,000
Printing and direct mailing $5,000
Newspaper and other paid advertising $2,000
Kick Off Sunday Preparation *(Welcome Center, Banners, Name tags, Potted Plants, Decorations, Food for first several coffee hours, soloists, hired nursery care)* $3,000

CLUSTER AND DISTRICT INVOLVEMENT

It is our hope that the cluster, and even the district will adopt a Lazarus church near it as a mission project. Surrounding churches could support the New Church start by:

- Holding it up in constant prayer
- Writing letters of support, especially during the wilderness time and first few weeks of the new start.
- Providing people to assist in the phoning campaign.
- Providing special music or child care during the early weeks of the new start.
- Supporting it financially as a mission project.

LAZARUS NEW SITE SELECTION*

During this entire process, the pastor (and eventually a building committee) will want to be actively seeking potential sites for the new church. When the pastor receives training (at the Jesse Lee Institute or any other national church planting training event) he or she will be given extensive instruction regarding what to look for. However, in summary, here are a few things to keep in mind while seeking out a site:

- Minimum acreage (6 to 10 buildable acres)
- A lot that fits your vision for future ministry
- Visibility and accessibility
- Projected growth for that area
- Cost of development
- Availability of sewerage & water
- Conservation Concerns (wetlands, etc)

© 2018 Robert O. Crossman, www.UMNewChurch.org

You should spend the money to hire a reliable site engineer to help you answer many of these questions. Also, if there is no land available that meets your needs on the "main road", what could you do with the property that could draw attention to it (i.e. Is there room to develop some recreational space which could be open to the public?)

*It is possible that your vision for ministry may include staying in rented space over the long term. However, assuming your vision requires locating in space of your own, you will want to keep these things in mind

PITFALLS

There are a few pitfalls in this process that are especially easy to fall into if we are not very careful. Although some of them will be tempting at the time, they will all severely hamper the future ministry and growth of the church.

- **Don't assume anyone can lead this process.** This is a specialized ministry for which some pastors will be gifted, and some will not. By the same token, these NCD pastors should receive national level training.
- **Don't let newcomers know where you are during the wilderness time (the 8 weeks prior to Kick Off).** Your church needs that time, it needs to be private, and it needs to be in a separate location.
- **Don't cut corners in the marketing.** Yes, it is very expensive and time consuming. Yes, you could save money. Yes, you could save time. But it will cost you in the long run.
- **Don't build too soon.** Many new church starts severely limit their future growth potential by building too soon and too small.
- **Don't burn people out.** Involve as many people as you possibly can in this process to avoid overworking the few.
- **Don't consider going back to Egypt.** There may come a time when you have not sold your old building, you are paying rent for another facility, and returning home looks very tempting. **Don't Do it!**

Steve Murray's article is reprinted with his permission granted April 24, 2017.

†††

Steve Murray is lead pastor of Rock Church with locations in Newburyport & Amesbury Massachusetts and Sandown & Plaistow New Jersey.

NOTE: This article reflects the personal opinions of the author and does not necessarily reflect an official position of Discipleship Ministries or Path 1.

New Church Handbook
Nuts & Bolts for Planting New Churches In The Wesleyan Tradition

"Planter Check List For a Partnership Multi-Site Strategy"

edited by Bob Crossman

A "Partnership Multi-site" involves two United Methodist churches, located several miles apart, joining together in vision and mission, working as a partnership team to become **one** vital church with **two** locations. This is, you might say, taking "connectional" to the next level.

While it might be tempting to move quickly, coming up with the idea in January and becoming one church in two locations by June - that would be a foolish goal. A partnership multi-site is kind of like two churches deciding to get engaged and planning to get married in nine to twenty four months. To borrow a phrase from the wedding ceremony, a marriage should not be "entered into lightly." *[Before committing to this partnership model, there are some serious cautions to be aware of. These are listed at the end of this article.]*

Some of the steps below are broad and others are more specific. These steps below are somewhat in a sequence according to time frame and priority, although lots of this will happen simultaneously.

The Partnership Multi-Site Strategy Between a Healthy Small UMC & a Large UMC

Points to Consider in the Early Gathering of Leaders

- **Purpose?**
  God must be glorified in all that we do.
  People must be honored and respected.
  Both of these churches belong to the Lord, and doing the Lord's will is all that matters.
  Two United Methodist churches, located several miles apart, are joining together in vision and mission, working as a partnership team to start a 'new faith community' in this mission field.

- **Transition?**
  Transition is a process. It starts at a known point, and aims to arrive at the future God has planned. It moves along certain benchmarks along the way, frequently evaluating progress, striving to be faithful to what God seems to be doing.

- **Change?**
  Change is often difficult.
  Each of the congregations will have a few key leaders who will be 'early adopters' in this transition. Their readiness to accept change will greatly

 © 2018 Robert O. Crossman, www.UMNewChurch.org

encourage the transition team at the outset. Many of the leaders of both campuses will, however, be 'late adopters' in the transition process. A small group in each church will probably not be able to make the transition, and they may choose to withdraw their membership.
Each congregation *(the larger church in particular)* will need to avoid behaving as if they always have the right formulas, or the right answers on 'how to do it.'
Each congregation will need to resist 'self-centered pride' in this new relationship, guarding against any failure to respect, honor and celebrate the long history of the other church.

In the "Engagement" Pre-Transition Time (typically in the early Spring)

- **Prayer**
  A partnership is not a mechanical process, but this is a spiritual process of responding to the Lord's will for these two churches. Surround this new partnership in prayer at both campuses through prayer cards, prayer walks, pastoral prayers, specific prayer for this new ministry at every church gathering, and a variety of other prayer experiences.
- **Pastoral leadership**
  In almost every case, the smaller location will be having a change of pastors. This might be someone already on staff at the larger church, or a new campus pastor appointed by the cabinet.
  Pray for the bishop and district superintendent in the pastoral appointment process, as a decision is made who will be appointed to be on the pastoral staff(s).

- **Build Bridges of Relationship that foster Christian love and fellowship.**
  The staff and lay leadership of each campus will be making numerous on-site visits of the sister campus.
  Invite each congregation to the 'other' campus for a planned time of fellowship.

In the Early Months of the "Engagement" Pre-Transition Time
(beginning in July)
Build Bridges of Relationship that foster Christian love and fellowship.

- Establish a "**TRANSITION TEAM**" to meet at the smaller campus composed of:
  - The new campus pastor, and the senior pastor.
  - 10 lay leaders (5 from each campus).

The Transition Team's purpose

- Prepare a covenant to be adopted by both councils or charge conferences. This written covenant should include a statement of purpose for this partnership, establish the initial time line, establish preliminary benchmarks, include discussion of building use and possible relocation, and shall state whether the agreement is seen as temporary, long term, or permanent.
- Establish procedures that facilitate a healthy relationship between the two campuses.
- Ask God for a vision for the new campus (*current site of the smaller church*) that is so big, it can not be accomplished without God's help.

- Enhance communication between the congregations, to coordinate schedules and building usage, and to coordinate cooperative programs.
- Prepare the way for the new pastor being appointed to be the campus pastor of this two campus ministry. Be cautious about moving too fast before the new pastor arrives.

Tasks of the Transition Team

- **Naming.** In almost every case the smaller location will get a new name. One advantage is to clearly communicate to it's constituents that a change has taken place. A second is to indicate to the mission field that their is something new happening in this location. Third, to leverage the existing good reputation of the large church in the community, often the name will be something like, "First UMC, west campus." For convenience, this article will call the new multi-site the "West Campus."
- Hold a series of 'home meetings' with the new west campus pastor and the senior pastor of the main campus.
- At each church, set a Sunday in late summer to recognize and celebrate the past history of each church, and pray for the future of the new ministry together.
- Sermons and Sunday school lessons may focus on themes of new vision, new core values, and the timeless Biblical truths about making disciples through the local church.

Build Bridges of Relationship that foster Christian love and fellowship.

After the new campus pastor is appointed and moved in:

- Clarify the primary 'mission field' of the west campus ministry to avoid miscalculating the 'target' audience. Demographic studies, direct observation driving and walking the neighborhoods, and surveys should be done to clarify current assumptions.
  Where do they spend their time?
  What do they spend their money on?
  What community and school activities do they participate in?
  What are the major competitors for the people's time?
  Where do they hang out?
  What hurts and struggles do they have?
  Did they grow up in church or are they completely unchurched?
  What advice might community leaders offer?
  What are other area churches doing?
  Who are area churches not reaching already?
  Is there a unique population niche the west campus might reach?
  Of course, the new campus ministry wants to reach everyone in the community, however, what slice of the community can the west campus reach best or first?
  What worship style, ministries, and discipleship system will best reach that slice of the community with the saving good news of Jesus Christ?

- Clarify the financial relationships and budgets.
  What about the offering?

 © 2018 Robert O. Crossman, www.UMNewChurch.org

Each treasurer and finance committee continues to operate. In some settings, the larger church treasurer serves both campus, but keeps "separate' books for each site.

- Loose plate offerings are immediately retained by the treasurer of the site where that worship service was held.
- Checks or offering envelopes addressed to that location, will immediately be retained by that local treasurer.
- Any check or envelope addressed to the 'other' campus, will immediately be transferred to the 'other' treasurer.

• Invite and welcome members from the main campus to come alongside the west campus pastor, and join with the west campus. Those invited must have: a) a sense of God's call to this initiative; and, b) have a humble, servant's heart. Some may decide to stay with the new campus. Some may decide to serve for two years and return to the main campus.

• Establish early 'taste and see' ministries that can quickly and easily be established at the smaller west campus, with leadership and participants from both campuses, to "test" effectiveness is reaching the mission field:

- New adult bible studies (Disciple, Christian Believer, Beginnings or Alpha).
- Aerobics, kick-boxing, personal finance classes, parenting classes, etc.
- Stephen Ministry.
- Twelve-step recovery groups.
- Children's carnival, outdoor picnics, outdoor concerts, etc. specifically designed for the people who live in the west mission field.
- Servant evangelism to introduce the west campus to the community.

• Determine if any building improvements need to be made at the new west campus.
For example, in 2005, when St Paul UMC established a daughter congregation in the old Wyatt Memorial UMC building $1\,^{1}/_{2}$ miles away, $30,000 was spent remodeling the outside of the building, new glass wall, entrance covering, exterior paint color, landscaping, signage, and sidewalks. This was done, primarily so that the community was aware that something new was happening in that old building.

• Determine when to 'go public' with a launch Sunday at the new west campus. Announce the launch primarily through personal invitations and networking, but don't neglect to consider targeted Facebook ads, community zip code saturation mailings and other methods. Encourage both congregations to personally write, call and invite friends and family to attend worship at the new west campus.
Before the big public launch happens, all the essential ministries must be in place and functioning smoothly.

This might take three months to twenty-four months. Do not launch too soon! *(See Jim Griffith's book, "Ten Most Common Mistakes made by New Church Starts.")*

In some ways, you might say we are remodeling a house. We are bringing in new life, new ideas, new materials, and hopefully new money. We will need to recruit workers (from both congregations), lay a new foundation (infusing new DNA, prayer, vision), then begin to construct new systems: hospitality, discipleship small groups, outreach, and worship. Put on finishing touches (spruce up the church facilities and foster spirit of enthusiasm). Then have a big open house! (send invitations [mass mailings], personally invite, any way to get word out and people in).

Really this partnership is always going to be a work in progress, but there comes a point when it is best to make a push to invite the community to come. I'm hesitant to recommend that you send out a mailer immediately, and get a big crowd until there is confidence that they will have a good experience, be warmly welcomed, and offered a fruitful discipleship system. Laying the foundation and constructing the new framework is going to take some time, but if done well blessings will flow. Be ready for growth that can take off and keep going. At the same time, don't take too long and lose the momentum and excitement of this new thing. So, I guess I am proposing that a good time would be at the start of the new school year. That gives a few months to get ready but not too long. Also, it is important to launch at a time during the year when people tend to be more open to making a decision to begin attending church.

The new west Campus pastor may want to establish a dozen additional teams that are focused on the launch of this new ministry at the west campus.

This enlarged launch team may include such groups as:

- Intercessory prayer team. Your future congregation will look like this team. This team will anoint and pray for the empty chairs, pray for the lost, pray for those the Lord wants to come to the new west campus, they pray in each of the empty rooms on Sunday morning,
- Worship planning team, worship leader, and pastor to plan 6 to 8 weeks in advance. On the first public launch Sunday, you need to have the next 7 or eight Sundays already "in the can" with every song, drama, video, and sermon complete. This team has a representative from most of the other teams. Most campus have to pay worship leaders because they are so rare.
- Music team. Implement the music program. Plan the music. The performers don't have time to get all the charts together, etc. This team overlaps with the praise team below.
- Praise team, The actual singers and musicians. Three or four with voices and microphones. Don't even think of starting worship if you don't have those key musicians in place. Sometimes you have to pay some of your musicians, sometimes you don't.
- Drama team. A drama program if you have one.
- Video team. Selects videos and does the editing.
- Electronics team. Operate sound and video equipment. This is usually a large team.
- Logistics team. Set up and take down every Sunday morning with about 20 people on this team. Great if you eventually have two teams that can rotate schedules weekly or monthly.
- Publicity team. Advertising. Facebook targeted ads. Handouts

 © 2018 Robert O. Crossman, www.UMNewChurch.org

- Hospitality team. Food, name tag, greeters, usher people to the nursery.
- Special events team. Secure special guest, speakers, performers, testimony by star football players that will bring "people in the seats." It's far easier to witness to people when they are in your seats.
- Culture surfers team. What is hot and what's not. Meets at Star Bucks and keeps worship planning committee in touch with current issues in the community and culture.

Additional Points to Consider

The Book of Discipline? The 2016 Book of Discipline does have guidelines when local UM churches share a building in multi-ethnic and multi-language settings.

Some of the following guidelines may be applicable to your setting.

The District Superintendent

"The district superintendent must consent to any such action before implementation..." ¶2551

The District Board of Church Location and Building

"The district board of church location and building must be informed of such action..." ¶2551

A Covenant - The Charge Conference(s)

"By action of the charge conference(s) involved, a covenant relationship shall be mutually agreed upon in written form and shall include a statement of purpose for sharing the facility and shall state whether the agreement is seen as temporary, long term, or permanent..." ¶ 2551.1.a

Structure - Mutual Representation

Will each campus maintain its own separate structure?

It may be best for each campus to retain its own Council, Pastor-Parish Relations, trustees, and finance committees.

"The covenant relationship may provide for mutual representation on such bodies as church council and other committees and work groups. The board of trustees... The purpose of this arrangement is to enhance communication between the two or more congregations, to coordinate schedules and building usage, to involve the congregations in building maintenance and care under supervision of the board of trustees, and to coordinate cooperative programs..." ¶ 2551.1.a

Money? Rent?

"No United Methodist congregation shall pay rent to another United Methodist church. However, each congregation should be expected to pay a mutually agreed share of building expenses." ¶2551.1.b

Sharing the Same Facility?

"Congregations that share the same facility and other properties are encouraged to organize and share intentionally in some mutual ministries to strengthen their relationships and their effectiveness when focusing on the same objectives. Cooperative programs may be developed that enhance the ministry of both congregations and their witness to the love of Jesus Christ in the community. Such programs may include joint bilingual worship services and Christian education programs, fellowship meals, and community outreach ministries." ¶2551.1.c

"Each congregation in a shared facility is strongly encouraged to accept an interdependent relationship in reference to use of the facility. Such a relationship affirms cooperatively planned and executed programs and activities as well as independently planned and executed programs and activities. Thus, scheduling programs and using the facility will be implemented in a manner that contributes to the positive growth of each congregation." ¶2551.1.d

What if a problem develops in the future we can not mutually negotiate? How do we end this relationship?

The following references in the 2016 Book of Discipline may be applicable:

- "In situations where local congregations and / or ministries that share facilities cannot negotiate decisions that are supportive mutually by each congregation or ministry, the district superintendent shall consult with the leadership of each congregation and / or ministry prior to the implementing of any decision that may adversely affect the future of either congregation or ministry..." ¶2551.1.e
- "Ninety-day notification of intent to terminate the covenant relationship shall be made to the district superintendent and to the other parties in the covenant relationship. This termination shall require the consent of the district superintendent following consultation with the parties involved..." ¶2551.3

Cautions About The Partnership Multi-site Model

The reason most conferences are now using the Lazarus model more than partnership, is because 99 times out of a 100 when a congregation is declining in the midst of a growing population, something is "wrong" and DNA is so toxic that the only viable option is to allow the declining church to close. In many of these situations the smaller church has lost its affinity to the mission field around it, and affinity is something difficult to recreate.

On too many occasions, no matter what is officially said to the declining congregation, what they 'hear' is, *"If we are willing to change our name, the big rich church is going to spend $150,000 to fix up our building, but NOTHING else will really change."*

The partnership model only works successfully in those rare occasions when the declining congregation is still truly healthy, has great DNA at its core, does not have toxic behavior patterns, and feels called by God to actually relaunch as a new church in relationship with a large healthy congregation as a partner.

†††

NOTE: This article reflects the personal opinions of the author and does not necessarily reflect an official position of Discipleship Ministries or Path 1.

 © 2018 Robert O. Crossman, www.UMNewChurch.org

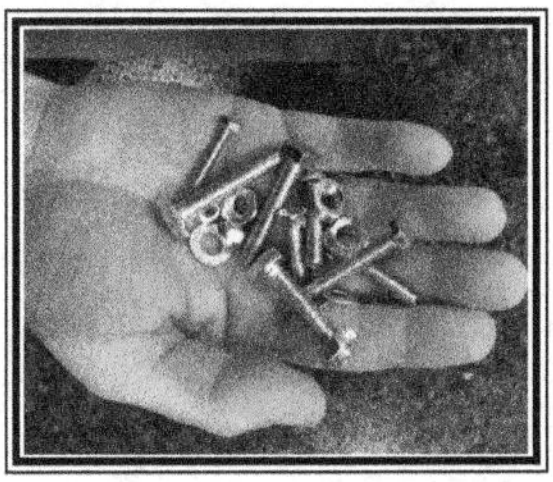

New Church Handbook
Nuts & Bolts for Planting New Churches In The Wesleyan Tradition

"Planter Check List For a Merger Strategy"

by Bob Crossman
including material from the East Ohio Conference

A merger is the joining together of two or more congregations to become one. Most annual conferences consider "vital mergers" to be a new church, but do not consider "basic mergers" as a new church. The basic merger's primary intent is for mutual survival. The vital merger's primary intent of providing greater mission and ministry to the community.

Advantages of Merging (Basic or Vital)

- Strength in numbers. A congregation of 400 may have the potential for more ministry and community impact than two churches of 300 and 100 each.
- Worshiping congregations already exist along with structures for ministry.
- Facilities at one of the locations may be in a great location and well maintained.

Disadvantages of Merging (Basic or Vital)

- DNA of two congregations may be so distinct that they are difficult to merge.
- Having a shared vision might be difficult.
- Attitude of superiority/inferiority on the part of one or both of the churches.
- Congregations may have difficultly agreeing which property to sell, or have difficulty agreeing to sell both properties and both move to a new location.

Of course, as United Methodist we have method for merging two congregations in our Book of Discipline ¶2546:

"¶2546 *Merger of Local United Methodist Churches* - Two or more local churches, in order to more effectively fulfill their ministry (¶201-204), may merge and become a single church by pursuing the following procedure:

1) The merger must be proposed to the charge conference of each of the merging churches by a resolution stating the terms and conditions of the proposed merger.
2) The plan of the merger as proposed to the charge conference of each of the merging churches shall be approved by each of the charge conferences in order for the merger to be effected, except that for a charge conference that includes two or more local churches, the required approval shall be by the Church Local Conference of each local church in accordance with the requirements of ¶2527.
3) The merger must be approved by the superintendent or superintendents of the district or districts in which the merging churches are located.

4) The requirements of any and all laws of the state or states in which the merging churches are located affecting or relating to the merger of such churches must be complied with, and in any case where there is a conflict between such laws and the procedure outlined in the *Discipline*, said laws shall prevail and the procedure outlined in the *Discipline* shall be modified to the extent necessary to eliminate such conflict.
5) All archives and records of churches involved in a merger shall become the responsibility of the successor church."

For details on the process of selling one or more of the buildings or property, see ¶2540-2543.
There may be additional disciplinary paragraphs that relate to the merger process.

†††

The following Guidelines were developed by the East Ohio Conference, Board of Congregational Development.
They only officially apply to the East Ohio Conference, but they may be applicable in other Annual Conferences.

MERGING TWO CHURCHES INTO A VITAL CONGREGATION

The merger of two or more congregations is one approach to becoming a "vital congregation." The combined church will have more resources, both human and financial, to make a greater impact on the community. Merger should not be considered as a final step for declining to dying churches. This will result in one merged church in poor health. A healthy merger resulting in a vital congregation will have a new mission and vision for new ministry taking place.

A biblical and theological rationale should be the driving reason for merger. In deciding whether a merger should occur, one question should be answered: "What new ministry will this new merged church bring that either congregation could not do by itself." Merger should bring new life, resurrection, for new energy and new ministry in reaching new generations with the Gospel.

The merger of two congregations can be compared to a marriage. Both parties bring their own personalities, their own character flaws, their own history and tradition. In a marriage these areas are understood and worked through (*although often not without conflict*). The new merged church must bear this in mind, and work through the differences.

As in a marriage, housing is an important issue. Where will the newly married couple live? In the merger of a church this is a major decision. It is always best to start with a new facility. This avoids "ownership" or "turf" issues. Bill Easum writes: ***"The only mergers that result in more people in worship two years later are those where each church sells its property and builds a new church on a new site altogether. The church must have a new name. Any other method results in less people in worship two years later."***

Excellent communication must be a continual part of the merger process.

 © 2018 Robert O. Crossman, www.UMNewChurch.org

Communication with the district superintendent is necessary. Communication with the congregation is mandatory. Regular updates should occur through written and verbal means. (*Written in the church newsletter or weekly bulletin, and verbal from the pulpit, and town-hall style meetings*).

A merger document must be prepared. This is written by a merger committee of equal representation from both (*all*) churches, and only after approval has been given by the district superintendent.

Once the merger document is complete, and has the approval of the superintendent, it should be presented to the congregation for discussion, debate and decision. The final decision to merge will occur at a special charge/church conference called by the district superintendent.

After the merger is approved by the charge/church conference of both (*of all*) churches involved in the merger, the document is presented to the bishop for final approval.

TWO TYPES OF MERGER:

Basic Merger

The basic merger's primary intent is for mutual survival. The merging of two or more congregations is because either or both can no longer provide adequate ministry, or financing to continue adequate ministry. The merged church will reside in one of the existing church buildings. All money, endowments and property become the sole ownership of the merged church.

Vital Merger - a new church start

A "vital merger" is completed with the primary intent of providing greater mission and ministry to the community. This may result from a desire to reach a new target audience or people, or possibly to be better stewards of the resources.

To be considered a vital merger and a new church start, the following must be part of the merger plan.

- The pastor must be enrolled, or have completed, the New Church Leadership Institute and/or Basic Training Boot Camp.
- The churches must sell all property and relocate into a new location.
- There must be a focus on new mission and ministry. What will this new, vital church offer that neither of the former churches could?
- The new church needs a new name. The new name can not be a combination or variation of the old names.

Guidelines for Vital Church Merger

1. The local churches contact the district superintendent stating the desire for a merger to take place.
2. The district superintendent establishes a date for an initial meeting with key leadership from both churches. It is recommended that the conference minister for new church starts be invited to this initial meeting.
3. Prayer must play a central role in the merger. Discernment of God's will and

direction are necessary. No movement on the merger should take place without clear leading from the Holy Spirit and the consensus among the leadership to move forward.

4. A demographic study should be completed for both of the existing church communities, as well as for potential relocation sites.
5. Once approval has been given, the exploration of a merger should proceed, and a transition team should be established. The transition team should be made up of equal representation from each church, consisting of ten to twelve members, and be led by a capable leader respected by the people of both churches. (*A co-chair position is recommended.*)
6. Create numerous opportunities for both congregations to get to know one another. Organize joint worship experiences, celebration events and opportunities unrelated to the discussion of the proposed merger.
7. The transition team creates a merger document for presentation to both congregations.
8. It is highly recommended that the merged congregation sell both church buildings and move to a new location. (*However, this information is not a part of the official merger document.*)
9. The Transition Team will hold regular "town-hall" style meetings to inform the congregations of the progress of the merger document and answer questions concerning the future of the new church.
10. Once the merger document is completed, a copy should be forwarded to the bishop, the district superintendent, and to the minister for new church starts.
11. When adequate information has been communicated to both congregations, and the expectation exists that approval will be given by both congregations, the district superintendent is to be contacted to schedule Church Conferences with both congregations.
12. Upon approval of the bishop, and both church conferences, a date will be set for the merger to occur.
13. We recommend that the new merged church be incorporated immediately, and all legal papers be in order.

For more information about Vital Mergers, purchase *"Vital Merger: A New Church Start Approach That Joins Church Families Together"* by Dirk Elliott at www.vitalmerger.com

†††

NOTE: This article reflects the personal opinions of the author and does not necessarily reflect an official position of Discipleship Ministries or Path 1.

© 2018 Robert O. Crossman, www.UMNewChurch.org

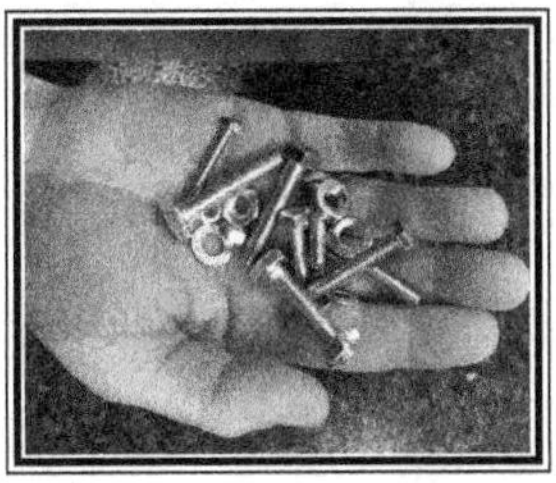

New Church Handbook
Nuts & Bolts for Planting New Churches In The Wesleyan Tradition

"Sharing Facilities: What Are The Best Practices?"

by Bob Crossman

If you are thinking about starting a new church, and sharing facilities with an existing church, the United Methodist Church has a method for doing just that. The 2016 Book of Discipline outlines how issues relating to any shared facilities should be handled.

While it is true that ¶ 2551, reprinted below, refers to multi-ethnic and multi-language settings, it seems to me that these are wise words that should apply to ALL instances of two congregations sharing the same facilities.

¶ 2551 *Covenant Relationships in Multi-Ethnic and Multi-Language Settings* -- Ministry in The UMC tradition is about partnership and mission. In situations where a local church or churches share a building with a congregation or with another group performing ministries in different languages and / or with different racial and ethnic groups, it shall be in accordance with ¶ 202, 206, and 212. The district superintendent must consent to any such action before implementation. The district board of church location and building must be informed of such action.

1. If the congregations are United Methodist, the following **shall** apply:

a) by action of the charge conference(s) involved, a covenant relationship **shall** be mutually agreed upon in written form and **shall** include a statement of purpose for sharing the facility and shall state whether the agreement is seen as temporary, long-term, or permanent.

The covenant of relationship **may** provide for mutual representation on such bodies as church council and other committees and work groups. The board of trustees of the church that holds title to the property **may** form a property committee composed of representatives of each congregation. The purpose of this arrangement is to enhance communication between the two or more congregations, to coordinate schedules and building usage, to involve the congregations in building maintenance and care under supervision of the board of trustees, and to coordinate cooperative programs.

b) The covenant relationship **shall not** require that a United Methodist congregation pay rent to another United Methodist church, or

© 2018 Robert O. Crossman, www.UMNewChurch.org

a United Methodist community of faith or a social ministry. The financial relationship established in the covenant is neither intended to generate profit nor to support the general budget (other than appropriate normal operating costs) of the receiving local church or any other entity involved in the sharing of the facilities.

c) Congregations that share the same facility and other properties are encouraged to organize and share intentionally in some mutual ministries to strengthen their relationships and their effectiveness when focusing on the same objectives. Cooperative programs may be developed that enhance the ministry of both congregations and their witness to the love of Jesus Christ in the community. Such programs may include joint bilingual worship services and Christian education programs, fellowship meals, and community outreach ministries.

d) Each congregation in a shared facility is strongly encouraged to accept an interdependent relationship in reference to use of the facility. Such a relationship affirms cooperatively planned and executed programs and activities as well as independently planned and executed programs and activities. Thus, scheduling programs and using the facility will be implemented in a manner that contributes to the positive growth of each congregation.

e) In situations where local congregations and / or ministries share facilities cannot negotiate decisions that are supportive mutually by each congregation or ministry, the district superintendent shall consult with the leadership of each congregation and/or ministry prior to the implementing of any decision that may adversely affect the future of either congregation or ministry.

2. If a United Methodist church is sharing with a congregation of another denomination, the following should apply:

a) Prior to agreeing to share facilities with a congregation that is not United Methodist and is of a different ethnic or language background, the United Methodist pastor and the district superintendent **shall** first contact district and conference congregational development agencies and ethnic leadership to explore the possibilities of organizing as an ecumenical shared ministry or a new United Methodist congregation with that ethnic or language group.

b) If it is decided that the United Methodist Congregation and the congregation of another denomination should share facilities, as a part of the covenant of mission, a property-use agreement **shall** be negotiated in writing in accordance with ¶ 2503; this agreement **shall** have the consent of the district superintendent and shall be approved by the United Methodist charge or church conference. Shared activities **may** be entered into to enhance the ministry of both congregations. A liaison committee to both congregations **may** be appointed to resolve conflicts, clear schedules, and plan cooperative activities.

3. Ninety-day notification of intent to terminate the covenant relationship

 © 2018 Robert O. Crossman, www.UMNewChurch.org

shall be made to the district superintendent and to the other parties in the covenant relationship. This termination **shall** require the consent of the district superintendent following consultation with the parties involved.

4. The district committee on religion and race **shall** monitor consultations and plans related to the transfer or use of property to ensure fairness and equity in situations involving two or more local congregations or ministries.

Additional guidance is found in the United Methodist Churches General Council on Finance and Administration (GCFA) Legal Manual, Part II, pages 12-13 on "Sharing Facilities."

The sharing of church buildings by congregations of differing racial, ethnic, and/or linguistic backgrounds presents its own unique set of challenges. In recognition of the increasing use of these arrangements, ¶ 2551 is designed to ensure that fairness and orderly procedures prevail. Consent of the district superintendent to such arrangements is required, as is notification of the district board of church location and building. Shared facilities arrangements between United Methodist congregations require a mutually agreed-upon written covenant relationship, passed by both charge conferences, that includes a statement of purpose and a reference to the length of time the arrangement is expected to run.[35] The purpose of the covenant is to enhance communication, facilitate coordination of schedules and building use, provide for cooperative building maintenance, and coordinate cooperative programs.[36] While mutually agreed upon sharing of expenses is acceptable, payment of rent by one United Methodist congregation to another is prohibited.[37]

If a congregation seeks to share facilities with another, non-United Methodist congregation of a different ethnic or linguistic background, it must first consult with the pastor and the district superintendent.[38] In these scenarios, a written property-use agreement must be created.[39] This agreement must be approved by the district superintendent and the charge or church conference.[40]

All shared facilities arrangements, whether they are with another United Methodist congregation or with another denomination, require a 90 day notice, to the district superintendent and to the other parties to the covenant relationship, whenever a United Methodist congregation intends to terminate the arrangement.[41] The district superintendent must consent to the termination.[42]

---

[35] ¶ 2551.1a.
[36] Id.
[37] ¶ 2551.1b.
[38] ¶ 2551.2a.
[39] ¶ 2521.2b.
[40] Id.
[41] ¶ 2521.3.
[42] Id.

SAMPLE #1
COVENANT AGREEMENT

The Ebenezer United Methodist Church Building and Relocation Committee, trustees, and members, received approval from the district superintendent to seek a temporary location for worship and ministry, until Ebenezer UMC, has the opportunity to build a new church facility. Therefore, Ebenezer UMC enters into this covenant agreement with Wesley UMC, to temporarily share the Wesley facilities. The covenant agreement was approved at both church's annual charge conferences.

MISSION

The missions of both churches are very similar. We, the members of Ebenezer UMC are committed to serving the needs of our local community. We the members, of Wesley UMC, believe it is God's vision for us to introduce the people within a 5-mile radius of this church to Jesus Christ, by communicating God's love to them through ministries that respond in relevant ways to their needs and concerns, to provide ministries that will guide growth in Christ, and deploy them in ministry.

Sample

POLICY

- The Ebenezer UMC trustee board, Administrative Board/Council, Local Church Building and Relocation Committee, and pastor have received and read the Wesley UMC policy for use of facilities and have agreed to abide by all guidelines.
- The Ebenezer and Wesley pastoral leadership will be responsible for communicating and coordinating all church scheduling, which will contribute to the positive growth of both church congregations.
- It will be the responsibility of the Ebenezer UMC and Wesley UMC Board of trustees to schedule and facilitate the cleaning and maintenance, of the church facilities.
- Ebenezer UMC and Wesley UMC both agree to pay 50% of all utilities and maintenance (to include repairs or replacements of equipment, etc.) while in this covenant agreement.
- Quarterly meetings will be held between the two boards of trustees to discuss any issues. It will be the responsibility of the board of trustees of both congregations to review and amend this covenant agreement every six months. All amendments will be written and decided on by the board of trustees of both congregations, and a copy of this agreement will be kept in the trustee file for both congregations and the district superintendents office.
- Annually this covenant agreement, between Ebenezer United Methodist Church and Wesley United Methodist Church, both of Conway, Arkansas, will be reviewed.
- Ninety-day notification of intent to terminate the covenant relationship shall be made to the district superintendent and to the other parties in the cov-

© 2018 Robert O. Crossman, www.UMNewChurch.org

enant relationship. This termination shall require the consent of the district superintendent following consultation with the parties involved.

MINISTRY

It shall be the responsibility of the Pastoral leadership and the Committee on Lay Leadership of both congregations to oversee that the existing ministries of both churches are providing effective outreach programs. It shall also be the responsibility of the pastoral leadership and the Committee on Lay Leadership, to initiate and oversee programs to include: joint worship services; joint Christian education programs; fellowship meals; and joint community outreach ministries. *{Signature lines were at the bottom of this agreement for all the members of both boards to sign.}*

SAMPLE #2

Sample #2 below appears to be a document written by the senior pastor of the larger church, and not a document approved by the two charge conferences. It appears to be rather one sided.

FIRST DRAFT
OF A COVENANT AGREEMENT

VISION

The vision that God has placed on my heart concerning the partnership between Zion UMC and First UMC is that both churches will be intentional at working together in the areas of: Bible study, evangelism efforts in the community, fellowship events, joint worship services together, mission work, spiritual retreats, training events together, and youth events. The Zion UMC/First UMC Partnership Team (representatives from both churches) and myself will be responsible for strategically planning these events with the proper follow-up and action demonstrated towards these areas.

Sample

PURPOSE

When I think about the word partnership and what that word means in this context, my first impression is that there are two churches that have agreed to be in relationship with each other and both of those churches bring something to the table that is going to benefit each party involved. It is my belief that both Zion UMC and First UMC can benefit from this partnership, but before we get to far ahead of ourselves, there is a reality that each of us most understand. The truth of the matter is that if Zion UMC is not strengthened, then there will not be a partnership that will exist, because there will no longer be a church called Zion. So with that being said, I truly think that at this point in time, the purpose of the partnership should be focused on getting Zion UMC stronger. First UMC is a strong and viable church that I believe is fine and will be fine for years to come. Zion UMC is weak, but if there is not a genuine effort towards turning the church around, she will die.

MAIN THINGS THAT NEED TO TAKE PLACE IN THE PARTNERSHIP

- Agreement for Zion UMC to use space at First UMC when it is available for programs.

- Agreement to let me have the freedom to recruit 10-15 people from First UMC to come for worship services and attend other programs at Zion on a full-time basis. This will help Zion UMC to reach the mass of people that is so critically needed in turning the church around. Once Zion has reached an attendance of 200 adults in worship, the people from First UMC can return.

- Agreement to let Zion's youth have the opportunity to come and participate at youth functions at First UMC at least twice a month. Note: This does not mean that Ebenezer's youth will not have their own youth program, but to give the two groups opportunities to build relationships as well as grow and learn more about each other and to become better disciples of Jesus Christ.

CONCLUSION

This concludes my summary concerning the partnership and my understanding of it as well as some things that need to take place. As I stated in my introduction, I do not have all the answers, in fact I am learning how to do this as I go. It is my belief that God will give each of us the help that we need if we truly seek him for the answers. I ask that each of you be in prayer with me concerning the partnership and always feel free to give me a word from the Lord that will be helpful in moving us forward.

†††

NOTE: This article reflects the personal opinions of the author and does not necessarily reflect an official position of Discipleship Ministries or Path 1.

Sample

 © 2018 Robert O. Crossman, www.UMNewChurch.org

IV. How Do I Engage the Community and Invite People to my New Church?

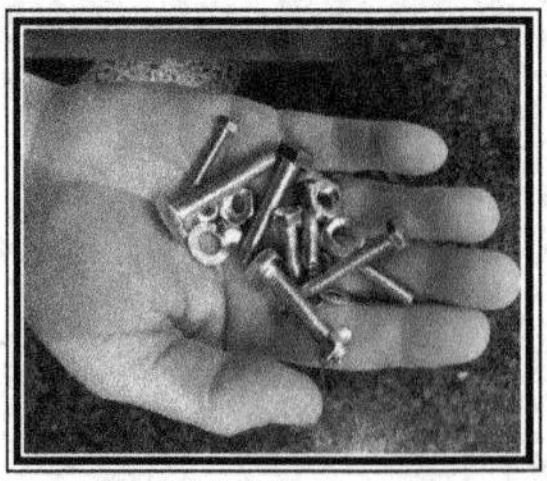

New Church Handbook
Nuts & Bolts for Planting New Churches In The Wesleyan Tradition

"What Might A Ministry Plan in a New Church Look Like?"

by Bob Crossman
including material by George Hunter, Junius Dotson and Craig Kennet Miller

In this article you will find three different suggestions on the content of an effective church planter's ministry plan: one designed by George Howard, a second by Craig Miller, and a third by Junius Dotson and Craig Kennet Miller. Scan through these three different formats and chose those portions that you discern will be most helpful as you begin to plan your ministry of planting.

When George Howard was Director of New Church Starts in the West Ohio Conference, he developed these thirteen questions as a framework for new church planters as they began to write their ministry plan for launching a new church.

- Where did you grow up? What type of community was it? Your answers to this might be a good indication of the kind of community where you have the natural affinity to start a new congregation. Describe your natural affinities.
- Discover the pool of humanity for the area where you feel called to start a church and write a two-page contextual analysis demonstrating your grasp of key demographic information.
- Who is your target group for the new church?
- Describe the felt needs of the target group that will drive your start up decisions.
- Write a brief mission statement for your church.
- Describe your local launch team and how you will recruit them.
- What are the core values of the new church (and how does your lifestyle currently reflect them)?
- What new start model would you recommend to be used in this setting?
- What are your 6 month, 1 year, 3-5 year, and 10 year goals?
- Describe the outreach or advertising approach you will use to initiate the start.
- What will your discipleship system look like and how will you put it into place?
- Describe the worship experience people will have at your services and demonstrate how this reflects cultural relevance and your particular demographics.
- Give the general steps for how you would follow up on a visitor in your setting.

© 2018 Robert O. Crossman, www.UMNewChurch.org

The goal of this process is for you to present the church start and growth concepts that you have been hearing and discussing. You are to pull together the concepts with your understanding of who you are and where you believe you could effectively plant a new congregation.

†††

Craig Miller developed the following information as a framework for new church planters as they begin to write their ministry plan for launching a new church.

Tips for Listening to God

- Create a prayer letter or email letter that you send at least once a month to people who agree to be in prayer for this ministry. Include your district superintendent, conference staff person related to new church development, and the bishop on this list.
- Find at least one prayer partner in your area with whom you meet at least twice a month.
- Find a mentor or coach who holds you accountable for your spiritual growth and development as well as for the steps related to the new church start.
- Who is praying for this new ministry? (list their names)
- Who are your prayer partners? (list their names)
- Who is holding you accountable for your spiritual growth?
  (list their names)

Spiritual Life of the Pastor

As a new church pastor you are creating the normative expectations for spiritual growth in your congregation. Many new church pastors set aside one day a week for prayer, reflection, and visioning *(this is not a day off)*. Later, when you move to weekly worship, this becomes a day for prayer and sermon preparation. Your prayer life, physical health, artistic pursuits, and relationships have a direct influence on the spiritual life of your leaders. Build in the time and experiences that sustains you and connects you to God and others.

What is YOUR plan for YOUR personal continued spiritual growth and development?

- How do you connect with God? *(check all that apply)*
  - __ Day apart
  - __ Family prayer
  - __ Daily devotion
  - __ Worship with other congregations
  - __ Meeting with a prayer partner or coach
  - __ Other: ______________________________
- How are you connecting with others? *(check all that apply)*
  - __ Time alone with spouse or friend
  - __ Family night/day
  - __ Focused time with your children
  - __ Regular connection with extended family
  - __ Time with friends outside of church
  - __ Other: ______________________________

- What arts feed your soul? *(check all that apply)*
  __ Playing musical instrument or singing __ Writing
  __ Dance __ Drawing __ Gardening
  __ Other: ____________________________
- How are you taking care of your body? *(check all that apply)*
  __ Walking/running __ Active in a sport
  __ Healthy diet __ Aerobics
  __ Other: ____________________________
- Reflect on the Wesley's "Means of Grace" (¶72, The Book of Discipline)
  - The public worship of God - Christian conferencing
  - The Lord's Supper - Family and private prayer
  - Searching the Scriptures - Fasting or abstinence
  - The ministry of the Word, either read or expounded

Based on the means of grace, complete the **Spiritual Leader Checklist** below:

Spiritual Leader Checklist

__ I say grace before each meal.
__ I set aside a time to pray each day.
__ At least once a week, I pray out loud with another person (a family member, a friend, a person at work or church).
__ I read at least one verse of Scripture every day.
__ I attend worship at least three times a month.
__ At least twice a month I meet with a group of people to pray, reflect on Scripture, and build one another up (small group, Sunday school class, prayer group, etc.)
__ I take Communion at least once a month.
__ At least once a month I give of myself to others. (I volunteer at a homeless shelter or soup kitchen, visit in a nursing home, tutor a child, visit a prisoner, mow a neighbor's lawn, etc.)
__ I fast once a week (I give up food for a period of time or do a media fast and go without electronic media – TV, radio, etc. – for a day.)
__ As part of every meeting at church, we spend 10-15 minutes praying together and reflecting on a Scripture passage.

Central to the life of any congregation is its leadership. What happens in the launch team affects the life of the whole congregation - *"The congregation will look like your launch team."* The launch team is made up of those leaders who are responsible for the spiritual life of others in your congregation. These range from Sunday school teachers, small group leaders, elected members of boards and committees, to staff.

 © 2018 Robert O. Crossman, www.UMNewChurch.org

Spiritual Life of the Launch Team

What spiritual disciplines will your launch team be expected to practice?

(check all that apply)

__ Weekly worship
__ Daily Bible reading
__ Service to others
__ Fasting or abstinence
__ Family prayer
__ Daily prayer
__ Receive the Lord's Supper __weekly; __monthly
__ Other: ______________________________

Spiritual Gifts Assessment

(After taking the Spiritual *Gifts Assessment Tool* at UMC.org fill in the three spaces below with what you have learned.)

Primary Gifts: ______________________

Secondary Gifts: ______________________

Spiritual Gift Cluster(s) ______________________

What does does the spiritual gifts assessment say about you and about the type of team you need to create to work with you?

What will be the core values of your congregation?

What will be the vision of your congregation?

Demographic Context for Ministry

Ministry does not take place in a vacuum. Your congregation will be in a unique location and have its own history. To help plan for your first two years in a new church setting, think in concrete terms. Begin by naming a community where you might actually have the natural affinity to start a new church in that community. It might not, of course, end up being the actual community where a new church is started, but by naming a location it helps to give reality to this process and ground your plan to the kind of setting where you feel best called to start a new congregation.

1. **Demographics in the community**

	Community	Launch Team
Racial Ethnic Makeup	____________	____________
Languages spoken	____________	____________
Age	____________	____________
Income level	____________	____________
Marital Status	____________	____________

2. **Demographics by walking around**
Tip: Go to several restaurants in your target area.
- How are they positioning themselves? (Whom are they trying to reach?)
  - Atmosphere
  - Dress code
  - Type of food
  - Music in the background
- Do the customers reflect the neighborhood?

- How well do the waiters and staff reflect the customers?
  - Dress code of the waiters and staff?
  - Attitude of the server?
  - Do they know the menu?
- Service
  - Did you feel welcomed?
  - Was the food prepared as you requested?
  - Was it served on time?
- What implication does this have about your church?

3. **Church Visit Survey**
(make additional copies of this section, one for each church visited)
Assignment: Go to several different churches. Be sure to include the newest churches in your target area. Visit several denominations.
- How did you find out about this church?
  - Facebook - personal contact - church sign
  - website - phone book - advertising
  - Other: ____________________

• What impressions does the name of the church give you? Does the name of the church accurately describe the ministries or people involved? Any thoughts about why they chose that particular name for their church?

 © 2018 Robert O. Crossman, www.UMNewChurch.org

- Where is the church you visited meeting?
  - Church sanctuary
  - School: __High School __Middle School __Elementary School
  - Church fellowship hall
  - Movie Theatre
  - Church chapel
  - Converted Office Space
  - Other: ______________________________

- Describe the people who they are reaching
  - Age
  - Ethnicity
  - Dress code
  - Economic Status
  - Age of cars in parking lot
  - Other: ____________________

- Childcare/Nursery (check those that apply)
  - Easily found
  - Friendly teachers
  - Clean rooms
  - Check-in system for security
  - Smell
  - Are toys new and unbroken
  - Security
  - Check in / check out procedures
  - Other observations: ____________________

- Hospitality (check those that apply)
  - Was parking adequate and assessable
  - Directional signs and/or banners for rooms
  - Could you easily find the rest rooms
  - Comfortable seating
  - Is the nursery near the worship space
  - Printed information about the church available
  - Friendly greeters
  - Clear directions for order of worship
  - Quality of content on the screen
  - How do they gather contact information of guest
  - How did they handle announcements
  - Friendly worship participants
  - Personal invitation to other activities
  - Friendly pastor and Staff
  - Other: ____________________

- Worship experience:
  - What was the format of worship?
  - Style of music?
  - Did all elements of the worship flow together?
  - Was it uplifting?
  - What was the main message?
  - What did you learn?
  - What needs improvement?

- What makes them unique?

- What alternatives are they offering when compared to the other churches you've visited?

- Reflecting on your visit at this church in general, what have you learned that will help in starting your new church?

4. Summary of Demographics

- Combine data and write a summary of the primary demographic group in the area. Include items like greatest needs, hopes, and dreams.

- Combine data and write a summary of the secondary demographic group in the area. Include items like greatest needs, hopes, and dreams.

- What are the major competitors for people's time in these groups?

- What are existing churches offering to these groups?

5. Define the Characteristics of your New Church Community of Faith

- What alternative do you offer to what is already available?

- Identity and purpose (Who are you? What makes you unique?)

Creating the Discipleship System in the First Few Years

The discipleship system includes everything that you do to help people connect with God and grow in their faith in Jesus Christ. Typical components of a discipleship system would be worship, Christian education, community service and outreach. Answer the following questions.

1. What are the essential beliefs of the Christian faith?
   What are the essential beliefs of the United Methodist Church?

2. What spiritual disciplines will active members of this faith community practice? How will you encourage this?

3. What will you offer for newcomers for the first three years they are involved in the life of your congregation? (classes, seminars, experiences, ministry opportunities, worship, etc.) Describe each.

4. How do all of these components work together so that a newcomer knows how to get plugged in?

 © 2018 Robert O. Crossman, www.UMNewChurch.org

5. What will you offer for spiritual growth and leadership development for long-term members and participants in your faith community? (someone who stays longer than three years) Describe.

6. How will you create new faith communities for new people groups? (A people group may be a generational, racial ethnic, and/or language cultural group.) Describe.

7. How will your congregation incorporate celebrative worship, small groups, and fellowship/instruction groups in the life of the congregation?

8. What is your discipleship system for children and youth?

9. Rather than using the term *contemporary or traditional,* describe the worship experience(s) you believe will have an affinity with your target audience?

10. Describe the people who will come for worship. If you plan more than one worship experience, how are they different?

11. How would you describe the preaching style of this/these experience(s) you believe will have an affinity with your target audience?

First-Year Plan of Action for Your New Church

As you prepare to start a new church, think through your plan of action for the next year.

1. What is the greatest opportunity for spiritual and numerical growth for your new congregation?

2. What is the biggest obstacle that might prevent you from taking advantage this potential for spiritual and numerical growth for your new congregation?

3. As you think about the future, where do you hope your congregation will be:

   Three months from now?

   Six months from now?

   One year from now?

   What are the five most important things you need to do to move your congregation toward becoming a disciple-making faith community?
   a.

   b.

   c.

   d.

   e.

   What do you need to change about yourself in order to help make this happen?
   a.

   b.

Ministry of Time *"There is a time for everything..." Ecclesiastes 3:1*

- As a new church pastor, the way you use your time is a witness to others. The spiritual and numerical growth of a church is dependent on the pastor's willingness to let go of the ministry and allow laity to be in ministry.

- Who holds you accountable for your time?

- Set aside one day for visioning and prayer.

- Share and develop this with your family and/or close friends before you start.

 © 2018 Robert O. Crossman, www.UMNewChurch.org

- In the chart below, plan your typical week in blocks of time:
  - office hours
  - leadership development
  - contact hours
  - time off
  - family, spouse, children, friends
  - contact hours
  - tasks (nuts & bolts)
  - personal spiritual growth
  - personal time (exercise, play)

	Morning	*Afternoon*	*Evening*
Monday			
Tuesday			
Wednesday			
Thursday			
Friday			
Saturday			
Sunday			

Strategic Time Line - Launch in 5 months (example)

TIP: Set launch worship date, and work backwards from that date.

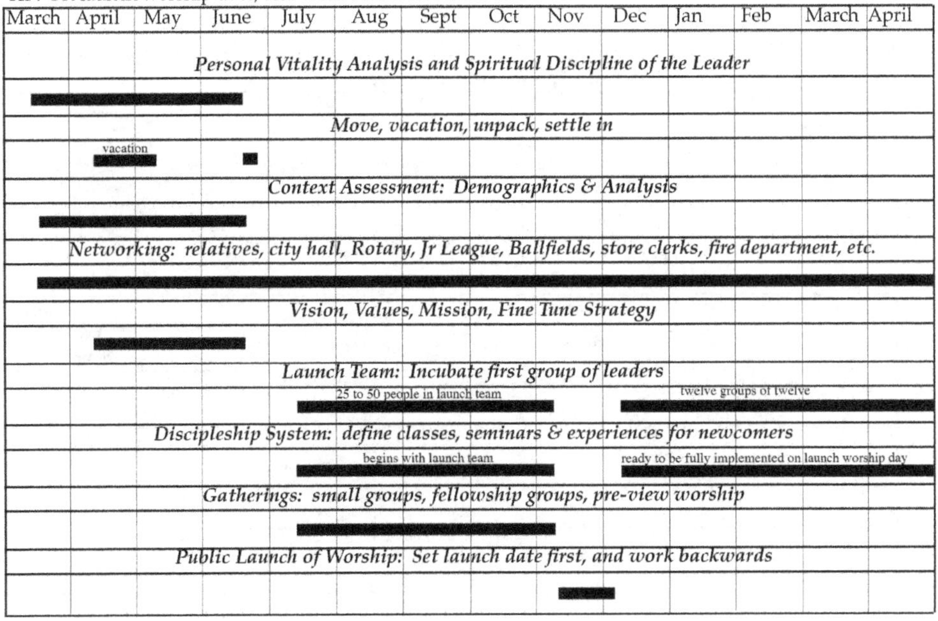

Strategic Time Line - Launch in 9 months (example)

TIP: Set launch worship date, and work backwards from that date.

Activity	July	Aug	Sept	Oct	Nov	Dec	Jan	Feb	March	Apr	May	June	July	Aug
Personal Vitality Analysis and Spiritual Discipline of the Leader	■													
Move, extended vacation, unpack, settle in	■													
Context Assessment: Demographics & Analysis	■	■												
Networking: relatives, city hall, Rotary, Jr League, Ballfields, store clerks, fire department, etc.	■	■	■	■	■	■	■	■	■	■	■	■		
Vision, Values, Mission, Fine Tune Strategy			■	■										
Launch Team: Incubate first group of leaders - twelve groups of twelve					■	■	■	■						
Discipleship System: define classes, seminars & experiences for newcomers (begins with launch team ... ready to be fully implemented on launch worship day)				■	■	■	■	■	■	■	■	■	■	■
Gatherings: small groups, fellowship groups, pre-view worship					■	■	■	■	■					
Public Launch of Worship: Set launch date first, and work backwards										■				

Strategic Time Line - Launch in 15 months (by Don Smith, vitalconnections.com)

TIP: Set launch worship date, and work backwards from that date.

July	Aug	Sept	Oct	Nov	Dec	Jan	Feb	March	Apr	May	June	July	Aug	Sept	Oct
Networking begins • in mother church (if mother daughter model) looking for potential Launch Team members • in the mission field: relatives, city hall, Rotary, Jr League, ballfields, store clerks, fire department, etc. looking for potential Launch Team members															
		Launch Team Gathering		Launch Team Gathering		Launch Team Gathering		Launch Team Gathering		Launch Team Gathering		Launch Team Gathering			
		Taste & See Event				Taste & See Event				Taste & See Event					
				Pre-View Worship Christmas Eve				Pre-View Worship Easter Sunrise				One Pre-View Worship Service	Two Pre-View Worship Services	**Launch Worship Season Begins**	
		2 Task Groups formed to do Taste & See Event			2 Task Groups formed to do Taste & See Event			2 Task Groups formed to do Taste & See Event							
			2 Task Groups formed to hold Pre-view worship			2 Task Groups formed to hold sunrise worship									
											Multiple Task Groups formed to implement the Launch Worship Season adding one or two groups each month beginning in April.				
		Begin establishing on-going small discipleship groups, adding about one of these groups every other month beginning about October	1 group		2 groups		3 groups		4 groups		5 groups		6 groups		7 groups

© 2018 Robert O. Crossman, www.UMNewChurch.org

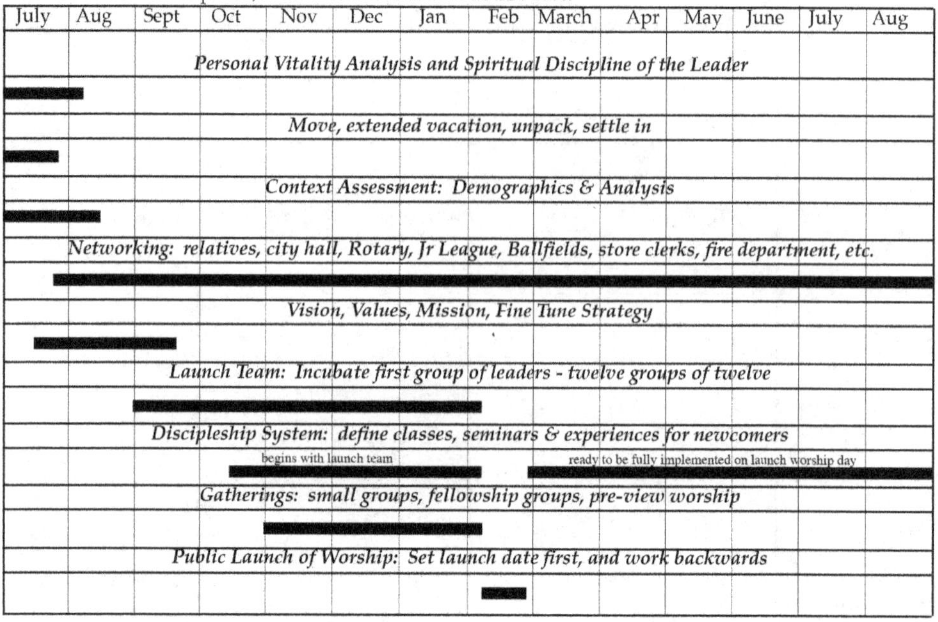

YOUR Strategic Time Line - Launch in __ months

TIP: Set launch worship date, and work backwards from that date.

July	Aug	Sept	Oct	Nov	Dec	Jan	Feb	March	Apr	May	June	July	Aug	Sept	Oct

CHURCH PLANTING WORKSHEET
First Steps: Setting the DNA

Developed by Junius Dotson and Craig Kennet Miller
Reprinted here by permission of the authors, Junius Dotson and Craig K. Miller granted on October 10, 2017.

As you prepare to develop your congregation, here are key questions for you and your core group to consider.

Leadership (Seed Profile)

Call: What has God called you to be?

Chemistry (DNA):
Core values =These articulate why you do what you do – the non-negotiables in your life.

Personal vision =As you live out your calling, this is a picture of the preferred future.

Personal mission =This is the composite of your core values that articulates what it is that you are doing in general terms.

Connection (seed root):

To God:
Spiritual Disciplines

Spiritual type

To Others:
Who is praying for this new ministry?

Who are your prayer partners with whom you can share personal issues and concerns?

Who is holding you accountable for your spiritual growth and development?

 © 2018 Robert O. Crossman, www.UMNewChurch.org

Competencies (seed leaf)

What are your spiritual gifts?

What are your greatest strengths?

What are your greatest weaknesses?

Character (seed Coat)

Your personality

Your leadership style

Your world view

Listening to God

Who is praying for this new ministry?

Who are your prayer partners with whom you can share personal issues and concerns?

How are you setting aside time for prayer, searching the scriptures, reflection, and visioning?

Who is holding you accountable for your spiritual growth and development?

To what spiritual disciplines will you and your congregation practice?

Wesley's "Means of Grace"

- **The public worship of God**
- **The ministry of the Word, either read or expounded**
- **The Lord's Supper**
- **Family and private prayer**
- **Searching the Scriptures**
- **Fasting or abstinence**
- **Christian conferencing**

Who are you best able to communicate with?

What is the biggest gap in the above that you must make sure is covered by members of the launch team? (If you are great at casting a vision but lousy at the details, you need some detail type people)

Listening to your Community

- What is currently being offered in your community for spiritual growth and formation?
  - Denominations
  - Worship styles
  - Groups already being reached
  - Theological perspectives
  - Worship size
  - Discipleship process
  - Visitor follow-up
  - What is highly effective?
  - What is a major turn-off?
- What are the gaps?
  - Denominations
  - Worship styles
  - Groups not being reached
  - Theological perspectives
  - Worship size
  - Discipleship process
  - Visitor follow-up

 © 2018 Robert O. Crossman, www.UMNewChurch.org

- What are the major competitors for peoples' time?

  - Children's and youth sports

  - School daily and yearly schedule and time:
    (for example you would not want to launch your worship service on a weekend that schools have a Friday off)

  - Commuting to work

  - Addictions (gambling, alcohol abuse, drugs, etc.)

  - High school, university, and pro sports
    (not good to launch on the Sunday your home team is in a playoff)

  - Other

- What are the major influencers of culture in the community?

  - Major employers

  - Major corporations

  - Universities or colleges

  - College or pro sports

  - Kinds of entertainment options
    (kayak, biking, riverboat gambling, theatre, symphony, etc.)

  - Major influential denomination in the community

  - Other

- Who are the primary people groups?

  - Racial ethnic groups

  - Language groups

  - Immigrant groups (i.e. new residents from California who have moved to Las Vegas/people who have moved from a different country)

- Generations

- Age Groups

- Economic groups (lower, middle, or high income)

- Types of work (blue collar, white collar, service, professional)

• Who are key leaders for you to contact and be in conversation about community needs and issues?

- Superintendent or Principals of local schools

- Mayors and other elected officials

- Police chief, fire chief

- Local city planning department

- Service organizations

- Print shop owners

- Social services

- Medical professionals

- Pastors

- Other

Creating a Vision for the Congregation

• What makes us unique? What is our "Niche"?

- Denomination

- Worship style(s)

- Groups we are going to reach

- Theological perspective

- Worship size

 © 2018 Robert O. Crossman, www.UMNewChurch.org

- Discipleship process

- Visitor follow-up

- How will the new church develop understanding of shared memory and identity? (Internally and externally – core group and newcomers)

  - Who are we as God's people?

  - Who are we as a church?

  - Who are we as United Methodists?

  - Who are we as a congregation?

  - What are our core values?

  - Who are you trying to reach?

  - What is your target audience (be specific and carefully defined)?

  - Construct a profile of the person we are "most likely to reach."

How will we get the word out?

- How will we communicate?

  - Our existence?

  - The benefits?

- How will we communicate the Vision (internally and externally – core group and newcomers)?

  - Interpersonal communication

  - Publications

  - Ministry events

  - Bible studies (images)

  - The meaning of the church name you've chosen

  - Slogan you've chosen that captures the vision and the core values

Ways to disseminate information:

- social media
- e-mail
- newsletters
- notes/letters/postcards
- CD's
- newspaper articles
- flyers
- prayer chains
- posters
- voice mail
- web sites
- direct mail pieces
- Sunday service program
- DVDs
- banners
- verbal announcements
- bulletin boards
- press releases

How will people be able to contact the pastor and the church:

- phone
- text
- cell phone
- web site
- e-mail
- stop by pastor's office/home
- facebook
- other

What will you put on your connect/business card?

How will we follow-up visitors?

And last but not least:

when is your day off?
how will you protect family time?
how will you protect date night?

SECOND STEP: PREPARING FOR THE LAUNCH

Self-Care

- Identify to the congregation your day off and the day you do your sermon and worship preparation.
  How will you hold to these days so that people will respect your time?
- Develop a weekly and monthly calendar that shows how you will spend your time.
  Share with your family and accountability group.
- Develop an accountability group.
- Create a prayer group of people outside of your local ministry to keep you and your ministry in prayer.
- Find a mentor, someone who has started a church in the past, who you can call on for advice and support.
- Protect your family time.
- Pray daily for guidance and wisdom.

© 2018 Robert O. Crossman, www.UMNewChurch.org

First Steps to Launch Weekly Worship

- Get to know your community

Use the following survey as a way to learn about the people who live in your community. Pick out a neighborhood and go door to door. Or set yourself up in front of a grocery store and invite people to take a survey. Plan to do at least 100 of these surveys yourself. This is about the only way you will begin to see who will be part of your future congregation. Robert Schuller, Bill Hybels, and Rick Warren all started their ministry in their new communities by conducting a house to house survey. One denomination gives the new pastor of a new church a pair of shoes and instructs them to knock on 1,000 doors.

The Survey

_ Are you active in a local church? (If yes, go to the next house or person)
_ Why do you think most people do not go to church?
_ What is the greatest need in the community?
_ What advice would you give to me as a Pastor (or new church starter)?
_ Would you be interested in finding out more about our church? (If he or she says yes, write down the address for future contact.)

- Visit other churches in the area to see what kind of worship experiences are being offered. Look for what is working? What is not working? What is not currently being offered?

- Get a demographic printout of your community. Your annual conference should have access to this kind of information at MissionInsite.

- Do a drive around and a walk around survey of the area to see what fits and does not fit with the demographic picture.

- Talk to key leaders in the community. Find out where future growth will take place, what is happening in the school system, what are the most important needs and what opportunities are available to be in service.

- Check out traffic flow on work days and at the time you are planning to offer your first worship experience.

- Design your discipleship system. Develop or find a resource that you will use for developing the launch team of your new congregation. Develop the ongoing classes or experiences that will help people grow in spiritual maturity.

Identify Type of Church Start
That Will be Most Effective In your Mission Field

- Small Group Start
  Starts with a launch team and moves toward establishing eight to twelve small groups before the launch of the first public worship service.

- Worship-Centered Start
  Starts with a launch team who develops and resources a worship service to draw and attract new people to the church. After the public launch a small group/discipleship system is put in place.

- Community-Based Start
  Starts with a launch team who identifies felt needs in the community and develops ministries to meet those needs. After reaching a critical mass, they will launch the public worship service.

- Parenting-Church Start
  An existing church launches a new church. The church planter develops a launch team with existing members and develops a new congregation using one of the above listed models.

Gathering The People

- First meetings and event establish who you are. Start everything with prayer.

- Design first gatherings as the first part of your discipleship process.

- The first goal is to establish a healthy launch team: a healthy launch team is a Christian community that supports, prays, and works together as a team.

- Make sure your launch team reflects the people group or people groups you see as the future make-up of the congregation. YOUR CONGREGATION WILL LOOK LIKE YOUR LAUNCH TEAM!

Site Selection for Worship

Decide on the space you will need for gathering. What space do you need for office and small groups.

For large gatherings you can check out the following:

- Schools: A high school or middle school is preferable because youth in middle school or high school feel like they re going backward when they go to an elementary school.
- Warehouse
- Strip malls
- Movie Theater, Dinner Theater, or Playhouse
- Share facilities with existing church, or obtain closed church's facilities

 © 2018 Robert O. Crossman, www.UMNewChurch.org

Office space:
• Strip malls or an office building. Make sure you have meeting space for music rehearsals and a room for childcare when you hold meetings.

Obtain Equipment

- Computer with color printer.
- Music System that can handle electric keyboards, guitars, and bass as well as vocals.
  - CD or tape deck for playing music as people enter or for solos.
  - Keyboard with MIDI – MIDI means you can connect your keyboard with another keyboard or a computer. A professional keyboard can play organ music as well as piano and a wide variety of instruments. Look to spend about $2,000 and up for a professional quality instrument.
  - Drum set – (this is for a church that will have a praise band.) Your best bet if you can afford it is an electric drum set because you can adjust the volume of the sound to fit the size of room. You're more likely to find a drummer if you provide a drum set.
- Screen and Data Projector to project PowerPoint or MediaShout presentations for use for singing or showing announcements. They also can be connected to a laptop for projecting videos.

Obtain Licenses
(see article *"Do We Need a Music and Video License?"* in chapter ten)

Church Music License for printing or projecting words of songs: www.ccli.com

Also check out the worship section at www.umcdiscipleship.org for an updated list of companies that provide licenses.

Motion Picture Licensing Company that allows you to show video tapes in worship 1-800-515-8855

Staff

- Music person is primary: The kind of music you offer will determine who comes!!!

- Look for an administrator who will help you coordinate the growth of groups and ministries in the congregation.

Money

- Develop a budget for the first two years. Plan to share this with your core group and with denominational staff who are working with you.

- Develop a process for receiving funds: In the United Methodist Church you might ask the treasurer of the district or the annual conference to handle and process funds until you are all well enough established to have your own treasurer.

- Look for opportunities to share your vision for this new ministry with people who would be interested in helping to fund the work. Ask other churches or people to buy specific pieces of equipment for the project. Develop large donors who will begin to see this as part of their giving ministry.

Launching The Public Ministry

- Have a discipleship system in place before you start.

- Plan the first ten weeks of worship. Lay out the themes and scripture.

- Start your first worship service when you know that you will have at least 150 to 300 people in worship. Some congregations develop a small group system of eight to ten groups and bring them together for the first time at the launch. Others do phone marketing or mass mailings. Many do a combination of the two.

- Style of worship is key – who are you trying to reach?

- Determine dress code – people in leadership (musicians, greeters, speakers, liturgists, and speakers) model who are welcome in the worship experience.

- Have people in front who are in the same people group you are attempting to reach. Take into account gender, ethnicity, and age. Leadership for the worship service (musicians, liturgists, and speakers) model who are welcome in the worship experience.

- Have a dress rehearsal of the service the week before it is offered at the site.

Children & Youth

- Offer quality childcare and church school for children.

- Develop a system for checking in all children who are in church school. (One idea - laminate number cards that a parent takes with them after they have checked the child in. Make them small enough to fit in a shirt pocket. After worship children are released to the person who has the card. When finances allow, get a beeper system like restaurants use.)

- Develop a discipleship system for children and youth.

People show us, now what do I do?

- Follow-up with a letter from the pastor and a visit or phone call from a lay member or pastor of the church. Develop a system to tell whether visitors are returning. If they are not coming back, try a different way of following

© 2018 Robert O. Crossman, www.UMNewChurch.org

up or change the people who are making the contacts.
Keep careful track of people as they come and they respond to your ministry

- Develop your own registration card that includes a spot to identify if they are a visitor, an attender, or a member. Have a section for prayer concerns and for interest in classes or ministry opportunities. See Rick Warren's book, *The Purpose Driven Church,* page 261 for a good illustration of this.

- Develop a weekly electronic newsletter and Facebook site to keep visitors, attenders, and members informed.

- Invite people to small groups, Bible studies, and ministry opportunities.

Resources by the Authors

Dotson, Junius,
Developing an Intentional Discipleship System: a Guide for Congregations, 2017, Discipleship Resources

Miller, Craig Kennet
7 Myths of the United Methodist Church
Baby Boomer Spirituality: Ten Essential Values of a Generation
Boomer Spirituality: Seven Values for the Second Half of Life
Contemporary Worship for the 21st Century: Worship or Evangelism?
Creating a Culture for Innovation: An ILP Three-Hour Seminar
Encounters with Jesus: A Group Study in Baby Boomer Spirituality
Forty-Sixty: A Study for Midlife Adults Who Want to Make a Difference
Gen2Gen: Sharing Jesus Across the Generations
iKids: Parenting in the Digital Age
Innovative Leadership Project Guidebook 2.0: Values, VAP-IT, Discipleship System, Futurecasting
Innovative Leadership Project: Guidebook 3.0
Making God Real for a New Generation: Ministry with Millennials Born from 1982 to 1999
Next Church Now: Creating New Faith Communities
Sharing Jesus Across the Generations by Craig Kennet Miller
Teamworks: Creating A Discipleship System
TeamWorks: Connecting with Your Community
TeamWorks: Futurecasting
TeamWorks: Spiritual Life of the Leaders

Additional Resources

Hamilton, Adam, *Leading Beyond the Walls: Developing Congregations with a Heart for the Unchurched*, Abingdon

Melton, Joy Thornburg, *Safe Sanctuaries: Reducing the Risk of Child Abuse in the Church*, Discipleship Resources

Reeves, Michael, *Extraordinary Money! Understanding the Church Capital Campaign*, Discipleship Resources

Warren, Rick, *The Purpose Driven Church*, Zondervan

Warren, Rob, *Reconnecting*, on DVD, Abingdon Press

Wills, Dick, *Waking to God's Dream: Spiritual Leadership and Church Renewal*, Abingdon **Press**

†††

Reprinted here by permission of the authors, Junius Dotson and Craig K. Miller granted on October 10, 2017.

†††

NOTE: This article reflect the personal opinions of the author(s) and does not necessarily reflect an official position of Discipleship Ministries or Path 1.

 © 2018 Robert O. Crossman, www.UMNewChurch.org

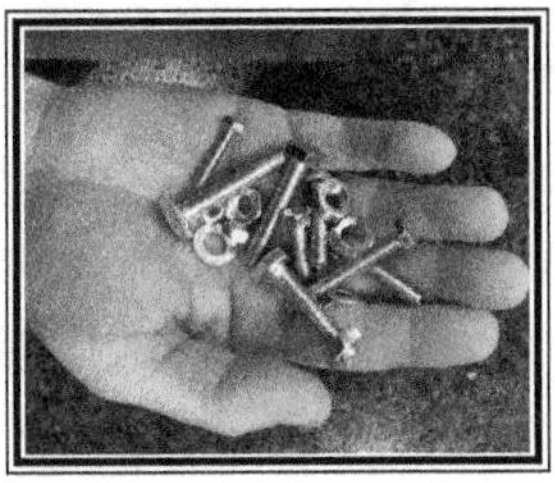

New Church Handbook
Nuts & Bolts for Planting New Churches In The Wesleyan Tradition

"Do I Need a Prayer Team?"

by Bob Crossman
including material by Kevin Kloster

You are about to embark on a ministry that will require more than the strength of your hands and the sweat of your brow. Church Planting will require your mind to be a mind in harmony with the mind of Christ, your mouth to be a mouth through whom Christ speaks, and your hands to be hands through whom Christ touches your mission field. You will need to be in touch with the one who said, *"I am the vine and you are the branches."* (John 15:5)

Your personal prayer life and spiritual disciplines will be an essential part in preparing you and sustaining your ministry as a new church planter.

You may have made it this far in your spiritual journey without a prayer team supporting you. Believe me, you are about to embark on a journey where you must have friends, family and colleagues surrounding you in prayer.

Build a team of prayer warriors to surround you and support your church planting ministry. Recruit 6 to 12 people among your family, friends and colleagues who live OUTSIDE your new church's mission field. They need to live out of town because at times you will have confidential prayer concerns that do not need to be shared within your launch team. You could have a second, local, prayer team if you wish, to whom you would send less intimate or confidential prayer request.

Send them an invitation, or contact them personally and ask if they would be willing to receive prayer request from you, and that they would pray DAILY for you and your new ministry.

On the following pages you will find a sample of how you might begin with an initial personal email, and then a weekly follow-up email.

I would anticipate that your contact with your Prayer Team would be weekly prior to moving day, perhaps monthly the first six months and then quarterly following that.

Sample:
Initial Email from a new planter:

From: "Kevin Kloster"
Subject: Prayers
To: "Bob Crossman"
Dear Bob,

As you know I am starting a new United Methodist Church in Maricopa, AZ. Starting a new church is, quite frankly, hard work. It is also high risk. I've done it once, call me crazy, but I'm doing it again! I'm not so crazy as to think I can do this alone. There is no way I can be successful without the undergirding and support of prayer. The early church was bathed in prayer. I believe prayer is one of the reasons that it grew and flourished. Acts 1:12-14 reads,
"Then they returned to Jerusalem from the mountain called the Mount of Olives. It is near Jerusalem, about half a mile away. When they came into the city, Peter, John, James, Andrew, Philip, Thomas, Bartholomew, Matthew, James (son of Alphaeus), Simon the Zealot, and Judas (son of James) went to the second-story room where they were staying. The apostles had a single purpose as they devoted themselves to prayer."

I am asking you to pray for this new church, for the people of Maricopa who do not attend church, and for Tracy and myself. We need your prayers! I am creating an email prayer letter that will get sent out once a week with specific prayers and answers to prayer. Your prayers, I believe, can help expand the kingdom of God by reaching new people for Jesus Christ. All I ask is a minute or two of your day to lift up this new church, as well as Tracy and I.

If you are willing to pray for us I will add you to the email prayer letter and you will start receiving it once a week. Tracy and I thank you in advance for your prayers! Please reply to this email and let us know if we can add you to the list of people praying that God will do an amazing thing through us so that we can touch the lives of people with the message of God's love, grace, and guidance.

Peace to you,
Kevin and Tracy

The material by Kevin Kloster
is used by permission granted on
April 2, 2017.

© 2018 Robert O. Crossman, www.UMNewChurch.org

Prayers for New UM Church Start in Maricopa, AZ

Dear Bob,

We'll we made it. We're all moved in a working away! Thanks for agreeing to pray for Tracy and I and the people of Maricopa as we begin to gather people within this new church.

Each week I will send you an email about the specific prayers I request from you. I will also list the answers to prayers that I've seen. Together we will witness Go at work in Maricopa. There is no way I can do all that needs to be done without your prayerful, daily support behind the scenes. I trust that you will pray daily for this new church start...maybe in the shower, driving to work, at the fitness center, before dinner, or as you fall asleep at night.

I can't imagine a more difficult, more challenging task than starting a church from scratch. It is a task, however, that with your prayers we are bound and determined to accomplish.

Be Ever Surrounded By God's Presence,

Rev Kev

Financial Support

Some of you have already supported this new ministry with your finances. Tracy and I thank you so much for your generosity. The big expense we have now is a web page. Web pages are the new front door to churches. I am researching which company to use so that we can have a "kick butt" web site. If God so moves you to help us out on the finanical side of things you can send your check to:

Randy Bowman, Treasurer
The Desert Southwest Conference of the United Methodist Church
1550 E. Meadowbrook Ave.
Phoenix, AZ 85014-4040

Makes checks out to the Desert Southwest Conference of the UMC and mark the memo area MARICOPA NEW CHURCH.

Join Our Mailing List!

Prayer Requests

This week I will be contacting each of the people who, thus far, have expressed a desire to participate in this new church start. I have twenty one people to hook up with this week. I'm sure they will have questions about me, just as I will about them.

Please pray that they are coming for the right reasons... not so much for themselves but to help us reach unconnected, unchurched people. Pray that God will work in their hearts to have a passion for reaching unchurched people. Pray that I might have wisdom to know if God wants any of these people to serve on my lead team.

*Sample: 3rd Email from a new planter**
Of course your prayer request can be within a simple email or private facebook page.

CITY OF MARICOPA
PROUD HISTORY • PROSPEROUS FUTURE

Prayers for New UM Church Start in Maricopa, AZ

Dear Bob,

This week marks the second week on the ground. Last week was a great week. Thanks a ton for praying!! Here is just a few of the kind of people who said yes to this great adventure. Let's start with the oldest. An 83 year old couple who I hooked up with last week are like big time excited to help with the new church. They said, "*Reverend, we don't have much money and can't knock on doors but if you need something you ask and if we can do it we will!*" Later in the week she brought me to her ladies group so I could introduce myself and talk about the new church. He gave me a tour of the clubhouse and made sure everyone knew why I was there.

I spent an evening with an amazing couple who have two kids, grades 4 and 6. She has experience as a Director of Christian Education. He has experience with audio-visual equipment. A lot of experience. Great people. Go getters.

Spent another evening with a young couple in early 20's. He wants to do Student ministry. She will do whatever. They are gung ho to get a new United Methodist Church in Maricopa.

This is a short week. I have to teach in Orlando, FL to a group of people on church planting. Should be a blast. When I get back we will hold our first informational meeting with all the people in one room. They get to see who everyone is for the first time. Can't wait to feel the energy!

Be Ever Surrounded By God's Presence,

Rev Kev

Join Our Mailing List!

Prayer Requests

I have had a hard time getting into see all the principals in the schools. I've met like 2 out 6. They are really busy as school starts next week. I did meet with the Superintendent of schools. Nice guy. The police chief hasn't gotten back to me either. I would invite you to pray that these people might open their hearts to at least a brief introductory meeting.

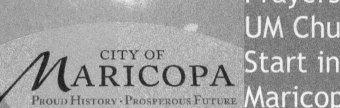

Continue to pray for me that I might be able to build lots of relationships with unchurched and unconnected people in Maricopa. My spirits are high. I'm feeling spiritually strong in the Lord. Life is good.

WANTED: More People Praying

© 2018 Robert O. Crossman, www.UMNewChurch.org

Sample: 4th Email from a new planter

Dear Bob,

This last week was a different week for me. I spent the last 7 days learning from and teaching potential church planters. It was great to spend time with people who feel called by God to start new churches. It did, however, take me away from here. I did get some good leads though while I was there! I followed up on one the other day. This guy has never, ever been to church. I left him a message on his cell and planned on calling him back later. After my devotions this morning, I prayer, "God, send me a person you want me to talk to today." One minute later, this guy called me back! We are meeting later this week for supper at a local restaurant. God is good!

I asked you to pray last week for some help breaking into the school system. I received an email saying the schools were looking for flag football coaches. Not exactly what I had in mind but if God is using this as an in to the schools then I'm signing up to coach kids how to play flag football! Also, I was invited to be a cub scout pack chaplain. God is good!

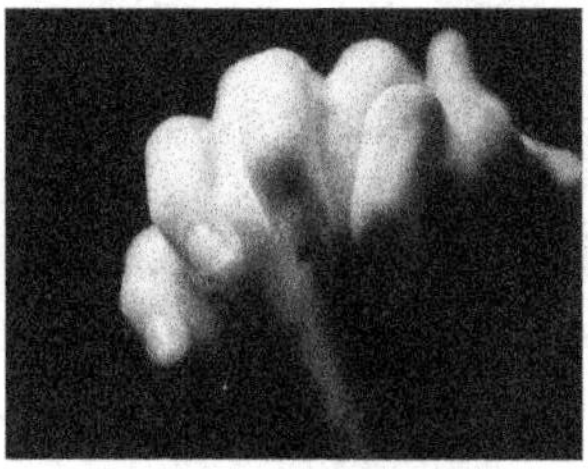

Finally, I asked you to pray for some kind of entry into the police chief's office. I received a phone call last week from a Sgt. who invited me into his office. We talked and I filled out an application for being their volunteer police chaplain. Don't know if I will get it but we got in! God is more than good. God is great!

Be Ever Surrounded By God's Presence,

Rev Kev

also start our outreach activities in the next few weeks as well. Though the Conference is paying my salary and expenses I have very little money to do outreach with. This money I have to raise on my own. Around $25-$50,000 is needed to grab the attention of people in Maricopa. If you can help, I would be deeply grateful. More importantly, you would be doing a huge part in reaching the lost and disconnected people within Maricopa. I promise that every dollar you give will go straight into reaching people through outreach and service events. Nothing will go to administration or overhead. All of it will go toward reaching people for Jesus. Please help by sending your checks to:

Randy Bowman, Treasurer
The Desert Southwest Conference of the United Methodist Church
1550 E. Meadowbrook Ave.
Phoenix, AZ 85014-4040

Makes checks out to the Desert Southwest Conference of the UMC and mark the memo area MARICOPA NEW CHURCH.

...and know, we're VERY grateful!

Join Our Mailing List!

As you continue your prayers, please pray that my heart might be open to all those people who are unchurched. Give me eyes to see them and the courage to walk across the room and talk with them. Ask God to put the people God wants me to reach in front of me and give me eyes to see them.

I will be pulling together about 30 of us next week for our first launch team meeting. Pray it goes well! Pray that people will be open to serving and getting out into the community doing service, mission, and outreach projects that will help grow this new body of Christ!

Prayer Matters!

start in Maricopa! The list needs to grow. Forward this email to your friends and family and ask them to join us as together we join God in this exciting of adventure of church planting!

*Sample: 5th Email from a new planter**

Of course your prayer request can be within a simple email or private facebook page.

CITY OF MARICOPA
PROUD HISTORY • PROSPEROUS FUTURE

Thanks for praying!

Dear Bob,

We'll the name should soon be announced. Hopefully, next week you will see our new name for this up and coming church as well as some pictures of its newest people. Some 40 people will be gathering this Sunday for our first ever church gathering! I am pumped! We have 30 plus adults and 10 children as part of the church family right now.

This Sunday people will meet each other for the first time. We'll spend time getting to know each other, have our first potluck meal, talk about the dream and vision of this church, and start small groups and outreach activities as a group.

In the sidebar to the left you will see my prayer requests for the week. Thanks again for keeping Tracy and I and this new church start in your prayers. We continue to feel strong and very much supported by you and the people we've met here. God is just incredibly awesome.

Be Ever Surrounded By God's Presence,

Rev Kev

p.s. i meet for the first time with my cub scouts as their chaplain this thursday. and, i am pretty sure i am in with the PD as their chaplain. did the finger print thing yesterday so if i am not wanted for something i didn't know i did - i am in! if i am wanted for something i didn't know i did please visit me at maricopa county jail. pray i don't get the tent city!

Prayer Matters!

70 some people are now praying for us. Please pass this along to anyone who you think would add us to their prayers.

Join Our Mailing List!

Here are the prayer concerns for this week:

1. Wisdom for me planning the first gathering.
2. Prayers for the Cabinet as they contemplate the name for this new church.
3. Peace for those who come on Sunday full of excitement but not yet knowing anyone.

© 2018 Robert O. Crossman, www.UMNewChurch.org

Sample: 6th Email from a new planter

October 1, 2008

Thank You for Your Prayers and Amazing Support!

Dear Bob,

Tracy and I want to say thank you for your continued prayers and support. We get emails and phone calls from many of you simply checking up on us. You have no idea how much that means to us! We wanted to bring you up to speed on what's happening and how we are doing so you get this separate and special email! It's not going out to the people of Journey Church - just you!

So, How are Tracy and I Doing?

Starting a new church is simply hard, tiring, grinding work. Looks like it by the picture doesn't it? Tracy and I took a short trip to San Diego to enjoy some R and R. Usually, my days start at 7:30am and go to 4:00pm. Then I work out at the gym until 5:30pm. Then home for supper and I continue to work most nights until 10:00pm. My spirit is strong and I feel energetic and healthy. My faith is unwavering in the belief that God is doing something incredibly amazing in this place and through us. I am meeting with people almost every day for lunch or dinner or coffee. The gym workout helps manage the weight!

So, How's the Church Doing?

We've been on the ground just over 10 weeks and we are half way to our goal of 125 people by Christmas. We currently have 63 people on board with several others on the prospective list. Last night was huge for us. Tracy and I took the President of the Chamber of Commerce and his wife for dinner. I met him two weeks ago and started developing a relationship with him. They are well-respected, well-known connectors in the community. After dinner I made my pitch and they are in! She is coming on board my launch team and has amazing ideas. Church hasn't been a part of their lives for many, many years. Their presence will no doubt speed our growth.

I have two fantastic women who are running JourneyKIDS, our ministry to children. You've read about them in the newsletter and can see for yourself how blessed we are to have them with us.

Yesterday, I was called in as the Police Chaplain to deal with a suicide of a prominent member of the community who was employed at City Hall. I conducted a crisis intervention with members at City Hall so that they could begin to process their grief. It was ministry and it was great exposure for our church.

We have a young man with us now who has never been in church. I don't get how this happened other than your prayers lead him to us. Out of the blue he called me to talk. He was very suspicious, very skeptical, very cautious as we talked. I asked him why he called and he said," I feel like something is missing in my life and I can't explain why but you were the name I called." I gave him his first Bible and today he is on my lead team. He helps us see things from a totally unchurched perspective.

All of this is to say, Tracy and I are grateful for your prayers and support. You are helping us to reach people who have not been reached before. I believe we will have more than 125 people by Christmas. I believe we will reach more unconnected, unchristian people then we ever imagined. I believe it's happening because God is working in the lives of people, because I am working my tail off, and because you are with us on the Journey prayfully, lovingly, supporting us.

Kevin Kloster

© 2018 Robert O. Crossman, www.UMNewChurch.org

After about 6 weeks in the new mission field,
the planter began a weekly email to the new congregation...

In This Issue
The Journey begins..
How to Financially Support the Journey
Spiritual Gifts Inventory

The Journey Begins...

36 people met for the first time to share a meal, meet one another and step onto the path that will create a new United Methodist Church in Maricopa. 13 families were present. 5 families were unable to attend. It was absolutely a blast!

How to Support Journey Church

As a new United Methodist Church we are financially supported by the Desert Southwest Conference of the UMC. The Conference pays my salary and expenses for the first couple of years and gives us a little extra for programming. It's up to us to give so that we can do all the outreach and programming that's needed to offer great things to our community.

Because we don't "manage" our own financial resources until January 1st we need to send our offerings to the Conference office. Just as you would normally place an offering in the plate at a church, our offering, for the next few months, goes in an envelope and gets sent to:

Desert Southwest Conference of the UMC
Att. Randy Bowman
1550 E. Meadowbrook Ave. Phoenix, AZ 85014

Write the check out to <u>Desert Southwest Conference of the UMC</u> In the memo area write: **MARICOPA NEW CHURCH START.**

Dear Bob,

Welcome to the first edition of Journey E-Updates. Each Monday you will receive this email with all the exciting events and activities happening at Journey UMC. Please forward this to anyone interested in the Journey!

Take the Spiritual Gifts Inventory

As we discussed on Sunday, we will place people in ministry positions based upon spiritual gifts, personality styles, and passion. Pastor Kevin wrote a spiritual gifts inventory that is being used by the United Methodist Church. It's easy to use and will give your results to you immediately. Click <u>here</u> to take the inventory. In the conference box write DSW. Please email your results to <u>Pastor Kevin</u>. Thanks!

JourneyKIDS

Here are some of the Journey Kids! Not everyone was pictured because I took this one early in the gathering. We will get them all in the next picture!!

Journey Goes on a Worship Tour

If you don't already have plans for worship this Sunday then join us as we start the church tour around Maricopa. This Sunday we will worship together at Church of Celebration at 9:00am. They are located at the Maricopa Elementary School
18150 N. Alterra Parkway
(Corner of Bowlin & Alterra Parkway)

We'll worship together and then anyone who wants to do brunch can join us as we talk about what we learned, what we liked and what we didn't like. This will help us learn about the variety of worship styles in Maricopa so that, when the times comes, we can create our own style.

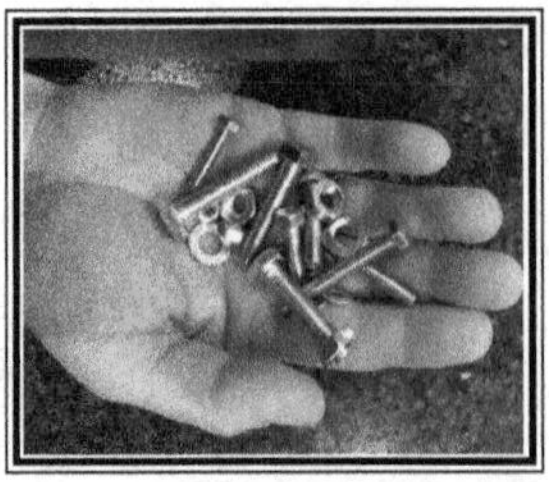

New Church Handbook
Nuts & Bolts for Planting New Churches In The Wesleyan Tradition

"Networking: Finding People - Part One"

by Bob Crossman

During my first fifteen years under appointment as a United Methodist pastor, I served a variety of congregations that were each about 100 years old. My primary responsibilities beyond preaching, was to be the pastor, the chaplain, the shepherd of the flock, and to respond to those who paid my salary.

The advice passed down to me from five generations of my Crossman forefathers who each grew up in parsonages - I was to care for my flock; to visit in the homes of my board members; and to visit in the homes of the 20 households who were the largest financial contributors.

The idea of networking or working to find new people for my church was simply not a priority.

After a dozen years, I was disappointed in the fruit of my ministry. While I served Pottsville UMC the worship attendance was steady at 43. While I served the Viney Grove and Prairie Grove circuit the worship held steady at 160. I had conducted several dozen funerals, and received several dozen new households - yet the net result was stability. Through my pastoral care I had expected my churches to grow, but they did not. That compelled me to return to seminary and receive a Doctor of Ministry in Evangelism and Wesleyan History. In those three years, Dr. George Hunter, David Watson and Richie Hogg taught me the fundamentals of Wesleyan evangelism and making new disciples.

In the fifteenth year of my ministry, I was appointed to be Associate Pastor of a 600 attendance congregation. My title was, "Minister of Evangelism." My responsibility was to respond to worship visitors, lead them toward the membership vows, and support them during their first six months as members until they had developed the holy habit of regular worship attendance and had become involved in a variety of small group ministries.

I was good at that job. My primary work involved:

- Develop a team of 150 laity who were committed to each bring at least 1 person into active discipleship in the coming year. *(Our was to receive 150 new people per year.)*
- Offer the new members class on a repeating eight week cycle that I had designed during my Doctor of Ministry in Evangelism work with Dr. George Hunter and Dr. David Watson.

 © 2018 Robert O. Crossman, www.UMNewChurch.org

- Respond by telephone on Sunday afternoon with every worship visitor (we averaged about 80 visitors each Sunday) keeping careful written records on each household.
- Hand address one of a series of seven different brochures to each visitor, with a personal note inviting them to return the next Sunday.
- Match each visiting household with a small group, and having a contact person from that small group telephone the visitor mid week with an invitation to participate in their small group.
- Relay contact information weekly to the appropriate staff member that might relate to that particular visiting household: Christian education, college minister, singles minister, children's minister, or youth minister.
- Contact regular worship visitors by phone if they had missed two consecutive Sundays.
- New members were telephoned on the anniversary of their joining (3, 6, 9 and 12th month) by a friendly team of evangelism committee members;
- Watch the "back door" by accurately recording attendance for all member households.
  - If they missed four consecutive weeks, a team of laity would make a friendly telephone call.
  - If they missed eight consecutive weeks, one of the pastors would make a second call.

In 1992 I received sixty-two households into the church, along with twenty-nine confirmands. I received a letter of commendation from the conference lay leader for leading that church to be in the 92nd percentile of Arkansas congregations, showing growth in professions of faith, average Sunday school attendance, average worship attendance, and growth in church membership.

These years as an associate did not teach me how to find new people from scratch - but I did learn more about responding to worship visitors in a winsome way. My ministry style was beginning to move in the right direction. Those years as "Minister of Evangelism" were a paradigm shift in the way I spent my time in ministry. My primary job description was no longer "pastor to my flock" but rather centered around responding to worship visitors and inviting them in winsome ways to join the journey toward becoming a faithful disciple of Jesus Christ.

Unknown to me, the Lord was preparing me to be the pastor of a new church start.

In my fifth year as "Minister of Evangelism" on that large church staff, Bishop Richard Wilkie appointed me to a be the pastor of a new church. The Lord was leading me to another paradigm shift in my ministry.

Before moving day, I decided that my primary focus in this new church would be to find *lost sheep*, to welcome *prodigals* home, to build and increase worship attendance, and to increase the population of heaven. This task consumed and deserved all my creativity, all my prayers, all my time, all my energy.

The content of this article has developed out of:

- the experience of being a new church planting pastor.
- having the primary responsibility of "putting people in the seats" on Sunday
- developing a system that would invite them to not just attend but to join the journey toward becoming a deeply devoted Disciple of Jesus Christ.

I believe that a healthy new church does not consist of just 50 or 500 deeply devoted disciples, but instead has people at many levels of involvement.

- First, every healthy church needs a large group of people who think favorably of the new church, know of its existence, but **have never attended** any event or worship service of the new church. You might say that they are just peeking through the stained glass windows. These people are not to be thought of or treated as deadbeat, freeloading, cheap grace, tag alongs. Rather, these people are the future of the church - they are prospects - praise God that there is a spark, a flicker of a flame inside of them - they are the next potential wave of deeply devoted disciples.
- Secondly, every healthy church needs a large group of people who have been to at least one event or worship service, or had at least one face to face contact with the pastor or key lay leadership. Perhaps they brought their children to a free carnival, Easter egg hunt, attended Christmas eve candlelight, or attended the Easter sunrise service. If you are serving an established church, perhaps they attended a wedding or funeral at the church, their kids are in your Boy Scouts or Girl Scouts, or they dropped their young children off at your Vacation Bible School. These households might even claim your church as "their" church, but they are not members yet, nor have they attended with any regularity. You probably don't even know their name yet.
- Third, every healthy church needs a group of people who participate at least **twice a year** in worship, or in a service ministry of the church. They are perhaps your Christmas, Easter and Mother's Day crowd.
- Fourth, every healthy church also needs a group of people who participate at least **twice a month.**
- Fifth, every healthy church needs a group of disciples, who are in worship and Christian education **every week**. You might be referring to them as your "two hour" disciples (one hour of worship, one hour of Sunday School).
- Sixth, every healthy church needs a group of saints, who are in worship every Sunday without fail and involved in many ministry and service opportunities... striving to become deeply devoted disciples, perhaps getting close to tithing 10% of their time and money.

If you are starting a new place for new people, one of your first tasks is to look for ways to add people to the "fringes" of the new church; to find people to be committed to the new church at various levels; AND in the process, begin to develop your initial launch team for new church or faith community.

See chart on following page...

© 2018 Robert O. Crossman, www.UMNewChurch.org

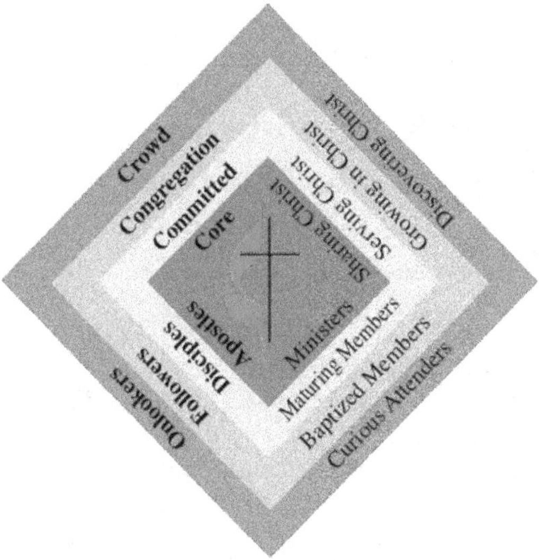

Steps of Commitment... A New Testament Pattern

Onlookers, "The Edge" - In Jesus day, these were the people on the outside, who were watching and observing the event. They gathered on the mountain to listen and eat a piece of fish & bread, but when Jesus moved on to the next village, they simply went back home.

Followers, "The Congregation" - this included those who watched, but were also interested enough to follow Jesus to the next town.

Disciples, "The Committed" - were the committed who followed Jesus from town to the next town to the next town, and also embraced the teachings of Jesus.

Apostles, "The Heart" - were those who took responsibility for the fellowship.

How do people move from the Edge to the Heart?

- **Onlookers, "The Edge" -** Onlookers move toward followers, as they begin to attend events, inquire about Christ, and occasionally attend worship.

- **Followers, "The Congregation" -** Followers move toward discipleship, as they become regular attenders of worship and begin participate in occasional short-term classes designed just for newcomers. These occasional short-term classes might include topics such as: Get Acquainted with the Bible; Get Acquainted with Jesus; or Get Acquainted with the Christian Faith. After these classes, many become ready to take the vows of membership, *"To support the church with my prayers, presence, gifts, service and witness."* They might also begin to attend traditional Sunday School classes or small home based ongoing life groups.

- **Disciples, "The Committed" -** Disciples move toward Apostles, as they develop a solid commitment to prayers, presence, gifts, service, witness, and reading the Bible. *{pray daily for the church, every Sunday attendance in worship and Sunday School, giving the tithe to the Sunday offering, giving time to serve the Lord, and reading the Holy Scriptures daily.}* Completion of Disciple Bible Study in your congregation may be the primary way Disciples move toward the core.

- **Apostles, "The Heart" -** The Core, are faithful Disciples committed to sharing the Good News with others. They have also moved into positions of serving the Lord through this church *(such as the choir, leading a small group, serve on the council or helping in the nursery)*, tithing financially, and also serve by witnessing and inviting others to join them in this journey toward faithful discipleship.

†††

New Church Handbook
Nuts & Bolts for Planting New Churches In The Wesleyan Tradition

"Networking: Finding Even More People - Part Two"

by Bob Crossman

NETWORKING in your mission field:

Jesus said, *"A farmer went out to scatter seed. ... Other seed fell on good soil and bore fruit, in one case a yield of one hundred to one, in another case a yield of sixty to one, and in another case a yield of thirty to one. Everyone who has ears should pay attention."*

Matthew 13: 3-9

Below you will find a long list of possible ways for you to *test the soil* in your mission field to determine where the soil is good and where it is rocky. They are ways for you to sow seeds in your mission field to discover where your ministry may take root, grow, and produce a bountiful harvest for Christ.

Determine what slice of the community you have a natural "affinity" to reach, and then to determine ways you might network with that slice of the community.

Don Smith suggests that the following questions might help you to determine where your networking might be the most effective:

- What are YOUR hobbies and interests and where could you connect with others that share those interests?;
- What is your household situation and how can your children's or spouse's connection to the mission field become an opportunity to network?;
- Where are the places that people in your community gather?; and
- What are the annual events that draw large crowds in your ministry context?

The following questions might lead you to the right people with whom to network with in your mission field:

- Who are the people who hold a vast amount of indigenous knowledge for your context?
- Who are the "power brokers" - people you need to meet as soon as possible?
- Who are the "connectors" - people who know a lot of people and will serve as a "walking billboard" if they get excited about the new church?

 © 2018 Robert O. Crossman, www.UMNewChurch.org

In your discernment process, you might ask several key questions, such as,

- *What subgroup or culture might God be calling me to establish a new expression among?*
- *Who are my friends and acquaintances who never attend any church, temple or synagogue?*
- *Is there a particular group already connected with one of the ministries I'm involved with?*

Remember that ministries which truly bless a community often arise out of conversations where you listen for the hopes and dreams of people in your community.

Below you will find a list of various ways planters have answered these questions in their particular mission field: ***(NOTE: These are not simply opportunities to do ministry to groups, but rather opportunities to network and gather people for the "new thing" you intend to start.)***

- Junius Dotson developed a "**referral card**" to give out. It was a self-addressed, stamped post card. On the reverse side it said, *"I would like to refer the following person to you and your new church. Name __, Address __ Phone __. Please tell them that I referred them to you. My name is __ my address __ my phone__."* He gave out hundreds of cards to people he met, asking if they might know someone who might be interested in being part of a new church in town.

- If you have a business background, you might join the **Rotary club, Chamber of Commerce or any notable civic club**, where you will actively tell your new church story, and look for people who might want to join you. As a planter in Ottawa, Kansas, Kent Melcher found that as an officer in the chamber of commerce, he attended every Ribbon Cutting for new businesses, and every monthly Chamber "coffee" in existing businesses. The chamber helped him to make connections with community leaders and new business leaders from every segment of the community.

- Visit every **funeral home director** in town. Make yourself available for funerals for families with no church affiliation. Adam Hamilton found this to be a great way to connect with people who were not active Christians, yet in a season of life when they were open to spiritual things. Who attends the funeral of sinners? Sinners. *(Did you know Church of the Resurrection started in a funeral home?)*

- Based on your background and affinities, other community groups that you might join to network in might include: **United Way, fraternity, sorority, Junior Auxiliary, Welcome Wagon, Kawanis Club, PTA, cattlemen's association, country club, Jaycees, scouts,** etc.

- Make an appointment to visit the **other pastors in town from your denomination.** Tell them your story, and invite their prayer support. Make an appointment to

© 2018 Robert O. Crossman, www.UMNewChurch.org

visit pastors of other denominations in town, for much the same reasons. These pastors may also have names for you of people who visited, but did not connect with their particular style of church.

- Drop by the **fire department and police department** occasionally to introduce yourself, tell your story, ask if they personally might be interested, or be able to refer you to a friend, relative, associate or neighbor who might be interested in being part of your new church. Kent Melcher suggest that if you have the temperament and training for it, you might become a police or fire chaplain.

- Make an appointment to visit any **business owners** you might have a natural affinity with. One of the Hispanic planters in Kansas talked to a local meat-packing company and became a paid chaplain for the Spanish speaking workers. All the compensation was paid directly to the new church start's budget, saving both the planter and the company taxes (no W-2 for the planter, and a charitable contribution for the company).

- Make an appointment to visit several community leaders to tell them your story, ask if they personally might be interested, or be able to refer you to a friend, relative, associate or neighbor who might be interested in being part of your new church.

mayor	**Deputy Mayor**
chief of police	**Chief of Fire Department**
postmaster	**Bank Branch Managers**
realtors (all of them)	**Bank President**
superintendent of schools	**president of the chamber of Commerce**

principle *(High School, Middle School, and Elementary)*
Utility Office Managers *(where newcomers sign up for water, electricity, trash pick-up, gas, or phone)*

In my new church start,
the first family to join was Michelle, the largest volume Realtor in town.
Over the next five years Michelle brought more new members into the church that I did.
The second family to join was the new bank president in town,
which gave my new start great credibility in the community.
Once we launched worship, he was a greeter and his wife
taught the children's Sunday School class.

Bob Crossman

- Where does your target audience spend their time? Where might you meet people, introduce yourself, tell your story, ask if they personally might be interested, or be able to refer you to a friend, relative, associate or neighbor who might be interested in being part of your new church.

© 2018 Robert O. Crossman, www.UMNewChurch.org

Concession stand at the ball field *(football, baseball and soccer)*
"Bob's Grill" *(where the police, and pick-up truck crowd eats lunch)*
County Fair or Festivals *(depending on policies of the sponsoring groups, secure booth space, but make sure to do it with excellence.)*
Square Dancing *(In Prairie Grove, hundreds of 3rd through 12th graders, take great pride to practice and compete in the annual Square Dance competition connected with the County Fair. A great place for the new church planter to work the crowd.)*

Starbucks	**Parades**
Golf course	**Barrel Racing or Rodeo or Trail Rides**
Pow-Wow	**City Park**

- Ask the mayor if the **city council has a chaplain.** *Weekly in one mission field, on the public cable TV, the mayor opens the City Council meeting by saying, "As we begin, I have asked the pastor of the new Methodist church forming in town, to give our opening prayer and to serve a Chaplain of our City Council." The council meeting is broadcast live and rebroadcast four or five times each week giving free exposure for the planter and the new church that is forming.*

- Support the **city council** with a free meal once a quarter before their meetings.

- Volunteer as a **crossing guard** for the local elementary school. *Don Smith did this every Friday for several years learning the names of the children, and getting recognized at PTA meetings.*

- Volunteer as a **story teller / reader** at the public library and / or elementary schools (but only if you're gifted at it.) Kent Melcher also suggests that if you have an unusual talent or skill, volunteer to provide a program at the library or schools.

- Looking for Native Americans who might not have a church home, David Wilson invited Native Americans to join a **basketball team and a baseball team** to play in the city league. He also put up a booth at pow-wow.

Who do you believe God is calling you to reach?

In the initial phases of your new church start, rather than attempting to appeal to or reach everyone in your community, spend time clearly discerning which particular group of people within your mission field God is calling you to reach with this new ministry.

†††

NOTE: This article reflects the personal opinions of the author and does not necessarily reflect an official position of Discipleship Ministries or Path 1.

New Church Handbook
Nuts & Bolts for Planting New Churches In The Wesleyan Tradition

"50 Ways to Missionally Engage Your Mission Field"

by Bob Crossman

Introduction

Perhaps it may be true that twenty years ago a new or established church only needed to offer inspiring worship with great music to spark a word of mouth process that would bring new people, causing the church to grow and prosper.

However, today in an increasing number of mission fields, people are seeking more than inspiring worship with great music. In an increasing number of mission fields in the USA, even the nones, lost sheep, prodigals, and prospects somehow understand the heart of Matthew 25 and John Wesley's "Works of Mercy." Out of this intuition, they are only inclined to be a part of a church that is authentically "doing something," and getting blisters in Jesus' name.

How can our churches, both new and established, continue to be faithful to Matthew 28 *(go make disciples, teaching and baptizing)* while experiencing an increasing faithfulness to Matthew 25 *(feed the hungry, cloth the naked, welcome the stranger, and visit the prisoner)*?

In this context, I offer these "50 Ways to Missionally Engage Your Mission Field."

Discovering Your Mission Field - Listen and Learn

1. You can not accurately discover your mission field if you only sit at a strategic planning table reading demographic reports. Demographic reports such as MissionInsite's Quadrennial Report and Executive Report with Mosaic Types will give you hypothesis that must be checked out and tested in live conversations. Test these demographic hypotheses by walking around and spending time with the people who live in your mission field.

2. To begin this process - start with building relationships and trust. Do not start with big events with large numbers.

3. Ministries that fruitfully bless communities in Jesus' name often arise out of unorganized, crazy and chaotic conversations where we listen for the hopes and dreams of people within a mission field.

 © 2018 Robert O. Crossman, www.UMNewChurch.org

4. Discover ways to spend time with individuals in your mission field. You might even sit in a park, diner or coffee shop. Hannah Estock sat at Venice Beach, California with a sign that read, *"Tell me your story and I will give you a dollar."* Hannah was busy all afternoon, and a line of people formed to tell their story to Hannah. Engage with the people who accept your invitation, and slowly listen to their stories.

5. As you listen don't let your pre-set ideas or pre-conceived notions shape the conversation. Rather, simply listen for the challenges, hopes, longings and dreams of your neighbors. Be willing to actively listen.

6. Introduce yourself to the mayor, city administrator, chief of police, superintendent of schools, fire department chief, and school principles. These people have tremendous influence in your mission field, and they need to know who you are, what your are doing, and that you want to help the mission field.

7. Following Nehemiah's example (Nehemiah 1:4), out of love and compassion for the mission field, spend significant time mourning over the brokenness, confessing the sins of the people, fasting, and prayer before the God of Heaven.

Tools for Building Incarnational Relationships of Trust

8. Frederick Buechner, in Wishful Thinking: A Seeker's ABC's writes, *"The place God calls you to is the place where your deep gladness and the world's deep hunger meet."*

9. Engage a team to engage in these relationships, thereby multiplying the quantity and quality of this discovery process.

10. As a covenant team, hold each other accountable in the faithful practice of spiritual disciplines.

11. Within the context of the programs already in place within your church, discover ways to create spaces for the possibility of incarnational relationships to happen. Perhaps with...
    12. The participants in your English as a second language program;
    13. The neighborhood youth who play basketball in your parking lot;
    14. The parents who bring their children to your annual Easter egg hunt;
    15. The households who utilize your food pantry and clothing bank;
    16. The household who lives next door to the church;
    17. The neighbors who participate in your community garden project;
    18. The families who receive your annual Thanksgiving baskets;
    19. The men who sleep under the Broadway Bridge each evening

20. The residents of your local battered women's shelter;
21. The youth in the local Boys and Girls Club after-school program;
22. The recipients of your annual Angel Tree program.
23. Your church's custodian and lawn care workers.

24. Observe and listen to an increasing number of private individuals and public officials. Determine if there are clusters of the most pressing themes, dreams and challenges that face the people in your mission field.

Boundaries and Conflict

25. Rather that approaching all of your local programs, start with the possibility of changing ONE of your missional gestures into a missional engagement.

26. Learning from that first attempt, expand the invitation for incarnational relationships to a second and third ministry.

27. Your coach can help you address the need for boundaries within these relationships so they do not merge with the personal lives of your team members, and become exhausting.

28. Your coach and spiritual director can help you address the conflict that will arise as multiple passions (priorities) develop within the church out of these incarnational relationships.

Organizing Through One to One Relationships

29. As the number of significant relationship encounters grow, continue to be open to creativity, risk, and the dream of transforming brokenness.

30. The journey toward a dream of transforming brokenness, should include two core principles: (see #31 and #32 below)
31. Be clear on what you are attempting to change.
    - What issues, suffering, injustices, challenges or inequalities are you attempting to change? What are the concrete improvements in people's lives that will happen as a result of your work on this potential issue?
    - From among this list, which of these might be winnable, easy to understand, have a clear time-frame, non-divisive within your church, and consistent with your values and vision?

32. Be clear on what you are building.
    - How are you creating and sustaining teams of leaders who can take action together for that change?
    - How are you discerning who is passionate about justice, has a vision for change, or is interested in service?

 © 2018 Robert O. Crossman, www.UMNewChurch.org

- Have you connected with civic groups, community leaders, local businesses, companies, organizations, and the shakers and movers in your mission field?
- Create the team by face to face conversations, listening for their passion, vision, and stories - then inviting them to help you.
- Rule of 1/3's: You will need to have face to face contact with 63 people to find 21 who are willing to engage, and find 7 out of the 21 who will be fully engaged in the team's project.
- Begin a "domino effect" by empowering and inspiring these early team members to extend the invitation to additional team members.
- Strive to *bring the church council and congregation along* so the team does not get too far ahead, and thereby loose support from the host church.

33. Determine which of these clusters of the most pressing themes *(including dreams and challenges that face the people in your mission field / community)* are already being addressed by other programs and agencies. There is no need to reinvent the wheel if you can partner with another group or agency with whom you have common missional objectives.

34. New churches will need to be sure they act their age and not take on missional ministries to the level that it distracts from the journey toward survival and sustainability. If the new church survives and thrives, then at that point it will have the people and financial resources to have even greater missional impact.

35. Smaller membership churches, in order to more fully respond to the missional needs they discover, may need to find partners that can provide the additional people and financial resources.

36. As you begin to respond to the brokenness revealed in the conversations and relationships, consider starting both direct mercy ministries and ministries that address the root causes of brokenness.

Principles of Team Building and Effective Coalitions

37. A team is MORE THAN
    - An email list or listserve.
    - A committee that does little outside of meeting times.
    - A group of people mandated by some other power to be on a committee.
    - A group of people that are more interested in being the representative or some other role in a structure than in building relationships and doing real work with others.
    - A group that is disconnected from the people affected by the issue they are working on.

38. An effective team works together to come up with a common vision for this work and ministry. They are also clear about their shared passions, dreams, and hopes for change. An effective team can answer: *"One year from now, what is the concrete change in people's lives we want to see?"*

39. An effective team cares so deeply about this ministry, that they actively invite others to be part of this team. Two team members may have an idea, but two people can not sustain an ongoing ministry. Send the two to gather five people who are willing and able to engage, and then send the five to gather twelve. Typically at least twelve people are needed to sustain most ongoing projects.

40. An effective team thinks of creative ways to engage the entire congregation and community in this ministry, not just themselves and those who would usually participate.

41. An effective team uses "we" language instead of "I" language when talking about this ministry.

42. An effective team quarterly reviews and re-engages with their common vision, passion, dream, and hope for change.

Adding Discipleship to Community Relationships

43. Lack of positive relationships and unintended *us and them* attitudes have resulted in many churches frustration that hundreds of people each year visit their food bank or clothing bank or social justice ministry, but none of those same people ever attend their worship services on Sunday.

44. Some congregations have discovered that new people are uncomfortable entering a building that is three steps nicer than their apartment, or when cars in the parking lot or the dress code of the congregation are three steps nicer than those whom they are trying to begin reaching in their mission field. Asking members to drive their truck instead of their new car, and wearing casual clothes instead of their "Sunday best" has helped some congregations more warmly welcome their neighbors to worship.

45. A congregation in Wichita, Kansas offers a 30 minute worship after their English as a Second Language program each week. About 125 of the 150 ESL participants stay for worship each week.

46. In central Virginia, a new rural church, working with de-churched people, began as a movement to love and care for neighbors, GED classes and a thrift store. Only after the community relationships were built, did they begin to offer worship.

 © 2018 Robert O. Crossman, www.UMNewChurch.org

47. Mike Breen with 3DM has an amazing program of beginning with social justice program in a community, gathering 50 to 80 people in that program. Within 18 months, five to twelve of this group are ready to huddle around exploring spirituality and explore what it means to look at the world through the eyes of Jesus.

48. Several churches in the Dallas Metroplex have added Bible studies and worship at 10 am midweek or Saturday inside their clothing bank room, primarily directed toward households that have been using the clothing bank.

49. A congregation in Dayton, Ohio added a donut and coffee table to their weekly food and clothing bank. A church member with the gift of warm hospitality serves as the donut hostess. She invites each person to stay for the thirty minute Bible study that morning.

50. A congregation in Escondido, California discovered that inadvertently their food and clothing bank was communicating *"you are not worthy to come to worship, but you can come around to the back door and we will give you a handout."* As a result, very few people were attending their Spanish language worship service. They turned their program upside down, and now the cutting edge into the mission field is *"come to worship."* Today, their worship attendance, food bank and clothing bank have all grown exponentially.

†✝†

NOTE: This article reflects the personal opinions of the author and does not necessarily reflect an official position of Discipleship Ministries or Path 1.

© 2018 Robert O. Crossman, www.UMNewChurch.org

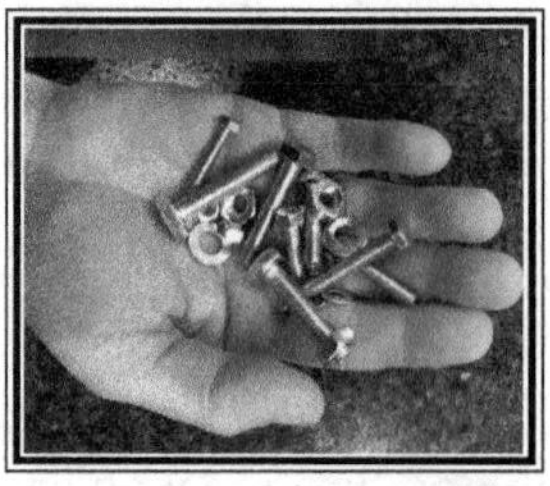

New Church Handbook
Nuts & Bolts for Planting New Churches In The Wesleyan Tradition

"Do I Need a Website, Facebook, Blog... ?"

by Bob Crossman

Do I need a website, Facebook or blog?

Your mission field will tell you the answer.

In almost every mission fields the answer is YES! Increasingly, Facebook and other social media are replacing the web site as the initial on-line contact.

In most mission fields today people refer to the internet and Google the same way our parents once referred to the Yellow Pages.

In some mission fields, if your new church is not on the internet, your church is invisible and does not exist. In an increasing number of mission fields, the social network is rapidly becoming a staple.

When Pew Research Center began tracking social media adoption in 2005, just 5% of American adults used at least one of these platforms. By 2011 that share had risen to half of all Americans, and by January of 2017, 69% of the public uses some type of social media. In January of 2017 the Pew Research Center reported that *"Facebook is the most-widely used of the major social media platforms, and its user base is most broadly representative of the population as a whole. Smaller shares of Americans use sites such as Twitter, Pinterest, Instagram and LinkedIn."*

Ed Stetzer of Lifeway Research says, *"If people are going to consider your church, they're going to consider it first online. They're going to wonder: 'What is it like? What is going on?' And if you don't tell them on line, they're not going to come... Church requires feet and faces, not just electrons and avatars. Social media can be the tool, but not the goal."*

Lifeway Research's 2011 survey of 1,003 protestant churches found that while 78% have a website, less than half of those congregations use their sites for interactive purposes like obtaining and distributing prayer requests (43%), registering people for events and activities (39%) and automating more church processes (30%). A full

 © 2018 Robert O. Crossman, www.UMNewChurch.org

91% provide information to potential visitors online and 79% provide information to the congregation. The found that 57% encourage increased attendance and involvement among the congregation and 52% solicit interest in ministry or volunteer opportunities. The study also found differences in the frequency of website usage. They found that 40% of churches with websites update their sites once a week. 15% update more than once a week. But nearly half of churches with websites (42%) update them once a month or less, including 7% that update once a year or less.

Lifeway's survey also found that 47% of churches actively use Facebook. They found that 81% percent of congregations with 500 or more in average worship attendance use Facebook, compared to 27% of churches with one to 49 attendees. Also, 43% of churches with 50 to 99 attendees use Facebook, as do 46% of churches with 100 to 199 attendees and 56% of churches with 200 to 499 attendees.

Lifeway Research reports that among churches that utilize social networking tools, 73% use them for interacting with the congregation, 70% for distributing news and information in an "outbound only" manner, 52% for fostering member-to-member interaction and 41% for managing the church's group ministry. A majority (62 %) of churches that utilize social networking tools use them to interact with individuals outside the congregation.

According to a 2012 nationwide research study by Phoenix-based Grey Matter Research, more than 17 million non-churchgoers visited the website of a local church or place of worship in the past 12 months. Yet many sites fail to easily provide the information these visitors are looking for. Twelve percent of all American adults have visited the website of a church or other local place of worship within the past thirty days. Twenty two percent of all American adults have visited the website of a church or other local place of worship within the past six months.

They also found what people do on the web sites of places of worship:

- Check to see the times of services, 43%;
- Check what activities are offered, 29%;
- Look for a map or directions to the church, 28%;
- Watch streaming video, 26%;
- Listen to streaming audio, 26%;
- See the church's religious beliefs, 22%;
- Request prayer, 18%;
- Download a podcast, 15%;
- Check what denomination or group the church belongs to, 15%;
- Send a message to the pastor or leader, 12%;
- Post on a bulletin board or forum, 5%.

The web presence for your new church can be simple - one page only, giving the pastor's email address, and worship date/time/location. **The planting pastor should not be spending hours each week building a web site**. Initially keep the web site simple so that you can use more of your creativity and time with personal networking to reach new disciples. As the launch team grows, someone on the team may have web design skills to build the site beyond the initial single page.

Before you dive into a website and Facebook you might consider having someone on your launch team enroll in one of the on-line training resources listed at: www.umcom.org/learn/all-training-courses. The United Methodist Communication's (UMCOM) online training resources will help your lay person understand how a web ministry can be part of the bigger picture of your church's outreach, and explain the theological and practical basis for maintaining a web ministry.

†††

NOTE: This article reflects the personal opinions of the author and does not necessarily reflect an official position of Discipleship Ministries or Path 1.

 © 2018 Robert O. Crossman, www.UMNewChurch.org

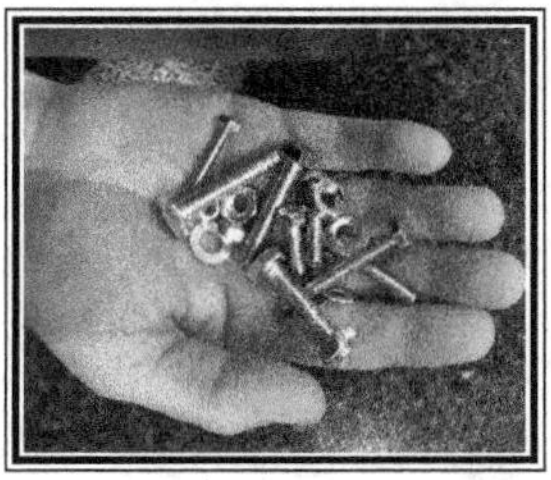

New Church Handbook
Nuts & Bolts for Planting New Churches In The Wesleyan Tradition

"Social Media Ideas & Cautions"

by Bob Crossman
including material by Kent Melcher, Natalie Bannon & Jeremy Steele

Is your email address Cannabis@hotmail.com or partygirl@hotmail.com?

Do you frequently post on Facebook, Twitter, Instagram, or Pintrest your opinions about the president of the United States?

Did you a post selfie the last time you were intoxicated?

Deployed to start a new church in a "deep red state," did you take a public front row position at the small gay rights parade in your town?

Upon hearing of your new appointment, did you actually post on your personal Facebook page your personal regret about being deployed to such a red neck town?

Did you really do those things?

Does your use of social media accurately reflect the image you want to project to your mission field?

Does your use of social media accurately reflect the vision & mission God has given you for the new church you've been deployed to launch?

Do you agree for the sake of the mission of Jesus Christ in the world and the most effective witness of the gospel, and in consideration of your influence as a pastor in the church, to make a complete dedication of yourself to the highest ideals of the Christian life, and to this end agree to exercise responsible self-control by personal habits conducive to bodily health, mental and emotional maturity, fidelity in marriage, social responsibility, and growth in grace and the knowledge and love of God?

Read the articles on the following pages for guidelines on responsible use of social media. You will find great ideas for using social media to make a positive connection with your mission field.

Jeremy Steele is Teaching Pastor at Christ UMC in Mobile, Alabama. jeremywords.com

"7 Tips to Draw Visitors with Social Media" by Jeremy Steele

You cannot log onto any site without seeing "recommendations." Sometimes, they are generated by a computer, sometimes by your social connections, but it is clear that we are looking more and more to "recommendations" to guide our decisions.

Though we often ask people to invite their friends and coworkers to church, churches tend to miss asking them to recommend their church via social media platforms. Here are seven ways to give congregants what they need to easily make those social recommendations.

1. **Ask congregants to check-in or post to social media**
   Take a moment to get to know Google Business so all your information shows up correctly when people search for it. Make sure your address on your Facebook page is listed correctly so people can check-in to church.

   Ask people directly to check in during announcements. Give congregants permission use their cellphones during worship. During specified times, they can post shareable moments on social media, take polls about the sermon topic and even use certain apps designed to enhance worship.

2. **Create "tweetable" links to share**
   At clicktotweet or Share Link Generator, you can easily create a message that you want readers to tweet. Click "generate link" and embed that URL in a link that says, "Tweet This." Share this link in all appropriate landing pages and emails. Whoever clicks on the link will then see the properly formatted tweet added to his or her Twitter status box! Simplifying the tweet process for users can significantly increase readership and shares.

3. **Create "tweetable" quotes**
   Learn the strategies for creating "tweetable" quotes (280 or fewer characters) summarizing your content's main point. Find a good quote from a prominent United Methodist figure and add it to your piece. Prepost a prayer that helps people begin processing some of the bigger issues with which you will wrestle on Sunday or in small groups.

   Enlarge, bold or highlight these special callouts, using colored content boxes. Next, place the "Tweet This" link, covered in Point 2, next to the quote. Now sit back and watch the analytics, as your content soars through the Twittersphere.

   Create "tweetable" quotes on your church website or blog and watch as your content soars through the Twittersphere. TWEET THIS TWEET THIS

 © 2018 Robert O. Crossman, www.UMNewChurch.org

If you don't want to be held down by the 280-character limit, create a Twitter image that is easily retweetable.

4. **Make sharing easy**
   One of the best ways to allow your members to reach out is to make your entire website quickly and easily sharable. Though many site providers include some version of this in their templates, it is not always front and center. If you need to improve your site's sharability, you can use the free service Share This to auto-generate the code that will add a sharing bar to the side of every page.

   You may also incorporate some of these social media sharing techniques during worship service to help your sermon or small group lesson teach all week long.

5. **Make "Instagrammable" slides**
   If you lay out your main point slides so that they are beautiful and will look right when cropped to a square, people will be able to snap a quick picture of them while you are talking and post them to Instagram. You might pull out your phone and say, "I need to take a picture of this to Instagram later." Since many people will be too far away to take a good picture, just suggest they share the image you just took. At some point during service, after you've posted the image on Instagram, tell everyone how they can share the image. Learn other creative ways to use Instagram to promote church events.

6. **Post a teaser video**
   Do you have a particularly interesting topic coming up? Take a moment to record a brief, attention-grabbing video that highlights the subject on which you will focus and share it on Facebook and Twitter. You will be surprised at how many people share and comment on these before and after your sermon.

7. **Advertise hashtags and account names**
   What the heck's a hashtag? Well, after you find out, put them along with account names (like @unpretending on Twitter) on all bulletins. If you have screens in your service, use them to tell people how to tag the church in their posts.

Source: umcom.org/mycom, reprinted by permission of Darby Jones on Jan. 26, 2018.

†††

Social Media and The Pastor

by Kent Melcher, Great Plains Conference

In an increasing number of mission fields across the United States, social media such as Facebook and Twitter are effective ways to follow up networking contacts and the laity in your congregation. Social media is not a fad, it has become a fundamental shift in the way we communicate.

It is recommended that if you are using social media, you have two accounts:

- a **personal** set of social media that only family and intimate friends outside the mission field can access; and
- a **public** set of social media for your mission field.

The purpose of having these two separate accounts/profiles is to create a line of privacy and maintain healthy boundaries with youth and real family, friends and colleagues.

Concerning Your Use of Public Social Media:

- Only use social media for positive or factual posts about your new church start. Social media can generate enthusiasm when planters tell stories of vital ministries being done, people responding to the love of Jesus Christ, lives transformed, and events that are planned to extend the Kingdom. Social media should encourage people to respond with positive comments, which then appear on their own Facebook pages, which then elicit positive comments from others that appear on their pages, and thus multiply exponentially as more and more people post on their pages.
- Constructive criticism should be communicated privately, not through social media.
- Use your best judgment when engaging in social media activities and be on guard against actions and discussions that could harm the interests of our church.
- Remember that what you write will be public, and potentially for a long time.
- Even when engaging in social media for personal use, your comments may be viewed as a reflection on the church.
- Do not publish the personal information of others without their permission or, in the case of minors, written permission of their parents.
- Do not tell secrets – respect the confidentiality of matters that are shared with you in confidence, or that are meant to be kept confidential by the nature of your work, ministry or volunteer mission. In the use of email, make every effort to never use blind copy - rather be open and transparent and use cc instead of bcc.
- Social media pages open to church members and general public should be governed by a strict set of ethical guidelines in line with United Methodist theological positions. In front of the church, in the community, in fact at all times the pastor is engaged in any public activity, including social media, that pastor is "on stage," and is seen as a representative of the UMC. Therefore, pastors and church staff should faithfully portray what our church stands for, according to Discipline, including the Social Principles.

  That is not to say that pastors/planters may not disagree with UM positions. But if they do, those disagreements should be discussed/debated within the connection, not publicly on social media.

  If you are only "nominally" United Methodist, or have theological positions that contradict United Methodist statements on baptism (for example) you

 © 2018 Robert O. Crossman, www.UMNewChurch.org

should have the integrity to be honest with your district superintendent and not accept an appointment to pastor an existing or to start a new United Methodist church.

- It is NEVER appropriate via social media to complain, express frustration in any way, or to confess discouragement. For example, one pastor, upon hearing of their upcoming appoint to a remote town, posted on their Facebook page, *"I've been appointed to Podunk!"* People in the new appointment saw the post, complained to the district superintendent, and the appointment was withdrawn. Other pastors have posted negative comments about parishioners in their congregations, or radical political comments, or have expressed their own depression and discouragement with their churches and appointments.
- When pastors / planters have personal / professional struggles, they should take those frustrations to their spiritual directors, therapists, district superintendents, or confidants, and deal with them there - not on social media.
- One of the concerns is who Facebook users "befriend." Personal information, including "family stuff," struggles regarding spiritual, emotional or physical issues, should be posted on a private page, open only to family and close friends, but never on a public page that is open to church members or the general population.
- Remember that what you write is public. You should always assume that it will be read by your boss, your co-workers, church volunteers and attendees, other church leaders, your parents, your children, your spouse, your friends, your 'enemies" and the attorney for the person who does not like you. Ask yourself if you are comfortable with all of these people reading what you plan to post.
- If you are a long-time Facebook or Twitter user, what you posted several years ago, when you were in college for example, may no longer be appropriate now that you represent your congregation and the United Methodist Church. While those posts may still exist in cyberspace, it is best to delete any questionable posts from your current Facebook account or website.

The material by Kent Melcher is used by permission granted on April 2, 2017.

†††

"5 Social Media Guidelines for Churches"
by Natalie Bannon

Natalie Bannon is a writer for United Methodist Communications.

Sometimes the most difficult part of managing social media is figuring out how to actually use it to effectively build relationships without crossing any lines. We encourage you to use the following guidelines to help you craft a social media policy tailored to your ministry.

First and foremost, LISTEN. Make sure someone is regularly monitoring all of your ministry's social media accounts. It's okay to use scheduling tools to post or "tweet" in advance, but make sure someone is monitoring comments and messages at least daily, if not more frequently. This ensures that you answer each question and concern in a timely manner.

Secondly, it's important to RESPECT PRIVACY. We all know that posting photos from church events is a great way to get likes and comments from members and even potential visitors. However, some people might not want photos of themselves or their children online. Always ask permission or consider a photo release. The same goes for prayer requests. Make sure the person in need is okay going public with any sensitive information.

Next, ASK PERMISSION before posting photos you didn't snap. Aside from helping you avoid any costly copyright issues, it's a simple courtesy that can help you build relationships to get more content in the future. There is an exception though. If a photo is already posted on Facebook, it's perfectly acceptable to go ahead and click "share." The share button is one of the best ways to create new relationships.

Next, THINK BEFORE YOU POST. Once it's out there, there's no "delete" button that can make a misguided post disappear forever. Consider the following questions from the get-go: Is your message in line with your reputation as a loving and welcoming church? Can it be misinterpreted in an offensive manner? Still not sure? If you have any reservations, it's better to be safe than sorry.

Finally, CREATE A SOCIAL MEDIA POLICY. Outline a set of rules for those managing your social media presence. This policy could include a variety of considerations such as how often your administrators will post, how often they should monitor comments, use of good judgment, transparency and tone of voice.

United Methodist Communications has a great online course that can help you get started. It's called Communicating Faith in the 21st Century. Learn more at umcom.org/training. And if you have any questions, send a message on Facebook or drop us an email to umcom@umcom.org. We're happy to help!

Source: umcom.org/mycom, reprinted by permission of Darby Jones on Jan. 26, 2018.

†††

6 Questions Every Church Social Media Policy Should Answer

by Jeremy Steele

You've probably already implemented a safe sanctuaries policy to ensure your church is a safe place for children, youth and elders to experience fellowship and the abiding love of God. Consider developing a complementary social media policy.

The questions below will help you get started by guiding you through the process of discerning exactly which boundaries are most appropriate in your context.

 © 2018 Robert O. Crossman, www.UMNewChurch.org

1. **Should social media platforms be treated differently?**
Though they are all grouped together, it doesn't take long for users to see that Facebook, Twitter, Pinterest and others are unique services. Where Twitter has a completely unfiltered feed focused on short "updates," Facebook shows what it thinks you want to see hoping you will engage in more relational activities. On the other hand, Pinterest drills down into idea sharing and engagement around those ideas.

   Beyond the technical distinctions, depending on your context, each social media platform can be perceived and engaged with differently. That is why is it important to think through this question at the outset. Are these services used or perceived differently enough to deserve unique consideration, or is it safe to link them together?

2. **Who initiates the network connection, and are any off-limits?**
With words like "follow" and "friend" used to describe these connections, it is easy to see that people can have strong real-world parallels that might color, for example, how they see an adult volunteer connecting online with a teenager. If this is a sensitive issue in your context, require any connections to be initiated by the younger party. Afterwards, you might require the adult to ask permission from a parent. Depending on the social media platform, you might even make connections between adults and kids off-limits. For instance, there is no reason an adult and child should connect on Snapchat. This is a service that allows users to send messages that vanish. Users set a time limit for how long recipients can view their message, after which it is hidden from the recipient's device and supposedly deleted from Snapchat's servers. You can see how Snapchat could quickly become the center of a scandal.

   Think about these types of scenarios and realize that churches must be careful not to over-limit online interaction as the Internet can be a powerful tool for ministry and a way to be seen quickly by those who never come to church.

Church social media policy:
How should adults "follow" or "friend" teenagers?
Who should initiate connections?

---

3. **What types of communication should and should not happen privately?**
Most online network platforms have both public and private ways to communicate. Some areas of concern could be sharing medical information via a prayer request, giving negative feedback, and disciplining inappropriate behavior. Some churches make the rule that whatever is appropriate in public in the physical world is appropriate in the virtual world, while anything that calls for a private conversation should occur in person, which is then subject to the standard safe sanctuary policy. That is simple, but you will likely want to give specific guidance based on your church culture.

4. **What sorts of images are OK to post?**
There are tons of issues around posting images of minors from events, as well as what parents may think of how volunteers spend their free time. This is a good time for you to talk to a lawyer regarding media releases, what boundaries you must enforce legally and what is your prerogative to decide. Likewise, it is equally important to think through the types of character traits you hope to see in volunteers.

It can be as simple as saying that staff can only post pictures of kids for whom you have a media release and that all images posted by volunteers should illustrate the same standards of behavior you expect from them in the rest of their life. Depending on your location, it may be important to talk about what sorts of images from the weekly beach devotion are within the safe zone in regard to the apparel people wear in different contexts. Whatever you decide, know that images are a place of particular concern for many.

5. **When should something be deleted?**
With the advent of auto-deleting services like Snapchat, this may be difficult to define globally, but it is important to consider when deleting a post could make an act better or worse. The perception that people are covering up something may be far worse than the post and an apologetic comment ever could be. Some churches ask volunteers not to delete posts until a staff person has approved it, and some leave it to the volunteer's discretion. The goal here is to make sure you think through how you deal with the perceptions created by deleted posts.

Church social media policy:
Deleting a post may make things worse.
Apologetic comments may be the best solution.

---

6. **What privacy settings will we use?**
For groups that will deal with children, setting the privacy to "secret" instead of "closed" will ensure they do not show up in search engines. Location settings should also be private so locations of children are not shared inadvertently. Privacy is key, but it extends beyond the settings pane to the content being posted, especially when names are used. As a rule, the names of children should not be posted.

Church social media policy:
Location settings should be private
so locations of children are not shared.

Most people have a strong, gut-level reaction to many of these questions, but they are far from universal. When you assemble your team to look at these questions, make sure you have diverse representatives that include young people, adults/

 © 2018 Robert O. Crossman, www.UMNewChurch.org

parents and older adults. You may be surprised at how differently these groups perceive what is happening online and will come out with a much stronger policy as a result of this diversity of input.

Once you consider these questions, it is time to create the written document. You might try looking at the following sample social media policy:

The Frazer UMC Employee Handbook
Montgomery, Alabama • Updated Sept. 7, 2010
SOCIAL MEDIA & NETWORKING WEBSITES

A. Personal Web Sites / Social Media

Personal web sites, blogs and social media (hereafter referred to collectively as social media) have become prevalent methods of self-expression and community interaction in our culture.

1. **Representation of the Church**
   Frazer UMC respects the right of employees to use social media during non-working hours. However, because the nature of these sites is essentially public, certain guidelines apply in the same manner as if the employee were speaking in person to a public gathering. Thus, if an employee is identifiable as a Frazer UMC employee on a social media site (their own, or as a public contributor to someone else's), he or she must adhere to the following guidelines:
   - Communicate in a manner that honors Christ and demonstrates His love for others. Our responsibility to lead the church by example as followers of Jesus includes the online realm of social media.
   - Uphold Frazer UMC's value of respect for the individual and avoid making defamatory statements about Frazer UMC employees, members, and others.
   - Do not disclose any information that is confidential or proprietary to Frazer UMC. Examples of confidential information include members' financial information and giving records, medical information, and personal or family problems you may become aware of during the course of your work. Requests for prayer should be made public only if you have express permission from all those affected by the information you release.
   - Make it clear to the readers that the views expressed are yours alone and that they do not necessarily reflect the view of Frazer UMC.
   - Employees are expected to show a duty of loyalty to Frazer UMC. The use of good judgment and discretion is expected.

2. **Use of Time and Equipment**
   Employees may use Frazer equipment to access social media during work hours if the nature of their job duties and ministry responsibilities include interacting with members of the congregation and the community to

promote our mission to worship, win, disciple and serve.

Employees should not use work time or Frazer UMC equipment to access social media for personal use.

Communication over the Frazer UMC network is not considered private and the church reserves the right to monitor such internet activity. Note that in certain situations the church may be legally compelled to access and disclose information sent over our network.

If social media activity is seen as compromising Frazer UMC or interfering with the employee's job, the employee may be asked to cease such activity and may be subject to counseling and / or potential disciplinary action.

B. Church-Sponsored Web Sites / Social Media

Church-authorized social networking and blogging is used to convey information about Frazer UMC, raise awareness of church activities and events, communicate with members, and otherwise work toward our mission to worship, win, disciple and serve to the glory of God. When communicating through social media, Frazer UMC must ensure that the content and style used maintains our identity, integrity and reputation. The following guidelines apply to social media when authorized by Frazer UMC and done for church-related purposes:

1. **Creating Sites**
    - Only authorized employees may create sites that represent Frazer UMC or any of its ministry areas. "Sites" include creating groups or pages within social media.
    - Authorized employees are the director of communications and those approved by the director of communications.
    - Official sites must have more than one staff member as an authorized administrator and employees are required to turn over passwords and administrative privileges in the event they leave employment at Frazer UMC.

2. **Posting Content**
    - Only authorized employees may post content to church sites. "Posting" includes using church sites to make announcements, distributing media, and initiating topics of discussion.
    - The publication of confidential information is prohibited.
    - Employees are expected to comply with copyright laws and avoid plagiarism. Any copyrighted information where written reprint information has not been obtained in advance cannot be posted.
    - If uncertain about any information, material or conversation, discuss the content with the director of communications.

3. **Commenting**

    If employees participate in discussion on church-sponsored social sites by commenting on posts, the following guidelines should be observed:

© 2018 Robert O. Crossman, www.UMNewChurch.org

- Employee comments should only be factual or positive in nature. Constructive criticism should be communicated privately, not through social media.
- Comments should be worded with great care to avoid unnecessarily offending any group or individual. Employees who are perceived as offensive, even if that is not their intention, may be asked to attend training and/or asked not to comment on church sites.
- Only authorized employees should attempt to respond to a comment that is critical of the church or a church leader, and/or may be deemed obscene or offensive.
- Employees should report any concerns about inappropriate comments to the director of communication or coordinator of digital ministry.

4. **Unofficial Sites**

Frazer UMC cannot control and cannot be responsible for sites started by non-employee subgroups of the church on their own initiative (e.g. classes, small groups, or individual church members). However, employees who have a position of leadership in a ministry area are expected to:

- Use their influence to encourage groups and individuals in their area of ministry to communicate online in a manner in keeping with the mission and values of the church.
- Advise groups and individuals not to represent themselves as official church sites.
- Report any unofficial sites which they become aware of that are not acting in keeping with the mission and values of the church to the Director of Communication to determine if further action is necessary.

Source: umcom.org/mycom, reprinted by permission of Darby Jones on Jan. 26, 2018.

†††

Recommendations for Use of Email or Texting or twitter from the Episcopal Diocese of Connecticut

- Email can be an appropriate and effective means of communicating basic factual information such as the time of an event, agenda for a meeting, text of a document, etc.
- Email is not an appropriate communication method for matters that are pastorally or legally sensitive, emotionally charged or require extensive conversation.
- If an email message is longer than a couple of sentences, then the matter might more properly be addressed via live conversation.
- Humor and sarcasm can be easily misinterpreted in an email.
- All email users should take a moment to consider the ramifications of their message before clicking on the "send" or "reply to all" button.

†††

Recommendations For Video Chats, Blogs or Video Blogs from the Episcopal Diocese of Connecticut

- Adults should refrain from initiating video chats with youth or children.

- Participants in a video chat or blog should consider what will be shown in the video such as surroundings, clothing, state of dress, etc.

- All transcripts of on-line text chats, video chats, blogs or video blogs should be saved when possible.

- All clergy and adults engaged in ministry with youth should consider the content and nature of any post that will be read by or visible to youth. Your voice is often considered the voice of the church.

- If an adult chooses to accept friend requests from minors or youth who are associated with their community of faith, other adult leaders must have full access to all aspects of that adult's profile and correspondence.

- Adults who want to connect via a social networking website with youth to whom they minister are strongly encouraged to set up a closed group account that youth may join. Youth requesting to "friend" an adult can then be invited to join this group rather than be accepted as a friend on an adult's personal profile account. The purpose of these two separate accounts / profiles is to create a line of privacy and maintain healthy boundaries with youth and real family, friends and colleagues.

- Any material on any site (whether affiliated with the church or not) that raises suspicion that a child has been or will be abused / neglected / exploited should be immediately reported to the clergy and / or the department of children and Families. If the material is on a church affiliated site, that material should be documented for church records then removed from the site after consultation with DCF and / or police.

†††

NOTE: These articles reflect the personal opinions of the author(s) and do not necessarily reflect an official position of Discipleship Ministries or Path 1.

 © 2018 Robert O. Crossman, www.UMNewChurch.org

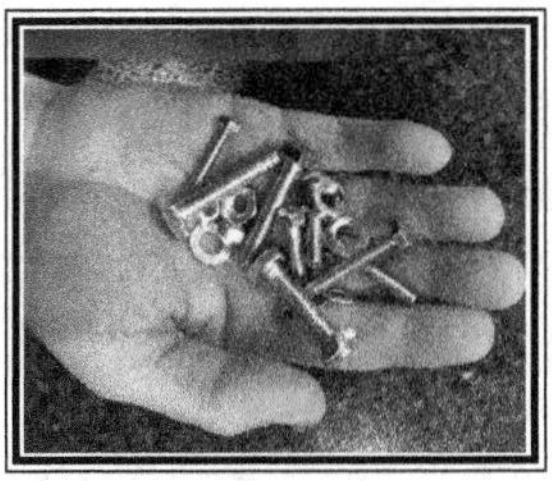

New Church Handbook
Nuts & Bolts for Planting New Churches In The Wesleyan Tradition

"50 Ways to Increase Worship Attendance"

by Bob Crossman

Introduction: Why is this our topic?

- In the central part of the United States, if the 20 houses on your street are typical: 5 of your neighbors will attend worship this Sunday; 10 will attend worship before the month is over; 15 will attend before the year is over; and 5 will NOT attend any church, temple or synagogue this year. In the Northeastern and Western states, worship attendance patterns are even weaker.
  - Agree with me today that God is not happy with those numbers, and that God desires for EVERYONE to become a faithful disciple of Jesus Christ.
  - Agree with me today that God desires to work through EACH OF US to spread the Good News of Jesus Christ.

- In the United States, on a typical Sunday, 250 million people (82.5% of the population) stay home. Source: *American Church Research Project*

- Could it be that many of these 250 million are today's "lost sheep" and "prodigal" sons and daughters that Luke 15 invites us to reach?

- Do not let the size of your congregation keep you from inviting others to join you. Whether your church has 12 people on Sunday or 1,200 people on Sunday, you have a wonderful gift to offer your friends, relatives, associates and neighbors who do not yet attend worship faithfully. It is a gift from Jesus Christ: forgiveness for their sins (Romans 3); a life filled with the increasing fruits of: "love, joy, peace, patience, kindness, generosity, faithfulness, gentleness, and self control." (Galatians 5:22 NRSV); the promise of eternity in heaven (John 14: 1-3); and a pathway toward becoming a deeply devoted disciple of Jesus Christ.

- Adam Hamilton, pastor of Kansas City's UM Church of the Resurrection, (Leading Beyond the Walls, chapter 2) suggests that the leadership of your congregation needs to be clear about answers to three questions: 1) Why do people need Jesus Christ? 2) Why do people need the church? 3) Why do people need your particular church? He suggest that these might be the topic of a sermon series and an intensive study by the leadership of your congregation.

- If you keep doing what you've been doing, you are probably going to keep getting the results you been getting. *If you are currently getting great results, keep doing what your doing... if not, you might consider a few changes.*

Why work to increase worship attendance?

- If your motivation is to save the lost, to welcome the prodigal back home, to increase the population of heaven, God will honor and bless your efforts.
- If your motivation is to get a few extra folks to help with the Sunday offering – that motivation is self-serving, empty and hollow, and does not honor the Lord.

There are only two ways to increase worship attendance:

- To have your current members attend more often.
- To invite new people to start attending worship.

Some of the 50 ideas on the following pages will work in your particular church. You are invited to review the list below, and to discern the one or two ideas that fit your unique setting, the nature of your local church, and your own unique personality.

Improve the Attendance of Current Members

1. Strive to increase the number of times current members are in worship each year. Start with yourself.
2. At least once or twice each year, perhaps in the New Year's resolution season, teach and preach the importance of faithful worship attendance.
3. Invite church members to make a written commitment to grow one step toward faithful attendance.
4. Include a commitment to faithful worship attendance as part of a holistic annual stewardship commitment.
5. Keep a record of attendance and monitor it.
6. Know that it is important to respond to absentees before they drop out of active attendance. Once a regular attender misses six consecutive weeks, it is hard for them to return to the habit of consistent Sunday worship.
7. Form a worship membership care team to review attendance within 24 hours of each service.
8. Send a handwritten note (signed by the membership care team, not the pastor) to anyone who has missed three Sundays in a row. Say, *"Looking through the attendance slips, we've missed your name! Hope to see you next Sunday."* In a smaller church, the wording can be more personal.
9. Ask a personal friend (a choir mate, Sunday school class member, or someone who sits in the same pew) to telephone people who have missed four Sundays in a row. "Hi John. We've noticed that Fred has missed church the last four Sundays. Would you telephone him this evening to say 'I've missed you'?"
10. Maintain a loving, invitational relationship with those who have been absent for five or more Sundays. Never be judgmental.

 © 2018 Robert O. Crossman, www.UMNewChurch.org

11. Know that is often very difficult to return to worship after the death of a loved one. Form a grief support team to send handwritten notes monthly until the family has returned to regular Sunday attendance.

12. Telephone every household in the church and everyone who has ever visited to invite them to some special event four times a year. Say, "Hi, We are calling everyone related to First Church this week, reminding everyone that this Sunday the choir is singing the Messiah. I hope you will be there."

Invite New People to Attend Worship

13. Decide today to open your minds, hearts, and doors to new faces, even if it means changing your music, sermon content, Sunday School, and enlarging your personal circle of Christian friends.

14. Pray for the unchurched in your community. Pray for children being raised outside the church, couples in marriages that don't have Christ at their center, etc. But pray also for specific families, individuals, friends, relatives, associates, and neighbors by name every day.

15. Know that personal invitations are the most effective method of increasing worship attendance. Invest sixty seconds once a week to invite someone to attend worship with you.

16. Continue to invite a person every two months even if they decline your invitations. Those invited may eventually come to a season of life when they are receptive to attending worship. Regular invitations are more likely to overlap one of these seasons.

17. If you have a worship bulletin, use it as an invitation tool. Keep Sunday's bulletin in your car or on your desk until you have given it to someone along with your personal invitation for them to join you in worship.

18. At least once a year, perhaps in the pre-Christmas season, preach and teach the importance of becoming an inviting people. Invite the congregation to make a written commitment to grow one step toward faithful inviting and witnessing.

19. Distribute to members simple printed invitations during the Christmas and Easter seasons that they can give to family and friends. Print at the top of the card, "If you are not active in a church, worship with us this season."

20. Have a "bring a friend day" or "F.R.A.N." day *(a church-wide effort to bring a friend, relative, associate or neighbor)*. Select a Sunday when something special is happening, such as homecoming, the start of vacation Bible school, or Christmas eve. Prepare as you would for company coming.

21. Know that the people who are on the fringe of your church are your future, your prospect list, and your next potential generation of deeply devoted disciples. Avoid the tendency to belittle or alienate those who are not yet fully committed disciples.

© 2018 Robert O. Crossman, www.UMNewChurch.org

22. Find ways continually to invite those on the fringes of your church. *(Such as those who have come to the church for a wedding, a funeral, or to vote and those who already worship a couple of times a year.)* Do not drop them from the newsletter or membership list.

23. Distribute door hangers in target neighborhoods near your church. It is more effective to cover the same 500 doors six times a year, than to do 3,000 doors one time.

24. Send mass mailers to targeted postal routes near your church 6 to 8 times a year. *(Post Office can help you determine which routes cover your mission field.)* The back-to-school season, pre-Christmas, and pre-Easter times are logical for these mailing.

25. Have a web site. In most of our mission fields people now use the internet and Google the same way our grandparents used the Yellow Pages. Web presence can be very simple, a single page with a map, worship times, simple welcoming invitation, and contact information.

Make Your Church Visible and Attractive

26. Purchase permanent roadside directional signs to point the way to your building. If your building is not on the main highway, install a prominent sign on the highway.

27. Purchase temporary yard signs to put out for a few days and then remove. They catch the eye and are relatively inexpensive. They should be very simple with little wording, such as: "Worship 10 a.m. Sunday. You're Invited." "Easter Sunday 11 a.m. You're Invited"

28. Don't hide your cars. If there is parking in front of the building, use it. Cars in the parking lot let the community know that something important is happening at your church.

29. Make a good first impression through the appearance of your building and landscaping. A well cared for exterior lets guests know that you are expecting company.

30. Clearly indicate the main entry to your building so that worship guests can find it easily.

31. Reserve and mark the best parking spaces for guests. The pastor, staff, and church officers should park on the edge of the parking lot, leaving the best spaces for others.

32. Make the nursery the nicest room in the church to attract and keep families with young children. It should be clean and well equipped, in an easy-to-find location close to the worship space, and staffed with adults. As your church grows, you will need pagers, check in and check out procedures, and nursery staff wearing uniforms with a photo ID.

 © 2018 Robert O. Crossman, www.UMNewChurch.org

33. Have clean, neat Sunday school rooms for children. The Sunday school program should be well-staffed and well-resourced.

Welcome Worship Guests Warmly

34. Greet guests when they first arrive in the parking lot. Give a couple of people orange vests and have them wave and smile as cars pull in. On rainy days, they can escort people to the door under a church umbrella. If the lot is large, they can drive folks to the door in golf carts.
35. Greet guests as they arrive at the door, saying "Good to see you. Glad you are here." Do not ask for their names as many guests are cautious and prefer anonymity. The larger the church, the more this is true.
36. Clearly mark directions to the rest rooms, nursery, and worship rooms. In a large building with a complicated layout, have greeters stand at the intersection of hallways ready to escort guests who are unsure about finding their way.
37. Find a way to acknowledge and welcome guests in worship without singling them out or embarrassing them. In many communities, guests prefer to be anonymous so don't ask them to stand and introduce themselves.
38. Have an easy readily available method for worship guests who wish to give you their name and contact information.
39. Practice the "circle of ten." Encourage church leaders to personally greet everyone -- member or guest -- who may sit within ten feet of them on Sunday with a simple "good morning" or "glad you are here today."
40. Know that guests typically leave the building within three minutes after the service. Encourage church leaders to follow the "rule of three," devoting the first three minutes after the benediction to speaking with people they don't know before speaking to family and friends.
41. Have greeters at all the exits, smiling, shaking hands, and simply saying to members and guests as they leave, "Glad you were here. I hope to see you next Sunday."
42. Start a "first friends" ministry as a way to reach a new age, racial, or cultural group. Train a pool of people, from a variety of ages and stages of life, to watch for first time guests, sit by them, treat them to lunch, and telephone them the next Saturday inviting them to Sunday worship.

Make Worship Accessible to Newcomers

43. Make your worship bulletin or screens visitor friendly. Include the actual words, or at least the page numbers, for any songs or responses commonly known to members but not newcomers.

44. Preach sermons that don't assume familiarity with the inner workings of the church or a high level of previous biblical knowledge.

45. Present all musical offerings well and in a style most likely to appeal to worship guests.

46. Consider adding an additional worship service to reach new people who would prefer a different time; or to reach new people who would prefer a different style of worship and music.

47. Start a new church or a second worship site at a different location as a way of increasing attendance.

Follow Up with Visitors

48. Develop a systematic plan for following up with visitors after their first, second, and third visits.

49. One model includes:
    - follow up with first-time visitors with a doorstep visit before 3 p.m. that same Sunday, a letter or telephone call from the pastor within 2 days, and placement on the newsletter and email lists;
    - follow up with second-time visitors with telephone call within 36 hours from someone related to the visitor's interests or needs – for example, a youth minister, or Sunday school teacher, or choir director; and
    - follow up with persons who visit a third time with a telephone call to request a home visit.

50. Invite newcomers who have visited in recent months to an informal coffee with the pastor or other social gathering that includes fellowship and information.

†††

This list of 50 ways by Bob Crossman is also available at the web site of the Lewis Center for Church Leadership: www.churchleadership.com and on Bob's website: www.UMNewChurch.org

NOTE: This article reflects the personal opinions of the author and does not necessarily reflect an official position of Discipleship Ministries or Path 1.

 © 2018 Robert O. Crossman, www.UMNewChurch.org

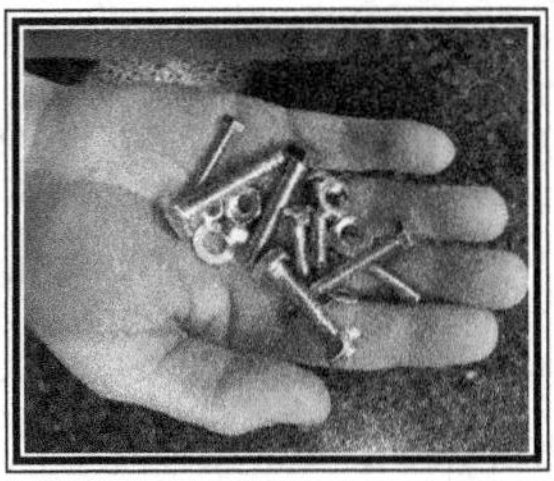

New Church Handbook
Nuts & Bolts for Planting New Churches In The Wesleyan Tradition

"10 Ways to Avoid The Summer Slump"

by Bob Crossman

I love the summer because the days are longer, with 12 to 13 hours of daylight. Physically, I enjoy waking up at 6 am with the sun in the summer, instead of waking up in complete darkness during the winter months.

Practically, I enjoy driving home after work in the sunshine, with 2 or 3 hours of daylight still left to spend time outside with family.

I love the summer months because the snow and ice are gone! As a youth in Minnesota, I did earn money shoveling snow for half a dozen neighbors in the winter. However, personally I took greater joy earning money by mowing their lawns in the summer.

For the local church many church leaders dread the summer months because historically May to August are the lowest attendance months, the smallest offering months, and the weakest in music ministry.

Historically May to August are the lowest attendance months, the smallest offering months, and the weakest in music ministry.

A century ago, when much of the US economy was agriculturally based, and fields were worked by hand, perhaps it made sense for the community church to "cut back" in the summer. On every good weather day from spring till harvest, every hand was needed in the fields. Without them the family might lose the farm, starve during the long winter, or not have the financial resources to plant next spring.

In this century, however, generally the US economy is not so dependant on the family farm, and very few family farms are entirely driven by manual labor. Instead of agricultural demands affecting church participation, today the summer is challenging for churches because of an increased number of things contending with for people's time. Today summer schedules are more likely filled with extended vacations, sports, family reunions, repair projects around the house, vegetable garden maintenance, and lawn care.

These summer activities are optional, not mandatory. Yet, many of our churches still operate on the notion that the summer slump is inevitable, and almost adjust the church's program in such a way as to encourage the summer slump to continue year after year. It almost seems like a self-fulling prophecy. Churches do this in several ways:

- Combining worship services, cutting back from two worship services to one;
- Giving the choir or music team "the summer off";
- The pastor taking the month of August off for vacation; and
- Canceling dozens of programs during the summer months, closing the church doors except for Sunday morning worship, youth activities and Vacation Bible School.

I have several concerns about this repeating summer pattern, and accepting this pattern as inevitable.

First, in many mission fields the summer months are the prime "church shopping" months. Historically, about two-thirds of households who relocate, do so between mid-May; and August. When they visit churches who have basically closed for the summer, those churches make a poor impression on the prospective households who drop in on Sunday.

Second, a significant number of people are creatures of habit. When church ministry opportunities are radically cut back during the summer, and congregants are encouraged to find non-church activities to fill their summer, a significant number of those who were regular participants in the spring, will not quickly return to faithful attendance in the fall.

Third, the church is indirectly making a statement that Christian discipleship appropriately takes a back seat to summer sports, weekends at the lake house, and yard work.

Fourth, the momentum within the church family that was building from Thanksgiving to Easter, is hard to resurrect in September when congregants have taken six to twelve weeks "off" during the summer.

But does the summer slump pattern have to happen? Is it inevitable?

I believe the answer is "no."

Is the summer slump inevitable? NO!

Let me suggest several ways we can decide to have a summer **bump**, instead of a summer **slump**.

First, be clear about your **motivation** for planning for a summer bump. If your motivation is to save the lost, to welcome the prodigal back home, to increase the population of heaven – God will honor and bless your efforts. If instead, your motivation is to get a few extra folks to help with the Sunday offering during the summer months – that motivation is self-serving, empty and hollow, and does not honor the Lord.

 © 2018 Robert O. Crossman, www.UMNewChurch.org

Second, instead of only aiming to maintain momentum in the summer, aim to **gain momentum** during the summer. Over the span of multiple weeks in the spring, cast a vision to your staff, lay leaders and congregation to have a summer **bump**, instead of accepting a summer **slump** as inevitable.

Third, have more **special Sundays** during the summer that attract a crowd of regulars and are attractive to potential new comers. Consider making "special Sundays" out of summer events that are naturally attractive in your particular mission field. It might be Mother's Day, Memorial Day, graduation, Father's Day, July 4th, youth Sunday, children's Sunday, back to school blessing of the back-packs, blessing of the animals, Memorial Day, appreciation of local firefighters, appreciation of local police, appreciation of local school teachers, or summer events that are unique to your local community.

Fourth, **celebrate** important spiritual moments during the summer. When youth leave for church camp or mission trips, take time in your worship services both to send the group off and again on the next Sunday to welcome their return. By commissioning upon departure and celebration upon their return, you help to recognize the spiritual impact such retreats often have. If your church typically has an increased number of first time guest in the summer, have a different member take two minutes in the service, every Sunday, to share "why I love this church."

Fifth, consider **adding to the number of worship services** instead of reducing the number during the summer. If you are in a mission field where 25% of your congregation spends the summer weekends at their lake house, consider adding Monday or Tuesday evening worship to your summer schedule. This Monday or Tuesday evening worship is a repeat of Sunday's sermon, because it's designed for those who were out of town on Sunday. When weather permits, perhaps this additional service is outside on the church lawn. Don't forget to receive an offering at these additional worship services.

Sixth, as much as possible, continue a **full schedule** during the summer months, instead of assuming the majority of the program will be cancelled for the summer. For the small groups that continue to take the summer off, challenge them to devote one weekend a month during the summer to volunteer in an inner city mission project. Challenge people to devote part of their vacation to join a mission trip.

Seventh, look for ways appropriate to your mission field, to **expand the church's schedule** during the summer. Perhaps adding ice cream socials, music concerts, or a family day at the local city park.

Take advantage of the beautiful weather by hosting lunch on the church lawn following the service. Don't try to shoulder the whole cost yourself, though. Most people are willing to contribute by bringing a side dish, drinks, or a dessert. Shorten your service to keep the time commitment manageable, and make a rain plan just in case.

Eighth, work to continue or better yet, increase the amount of **music** in worship. It takes a good deal of persistence to make this shift, and often the choir director is the main driver of taking the summer off. If the choir director can be convinced of the value of offering strong music during the summer, the choir will typically follow suit and sing all summer.

There might be several aspiring Christian artists in your town who would be available to fill in on a Sunday morning for a small honorarium and the permission to sell CDs. Also, in today's economy you might be surprised how inexpensively you can book a fairly well known Christian artist.

Ninth, be sure that you have **on-line giving** and **automatic bank drafts** available, for those who will be traveling during the summer.

To acknowledge and encourage on-line giving year round, in one church the pastor sends this email: *"Hey John, Thank you for giving on line this week. In fact, it's our preferred method of giving at the church! It allows us to be better financial stewards because its safe, secure, and provides better accountability. If you have any questions about online giving or how you can automate your gift, don't hesitate to contact Mark Norman in the church office. Blessing, Pastor David."*

After sending this email, they have found that the majority of recipients begin giving online frequently, and this helps to increase summer giving even among households that are absent a few weeks.

Tenth, encourage pastors and staff to **spread their vacation** throughout the year instead of taking four or five consecutive Sundays in the summer. I've read of one pastor who set several worship attendance records by intentionally planning some of his best sermon series for the summer, and also inviting several notable Christian sports figures from the nearby university to give their testimony during the service.

Whatever you decide to do this summer, don't let the summer slump dampen your enthusiasm. Don't miss a great opportunity this summer to make new disciples! Do something intentional! Even though many in your congregation may be distracted by the typical summer activities, God may desire to do something powerful through your ministry this summer. If you plan to have a summer **bump**, instead of accepting the summer **slump**, in the process you just might discover a unique way to reach your mission field that you may decide to continue year round.

I wonder, in your particular mission field, what can you do to plan for a summer bump instead of a summer slump?

†††

NOTE: This article reflects the personal opinions of the author and does not necessarily reflect an official position of Discipleship Ministries or Path 1.

 © 2018 Robert O. Crossman, www.UMNewChurch.org

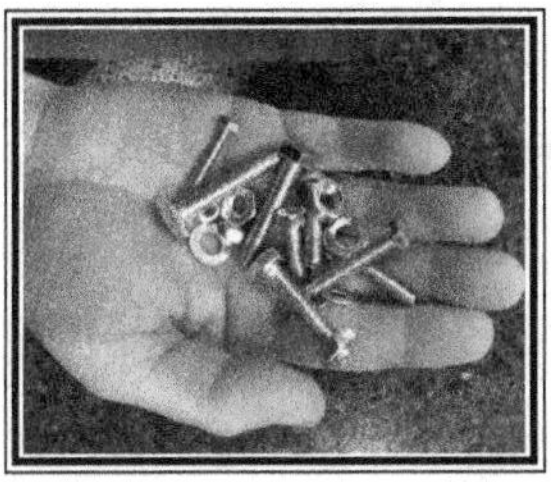

New Church Handbook
Nuts & Bolts for Planting New Churches In The Wesleyan Tradition

"Navigating Worship Attendance Barriers"

by Bob Crossman

What has been happening at **your** place recently? Are you finding your way toward your goal?

Has your new church lost it's power, vitality, drive and excitement?

Is your new church continuing to thrive with growth, professions of faith, baptisms, growing worship attendance, new ministries, and new outreach into your community?

Or, has your new church already started shrinking, dying, holding on, treading water, gasping for breath?

Your new church may only be three years old, but you might need to think about "transforming your church" if you have to struggle just to keep your church "moving" ... if it feels like your stuck in the mud and it takes tremendous effort to move forward.

You might need to think about transforming your church if...

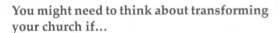

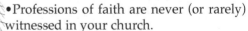

- Professions of faith are never (or rarely) witnessed in your church.
- Worship attendance has declined for months or maybe years.
- Membership has declined for months or maybe years.
- No one knows or can remember the church's vision statement

- Your baptismal font is dry, and has been dry for months or maybe years
- There are lots of children & youth in the neighborhood, but not in your church.
- "Faces" in the neighborhood look different from the "faces" in church
- You can't financially make payroll, keep up with the insurance or maintenance needs

You might also need to think about transforming your church if this is a photo of your launch team or church council members.

Is it possible for your new church to be "transformed" and to "come alive" again?

Oh, yes. There is a way… there is **hope**!

What is a healthy & vital transformed church?

- It is a faith community dedicated to helping people meet, know and serve Jesus.
- It is a congregation that expresses care and compassion for both its members and its community.
- It has leaders that know, own and live out the clearly-stated mission, vision and values of the church.
- It experiences numerical and spiritual growth.
- It has worship services that both inspires long-term members and is meaningful to first time guests.
- It has a warm, welcoming environment and numerous opportunities for people to develop deep personal Christian friendships.
- The ministry of the church results in new people coming into a personal relationship with Jesus.
- It is both rooted in the historic theology of the Church and willing to try new ways to share the good news of Jesus with those not **yet** involved in a church.

 © 2018 Robert O. Crossman, www.UMNewChurch.org

What is a healthy & vital church?

It is **your** new church - or at least it can be!

God calls every church to be a healthy, vital church. Small, large or mid-size, every church can be filled with spiritual energy and life.

New or celebrating its 100th birthday, every church can reach new people with the life-changing message of Jesus.

Rural, suburban, urban, or open country - every every church can be filled with joy, hope and peace.

It is the destiny desired by God for every church. Becoming healthy and vital should be the goal of every church. Anything less and the church is trading the power of the Spirit for mere existence.

Healthy & Vital churches come in many different sizes.

In the entire USA, this the average worship attendance on Sunday morning:

Percentage of Churches in Each Attendance Category

75 or less	75 to 200	200 to 500	500 +
50%	30%	17%	3%

There are healthy, vibrant, alive churches in each size cluster. **It is wonderful to have a variety of church sizes!**

However, I have two concerns for the church who says to me, *"We don't want anyone else coming to our church. We like it the size it is."*

My first concern is that 20% to 30% of your neighbors **never** attend any church… they are the "lost sheep" and the "prodigal sons and daughters" that Luke 15 invites us to search for and to welcome home.

My second concern is that in many of these churches the attendance is **not** holding steady - rather, it is slowly declining.

Is this the trend in your church?

If the current trend continues, what will be happening at your place in two years... in five years?

Do you want your future to be different than that?

Do you want to transform your church, so the future is different?

Are you ready to transform?

Transformation

Don't be conformed to the patterns of this world,
but be transformed by the renewing of your minds
so that you can figure out what God's will is—

So often we use phrases like "grow a church" or "move a church forward." Mike Roberts reminds us that phrases like this can carry the connotation of moving the "same" church to another level, when it fact is must become a "different" church.

The best words to describe such growth are "transition" or "transformation."

Reversing a pattern of decline is **not** just a matter of increasing attendance or starting a new program. Rather, it is changing the culture of the congregation, internal leadership structures, decision making processes, communication styles, and relational orientations.

The challenge is great, which is why many new churches *(as well as traditional congregations)* tend to hit an attendance ceiling… leaving hundreds of people in the community without a 'church home.'

Are the other United Methodist Churches in town declining?

Working with long established churches across the country, in every corner of this country... one phrase I hear frequently is this: *"We used to... "*

We used to be alive and vibrant,
have a 75 in our youth group,
have monthly church dinners
have six music teams and a crowded nursery
have small groups every night of the week
have three full-time pastors
have two worship services to hold the crowd
We used to...

How does "used to" happen?

It is usually a slow process of shrinking and holding on. Churches that are 'shrinking' or 'holding on' are often wondering:

"Who is killing my church?
Who is holding my church back?

I want to propose, that it's not who they think it is.

 © 2018 Robert O. Crossman, www.UMNewChurch.org

Steve Compton, author of *Rekindling the Mainline*, attempts to answer the question, *"What is causing many of our main line churches to decline?"* (That includes Methodist, Presbyterian, Lutheran, Episcopal, and Disciples of Christ.) Steve Compton writes that across America, new churches were first established where people were moving to. In the 1800's circuit riders established churches in frontier and farming communities. A church was built where ever a post office, school, or general store was found. My next door neighbor tells the story of how his grandfather started 87 new churches in western Tennessee, saying *"There was always a new village five miles down the road that didn't yet have a church."*

During the 1900's, people began to move from the farm to the new factory or mill towns. New churches were started there. These old Methodist churches were "family related." They had 50 to 100 people on Sunday. They had been sustained through the years by the children taking up the parent's place as the years passed. Everyone looked up to grandfather or grandmother as the alpha leaders, surrounded by their children, grandchildren and great grandchildren.

These old methodist churches grew by "bedroom evangelism." They were sustained by biological growth, giving birth to children and keeping those children on the farm. These were very self-contained congregations. This was the Methodist way. No evangelism committees were needed. This system worked through World War II.

Something changed during and after World War II. Our young adults were drafted and sent off to Europe or the Pacific Islands. That experience of war was so horrific, they were changed by the experience and the horrors they witnessed.

These young former soldiers remembered how their parents and grandparents worked long hard hours on the farm, yet were barely able to provide for their families during the depression. Many of these young adults, returning from WW II, decided to leave the family farm permanently. After the war, the GI bill provided a college education for these young adults. These soldiers moved to town, leaving the home community to attend school, and never moved back home.

In the 1950', 1960's and 1970's the older grandparents were left alone in the old church. The population of the town today may be larger than it was in the 1930's but the three founding families in the church are smaller... so the church is smaller.

That pattern is still continuing. Our teenagers graduate from high school, go off to college, and find a job in the big city. They do not come back to the family farm or business.

Why are so many of our churches shrinking in size? Steve Compton suggest that it is **not** because of liberals or conservatives in the UMC. It is **not** because of the Conference. It is **not** because of ineffective pastors. But rather, in most of our churches across the country, there has been a change in our demographics and the breakup of the old family-perpetuated systems that once held our churches together for generations.

This trend is most visible in our open country churches. The majority of our churches are now located in empty communities, where very few people live. The pews are near empty, and filled with a single generation. They are holding it together... retirees in their 70's... in ten years they will be in their 80's... I fear that we will soon experience a tremendous number of these churches asking permission of the district to close. We will not have a United Methodist presence in 100's of communities.

Signs of Hope Emerging

Is there hope for these county seat or open country churches?

Yes! If we are going to grow, we must stop passively waiting for people to walk into the doors of our churches.

We must stop relying on the old system of biological growth.

We must adapt a new system of actively inviting our friends, relatives, co-workers, school mates to experience Jesus Christ and come to worship with us.

Some of our United Methodist Churches are Growing!

For example, in my last study of Arkansas worship attendance,
1/3 of the churches were growing...
100 of them by more than 20% in the previous 5 years.

The growing churches among us are typically growing for one of three reasons:

1. They are reaching the unchurched and de-churched - starting with their friends, relatives, co-workers and neighbors. In the central part of the U.S.A. about 20 to 30% of the population never attends worship. An additional 30 to 40% are only somewhat involved with their faith.

The fields are ripe and waiting for the harvest!

---

2. They are reaching the younger generation. In this part of the country the aver-

 © 2018 Robert O. Crossman, www.UMNewChurch.org

age age of the community is about 35. In this part of the country about 20 to 30% of the population is under 18. The average age in most of our pews is far higher.

The fields are ripe and waiting for the harvest!

---

3. They are reaching your multi-ethnic population. In this part of the country, almost every community is becoming ethnically diverse.

The fields are ripe and waiting for the harvest!

Are you ready for transformation?

Let me share with you a true story about how difficult transformation can be: At a United Methodist church in a small Arkansas town of 200, 18 people received my dad as their new pastor. My father was 52 years old when he entered the ministry and this was his first appointment - a 3 point circuit.

- My dad went door to door: *"I'm the new United Methodist pastor. If you don't have church home, we would love for you to attend this Sunday."*
- My dad went to the post office frequently at 9 am when the mail was put out: *"I'm the new United Methodist pastor. If you don't have church home, we would love for you to attend this Sunday."*
- My dad volunteered to sack groceries and pump gas at the family owned general story in town: *"I'm the new United Methodist pastor. If you don't have church home, we would love for you to attend this Sunday."*

Worship attendance grew every week, growing from 18 to 40 to 60 by Thanksgiving. About Christmas time, one Sunday evening at the church, eating pecan pie and drinking coffee, one of the newcomers said, *"You know, the window sills are so dark. The varnish has turned black. My husband and I would be glad to strip them and varnish, or paint them white. I think it would brighten up the room so much."* Hearing that, one of the original 18 members stood up and said, *"We don't need you newcomers telling us what color to paint our window sills."*

That was at Christmas. Do any of you have the gift of prophecy? Tell me, what the attendance was by Easter? You are right - only 18 attended the next Easter.

They had successfully run the new folks off.

Then it was a church of 18.

Now it stands an empty building.

A few years later, after several funerals and several more with failing heath among the 18, they told the district superintendent that they were closing. Today, there is an empty building. It hasn't been painted for two decades. They didn't realize it, but that Sunday night the 18 had said in effect, *"We would rather die than change the color of our window sills."*

Hope

God has given our churches, even in their old age, an opportunity to leave a legacy by doing evangelism that opens the doors to the community and allow these new neighbors to sit in our empty pews, grow to be the leaders of the church, and to count our money.

The challenge is to reach out to them. To do that, is going to require us to be a different church. But the change is difficult!

Navigating Past Worship Attendance Barriers

For growth in worship attendance to happen, you will discover that other things need to change too. Some churches have noted a repeating worship attendance pattern. Their attendance will:

- Grow from 80 to 120... and then back to 80, or
- Grow from 150 to 200, and then back to 150, or
- Grow from 350 to 450, and then back to 350.

What's going on? Why can't some churches sustain the high level and even continue growing to a higher level? In some cases, it is because the churches internal systems are designed for the smaller size. It is "nature taking it's course." Attendance will drift back to a more comfortable size that fits the internal system.

Different Size Churches Function Differently.

The basic idea is that different size churches function differently. And in fact, churches seem to cluster in different sizes. Several studies have been done of church size. They have grouped churches into various clusters.

Steve Compton

- 5 to 50 - single cell family size
- 50 to 150 - pastoral size
- 150 to 350 - program size
- 350..500 to 1,000 corporate size

Arlin Routhage

- Family (2-50)
- Pastoral (51-150)
- Program (151-350)
- Corporate (351 – up)

Lyle Schaller

- Fellowship "cat" (5 to 40)
- Small "collie" (35 to 100)
- Middle "garden" (100 to 175)

 © 2018 Robert O. Crossman, www.UMNewChurch.org

- Awkward "house" (175 to 225)
- Large "manager" (225 to 450)
- Hugh "ranch" (450 to 700)
- Mega church "state" (700 and up)

While the cluster sizes are not carved in stone, most seem to agree that to "move up to the next level in worship attendance" is a **transition**. If you move from the 40's to the 140's on Sunday more happens than just having 100 additional people sitting in the pews.

Let's take a look at characteristics of each size cluster. Reflect on what might have to happen internally to transition to the next size cluster.

The Single Cell (Family) Size Church

The single cell or family size church typically has up to 50 in average attendance.

By definition, everyone does everything together. In a new church, the pastor is in the center of the church. Everything is connected to the pastor. The new church start pastor is in charge, controls *or does* everything, and attends everything.

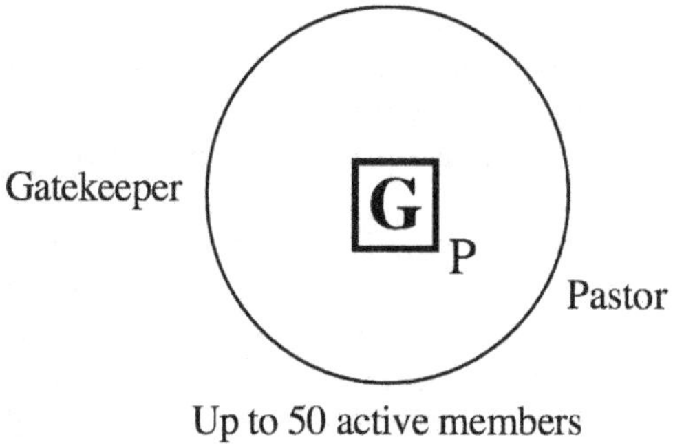

In a small long-established congregation, the gatekeepers are in the center of the church. An individual or group of people keep the church family together. The gatekeepers are often descendants of the original founding families. They are essential to keep the church healthy. They are the 'parents' of the church. Through the years they made sure the propane tank gets filled, lawn mowed, building painted, literature ordered, apportionments get paid, and that there is enough money to pay the preacher each month. In this size older church, the pastor is not in the center, and not in charge, but does stand near the gatekeeper. The pastor is a person of great authority. Along with the gatekeeper, they will lead the church. The pastor must be the pastor to the gatekeeper, and church family chaplain to care for the spiritual needs. The gatekeeper will take care of administrative issues and disputes. Newcomers are only welcome when the gatekeeper gives the nod. The gatekeeper is not an evil person. The gatekeeper does everything they can think of to keep their church alive.

What does the road from 50 to 150 on Sunday look like?

First, the key lay leadership has a growing love for the F.R.A.N.'s *(Friends, Relatives, Associates at work/recreational/business/school, and Neighbors)* and the 'prodigals" and 'lost sheep' in their community.

Second, this love is so great, that the key lay leadership is willing warmly invite their network to engage in some facet of the church, to expand their circle of Christian friends, and to scoot their chairs closer together. When guests arrive at a church event, they are warmly welcomed into the life and leadership of the church.

Third, the number of quality small discipleship groups must continue to increase, so that when you reach 150 in attendance, people still say, *"This is the warmest, friendliest, caring church I have ever been a part of."*

Fourth, increasing higher levels of excellence in **all** areas of ministry: music, children, youth, young adult, family, retiree, facilities, preaching, worship, missions, education, small groups, spiritual development and so on.

Fifth, in new churches the pastor must allow the laity to discover the joy of being in ministry and service. In new churches key laity are vetted and trained to oversee ministry areas of the new church. A collection of teams of 4 to 10 each plan and implement ministry in one of the various ministry areas: nursery, children, youth, small groups, music, hospitality, set-up, tear down, and financial accounting.

This sixth area in older established churches involves the pastoral leadership beginning to move from part-time to full-time, and the laity begin to allow the pastor to be the "pastor in charge." Typically, the old lay led system can not provide the level of support needed by 75 to 100 people on Sunday.

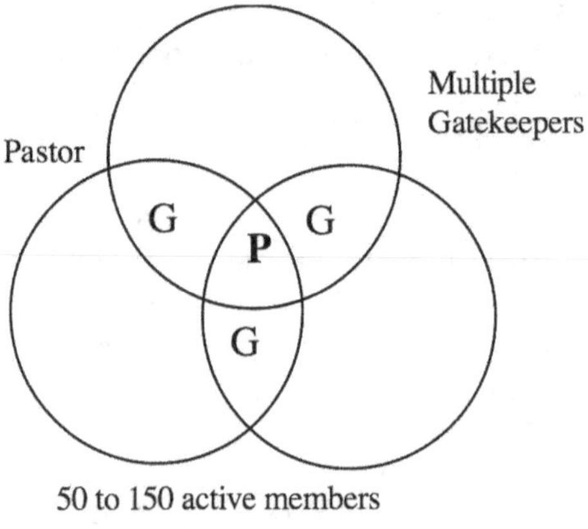

The Pastoral Size Church -

The pastoral size church typically has 50 to 150 in average attendance.

In new and in old congregations this size, the pastor is the one who initiates much of what happens. The pastor is directly involved in administrative and program issues. Newcomers join when the pastor remembers their name on the second visit, preaches a decent sermon, and visits them at home.

 © 2018 Robert O. Crossman, www.UMNewChurch.org

There are multiple gatekeepers, each leading a group such as retirees, young families, music, children, single adults, building maintenance, lawn care, etc.

The church will often cap off at 100 in worship attendance without part-time staff or significant lay leadership. *(Typically it takes about 1 full time pastoral or ministry program staff member for every 100 in attendance.)*

In older established pastoral size churches the pastor moves from part-time to full-time. As time passes, the pastor becomes the center of the church because it is to large and complex for a volunteer lay person to stay connected to all the different facets of the church.

What does the road from 150 to 350 on Sunday look like?

First, the pastor and lay leadership has a growing love for the F.R.A.N.'s *(friends, relatives, associates at work/recreational/business/school, and neighbors)* and the 'prodigals" and 'lost sheep' in their community.

Second, this love is so great, that the key lay leadership is warmly inviting their network to engage in some facet of the church, expanding their circle of Christian friends, and moving their chairs closer together. When guests arrive at a church event, they are warmly welcomed into the life and leadership of the church.

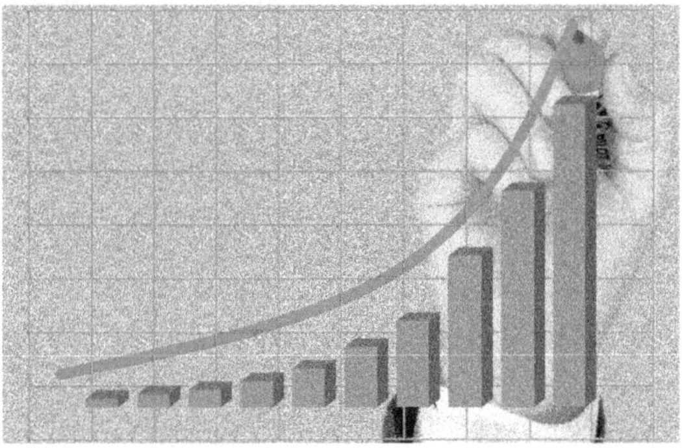

Third, in moving from 150 to 300, there is an increasing higher level of excellence in all areas of ministry: music, children, youth, young adult, family, retiree, facilities, preaching, worship, missions, education, small groups, spiritual development and so on.

Fourth, the church begins to "staff for growth." They hire part-time staff in children, youth, music and visitation areas. Typically, 40 hours of pastoral and ministry staff is needed for every 100 in worship. So, a church with 220 in worship might have one full-time pastor, and a 20 hr per week part-time children, youth and music staff in addition to part-time office and custodial staff.

Fifth, the number of quality small discipleship groups must continue to increase, so that when you reach 350 in attendance, people still say, *"This is the warmest, friendliest, and caring church I have ever been a part of."*

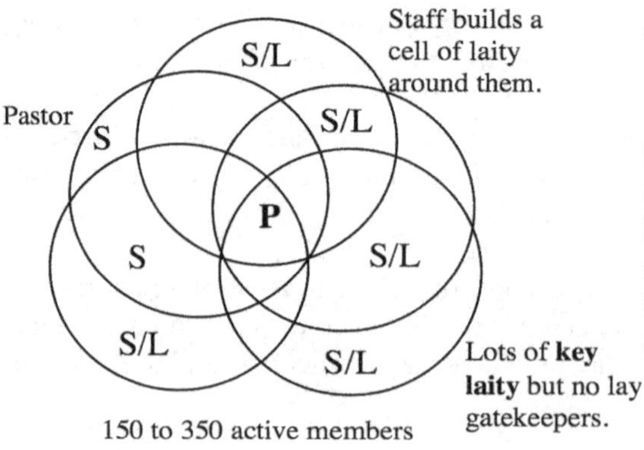

The Program Staff Size Church

The program staff size church typically has 150 to 350 in attendance. The pastor is the vision bearer, spiritual guide, and has a close relationship with the staff, so that the church does not develop competing cells.

The pastor does not know everyone or know everything that is going on. If the pastor knows everything that is going on, there isn't enough going on. The paid staff will have strong relationships with the laity and new comers long before one develops with the pastor. Newcomers may join through the music ministry and build relationships through the staff music minister, and may decide to join the church before they have ever met the pastor in person.

Each worship service becomes a circle, the youth group becomes a circle, the music ministry, key small groups, mission teams, etc. So the church becomes more complex.

It takes about one full time pastoral or ministry program staff member for every 100 in attendance. The church will often cap off at this size without additional pastoral staff or significant lay leadership involved in active pastoral care.

What does the road from from 350 to 750+ in attendance look like?

First, the number of quality small discipleship groups must continue to increase, so that when you reach 750 in attendance, people still say, *"This is the warmest, friendliest, and caring church I have ever been a part of."*

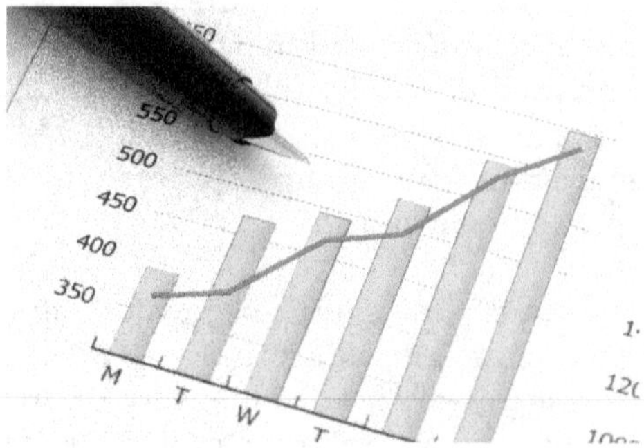

Second, the role of the senior pastor changes. The senior pastor spends less time as chaplain of the congregation, and more time in leading the church instead of managing the church. More time vision casting with key laity and staff, supervising staff, and leading worship to a higher level of excellence. One pastor can be the chaplain for a worship attendance of 75 to 150, but there are not enough hours in the day for one pastor to provide that level of pastoral care to 500 people.

 © 2018 Robert O. Crossman, www.UMNewChurch.org

For example, in a small church of 75, the pastor may sit with the family for six hours during a member's gall bladder surgery, or even the gall bladder surgery of a member's next door neighbor.

In a church with 1,000 in attendance, other staff or laity sit with the family during the 6 hours of a member's surgery. However, the pastor or staff do not sit with the family during the surgery of a member's next door neighbor. If your church is going to grow from 350 to 750, many pastoral care responsibilities must picked up by other paid pastor staff and trained laity.

Third, the church needs to staff for growth. Don't wait until you desperately need a full time children's minister. Instead, go ahead and hire the full time children's minister so that you can grow from 100 children in the program to 200 children in the program.

Fourth, there must be longer tenure pastoral and lay staff.

Fifth, there must be an increasing higher level of competence among lay and clergy staff. The staff should feel personally and internally called by God to this ministry, and they are driven to do what ever it takes to make disciples in Jesus' name.

Sixth, higher salaries to achieve longer tenure and higher competence.

Seventh, lay leadership must be condensed into committed smaller groups rather than large committees. The church council of a church of 25 often has 25 people on it. The church council of a church of 150 often has 40 people on it. While active, vital, growing churches of 500 may have 100's of people in ministry teams, the primary church council may have only nine people.

Eighth, if a church is going to move from 350 to 700, there must be increasing higher levels of excellence in all areas of ministry. *(music, children, youth, young adult, family, retiree, facilities, preaching, worship missions, education, small groups, and spiritual development.)*

Ninth, the mother church expands by opening satellites or second campuses, to reach different mission fields across town.

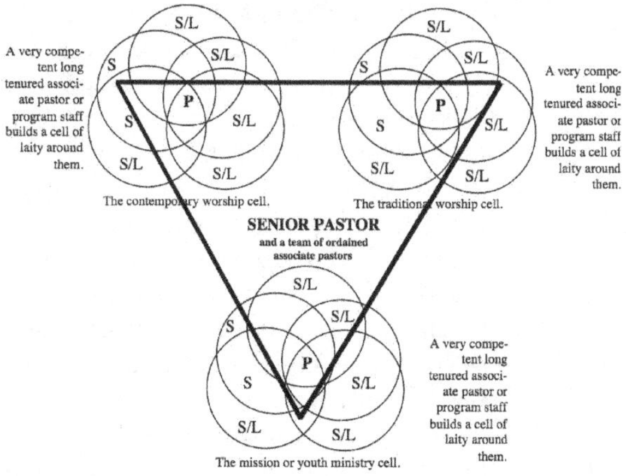

The Corporate Size

The corporate size church typically averages 350 to 1,500 in average worship attendance.

Similar to the program size, but more pastors are added and the number of circles becomes more complex. The glue that sticks people to the church? People still find their place in a small group. It remains the 'warmest, friendliest, caring church' they have ever been a part of, because of their small group.

IN SUMMARY

Strengths & Challenges of SMALL Churches

Mike Roberts points out some of the strengths & challenges when comparing smaller and larger churches.

- Some RELATIONAL strengths in a small church
  - Sense of intimacy
  - Sense of personal responsibility
  - Sense of ownership
  - Personal attention
  - Accountability by God's people
  - High degree of lay involvement
- Some RELATIONAL challenges in a small church
  - Inferiority complex
  - Limited resources
  - Suspicion of newcomers
  - Difficulty incorporating others if they are older or younger, different economic level, different social standing, or different ethnicity.
  - Sabotage of growth (sometimes well intended)
  - Patriarchs and matriarchs who hold the church together are afraid that if 25 more people started to attend - they very spirit and heart that makes this church special may disappear.

Strengths & Challenges of LARGE Churches

- Some RELATIONAL strengths of a large church include:
  - a sense of participating in something important
  - when the parking lot is overflowing
  - when 100, 200, 500 or 1,000 people in the room
  - There is a critical mass & excitement
  - Sense of possibility and opportunity
  - Multiple staff specialists
  - Quality in facilities
  - Variety and Diversity
  - Multiple programs
  - Possibilities for growth
- Some RELATIONAL challenges of a large church include:
  - Incorporating new people
  - Closing the back door too.
  - Establishing a unifying purpose & vision
  - Creating opportunities for belonging
  - Becoming a "club" without a Biblical focus
  - Compartmentalized areas of ministry where turf battles and competition for resources is the norm – rather than a sense of mutual interdependence and support and a unified purpose.

© 2018 Robert O. Crossman, www.UMNewChurch.org

ADDITIONAL THOUGHTS

Organizational Dynamics

A large church is not simply a small church with more people. It is "an entirely different kind of animal." ... not better, just different. Failure to recognize these differences can be disastrous.

Planning to move up off a plateau in size can be very difficult. Why?

- growth means bringing strangers into your small, intimate fellowship.
- growth requires a change in the basic organizing principle from a network of one-on-one relationships to a network of groups and organizational ties to a larger administrative structure.

Newcomer Dynamics

Family Church – incorporates new members the way a family does – by birth, marriage, and adoptions. *"I like the family feel."*
Newcomers become members when GRANDMOTHER 'adopts' them.

Pastoral Church – incorporates new members mostly through a relationship with the pastor. *"I'm looking of a congregation where the pastor is available and knows me."* Newcomers become members when the PASTOR 'adopts' them.

Program Church – attracts new members through programs
(choir, youth ministry, children's ministry, small group ministry, etc).
"We are interested in finding activities for our children."
Newcomers become members when a PROGRAM 'adopts' them.

Corporate Church – attracts new members through high quality resources, worship, and ministries. *"This church has something great to offer everyone."*

REFLECTION

Why are we the size we are now?
Is it true that different size churches function differently?
Do you really want your church to grow?
Do you believe God wants your church to grow?
What is holding you back?
Is your church ready for transformation?
What might we have to change to break into the next size cluster?
What must we do in order to grow?

NOTE: This article reflects the personal opinions of the author and does not necessarily reflect an official position of Discipleship Ministries or Path 1.

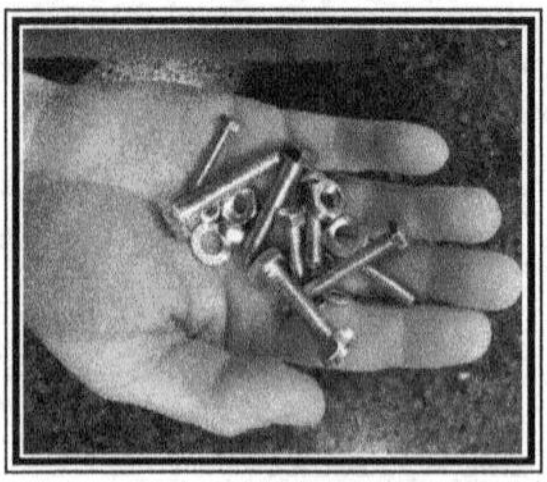

New Church Handbook
Nuts & Bolts for Planting New Churches In The Wesleyan Tradition

"When Should We Start A 2nd Worship Service"

by Bob Crossman
including a lengthy article by Ed Fenstermacher

Lyle Schaller, speaking some years ago to a district workshop in Fayetteville, Arkansas asked:

> *"If your business was only open for one hour, between 11 and noon on Sundays, do you think you would increase your client base by also being open from 9 to 10 am on Sundays and also perhaps Monday evenings at 7 pm?"*
>
> *"If your business only offered hamburgers and french fries, do you think you might increase your client base if you also started to offer chicken nuggets or even salad?"*

Lyle Schaller went on to encourage the workshop participants to consider having multiple worship services each week, offering a variety of worship styles, designed to reach a larger portion of our mission fields for Christ.

Lyle Schaller's position made sense to me, and he was a major contributing factor to my new church starting with the intention of eventually offering five worship services each week with five different worship styles.

And that is exactly what we did.

Below I've reprinted Ed Fenstermacher's article, *"Are You Starting A New Worship Service?"* He offers excellent advice on how to start a new service.

The following material by Ed Fenstermacher is used by permission granted on October 14, 2017.

Are You Starting A New Worship Service?

by Ed Fenstermacher, Indiana Conference

When should you start another service?
- When your attendance fills 50-80% of your sanctuary's seating.
- When you want to reach a new group of people.

Barriers to overcome
- The desire to be one congregation; to know everyone.

 © 2018 Robert O. Crossman, www.UMNewChurch.org

- The fear of the new service changing the old one/s (e.g. choir no longer participating each week, some people no longer attending the older service, having to change the time of the older service).

Overview of Steps to Take

- Clarify why you are starting another service.
- Clarify your target group.
- Recruit a planning team that is made up of a majority of people that is like this target group.
- Design a service that is tailored to the target group.
- Determine the time, place, and proper attire for participants.
- Recruit leadership, especially music and child care (if the target group has children). Leadership should be similar (e.g. in age, education, economic level, culture, etc.) to the target group.
- Set your initial attendance goal and develop a marketing strategy to meet that goal.
- Develop an intentional visitor follow-up and assimilation strategy.
- Develop and be ready to implement a Discipleship System in the early weeks for attendees who are looking for additional settings to grow as disciples (i.e. small groups, Sunday School, etc.)

Rules of Thumb

- The majority of churches adding an alternative service experience at least a 20% worship increase.
- The best time to reach most unchurched people is still Sunday morning.
  - The majority of mainline attendees prefer services that end by noon.
  - Typically if the service is targeting charismatics, Hispanics, or African-Americans, services can be over an hour; otherwise, the preference commonly is sixty minutes.
  - Few parents with small children arrive at church before 9:00am.
  - Early services--8:00 to 8:30am--attract more senior adults.
  - College students and young singles prefer services scheduled at 10:30am or later.
  - Unchurched young couples with preschool children show up in larger numbers at "contemporary" worship services scheduled simultaneous with Sunday school.
- The best time to start a new service is anytime between September 1st and the first Sunday of Advent.
- Changing worship schedules each summer (even in smaller churches) will result in a lower overall worship average.
- Most non-Sunday morning services (in Protestant churches) will average no more than 50 people.
- Saturday-night services tend to attract:
  - older persons who like a slower pace,
  - childless couples,

- pilgrims, seekers, searchers,
- young never-married adults,
- two-church couples,
- recent empty-nesters,
- former Roman Catholics (typically 30% of those who attend).

- However, one out of six unchurched adults work on Sundays (according to George Barna).
- Worship attendance will typically drop 50% the second week of a new service (especially if you rely on mass marketing to do the initial inviting).
- Depending on your sanctuary's size and community, the minimum needed to launch a service that will grow is between 100 and 400 people. (These figures will drop to between 50 and 200 initially.)
- The younger your target group...

- the larger the initial service's attendance must be,
- the more important (and louder) the music is,
- the faster paced and more visual (few readings, more drama, dance, & video) the service must be,
- the more casual the service must be (including dress),
- the more celebrative (as opposed to meditative) the service must be,
- the more expressive and participatory the service must be.

Experiences of Other Churches

- Sometimes the leadership (including for the music) emerges after the service is launched.
- Using professionally-produced music accompaniment (e.g. CD's or I Worship) in lieu of a live band or a keyboardist has been done successfully.
- Churches have successfully started new services without existing members (or choirs) participating.

Launching a New Worship Service?
Recommended Steps to Take

Prayer

I can not overstate how important it is to have the church intentionally praying for this effort. If you don't already have groups and/or individuals praying specifically for this effort, I encourage you to do that right away.

Identify Target Group

Before you make any decisions (e.g. when and where the service is to be held, its style and format, even its name), it is important to know who you sense God is wanting you to especially reach. Of course, the service will be open to anyone; however, the reality is that it will be especially inviting and inspiring for a certain type of person. The more you clearly you can describe that person, the easier it will be to design a service for them, and as a result, you'll be more likely to reach them.

- A church will typically attract is people like themselves. You may want to

 © 2018 Robert O. Crossman, www.UMNewChurch.org

describe the type of people your church naturally attracts. If you sense God is calling you to reach a different group of people, you will probably have to take extra care in designing the service (when, where, its style, how the invitations are shared, etc.).

- The target group could be determined by matching those God already is bringing to your church (e.g. Sunday morning newcomers, those you reach through the week, during vacation Bible school, etc.).
- The target group also could be identified using the community's demographics. Keep in mind that you do not need to target the largest demographic lifestyle groups in your community.
- Who ever you determine your target group to be, I encourage you to write down a description of that group (e.g. where they're at on their spiritual journey, their mindset, their unique needs, their music preferences, etc.).

Build Your Launch Team

The launch team will help answer the questions regarding when and where the service will meet, determine when it will be launched, the design of the service, how to get invitations out, setting a budget, dealing with logistical issues such as child care, parking, set-up, technology needs, etc. Set a goal to have at least half your launch team reflect your target group.

Define What a "Win" Looks Like

In order for everyone to have a clear understanding of what the church hopes to establish, the launch team needs to describe how the church will know if its new service is successful. What are the metrics that will determine whether or not the service should be continued or not? This needs to be clearly defined before the service is ever launched, that way the expectation is clear to everyone and it will be easier to determine the service's viability.

Determine Your Launch Strategy

There are two basic approaches you can use to launch the service.

One is to focus on developing relationships with your target group (e.g. one-to-one conversations, listening sessions, small groups, etc.) before you start the service. These can take as much as six months to two years to do.

The second is to rely primarily on word-of-mouth and marketing to launch the service and then to develop relationships once they attend. The advantage of the first approach is that it provides a more solid congregation when you launch. The downside is that it takes more time (six month to two years). Your launch team needs to decide which approach it will take.

Establish Task Force Teams

The next step is for the launch team to identify all the tasks that will need to be done. They might fall into the following 7 areas:

© 2018 Robert O. Crossman, www.UMNewChurch.org

- Prayer support.
- Worship design.
- Logistics (parking, technology, set-up).
- Child care.
- Publicity/invitations.
- Hospitality/discipleship of newcomers.
- Finances.

Identify who will head up each of these areas and have them establish an implementation time line. (An example of a time line for an effort to launch an off-site worship service is printed on the following page.) Your goal should be to fill 90% of your leadership/helper slots for each task area by the public launch of the new service.

Sunday Morning Schedule

If the launch team (or church's worship team) determines that the new service should be held at the church on a Sunday morning, make sure adequate parking is available. If you need to adjust the present worship times to fit the new service into the schedule, it is advised not to move the present times more than 30 minutes either direction. Make sure those having to accommodate the new schedule clearly understand why the change is important and provide them with ongoing updates as to the positive results due to the change (e.g. short videos of the new service being shown at the original service/s).

Critical Mass

As I said, it is extremely important to have your worship meeting space always at 50% or more of the room's capacity. Otherwise, it will feel as though there is a lack of energy and the service won't be as attractive to newcomers. This means that you won't want to launch the service until you know you'll be able to consistently fill half (or more) of the seats.

Launching Your Service

It is recommended that you do a soft launch of your service to work out the bugs before doing your public "official" launch. During this time, which could be as many as three months, you can begin your marketing effort for your public launch date. Word of mouth is by far the best way to reach people. Encourage core attenders to the soft launch services to identify three people they know who would like the new service, have them pray for them, then set a date each month that they are encouraged to intentionally invite them to attend with them. Have attenders to the soft launch provide feedback on the various components of the service and make ongoing adjustments to improve the experience.

Following Your Launch

Make sure to implement your system to welcome and involve new attenders. Invite the newcomers to fill the remaining 10% of the leader/helper slots in your

 © 2018 Robert O. Crossman, www.UMNewChurch.org

matrix. Continue to engage newcomers by inviting them into missional and discipleship opportunities as well. At some predetermined point/s (e.g. 6 months, 12 months), evaluate the new service, referring back to your description of what a "win" would look like. Make adjustments as needed.

Sample Launch Time Line

Month 1

- Clarify your vision for the new service. Who is God calling you to reach?
- Establish a pray team (at least 3 persons) to pray.

Month 2

- Put together a design team (5-12 people), at least half of whom represent the target group.
- Identify all the potential prospects that are in the target group (e.g. preschool families, vacation Bible school participants, scout families, etc.). Invite them to a focus group.

Month 3

- Hold focus groups with your prospects testing your vision for the new service. Help them determine when and where the service should be held and its style, whether it should be designed to include children and food. Ask the focus group for others who might be interested in the service and hold a focus group with them. Add all of them to your prospect list.
- Refine your vision accordingly. Define what a "win" will look like.

Month 4

- Further refine your worship design and establish needed task teams using a leadership matrix. Begin recruiting the needed leaders from your prospect list.
- Begin internal communication in the church about the service and the leadership and volunteer needs.

Month 5

- Finalize the budget and develop the marketing/outreach plan.
- Continue to fill the leadership volunteer matrix.

Month 6

- Hold a pre-launch worship service and evaluate.
- Begin to implement the marketing/outreach plan. Get children's ministry and hospitality plans finalized. Develop a newcomer follow-up/assimilation plan that includes getting them involved in discipling opportunities.

Month 7

- Hold another pre-launch worship service and evaluate. Include the hospitality and children's ministry components.

- Lead the church in a special prayer effort for the new service. Collect prospects' contact information and share with the marketing outreach team.

Month 8

- Hold a final pre-launch worship service with all components in place and evaluate.
- Continue to implement the marketing outreach plan and finalize the follow-up assimilation process for newcomers.
- The leadership matrix should be 90% filled.

Month 9

- Publicly launch the worship service. Evaluate and celebrate.
- Implement the follow-up process for newcomers.

Month 10

- Begin inviting newcomers to fill vacancies on the leadership matrix and to serve.
- Continue evaluating all components of the service, continue the marketing outreach.
- Begin inviting participants into discipleship opportunities.

At a predetermined date (e.g. 6 months or 12 months after launch) Evaluate the service against the definition set in month 3 of a "win." Decide whether to continue the service.

Notes on time line:

There are two ways to approach this time line. One is to set a firm public launch date and follow the above time line. A second is to have a tentative launch date and once the leadership matrix is 90% filled the public launch date will be firmly established.

Some churches will want to first establish discipling groups and recruit newcomers to participate in them. Once a predetermined number of these groups have been established, a date for public worship is set and the above time line is used.

This material by Ed Fenstermacher
is reprinted here by permission granted on October 14, 2017.

NOTE: This article reflects the personal opinions of the author
and does not necessarily reflect an official position of Discipleship Ministries or Path 1.

© 2018 Robert O. Crossman, www.UMNewChurch.org

V. What Are Some of the Most Fruitful Behaviors of New Church Planters?

New Church Handbook
Nuts & Bolts for Planting New Churches In The Wesleyan Tradition

"Have An Active Relationship With a New Church Coach"

by Bob Crossman

Ed Stetzer, author of *"Viral Churches: Helping Church Planters Become Movement Makers,"* and the Billy Graham Chair of Evangelism at Wheaton College, has found that **the one** consistent element present in successful and fruitful new church starts is that the planter has a positive relationship with a coach twice a month during the first six months, and monthly thereafter.

Jim Griffith *(founder of Griffith Coaching)* is the wisest person I know when it comes to coaching new church planters. Much of the following content is appropriately credited to him.

Planting a church can be a wonderful, exciting experience; it can also be a lonely, discouraging journey. Because of this, it is important that every church planter have a relationship with two special people – a mentor and a coach. The two roles are very different and each addresses particular elements in the life and ministry of the planter.

Mentors are spiritual friends and gentle guides. They are wise people with years of ministry experience. Their focus is on the spiritual life of the planter and the well being on the planter's family. Mentors do not need to have been planters nor do they need to be knowledgeable about all aspects of church planting. Their role is not to teach or give advice about how to plant the church but to care and give advice on how to live. Mentors are usually either sough out or discovered – they are almost never assigned. Mentors may be part of the denominational system but this is not a requirement. A mentor is rarely also the supervisor of the church-planting project. The two roles are different; in fact, they can even be contradictory. It is best to keep these two roles separate. Denominations can assist planters by:

- Encouraging pastors to make themselves available to meet with planters and, thus, facilitate the process through which planters often discover mentors.
- Clearly define the role (expectations and obligations) of a mentor.

Coaches are teachers and skill builders. They are people with the ability to help others perform at a higher level. Their focus is on the day-to-day activity of the planter and the development of the church-planting project. Coaches do not necessarily need to have been planters but they need to be familiar with all aspects of church planting and they need to understand human behavior and personality.

 © 2018 Robert O. Crossman, www.UMNewChurch.org

The role and value of a coach

- Asks questions that no one else is asking, guiding the planter to think more deeply and with greater clarity about the church planting project.
- Helps the planter see what would otherwise not be seen. This helps the planter to clarify the vision.
- Provides an outside ear and voice for both the planter and the church planting system.
- Adds expertise and information to the church planting process.
- Assists the planter and the church planting system to reach their goals.
- Serves as a compassionate, secure and confidential outlet to vent frustrations and problems.
- Provides a clear line of communication between the planter and the sponsoring agency.
- Conducts reality checks on the planter's vision, values and strategy.
- Walks with the planter through conflict when it arises.
- Helps the planter implement the master plan in proper sequence.
- Works with the planter to develop strategies for recruiting, launching and fund-raising.

A coaching relationship is fostered by some sense of affinity between the planter and the coach. For this reason, assigning coaches can be problematic. Providing planters with some form of input into the selection process can prove helpful.

Coaches may be part of the denominational system but this is not a requirement. Coaches are rarely also the supervisor of the church planting project. The two roles are different. In fact, they can even be contradictory. It is best to keep these two roles separate. Denominations can assist planters by:

- Identify an approved group of coaches from which the planter may choose.
- Clearly define the role (expectations and obligations) of a coach.

Some people may question the need for coaches for church planters or for pastors in general. The answer to this question is straightforward. Natural talent and acquired knowledge are great tools for leaders who desire to plant a church or lead a church towards growth, vitality and faithfulness. These tools alone, however, may not be sufficient. The missing element is often the presence of a coach.

Just as great athletes with multi-million dollar contracts need great coaches for maximum performance, so do great leaders of vital congregations.

Retaining the services of a coach is a sign of strength, not a sign of weakness. It is recognizing both that each person is unique and that no person knows everything.

© 2018 Robert O. Crossman, www.UMNewChurch.org

While **spiritual friends** help us develop our spiritual lives and **mentors** help us develop our personal and professional lives, **coaches** help us perform better. Coaches are part trainer, part behavior analyst, part motivator, part accountability partner, part reality detector and part resource provider. Coaches help leaders clarify their goals, better define the context in which their decisions are made, explore possible options for reaching their desired outcomes and provide support and resources once strategic decisions are made. A coach can assist with defining reality and contemplating possible action plans but leaves the responsibility for decision-making with the person being coached. Coaching may be formal or informal, paid or free, involving a contract or just a verbal agreement.

With hard work and some natural talent, most leaders can be above average. With the assistance of a coach, leaders can become outstanding!

Professional coaching in a church-planting situation is usually provided on a contract-basis. The contract will usually specify the terms and extent of the coaching relationship. Typical elements of a coaching contract include the following:

- The length of the contract (usually 6-18 months).
- The method of contact between the planter, they sponsoring agency and the coach (usually via email and / or phone with in-person meetings arranged as needed).
- The frequency of contact between the planter and the coach (often one or two phone calls or meetings per month with email as-needed).
- The fee schedule for the contract (this varies greatly but is often between $100 - $300 per month with on-site visits at an additional fee).
- Any reporting requirements of the sponsoring agency.
- A clear delineation of the role of the coach.
- A statement of sponsoring organization's expectations, their anticipated timeline and their definition of success.
- Any other items which the planter, coach, sponsoring agency and / or launch team members feel need to be added and to which all are in agreement.

The presence of a good coach does not guarantee the success of a church plant nor does the absence of such a coach guarantee the failure of a church plant. The presence of a coach does, however, increase the likelihood of success. Additionally, a coach can help the church-planting system to refine its efforts and improve its process. A coach can, and probably will, save a church planter and the sponsoring organization many times their investment in the coaching contract.

Contact your conference director of new church starts or director of congregational development for recommendations on who you might engage as a coach.

†††

NOTE: These articles reflect the personal opinions of the author(s) and do not necessarily reflect an official position of Discipleship Ministries or Path 1.

© 2018 Robert O. Crossman, www.UMNewChurch.org

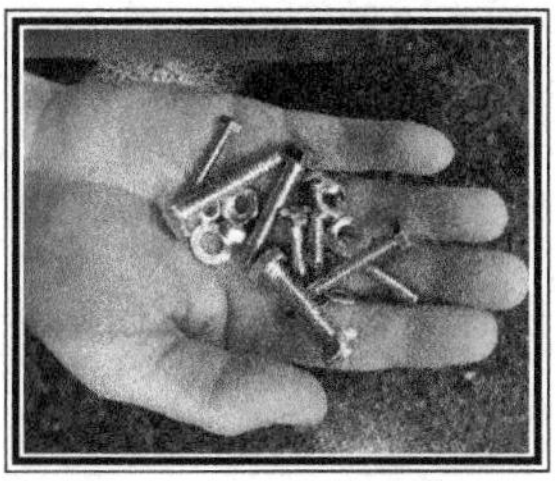

New Church Handbook
Nuts & Bolts for Planting New Churches In The Wesleyan Tradition

"Behaviors of The Most Fruitful New Churches"

by Bob Crossman

In 2015 the Path 1, Discipleship Resources was a major sponsor of the largest and most thorough survey on church planting in the U.S. since 2007. The survey was conducted by Lifeway Research between May and August of 2015, asking well over 12,000 church planters to participate in a 30 minute online survey.

These 12,000 new church planters represented 17 different denominational and church planting organizations, including: Assemblies of God, Baptist Missionary Association of America, Center for US Missions - Lutheran Church – Missouri Synod, Christian and Missionary Alliance, Church of the Nazarene, Converge Worldwide, Evangelical Free Church of America, Free Methodists, International Pentecostal Holiness Church, Missionary Church, New Thing Network, North American Mission Board – The Southern Baptist Church, Presbyterian Church in America, Project Jerusalem, Path1 - The United Methodist Church, Vineyard Church, and The Wesleyan Church.

United Methodist financial sponsors of this survey included: Path 1, and the following annual conferences: Arkansas, Northwest Texas, North Texas, North Georgia, Kentucky, Central Texas, Illinois Great Rivers, South Georgia, Eastern Pennsylvania, Oregon-Idaho, Baltimore-Washington, New England, Peninsula-Delaware, Western Pennsylvania, and Susquehanna.

Over 1,200 planters completed the survey, of which 843 fit the criteria of being planted since 2007 and still open today. The survey offered analysis of these 843 church plants, of which United Methodist planters represented 11.5% of the responders.

Several initial observations among the United Methodist church planters who completed the survey:

- 73% white/caucasian; 19% Hispanic/Latino; 6% Asian/Pacific Islander; and 2% Black/African American.
- 50% intentionally sought to reach a cross-cultural or multi-ethnic group of people.
- 23% of the church plants surveyed are multi-ethnic.
- 79% hold primary worship on Sundays; 21% on weekdays; 5% on varies week to week; 1% on Saturday.
- 39% of the planters work on planting more than 60 hours a week; 42% work

40 to 59 hours a week; 9% work 20 to 39 hours a week; and 9% work less than 20 hours a week.

- The typical UM new church received grants totaling $226,289 in the first 5 years from Conference, District and other sources.
- The typical UM new church received received $601,485 in the first 5 years from its offering plate.

The survey revealed several factors that contributed to each of the following benchmarks:

Higher Worship Attendance
Witnessed More New Decisions for Jesus Christ
Have a Majority of Unchurched in the Congregation
Reaching Financial Self-Sustaining Status
Multiplying By Starting Another New Church

This study identified significant factors with correlation, not causation, to reaching these benchmarks. In other words, churches that reached these benchmarks had these factors in place – however, simply adding these factors to a new church's activities will not necessarily cause a struggling new church to automatically reach the benchmark. The reality is that cause and effect can be indirect and due to a third factor such as the vision, heart, passion or motivation behind the use of the activity itself.

Simply adding these factors to a new church's activities will NOT necessarily cause a struggling new church to automatically reach the benchmark.

What factors are present in the new churches that witnessed higher worship attendance?

{Note: United Methodist new churches exceeded the average attendance of the typical new church in each of the first five years. In year one, UMC churches averaged 53, while the typical new church among the seventeen denominations averaged 51. By the 5th year, UMC churches averaged 175 while the typical church averaged 146 in worship.}

Among the 17 denominations of new church planters with the highest worship attendance, there were five groups of contributing factors:

1. **Highly public presence visible to the community**
   A. Churches that met in public school average 187 in 4th year. Those who met elsewhere averaged 94 in 4th year.
   B. Churches that met in warehouse/industrial space average 238 in 4th year. Those who met elsewhere averaged 111 in 4th year.
   C. Use of mailers as one of top 3 forms of publicity average 173 in 4th yr. Those that didn't averaged 110 in 4th year.
   D. Use radio or television as one of the top 3 forms of publicity average 208

 © 2018 Robert O. Crossman, www.UMNewChurch.org

4th year. Those that didn't averaged 120 in 4th year.

2. **Commitment to multiplication permeates their culture**
   A. Churches that planted a daughter church within first 5 years averaged 204 in 4th year. Those who did not birth another new church averaged 98 in the 4th year.
   B. Churches that financially contributed to other new church plants averaged 150 in 4th year. Those who do not averaged 80 in the 4th year.
   C. Partnering with another organization to plant another church averaged 156 in 4th year. Those who do not averaged 94 in the 4th year.
   D. Leaders invest in or mentor other new church leaders at least quarterly avg. 167 in 4th year. Those who do not averaged 85 in the 4th year.
3. **Generous support of planter compensation from denomination whether its full, half or part-time**
   A. Churches whose planting leaders received a minimum of a month-long training by their denomination averaged 247 in the 4th year. Those who did not receive training averaged 120 in the 4th year.
   B. Church planters who received financial compensation averaged 142 in the 4th year. Those who did not receive financial compensation averaged 59 in the 4th year.
   C. Church planter "feels" compensation adequately meets needs average 162 in 4th year. Those who do not, averaged 93 in 4th year.
   D. Health insurance provided for the planter averaged 155 in the 4th year. Those without health insurance averaged 104 in 4th year.
   E. Experience of planting meets expectations of the church planter averaged 146 in the 4th year. Those who did not, averaged 102 in 4th year.
4. **Leadership development**
   A. Churches that have new member classes averaged 139 in 4th year.
   Those who did not hold new member classes averaged 98 in the 4th year.
5. **Rapid financial self-sufficiency**
   A. Church being financially self-sufficient within three years averaged 138 in 4th year. Those who did not, averaged 85 in 4th year.

What factors are present in the new churches that witnessed more new decisions for Jesus Christ?

{Note: United Methodist planters exceeded the typical new church in the reception of new decisions for Christ. While the typical new church witnesses 78 new commitments in the first 5 years, United Methodist planters witness 84 new commitments in the first 5 years.}

Among the 17 denominations of new church planters that witnessed more new decisions for Jesus Christ there were four groups of contributing factors:

1. **Highly public presence visible to community**
   A. Church uses public school, industrial or warehouse space as worship site had 23 new commitments in 4th year.
   Those not in public school had 14 new commitments in the 4th year.
   B. Church uses industrial or warehouse space as facility had 56 in 3rd year

and 33 in 4th year. Those not in a industrial or warehouse had 15 new commitments in 4th year.

C. Churches that use podcasts as a form of communication had 27 new commitments in 4th year.
Those who do not use podcast had 14 new commitments in 4th year.

D. Churches that use mailers as one of their top three forms of publicity had 28 in 4th year.
Those who do not use mailers had 14 new commitments in the 4th year.

E. Use contact management system as form of electronic communication had 24 in 4th year.
Those who did not had 16 new commitments in the 4th year.

F. Use podcast as regular form of electronic communication had 27 new commitments in 4th year.
Those who did not had 14 new commitments in the 4th year.

2. **Intentional outreach activities and programs**

A. Conduct revival meetings as an outreach activity (predominately in ethnic churches).

B. Regularly mails church invitations as outreach activity had 20 new commitments in 4th year.
Those who did not, had 15 new commitments in 4th year.

C. Churches using sports league as a form of outreach, had 23 new in commitments 4th year.
Those who did not use sports had 15 new commitments in theirs.

3. **Intentionally developing lay leaders – unleashing laity for ministry**

A. Churches that offer a leadership development plan for lay members had 22 commitments in 3rd year and 19 commitments in the 4th year.

B. Churches with out leadership development plan had 11 and 12 commitments in the 3rd and 4th year.

C. Church having a proactive stewardship development plan enabling the church to be financially self-sufficient had 20 new commitments in 4th year. Those who did not, had 12 new commitments in 4th year.

4. **Preparation for multiplication**

A. Church becomes financially self-sufficient within three years had a total of 62 new commitments by the 4th year.
Those who do not, had a total of 55 new commitments by 4th year.

B. Church provided financial compensation for church planter had 18 commitments in 4th year.
Those who do not, had 12 new commitments in the 4th year.

C. Church plants a daughter church within 1st five years had total of 106 new commitments by the 4th year. Those who do not plant another church, had a total of 46 new commitments by 4th year.

D. Church staff invests (mentors, trains, interns, residency, coaches, etc.) in new or potential church planters at least once a quarter had 22 new commitments in the 4th year.

 © 2018 Robert O. Crossman, www.UMNewChurch.org

Those who do not, had 11 new commitments in the 4th year.

What factors are present in new churches who have a majority of unchurched attending worship?

{Note: United Methodist new churches outperformed the typical new church in reaching the previously unchurched and those who were unchurched for many years. In the typical new church, 42% of worship attendees were unchurched or unchurched for many years. In United Methodist new churches, 52% of worship attendees were unchurched or unchurched for many years. In the typical new church, 43% of attendees were previously part of other existing churches, while in United Methodist new churches only 34% of attendees were previously part of other existing churches.}

Among the 17 denominations of new church planters who have a majority of unchurched attending worship, there were two groups of contributing factors:

1. **The survey indicates that churches that simply *"do something"* are more effective than churches who don't. It also indicates that churches who create opportunities for the message of Christ to be shared with unchurched people are the most effective in reaching the unchurched.**
   A. 37% that use a community hall or recreation center as a facility have a majority unchurched attendees. 33% of those not using community hall have a majority unchurched attendees.
   B. 38% that use a contact management system as a regular form of electronic communication. 33% of those who do not use contact management system have a majority unchurched.
   C. 37% that use podcasts as a regular form of communication have majority unchurched attendees. 33% of those who do not use podcasts have majority unchurched attendees
2. **Have an intentional strategy to use techniques that lead to increased number of unchurched people engaging with the new church.**
   A. 44% conduct revival meetings as an outreach activity (predominately ethnic churches). 33% of those who do not conduct revival meetings have majority unchurched attendees.
   B. 50% who launch affinity group meetings for people in the community (Bunco nights, Monday Night Football, Movie Nights, etc.) have majority unchurched attendees. 33% who don't launch affinity groups have majority unchurched attendees.
   C. 45% who use door hangers or flyers as a form of outreach, are majority unchurched. 31% of those who don't use door hangers have majority unchurched attendees.
   D. 45% who use door-to-door outreach as a primary strategy for launch, are majority unchurched. 33% of those who don't use door to door have majority unchurched attendees.
   E. 37% who use special events for kids as a primary form of outreach, are majority unchurched. 30% of those who don't have special kids events have majority unchurched.
   F. 38% who use prayer walking in preparation for their launch, are major-

ity unchurched. 33% of those who don't use prayer walks have majority unchurched attendees.

G. 38% who use outreach Bible studies as a form of outreach, are majority unchurched. 30% who don't use Bible studies for outreach are majority unchurched.

H. 46% who use sports leagues as a primary form of outreach, are majority unchurched. 32% who don't use sports leagues have majority unchurched attendees.

What factors are present in new churches who have become financially self-sustaining by year five?

{Note: *United Methodist new churches were less likely to become self sustaining within five years. In the typical new church, 64% were financially self-sufficient by year 5. While in United Methodist new churches, 42% were financially self-sufficient by year 5.*}

The survey also clearly indicates that if a church does not become financially self-sufficient by year 5, it is UNLIKELY that it will ever become financially sustainable.

Among the 17 denominations of new church plants that became financially self-sustaining in the first five years, there were four groups of contributing factors:

1. **Prioritize a public presence**
   A. 71% of churches putting sermons online as a communication tool are self-sufficient within 1st 3 years. Those that don't, 57%.
   B. 74% of churches using school as a meeting space are self-sufficient within 1st 3 years. Meet elsewhere, 60%.
   C. 75% Use newspaper or other print ads to communicate news of a new church in the community. Those that don't, 63%.
2. **Focus on new member assimilation to develop leaders well**
   A. 71% of the churches holding a new members class are self-sufficient within 1st 3 years. Those that don't, 53%.
   B. 68% who develop a leadership training plan for their members are self-sufficient within 1st 3yr. Those that don't, 57%.
3. **Handle money well**
   A. 72% of the churches that develop a proactive church stewardship to move the church to self sufficiency. Those that don't 53%.
   B. 71% of the churches that financially contribute to other church plants. Those that don't 54%.
   This seems counterintuitive. This study seems to indicate that if the focus is not on self, but beyond self to create even more new disciples by starting more new churches, it leads to greater generosity among attenders.
4. **Multiplication focus**
   A. 72% of the churches who plant at least 1 daughter church within the first 3 years are self-sufficient within 1st 3 years. Those who don't, 62%.
   This seems counterintuitive. This study seems to indicate that people give to vision. When pastor leads church to have a big vision for expansion and multi-

 © 2018 Robert O. Crossman, www.UMNewChurch.org

plication, and the church commits to that vision, churches are more likely to give sacrificially, increasing the likelihood they will reach financial self-sufficiency.

What factors are present in churches that have multiplied by starting another new church within the first five years of their existence?
{Note: United Methodist new churches under perform in this area when compared to the typical new church. In the typical new church, 22% have started a daughter church within 1st 5 years. In United Methodist new churches, 13% have started a daughter church within 1st 5 years.}

Churches that give birth and start another new church within the first five years prepare, plan, and execute their strategy to not only see a new church begin, but to give birth to additional new churches.

Among the 17 denominations of new church plants giving birth to another new church in the first five years, there were five groups of contributing factors:

1. **Very visible, both publicly and digitally**
   A. 27% Use a church building, industrial or warehouse as a facility, give birth with in the first 5 years. 20% of those who use different type facilities give birth within the first 5 years.
   B. 26% Use mailers to publicize the news of a new church in the community. 19% of those who don't use mailers.
   C. 23% of those who promote new church using internet, websites and email blasts. 19% of those who don't use internet.
   D. 36% of those who post a blog as a regular form of electronic communication. 16% of those who don't blog.
   E. 40% of those who use a contact management system as a regular form of electronic communication. 19% of those without such a system.
   F. 25% of those who post sermons online. 17% of those who do not post sermons.
   G. 40% of churches that utilize a podcast as a means of communication. 16% of those who do not utilize podcast.
2. **Intentional programs and activities**
   A. 27% who conduct regular revival meetings give birth to another church within 5 years. 20% of those without revival meetings give birth to another church within 5 years.
   B. 34% who have sports league activities as an outreach. 19% of those without sports activities.
3. **Commitment to discipleship, member and leadership development**
   A. 26% of new churches that practice one-on-one discipleship. 14% of those who do not practice one-on-one discipleship.
   B. 26% of new churches that require a membership covenant for anyone joining the church. 16% of those who do not require a membership covenant.
   C. 24% who offer a new member's class. 16% of those who do not offer a new member's class.
   D. 24% who offer evangelism training including one-on-one training or a class or workshop 18% of those who do not offer evangelism training.

E. 26% of new churches that have an intentional stewardship plan. 13% of those who do not have stewardship plan.

4. **Plant and planter preparation**
   A. 25% of new churches receiving denominational funding will give birth within 1st 5 years. 12% of those who do not, will give birth to another church within 1st 5 years.
   B. 31% of new churches that receive outside funding from a sponsor or church. 10% of those who do not.
   C. 25% of churches that obtain demographic analysis and assessment of the community. 14% of those who do not.
   D. 32% of churches that receive demographic and or research expertise. 12% of those who do not.
   E. 29% whose planter attends conferences on church planting. 15% of those who do not.
   F. 26% of Planters assessed by a denomination or church planting network. 12% of those who are not.
   G. 26% of Planters who enlist several personal prayer partners prior to starting the new work and continuing to engage their prayer support during the 1st year of the new church work. 9% of those who do not.
   H. 26% of Planters actively engaged in a plan of personal spiritual formation during the duration of the new church start. 13% of those who do not.
   I. 29% of Planter's experience meeting their expectations. 13% of those who do not.
5. **Intentional about creating specific pathways to make multiplication happen**
   A. 35% of Church that partners with another organization to plant another new church. 8% of those who do not.
   B. 31% of churches that contribute financially to other church plants. 6% of those who do not.
   C. 32% of churches who regularly communicates to the whole congregation a commitment to start another new church. 11% of those who do not.
   D. 36% of Churches whose staff invests (mentors, trains, interns, residency, coach, etc.) in new or potential church planters at least once a quarter. 8% of those who don't.

Conclusions...

- Many of our new church plants are effectively making new disciples of Jesus Christ.
- By comparison, our new churches are faithfully reaching the unchurched. In a typical new UM church, 52% of worship attendees were unchurched or unchurched for many years. *(Other denomination starts report only 42%.)*
- By comparison, our new churches are faithfully receiving new commitments. In a typical new UM church, 84 new commitments are witnessed in the first

© 2018 Robert O. Crossman, www.UMNewChurch.org

5 years..*(Other denomination starts report only 78.)*

- By comparison, our new churches are successfully attracting worship attendees. In a typical new UM church, worship attendance averages 175 by the 5th year. *(Other denomination starts report only 146 in attendance.)*
- We need to improve our ability to reach financial self sustainability. In a typical new UM church, only 42% are by the 5th year. *(Other denomination starts report 64%.)*
- We need to improve our multiplication. Only 13% of our new churches have given birth to an additional new church by 5th year. *(Other denomination starts report 22%.)*
- Based on the reports from these 17 denominations, Church Planting is no longer on the fringes of the church, but is now vital strategy for reaching more new disciples, more younger disciples, and more diverse disciples.

Summary

In summary, United Methodist new church starts were more vital and fruitful than the typical new church in several areas including: 1) having a higher average worship attendance every year of the first five year; 2) witnessing more new decision for Christ; and 3) having more unchurched attending worship.

United Methodist new churches under-performed, when compared to the typical new church in two areas: 1) reaching financial self-sufficiency within the first five years, and 2) multiplying by giving birth to start another new church within the first five years.

Note: This study identified significant factors with correlation, not causation, to reaching these benchmarks. In other words, churches that reached these benchmarks had these factors in place. However, simply adding several of these factors to a struggling church's activities will not necessarily cause that struggling new church to automatically reach the benchmark. The reality is that cause and effect can be indirect and due to a third factor such as the vision, heart, passion or motivation behind the use of the activity itself.

Recommendation

While the presence of these factors do not "guarantee" positive results, we recommend that planters and launch teams with the vision, heart, passion and motivation to reach these 5 benchmarks – test these factors to discover if they might prove fruitful in their particular mission field.

We are just beginning to unpack the results of this survey. There is more to come as we dig deeper into this research.

†††

NOTE: This article reflects the personal opinions of the author and does not necessarily reflect an official position of Discipleship Ministries or Path 1.

New Church Handbook
Nuts & Bolts for Planting New Churches In The Wesleyan Tradition

"Be a Multiplying New Church"

by Bob Crossman

Path 1, at Discipleship Ministries, defines a new church as follows: *"A new congregation is a newly organized faith community that is committed to making disciples of Jesus Christ and includes regular community worship, is theologically Wesleyan,* ***is willing to plant a new congregation in its first decade****, has an effective discipling system, demonstrates faithful stewardship, does community outreach, and receives new members. A new church is more than a mission project, a new worship service, or the construction of a new building."*

Path 1, at Discipleship Ministries, invites every new church to implant a critical piece into their DNA: a commitment to sponsor (give birth to) another new church within the first few years of the new congregation's life.

This multiplying DNA was once a vital part of what it meant to be Wesleyan. In the 1800's our Methodist laity and circuit riders felt a compulsion to start a sister congregation if there was a community nine miles away with a school, livery stable, post office or mercantile. For circuit riders in the 1800's, success was turning their 15 point circuit into a 20 point circuit.

In the 1940s and 1950s, all across our nation, the old First UMCs downtown were naturally giving birth to new congregations to reach those moving out to the suburbs. Many of these new suburban congregations were called Wesley UMC, Asbury UMC, or Trinity UMC.

Path 1 invites our new churches to rediscover the circuit riders' DNA. In response to the changing demographics of the United States we have the opportunity make disciples of more people, more younger people, and more diverse people. *"New Places for New People"* is a national goal of the United Methodist Church to start 500 new churches, 5000 new faith communities, and 50,000 new groups for new people between 2017 and 2020. In the years after 2020, the goal is to move even closer to starting one church a day.

As you dream about your new church... as you begin to think of core values... as you begin to form benchmarks for your ministry - include, *"we will sponsor and give birth to a second new United Methodist Church within the first five years."*

Two great second-site stories are available on video. You can find them through Google *"UMTV: Church in a Diner,"* and also *"UMTV: Bowling Church"*

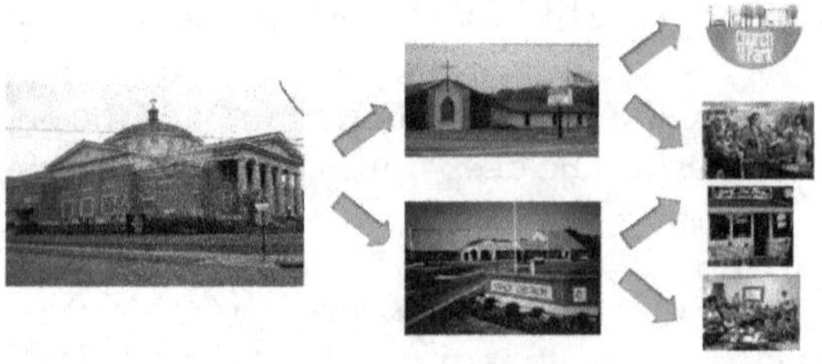

See also the article, *"What are some of the strategies for staring a new church?"* in chapter three.

 © 2018 Robert O. Crossman, www.UMNewChurch.org

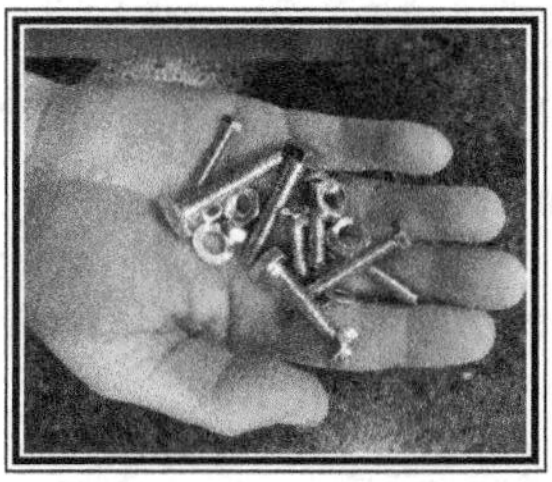

New Church Handbook
Nuts & Bolts for Planting New Churches In The Wesleyan Tradition

"Be a Theologically Wesleyan New Church"

by Bob Crossman

Francis Asbury

John Wesley

Path 1, General Board of Discipleship, defines a new church as follows: *"A new congregation is a newly organized faith community that is committed to making disciples of Jesus Christ and includes regular community worship, is* ***theologically Wesleyan****, is willing to plant a new congregation in its first decade, has an effective discipling system, demonstrates faithful stewardship, does community outreach, and receives new members. A new church is more than a mission project, a new worship service, or the construction of a new building."*

Path 1, General Board of Discipleship, invites every new United Methodist Church to be "theologically Wesleyan."

With our growing population and the vast number of unchurched in the United States, there is a need for many different kinds of new churches to start across the country: Assembly of God, Southern Baptist, Lutheran, Roman Catholic, Unitarian, Orthodox, Disciples, Anglican, Episcopal, United Methodist, Presbyterian, Holiness, and non-denominational too. With the increasing number of new immigrants into the United States, there is also a need for new Hindu, Buddhist, and Jewish congregations. However, as a United Methodist denomination, we are only directly working to start new churches that are faithful to our understanding of Wesleyan Theology.

What is a "theologically Wesleyan" church?
It is a church whose preaching and teaching
are in harmony with the basic theology
of the United Methodist Church.

Our Wesleyan theology is a wonderful gift from our tradition. We have an historic seamless blend between vital piety and social justice. Our stance on gender equality, racial equality, and the ordination of women brings great strength to our missional task. Our flexibility in baptism (infant, child, youth or adult) (sprinkling, pouring, or immersion) allows us to reach new people from a variety of denominational backgrounds. Our pastoral appointive system allows the United Methodist Church to deploy pastors to start new churches in new places, gives our pastors great freedom in the pulpit, and helps to insure that every new church has a pastor.

When I hear from a superintendent, church developer, pastor or layperson regarding one of our new churches being "non-Methodist," it almost always relates to the issue of style and that person's pre-conception of what a United Methodist Church should "look like" in worship, music, Christian education, etc.

- Can a new church that uses sermon series instead of the lectionary be United Methodist? Of course!
- Can a new church in which spiritual formation takes place in small groups in homes rather than in traditional Sunday School classrooms still be United Methodist? Certainly!
- Can a United Methodist worship service be held in a rented elementary school cafeteria, diner or bowling alley? Yes!
- Can a United Methodist sermon be delivered by a preacher dressed in "business casual" instead of a pulpit robe?
- Can a United Methodist congregation sit at tables and chairs instead of pews on Sunday morning?
- Can a United Methodist congregation celebrate the Christmas and Easter season but not particularly notice when "Christ the King Sunday" occurs in the Christian Calendar?
- Can the Wesleyan doctrine be manifested in a variety of creative, non-traditional ways in the ministry style of our new churches? I believe the answer is, "yes."

What is a new United Methodist Church? Path 1, General Board of Discipleship, defines a new church as follows: "A new congregation is a newly organized faith community that is committed to making disciples of Jesus Christ and includes regular community worship, is theologically Wesleyan, is willing to plant a new congregation in its first decade, has an effective discipling system, demonstrates faithful stewardship, does community outreach, and receives new members. A new church is more than a mission project, a new worship service, or the construction of a new building."

The cutting edge of being "theologically Wesleyan" is not about architecture. In the early years of the Methodist movement, worship took place is a variety of structures and settings. The Wesleys did preach in the tall steeple sanctuary at Christ College, but in response to their mission field they also preached and held worship in city parks, cemeteries, coal mines, prisons, factories, and textile mills.

 © 2018 Robert O. Crossman, www.UMNewChurch.org

Wesley was uncomfortable in those informal settings, but his passion to reach the unchurched was even stronger. New United Methodist Churches continue the Wesleyan tradition of holding worship in a variety of places in response to the new mission fields they are committed to reaching. New United Methodist churches occasionally are able to inherit buildings abandoned a decade ago. But more often, new church pastors are seeking initial worship sites that match the target audience of the new church: elementary schools, day care centers, Wesley Foundations, public libraries, banks, movie theaters, commercial office strip centers, hospitals, restaurants, bars, parks, recreational facilities, and even funeral homes. Some of our new churches intentionally stay in these settings for five years, ten years, or longer before even considering the possibility of site purchase and new construction. Bill Easom, in his book, *The Nomadic Church,* invites new churches to even consider becoming "nomadic" churches that never have a permanent site. I believe that John Wesley would be proud.

It's interesting that in the American Colonies, early Methodist chapels were simple and without traditional architectural elements. When Francis Asbury first visited a new building the Methodist erected in New England, he was shocked to discover a steeple! He is quoted as expressing his distress at the traditional colonial architecture, saying, *"If this distressing trend continues, the next generation of new Methodist chapels will not only include steeples, they will have organs and pews."*

The cutting edge of being "theologically Wesleyan" is not about pulpit robes. When Francis Asbury sent circuit riders to start new churches across the American colonies, he did not expect them to carry pulpit robes and stoles in their saddle bags. In new church settings, our pastors are seeking a dress code that matches the mission field they have been sent to reach. In my first student appointment, I intended to wear a pulpit robe like the pastor in my home church. However, only the larger church on my circuit was open to this. The three open country congregations let me know that "our preachers have never worn one of those."

The cutting edge of being "theologically Wesleyan" is not about a particular style of music. Many of our United Methodist congregations that started in the 1920's, during the height of Fanny Crosby's popularity, often still cling to their tradition of only singing from the Cokesbury Hymnal (which was copyright in 1928).

One of my United Methodist congregations on the circuit still sang from a "shaped notes" hymnal, and held annual Singing Schools on reading shaped notes. Many of our district superintendents have discovered that the churches in their district do not all sing the same tempo, to the same instrument, nor have the same list of favorites.

Our new churches today, continue this Methodist tradition of having a musical style that appeals to the target audience they have been appointed to reach, while still being sensitive to singing words that reflect our wesleyan theology.

For the purpose of this article, the cutting edge of being "theologically Wesleyan" is more about doctrine than style. In this discernment phase of your ministry, before accepting an appointment to start a new United Methodist congregation, you might want to reread Part II of our Book of Discipline: "Our Distinctive Heritage as United Methodist," "Our Distinctive Wesleyan Emphases," "Doctrinal Standards and General Rules," "Articles of Religion of the Methodist Church," "Confession of Faith of the Evangelical United Brethren Church," and "Our Theological Task." These articles are printed in every copy of The Book of Discipline, and at www.umc.org click on "Our Faith" and then "Beliefs."

After reading the following two articles,
if your heart beats fast for Wesleyan Theology,
continue your discernment about the possibility
of receiving a new church planting appointment.
But, honestly,
if your theology is not Wesleyan, I encourage you to have the integrity
to transfer to a different denomination that reflects your theological preference.
Bob Crossman

Practically speaking, it is the United Methodist church who has appointed you and gave you financial aid, and therefore has the right to expect that you will be faithful to your annual conference's policies, to the Book of Discipline, and to our Wesleyan theological heritage.

†††

The following two articles, "Distinctive Wesleyan Emphasis" and "Basic Christian Affirmations," are reprinted here from the Book of Discipline, ¶101.

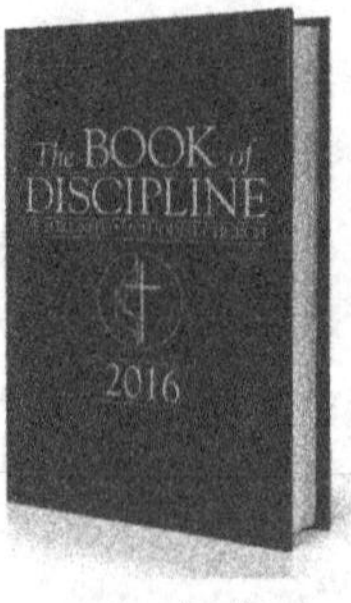

"Distinctive Wesleyan Emphasis"
From The Book of Discipline of The United Methodist Church, ¶101

Although Wesley shared with many other Christians a belief in grace, justification, assurance, and sanctification, he combined them in a powerful manner to create distinctive emphases for living the full Christian life. The Evangelical United Brethren tradition, particularly as expressed by Phillip William Otterbein from a Reformed background, gave similar distinctive emphases.

Grace pervades our understanding of Christian faith and life. By grace we mean the undeserved, unmerited, and loving action of God in human existence through the ever-present Holy Spirit. While the grace of God is undivided, it precedes salvation

 © 2018 Robert O. Crossman, www.UMNewChurch.org

as "prevenient grace," continues in "justifying grace," and is brought to fruition in "sanctifying grace."

We assert that God's grace is manifest in all creation even though suffering, violence, and evil are everywhere present. The goodness of creation is fulfilled in human beings, who are called to covenant partnership with God. God has endowed us with dignity and freedom and has summoned us to responsibility for our lives and the life of the world.

In God's self-revelation, Jesus Christ, we see the splendor of our true humanity. Even our sin, with its destructive consequences for all creation, does not alter God's intention for us—holiness and happiness of heart. Nor does it diminish our accountability for the way we live.

Despite our brokenness, we remain creatures brought into being by a just and merciful God. The restoration of God's image in our lives requires divine grace to renew our fallen nature.

Prevenient Grace—We acknowledge God's prevenient grace, the divine love that surrounds all humanity and precedes any and all of our conscious impulses. This grace prompts our first wish to please God, our first glimmer of understanding concerning God's will, and our "first slight transient conviction" of having sinned against God.

God's grace also awakens in us an earnest longing for deliverance from sin and death and moves us toward repentance and faith.

Justification and Assurance—We believe God reaches out to the repentant believer in justifying grace with accepting and pardoning love. Wesleyan theology stresses that a decisive change in the human heart can and does occur under the prompting of grace and the guidance of the Holy Spirit.

In justification we are, through faith, forgiven our sin and restored to God's favor. This righting of relationships by God through Christ calls forth our faith and trust as we experience regeneration, by which we are made new creatures in Christ.

This process of justification and new birth is often referred to as conversion. Such a change may be sudden and dramatic, or gradual and cumulative. It marks a new beginning, yet it is part of an ongoing process. Christian experience as personal transformation always expresses itself as faith working by love.

Our Wesleyan theology also embraces the scriptural promise that we can expect to receive assurance of our present salvation as the Spirit "bears witness with our spirit that we are children of God."

Sanctification and Perfection—We hold that the wonder of God's acceptance and pardon does not end God's saving work, which continues to nurture our growth in grace. Through the power of the Holy Spirit, we are enabled to increase in the knowledge and love of God and in love for our neighbor.

New birth is the first step in this process of sanctification. Sanctifying grace draws us toward the gift of Christian perfection, which Wesley described as a heart "habitually filled with the love of God and neighbor" and as "having the mind of Christ and walking as he walked."

This gracious gift of God's power and love, the hope and expectation of the faithful, is neither warranted by our efforts nor limited by our frailties.

Faith and Good Works—We see God's grace and human activity working together in the relationship of faith and good works. God's grace calls forth human response and discipline.

Faith is the only response essential for salvation. However, the General Rules remind us that salvation evidences itself in good works. For Wesley, even repentance should be accompanied by "fruits meet for repentance," or works of piety and mercy.

Both faith and good works belong within an all-encompassing theology of grace, since they stem from God's gracious love "shed abroad in our hearts by the Holy Spirit."

Mission and Service—We insist that personal salvation always involves Christian mission and service to the world. By joining heart and hand, we assert that personal religion, evangelical witness, and Christian social action are reciprocal and mutually reinforcing.

Scriptural holiness entails more than personal piety; love of God is always linked with love of neighbor, a passion for justice and renewal in the life of the world.

The General Rules represent one traditional expression of the intrinsic relationship between Christian life and thought as understood within the Wesleyan tradition. Theology is the servant of piety, which in turn is the ground of social conscience and the impetus for social action and global interaction, always in the empowering context of the reign of God.

Nurture and Mission of the Church—Finally, we emphasize the nurturing and serving function of Christian fellowship in the Church. The personal experience of faith is nourished by the worshiping community.

For Wesley there is no religion but social religion, no holiness but social holiness. The communal forms of faith in the Wesleyan tradition not only promote personal growth; they also equip and mobilize us for mission and service to the world.

The outreach of the church springs from the working of the Spirit. As United Methodists, we respond to that working through a connectional polity based upon mutual responsiveness and accountability. Connectional ties bind us together in faith and service in our global witness, enabling faith to become active in love and intensifying our desire for peace and justice in the world.

© 2018 Robert O. Crossman, www.UMNewChurch.org

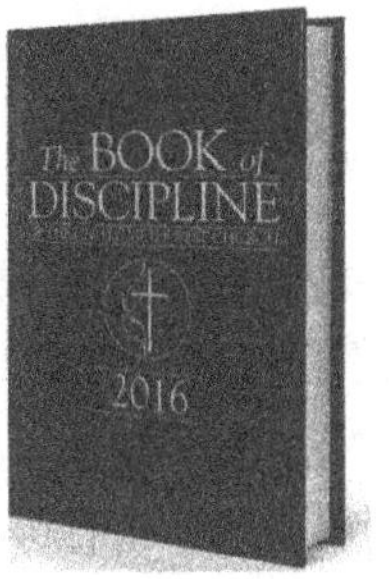

†††

"Basic Christian Affirmations"

From The Book of Discipline of
The United Methodist Church, ¶101

With Christians of other communions we confess belief in the triune God—Father, Son, and Holy Spirit. This confession embraces the biblical witness to God's activity in creation, encompasses God's gracious self-involvement in the dramas of history, and anticipates the consummation of God's reign.

The created order is designed for the well-being of all creatures and as the place of human dwelling in covenant with God. As sinful creatures, however, we have broken that covenant, become estranged from God, wounded ourselves and one another, and wreaked havoc throughout the natural order. We stand in need of redemption.

We hold in common with all Christians a faith in the mystery of salvation in and through Jesus Christ. At the heart of the gospel of salvation is God's incarnation in Jesus of Nazareth. Scripture witnesses to the redeeming love of God in Jesus' life and teachings, his atoning death, his resurrection, his sovereign presence in history, his triumph over the powers of evil and death, and his promised return. Because God truly loves us in spite of our willful sin, God judges us, summons us to repentance, pardons us, receives us by that grace given to us in Jesus Christ, and gives us hope of life eternal.

We share the Christian belief that God's redemptive love is realized in human life by the activity of the Holy Spirit, both in personal experience and in the community of believers. This community is the church, which the Spirit has brought into existence for the healing of the nations.

Through faith in Jesus Christ we are forgiven, reconciled to God, and transformed as people of the new covenant.

"Life in the Spirit" involves diligent use of the means of grace such as praying, fasting, attending upon the sacraments, and inward searching in solitude. It also encompasses the communal life of the church in worship, mission, evangelism, service, and social witness.

We understand ourselves to be part of Christ's universal church when by adoration, proclamation, and service we become conformed to Christ. We are initiated and incorporated into this community of faith by Baptism, receiving the promise of the Spirit that re-creates and transforms us. Through the regular celebration of Holy Communion, we participate in the risen presence of Jesus Christ and are thereby nourished for faithful discipleship.

We pray and work for the coming of God's realm and reign to the world and rejoice in the promise of everlasting life that overcomes death and the forces of evil.

With other Christians we recognize that the reign of God is both a present and future reality. The church is called to be that place where the first signs of the reign of God are identified and acknowledged in the world. Wherever persons are being made new creatures in Christ, wherever the insights and resources of the gospel are brought to bear on the life of the world, God's reign is already effective in its healing and renewing power.

We also look to the end time in which God's work will be fulfilled. This prospect gives us hope in our present actions as individuals and as the Church. This expectation saves us from resignation and motivates our continuing witness and service.

We share with many Christian communions a recognition of the authority of Scripture in matters of faith, the confession that our justification as sinners is by grace through faith, and the sober realization that the church is in need of continual reformation and renewal.

We affirm the general ministry of all baptized Christians who share responsibility for building up the church and reaching out in mission and service to the world.

With other Christians, we declare the essential oneness of the church in Christ Jesus. This rich heritage of shared Christian belief finds expression in our hymnody and liturgies. Our unity is affirmed in the historic creeds as we confess one holy, catholic, and apostolic church. It is also experienced in joint ventures of ministry and in various forms of ecumenical cooperation.

Nourished by common roots of this shared Christian heritage, the branches of Christ's church have developed diverse traditions that enlarge our store of shared understandings. Our avowed ecumenical commitment as United Methodists is to gather our own doctrinal emphases into the larger Christian unity, there to be made more meaningful in a richer whole.

If we are to offer our best gifts to the common Christian treasury, we must make a deliberate effort as a church to strive for critical self-understanding. It is as Christians involved in ecumenical partnership that we embrace and examine our distinctive heritage.

†††

NOTE: This article reflects the personal opinions of the author and does not necessarily reflect an official position of Discipleship Ministries or Path 1.

 © 2018 Robert O. Crossman, www.UMNewChurch.org

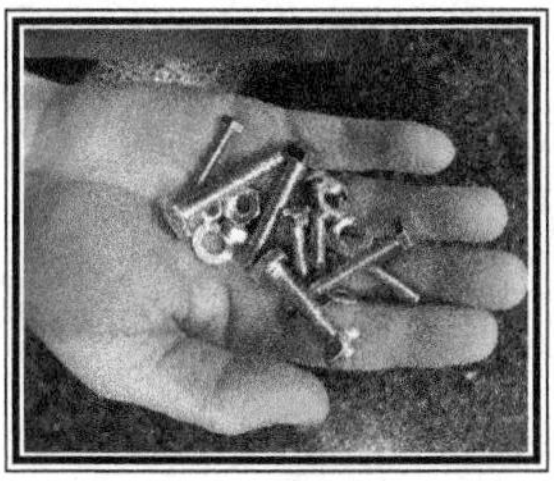

New Church Handbook
Nuts & Bolts for Planting New Churches In The Wesleyan Tradition

"Be Proud to Be United Methodist"

by Bob Crossman

Path 1, General Board of Discipleship, defines a new church as follows: *"A new congregation is a newly organized faith community that is committed to making disciples of Jesus Christ and includes regular community worship, is theologically Wesleyan, is willing to plant a new congregation in its first decade, has an effective discipling system, demonstrates faithful stewardship, does community outreach, and receives new members. A new church is more than a mission project, a new worship service, or the construction of a new building."*

Don't hide the fact that you are a United Methodist Church! Use the cross and flame logo and the words "United Methodist" in all your marketing and signage.

Why? A September 2011 study by the South Baptist Research group, found that United Methodist are held in a more favorable regard by the U.S. public than Southern Baptists, Catholics, Mormons, or Muslims. This reinforces the April 2008 research by the Gallop Panel which determined that Methodist have the **highest positive ratings** and the **lowest negative ratings** of religious and spiritual groups in the United States, ranking higher than Baptists, Catholics, Jews, Evangelicals or Fundamentalists.

Non-United Methodist new church starts may want to hide their denominational or para-church affiliations, and perhaps rightly so because their negatives are so high.

You may have new church starts in your community who are only known as "The Living Church" or "The Family Church" or "First Church Memphis." Those churches may even hide their denomination in any church printing, worship bulletins, newsletters, web site, and church signage. Worship guests must attend frequently and persistently ask questions to finally hear, in hushed apologetic tones, the truth. That does not seem honest to me, and lacks integrity.

However, as United Methodists, if we want to be the most effective inviting new people to become disciples of Jesus Christ for the Transformation of the World, we should proudly display the cross and flame logo, and the word United Methodist, on all our signs, printing and marketing. With such a positive and winsome public image across the nation, why would any new United Methodist Church desire to hide its true identity?

In a telephone interview,
Jim Griffith said, ***"While there is clearly an "anti-denomination movement," United Methodists are one of the rare church bodies with a positive image. It's just a bad idea to keep your Methodist affiliation a secret.***
www.griffithcoaching.com

In the 2008 study, only four percent of the United States population gave United Methodists a negative rating. Ninety-six percent of the 1,005 persons (adults 18 and older) interviewed during the March 2008 poll, had either a positive or neutral view of Methodists. United Methodists are one of the four U.S. religious groups with strongly positive ratings. The others are Jews, Baptists and Catholics. Broader groups of "evangelical Christians" with 16 percent net positive and "fundamentalist Christians" with a 10 percent net positive did not fare as well, according to an analysis of the survey. Methodists received the highest marks in the total positive and net positive categories of the survey of "Americans' Views of U.S. Religious and Spiritual Groups," with a 45 percent net positive rating. Forty seven percent of the respondents gave United Methodists a "neutral" rating. As a matter of comparison, Jews had a 42 percent net positive rating, Baptists 35 percent, and Catholics 32 percent.

In the 2011 study, 62% had a favorable view of United Methodists, the highest positives in the study. United Methodists also had the lowest negatives in this 2011 study.

The 2011 study included 2,144 respondents, conducted by Lifeway Research. This study was conducted in September 2011 after the president of the Southern Baptist Convention appointed a task force to consider a possible name change for the 166-year-old denomination.

The March 2008 poll, was a random, demographically weighted poll, asking a representative sample of Americans whether they had a positive, negative, or neutral view of each of 10 spiritual or religious groups in the United States. The Gallop Panel is weighted so that it is demographically representative of the U.S. adult population. For results based on this sample, one can say with 95% confidence that the maximum margin of sampling error is plus or minus four percentage points.

In the years ahead public opinion of the United Methodist Church may change nationally. In your particular mission field, general opinion of the UMC may be negative. You will have to test your mission field to find out. Nationally, according to the most recent studies available, the UMC is one of the rare church bodies with a positive image. You can display the cross and flame and the name "United Methodist" proudly.

†††

NOTE: This article reflects the personal opinions of the author and does not necessarily reflect an official position of Discipleship Ministries or Path 1.

 © 2018 Robert O. Crossman, www.UMNewChurch.org

VI. Ready to Give Birth?

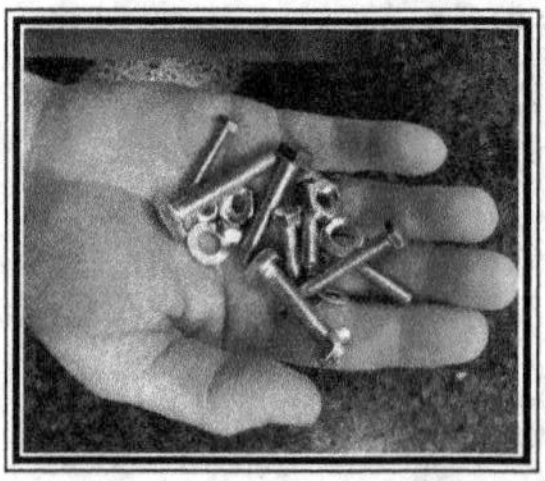

New Church Handbook
Nuts & Bolts for Planting New Churches In The Wesleyan Tradition

"Getting Ready to Plant"

PATH1

Congratulations! If your congregation is considering seriously its call to multiply, it is stepping out of the norm for many typical American churches. The very fact that you would enter into a serious conversation around the possibility of planting a new church places you into a very special category among churches. A multiplying movement of churches planting new churches was quite the norm for first century congregations we read about in the Book of Acts. Even today there is no better way to reach more people, more young people, more diverse people in our communities than to plant a new congregation.

A new congregation is simply a newly organized faith community that is committed to making disciples of Jesus Christ and:

- Includes regular community worship and celebration of sacraments.
- Practices Wesleyan theology.
- Has an effective discipling system.
- Receives new members.
- Demonstrates faithful stewardship.
- Is deeply involved in community transformation.
- Is willing to plant a new congregation in its first decade.

Existing congregations can plant new churches in a variety of ways. Each planting opportunity, and methodology, will vary by context. The 10 most common planting strategies used in America today include: peer church, multiple partner, multi-site expansion, shared facility, closed/reopened facility, connectional parachute drop, vital merger, house church, Elijah/Elisha, and surprise birth.

More information on these strategies is included in the article, *"What Are Some of the Strategies or Models for Starting a New Church?"* in chapter three of this handbook.

Regardless of the strategy chosen to plant a new congregation – your church and its leaders need to be ready for the task of planting. Is your church ready to plant? How can you assess this? And if your church is not quite ready, how can it get ready for such an endeavor? What strategy will you follow to make it happen?

 © 2018 Robert O. Crossman, www.UMNewChurch.org

Fit matters! Your church might be wonderfully prepared to plant following one kind of strategy and woefully unprepared to plant following another. Few churches, if any, will ever be ready to plant in ALL of the ways imaginable. However, many churches can plant IF they are willing to nurture and develop some standard core competencies and then choose a strategy that is suitable to their unique church strengths, ministry opportunities, and community context.

It is important when assessing a church's readiness to plant to examine these five key areas:

1. Leadership readiness
2. Vision/Mission alignment
3. Evangelistic aptitude
4. Passionate spirituality
5. Cultural attitudes

In almost every situation, there will be some cultural differences between the groups we seek to reach with the new church than the groups we are reaching effectively with the existing church. The differences between the partner church and the projected population in the new church could center around any or all of the following themes: generation, ethnicity, educational levels, socio-economics, language and world view.

Though these five key areas are not listed in any particular order, we believe each is critically important. The stronger a partner church is within each of the five key areas, the healthier the plant will be. Strengthening weak areas before undertaking the work of planting is strongly recommended. Significant dysfunction or un-readiness in any of the five key areas can greatly diminish your church's effectiveness in this effort.

Jesus told a parable about how important it is for us to be ready before we launch into any significant project for God:

"Is there anyone here who, planning to build a new house, doesn't first sit down and figure the cost so you'll know if you can complete it? If you only get the foundation laid and then run out of money, you're going to look pretty foolish. Everyone passing by will poke fun at you: "He started something he couldn't finish!"
Luke 14:28-30, The Message

Path 1 recommends a process of discernment for all prospective partner churches, so that if they choose to plant a new church, they will do so well prepared and ready to build something that will be viable, sustaining and equipped to multiply.

This discernment process involves the following elements:

1. **Discerning God's call**
   This conversation formally raises the possibility of planting a new congregation. It may begin in several different places and be initiated by diverse people. Every year, new United Methodist churches begin because of lay initiative, senior pastors who lead their churches to consider planting another church or because a prospective planting pastor dares to share a vision that God has given them for this kind of ministry. New United Methodist churches are started because of the faithfulness and vision of a district superintendent or because God has placed a vision for this in the hearts of conference staff people. Regardless of who begins the conversation, ultimately a group of God's people must finally evaluate the possibilities, dream great dreams, and sense the Spirit of God in the midst of their discernment.

2. **Readiness assessment**
   Just as it is important to assess prospective church planters to verify their call, Path 1 encourages prospective planting congregations to further explore theirs. Path 1's "Readiness to Plant 360" is a web-based tool that allows a congregation to gain a comprehensive sense of their strengths as well as those areas that need improvement in order to be a successful partner in planting a new church.

3. **Season of preparation**
   a. Develop a customized plan, with assistance by a conference-designated person or a Path 1 coach, that is based upon the results of the "Readiness to Plant 360". Your plan may include one or more of the following elements:

      i. Establish a planting prep team made up a mix of persons from the partner church that is passionate about participating in the new faith community as well as those who simply carry credibility with the other leaders of the partner church.

      ii. Address one or more areas of weakness indicated by the "Readiness to Plant 360" to increase viability and ease of planting. It is important to involve your district superintendent, a conference staff person or coach in this process.

      iii. Identify potential leaders for the new plant and help them to get involved

 © 2018 Robert O. Crossman, www.UMNewChurch.org

in discernment and equipping experiences for potential new church planters. (Always, always, always – leader identification should be coordinated with your district superintendent and the conference staff person responsible for new church starts. If you anticipate asking for an appointed pastor for the new church, ultimately the district superintendent and bishop will assign the pastor, usually in consultation with your church's planting prep team and the conference staff person responsible for new church starts. If your church anticipates utilizing a lay pastor, an existing staff member or your appointed associate pastor, please clarify early in the process that your district superintendent is amenable to this plan.)

iv. Send a team of people to the partner church ministry track at the School of Congregational Development. It is highly recommended that the lead pastor of the partner church attend with this team. This is a five-day, multi-faceted, high-energy event, held annually in late July through early August. The location moves to a different US city each year.

v. Regional training opportunities. There are currently three annual regional events, sponsored by coalitions of regional United Methodist leaders, focused on skills, best practices and ministry stories from the world of new church development. These range from two to three days in length and are currently being held in Arkansas, Virginia and Washington State. For more information, go to path1.org/events

vi. Discern where God may be calling you to plant a new place for new people. Major providers of community demographic information include MissionInsite and Percept. Your annual conference may have a contract with one or both of these companies. Path 1 is in a partnership with MissionInsite and may be able to provide limited assistance to your annual conference in discerning demographic trends and opportunities in your community.

b. Planting prep team and conference staff person responsible for new church starts decide together the appropriate planting strategy, in light of the community context. This could involve your church as the primary planting partner – or it could involve a community of planting partners (multiple congregations and/or campus ministry groups or other entities). The district superintendent needs to be involved in this conversation.

c. Planting prep team, conference staff person responsible for new church starts and district superintendent follow annual conference process for making a recommendation to the cabinet. The recommendation will include funding strategies, strategic plan for the plant, church planter profile and compensation package.

d. Since almost all new churches are to some degree cross-cultural, the congregation needs to prepare itself in additional ways that include something like Pentecost Journey (a resource for preparing to plant a church that is different ethnically) or inviting a recent planting team (one that has planted a church with the type of people you envision) to spend time with your planting prep team.

4. **Forming the planting stakeholders group**
In the United Methodist Church, planting is never a solo act. This stakeholder's group ensures that the project is in conversation and United Methodist connection beyond your local church. The group gathered around the planting table should include:

a. Planter pastor (if he/she has been appointed or designated already)

b. Coach selected by the planter pastor and conference staff person responsible for new church starts to the project

c. Senior pastor of partner church

d. District superintendent

e. Conference staff person responsible for new church starts

f. Three to five lay members of the partner church(es). (Please try to avoid persons with control issues or an 'axe to grind.')

g. District committee representative (if there is a district new church committee)

h. Relevant cultural resource person(s) – someone who knows the population you are seeking to reach (could be a community leader or a person who is an expert in the particular demographic)

Note: A stakeholders group will be critical in cases where a large amount of funding is coming from beyond the partner church and the launch team of the new church. In cases where there is no funding beyond the local people involved in the plant, the stakeholders meetings will be less frequent, and can often be accomplished by conference calls.

The first meeting of the stakeholders ideally occurs three months prior to the commencement of the planter's appointment (typically by late winter/early spring). At the 18 month review (one and a half years after the planter begins on-site work) it is determined whether or not the group needs to continue its work.

 © 2018 Robert O. Crossman, www.UMNewChurch.org

This stakeholders group will function somewhat like a staff parish relations committee for the planter and family. Roles will include: vision-keepers for the project, keeping the project on track with the agreed-upon plan, establishing and monitoring benchmarks for project evaluation and interpreting back to the key stakeholders how things are going. This group may be the ones who write grant applications and renew such requests annually. This group should commit to monthly meetings for the first 3 months of the planter appointment and quarterly for the next year.

The planting pastor, senior pastor and coach continue to meet on a regular basis, even as the project management team begins to meet less frequently.

In most new church projects, the planting pastor and team seek to gather a launch team (which may involve gathering small groups and developing ministry teams) prior to the commencement of weekly worship services. As the attendance grows, the church will begin to develop a committed cadre of leaders and financial givers to sustain the church. The district superintendent, conference staff person responsible for new church starts and coach will work in consensus as to when the right time will be for the church to officially organize as a United Methodist congregation (with the exception of those projects where it is determined in advance that they will remain as connected campuses with the partner church.)

†††

Reprinted here by permission of Bener Agtarap granted on January 26, 2018.
Source: www.Path1.org

PATH1

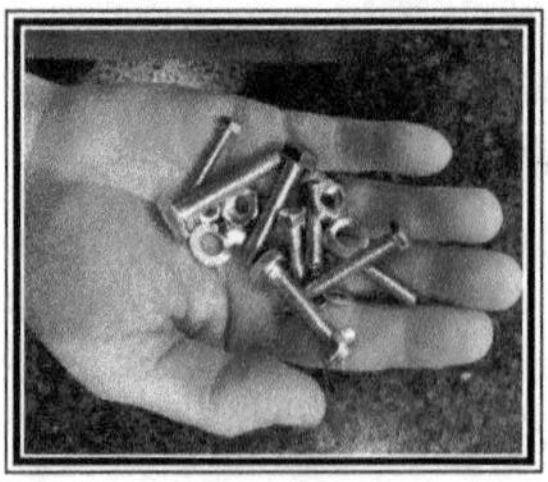

New Church Handbook
Nuts & Bolts for Planting New Churches In The Wesleyan Tradition

"Is My Church Ready to Give Birth or Sponsor a New Church?"

Are we ready to plant a new faith community?
Readiness to Plant 360

Go to: www.readiness360.info

Your Capacity in These 5 Areas Determines Whether Planting will be Fruitful or Frightful.

Leadership readiness
It is critical that leaders cast vision, walk the talk and have a clear understanding of how planting a new church is central to the church's mission and vision. Have key leaders of your church embraced the value of letting go of some leaders and/or some money in order to plant a new congregation or campus?

Vision/Mission alignment
The degree to which your church consistently prioritizes investment of its resources (time, talent, treasure) according to its Biblical vision and mission indicates readiness in this dimension. Do your plans, major initiatives and pruning of ministry stem clearly from a Biblical vision, mission and drive for fruitfulness?

Evangelistic aptitude
Good habits and skills for leading new persons into a relationship to God through Christ and strengthened by regular church participation is vital. How often does your church faithfully exercise its evangelism muscle?

Passionate spirituality
All of the great church planting movements worldwide are marked by a deep love for God and a surrender to what God is seeking to do through human beings. Does a spiritual fire burn within the hearts and souls of your church's key leaders?

 © 2018 Robert O. Crossman, www.UMNewChurch.org

Cultural openness

Churches that exhibit fortress behaviors or who spend excessive time mourning social change often have difficulty sharing life with new kinds of people. Does your congregation exhibit a capacity for embracing new cultures (e.g., socio-economic, racial/ethnic, generational, etc.)?

What are the benefits of using the Readiness 360?

Starting a new faith community is an entirely different undertaking than starting a new ministry. It requires unique assessment and preparation. Unfortunately we've seen well-intended "mother" congregations begin competing with or smothering "their" new congregation. And "church within a church" strategies have all too often yielded hostile behavior instead of radical hospitality and intentional, appropriate support.

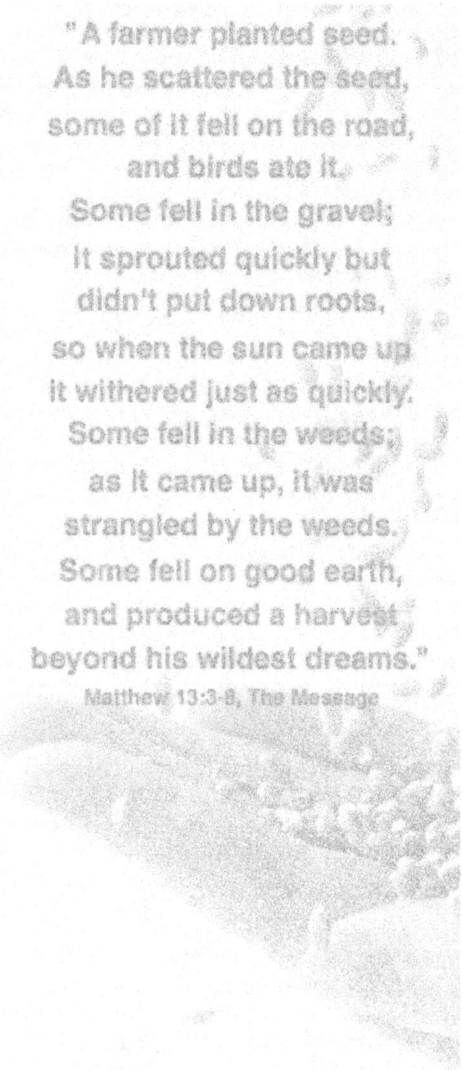
"A farmer planted seed.
As he scattered the seed,
some of it fell on the road,
and birds ate it.
Some fell in the gravel;
it sprouted quickly but
didn't put down roots,
so when the sun came up
it withered just as quickly.
Some fell in the weeds;
as it came up, it was
strangled by the weeds.
Some fell on good earth,
and produced a harvest
beyond his wildest dreams."
Matthew 13:3-8, The Message

The benefits of using the Readiness to Plant 360 as a part of your discernment and preparation process include:

Increased awareness of cultural and behavioral practices that improve planting success.

Understanding what your congregation needs to focus on in order to be better positioned to plant.

Shared language that helps with aligning your congregation around the vision of planting new places for new people.

The congregational 360 expands the ownership of the assessment and alignment process.

Low cost and high return on investment of time and money through the web-based survey and easy to understand report.

Readiness 360 Next Steps

1. Purchase your Readiness to Plant 360 (available at cost to United Methodist Congregations) via web or by phone: 1-866-721-0177. Customization is available at additional cost.

2. Upon payment you will receive:
   a. a link and to the online survey for distribution
   b. promotion templates to get the word out about the process

3. Distribute a link to 25-100 people who are very familiar with your congregation and who represent a variety of stakeholders in your planting process.

4. After designated members of your congregation take the Readiness 360, you will receive:
   a. a customized, detailed report
   b. links to suggested resources or next steps

5. Review and interpret results of the Readiness 360 using the detailed report as a basis.

Are we ready to plant a
new faith community?
Readiness to Plant 360

A Path 1 Readiness 360 Associate is available to review the results with you, provide ideas and resources for strengthening specific areas and customize your next steps for planting as needed.

Q: What is the Readiness to Plant 360?
A: A web-based tool used by key people in your congregation and potential stakeholders in the new plant to provide input about your church from their vantage point. The resulting report provides feedback to the leadership of your congregation about its capacity in each of the five critical areas for becoming a successful partner church. But this assessment is just one step in the process. Learn more...

Q: How many people can take the Readiness 360?
A: Up to 100 people are included in the price of the instrument and there is no limit on how many more may participate (extra charges apply). However it is

 © 2018 Robert O. Crossman, www.UMNewChurch.org

our experience that 25-30 invested, diverse leaders yield good results.

Q: We scored low in a particular dimension. Does that mean we should not consider planting?
A: NO! A low score simply indicates an area that may need to be strengthened. If you have discerned that God is calling you to plant a new congregation, use the feedback from the report to learn what you might work on to fully develop each of the five dimensions before planting.

Q: How is this tool different than Natural Church Development (NCD)?
A: NCD is a statistically validated tool for helping congregations assess and strengthen their weakest areas so they can grow in their overall ministry effectiveness. The Readiness to Plant 360 is the first tool of its kind designed to help a congregation specifically assess its readiness to plant a new church. As part of our testing phase we are seeking to partner with congregations who have: a desire to plant a new church, recently used the NCD process, and are willing to help us test this tool against their NCD results. Contact us if you are interested in participating in this aspect of the study.

Questions? Comments? Suggestions? Path 1 would love to hear from you!
Call us during business hours Monday thru Friday at 1-866-721-0177
or email us at service@readiness360.info

Reprinted here by permission of Bener Agtarap granted on January 26, 2018.
Source: www.Path1.org

PATH1

© 2018 Robert O. Crossman, www.UMNewChurch.org

VII. What Are Some of the Common Mistakes I Should Be Aware Of?

New Church Handbook
Nuts & Bolts for Planting New Churches In The Wesleyan Tradition

"What Are The Most Common Mistakes?"

One of the best reads for church planters and launch teams is a book by Jim Griffith and Bill Easum, "Ten Most Common Mistakes Made by New Church Starts" available from www.cokesbury.com Below is a brief summary of those ten mistakes from the book.

Mistake Number One: Neglecting the Great Commandment in Pursuit of the Great Commission

In their zeal to pursue the Great Commission, too many church planters ignore the One for whom they're planting the church – God. Church planting can be so all consuming that planters are seduced into thinking that they can put it before all else because they are doing God's will. But nothing should come before our love for God. Replacing the Greatest with the Great, makes "God Work" a mistress of the most damaging kind.

The Fix: Don't think your church plant will feed you spiritually. It won't. If you're more in love with your church plant than God, stop in your tracks and return to your first love. Do it now! Set aside everything and get focused once again on the Greatest Commandment. Don't replace the "Greatest" with the "great."

Mistake Number Two: Failing to Take Opposition Seriously

Make no mistake, opposition always occupies a church plant and failure to recognize it when it rears its ugly head is usually fatal. Opposition comes from several directions. It can come from within the church or those new people who want to recreate the church they just left or from the launch team who feel neglected as the church grows. Or it can come from the culture in the form of resistance by city officials. And the opposition can be spiritual because starting a new church is not a benign activity – it threatens all that is evil in this world.

The Fix: Carefully hand-pick an intercessory prayer team outside your circle and mission who have the spiritual gifts to hold you, and your family up before God and pray for your guidance, wisdom, and the grace to lead.

Mistake Number Three: A Love Affair With One's Fantasy Statement Blinds the Planter to the Mission Field

Many church planters are so in love with their dream church and their mission

 © 2018 Robert O. Crossman, www.UMNewChurch.org

statement that they are blinded to the realities of the mission field around them. Their formula for success doesn't match the needs of the mission field and they are unable to adapt. They are so in love with their fantasy church that they forget to examine their real life mission field. They never contextualized their strategy because their methods are sacrosanct.

The Fix: Fall more in love with the people in your area than with your fantasy church. Doing so will allow you to adapt your dream church to the context.

Mistake Number Four: Premature Launch

Going public with an insufficient "critical mass" of people quickly moves from the "euphoria" of birth to the nightmare of realizing "Sunday follows Sunday, follows Sunday, follows Sunday, follows Sunday." What started out so full of hope quickly shifts to crisis-mode, focusing on survival. The group now faces the daunting task of resisting the downward pull because the new church lacks sufficient infrastructure and development to survive on such limited resources.

The Fix: Don't launch publicly until you have gathered enough people and money that you are sure that the second Sunday after launching you still have enough critical mass to thrive on into the future.

Mistake Number Five: Evangelism Ceases After the Launch

Many planters act as if evangelism is a phase a church goes through on its way to maturity. Not so! Evangelism must be embedded as part of the DNA of the plant for it to be successful, much less biblical. Planters also become sucked into "doing church" and taking care of the members rather than focusing on the unchurched and being visible in the community.

The Fix: Pastor, it's all up to you. You must keep yourself and the people focused on the primary goal of any biblical church: reaching those who don't know Jesus. You must not allow maintaining the church and caring for the members to take the focus off of evangelism.

Mistake Number Six: No Plan for the Other Six Days of the Week

Churches that plateau at one hundred and fifty participants usually do so because they put too many eggs in the basket of Sunday worship. Everyone's attention is on Sunday morning worship and they fail to develop a process to connect people to each other and to God throughout the week. It's just, "Come to the show" with little thought given to the relational aspects of developing the spiritual community.

The Fix: Pastor, don't hoard all the ministry. Learn how to hand-off all the actual hands-on ministry to others. Remember, you are the equipper, not the doer. And as the church grows, when people begin to complain that they don't have access to you anymore, tell them to grow up or find another church!

Mistake Number Seven: Fear of Talking About Money Before It's Too Late

Too many planters start their campaign to plant a church by committing one of the "unpardonable sins" of church planting – failure to calculate the financial cost during the start-up phase of the work. This is one mistake from which most church plants cannot recover. They raise just enough money to "give birth" and create a splash on the scene. However, once the plant is launched, the lack of financial reserve and thinking through cash flow poses a great threat to most new plant's survival. Naively, both planter and supervisor reason that "once the church gets up and running, we can take an offering and begin to off set our expenses." But once the new church launches, costs escalate: facility rental, child-care, printing costs, meetings, advertising, and mailings. And if the launch is successful, the money issue gets worse – more people actually increase the cash drain, thus accelerating the demise of the church. Bottom line: Growth has to be fed.

The Fix: Pastor, you are the primary money raiser. If you can't do this, don't plant. Don't wait until you are out of money; constantly disciple people, and that means teaching people how to give. Never beg. Instead, send letters to everyone you know and ask them to support your vision. Then once you've set the example, encourage your launch team to not only tithe, but to ask their networks for support as well.

Mistake Number Eight: Failure of the Church to Act Its Age and Size

Trying to act as if the church is ten years old when its actually less than a year old usually kills a plant. Why? It tries to do too many things and provide ministries for everyone when it doesn't have the talent nor the funds to do quality ministry. On top of that, it burns out the staff who are run ragged. Aggressive planters will push their team into programs and plans that they aren't ready to undertake, and because the team deeply believes in their pastor's vision, they push ahead and clean up behind the planter. Great plans – but they were plans that didn't fit – yet. They need time to grow up into them.

The Fix: Decide on the essential ministries for your particular mission field and delay all others until they are necessary. Over time, you'll layer in new ministries and expand what you off er as you grow.

Mistake Number Nine: Formalizing Leadership Too Soon

The last thing a new plant needs is more leaders. What a planter needs in the beginning are people who will show up and do what you ask them to do. Formalizing leader ship too soon always hinders the growth of a plant. The organization of the plant needs time to fi nd its indigenous roots in the mission field and for future leaders to prove themselves on the battle field.

The Fix: Set up a task force, or advisory team, or an ad hoc group, but don't call it a board and turn them into a group from which you have to get permission

© 2018 Robert O. Crossman, www.UMNewChurch.org

to act. You don't need any form of a board in the early years. When you do go to a board, keep it as small as possible. The smaller the board, the larger the church has the chance of becoming. It's not unusual today for a church of ten to twenty thousand to have three people on their board. And don't charter or develop by-laws or a constitution until it is absolutely necessary.

Mistake Number Ten: Using the "Super Star" Model as the Paradigm for All Plants

"Cut and paste" plants seldom do well. Just because the Willow Creek model worked in South Barrington doesn't mean you can photocopy it in Athens, Georgia. Too many planters go to a conference in a mega church and say to themselves *"This is the kind of church I want to plant."* The problem is that type of church might not fit the demographics of the city in which the planter is going to start the new church. The context needs to dictate the model.

The Fix: Never attempt to replicate what some other church is doing. Instead, plant your church out of your personal reflection, fine tuned by mentors and trainers, and adapted to the people in the mission field.

Well, these are the top ten most common mistakes made by church planters and a brief word on how to fix the mistake. Of course the book goes into far more detail. So, if you find yourself making one or more of these mistakes and want to get out of the mess you're in, grab a copy of our book *"Ten Most Common Mistakes Made by Church Starts"* and you will find ways to correct your mistake. Good planting.

NOTE: This article reflects the personal opinions of its author and does not necessarily reflect an official position of Discipleship Ministries or Path 1.

Copies of the book are available from www.cokesbury.com or your favorite book retailer.

New Church Handbook
Nuts & Bolts for Planting New Churches In The Wesleyan Tradition

"11 Ways to Avoid Burnout: Caring for Self"

by Bob Crossman

including portions of Craig Miller's "Spiritual Inventory"

I entered the ministry in May of 1973. I left the ministry fourteen years later on December 31, 1987.

I decided to be a lay person and move to Conway, Arkansas. I left the ministry for the health of my family and my marriage. We took our life savings and started a business. The business prospered and grew to have six employees. That business is still open, and my oldest son owns and operates the business now.

In 1990, I re-entered the ministry, and accepted a part time appointment. In my re-entry to the ministry, I had **new** priorities that centered on having a healthy marriage and healthy family with my two sons.

Is there stress in pastoral ministry?

Oh yes.

Sometimes we are appointed to a ministry setting that isn't a natural fit.

- The laity's expectations are not a natural fit to our preferred leadership style.
- Our kids may not like the school system.
- Our spouse may not like the community (or the people in the church).

Sometimes we wonder...

Will anyone show up on Sunday?

Will Christ reach any new people through me?

Some days as a pastor start out great, but then sometimes they don't end that way.

There are many kinds of stress, including good-stress and dis-stress, but they both have the same effect on our bodies.

Good Stress might include: getting married, pregnancy, new children in the family, getting a new job, major increase in salary, buying a home, outstanding personal achievement, change in personal residence, or a vacation.

Bad Stress might include: death of a spouse, divorce, marital separation, death of a close family member or friend, personal injury, illness, illness in the family,

 © 2018 Robert O. Crossman, www.UMNewChurch.org

loss of a job, new house or car payments, son or daughter moves away from home, trouble with the in-laws, financial trouble, or major sin.

Consequences Stress might include: perception level decreases, loss of perceived options resulting in bad decisions, regression to infantile behavior, getting locked in destructive patterns of behavior, acting in ways that are counter to 'who we are,' fatigue, physical illness, addictive behaviors or abusive behaviors.

Is there **hope**?

Oh, yes!

How do you take care of your self, your family, and your congregation when you are under so much stress?

As a pastor, I discovered several ways to: care for my self, care for my family, and care for my congregation. Perhaps one of two of these might help you.

First, Time Management

I decided that since I am paid full time I must work at least 40 productive hours a week. Watching ESPN with a Bible in my lap did not count toward my forty hours.

I decided that the physical and emotional stress of working more than 60 hours a week was detrimental to my health, my ministry, and to my family.

I decided that it was important for my health to take four weeks of vacation every year and in addition, once or twice a month to have an excellent guest preacher in the pulpit.

I decided to only check my email at 11 am and again at 4 pm. I was going to set priorities, do first things first, and not let email distract me.

I would strongly recommend not to check your email or smart phone first thing in the morning.

Better yet, turn your cell phone off until 11am.

For the same reasons, don't answer your phone every time it rings... let it go to voice mail.

I decided that if I am in the middle of a creative time of sermon preparation, not to answer my cell phone. I found it was hard to recreate that creative moment.

Train your assistant to say, *"Rev. Crossman is not able to take any calls at this time. Would you like him to call you back at 11 am?"*

It is amazing how many people decide it really wasn't important after all and they don't leave a message on your cell phone or with your assistant.

If they don't leave a voice mail, don't call them back.

Evenings are for family time and time to slow down for the evening's rest. When the cell phone rings at 9 pm consider letting it go to voice mail instead of instantly answering. Your family needs your attention this evening more than the church member who calls you at home to bend your ear for an hour. Check your voice mail late in the evenings, make a habit of not returning those calls until 10 am in the morning unless it is a true emergency.

The same applies to social media and text messages.

I also decided not to sit at the hospital for 8 hours with the Presbyterian family who lived next door to one of my members.

I engaged a retired woman in the church to be my volunteer prayer list coordinator and hospital visitor. I would be at the hospital at 6 am for the heart surgery, but she came at 8am and I passed the responsibility to her.

When my new church grew to 375 in attendance on Sunday I hired a retired elder in the congregation, Rev. Robert Winter, for the salary of $50 for 5 hours, and later $100 for 10 hours a week. In today's dollars you should double or triple those amounts.

Second, Exercise and Weight Control

On vacation one year, I visited a new church on Sunday morning. When the preacher walked out, my first thought was: he is fat.

My second thought was: he is the same size as me.

I decided that being 60 pounds overweight affected my health and the perception of worship visitors. I started working on exercise and weight control. I went from 225 to 175 pounds and kept it off while I was a new church pastor.

I'm still working on this...

Third, Have a Hobby

I decided I needed some kind of distraction so that I wasn't thinking about work 24/7. Actually my wife made that decision. Several mornings she found that I had not come to bed, but had instead fallen asleep with my face pressed into the keyboard of my laptop. Eventually she said, *"You have to have a hobby. You can't work seven days a week."*

I tried golf with my father in law.

I tried fishing and woodworking with my dad.

I ended up resurrecting my old postage stamp collection as a distraction. I found a great distraction in organizing a stamp album and moving those little pieces of paper around for an hour or two.

 © 2018 Robert O. Crossman, www.UMNewChurch.org

Fourth, Develop New Friends

In the first years of planting a new church, my 'old' friends didn't enjoy being around me.

They would ask, *"How's it going?"* I would answer, *"Amazing. I baptized an 89 year old yesterday, two households joined the church, and six new households were first time guests."*

That wasn't what they wanted to hear. Instead, they wanted to play the old games of *'ain't it awful', 'the music minister is crazy,'* and *'I never know where youth minister is.'*

Some of my clergy friends openly wondered if I was "Methodist enough" or that I was preaching "cheap grace." One of my clergy friends said, *"Bob, I'm concerned about you. Methodist just don't witness that many professions of faith, baptisms, or worship attendance worship growth."*

I had to develop a new group of friends who were also experiencing great growth in their ministry and who celebrated the work of the Spirit in my new church.

Fifth, My Spiritual Life

I decided that I could not keep 'giving the Spirit away' without intentionally receiving the Spirit in new and renewing ways. I found a couple of 'preachers' out of state, and I faithfully listened to their sermons each week. They became my 'preachers' and their CDs were playing in my car constantly.

Occasionally, I would sit on the back row at the Pentecostal Church... and just soak in the Spirit.

When my new church grew enough to have a staff, on Wednesday mornings I invited others *(district superintendent, conference staff, or colleagues in the ministry)* to hold staff worship, so that as a staff we could all sit together and worship without distraction.

Sixth: Integrity

I was blessed to have my parents join and faithfully attend my new church. Occasionally on Mondays my dad would stop by for coffee. He would ask, *"Do you really believe what you said yesterday? I just don't see that in the way you spend your time."*

He was right, and I deeply appreciated that he was honest enough to call my hand.

Some of my stress in ministry had to do with a personal lack of integrity - a lack of harmony between what I believed, what I preached, and the way I lived.

I wondered if people could tell I wasn't always living on Monday what I had preached on Sunday? And so it was back to the basics for me.

What would my personal spiritual disciplines be? What spiritual disciplines would I expect of new members, and of the leaders in the new church?

I found and adapted Craig Miller's "Spiritual Inventory" and began to us it personally and in my relationship with the lay leadership of my congregation.

Spiritual Life of the Leader

As a new church pastor you are creating the normative expectations for spiritual growth in your congregation. Many new church pastors set aside one day a week for prayer, reflection, and visioning. Later, when you move to weekly worship, this becomes a day for prayer and sermon preparation. Your prayer life, physical health, artistic pursuits, and relationships have a direct influence on the spiritual life of your leaders. Build in the time and experiences that sustains you and connects you to God and others.

What is **your** plan for **your** personal continued spiritual growth and development?

- How do you connect with God?
  __ Day apart
  __ Family prayer
  __ Daily devotion
  __ Worship with other congregations
  __ Meeting with a prayer partner or coach
  __ Other: ____________________

- How are you connecting with others?
  __ Time alone with spouse or friend
  __ Family night/day
  __ Focused time with your children
  __ Regular connection with extended family
  __ Time with friends outside of church
  __ Other: ____________________

- What arts feed your soul?
  __ Playing musical instrument
  __ Dance
  __ Other: ____________________
  __ Writing
  __ Singing
  __ Drawing

- How are you taking care of your body?
  __ Walking/running
  __ Healthy diet
  __ Active in a sport: ____________
  __ Aerobics
  __Other: ________________

 © 2018 Robert O. Crossman, www.UMNewChurch.org

- Reflect on John Wesley's "Means of Grace" (¶72, *The Book of Discipline*)
  ___ The public worship of God
  ___ The ministry of the Word, *read or expounded*
  ___ The Lord's Supper
  ___ Family prayer and private prayer
  ___ Searching the Scriptures
  ___ Fasting or abstinence
  ___ Christian conferencing

Based on the means of grace listed above, complete the Spiritual Leader Checklist below, giving yourself 10 points for each 'yes' answer.

___ 1. I say grace before each meal.

___ 2. I set aside a time to pray each day.

___ 3. At least once a week, I pray out loud with another person (a family member, a friend, a person at work or church).

___ 4. I read at least one verse of Scripture daily.

___ 5. I attend worship at our church at least three times a month.

___ 6. At least twice a month I meet with a group of people to pray, reflect on Scripture, and build one another up (small group, Sunday school class, prayer group, etc.).

___ 7. I take Communion at least once a month.

___ 8. At least once a month I give of myself to others. (I volunteer at a homeless shelter or soup kitchen, visit in a nursing home, tutor a child, visit a prisoner, mow a neighbor's lawn, etc.).

___ 9 I fast once a week (I give up food for a period of time or do a media fast and go without electronic media – TV, radio, etc. – for a day.)

___ 10. As part of every meeting at church, we spend 10-15 minutes praying together and reflecting on a Scripture passage.

___ TOTAL POINTS - *What does this 'score' say about you and about the type of team you need to create to work with you?*

Spiritual Life of the Launch Team

Central to the life of any congregation is its leadership. What happens in the launch team affects the life of the whole congregation. *"The congregation will look like your launch team."*

The launch team is made up of those leaders who are responsible for the spiritual life of others in your congregation. These include small group leaders, elected members of boards and committees, the staff, and the music ministry team.

1. What spiritual disciplines will your launch team be expected to practice?
   __ Weekly worship
   __ Daily Bible reading
   __ Daily Prayer
   __ Service to others: give examples ________
   __ Fasting or abstinence
   __ Family Prayer
   __ Tithing, financial gifts growing to the Biblical minimum of the 10% tithe
   __ Witnessing, inviting (friends, relatives, recreational associates, work associates, neighbors) to worship
   __ Receive the Lord's Supper
      __weekly
      __monthly
      ___Other: ________

2. Reflect on the degree to which you personally practice these spiritual disciplines (Holy Habits) that you expect your launch team to practice?

3. What does this say about your ability to inspire/lead your launch team to practice these spiritual disciplines?

What spiritual disciplines will you expect of yourself,

your launch team,

and your congregation?

For me, the integrity issue meant getting back to John Wesley's basics about "Holy Living" journeying toward sanctification, and the means of grace.

How could I with integrity lead my congregation through the Committed to Christ program, inviting them to be engaged in the journey toward sanctification and holy living – if I am not engaged in that journey.

So for me it began with prayers, presence, gifts, service and witness.

Prayer -

I spent time alone with the Lord. I would 'Pray over the Chairs' - following Adam Hamilton's pattern.

I turned off the talk radio and started praying while driving.

 © 2018 Robert O. Crossman, www.UMNewChurch.org

With integrity, how could I preach
on the importance of prayer, when I rarely prayed?

I stopped lying to my members. For years, at the door, when asked members asked me to remember something in my prayers - I lied. I said, *"Yes, I will."* But the truth is that thirty seconds later, after shaking a dozen more hands, I could no longer remember the prayer request.

So, I started keeping 3x5 cards in my shirt pocket. When someone asked me to pray, I immediately handed them a 3x5 card and said, *"If you write it down and put back in my pocket I will remember to pray for you."* After a month or so, the congregation caught on and they started sticking prayer request in my pocket.

To keep up with the requests, I kept the stack of 3 x 5 cards on my desk, and kept Post It Note summaries in my car and study at home. Eventually this grew into a sheet of prayer requests, and I invited the prayer warriors in the congregation to join me in the non-confidential prayer requests.

Presence -

I decided to bring my heart to worship, and not to just lead worship. I looked for mid week services to attend. On vacation I decided not miss worship.

With integrity, how could I preach
on the importance of worship attendance, if I only attended when
I got paid to be there?

Gifts -

Marcia and I began to 'turn our wanter down' and to step up toward 10% tithing year by year.

We discovered the joy of tithing.

During the church's building campaign, we discovered the joy of double and triple tithing.

Service -

I began to volunteer. I found myself weeding the flower bed, edging the church lawn, cleaning gravel out of the curb, cooking breakfast for the men's group, or putting out door hangers.

With integrity, how could I preach on the importance serving,
if I only served or volunteered when I got paid to be there?

© 2018 Robert O. Crossman, www.UMNewChurch.org

It's an integrity thing. Integrity is seeking a harmony between what I believe, what I said, and what I did.

Seventh: I clung to my spouse

I decided to cling to my spouse and not to get a divorce. I didn't want to give birth to a new church and loose my family in the process.

We took walks together.

We watched old movies,

We went on trips.

We shared our private feelings about the church with each other: hurts, fears, hopes, and dreams.

I decided to cling to my boys.

I made appointments with my sons, and I kept them.

I began to enjoy my boys' ball games.

I spent time with my sons on Boy Scout camp outs and took trips just with them.

I spent time doing things **they** wanted to do: canoeing, rappelling, and camping.

And, by the way, I did NOT loose my family in church planting a new church. It was a blessing to see my sons and their families in church on Sunday and see the ways they have found to serve through the church I was a part of planting.

Eighth: ministry plan

I clarified by own ministry plan.

I began the annual habit of preparing a formal Ministry Plan containing my vision, mission, core belief, goals, and objectives.

I decided that having a personal Ministry Plan, or a personal Vision Statement was vital, but **over rated**!

It was more important that I had **behaviors** that match.

It's an **integrity** thing, a harmony between what I believed, what I preached, the way I lived, and the way I worked.

Ninth: continuing education

I began to attend continuing education events three or four times a year, for three to five days each. I did this at my own expense because my church did not have the funds to pay for it.

I went on these continuing education trips so that I could offer my best to the

 © 2018 Robert O. Crossman, www.UMNewChurch.org

Lord; to discover the potential potholes I might avoid in the coming year; and to get away from the new church and retool and regain my perspective on the task ahead of me.

Tenth: lay leadership

As part of self-care:

- I admitted that I did not know everything.
- I admitted that I could not do everything.
- I admitted that IF my church was going to grow to the next level, I needed to share the leadership and train laity to step up.
- I intentionally shared ministry responsibilities with laity so that they could also experience the joy of serving and getting 'blisters for Jesus.'

If your new church is 18 months old and you are still unloading the trailer, making the coffee, and singing in the praise band
- you really need to stop -
and start immediately allowing laity to be in service and ministry.

I also began hiring part-time staff for 10 hours per week each.

Eleventh: the discipleship system

During the first few years of planting the new church, I had been focused on just increasing attendance.

It was time to clarify exactly what I understood the Lord expected from those who sought to follow: prayers, presence, gifts, service, witness and reading the Bible.

I developed an annual discipleship education emphasis called, ***Committed to Christ: Six Steps to a Generous Life***.

When the United Methodist Publishing House learned about my program from Clif Christopher, Abingdon Press decided to publish the program I designed. The kit, ***Committed to Christ: Six Steps to a Generous Life*** is available from www.cokesbury.com

I also discovered...

If a pastor works closely with a coach;

If the pastor and spouse spend time on their knees in prayer;

If the pastor practices some of these ways to care for self, family and congregation that I have just outlined; then the new church planter can discover that Jesus comes - even in the midst of storms to surround us with His love.

The year that my wife and I lost three parents to cancer within a ten month period, Jesus did come through the members of that new congregation.

I also discovered that we can not only

survive but become stronger

and victorious in the midst of planting.

Reflection:

- Write down three things you are going to do beginning this week to take care of YOURSELF.

  1. ____________________

  ____

  2. ____________________

  ____

  3. ____________________

  ____

- Write down three things you are going to do beginning this week to take care of YOUR FAMILY.

  1. ____________________

  ____

  2. ____________________

  ____

  3. ____________________

  ____

 © 2018 Robert O. Crossman, www.UMNewChurch.org

- Write down three things you are going to do beginning this week to take care of YOUR CONGREGATION.

1. ____

____

2.____

____

3. ____

____

†††

NOTE: This article reflects the personal opinions of the author and does not necessarily reflect an official position of Discipleship Ministries or Path 1.

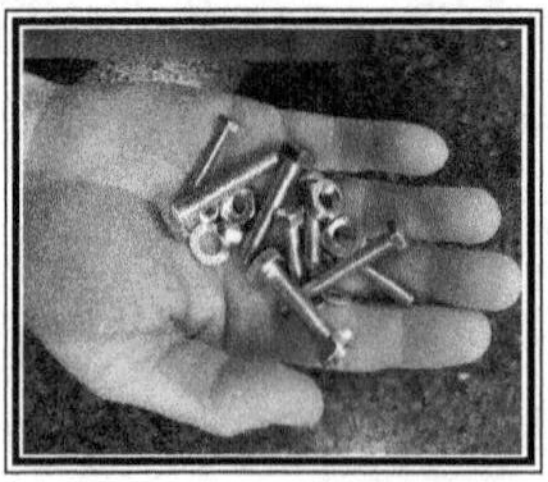

New Church Handbook
Nuts & Bolts for Planting New Churches In The Wesleyan Tradition

"What Should You Name Your New Church?"

Each annual conference has a different policy on this subject.

I have a suggestion. The new church should be named by the planting pastor (in cooperation with the district superintendent and conference new church staff person) before even moving to the new community. This timing avoids potential conflict over name selection among members of the future launch team, and helps to insure that the name will be one that reflects the new ministry.

What will be the name of your new church?

The "right" name you choose for your new church will not insure success, but the "wrong" name could prove to be detrimental to the future viability of the church.

Some new churches have names that reflect a biblical character or theme (St. Paul UMC, Living Water UMC, Cornerstone UMC, etc.). Great idea! However, a Biblical name, such as "Emmaus Road UMC" is a great Biblical name - but potential visitors will be looking for you to be located on Emmaus Road. A name such as "Transfiguration UMC" is a great insider word among Christians, but the word "transfiguration" has no meaning whatsoever to your mission field.

Other new churches have names from our Wesleyan heritage (Wesley UMC, Asbury UMC, Aldersgate UMC etc.). However, a Methodist name such as, "Discipline UMC" might give the wrong impression. A name such as "Quadrilateral UMC"or "Foundery UMC" are both great insider words among Methodist, but they have no meaning whatsoever to your mission field.

While still other pastors choose to name the new church after the city or town its located in. Naming your new church after the town may be a good idea. Such a name implies credibility, legitimacy, and stability. Or, maybe not. If your new church is

© 2018 Robert O. Crossman, www.UMNewChurch.org

in any of the following towns, you might want to consider a different name for your church: Bucksnort, Tennessee; Peculiar, Missouri; Hell, Michigan; Possum Grape, Goobertown, Toad Suck or Hooker, Arkansas.

I wonder, what would be a winsome name for your new church?

Before settling on a name, compare your list to the other church names in your mission field, and check the availability of potential domain names.

Thinking of naming your new church: Bucksnort UMC, Hooker UMC, or Possum Grape UMC ?
Think twice!

NOTE: This article reflects the personal opinions of its author and does not necessarily reflect an official position of Discipleship Ministries or Path 1.

 © 2018 Robert O. Crossman, www.UMNewChurch.org

VIII. What Do I Need to Know Before Selecting a Rental Site, Buying Land or Construction?

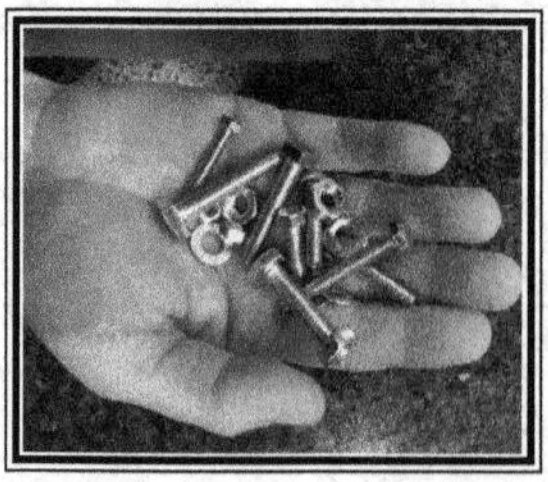

New Church Handbook
Nuts & Bolts for Planting New Churches In The Wesleyan Tradition

"Evaluating a Potential Site"

by Bob Crossman

It is very wise, and in most annual conferences REQUIRED, to have your district or conference chancellor (attorney) examine any lease or purchase agreement before you sign anything.

Also, your district superintendent and district board of church location and building will have to approve your new location before you sign anything.

Daniel Im and Todd Adkins suggest that when looking for a initial site to rent or lease, to first look for a place that is typically "dark" during the time and day you are planning to need the space. Spaces that are typically dark on Sunday mornings include performing arts venues, bars, larger nightclubs, cafes, schools, or colleges. *(www.newchurches.com, Podcast #187)*

Be cautious about thinking *"If I could just get ____, everything would be great, and all this pressure would stop."* Before you convince yourself that you must relocate or must purchase a building, it may be time, as Bishop Richard Wilkie would say, *"to reach out and grab your 'wanter' and turn it down.'* The fantasy or dream of having something we don't have can often skew our perspective and priorities. Moving to a different facility brings increased financial pressure, along with pressure from laity who now expect the church to become more like their former church, and offer the same programs they were used to.

When selecting a site, be careful about the personality of the new site. Does the new location have the same "vibe," ethos, personality, or appeal of your current location? How will the new location influence the culture of our existing congregation? Will the new location be attractive and winsome to the target audience you feel called to reach? What ways, in decorations or layout, can you reflect the positive attributes of your old location in this new site? What are the capacity limits of the local fire code for this particular room?

Before purchasing a building, be sure and have a competent professional building inspector check out the roof, heat/air systems, sewer system, termites, foundation, electrical system, and structure.

Before signing a long term lease, be sure and determine what your actual cost will be for monthly lease payment, renter's insurance, utilities, and any triple-net fees *(it is common for landlords to require lease holders to pay a percentage of the land-*

© 2018 Robert O. Crossman, www.UMNewChurch.org

lords property taxes, utility fees for common spaces and parking lighting, marketing for the shopping center, and maintenance for common areas). Also, be sure you have solid prices for any improvements, furniture, flooring, lighting and fixtures you will need to obtain.

You also want to relocate within your mission field, with demographics that match your target audience, with room to grow, great off-street parking in the front, and good traffic flow into and out of the parking lot and access on Sunday morning.

Be sure and study the facilities on Sunday morning during the actual time you intend to use it. A space may look different to you on Tuesday after work than on Sunday morning. What businesses will be your neighbors? Are they open and using your parking spaces on Sunday morning?

Finally, after all of the inspections, demographics, and finances appear to be in order, don't forget to kneel in prayer at the site of your future worship space. Do you sense that this is Holy Ground?

A great score sheet follows. Also see the article *"Site Location"* by John Southwick.

SITE SELECTION WORKSHEET

Source: Growing New Churches, Discipleship Resources
by Stephen Compton

Under each heading, select which characterization best describes the site being evaluated. Write in the point value indicated. Write in only one point value selection for each heading. Total all values at the end of the evaluation.

SITE SHAPE

A. Site is roughly square or rectangular (without being too narrow) in shape. _____ +10

B. Site is rectangular or oddly shaped but is of adequate size to accommodate all necessary buildings, parking, and recreational spaces. _____ +5

C. Site shape significantly reduces the available construction area and usefulness of site. _____ 0

SITE LOCATION

A. Site is situated on a major thoroughfare. _____ +10

B. Site is situated on an interior neighborhood street. _____ +5

C. Site is located on a dead-end street, cul-de-sac, or one-way street. _____ 0

SITE ACCESSIBILITY

A. Site has (can have) at least two driveways, each allowing ingress and egress to adequate space for parking, or site has adequate off-site parking (within two short blocks). _____ +10

B. Site has one two-way driveway or two driveways, each allowing for one-way traffic only. _____ +5

C. On-site and off-site parking is (will be) severely limited. _____ 0

SITE USABILITY

A. Site is unencumbered by major barriers to construction and use, such as flood plain surfaces, steep slopes, power lines, protective covenants, deed restrictions, etc. _____ +10

B. Site is somewhat encumbered by barriers or restrictions. _____ +5

C. Site is greatly encumbered by barriers or restrictions. _____ 0

SITE TRAVEL EXPOSURE

A. Site is located along a major corridor of travel that serves as the typical travel pathway for shopping, recreation, and work-related automobile traffic, and is situated more nearly toward the end of that pathway (near the travelers' destinations) than toward its beginning. _____ +10

B. Site is located more nearly toward the middle of the travel pathway. _____ +5

C. Site is located near or beyond the beginning of the pathway (the residential neighborhoods generating the traffic along the travel pathway). _____ 0

SITE SIZE

A. Site has adequate acreage to accommodate present and projected future needs for worship, fellowship, education, recreation and parking uses. _____ +10

B. Site is moderately restricted in size to accommodate present and future needs. _____ +5

C. Site is significantly limited in size and will require ardent attention and multiple use to accommodate present and future growth. _____ 0

SITE MISSIONAL ACTIVITY

A. Site characteristics (size, location, cost, accessibility, etc.) are excellently

© 2018 Robert O. Crossman, www.UMNewChurch.org

matched to the missional objectives of the congregation and to its resources. _____ +10

B. Site is somewhat well-matched to do the missional objectives of the congregation. _____ +5

C. Site is not well-matched to the missional objectives and the resources of the congregation. _____ 0

SITE COST

A. Site cost is significantly below market value or site is presently owned, without debt, and occupied by existing congregation. _____ +10

B. Site cost is at or slightly above market value. _____ +5

C. Site cost is significantly above market value. _____ 0

SITE DEVELOPMENT

A. Site development cost (grading, assessments, utilities, etc.) is minimal. _____ +10

B. Site development cost is moderately high. _____ +5

C. Site development cost is excessive. _____ 0

SITE NEIGHBORHOOD

A. Current or proposed land use of adjacent properties is not detrimental to the development of the mission of the congregation and may actually be complimentary to its mission. _____ +10

B. Current or proposed land use of adjacent properties is somewhat detrimental to the development of the mission of the congregation._____ +5

C. Current or proposed land use of adjacent properties is likely to be detrimental to the development of the mission of the church _____ 0

TOTAL _______________

GOOD SITE 75 -100 Points
MARGINAL SITE 50 - 70 Points
UNACCEPTABLE SITE 0 - 45 Points

This material by Stephen C. Compton is used by permission granted on October 14, 2017.

†††

NOTE: These article reflects the personal opinions of its author and does not necessarily reflect an official position of Discipleship Ministries or Path 1.

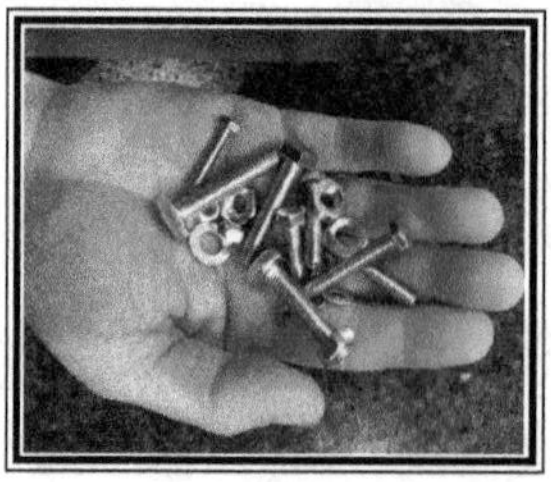

New Church Handbook
Nuts & Bolts for Planting New Churches In The Wesleyan Tradition

"Site / Location"

by John H. Southwick

Commercial real estate site and location consultants are highly skilled in their analysis of business locations for retail stores and restaurants. Church leaders considering new church starts, relocations, or even evaluating existing locations can benefit from the knowledge, experience, and systematic approaches used by the real estate professionals.

A valuable first step is to learn to distinguish between site and location. These terms are often used loosely and interchangeably although they have distinct meaning and applications. Site has to do with the size and shape of the property, the parking, the layout of the building(s) on the property, accessibility from the street, visibility to passersby, and attractiveness of the property. In essence the site is the property itself and its characteristics. Location, on the other hand, has everything to do with where the site is. Location includes market characteristics, population density, demographics, proximity to existing and prospective customers, position relative to competition, proximity to driving patterns, type of neighborhood, zoning, and general geography. A combination of a great site and great location are obviously a real boon to a retail establishment or restaurant, and to churches as well.

Business real estate professionals qualify a location through a number of grids. The first is to determine if the location fits the requirements as a trade area for the particular business. Are there enough of people who will buy the product or service in the area? This means more than just raw numbers, but seeks specific types of people who are known to use the product or service. Demographics are key here, including lifestyle analysis. Additionally, what sort of major streets and highways are present and how well connected is this area to the larger trade area? Is retail synergy possible? In other words are there businesses which complement their business which could help as a magnet for customers? A competitive assessment will be run. What competitors are near and throughout the trade area? What is the closest sister location? Do any competitors intercept customers before they get to the potential site? If we don't go here, who will?

Multiple sources of information are pursued. Credible demographic and lifestyle sources are used. School personnel are queried about their building plans, the anticipated growth in the area, and racial/ethnic makeup of the student body. Post

 © 2018 Robert O. Crossman, www.UMNewChurch.org

offices can often provide information about the opening of new delivery routes. Civic authorities can share any new developments in the works, along with annexations, and building moratoriums. Traffic engineering projects being considered can have a significant impact on an area.

Of course, seeking a location for a new church or for relocation of an existing one would require tweaking these qualifiers. Churches don't usually evaluate a population by looking for folks like the present church goers, but seek to find those people God is calling them to reach. "Competition" is not so much a factor for churches. Churches are usually distinct in their ministry styles, beliefs, and polities between denominations and do not locate near healthy existing churches (emphasis on healthy: churches not interested in reaching new people are not a factor) of the same denomination unless the new ministry will be notably different. Of course, if an area is saturated with healthy churches, this deserves consideration. Traffic patterns, growth, attractiveness, and/or ministry needs do play into the decision.

Once a desirable location has been determined, the next choice is the site. If no site can be found, it matters little how otherwise fabulous the location may be. When business real estate pros are looking at sites, the following perspectives are considered. Fieldwork is essential. Prospective sites are diagramed. Emotional attachment to a site is to be avoided. Advance research with maps, aerials, and demographics is very helpful. The site visit involves diagramming it, photographing it, driving the neighborhood, and taking detailed field notes. Some even use prepared survey forms to record the needed information. The site is viewed from a retail perspective, i.e., does it fit the mental picture of the prototype? Does it fit the specifications for parking and building floor space? What is the quality of the facility, if there is already a structure being considered? What is the quality of the potential site?

Most of the retail/restaurant evaluation tools work well for new church or relocation site consideration as well. Of course a huge factor is the cost. The perfect site may be simply unaffordable. One factor the business folks don't usually employ is prayer. Stories abound about churches having prayer vigils on prospective sites, as well as serious prayer off site, with the result of remarkable price breaks being offered. Sometimes land is even donated. By all means include God in the process.

The subject of new locations and sites realistically only impacts a relatively few United Methodist Churches each year. Hopefully this will increase in coming years. The denominational goal is to start 600 new churches in the next quadrennium. In addition to the new starts, some churches will relocate, so they will also deal with location and site. Another group considering new locations and sites are those churches looking to branch into multi-site ministries. However, most of our 32,000+ existing churches are not likely to relocate in any way. Even so applying some of the same evaluation may be useful in their existing locations and sites. A good look at the location may suggest some adjustment in ministry emphasis and style. Likewise a keen look at the site may suggest some alterations to make it more functional and appealing to those in the community.

Professional business real estate consultants place great value on site and location, but concede that some businesses are so strong, you can put them anywhere and people will do whatever it takes to find them and go there. Trader Joe's is a prime example. The same is true of churches. While we need to be very conscious of location and site, especially in new and relocating ministries, bringing new life and vitality to the ministries of existing churches can help them flourish, regardless of location and site.

This article by John Southwick first appeared in 2005, published by The Office of Research – Global Ministries UMC.

Reprinted here with permission of the author, granted on November 14, 2017.
pastorjohnsouthwick@centurylink.net

†††

NOTE: These article reflects the personal opinions of its author and does not necessarily reflect an official position of Discipleship Ministries or Path 1.

© 2018 Robert O. Crossman, www.UMNewChurch.org

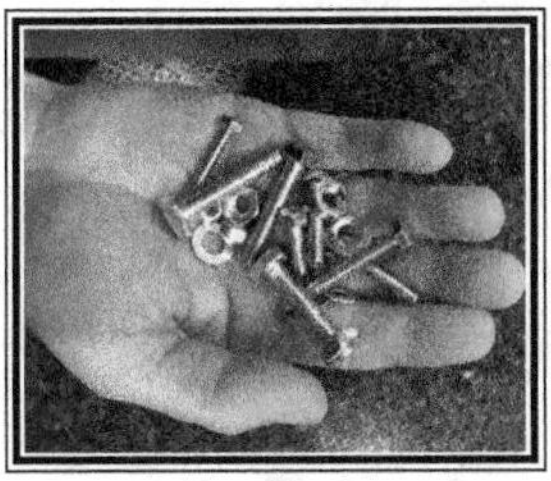

New Church Handbook
Nuts & Bolts for Planting New Churches In The Wesleyan Tradition

"When Do I Select a Building Committee?"

by Bob Crossman

- Years ago all of our churches were anxious and eager to appoint a building committee and break ground.

We were once operating
on the theory:
if you build it... they will come.

There are very few, if any, mission fields where that theory still works.

- If you are the kind of pastor who loves church construction projects... you've already starting sketching out the floor plan of your future phase one construction... and you have collected photographs of "the look" you have in mind for the exterior... **You just might be putting your energy in the wrong place!**

- If you are a new church pastor, or contemplating becoming one, your primary focus needs to be on people not bricks. You should be reaching new people, developing your launch team, multiplying the size of your launch team, developing ministry work groups, designing and forming a discipleship system, securing a site for launch worship, designing and holding taste-and-see events, designing and holding preview worship. Do not spend your creative energy planning and daydreaming about 'bricks and mortar." This advice has something to do with "keeping first things first" and "keeping the main thing the main thing."

***Your primary focus
needs to be on people not bricks.***

- In response to the rapidly escalating cost of land and construction across the country, it may be time to recover a piece of our Methodist heritage following the example of the church planting pastor in Jonesboro, Arkansas:

> In 1861, the first Protestant sermon was preached in Jonesborough *(later shortened to Jonesboro)* when Methodist circuit rider Rev. W.R. Foster *(appointed to the Gainesville Circuit)* held the first worship service in Fergus Snoddy's livery stable. In the fall of 1861, Rev. Foster returned to Jonesboro

and held a revival in the courthouse, witnessing twenty-four conversions. Through the following twenty-two years, Methodist worship services *(and Sunday School)* were held first at Snoddy's Livery Stables, then moved to the Craighead County Courthouse, in the summer months meeting in the open air of Courthouse Square, and were later welcomed to share the facilities of the Bethany Baptist Church in town. The congregation waited twenty-two years *(until November 10, 1883)* to purchase land on the corner of Main and Matthews Street. Actual construction on the wood frame structure Methodist building started in 1884, and on Easter Sunday of 1889, the building was dedicated by Bishop Charles B. Galloway.

- In the following article by Bill Easum and several related articles that follow from Circuit Rider, you may come to discover an interesting thought - **YOU DON'T NEED A BUILDING TO BE A CHURCH.** If the Lord provides you wonderful rental space that meets your ministry needs don't be in a hurry to trade that rental space for $1,000,000 debt.

†††

The Nomadic Church
Growing Your Congregation Without Owning the Building
by Bill Easum and Pete Theodore

A remarkable thing began happening in the final years of the twentieth century. God began directing more and more pastors to bypass the traditional method of planting churches and instead start "Nomadic Churches"—congregations that meet for years in temporary facilities without the cumbersome burden of huge debts incurred from buying land and property at the outset. They focus on building lives and communities instead of building with bricks and mortar. They are shackled to the majestic Builder, not chained to mere buildings.

Christian leaders of the emerging world aren't as tied to property and space as are the leaders of earlier generations. Many pastors are eager to take the gospel to the streets and don't have the money or patience for bricks and mortar. They're not willing to wait to tell the story, so the Nomadic Church is a Godsend to them and the countless people they reach.

The Nomadic Church

The nomadic church, sometimes called a portable church, is a local church that meets in someone else's space, which is not a traditional church building, for an extended period of time in order to conduct corporate worship and other ministries. The nomadic church is no longer the face of a few; it's a growing trend. Thousands of churches are started in the United States each year, and the vast majority of them rent meeting space, many for ten years or longer. That is more than twice

 © 2018 Robert O. Crossman, www.UMNewChurch.org

as long as a decade ago, and a growing number say they never plan on purchasing property. Consider the comment of Todd Wilson, executive pastor of New Life Christian Church (www.newlife4me.net) in Chantilly, Virginia: "We will consider getting our own property when the costs for renting begin to approach the cost of owning our own property." According to a comprehensive 1998 survey, almost 14 percent of all congregations in the United States. rent space in a school or other public facility. An even broader study in 2001 found that 10 percent of churches meeting in a church building rent that space from another church. That study also reports that of all faith communities begun since 1945, nearly half of them began in the 1990s. Because of the upsurge in the cost of construction and because of modifications in ministry philosophy, most of these churches remain without their own campus today. Our observations and networks indicate that this building less trend is only increasing since these recent surveys were published.

Two decades ago, some thought that these Nomadic Churches were smaller and catered to the lower half of the income structure. But no more. Today, they come in every size and reach every strata of American culture. In fact, with good reason many former negative perceptions of nomadic churches have begun to be shed in recent years.

New Hope Christian Fellowship (www.enewhope.org) in Honolulu, Hawaii, is one of the premier examples of a congregation choosing to remain in rented facilities. As of 2003, the average weekend attendance exceeds 1,500 people, including seven satellite sites, and the church still rents worship facilities for all its locations. They see their group of Levites, the crews who set up and break down each weekend, as one of the basic training grounds for future leaders of the church. Every Sunday morning from 2:00 to 5:30, a team of over a hundred people gather to set up for services in the rented Farmington High School, which accommodates up to 8,500 people.

In a 1999 interview with their pastor, Wayne Cordeiro, we asked why they were still in rented facilities even though at the time around five thousand people were worshiping with them each weekend. Cordeiro replied, "We did a study of what it would cost to purchase our own worship space. If we did that, we would not be able to spend the amount of money we need to spend on leadership development." The odds are that New Hope may purchase facilities sometime in the distant future, but they have still set a precedent that is hard to ignore.

And what can we say about influential churches like Bill Hybels's Willow Creek Community Church in Barrington, Illinois (www.willowcreek.org)? They spent their foundational years in rented movie theaters and are again renting meeting spaces for their expanding campuses. Or what about Saddleback Community Church (www.saddleback.com) in Lake Forest, California? That congregation shuffled between seventy-nine different places and reached more than 10,000 in regular attendance before erecting their first building. Legend is that it got to be a joke: people could attend, if they could find the church!

Because of churches like New Hope, Willow Creek, Saddleback, and many other thriving congregations, the nomadic church is no longer viewed as a second-class way to do church. Christian leaders of the emerging world aren't as tied to property and space as are the leaders of earlier generations. Many pastors are eager to take the gospel to the streets and don't have the money or patience for bricks and mortar. They're not willing to wait to tell the story, so the nomadic church is a Godsend to them and the countless people they reach.

It's our belief that the percentage of churches renting facilities will continue to grow and that more and more churches will opt to rent nontraditional facilities as long as possible. If that's the case, more research needs to be done to learn how to fortify these mobile congregations.

According to the U.S. Census Bureau, $7.3 billion was spent on religious construction in 2000, up to a hefty 89 percent from 1994. Every year the costs of land and construction increase. To fulfill the Great Commission, the number of new churches that must be planted requires a method that demands less initial capital than in the past. When we ask denominational leaders why they aren't starting new churches, they inevitably mention their lack of money. But money is a major hindrance only if you're eager to buy land and construct a building. In talking with dozens of leaders in charge of church planting for their constituencies, we've learned that it costs between five hundred thousand and a million dollars to plant a church the traditional way!

Disadvantages of a Permanent Building

Many church planters eagerly await the day when they cut the ribbon on a new church facility. That desire is understandable and there certainly are benefits to a building. We're not trying to suggest otherwise. But it is equally important to consider advantages of the portable paradigm and disadvantages of owning a permanent church facility. Here are a few major drawbacks to owning church property that you need to be aware of.

Costs. The capital needed to acquire land and then design, build, and maintain a permanent facility is astronomical. The closer you are to a population center, the higher the costs. And because land is a limited resource, its expense will only increase. Financial bondage is not uncommon for stationary churches.

Focus. The massive amount of limited resources that must be expended on land and facilities may produce more lasting results—spiritually and eternally—if invested elsewhere. Buildings too easily drive the direct the energies of a church. As long as you can meet somewhere, purposefully putting your money into more people, programs, and pastors will out-produce funding a building any day.

Limits. As much as buildings can initially boost a congregation's size, they can just as quickly limit it. Future grow this always limited by the present size of a facility, available parking, and zoning laws. In When Not to Build, Ray Bowman explains how church buildings can actually kill church growth.

Definition. Buildings can shape—or misshape—a church by communicating an inadequate image. Even the best designed building today can mis-define the essence or emphases of a church in a relatively short time. Then, you either suffer the consequences or go back to the drawing board and the money pit cycle.

Affections. Church buildings can foster misplaced affections. They can

 © 2018 Robert O. Crossman, www.UMNewChurch.org

produce unhealthy territorialism, a conviction that certain things ought never to be done in the building and certain others can be done only in the building, and even thinly veiled idolatrous building worship and ego stroking (consider the tower of Babel!). Sacred buildings are virtually universal inhuman religions, but Christianity does not require or endorse them—maybe for more reasons than meet the eye!

Outreach. Perhaps Stuart Murray (in Church Planting: Laying Foundations) expresses this one best: "Having their own building may encourage churches to operate with a centripetal ('come') rather than a centrifugal ('go') mentality in mission, inviting non-members on to church territory at times convenient to church members, rather than going into society to meet people on neutral territory, reversing the apparent thrust of mission in the New Testament."

Multiplication. Churches that have invested enormous amounts of money in buying land and building on it may warily view a proposal to use the building less in order to start a new church elsewhere. After all, redirecting financial assets may mean less ability to upkeep the present building. Mission can be minimized by maintenance.

Effectiveness. A building can't solve non-building problems, and mortar won't accomplish what ministry should accomplish. This is because buildings do not minister; only people do. Leaders too frequently expect a building to do things it never can—and they and their ministry suffer for it.

Churches that have learned to be effective without a permanent home are more likely not to be sucked into these pitfalls if and when they do build. That's why it is so critical to immerse a young congregation in a prudent, biblically balanced perspective on mission, people, buildings, service, and finances. It also helps for Nomadic Churches to know that it's not all rosy on the other side!

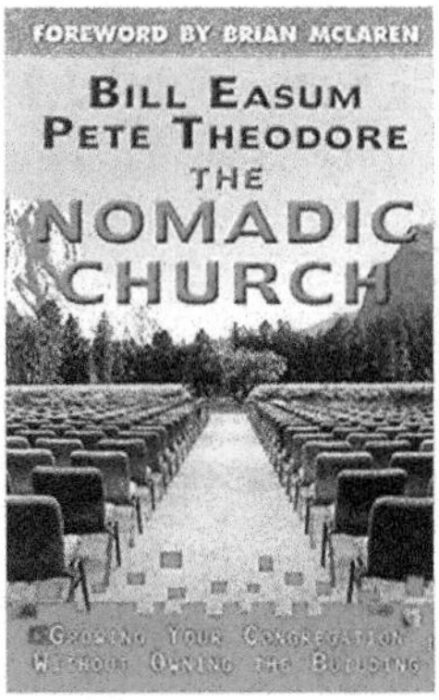

Adapted and excerpted from The Nomadic Church by Bill Easum and Pete Theodore.(Abingdon Press, 2005) Used with permission.

Bill Easum is a president and senior managing partner in Easum, Bandy and Associates, a church consulting and nurturing firm. He is the author of several books, including Unfreezing Moves and Put on Your Own Oxygen Mask First, both published by Abingdon Press. Pete Theodore is Pastor of Teaching at Rolling Hills Community

You can order The Nomadic Church at www.cokesbury.com

Excerpted from the Nov/Dec 2006 edition of Circuit Rider,
a publication of Abingdon Press, © 2006
Used by permission. All rights reserved.
You can subscripe to Circuit Rider and view back issues at:
http://www.ministrymatters.com/circuit_rider/

†††

NOTE: These article reflects the personal opinions of its author and does not necessarily reflect an official position of Discipleship Ministries or Path 1.

Wasted Space
Wasted Opportunity
by Dan R. Dick

A church that attracts a large number of people, offers a wide variety of programs, is financially sound, and provides engaging worship is generally considered to be a "successful" church. Common measures of success are full pews and parking lots on Sunday morning, relatively full collection plates, a full slate of hired and elected congregational leaders, and a growing—if not stable—membership roster. Each of these factors contributes to the measure of a church's effectiveness, but there is another factor— much less obvious—that reflects deep and significant vitality: the use of space.

American Protestant churches are among the greatest space wasters of all public-use facilities.

The vast majority of sanctuaries—huge open spaces—are used only two or three hours a week. The majority of rooms designated for Sunday school classes are used one hour each week. Fellowship halls stand empty 90–95 percent of the time. Church parlors are often used once or twice a month, and many church libraries haven't seen any action since the late 1970s. In churches with declining involvement, once trafficked rooms now serve as storage areas. In a recent survey conducted by the General Board of Discipleship, two of every three churches (64 percent) report having rooms that stand empty on a regular to constant basis. Paradoxically, almost half of these churches are planning to expand or relocate to create more space for ministry. One church with fourteen empty Sunday school rooms just completed construction of a four million- dollar Christian Life Center that is used approximately twelve hours a week on average. Of all the practices of congregational stewardship, our understanding and use of space is perhaps the worst. Churches that provide a powerful and healthy usage model do so by overcoming five critical limiting factors. Each factor poses a unique constraint causing church facilities to be under utilized and ministry potential to remain unrealized. These factors are:

- territorial protection of space;
- an "us/them" mentality that prevents sharing space with those outside the congregation;
- a lack of vision for missional ministry and outreach;
- a strong sense of "church" happening only on Sunday;
- pride of architecture and status.

Territorial Protection of Space

In almost every church in existence, different segments of the congregation claim for themselves discreet, exclusive, and private space. Kitchens, parlors, Sun-

 © 2018 Robert O. Crossman, www.UMNewChurch.org

day school rooms, meeting rooms, and fellowship halls are just some of the areas that can become battlegrounds in local churches. Heaven help the poor person who dribbles punch on the parlor rug or fails to put the coffee urn back in the "right" place. Youth and young adults are often relegated to less-favorable spaces in the church, and they are expected to stay "where they belong." Until a congregation's members can learn to share, facility space is a limiting factor instead of a resource for ministry and service.

Leaders in many congregations relate that territorial issues are generally hidden, unspoken, and unexplored until there is a violation. Then they become a trigger for conflict. The best time to explore the use of shared space is when there are no controversies. One church navigated a re-visioning of space usage by referring to the whole church facility as "God-space." This allowed them not only to learn to share within the congregation but also moved them to see new possibilities of sharing their facility with their community.

An "Us/Them" Mentality

Many congregational members view their church building as . . . their church building. The only people who have any right to use the facility are church members. Overcoming this divisive, non-inclusive mind-set is a huge hurdle to clear for many local churches. A large number of churches define their ministry as what they do for, provide for, and offer to others. Occasionally, a church may open space to a day care center, a thrift shop, or a soup kitchen, but even in these cases there is a clear "landlord/tenant" relationship rather than a true partnership in ministry. The goal of many growing congregations is to expand the number of ministries they can provide, but they only consider those that they own and control as "ministry."

Every community has a wide variety of social, relief, crisis, and assistance agencies with limited resources. Space— adequate facility—is usually one of the greatest needs. The services and programs these agencies provide align very clearly and closely with the mission and ministry of most churches. The opportunities to marry skills, knowledge, and expertise to under utilized church space are almost limitless. Churches with strong, workable partnerships in their communities create these relationships from a strong vision for ministry with the community.

When the church building is viewed as the center and location of ministry, leaders do all they can to draw as many people as possible into the building. However, when the field of opportunity for ministry is located in the community, the church building pales in comparison. It is seen as a resource for ministry rather than a key focus of ministry.

Too many congregations offer most—if not all—of their ministries and programs to the existing membership. This inward vision for ministry may be powerful and comprehensive, but it is still one dimensional. Until a congregation develops a broad vision for ministry—not only for others and to others, but with others—it is limited in the way it envisions the use of space.

"When we started thinking in terms of sharing ministry—doing ministry with other people—it freed us to dream much bigger dreams," one pastor reflected. "There are so many needs that we cannot begin to fill by ourselves, but when we link our resources with those of others, virtually nothing is impossible to us. I'm not sure why nobody ever taught us this in seminary."

This is a simple, rational, and sensible idea—together we are capable of much more than we are on our own. This is as true of congregations—and their community counterparts—as it is of individuals. Many congregational leaders claim that the turning point came by asking, "What does God want us to be doing" instead of "What can we do for God?"

Church Happens Only On Sunday

The lay leader of a midwestern United Methodist Church tells the story of a congregational epiphany when a new member asked the congregation's leaders what it would take for every room in the church to be used every day of the week: "We never thought about the church building being used seven days a week, fifty-two weeks a year. It changed our entire way of thinking about church."

The vast majority of Protestant churches in North America hold one (or possibly two) services in the sanctuary in a given week. Most Sunday school rooms are dedicated space, for use only by the class that meets there. The myth is that large churches are seven-day-a-week churches; activity depends on size. However, a growing number of smaller congregations— one hundred members or less—offer worship services every day of the week and hold multiple classes and studies throughout the week. Additionally, they offer tutoring, health screening, counseling, skills training, and a host of other services every day.

Pride of Architecture and Status

Among the most perplexing stewardship issues concerning the use of church space are the number of churches that are considering expansion, building, or relocation at a time when they are not using the space they already have. The pastor of a growing southeastern church provides a representative opinion when he says, "We want big, new, and beautiful. An old, failing church does nothing to honor God. People in our culture, especially baby boomers, will not settle for anything but the best. If we want to grow we need the biggest church, with the latest equipment, a state-of-the-art nursery, and abundant parking close to the building. The only way to be the best is to keep ahead of the competition."

This is a matter of values. When the church building is viewed as the center and location of ministry, leaders do all they can to draw as many people as possible into the building. However, when the field of opportunity for ministry is located in the community, the church building pales in comparison; it is seen as a resource for ministry rather than a key focus of ministry. There are church buildings—big and small, old and new, in prime locations and out of the way places—that are excellent stewards of space, using what they have to the utmost.

 © 2018 Robert O. Crossman, www.UMNewChurch.org

There is one other powerful argument against using church buildings for ministry: insurance and liability. Conversations with lawyers and insurance agents lead to one simple response— baloney! If there is a ministry need and a partnership opportunity—even in this litigious and contentious age—there is a viable way to provide adequate protection.

The church exists for one purpose: ministry. The more ministry we can do, the better we can honor and glorify God. The best way to expand our ministries is to open our doors and use every resource at our disposal, including the church building, to serve the greatest number of needs. An important function for leaders of every congregation is to explore space considerations: territoriality, the "us/them" mentality, the vision for ministry, the use of the facility seven days a week, and the importance of architecture versus stewardship and service.

Dan R. Dick is the research coordinator for the General Board of Discipleship and a clergy member of the Greater New Jersey Annual Conference.

You can order
Beyond Money
at www.cokesbury.com

Excerpted from the Nov/Dec 2006 edition of Circuit Rider,
a publication of Abingdon Press, © 2006 Used by permission. All rights reserved.

You can subscripe to Circuit Rider and view back issues at:
http://www.ministrymatters.com/circuit_rider/

NOTE: These article reflects the personal opinions of its author
and does not necessarily reflect an official position of Discipleship Ministries or Path 1.

Shaping Welcoming Spaces
by Susan Eaton Mendenhall

We shape our buildings and afterwards our buildings shape us." These words of Winston Churchill continue to teach by example as we enter public buildings, churches, and even our homes.

Anyone new to a space instantly asks three questions. These questions move through us very quickly and often are not recognized by our rational mind, but are definitely experienced in our bodies.

Do I feel safe? Safety may be physical and/or emotional. Am I able to see well enough to navigate the space? Does the space look/feel safe for me to enter? Why is no one here? This is not what I expected when I saw the exterior sign—it does not match what is inside.

Do I feel welcome? Are the people happy and engaging? Does the décor look inviting and well maintained? Does the space allow me to engage it as I am ready—giving me space to breathe and adjust?

What is expected of me? I'm here! What is next? Am I to check in with someone, help myself? Are there signs that direct me in my decisions/questions?

If we are not able to navigate through these three questions easily and effortlessly, we may choose to leave. If we stay, our general nature may be tentative or protective. Abraham Maslow created a pyramid called the Hierarchy of Needs, suggesting that human beings are motivated by their unsatisfied needs. Our very first need is to feel safe and secure. Until this is satisfied it is difficult to explore community and spiritual growth. Perhaps another way to engage these three questions is by **creating an environment for people to feel safe, included, and informed.** Have we thought of this as we create and shape our church spaces?

First Impressions

These days first impressions often start with the church web page. More and more "church guests" are doing their homework on the Internet. Here is where they might see a view of the building, pictures of the staff, and a list of activities. A great impression is made if the web design is engaging, allows for easy navigation, and has a clean look. Put things on your web site that a new person would want to know. Perhaps a blueprint of the church and directions to the site. This allows someone new to know where to park, where to enter the building, and how to locate rooms. Too many bells and whistles on a site can be annoying and may feel invasive to some people. Keeping the web information up to date is one way a church says, "We are alive, vital, and ready for YOU".

New people notice everything! We may no longer "see" what is truly there because it is now familiar. New people are looking for 'clues' to this unknown place and its people. Everything speaks. Look at your facility with the eyes of someone new.

- Is the **main door** clearly known? Do the doors encourage one to enter? Through what door do the members enter? What door would someone new

 © 2018 Robert O. Crossman, www.UMNewChurch.org

be likely to enter? Being able to see into a building through glass paneled doors assists a person in early navigation.

- Once inside, **what first catches the attention**—coat-rack, bulletin board, artwork, clutter, smells . . .?
- What three **signs** are first seen? What do they communicate? In what condition are they? Are they important to someone new?
- List **what is located in the first 10 feet** of entering the main door. Name all that happens in this area.
- **Where do people gather?** What causes them to gather? Is there enough space? What might be needed to enhance this experience?
- What parts of the building **appear cluttered**? Why? Are there items that are broken/past their prime or could be thrown away?
- **What about the building embraces the present and says that it is moving into the future?** What indicates that the facility and ministries might be living too much in the past? Are artwork and furnishings up to date? Is signage uniform and easy to read?

Gathering Spaces

I call gathering spaces (frequently the first place we enter) the "room of introduction." Here is where the personality of the church is first explored. How do you wish to introduce yourself? Notice how people move through this space. Remember that people—their attire, gestures, and voices—make a room seem full. Keeping all furnishings and displays at a minimum allows the energy of the people to be the accessory. Gathering spaces hold the diversity of people's lives. Tasks and emotions happen in this space. This is where people are trying to find a person, allow a child to move more freely, greet a visitor, have a conversation, or pass through to another part of the building. Laughter, joy, concern, anxiety, and frustration accompany these tasks. To allow emotional space for these many tasks and emotions, take care that the area is not filled with excessive furnishings.

Experience shows that renewal
of the building and enlargement thereby
of its capacity for hospitality and service, has led to the renewal
of the worshipping community in that place, and to growth in
numbers as well as in maturity of faith.

Richard Giles
Re-Pitching the Tent

People are also looking for information in gathering spaces. Signage is very important. Directional signs for rest rooms, nursery, offices, and the sanctuary are best positioned above the heads of people so they can be seen when the space is full. Try to keep all signs throughout the building with a similar look. Not only does this provide a harmonious feel to the building, but gives confidence to a new person of knowing what to look for as he moves through the building. Where pos-

© 2018 Robert O. Crossman, www.UMNewChurch.org

sible use the international signage as this is very well identified and understood.

Gathering spaces are also places of waiting. Providing comfortable chairs as room allows and adding a complementary table to rest a beverage is welcomed hospitality. Having a variety of lighting possibilities allows for different moods and uses of this space. A combination of table lamps, overhead, wall sconces all invite this area to be public as well as more intimate for personal reading or visiting with a friend.

Hospitable Worship Space

Worship space that offers flexibility is another form of hospitality. Think through the many ways the space will and could be used. What appointments would be appropriate when the space is used for a concert, a dinner, or a business awards event? Consider the varied uses of the space in each liturgical season. How could the space be changed to allow the congregation to experience the season anew? Give thought to how technical images will be projected and make sure that art and symbols are not limiting this possibility. Maintain a rule of thumb that all furnishings in the chancel and sanctuary space are moveable, which allows for varied expressions in worship style, congregational size, and multiple usages.

Spiritual Welcome

Our spiritual sides are drawn to beauty and the natural world is beauty. Creating spaces that use and accent the natural woods, fibers, minerals, sounds, and lighting will open the spiritual dimensions and provide welcome for the soul. Use of healthy floor plants with sufficient space around them offers a restful expression. Eliminate plastic and artificial as much as possible.

Cluttered Versus Empty Spaces

One of the greatest tasks is keeping clutter to a minimum as well as discernment in accepting donations. Members will offer furnishings that are "used but in great condition" throughout the church's history. Usually these add to the element of clutter. Clutter depresses any space and us as we move through it. The description of the Upper Room prepared for the disciples is a good reminder of how to keep our church spaces . . . "spacious, furnished, and all in order." Clutter often happens because our culture is not comfortable with empty space. We want to fill it with "something." Be slow to add to empty places. Hallways might seem like empty space, but we forget that the movement of people takes room and creates energy. Hallways are also for spiritual, emotional, and physical transitions. As we move from one space to the next we change our intentions. Moving from worship to study to fellowship all requires a transition in thought. Allow the hallways to be simple and uncluttered to give people space to rest and re-group their thoughts. Use the rule of minimal appointments in as many places as possible. What makes the space in many monasteries so sacred and spiritual is that they have included only what is needed—nothing more. The simplicity of the space welcomes and offers room for our cluttered lives while at the same time helping us to focus.

 © 2018 Robert O. Crossman, www.UMNewChurch.org

Buildings speak a language.
- They tell us whether they are loved or ignored.
- They tell us of the energy and spirit of those who use them.
- They easily invite or distance someone new.
- They encourage or complicate new ideas.

Buildings speak a language.
- Some buildings look tired and out of date.
- Some buildings feel refreshed and vital.
- Some buildings have no place for silence to reside.
- Some buildings invite the soul to explore.

Buildings speak a language.
What is your building saying?

Susan Eaton Mendenhall, of DeForest, Wisconsin, has worked with the development of church and nonprofit ministries for thirty years. In 2002 she started Spatial Impact: Interpreting the Language of Space, a consulting service for businesses, churches, and homeowners at www.spatialimpact.com. Susan's articles on facility space have been published by several conferences and *Net Results* magazine.

Excerpted from the Nov/Dec 2006 edition of Circuit Rider, a publication of Abingdon Press, © 2006 Used by permission. All rights reserved.

You can subscripe to Circuit Rider and view back issues at:
http://www.ministrymatters.com/circuit_rider/

NOTE: These article reflects the personal opinions of its author and does not necessarily reflect an official position of Discipleship Ministries or Path 1.

Birthing Congregations in Nontraditional Spaces
by Rodney Thomas Smothers

A ride through any city or town will reveal ministries that now occupy spaces that we once referred to as storefronts. Today these storefronts have grown from former stores, offices, and mom and pop businesses into mega ministry centers that are now found in former theaters, big box stores, schools, and factories. The once easily recognizable facade of a church has been replaced by creative designs born out of convenience, zoning laws, and creative accommodations. Practical facility use and function are also driving this new look of ministry facilities. Vital churches today are so much more than Sunday morning worship centers only. The seven-day-a-week church provides space for worship, education, small group ministries, child care, senior care, youth activities, family athletics, and other ministries and services like Christian schools, bookstores, banquet facilities, and, in some cases, retail outlets that often provide additional streams of income to the ministry.

The once easily recognizable facade of a church has been replaced by creative designs born out of convenience, zoning laws, and creative accommodations.

Rodney Thomas Smothers

New ministries are particularly attracted to these multiple use buildings because they often come with ample off-street parking, an affordable lease arrangement that provides for additional space as the ministry grows, and zoning that is easier for church start-ups than acquiring new property. Often these spaces are found in locations where the infrastructure is already in place so that scarce start-up funding can be utilized for the greater ministry needs. For a new ministry, the more flexible the space—the better the facility. For many years in church development our goal was to define a successful new church start by the speed at which the first unit was built. Today our thinking has evolved. We understand that by leasing space we can grow into or move away from the rented space if growth exceeds the capacity of the present facility. Other factors that favor facility flexibility are the changing socioeconomic conditions that may shift the demographics of a new church start in such a way that its starting location may not be the best location for its permanent facilities. Another benefit of beginning new ministries in nontraditional spaces is the psychological impact that nontraditional spaces have on people who are not familiar with the church. Flexible creative space that is high on hospitality and low on tradition makes church a less imposing place for newcomers to new faith communities. Innovative facilities that provide for open access, emerging technology, and space where people can gather before and after the worship settings invite people to interact and build new community.

 © 2018 Robert O. Crossman, www.UMNewChurch.org

Mothering and Multi-Site Models

Nontraditional facilities are also becoming popular among existing congregations that are "mothering" new congregations or launching multiple ministry sites. Congregations that pursue the birthing of a new congregation must be spiritual healthy, financially viable, and missionally minded. They see the expansion of the kingdom of God as a calling that can be met through their commitment of resources, knowing that they have been chosen and equipped to bring multiplication to the Body of Christ. This approach to kingdom expansion has various approaches. Daughtering, satellites, multicampuses, and adoption are just a few of the methods that have been used successfully.

Multicampus ministry is often used to extend a congregation's current capacity. Though the additional site might have as its primary target group another demographic or seek to extend capacity to the same demographic by physically replicating itself in another location, its central administrative control remains with the mother congregation. Mothering new congregations, however, has as its long-term goal the sponsorship of a new congregation that will become healthy enough to become a fully self-sustaining ministry on its own. First United Methodist Church and Windsor Village, both located in Houston, Texas, stand as models that are working well. In First Church's case, a new campus in an outlying area was sponsored and has become a fully selfsupporting congregation. In Windsor Village's case, it has used the multicampus model and the adoption model of daughtering a church. These approaches have also provided great models for kingdom expansion.

Who Will Do Ministry With Us?

In the Baltimore-Washington Conference, we are approaching facility use with a different model in mind. We are inviting existing congregations that are geographically close to one another to share creative ministry options that utilize their existing campuses and all of the pastoral leadership in shared mission and ministry. In the past, a single pastor was assigned to a single charge and served multiple congregations; this new model promotes sharing of pastors and resources around shared vision, spiritual gifts, competencies, and joint use of facilities in an extended campus arrangement where facility use is determined by ministry need rather than a single congregation's desire alone. The benefits are numerous. The congregations benefit from the shared leadership of a team of pastors, and the laity begin to think about ministry as something that they do with others rather than something that they do with a silotype mentality.

In mainline denominations, Anglo new church developments have a much better track record of starting in temporary facilities while African-American new church developments

seem to do better in established facilities while Korean and Hispanic new church developments thrive in house church models, but expand rapidly once facilities are made available. The point is one size does not fit all.

Rodney Thomas Smothers

The congregations that need additional space most are not just large congregations. In fact, it could be said that our small- and medium-size congregations' greatest obstacle to growth is lack of expandable ministry space. What options are available? We begin our quest for additional ministry space by asking the question, "Who will do ministry with us?" Are there other congregations willing to share space? Are there potential partners in the community that are willing to share space like educational and civic organizations or county, city, or state-sponsored facilities? There are food establishments in our communities that would welcome our use of their meeting rooms and there are professional offices including funeral homes that are usually willing to partner with us to share space. And don't forget other religious organizations that don't use their worship or ministry space on the same days and times where we might wish to expand our ministry. And please don't underestimate the value of empowering house church meetings in your community.

Our creativity and focus on the changing landscape of ministry provides us with more options for ministry than we've had in the past. No longer is the church defined by its buildings alone. Affordable, user friendly space where relevant life changing worship takes place, effective small groups can meet, and efficient systems of nurture and care are enabled, works for most ministries. Rapidly changing ministry conditions make temporary space a good option for growing ministries. Some of our existing churches should consider sharing current sites or swapping ministry sites so that vibrant and growing ministries can be expanded. Any permanent new building should be developed with projected ministry needs in mind so that future ministry needs can be met at that location. Birthing new faith communities in nontraditional spaces requires strategic visioning, creative implementation and courageous commitments to try new methods. Every large ministry has used creative temporary ministry space to expand its ministry—it's good for evangelism and good for missional outreach.

Cultural Contexts

Changing ministry needs, changing demographics and changing socioeconomics are not the only factors that influence a congregation's decision to stay at its present location or move to another location. While we talk a great deal about multicultural and multiethnic congregations, we still have a long way to go in

 © 2018 Robert O. Crossman, www.UMNewChurch.org

mainstreaming our congregational response to this reality. With our communities becoming more diverse every day, opportunities for us to minister to people from multiple cultural contexts is going to drive greater understanding of how new faith communities can thrive in the midst of diversity.

In mainline denominations, Anglo new church developments have a much better track record of starting in temporary facilities while African-American new church developments seem to do better in established facilities while Korean and Hispanic new church developments thrive in house church models, but expand rapidly once facilities are made available. The point is one size does not fit all. Cultural, economic, social and political contexts also play a significant role in the birthing of new faith communities in nontraditional spaces.

The growing conversation around the "organic church movement" would suggest that purpose, passion, and innovation are more important than specific spaces. More than mere marketing, nontraditional ministry space should be first and foremost mission responsive, hospitality-attractive, and Christ-encounter intentional.

Dr. Rodney Thomas Smothers is currently the Director of Leadership and Congregational Development for the Baltimore-Washington Conference of the United Methodist Church. He is a popular consultant and coach, assisting conferences and new church planters across the country.

rsmothers@BWCUMC.org

Reprinted here with permission of the author, Rodney Smothers, granted on December 30, 2017.

Excerpted from the Nov/Dec 2006 edition of Circuit Rider, a publication of Abingdon Press, © 2006 Used by permission. All rights reserved.

You can subscripe to Circuit Rider and view back issues at: http://www.ministrymatters.com/circuit_rider/

NOTE: These article reflects the personal opinions of its author and does not necessarily reflect an official position of Discipleship Ministries or Path 1.

New Church Handbook
Nuts & Bolts for Planting New Churches In The Wesleyan Tradition

"Building Construction -What Does the 2016 Book of Discipline Say?"

A summary from ¶ 2544, 2016 Discipline

STEPS FOR A BUILDING PROJECT IN THE UNITED METHODIST CHURCH
by Bob Crossman

1. Establish a "study committee" to analyze the building needs of the church and community. Project the potential membership with average attendance, and write up the church's program of ministry.

2. Secure the written consent of the pastor and district superintendent to the building project. The study committee presents their study to the district board of church location and building for its consideration and preliminary approval.

3. After securing these approvals, the charge conference (made up of all members of the church council along with retired ordained ministers and diaconal ministers and presided over by the district superintendent) approves the building project and elects a building committee.

4. The building committee uses the information from the study committee to establish carefully the building facilities needed, develop preliminary architectural plans, secures an estimate of the proposed construction costs, and develop a financial plan for defraying the total cost of the building project.

5. The building committee submits a report to the district board of church location and building for its consideration and preliminary approval.

6. After preliminary approval by the district board of church location and building, a church conference (made up of all members of the church and presided over by the district superintendent) shall meet to approve the preliminary architectural plans, cost estimate, and financial plan submitted by the building committee. A majority vote of those present is required for approval.

 © 2018 Robert O. Crossman, www.UMNewChurch.org

7. After approval by the church conference, a capital funds campaign is held.

8. After completing the capital funds campaign, with sufficient pledges in hand, the building committee develops detailed plans and specifications, secures a reliable and detailed estimate of cost, and presents these to the District Board of Church Location and Building for approval.

9. After approval is received from the district board, then this is carried to the charge conference for its consideration and approval.

10. ONLY after all the 9 steps above are completed, the ground breaking and actual construction may begin.

The following pages give the official details.

**2016 Book of Discipline
The United Methodist Church ¶2544**

Margin Check List Boxes by Bob Crossman

¶ **2544.** ***Planning and Financing Requirements for Local Church Buildings***

1. If any local church desires to:

a) build a new church, a new educational building, or a new parsonage;

b) purchase a church, educational building, or parsonage; or

c) remodel an existing church, an existing educational building, or an existing parsonage where the cost of the remodeling will exceed 25 percent of the value of the existing structure or require mortgage financing, then the local church shall first establish a study committee to:

(1) analyze the needs of the church and community;

(2) project the potential membership with average attendance;

(3) write up the church's program of ministry (¶¶ 201-204); and

> All building construction, site purchases, or building purchases must go through this process. Remodeling must go through this process if it exceeds 25%...

These paragraphs from the Book of Discipline may be helpful in writing up a program of ministry as required in ¶2543.1.c.3. above.

¶ **201.** *Definition of a Local Church*- The local church provides the most significant arena through which disciple-making occurs. It is a community of true believers under the Lordship of Christ. It is the redemptive fellowship in which the Word of God is preached by persons divinely called and the sacraments are duly administered according to Christ's own appointment. Under the discipline of the Holy Spirit, the church exists for the maintenance of worship, the edification of believers, and the redemption of the world.

¶ **202.** *The Function of the Local Church*- The church of Jesus Christ exists in and for the world. It is primarily at the level of the charge consisting of one or more local churches that the church encounters the world. The local church is a strategic base from which Christians move out to the structures of society. The function of the local church, under the guidance of the Holy Spirit, is to help people to accept and confess Jesus Christ as Lord and Savior and to live their daily lives in light of their relationship with God. Therefore, the local church is to minister to persons in the community where the church is located, to provide appropriate training and nurture to all, to cooperate in ministry with other local churches, to defend God's creation and live as an ecologically responsible community, and to participate in the worldwide mission of the church, as minimal expectations of an authentic church.

¶ **203.** *Relation to the Wider Church*- The local church is a connectional society of persons who have been baptized, have professed their faith in Christ, and have assumed the vows of membership in The United Methodist Church. They gather in fellowship to hear the Word of God, receive the sacraments, praise and worship the triune God, and carry forward the work that Christ has committed to his church. Such a society of believers, being within The United Methodist Church and subject to its Discipline, is also an inherent part of the church universal, which is composed of all who accept Jesus Christ as Lord and Savior, and which in the Apostles' Creed we declare to be the holy catholic church.

¶ **204.** *Care of Members*- Each local church shall have a definite evangelistic, nurture, and witness responsibility for its members and the surrounding area and a missional outreach responsibility to the local and global community. It shall be responsible for ministering to all its members, wherever they live, and for persons who choose it as their church.

(4) develop an accessibility plan including chancel areas.
-The information and findings obtained by the study committee shall:
(a) form the basis of a report to be presented to the charge conference (¶ 2544.3);
(b) be used by the building committee (see ¶ 2544.4); and

- ❑ Done, Date______
- ❑ Both letters attached
- ❑ Does Not Apply

© 2018 Robert O. Crossman, www.UMNewChurch.org

(c) become a part of the report to the district board of church location and building (see ¶¶ 2544.5, 2521.1).

> ¶ **2521.** *Standards for the Approval of Building Proposals*- 1. The District Board of Church Location and Building shall review the plans of any church in the district which proposes to construct or purchase a new church or educational building or a parsonage, or remodeling of such a building if the cost will exceed 25 percent of the value of the building. Such proposal shall include a statement of the need for the proposed facilities, preliminary architectural plans, cost estimate of the project, and a financial plan for defraying such costs. Before finally approving the building project, the board shall determine that the preliminary architectural design and financial plans have been evaluated and approved by proper authorities. Building plans shall provide for equal access to persons with disabilities as per **¶2544.4.**

2. After the study committee finishes its work, the local church shall secure the written consent of the pastor and the district superintendent to the building project, purchase proposal, or remodeling project.

> ❑ Done, Date______
> ❑ Both letters attached
> ❑ Does Not Apply

3. In the case of a building project or purchase proposal, the local church shall secure the approval of the proposed site by the **DISTRICT BOARD OF CHURCH LOCATION AND BUILDING** as provided in the Discipline (¶ 2520.1).

> First meeting with District Board,Site approved?
> ❑ Done, Date______
> ❑ Copy of study attached
> ❑ Does Not Apply

> **¶2520.1** *Duties and Responsibilities of the District Boards of Church Location and Building - 1. Local Church Building Sites and Plans* - The board of church location and building shall investigate all proposed local church building sites, ascertaining that such sites are properly located for the community to be served and adequate in size to provide space for future expansion and parking facilities. (See **¶¶259.1, 2544.2**)

4. The charge conference of the local church shall authorize the building project, purchase proposal, or remodeling project at a regular or called meeting. Notice of the meeting and the proposed action shall have been given for not less than ten days prior thereto from the pulpit of the church, and in its weekly bulletin, newsletter or electonic notice or other means if required or permitted by local law.

> Charge Conf. approval?
> ❑ Done, Date______
> ❑ Copy of minutes attached
> ❑ Does Not Apply

   a) After approving a building project or a remodeling project, the charge conference shall elect a building committee of not fewer than three members of the local church to serve in the development of the

> Building Com. Elected?
> ❑ Done, Date______
> ❑ Copy of minutes attached
> ❑ Does Not Apply

project as hereinafter set forth; provided that the charge conference may commit to its board of trustees the duties of the building committee.

b) After approving a purchase proposal, the charge conference shall be deemed to have authorized and directed the board of trustees to proceed with the purchase. In the case of the purchase of a parsonage, the board of trustees shall either:

Only after completing all the above, may any land or buildings be purchased.
❑ Done, Date______
❑ Does Not Apply

(1) purchase a parsonage that has on the ground-floor level:
 (a) one room that can be used as a bedroom by a person with a disability;
 (b) one fully accessible bathroom; and
 (c) fully accessible laundry facilities; or
(2) purchase a parsonage without the accessible features for persons with disabilities specified above and remodel it within one year's time, so that it does have those features.

5.a thru 5.f:
❑ Done, Date______
❑ Does Not Apply

5. The building committee shall:
 a) use the information and findings of the study committee and any other relevant information to estimate carefully the building facilities needed, as the case may be, to house the church's program of worship, education, and fellowship or to provide for the present and future pastors and their families;
 b) ascertain the cost of any property to be purchased; and
 c) develop preliminary architectural plans that:
  (1) comply with local building, fire, and accessibility codes;
  (2) clearly outline the location on the site of all proposed present and future construction; and
  (3) provide adequate facilities for parking, entrance, seating, rest rooms, and accessibility for persons with disabilities, but providing for such adequate facilities shall not apply in the case of a minor remodeling project;
 d) provide on the ground-floor level of a newly constructed parsonage:
  (1) one room that can be used as a bedroom by a person with a disability;
  (2) a fully accessible bathroom; and
  (3) fully accessible laundry facilities;
 e) secure an estimate of the cost of the proposed construction;
 f) develop a financial plan for defraying the total cost, including an estimate of the amount the membership can contribute in cash and pledges and the amount the local church can borrow if necessary.

6. The building committee shall submit to the **<u>DISTRICT BOARD OF</u>**

 © 2018 Robert O. Crossman, www.UMNewChurch.org

CHURCH LOCATION AND BUILDING for its consideration and preliminary approval:

a) a statement of the need for the proposed facilities;
b) the preliminary architectural plans, including accessibility plans;
c) the preliminary cost estimate; and
d) the preliminary financial plan.

Second meeting with District Board:
❑ Done, Date______
❑ Copy of minutes attached
❑ Does Not Apply

2nd Church Conference:
❑ Done, Date______
❑ Copy of minutes attached
❑ Does Not Apply

7. After preliminary approval by the **DISTRICT BOARD OF CHURCH LOCATION AND BUILDING**, the pastor, with the written consent of the district superintendent, shall call a **church** conference, giving not less than ten days' notice (except as local laws may otherwise provide) of the meeting and the proposed action from the pulpit or in the weekly bulletin. At the church conference, the building committee shall present:
   a) the preliminary architectural plans;
   b) the preliminary cost estimate;
   c) the preliminary financial plan; and
   d) the building committee's recommendation.

   A majority vote of the membership present and voting at the church conference shall be required to approve the preliminary architectural plans, cost estimate, and financial plan and the building committee's recommendation.
8. After approval by the church conference, the building committee shall develop detailed plans and specifications and secure a reliable and detailed estimate of cost, which shall be presented for approval to the charge conference and to the **DISTRICT BOARD OF CHURCH LOCATION AND BUILDING.**

Third meeting with District Board:
❑ Done, Date___
❑ Copy of minutes attached
❑ Does Not Apply

9. After approval by the charge conference and **DISTRICT BOARD OF CHURCH LOCATION AND BUILDING**, the building committee may begin the building project or remodeling project. Written documentation substantiating the approvals of the charge conference and the district board of church location and building shall be lodged with the district superintendent and the secretary of the charge conference.

NOTE: Only after all 9 of the above requirements are met may the church begin the building or remodeling project. Copies of written documentation given to DS?

❑ Done,

The District Board of Church Location and Building.
¶2521.2. When the local church has secured final architectural plans and specifications and a reliable and detailed estimate of the cost of the proposed undertaking as provided in ¶2544.7, the board

❑ Done, Date____
❑ Does Not Apply

shall require their submission for consideration and approval. The board shall study carefully the feasibility and financial soundness of the undertaking and ascertain whether the financial plan will provide funds necessary to ensure prompt payment of all proposed contractual obligations and provide for the full financial support of the program ministries, including annual conference and general Church benevolences. It shall report its conclusions to the Church and to the cabinet in writing.

3. A final decision of the board approving purchase, building, or remodeling shall automatically terminate after a period of one year where no action has been taken by the local church to carry out such decision.

❑ Done, Date____
❑ Does Not Apply

10. In metropolitan areas, the building committee shall ensure that adequate steps are taken to obtain the services of minority (nonwhite) and female skilled persons in the construction in proportion to the racial and ethnic balance in the area. In non-metropolitan areas, the building committee shall ensure that racial and ethnic persons are employed in the construction where available and in relation to the available workforce.

❑ Done, Date____
❑ Does Not Apply

11. The local church shall acquire a fee simple title to the lot or lots on which any building is to be erected. The deed or conveyance shall be executed as provided in this chapter. It is recommended that contracts on property purchased by a local church be contingent upon the securing of a guaranteed title, and the property's meeting of basic environmental requirements of lending institutions and of local and state laws.

❑ Done, Date____
❑ Does Not Apply

12. If a loan is needed, the local church shall comply with the provisions of **¶ 2540** or **¶ 2541.**

❑ Done, Date____
❑ Does Not Apply

¶ 2540. *Unincorporated Local Church Property- Sale, Transfer, Lease, or Mortgage—* Any real property owned by or in which an unincorporated local church has any interest may be sold, transferred, leased for a term of thirty days or more (which shall include leases for less than thirty days if such a lease is consecutive with the same lessee), or mortgaged subject to the following procedure and conditions:

1. Notice of the proposed action and the date and time of the regular or special meeting of the charge conference at which it is to be considered shall be given at least ten days prior thereto from the pulpit of the church or in its weekly bulletin, newsletter or electronic notice, or other means if required or permitted by local law.

2. A resolution authorizing the proposed action shall be passed by a majority vote of the charge conference members (in a pastoral charge consisting of two or more local churches, the church local conference; see **¶ 2527**) present

© 2018 Robert O. Crossman, www.UMNewChurch.org

and voting at a special meeting called to consider such action.
3. The written consent of the pastor of the local church and the district superintendent to the proposed action shall be necessary and shall be affixed to or included in the instrument of sale, conveyance, transfer, lease, or mortgage. Prior to consenting to any proposed action required under this paragraph involving any United Methodist church property, the pastor, district superintendent, and the district board of church location and building shall ensure that: (a) full investigation shall be made and an appropriate plan of action shall be developed for the future missional needs of the community; (b) the transfer or encumbrance shall conform to the *Discipline*; and (c) the congregation, if no longer to continue as an organized local United Methodist Church, does not sell but may transfer title of its facilities to another United Methodist church or agency; and (d) the congregation, in case of relocation, first offers its property to a United Methodist congregation or agency at a price not to exceed fair market value. The district strategies or other missional strategies should include the ministries of both United Methodist congregations and the community where the existing facility is located. Certification by the district superintendent shall be conclusive evidence that the transfer or encumbrance conforms to the *Discipline*. The requirements of investigation and the development of a plan of action, however, shall not affect the merchantability of the title to the real estate or the legal effect of the instruments of sale or transfer.
4. Unless the charge conference directs otherwise, any contract, deed, bill of sale, mortgage, or other necessary written instrument needed to implement any resolution authorizing action regarding local church property may be executed by and on behalf of the local church by any two of the officers of its board of trustees, who thereupon shall be duly authorized to carry out the direction of the charge conference; and any written instrument so executed shall be binding and effective as the action of the local church.

❑ Done, Date____
❑ Does Not Apply

¶ **2541.** *Incorporated Local Church Property- Sale, Transfer, Lease, or Mortgage*—Any real property owned by or in which an incorporated local church has any interest may be sold, transferred, leased for a term of thirty days or more (which shall include leases for less than thirty days if such a lease is consecutive with the same lessee), or mortgaged subject to the following procedure and conditions:
1. Notice of the proposed action and the date and time of the regular or special meeting of the members of the corporate body—i.e., members of the charge conference at which it is to be considered—shall be given at least ten days prior thereto from the pulpit of the church and in its weekly bulletin, newsletter or electronic notice or other means if required or permitted by local law.
2. A resolution authorizing the proposed action shall be passed by a majority vote of the members of the corporate body present and voting at any regular

or special meeting thereof called to consider such action and a majority vote of the members of the charge conference, if the corporate members are different than the charge conference members.

3. The written consent of the pastor of the local church and the district superintendent to the proposed action shall be necessary and shall be affixed to or included in the instrument of sale, conveyance, transfer, lease, or mortgage. Prior to consenting to any proposed action required under this paragraph involving any United Methodist church property, the pastor, the district superintendent, and the district board of church location and building shall ensure that—(a) a full investigation shall be made and an appropriate plan of action shall be developed for the future missional needs of the community; (b) the transfer or encumbrance shall conform to the *Discipline*; (c) the congregation, if no longer to continue as an organized United Methodist church, does not sell but may transfer title of its facilities to another United Methodist church or agency; and (d) the congregation, in case of relocation, first offers its property to a United Methodist congregation or agency at a price not to exceed fair market value. The district strategies or other missional strategies should include the ministries of both United Methodist congregations and the community where the existing facility is located. Certification by the district superintendent shall be conclusive evidence that the transfer or encumbrance conforms to the *Discipline*. The requirements of investigation and the development of a plan of action shall not affect the merchantability of the title to the real estate or the legal effect of the instruments of sale or transfer.

4. The resolution authorizing such proposed action shall direct and authorize the corporation's board of directors to take all necessary steps to carry out the action and to cause to be executed, as hereinafter provided, any necessary contract, deed, bill of sale, mortgage, or other written instrument.

5. The board of directors at any regular or special meeting shall take such action and adopt such resolutions as may be necessary or required by the local laws.

6. Any required contract, deed, bill of sale, mortgage, or other written instrument necessary to carry out the action so authorized shall be executed in the name of the corporation by any two of its officers, and any written instrument so executed shall be binding and effective as the action of the corporation.

13. The local church shall not enter into a building contract or, if using a plan for volunteer labor, incur obligations for materials until it has cash on hand, pledges payable during the construction period, and (if needed) a loan or written commitment therefore that will assure prompt payment of all contractual obligations and other accounts when due.

❑ Done, Date____
❑ Does Not Apply

❑ Done, Date____
❑ Does Not Apply

 © 2018 Robert O. Crossman, www.UMNewChurch.org

14. Neither the trustees nor any other members of a local church shall be required to guarantee personally any loan made to the church by any board created by or under the authority of the General Conference.

❑ Done, Date____
❑ Does Not Apply

15. It is recommended that a local church not enter into a binding building contract without the contractor being properly bonded or furnishing other forms of security, such as an irrevocable letter of credit approved by the conference, district, or local church attorney.

❑ Done, Date____
❑ Does Not Apply

¶2545. ***Consecration and Dedication of Local Church Buildings*** - On acquisition or completion of any church-owned building, a service of consecration may be held. Before any church-owned building is formally dedicated, all indebtedness against the same shall be discharged.

†✝†

Recommended Resource List

From Cokesbury:

"Extraordinary Money: Understanding the Church Capital Campaign"
by Michael Reeves.
This book will help you understand
why you may need to consider hiring a capital funds firm,
such as Horizons Stewardship www.horizons.net
to direct your campaign.

"I've worked with Horizons Stewardship for years, and they are the best, without question."

Bob Crossman

---

†✝†

NOTE: The boxes inserted along the right side of the text of the Book of Discipline
reflect the personal opinions of the author
and do not necessarily reflect an official position of Discipleship Ministries or Path 1.

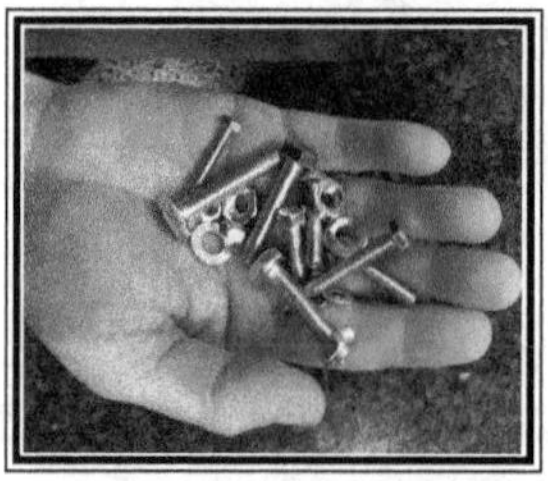

New Church Handbook
Nuts & Bolts for Planting New Churches In The Wesleyan Tradition

"Building Construction -Questions to Expect From Your District Board"

by Bob Crossman and Sam Dixon

You will have to appear before your District Board of Church Building and Location at least twice.
(Three times if your project also includes purchase of land.)

Questions to Expect From The District Board of Church Location and Building
by Sam Dixon and Bob Crossman

Mission

- What is the particular mission of your local church? How does this project help you to be more faithful to your mission?

Financial Questions

- What is the estimated cost of the total project, including all 'hidden' costs such as architect's fee, engineering, furnishings, permits, landscaping, telephone, utility connections, site preparation, contingency, etc.?
- Is a reasonable financial plan in place? What is it? *{Typically you need more than 60% of the total project cost in hand as cash or reliable three year pledges toward the building fund.}*
- How will increased operational costs (insurance, utilities, program expenses, custodian) be addressed?
- What has been the financial experience of the church for the past three years? What are the financial projections for the next three years?
- To meet the cost of the new project, will property currently held by the church need to be sold? If so, what is the plan for accomplishing that sale?

 © 2018 Robert O. Crossman, www.UMNewChurch.org

Land Use Questions

- Is the site conveniently located to serve both present and future church membership?
- How have all local building codes and zoning requirements been met? How large is the site?
- How much on-site parking will be available? What is the auto traffic pattern?
- Is there grade level accessibility to each level of the building? Can the site accommodate future expansion?
- How do future land acquisitions or sales on adjacent properties relate to this specific building program?
- Has an environmental audit been performed? Has the property ever had a gas station on it, or storage facilities for agricultural chemicals? Are there any environmental concerns on adjacent property?

Facility Questions

- Will the new construction / remodeling meet the present and future ministry needs of the church?
- Has the architect done a master plan "maxing out" the use of your site, so that this building phase is in harmony with future building additions? *This is to limit future problems such as, 'If we had only made the hallway one foot wider, then we could have extended the building another 50 feet... if the building were only over five more feet, we could have added an access drive to the kitchen..."*
- Is the facility easily accessible from the parking area?
- Are there adequate signs for the building and grounds? Can people easily orient themselves once inside?
- Do room sizes meet code requirements? Is there room for future growth?
- Is there adequate and appropriate space for storage?
- Are rest room facilities adequate and accessible to all?
- Is there a kitchen? How will it be used? Is it adequate for its intended purposes?
- Is there a fellowship hall? Is it of adequate size? Does it allow for proper storage of tables and chairs? Does it have a stage? Does it support the use of AV equipment?
- Is the size of the sanctuary appropriate? Seating capacity? Chairs or pews?
- How high is the chancel area? Is it fixed or flexible?
- How high is the ceiling in the sanctuary? What is the position of the choir and organ in the sanctuary?
- Is the sanctuary designed for multiple uses? Is there adequate storage in the sanctuary?
- Are rest room and nursery facilities easily available from the sanctuary?
- How wide are the corridors? Are there any dead-end corridors? How wide are the doors?
- Does the facility enable rapid and safe emergency evacuations?

- Where is the mechanical room in relation to the other rooms?
- Has the fire department and city approved the building and site plans?

Construction Questions

- Who is your contractor? Does the contractor have positive previous experience working with churches? How many of the contractor's church references did you personally call? Do you have a fixed maximum 'not to exceed' contract? Will volunteer labor be used?

- Does the architect have previous experience working with churches? How many of the architect's church references did you personally call? Have you visited those churches?
- What is the contractor and architect's cost estimates or final bids for the total project cost?
- Will the architect provide detailed plans and specifications? Will the architect monitor the construction project?
- Will the contractor consult with the architect during the design phase?
- How will change orders be handled by the church?

NOTE: These articles reflect the personal opinions of the authors and do not necessarily reflect an official position of Discipleship Ministries or Path 1.

In memory of Sam Dixon, who lost his life during the 2010 Haiti earthquake while engaged in mission with the United Methodist Committee on Relief.

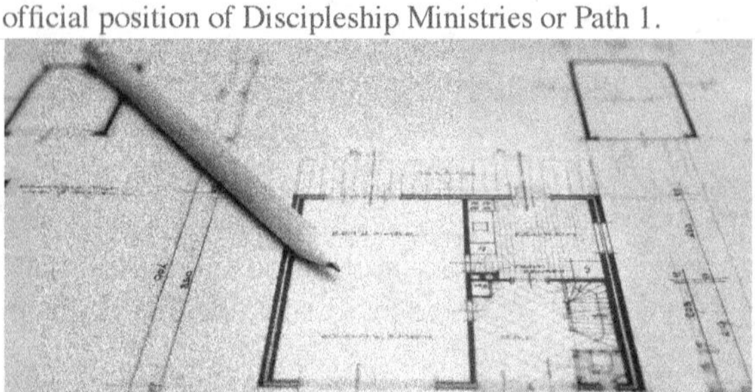

 © 2018 Robert O. Crossman, www.UMNewChurch.org

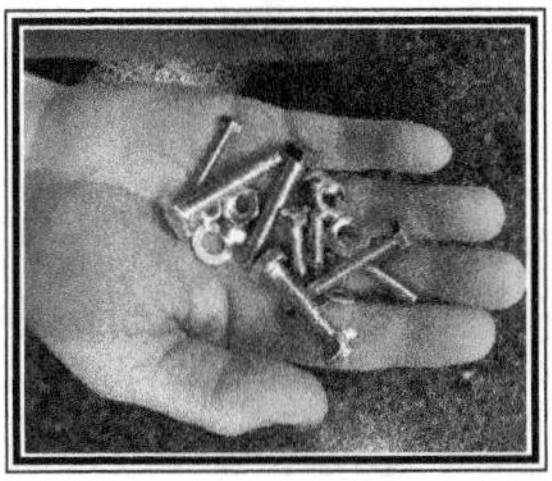

New Church Handbook
Nuts & Bolts for Planting New Churches In The Wesleyan Tradition

"Building Construction -Counting the Total Cost of Construction"

by Bob Crossman

**Are you thinking about a church construction project?
Counting the Cost...**

A Few Words About Cost & Debt

What ever you build, consider the Total Project Cost. If you ask your contractor or architect, *"What is this going to cost?"* they will often only tell you the construction cost. Construction cost is only part of the expense of building. As a church leader you need to know the Total Project Cost.

The Total Project Cost normally includes three things:

- the construction cost" to actually build the building, AND
- a 10% contingency fund, AND
- approximately an additional 25% for architect fees, city fees, utility hookups, fund raising costs, landscaping, parking lot, furniture, and fixtures.

Also, I strongly recommend that you enter into a contract with a Fixed Maximum Cost. You can't afford the risk of "cost plus." To be fair to your congregation, you must know a fixed maximum cost to the dollar before you ask them to vote on breaking ground

Let me suggest a few Rules of Thumb About Debt:

1. Building payments not funded by a capital campaign should not require more than 15%of the church's annual income.
2. A minimum of 1/2 to 2/3 of the total costs of the proposed building should be secured, either by cash in the bank or in reliable 3-year pledges.
3. Another way to see this: you don't want to go into long term debt more than three times your previous year's annual operating budget.
4. A capital funds program should be held to obtain pledges toward the support of the building project. These pledges should be collectible over a 3 year period. Church's sometimes can get the amount they need in 2 years, but on average 3 years will provide the maximum return in your investment in a capital campaign process. Except for very large gifts, in most cases a 5 year campaign brings in only a small amount more than a 3 year campaign, but you will receive the payout over 60 months instead of 36 months. Also, the longer the payout period, the greater the default rates because people move, change churches or die. Also, if you are not doing a excellent job of cultivating capital gifts from new persons, the longer the payout period the larger the number of persons in your church who have never been asked to give in your capital effort.

© 2018 Robert O. Crossman, www.UMNewChurch.org

5. Ideally, established congregations should borrow for a maximum term of 15 years. Doing so minimizes your interest expense and reduces your debt more quickly. It also provides you additional margin if your church were to experience a financial downturn because you still have room to ask your banker to temporarily increase your amortization term to up to 30 years to reduce your monthly payments until the downtown is over. If you are not able to safely cash-flow a 15 year mortgage, consider breaking your project into phases. Your congregation is likely to give twice the amount to build something than they will to reduce the debt, so you are almost always better off from an income perspective to build a little at a time than to build all at once.

Additional 'rules of thumb' about debt:

What ever you build, YOU will have to pay for. Of course we hope your new facilities will attract new people. But they will be new, and new believers need time to grow in their commitment to daily prayer, faithful attendance at worship, giving their time to serve the Lord, and giving their financial resources to support the church's ministry.

New people may give to your building debt, but they will NOT typically give sacrificially. YOU will have to pay for what you vote to build. Hopefully the new families will help to cover any 'short fall' that may occur as your current members move from town, experience a medical crises, or loss of income. Your Horizons Strategist can help you develop a process for inviting new people to contribute toward your capital campaign.

It is human nature that you will not receive 100% of the pledge amounts. Without an active follow up process over the collection period, you can generally expect to collect 70-80% .{Your faithful members may be transferred by their company, experience major medical crises, loss of employment, or drift away from active participation in the church.} Therefore, do not undertake debt greater than what 70-80% of your pledges will be able to cover on a monthly basis. If you work closely with your Horizons Strategist, and use their recommended follow-up plans, you can expect to receive closer to 85% to 105% of the amount pledged.

SAMPLE TOTAL PROJECT COST LIST

Your "real cost" are the TOTAL PROJECT COST.

The "construction cost" is only a portion of the whole picture.

Below you will find a real-life example. The contractor correctly said that "construction cost" would be $669,770. However, actual cost to the church was $1,016,312. See below for all the "soft costs" that must be added to give your congregation an accurate picture of what the project will really cost. Before asking for final approval from your Charge Conference, be sure you know THE TOTAL COSTS.

One MISTAKE this church made - they budgeted $0 for contingency - assuming that there would be no surprises, no add alternates, no additions to the project. They should have budgeted up to 10% for this - about $70,000 for unexpected contingencies.

 © 2018 Robert O. Crossman, www.UMNewChurch.org

You should anticipate bringing an abbreviated version of this page to your FIRST meeting with the District Board and Charge Conference. This is an actual sample of the financial page presented at the SECOND Charge Conference.

¶ 2544.5 *"The building committee shall submit to the district Board of Church Location and Building, for its consideration and approval, a statement of the need for the proposed facilities, and the architectural plans and financial estimates and plans."*

$669,770 includes:

Nabholz 7% fee, general Superintendent items, construction utilities, etc. Also: site preparation, testing, , asphalt paving, sidewalks, parking lot lights, concrete foundation and slab, pre-engineered structure with standing seam roof, brick and Dryvit on the exterior, sheetrock walls, interior wood doors in metal frames, insulated windows and aluminium entrances, acoustical ceilings, painting and finishing, millwork as shown - painted cabinets with plastic laminate tops, carpeting @1.50 sq ft , folding partitions - Hurcor 3800, electrical, plumbing, HVAC.

Estimate of dates & amounts due
Apr 15 - 32,000
May 15 - 64,000
Jun 15 - 131,000
Jul 15 - 224,000
Aug 15 - 129,000
Sept 15 -- 62,000

Permanent Financing Possibilities

We received competitive written bids from five banks in town: First National Bank, Nations Bank, First Community Bank and from First Financial Bank.

As of today...

The most attractive rate quoted was:
8% fixed 3 years, 15 yr amortization, no penalty for early payment

Project Cost & Projections {revised ___/__/20__}

COSTS YET TO COME:

Total Construction **(71.31/sf)**		669,770
Construction Performance & Payment Bond	10,000	
Architect Fee (6%+$300)(38,957-27,591=$11,366 *balance)*	11,366	
Conway Corp Utility Hookup	30,000	
Construction Interest (8.5%) *(with permanent Nov.1)*	10,500	
Construction Office *(8x16 storage building)*	1,500	
Landscape (required by city, perimeter) *(volunteer labor)*	3,640	
Landscape (around entrance to building) *(volunteer labor)*	2,014	
Exterior Sign, (Jap Burton, like 1st UMC NLR) *(his cost)*	5,300 *plus any brick work*	
Sound System *(waiting on better estimates, this is rough)*	6,000	
Window Treatments	0	
Contingency - soft cost & add alternates	0	
Playground Materials (volunteer labor)	1,500	
Closing Cost on Permanent Loan	2,500	

Furniture	31,236	
Total Soft Cost		115,556
TOTAL		**$ 785,326**

RESOURCES:

Cash on Hand January 17, 1996 — 274,995

(includes any grants received, all offerings & rummage sale receipts)
(includes $46,671.07 transferred from the general fund on 1/17/96)
(we have already paid: survey $650, campaign $10,812, architect $27,591, & taxes $12)
(we have already paid for the land @ $100,000 + interest)

New Funds Anticipated:

(2 months of regular Building Fund gifts before ground breaking)	16,800
(6 months of regular Building Fund gifts during construction)	50,400
(Anticipated Memorials/Gifts for Furniture & Fixtures & landscaping)	25,000

TOTAL RESOURCES RECEIVED BY MOVE-IN DAY, Oct. 1, 1996	367,195
plan to move from construction to permanent financing Oct. 1, 1996	
Debt Remaining on Move-In Day, December 1, 1996	418,131
Monthly payments on 15 year note @ 8% =	3,900
Monthly payments on 5 yr note @ 8% would be $ 8,276	

ASSUMPTIONS:

Although minimum monthly payment is $ 3,900, we will pre-pay as money comes in, at approximately $ 8,400 per month. *It's assumed that new growth in financial support will be limited to offsetting those who do not fulfill their pledge. However, it should be reasonable to estimate that future growth in financial support will be greater than this.* **At the end of the Grow With Grace pledges Oct. '98, debt remaining on the note should be less than $ 276,000** It will be necessary to have a 2nd capital funds campaign after we have been in the building for 12-18 months. The 2nd campaign will be to pay off the $ 276,000 debt + future interest. We may also be ready for the Phase II Children's Ministry Wing *{8 rooms , 3,888 sf @ $256,000 + 37 new parking spaces @ $28,000}* We may soon be ready for Phase II Adult Ministry, Office & Kitchen *{8 rooms , 3,888 sf @ $277,992 + 86 new parking spaces @ $44,000}*

Project Costs

Building Construction Cost	669,770
Soft Costs {fees, fixtures, utilities}	115,556
Building Children's Wing Modification {revised 2/7/96}	81,000
Fees for Children's Wing Modification {revised 2/7/96}	4,860
SUB -TOTAL	**$ 871,186**

The above amount does not include items already paid such as:
land $100,000; Interest on land note $2,022; Topo survey $650;

 © 2018 Robert O. Crossman, www.UMNewChurch.org

Grow With Grace Capital Campaign $10,812; Architect Fee to date $27,591; taxes $12; soil test $1,421; sign for land $220; bring sewer line to property line $2,173; and, survey $225 145,126

.... ***GRAND TOTAL*** **$ 1,016,312**

CONSTRUCTION COST ADJUSTMENTS:

deduction on insulation of perimeter slab ....<235.00>
deduction of interior signs from project
    <1,552.00> actual cost of signs $ 588.11..<963.89>
additional earthwork entrance and slab 14,874.00
additional to run 18" parking lot drain into city storm drain 6,200
additional to run wire to street sign 200

SOFT COST DETAIL

	Budget	Actual	Over/Under
Architect Fee {6% +300} {$38,957 - 27591 = $11,366 balance}	11,366		
we added $ 4,860 architect fee above with Children's wing	4,860		
Conway Corp Utility Hookup (Greg Dale)	30,000	16,551.20	<13,448.80>
Utility gift from Lanny (5 @ 843.64)	0		<4,218.20>
Construction Interest {8.5%}	10,500		
Construction Office (future general storage)	1,500	1,431.00	<69.00>
Construction Performance & Payment Bond	10,000		
Construction Building for Tools (future lawn mower building)	0	979.44	979.44
Landscape {required by city, perimeter of parking lot}{volunteer labor}	3,640		
2" caliper Maple & Oaks 22 @ $80= 1,760; 4' perimeter sod (tiff) 900 yards @ $1 = $900; Multi-trunk Crepe Myrtle 5 @ $40 = 200; seed (bermuda mix) $300; Top soil 4 loads @ $80 = $320; Skid loader one day rental $160			
Landscape {around entrance of building}{volunteer labor}	2,014		
3" caliper Holly or Conifer 1 donated; 10'-12' Crepe Myrtle 2 @ $70 = $140; 6'-8'Youpon Holly 2 @ $100 = $200 3 gal Azalas 19 @ $6 = $114; 1 gal Dwarf Barberry 5 @ $2 = $10 3 gal NeweSteven 3 @ $6 = $18; 3 gal Assorted (Dwf Youpon, Nana Nandina, Barbary, Dwf Spiroa, HellerHolly) 22 @ $6= $132; 1 gal Liriope bed 40 @ $1,50 = $60 12 yrd Hardwood Mulch, 1 load @ $200; Drain system $140; Sprinkler 1 1/4" back flow, out door 12 station approx $1,000			
Landscape - to extend sprinkler to all parking lot islands and along Hogan and Releigh	2,000.00	0 ?	2,000.00?
Lawn Care Equipment (mower donated by Betty Dunnaway) We will also need a small push mower for detail work close to building,	0		
Exterior Sign	5,300	? 2,000.00	< 3,200.00>
Sound System	6,000	? 6,500.00	? 500.00
Playground, phase I	1,500		
Exact design has not been determined. This amount would provide initial start up cost for ground cover, and some lumber for construction of equipment similar to that at many of the Conway schools.			
Postage	0	5.20	5.20
Storage for Windows	0	52.00	52.00
Closing Cost on Permanent Loan (est.)	2,500		
Furniture (detail list of furniture items attached)	31,236		

TOTAL SOFT COST {105,556 + 4,860 fees} ....$ 110,416

FURNITURE DETAIL

	Budget	Actual	Over/Under
Worship/Multipurpose Room			

Altar, Pulpit, Stand for Baptistry Bowl, 5 Kneel 8′ Rails,	3,000		
375 Chairs - for worship/Sunday School	12,000	11,231.26	<768,74>
20 Round mighty-lite tables, 60″, brown color,	1,600	2,268.00	668.00
3 rectangular mighty-lite tables, brown color, 30x72″	240	576.00	336.00
2 Round Table carts, hold 10 each @286	572	.00	<572.00>
Chancel platform, site built, volunteer labor, 12′x24′x24″ high	1,200	3,324.13	2,124.13
Brass communion ware to serve	240	0	
Foyer/ Lobby door mats (4) 4′x6′, @$40	160		
5 sled benches, oak w/fabric seat, 79″ long, @187	937	.00	<937.00>
information area - 1 chair	50		
information area - metal coffee cabinet w/sliding door storage under	150		
memorial book display with usher supply underneath	0		
information desk tack board	31		
Office 2 workstation desks @ 400, 2 chairs @100; 2 chair mats @20;	1,190		
Telephones 6 @ 50 (secretary, children, pastor, nursery, kitchen	300		
4 Wastebaskets (work room, secretary, child minister, pastor)	20		
Copier, 3,000 /wk avg., duplex, doc.feed, sorter, stapler	0	.00	.00
Pastor's Desk @$400; Chair @ $150; 2 side chairs @100 each; bookcases	1,100		
Custodian cart $180; Dust mop $22; Dust pan $18; Mop w/head $16;	311		
Back pack vacuum,	400		
Commercial carpet shampoo machine,	0		
Kitchen *{Ray Kordsmeier said our prices will be considerably lower than these}*			
dishwasher	450	180.00	<270.00>
refrigerator 26 cub ft with top freezer (will hold banquet trays)	1,000	755.00	<245.00>
ice maker (Scottsman, holds 50 lbs of ice, makes 35lb/day)	1,200	891.00	<309.00>
wastebasket	25		
stove & hood	500	226.00	<274.00>
Plates, drink cups, coffee cups, flatware {purchased with Bazaar funds)	0	.00	.00
Large pots, and pans (to be purchased with Bazaar Funds)	0	.00	.00
SUNDAY SCHOOL DEPARTMENT			
8 Chalk boards 4′x4′ @$65; 10 tack boards 3′x4′ @31; 10 wastebaskets @5880			
Nursery: 2 rockers @100 each; 3 cribs @ 150 each; 1 diaper bag shelf (free); toy chest @50			700
2 & 3 yr olds: 2 tables 30x60 adj legs @35 each; 2 teach chairs @38 each; 15 chairs 12″@12			326
4 & 5 yr olds: 2 tables 30x60 adj legs @35 each; 2 teach chairs @38 each; 15 chairs 12″@12			326
Grade 1 & 2: 2 tables 30x60 adj legs @35 each; 2 teach chairs @38 each; 15 chairs 14″@13			341
Grade 3 & 4: 2 tables 30x60 adj legs @35 each; 2 teach chairs @38 each; 15 chairs 14″@13			341
Grade 5 & 6: 2 tables 30x60 adj legs @35 each; 2 teach chairs @38 each; 15 chairs 18″@16			386
Youth room - 3 room dividers, free standing, 60x60 @ $100	300	.00	<300.00>
Grade 7 - 9 & 10 - 12: 30 chairs @32 = $960; *shown above within worship)*	0	.00	.00
Adult Classes: 3 metal coffee cabinet 32x18x42h @150	450		
Slinkard Class: no tables; 30 chairs @32 = $960 *(shown above w.worship)*	0	.00	.00
Slinkard Class: podium {will use Luxora Pulpit instead}	50	.00	<50.00>
Keith Class 30 chairs @32 = $960 *(total shown above within worship)*	0	.00	.00
Keith Class 3 tables @150 = $450 also for potluck food	0	.00	.00
Mitchum Class 30 chairs @32 = $960 *(total shown above within worship)*	0	.00	.00
TV and Cart (free from Bill Arnold) VCR $250	250		
Overhead projector	450		
TOTAL FURNITURE	**$ 31,236**		**<597.00>**

so far, furniture is $ 597 less than expected

© 2018 Robert O. Crossman, www.UMNewChurch.org

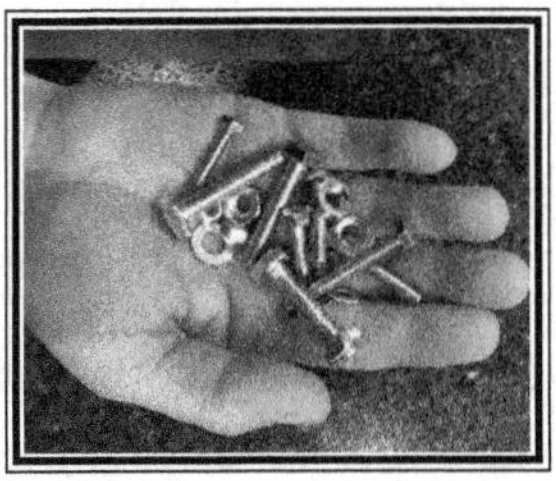

New Church Handbook
Nuts & Bolts for Planting New Churches In The Wesleyan Tradition

"Building Construction - Do You Need An Architect?"

by Bob Crossman

Do you need an Architect?

Yes. In most cases it is the law that you engage an architect (and safer than relying on your own design skills).

Check on your state law requirements. In Arkansas, for example, Architectural Act 17-15-302-b-2-c states that any church building with a market value of $100,000 or more SHALL be designed by a registered architect. The purpose of this law is to protect the health, safety and welfare of the general public.

Have your architect do a 'MASTER PLAN' of your site... to 'max out' your spaces...

As the years pass, and you experience additional growth, what might the next building expansion phase II, III, and IV be ten or twenty years from now?

This might keep you forward thinking, planning for growth, and avoiding mistakes.

It's like the young couple building their first new home... they may not be planning to have five children, but it is wise to plan for possible addition of another bedroom just in case, or the possible future addition of a 'mother in law' apartment. It may be possible for the young couple, without spending any money now, to build in such a way that future expansions fit in to the whole design and avoid expensive renovations just to make the house ready for the expansion.

You ~~might~~ WILL have to do your project in PHASES.

You probably want and need more than you can afford. It is wise to set priorities, and build first things first. Phases II, III, IV and V can complete the project.

You might say that it's Biblical: In Genesis, God had a wonderful vision... an awesome project he wanted to create... but even God did this in phases... One day at a time... not all on the same day!

Architect Fees

I think you will find that for new construction, 6% of construction cost is the typical fee requested by an architect. **A typical payment Schedule for architect services are as follows:**

A. Twenty percent (20%) of the fee is billed at the conclusion of the Schematic Design Phase.
B. Fifteen percent (15%) of the fee is billed at the conclusion of the Design Development Phase.
C. Forty percent (40%) of the fee is billed at the conclusion of the Construction

© 2018 Robert O. Crossman, www.UMNewChurch.org

Documents Phase.

D. Five Percent (5%) is billed at the conclusion of the Bidding Phase.

E. The remaining twenty percent (20%) is billed monthly during the Construction Phase pro-rated according to the percentage of construction completed.

F. The cost of the construction is billed monthly during the Construction Phase. The amount is based on the actual cost of the work completed during the preceding month less retainage.

Architectural Services

The services an Architect provides breaks down into the following six phases

1. **Programming**

   The Programming Phase consists of the gathering of information necessary to produce a design. This information is gathered through meetings between the architect and the building committee. The building committee and church staff are our best resources for determining the needs and wants of the church. The design of the building will be a direct result of an analysis of information received from those who know the church best.

2. **Schematic**

   The Schematic Design Phase translates the programming Design information into a preliminary plan. The phase concludes with an approved design and cost estimate. Presentation drawings, site plan, floor plan(s), views of the building, are provided for obtaining church approval and financing. Every step of the process will be reviewed and approved by the committee. Estimated costs will be presented early in the process and updated as the design progresses.

3. **Design**

   In the Design Development Phase, the architect will refine the Development schematic design by working out the structural and mechanical systems and finalizing the plans. It is the process of going from preliminary to precise. Minor changes in the design are expected.

4. **Construction**

   In the Construction Documents Phase the architect produces the Documents technical drawings and specifications that will be required to bid and construct your project. Architectural, structural, plumbing, heating/cooling and electrical plans are included. Engineering services such as sound, acoustical and civil are included as needed.

5. **Bidding/**

   The Bidding/Negotiation Phase includes assistance in the selection Negotiation of qualified contractors to bid on the project or, if preferred, a contracting firm with which to negotiate the contract. This phase concludes with the execution of a construction contract.

6. **Construction**

   The architect serves as your representative during the Construction Phase. This includes periodic job site inspections to ensure the construction adheres

© 2018 Robert O. Crossman, www.UMNewChurch.org

to the plans and specifications, review and approval of the contractor's pay requests, assistance in the selection of colors and finishes, meetings with the contractor and committee as required, and management of changes to the work. A final inspection is provided prior to your occupancy.

Typical Architect
Payment Schedule:

A. Twenty percent (20%) of the fee is billed at the conclusion of the Schematic Design Phase.

B. Fifteen percent (15%) of the fee is billed at the conclusion of the Design Development Phase.

C. Forty percent (40%) of the fee is billed at the conclusion of the Construction Documents Phase.

D. Five Percent (5%) is billed at the conclusion of the Bidding Phase.

E. The remaining twenty percent (20%) is billed monthly during the Construction Phase pro-rated according to the percentage of construction completed.

F. The cost of the construction is billed monthly during the Construction Phase. The amount is based on the actual cost of the work completed during the preceding month less retainage.

---

5 rules of thumb from Roger Patterson,
former General Commission Architect
for Evangelism and Church Growth.

Roger Patterson said that your first-time worship guests decide if they are going to come back in the NINE minutes BEFORE the call to worship or the first hymn.

1 After finding your address in the phone book, or by a telephone call to the church... can they find your building?
2 Is the parking lot out front, and large enough? Are 20 to 25% of the spaces empty?
3 Is there ONE main obvious entry that all visitors will naturally enter?
4 When they enter that door, do they enter a lobby that is 1/3 to 1/2 the size of your worship space?
5 In that lobby, without asking, can they find a hospitality counter with welcome food and a greeter? Without asking, can worship guests find the bathroom, nursery, worship room, educational rooms, and church office?

Your particular project may only be able to address a few of Roger Patterson's concerns but they are still good to keep in mind.

Basically, our buildings are not simply to meet 'our' needs, but they are also one of the ways we witness to the community… one of the ways we welcome seekers… **What does the building itself communicate?**

You only have one chance to make a first impression.

Look at your existing property:

Are there weeds in the flower beds?
Are the eves of the roof rotting?
Paint peeling off?
Sign needs repainting?

If so, what does that communicate about what happens inside?

Think about what kind of judgments YOU make based on the exterior of a restaurant, and the cars (or lack of) in the restaurant parking lot. By just looking at the exterior, you decide if you would enter; what kind of food they probably offer; what the meal is going to cost; how much of a tip you will need to leave; and whether the bathroom is clean or not. Amazing. You have a strong hunch about all of these things by just looking at the exterior of a restaurant. There is a good chance that your community makes the same judgements about your church just by looking at the exterior.

Look at your proposed construction... by just looking at the exterior, what will those driving by decide about what probably happens inside?

Another 'rule of thumb' about the appearance or quality of your construction:

It is said that people looking for a church to attend usually <u>feel most comfortable</u> in a building that is about the same quality construction as their home - or a bit nicer. It is also said that people looking for a church to attend usually <u>feel UNcomfortable</u> in a building that is poorer construction than their home.

Look at your proposed building, parking lot and landscaping. If this rule of thumb is true, which households in your community would probably feel most attracted to your facilities? Which households would probably be hesitant to enter?

If you are wanting to 'seek and save the lost' and make new disciples... you might want to keep this rule of thumb in mind.

NOTE: This article reflects the personal opinions of its author and does not necessarily reflect an official position of Discipleship Ministries or Path 1.

© 2018 Robert O. Crossman, www.UMNewChurch.org

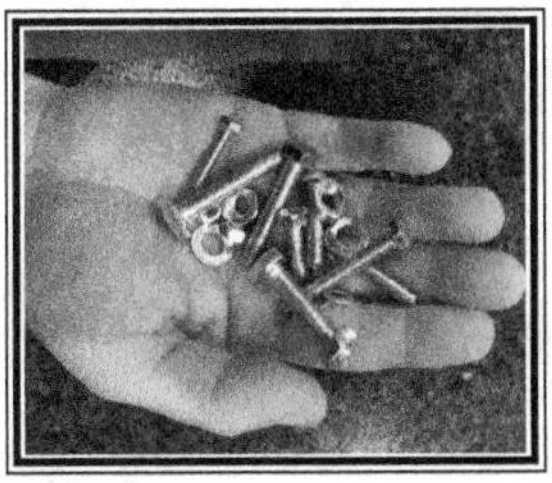

New Church Handbook
Nuts & Bolts for Planting New Churches In The Wesleyan Tradition

"Building Construction - Questions to Ask When Interviewing Architects"

by Bob Crossman

It is critical that you hire the right architect. This is one of the most important decisions your church will ever make. You may have a member whose son is a brand new architect and needs your business and a referral from your church - but you can not afford to take such a risk with the Lord's money.

You should research potential architects who have a good reputation for building the type and style of structure you are considering, and who are familiar designing within the total project cost you have in mind.

Plan to interview 3 or 4 of the most promising architects in front of the full Building Committee. Architects are use to this kind of process. Schedule each one 45 minutes for each architect, allowing 15 minutes between each for the committee to discuss what they have just heard. Try to conduct all 4 interviews the same evening or afternoon so your memories are fresh and can make accurate comparisons.

You need an architect you feel comfortable talking to over a cup of coffee when difficult situations arise during your project. You also need an architect who has *"practiced"* on many other church projects similar to yours. You can not afford to hire an architect to design your worship center, who has never designed one like you have in mind.

Introductory Questions

1. How long has your firm been in business?
2, How many architects does your firm employ?
3. What percentage of your firm's business is with churches?
4. If we hire your firm, who from the firm will the church be directly dealing with?
5. Is it the same person who will be designing the project?
6. If not, who will be designing it and what direct interaction will the church have with this person?
7. How long has that person been in business?
8. How many church projects like ours has this person done?
9. How many United Methodist projects has this person done, so we might be assured they understand the way most UMC's function?
10. Does this person have a specific design style, and how well does that style match what we are looking to build?
11. What are the most recent projects this person has completed?
12. When and where was the architect's most current project that is like ours?
13. Most likely, what we want and need will be more expensive than we can afford. Has this person worked with churches through Phases 1, 2, and 3?

© 2018 Robert O. Crossman, www.UMNewChurch.org

14. May we see examples of the architect's previous projects that are similar to our project, including sketches, photos, plans and budgets?
15. Should the church decide to hire their firm, may the church get the names, addresses, and telephone numbers of the clients for these previous similar projects? **(ACTUALLY CALL THESE REFERENCES!!!)**
16. Will you be using consultants, and how will they be paid?
17. What was the actual construction cost versus the architect's estimated cost for each of these projects, and how do they account for the variance?
18. *Our denomination suggests that we ask these three questions:*
    a. Does your firm carry insurance?
    b. What are the policy limits for each type of insurance you carry?
    c. What is the proposed mediation process for resolving disputes and will the architect agree to binding arbitration?

Concerning Your Particular Project

1. What are the most noteworthy challenges of the proposed project and how does the architect anticipate dealing with them?
2. How confident are you that your architect can meet our time constraints?
3. How will your architect gather information about our ministry space needs so that the most favorable design solution might be found?
4. What services will your firm provide during the construction project?
5. What are the phases in your proposed design process and how long should each take?
7. Since we are building phase 1, *(of what with the Lord's blessing may be 3 or 4 phases eventually)* we need your office to also give us a rough master plan, so that we are holding space to max out the use of the land available. Can your firm do this, and what is the cost for this service?
8. What will your architect provide to help us interpret the project to our congregation?
   (Computer 3D models, color renderings, line sketches, models, etc.)
9. What are the price differences between each of these these options you just mentioned?
10. Do you believe we are being realistic about our project's time line, budget, and building site?

Fees

1. What will be our fees for your services, and how do you calculate them?
2. Will you provide a fixed price agreement for each phase of this project instead of a percentage-based fee? *(Fixed price is usually better.)*
3. What is your schedule of anticipated payments?
4. If you hire consultants or engineers *(civil, structural, mechanical, electrical, geotechnical, testing and inspection, etc.)*, are their fees included in the architects quoted fee or are they separate services?
5. Are their reimbursable expenses we need to anticipate?
6. What additional cost should we anticipate for permits, impact fees etc.?
7. Will your firm provide construction cost estimates for the project?

 © 2018 Robert O. Crossman, www.UMNewChurch.org

8. What happens if the architect's construction estimates are not in line with construction quotes?
9. Who is liable for the cost of redesign if it is necessary to meet the construction budget?
10. Will there be additional charges for changes required by the building department or other government agency? If so, how are these charges calculated?
11. How are additional charges computed for design changes requested **by the church** after working drawings are already completed?
12. How are additional charges computed for design changes requested **by the contractor**?
13. Who is financially responsible for correcting errors and omissions in design and bids?
14. Our denomination also wants us to ask:
    • How might the church structure the contract so that the church has the ability to "walk away" from the agreement at the conclusion of any phase without additional cost or penalty?
    • How does the church insure they own and have the right to use the intellectual property (drawings, research findings, etc.) from each phase if we should decide to terminate our relationship with your firm?

Making the Final Decision

These following suggestions are excerpted from the book, *"Preparing to Build: Practical Tips & Experienced Advice to Prepare Your Church for a Building Program"* by Stephen Anderson.
It would be wise to order several copies of this resource.

Don't go by your feelings, check the references!
Call or visit each reference that each architect gives you.

Ask Each Reference the Architect Provides:
1. How well did the architect adhere to schedules?
2. How well did the architect live up to the expectation they set during the sales phase?
3. Did the project complete within budget? If not, why not?
4. Were you pleased with the architect's services and your working relationship with the architect? (Compare to the architects explanation to the same question)
5. Did the architect listen to your concerns and attempt to resolve them to your satisfaction?
6. Would you hire the architect again? Why or why not?
7. What problems surfaced during the project?
8. What were the architect's strong points?
9. What were the architect's weak points?
10. What would you do different the next time?
11. Ask each reference about other projects they know the architect was involved

with. This will give you some additional references to check.
Remember no one will knowingly hand out references that won't give a glowing report. Seeking other "off list" references may give you a more balanced viewpoint.

Subjective Issues To Evaluate And Consider When Hiring An Architect

These are questions that you may not always directly ask,
but may evaluate from the responses to other questions and actions.

1. DO THE REFERENCES INDICATE THAT WE SHOULD ENGAGE THIS ARCHITECT?
2. How interested is the architect in our project?
3. How much time and effort has the architect put into winning our business and earning our confidence?
4. How busy is the architect?
5. What do you feel sets this architect apart from the rest?
6. How well does the architect respond to being asked why you should hire them over someone else?
7. How well do your thoughts on why this architect may be the best fit for your church line up with their answer on why you should hire them?
8. How well has the architect performed in bringing projects to completion within the proposed budget on other projects?
9. How well does the architect understand our goals, priorities and constraints? 9. How good of a personality fit do you feel you have with the architect?
10. Does the architect have an "all or nothing" attitude towards the proposed services, or are they willing to offer services "a la carte" to help you meet our budget?
11. Are the agreements and pricing for services straightforward and easy to understand?
12. How well has the architect responded to your questions and communications in a timely and accurate fashion?

It is recommended you create a form (or several) with all the questions allowing each person on the evaluation team to rank each respondent's response on a scale of 1-10. If possible, visit the projects the architect has used as references for their services. This will provide an objective valuation for each applicant that should weigh heavily in the final decision and help eliminate personal feelings and preferences. As you may notice, many of the questions assume you have a good idea of what you want to build, why you need to build and what you can afford. If you cannot definitively answer these questions, it is premature to solicit the services of an architect or design/build firm.

†††

NOTE: This article reflects the personal opinions of its author
and does not necessarily reflect an official position of Discipleship Ministries or Path 1.

© 2018 Robert O. Crossman, www.UMNewChurch.org

IX. What About Discipleship Systems Within New Churches?

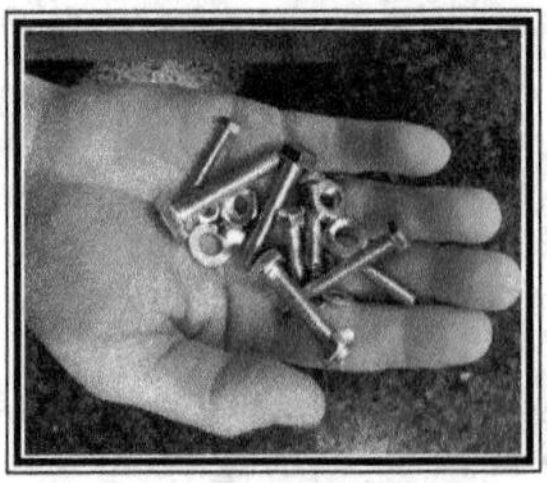

New Church Handbook
Nuts & Bolts for Planting New Churches In The Wesleyan Tradition

"How To Develop a Discipleship System"

by Tammy Garrison

Path 1, General Board of Discipleship, defines a new church as follows: *"A new congregation is a newly organized faith community that is committed to making disciples of Jesus Christ and includes regular community worship, is theologically Wesleyan, is willing to plant a new congregation in its first decade,* ***has an effective discipling system,*** *demonstrates faithful stewardship, does community outreach, and receives new members. A new church is more than a mission project, a new worship service, or the construction of a new building."*

Developing Discipleship Systems

By Dr. Tammy Garrison

A part of developing a new faith community is designing a discipleship system. There are lots of questions to explore and issues to understand in planning the way the people who become a part of the new church you start will grow closer to God and find places to live out their faith in ministry and witness. Developing the discipleship system can take as much if not more time and preparation as designing the worship experience. What follows are different aspects for consideration in developing discipleship systems. First comes a theological basis for discipleship from a Wesleyan perspective. Next is a working definition of what a disciple is. This is followed by a collective list of characteristics of disciple-making churches. Two models of discipleship systems are explored followed by cultural factors for consideration in putting a discipleship system in a new faith community together. The discussion ends with suggestions to consider as you begin to put the discipleship system for your church together.

A Theological Basis

Discipleship based upon a Wesleyan theology is the intersection of grace and sanctification. John Wesley's understanding of grace is three-fold: prevenient grace, justifying grace, and sanctifying grace. Although all three are evident simultaneously in a person's life, the focus of discipleship is primarily sanctifying grace. In sanctification we are made perfect in love. Sanctification and Christian perfection include works of piety and works of mercy. The goal of these works is holiness of the heart and of life, which includes love of God and love of neighbor. Works of piety as described by Wesley encompass worship, prayer, Bible study, and Communion. From the twenty-fifth chapter of Matthew, Wesley derives works of mercy, including clothing the naked, feeding the hungry, and visiting the sick and

 © 2018 Robert O. Crossman, www.UMNewChurch.org

imprisoned. These works of mercy and piety lead to holiness of the heart and of life because one is focused on things eternal that restore us to the image of God. This is the doctrine of the way of salvation as proposed by John Wesley, and our understanding of discipleship.

Sondra Higgins Matthaei, in her book *Making Disciples,* has explored Wesley's understanding extensively. She notes it is by grace that God invites us into a relationship that leads to holiness of heart and life. Matthaei also notes Wesley's particular emphasis that works of mercy and works of piety are transformational when our sole purpose is to seek God's heart.

Works of mercy and of piety are rote behaviors only, unless our one desire is truly to discover God's heart and grow in an intimate relationship with the Lord. In many of our congregations we have experienced individuals who do all the right things - attend worship regularly, participate in a small group setting, contribute both financially and through service to the church - and yet are not experiencing transformation. We ourselves may have been these individuals. However, Wesley makes it clear that we can participate in the things meant to bring us closer to God and to help us grow into mature disciples, but we are just going through the motions unless we truly and honestly are seeking to discover God's heart and participate in God's activity in the world in new ways throughout our lives.

A more recent source echoes John Wesley's insights into discipleship. Richard J. Foster, author of *Celebration of Discipline,* is well read and respected for his insights in the role of spiritual disciplines in cultivating holiness of heart and life. There are many similarities between Foster and Wesley.

Foster begins with the need for a great many professing people to move beyond the simple beginnings of faith in Christ. Foster identifies three groups of spiritual disciplines and explores practical ways to explore or implement these disciplines.

The first group he calls inward disciplines. These include meditation, prayer, fasting and study. These disciplines are more reflective in nature. The second group of disciplines, although possibly inward in nature, has an outward manifestation. These include simplicity, solitude, submission, and service. The third group features corporate disciplines that the church community engages in together. These include confession, worship, guidance, and celebration. Foster provides a brief overview of each of these and explores practical steps for engaging in all twelve disciplines. Foster offers an intentional focus on habits and practices within daily life that have the potential of bringing the Christian closer to God and God's purposes for life.

Foster is similar to Wesley in that he believes personal attitude is critical in determining the benefits of practicing spiritual disciplines. A person's greatest desire must be to discover the heart and mind of God. Without the ultimate desire to know God better, spiritual disciplines become rote practices of faith that will contain very little transformation for the individual.

Foster also recognizes that spiritual disciplines are a gift from God. They are the means through which we receive and experience God's grace. Foster emphasizes that the practice of spiritual disciplines is not the end within itself. The practice of spiritual disciplines does not make one a disciple, but provides tools through which a disciple experiences transformation. Keeping holiness of heart and life as the main priority both as a church and as an individual is vital to understanding discipleship and implementing discipleship systems.

In summary, discipleship is a gift of God by which we develop, through the power of the Holy Spirit, holiness of heart and life through works of mercy and works of piety. Holiness of heart and life happens when we engage in works of mercy and piety out of a desire to draw closer to God. Through the discipleship process we discover what it means to be a disciple, draw closer to God, seek to understand and know God's heart in order to fulfill Christ's purposes for ourselves and for the church.

A Working Definition

The purpose of a discipleship system is to provide a process through which people can grow and develop as disciples. While it is important to understand the process of developing holiness of heart and life through a discipleship system and the key components of such, it is also necessary to identify the end result of the discipleship process. In other words, we are addressing what is evident in a person's life as holiness of heart and life develops. Specifically, how a disciple is defined will help shape and determine the specifics of the discipleship system within the local church.

A biblical model for what it means to be a disciple can be found in the Gospel of John. A forum writer to the web-based resource Easum, Bandy, and Associates, notes that it would be nice if Christ had provided us specifically with a definition of what it means to be a disciple. Though Jesus doesn't do this, there are three places in John's Gospel where Jesus begins with the phrase "My disciples are"…" From these phrases we get a clearer idea of what it means to be Jesus' disciple.

In John 8:31, Jesus said, "If you remain in my word, then you are truly my disciples." In part this refers to reading the Bible and growing in knowledge of the faith. However, in the fifteenth chapter of John, Jesus defines further what it means to remain in Christ. "Remain in me, and I will remain in you. No branch can bear fruit by itself; it must remain on the vine. Neither can you bear fruit unless you remain in me."

Jesus is warning us not to neglect our spiritual health and invites us to draw closer to God. Jesus tells us that in order to have a productive spiritual life we

 © 2018 Robert O. Crossman, www.UMNewChurch.org

have to engage in the activities that lead to a vital growing relationship with Jesus Christ. This is the only way we produce the spiritual fruit of which Jesus speaks. To be a disciple means to submit oneself to discovering and maintaining a personal relationship with God in Christ through practices and disciplines that edify us and bring us closer to God. This includes such things as the works of piety John Wesley found crucial to discovering holiness of heart and life and the Christian practices as outlined by Foster. **A disciple is committed to such things as faithfully participating in worship, reading the Bible and praying daily, having a routine time of devotion and communion with God, faithfully being a steward of both talent and finances, and gathering with other Christians for encouragement, support, and accountability of one another.** A disciple practices works of piety to remain close to Christ and to bear fruit.

In John 13:34-35, Jesus also said, "A new commandment I give to you, that you love one another, just like I have loved you; that you also love one another. By this everyone will know that you are my disciples, if you have love for one another."

It is important to note in these verses that Jesus calls his disciples to love one another as he has loved us. We must remember that included in that circle are tax collectors, prostitutes, and sinners. Loving another the way Jesus loves us is not always easy. The disciples were called to build relationships with people very different from them and with whom they may have felt uncomfortable at times.

Christ's example is that of sacrificial love. **Being disciples means we develop holiness of heart and life for the purpose of preparing ourselves to give sacrificial love to others in sacrificial ways.** Through the washing of the disciples' feet, Jesus demonstrated how to humble ourselves and put the needs of others before our own. Ultimately he gave his life on the cross for ours and calls his disciples to pick up our crosses and follow him. Disciples demonstrate their love for God and for other people, and do so in sacrificial ways.

Jesus shares one thing more about his disciples. In John 15:8, Jesus said, "My true disciples produce much fruit. This brings great glory to my Father." What Jesus means by fruit has been interpreted and understood in different ways. The New Testament tells us much about bearing fruit.

One can judge a tree or a vine by its fruit or productivity. This is the presentation of fruits of the Spirit in our lives. In Galatians 5:22-23 we read, "But when the Holy Spirit controls our lives, the Spirit will produce this kind of fruit in us: love, joy, peace, patience, kindness, goodness, faithfulness, gentleness, and self-control. Here there is no conflict with the law." Evidence of the fruits of the spirit in our lives includes both inward and outward change, marked by both thoughts and behaviors, manifested through the priorities we"make in our lives. It is a change in what gets our time and attention. It is a shift to serving others and putting the needs of others before our own. It is a change in our hearts and a change in attitude toward life and other people.

Jesus speaks of yet another kind of fruit. We are also told in the scriptures that the fruit is ready for harvesting. The fruit of which Jesus speaks in this context are the least, the last, and the lost whom he seeks for the Kingdom. Jesus told his disciples in the fourth chapter of John, "Look around you! Vast fields are ripening all around us and are ready now for the harvest." As he spoke to his disciples on that day, he encouraged them to see the numerous people in need of the saving grace Jesus had to offer them. Following his resurrection it would become the responsibility of the disciples to share that saving grace with the world, bringing into the Kingdom of God all those who would hear and receive the Good News. As modern-day disciples, sharing the saving grace of Christ with others and doing what we can to usher them into a personal relationship with Jesus is what it means for us to bear fruit. "The harvesters are paid good wages," Jesus said," "and the fruit they harvest is people brought to eternal life. What joy awaits both the planter and the harvester alike!" Thus, as disciples, we are called to produce fruit in the form of people brought to eternal life in Christ. Great joy awaits both the Lord and us as we participate with God in this endeavor.

In his letter to the Roman church, the apostle Paul writes about producing fruit for Christ. "So this is the point: the law no longer holds you in its power, because you died to its power when you died with Christ on the cross. And now you are united with the one who was raised from the dead. As a result, you can produce good fruit, that is, good deeds for God." Here, Paul speaks specifically of good deeds. Paul's words reconnect us with John Wesley and holiness of heart and life that is a part of the discipleship process, particularly as it pertains to works of mercy. Paul's words remind us that a disciple feeds the hungry, clothes the naked, gives drink to the thirsty, visits the sick and imprisoned, and in addition shares the Good News of Jesus Christ. **Thus a disciple responds to those in need, bringing about healing and wholeness in the lives of others whenever possible.**

To summarize, the process of becoming a disciple involves three phases. A person makes an initial decision for Christ, grows in knowledge and spiritual practices, and produces fruit that glorifies God. The fruit of a disciple is internally manifested in a person's life through the gifts of the Spirit. The fruit of a disciple is also leading others to discover eternal life in Christ and performing good deeds for God, thereby meeting the needs of others.

Northwood Community Church, founded by Rev. Aubrey Malphurs, articulates the three phases of discipleship in this way: disciples are converted to knowing Christ as their Savior, are committed to Christ and growing in Christ, and are contributing to Christ by serving the body, sharing financial resources, and seeking the lost. What is interesting about Northwood Community Church is that it not only identified the goal and purpose of the individual and provided the basis for the specifics of the discipleship system, but also made the three aspects of the life of a disciple the basis for the vision and mission of the church. The DNA of the

 © 2018 Robert O. Crossman, www.UMNewChurch.org

church and the strategic goals of the church were defined and influenced by the specific definition of what a disciple is. For instance, the church's strategic goals for the fulfilling of its mission of developing faithful followers of Christ are:

1. To see people converted to Christ.
2. To bring people to a committed life in Christ.
3. To equip people to be contributors to Christ.

The image of a three-legged stool demonstrates the goals of Northwood Community Church. Becoming a disciple, the purpose and mission of Northwood Community, is represented by the seat of the stool. Supporting the stool are three legs labeled "conversion,"" "commitment," and" "contribution." For each leg of the stool, programming and short-term objectives flesh out Northwood Community's identity. Thus, the specific way in which Northwood Community defined the three aspects of becoming a disciple was not only formative in the development of the discipleship system, but was also formative in the very identity of the church community. As well as informing the make-up of the discipleship system, it also articulates a biblical model of discipleship that speaks about the very nature of the church. This has implications for local churches. Our understanding of what a disciple is and how we articulate that has a formative effect on the future of the church.

The Role of the Local Church

The local church has a vital role in personal discipleship journeys. Effective faith communities are combinations of small group gatherings and worship experiences through which people become mature disciples of Jesus Christ. It is important, then, to define or set parameters for the role of the local church and to explore examples of discipleship systems in local churches that have reported a degree of success in helping individuals develop as disciples.

What are the goals for which a church needs to strive to be able to meet the needs of new Christians as well as the seasoned church member? What are the criteria a church should have met in order to have a more than reasonable chance of helping seekers move forward in their Christian faith? To address key principles of discipleship systems, these questions need to be addressed.

A fundamental set of problems arises. The first is a question of vocabulary. No universal term exists to label or describe the congregation as the kind of church our local community of faith should be. In *Church For The Unchurched*, George Hunter calls such churches apostolic churches. Some have used the terms "healthy" or "growing" to label local churches that are effectively fulfilling God's purposes for the church. If the mission of the church is to make disciples of Jesus Christ, then our local congregations are called to be and to become disciple-making congregations.

The second problem that arises is one of criteria. What is the evidence by which we know we are on the right track and doing what God has called us to do as the church? What does a disciple-making church look like? What are the benchmarks we are trying achieve in order to be a disciple-making congregation?

Characteristics of Disciple-making Churches

The attributes identified as essential characteristics disciple-making churches should exhibit are as varied as the terminology used to define or describe what a church should be. A unified list of characteristics that would identify a disciple-making church is hard to find. Various combinations of literature suggest a list of ten characteristics (appearing in bold type in the following paragraphs) of disciple-making congregations.

Disciple-making churches are **permission-giving** and **entrepreneurial** churches, willing to do go to great lengths to reach people for Jesus Christ.

Disciple-making churches are **vision-driven**, and in everything they do in each of these essential areas they are motivated to strive for excellence and to offer the very best in the name of Jesus Christ. Disciple-making churches are driven and passionate about reaching people for Jesus Christ and providing the pathways for individuals to develop as mature disciples.

A church that is a disciple-making church also engages in **relational evangelism**. For many years in our recent past, event-related evangelism within the context of the local congregation, such as revivals, was effective in winning new converts to the Christian faith. Disciple-making churches recognize the need to create opportunities to develop relationships with unchurched people in order to reach them. They also recognize that relationship evangelism takes time and patience.

Disciple-making churches are **user-friendly** in their approach to worship and education. This means no one, whether newcomer or seasoned member of the church, is assumed to have any prior knowledge of the Christian faith.

Disciple-making congregations are **laity-driven** and **experience-based**. Disciple-making churches have reclaimed the importance of "a heart strangely warmed" as a part of the discipleship process. Disciples-making churches understand that the need for relationships is driving an experiential culture that seeks to engage the Holy and to escape feelings of isolation.

Disciple-making churches operate out of a model of **gifted leadership** and lay-driven ministry. They create ministry teams rather than committees. They start with determining the gifts and graces of each person and then develop the positions in ministry according to the people God has called to a particular faith community, rather than determining the ministries that need to take place and trying to fit people into ministry slots. Disciple-making churches empower the people who are passionate about the particular ministry to which God has called them rather

 © 2018 Robert O. Crossman, www.UMNewChurch.org

than trying to recruit people to fill pre-determined roles.

These churches engage in **holographic** and **holistic** programming. Being holistic means disciple-making churches make decisions based upon the mission field. These churches intentionally target the head, heart, and hands in making disciples, rather than just emphasizing a theological knowledge base of right-thinking and doctrine. Disciple-making churches realize that while some may experience transformation through a prayer retreat, others will be most touched through a hands-on service opportunity, while still others are best fed spiritually through scholarly work and biblical study. Being holographic means having an understanding that programming is not based upon templates, and that many aspects of the Christian life are targeted simultaneously in order to help people grow spiritually. In other words, disciple-making churches realize that "one-size-fits-all" programming is not beneficial for every situation. Disciple-making churches are needs-base driven.

These ten characteristics have been gathered from a variety of sources. No one resource in the literature contains all ten of these characteristics. However, they are similar to the list of essential qualities a church should exhibit in Christian A. Schwarz's *Natural Church Development*. Schwarz identifies eight essential qualities of healthy churches. The ten characteristics of disciple-making churches and natural church development principles demonstrate that there are differences between churches that are intentional about being disciple-making churches and those that are not.

Discipleship Models

A discipleship system can provide tools and a pathway for individuals who seek to fulfill the role of "disciple." Various theoretical and structural models depicting the process of discipleship growth have been developed. I will describe two models that influenced the design of this project.

The discipleship model developed by Rick Warren for Saddleback Community Church is probably the best-known. The image of a baseball diamond is used to illustrate the education and assimilation process by which members are to move to deeper levels of commitment. Each base represents a milestone of accomplishment, and success is defined as reaching all bases, (completing all four phases of the discipleship process.) Level One, or first base, is a move to membership and completion of the new member covenant. Level Two, or second base, involves an understanding of and commitment to developing spiritual maturity. Level Three, third base, requires discovery of a specific place of ministry within the church. An individual reaches Level Four or makes a home run through participation in faith sharing, both locally and through mission trips. At each level, four hours of instruction are to be completed and commitments are expected.

Dan Glover and Claudia Lavy describe a similar model in their book, *Deepening Your Effectiveness*. They divide the discipleship journey of an individual into four phases or sections. The four phases are Invitational Discipleship, Instructional Discipleship, Relational Discipleship, and Servant Discipleship. Glover and Lavy use a circle to illustrate the journey of becoming a disciple. Though somewhat similar, Glover and Lavy's phases differ from Warren's in terms of content and logistics.

In the Invitational Discipleship phase, Glover and Lavy broaden the discipleship process to include invitational worship and high impact hospitality. Glover and Lavy include everything a newcomer experiences, from entering the church parking lot to the worship experience to the follow-up received after attending worship. These aspects of the first phase of discipleship are implied in Warren's model but not specifically addressed in the manner or to the degree that Glover and Lavy include them as a part of discipleship development. Whereas the transition from one level to another includes a covenant card in Warren's model, Glover and Lavy suggest that every class offering should end with a written commitment from participants on what their next step will be. Warren marks the end of the first phase of his discipleship model with a membership class; Glover and Lavy suggest an orientation class that explores and explains the church's discipleship system.

Glover and Lavy's phase two, Instructional Discipleship, follows Warren's baseball diamond model in that it focuses on instruction in biblical knowledge in order to foster spiritual maturity. For Glover and Lavy, this level intentionally focuses on instruction and relationship-building through small group opportunities that consist of three kinds of offerings. The first are invitational small groups that provide a way for new members and worship guests to become connected; these classes teach theology, spiritual disciplines, and practical application of scripture. Next Glover and Lavy suggest a core belief class on the basic tenets of the Christian faith, entitled Christianity 101. The third small group offering is a core principle class that directly addresses the answer to the Senior Pastor's question, "What does a fully committed disciple look like as a result of being discipled in this church?" Glover and Lavy note that the purpose of the core principle class is to "transmit the DNA" of the church into the heart of the individual. It is at this time formal membership is addressed.

The next phase in Glover and Lavy's model is Relational Discipleship. Here Glover and Lavy make a distinction between Bible studies and fellowship gatherings that may create biblically knowledgeable or friendly individuals, but which may fail to create true disciples. Two types of activities are included at this level of discipleship. One is a small group ministry in which participants regularly address what is happening in their lives each week and what God is saying to them through these events. The second set of activities offered at this level are "Go and See" opportunities. This includes opportunities to serve in supportive roles in ministry and mission with training, encouragement, and mentoring. "Go and See" opportunities allow individuals to explore places of ministry and determine if they possess the skills, gifts, and calling for particular ministry areas. At this stage there

© 2018 Robert O. Crossman, www.UMNewChurch.org

is more planning and reflection than actual hands-on experience. Service experience increases in the fourth phase.

The final stage in Glover and Lavy's model is Servant Discipleship. Two opportunities also exist at this level. The first are called "Go and Make" opportunities. ""Go and See" opportunities evolve into "Go and Make" opportunities as individuals explore and discover the calling of God upon each life. Glover and Lavy advocate that people should not move into service prematurely. They feel it is important that individuals move through the first three stages before engaging in service at stage four. The second set of opportunities that are a part of Servant Discipleship involve one-on-one discipling opportunities. Not everyone will achieve this level in Servant Discipleship. At this point Glover and Lavy discuss leaders and leadership.

Warren's baseball diamond is more simplistic in some ways than Glover and Lavy's model. Both models are examples of modular training.

Tom Nebel and Gary Rohrmayer, in *Church Planting Landmines,* describe modular training as a systematic approach to teaching the skills necessary for discipleship. A key component of modular training is a coupling of a hands-on experience with a learning experience. The diagrams presented by Warren, Glover and Lavy suggest a linear process in which one level is completed before moving to the next level.

They consist of systematic progressions through four phases of spiritual growth, and both models represent a progression from prospective member through a period of development in knowledge and understanding, to participation in service to others. Both models include a final stage that focuses on witnessing to others and helping new people have faith in Christ.

All present the discipleship process in a linear fashion. While there is some realism in this, it is important to note that life is not always linear. Growth in discipleship comes in seasons and in overlapping cycles rather than following a linear progression.

A Paradigm Shift

The two models above are linear models of discipleship growth. Unfortunately, life doesn't happen in a linear fashion. Not only is life more complex, but changes in recent years seem to suggest adjustments may be necessary to our understandings about discipleship systems.

Robert D. Putman sheds some light on a cultural trend in our communities (including our churches) in his book *Bowling Alone.* He describes a unique set of cultural characteristics, including suburban mobility and sprawl, "a privatization of life," in which life for the suburban dweller centered inside the home, a desire to seek personal concerns and desires, and materialism. Putman notes the pursuit of all the things believed to make life full and enjoyable, such as better schools for the children, a nice home, cars of a certain caliber, participation by the children and youth in community sporting events and other enrichment activities, and a high level of consumerism.

Suburban mobility and sprawl, requiring lengthy commutes, has an impact on available time. Pressure from financial needs has grown. Technology, particularly television, effects our lifestyles and the amount of time families spend together. The largest impact on our dwindling social capital is the result of the passing of a more civic-minded generation.

In *Postmodernism,* Craig Miller creates a list of the current generation's motivational factors that deserve consideration. He notes the rapid technological development during the last half of the century; the speed of progress is exponentially faster. In relation to this, we live in the Information Age, but it is demoralizing our lives. No one can get away from it or turn it off. Television, Internet, radio, magazines: these are influencing us without our even being aware of it. Mass media is telling us what is most important in life, and what is most important is what sells. The primary filter of values and priorities for young people in the Twentieth Century was their parents. For the Twenty-First Century, computers, cable television, the Internet, music television, and virtual reality have become the filter. There are many priorities to choose from out there, and the one for us is the one that can best target us with its marketing strategy.

Both Putman and Miller also note that the changes in family structure play a part in the current

culture. The traditional family model has given way to the multifamily unit. A family may experience the process of blending and dissolution repeatedly. Siblings, half-siblings, and parents may all living in different homes. One month two children may be stepbrother and stepsister; the next month parents are divorcing, and they are no longer related. Youth and young adults of our times are having difficulty making sense about family and family relationships, which are filled with disruption, distortion and pain.

Also on the rise is the single-parent household, which comes with a unique set of problems. Often single parents cannot survive on one income and so must work two jobs to pay the rent and put food on the table. Essentially, children are left to raise themselves. Putman notes that the presence of more women in the workforce, regardless of the reasons, has affected the number of social activities in which families engage. Trends affecting both single mothers and working mothers have impact on our culture's social capital.

Putman identifies many noteworthy factors as contributing to the decline in

© 2018 Robert O. Crossman, www.UMNewChurch.org

participation in social events such as church groups or civic groups. However, as previously mentioned, Putman suggests that the biggest contribution to the lack of social capital is generational change. The civic-oriented generation is passing away. This generation's hallmark was their members' numerous group affiliations and participation within them. There has been a drastic decline in social activity within each new generation since the post-World War II era. Some as-yet-unidentified force has changed the frequency of participation and the commitment to groups and other organizations. Putman points to a conglomeration of potential factors that are part of a larger shift to more individualized thinking and a move towards materialistic value structures.

Generational groups are cyclical. A new civic generation is presently being born. However, Putman does not expect the new civic generation to match their grandparents and great-grandparents in levels of participation in social activity. Putman may be right in that the factors that both foster attitudes of individualism, materialistic pursuits, and lead to our increased isolation from one another, (i.e., television, technology, advertising,) are not going to decrease in presence or influence. Time will tell us how socially connected and civically involved the new civic generation is going to be.

Relating to decreasing social activity, Craig Miller points out that a feeling of security has also disappeared, an issue that Putman does not address. Miller describes not only a loss in sense of security but also an increase in the sense of fear. Putman's book was published before the terrorist attacks of September 11, 2001. That act of terrorism shattered the current generation's myth of security, bringing violence from others to our front doors. Even before that, though, American culture had become inundated by violent crime and violent images. It has become common place for our teenagers and young adults to lose a close friend or acquaintance to a shooting or other crime, to drunk driving, to suicide, or to accidental death. We must also note the especially traumatic effects of terror-evoking type of events such school shootings, mall shootings, the Oklahoma City bombing, and the Virginia Tech shooting. Even observers are changed by such events. Fear of violence has led to distrust, isolation, and loss of relationship. It may be appropriate to question whether all of us might be experiencing some degree of post-traumatic stress, even though we may not be involved personally in such events.

The mass media bombardment, the present landscape of family relationships, increasing consumerism, and a heightened sense of fear and distrust of others are some of the major contributing factors that result in relationally-deprived and isolated individuals. Much as Putman described, adults have moved to this community in an effort to provide a better lifestyle for their families, demonstrating an increased drive and focus on the material aspects of life. This enriched lifestyle, however, is characterized by debt, financial strain, over-scheduled children and youths, and parents working long hours to fund this active, yet increasingly private, lifestyle. The result is that the church must compete for time and attention.

The general shift in reduced social capital, to borrow Putman's terminology, in the last several decades includes active participation in the church and church groups. This holds tremendous implications for the church and discipleship growth through worship attendance, participation in service and fellowship activities, and small group participation as the church faces the future. Recently a church planter in another suburban area remarked that many in her community's culture do not recognize a need for the church. She thought perhaps this might be a common sentiment among those who are outside the church for one reason or another. Yet, even once they are willing to give the church a chance, they remain unconvinced that they need small group relationships and / or are reluctant to take the time necessary to engage in the activities that will help to develop relationships with other Christians and a greater intimacy with God. Yet, significantly, much of discipleship growth occurs in small group settings and requires a certain amount of active participation. What the current cultural trends mean for the future of discipleship models and systems is not clear, but the implications may be profound.

Myths About Discipleship

Putting discipleship models together with the realities of life creates some interesting hurdles for us to overcome as we put new faith communities together. What do we do when the models don't work as planned? Rick Warren understands that becoming a disciple is more complex than his model might suggest; he explores six myths about developing spiritual maturity. These myths reveal the nuances of the linear process of discipleship. When interpreted in the context of our current culture both within and outside the church, exposing these myths provide us with some interesting information concerning spiritual development.

The first myth is that spiritual growth occurs automatically once a conversion experience takes place. Spiritual growth must be intentional. Thus, I emphasized with participants attending the training seminar that the key to effective participation was dependent on each person's desire to seek God's heart.

The second myth is that spiritual growth is something for only a small select group of people, like preachers, who are expected to experience spiritual maturity. Both John Wesley and Robert Foster, as explored earlier, would insist that spiritual disciplines and faith practices can result in a closer relationship with God for every person. Practical behaviors and habits can be instrumental in spiritual maturity.

The third myth concerning spiritual growth involves the search for a quick path to spiritual maturity for most of our church members. Warren argues against the idea that spiritual maturity comes quickly on the heels of a conversion experience or as the result of a set of simple steps. He emphasizes that discipleship is a process. While each person must elect to participate for the purpose of growing closer to God, some people experience seasons in life in which intentional goal-setting for

 © 2018 Robert O. Crossman, www.UMNewChurch.org

faith growth is difficult at best. Warren's baseball diamond model will not work for everyone. Some people will experience spiritual growth without utilizing the model, and it is still possible for people to go through the motions of completing the process without developing spiritual maturity. It proves Warren's point that there is no one program or key that is going to provide quick gratification and spiritual growth. It takes time and effort, with the single purpose of growing close to God.

A trend in recent years has been an emphasis on "process" rather than on programming in understanding the pathway to spiritual maturity. In emphasizing the process aspect of discipleship, (although we are never completely through with spiritual growth and maturity,) we risk helping our members to excuse themselves from positions of leadership on the basis of inadequate spiritual maturity. By a well-meaning emphasis that we continue to grow in our relationship with God, we seem to have fostered the idea that one is never equipped enough or never perfected enough. To follow Rick Warren's model just discussed, many fail to round home plate. We need to watch the language that we use and do a better job of communicating that continued spiritual growth comes through the practice of *facilitating others*, through utilizing our abilities to help others in need, and through Christian witness.

Similarly, a fourth myth equates increased biblical knowledge with spiritual maturity. As an example, consider the Disciple Bible Study; this wonderful program has helped many people develop Christian maturity, yet some have taken all four Disciple classes and failed to engage in other behaviors that might be expected of a Disciple graduate. In addressing this myth, Warren cites that spiritual growth is measured by one's actions. The true measure of biblical knowledge would be, for instance, someone's giving sacrificially of time and talent to further the work of the kingdom.

Warren identifies as a fifth myth the idea that spiritual growth is personal and private. He notes that spiritual growth happens relationally. While we can experience growth in individual pursuits and practices, the complete experience of spiritual maturity also requires the context of relationships with God and with others.

The final myth Warren addresses is the conviction that all one needs is a deeper understanding or knowledge of the Bible in order to grow. Spiritual growth depends on a variety of internal and external experiences. As discussed previously disciple-building churches are holistic and holographic; in addition, different personality styles play a part in discipleship growth. The importance cannot be underscored enough of providing a variety of ways for people to experience closeness with God — not just through Bible study or small group offerings.

An excellent resource to understand how people connect to one another and the implications for discipleship systems is *The Search To Belong* by Joseph Myers. Myers explores the connection between small group participation, a sense of communal belonging, and discipleship growth. He notes that small group participation is often seen as a measurement for spiritual maturity. Churches frequently measure success in discipleship by the percentage of the congregation actively participating in small groups. Myers suggests that there are six myths about the expectations for small groups and their potential for discipleship growth. He has discovered that churches that aspire to have small groups as an important part of discipleship attract only thirty to fifty percent of their membership into such groups. Myers suggests that churches that strive to be churches of small groups instead of churches with small groups fail to understand how community functions.

Myers first explores the erroneous idea that more time spent in small group fellowship dictates a greater sense of meaningful belonging. In reality, the amount of time a person spends in small group fellowship is not in itself an indicator of deeper levels of discipleship. Myers uses as an example the story of a woman who was motivated to begin attending church by a short but significant encounter with a couple she met while vacationing; such episodic belonging can be meaningful and transformational. We must not ignore natural chemistry between people and organic relationship development.

A second myth equates a greater level of commitment by an individual with a greater sense of community. Standard requirements for small group function may fail to honor the reality that some people are seeking intimate and intensely personal relationships but that others may simply be looking for a sense of belonging. Faithful and regular attendance does not necessarily mean transformation of heart and life.

The third myth is that people will connect over a common purpose. The 1980's saw a rise in the use of vision and mission statements for business organizations and churches. Yet Myers reminds us that an organization's purpose statement does not guarantee a sense of communal belonging, nor is uniting with a church's vision the first motivating factor in why people become connected.

Myers also notes that it is a myth to believe that people with a particular personality style are more or less likely to find connection within a small group. The truth is that introverted or extroverted personalities neither enhance nor block our experience of belonging. What is important to remember is that prescribed programs and methods of belonging will not work for everyone. Extroverts do not necessarily find it easier to make friends or share spiritual intimacy; some introverts may experience significant connection through observation without openly participating. It is necessary to allow people to experience belonging in their unique ways.

 © 2018 Robert O. Crossman, www.UMNewChurch.org

The next myth Myers addresses requires a shift in understanding proximity as it relates to connecting. He notes that neighborhood proximity used to be a factor in fostering community; small groups formed around connections with neighbors.

People lived in the same community for longer periods of time. At one time in our history we sat on our front porches and visited with our neighbors who lived next door and across the street. We had deeper connections in the community in which we lived.

Yet Myers urges care in our digital age in defining proximity. Couples may initially meet through the Internet. Significant relationships may evolve through an Internet community created around a mutual interest, despite the fact that the individuals may not live near one another nor ever meet face-to-face. The role proximity plays in discipleship growth must be reexamined.

Finally, Myers addresses the concept that small group membership is necessary to the experience of communal connectedness. Myers's research has shown that churches with effective small group systems at best only have one third of their congregations actively participating in small groups. He notes that some churches hold small group participation as the most important or only mark of spiritual maturity. He cautions against aligning with this way of thinking. Myers notes that small groups have their place in discipleship systems, but he warns against the mistake of seeing small groups as **THE** discipleship system for a variety of reasons. Not everyone finds connections and develops relationships in structured small group settings.

Myers also suggests that churches frequently attempt to move people into intimate circles of belonging too quickly. Newcomers are expected to move from public to personal or intimate spaces without being given appropriate opportunities to connect naturally with others in social spaces. A strong focus on small group participation can even place pressure on church members to interact too intimately with others at inappropriate levels. Some more personal struggles need to stay within a small, select group of people determined by something other than a church's small group system.

Small group participation has its place in discipleship systems. Because we are created to be in relationship with God and with one another, it is impossible truly to grow as disciples without connecting with others in some way. We need such relationships for support and accountability. However, as a church body the intent must be to make disciples of Jesus Christ, not to become servants of any discipleship system. Current cultural trends and their implications for discipleship systems might be excellent areas for future research and exploration. Perhaps innovative discipleship systems such as Internet-based groups will be the result.

Discipleship Systems in New Faith Communities

Our journey leads us to consider the following in the discipleship systems we develop in our new faith communities:

1. Make sure that your discipleship system allows for adequate social time. Remember that discipleship and discipleship opportunities develop naturally. We will be very tempted to structure every activity that takes place or to discount any time our people spend together that does not contain prayer or Bible study. Fight the urge. Discipleship begins with relationship building and social times provide a natural place for relationships to develop. Therefore, social time is an important part of discipleship.

2. Consider personality styles when developing the discipleship system. Remember that not everyone will be drawn to prayer retreats nor want to be a part of a small group experience. In order to address this, a good discipleship system will have a variety of opportunities for everyone. I strongly recommend the *Commitment to Christ 2020* model developed by Dr. Bob Crossman. It not only addresses various aspects of discipleship, it also meets people where they are at.

3. Commitment to Christ invites us to make commitments for growth in seven different areas. Consider emphasizing one area for serious growth in the next year and encouraging maintenance commitments in the other areas. Most of us have a difficult time focusing on multiple growth goals simultaneously. However, in the vein of Natural Church Development, when we make gains in one area of our spiritual lives, we often experience growth in other areas as well.

4. Remember to create criteria that are concrete and measurable. This is for benefit of your people, not for you to be able to measure how many people are becoming disciples. People may complete the steps of your discipleship system and still not become disciples. Conversely, some may grow in their discipleship while never jumping through the hoops of your discipleship system. The true measure to determine the effectiveness of your discipleship system in the stories of transformation and changed lives. Concrete and measurable steps will encourage your new church members to invest themselves in the discipleship process.

5. Remember to remind your people frequently that they will only experience growth as disciples if their purpose is to discover God's heart. You cannot remind them of this enough.

6. Whatever model or method you choose, do not make the mistake of having your discipleship system consist only of small groups. If Joseph Myers is right, only one third of people who become a part of your church will connect through small groups. What about the other two thirds of your church? Small groups

 © 2018 Robert O. Crossman, www.UMNewChurch.org

should be one part of your discipleship system.

7. Remember that people go through seasons in their lives. Certain situations in life, like caring for an aging parent, will affect the ability of someone trying to participate in your discipleship system. How will you address their needs in a manner that will allow them to also grow as disciples?

8. This is a good time to review Rick Warren's model from moving from the crowd to the core. Warren's model is based upon a biblical model of those who followed Christ in the New Testament. Some were closer to Jesus and more intimately involved than others. While some of the people in our churches have life situations that will impact their ability to participate in your discipleship system, others will simply choose not to participate in whatever method or model you devise. While you may not choose such persons for positions of leadership, as their spiritual leader you are still responsible for their spiritual growth. How do you provide opportunities for growth for them?

9. Try to use invitational language that is compelling and compassionate, rather than appealing to people based upon commitment and expectation. Treat adults like adults. Jesus invites, but allows us to turn away.

10. Focus on high expectations of discipleship <u>not</u> on membership. One advantage of doing so is that you target the worship guest as well as the church member. Somehow we've placed a great deal of emphasis on making participation in the discipleship process criteria for membership. This creates several problems. Emphasizing discipleship rather than membership is a better choice.

11. In our desire to create humble hearts we have inadvertently encouraged our church members to feel they have never arrived. Following Rick Warren's model, we have created thousands of disciples who never reach home plate. Be sure to emphasize that disciples complete the process by serving in positions of leadership, as mentors, and as teachers.

12. Finally, the discipleship system you create will be shaped by two things. How you define what a disciple is will determine the shape of your discipleship process. Secondly, it will probably also be reflective of what was transformational in your life.

Dr. Tammy Garrison is an Elder in the Arkansas Conference.

This article is reprinted here by permission of the author granted April 4, 2017.

†††

NOTE: This article reflects the personal opinions of its author and does not necessarily reflect an official position of Discipleship Ministries or Path 1.

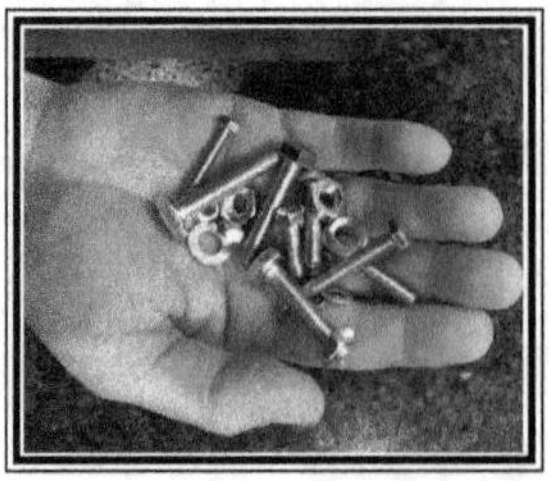

New Church Handbook
Nuts & Bolts for Planting New Churches In The Wesleyan Tradition

"Making Disciples, More Disciples, and Even More Disciples"

by Bob Crossman

> Path 1, General Board of Discipleship, defines a new church as follows: *"A new congregation is a newly organized faith community that is* ***committed to making disciples of Jesus Christ*** *and includes regular community worship, is theologically Wesleyan, is willing to plant a new congregation in its first decade, has an effective discipling system, demonstrates faithful stewardship, does community outreach, and receives new members. A new church is more than a mission project, a new worship service, or the construction of a new building."*

In two previous New Church Handbook articles, I discussed the topic of networking at length. The purpose of this article is to take the topic a bit deeper and to share a number of facets to the task of reaching more people. One of the first and primary responsibilities of the new church planter, as Jim Griffith puts it, *"is to put people in the seats, and then put more people in the seats."*

- If your motivation to reach more people is to save the lost, to welcome the 'prodigal' back home, and/or to increase the population of heaven, God will honor and bless your efforts. However, if your motivation is to get enough folks to cover your salary, to impress your bishop, and/or to make a name for yourself in the annual conference - those motivations are self-serving, empty, and hollow, and do not honor the Lord.

- Adam Hamilton (*Leading Beyond the Walls, chapter 2*) suggests that the planting pastor, and the launch team, need to be able to answer three questions: Why do people need Jesus Christ? Why do people need the church? And, why do people need your particular church? I would suggest that the planting pastor needs to develop short, fifteen second, clear, definitive answers to each of these questions. I would also propose that the launch team also needs to be able to respond to these questions in a quick, clear, articulate way when their friends, neighbors, co-workers and relatives ask.

- Pray! Pray until your heart aches and the tears flow. Pray for every child in your mission field being raised up outside the church. Pray for every marriage in town that doesn't have Christ as the center of that relationship. Pray for every church in town until every pew is filled every Sunday. Pray until every soul is saved. Pray until every lost sheep is found. Pray until every 'prodigal' son or daughter has

 © 2018 Robert O. Crossman, www.UMNewChurch.org

come to their senses, turned their hearts toward home, and have been welcomed back to church. Pray until every member of **your** extended family is an active disciple of Jesus Christ. Pray until your love for the unchurched, casts our your fear of witnessing to them about the saving good news of Jesus Christ.

- Pray specifically for five households. Begin by making a list of the last fifteen people you have encountered in your networking. Determine which five of those households have the greatest potential for responding to your invitation to be part of your new church start. For the next two weeks, pray for them by name every day. During weeks three and four, search for ways to interact in a casual way with each of the five households *(at your home or in public over coffee, breakfast, lunch, dinner, or at their place of work)*. During weeks five and six, directly invite them to be part of your new church start. Repeat this with a new set each week. As your launch team develops, inspire each of them to have their own list of five households they are praying for.

- Make an intentional effort to open your heart to the children in your new town who are being raised up outside of the church; to the single parents in town; to the families struggling to make financial ends meet; and to new residents who do not yet have a church home.

- Enlarge your circle of Christian contacts. Right now, you probably have three or four close, personal, Christian friends. *(former seminary classmates, fellow pastors across the district, family members)* The truth may be that you really don't want or need any more Christian friends. However, if you are going to be successful in inviting new people to become part of the new church you are seeking to establish, you *(and your future launch team)* will have to invite ten new people into your inner circle. This will not be easy! The Lord will bless and honor your efforts.

- I've read that the average United Methodist only invites someone to worship once every seventeen years. I have been unsuccessful in finding the source of this statistic. However, assuming it is partly true, simply decide today **not** to be an average United Methodist when it comes to the frequency of inviting.

- Every single day, place yourself in a setting where you can spend sixty seconds giving a personal invitation to each of three different people. Perhaps it is with your realtor, landlord, waiter, next door neighbor, haircutter, gas station attendant, standing in line at the post office, or store clerk. I am not suggesting a heavy-handed, door to door, end of times, Bible thumping street invitation. Rather, I am suggesting a natural, simple invitation. In three sentences, introduce yourself as the new United Methodist pastor in town, tell the purpose of your new church, and ask if they might be interested in being part of a new church.

- Give each person you meet a referral card. This might be a self-addressed post card. On the reverse side: "Pastor, I would like to refer you to someone who might be interested in your new church. Name: _____, address:_____ and phone: ______. Please tell them that I referred you to them. My name is ______, address_____ email ________________________________ and phone _____.

- Invite, invite, and invite again. As you begin to get settled in your new community and make networking contacts across the area, don't just invite each contact once. Instead, look for ways to follow up with each contact with repeated invitations. I am not suggesting that your 'pester' them until they finally surrender to your stalking. Rather, I am suggesting that you look for a variety of ways to follow up and repeat your invitation every month or so. Why? There are seasons of life when each individual is more receptive an invitation to be part of a church *(new or established)*. Those seasons occur when some event shakes their life and causes them to rethink life, how they spend their time on Sunday mornings, and their relationship to God. Such an event might be any of the following: new resident in town, new job, just married, just divorced, lost job, new major promotion, pregnant, miscarriage, abortion, new baby, child ready to enter kindergarten, grandparent has cancer, life-long friend dies from sudden heart attack, car accident, etc.
  If we only invite once, we are not likely to overlap one of these seasons. If we invite every month or two, we are more likely to have a positive response.

- You are searching for a few deeply devoted disciples to be on your launch team, but you are also searching for POTENTIAL deeply devoted disciples. Look for ways to increase the number of people who are on the fringes, people who have had some simple contact with you or your ministry. If you hold a community Christmas Eve candlelight service and out of the two hundred attendees you discover four deeply devoted disciples who join your launch team - praise God! However, do not neglect the other one hundred and ninety six. They are not cheap grace, free loading, tag alongs! They are instead, your prospect list - your future - your hope - the potential next wave of launch team members or new professions of faith. When these people on the "fringes" have the urge to be religious during the next year or two, pray that they will visit your new church.

  A healthy new church start has a central group of deeply devoted people on the launch team, but it is also surrounded by hundreds of people who have met the pastor, attended some 'elbow' event, read about the new church in the newspaper, heard about the new church from a co-worker, or read your saturation mailer invitation.

- Distribute invitation cards to everyone you meet. These might be the size of a traditional business card or slightly larger. It might read, *"If you are not active in a church in town, you might be interested in being part of a new church that is forming."* Below that, it lists pastors name, phone, email and a simple web site address where they might get more information.

© 2018 Robert O. Crossman, www.UMNewChurch.org

- In your networking, as you make contact with potential launch team members, look for ways to invite them to make a commitment to join your ministry. Make an appointment for coffee at their office or the local Starbucks, invite them to your home for lunch or dinner with your family. Find ways to have face to face contact every ten to fifteen days as you continue to cast the vision and tell the story your new church start.

- As your launch team develops and grows, inspire/lead/place DNA inside of them that reflects the basic principles and actions in the set of bullets listed above. Start a new faith community that has a passion to make NEW disciples, more disciples, more younger disciples, and more diverse disciples. In some mission fields, it is helpful for the pastor to meet monthly with the key laity to strengthen this process.

There are several new and old resources that might be helpful to read together, one chapter at a time:

Leading Beyond the Walls: Developing Congregations with a Heart for the Unchurched, by Adam Hamilton
Ten Most Common Mistakes Made by Church Starts, by Jim Griffith and Bill Easum
Membership to Discipleship: Growing Mature Disciples Who Make Disciples, by Philip Maynard
Rich Church / Poor Church, Keys to Effective Financial Ministry, by Clif Christopher
Shift: Helping Congregations Back Into the Game of Effective Ministry, by Phil Maynard
Five Practices of Fruitful Congregations, by Bishop Robert Schnase
Clip In: Risking Hospitality in Your Church, by Jim Ozier
The Race to Reach Out: Connecting Newcomers to Christ in a New Century, by Douglas Anderson and Michael Coyner

Resources directed more toward established congregations, which may have applicable chapters include:

The Church Growth Handbook, by William Easum
Twelve Keys to an Effective Church, by Kenneth Callahan
Checking Vital Signs, by Nancy Burgin Rankin and Beverly Bowyer Coppley
Deepening Your Effectiveness: Restructuring the Local Church for Life Transformation, by Dan Glover and Claudia Levy
44 Questions for Congregational Self-Appraisal and *44 Ways to Increase Church Attendance,* by Lyle Schaller

At Elbow Events, Pre-view Worship & Soft Launch Worship

- Test the gifts, graces, commitment, abilities of launch team members. Put together a small team to coordinate the essential elements for your first elbow event.

Depending on the nature of the event, you might ask a different person to put a team together for each of the following: hospitality team; intercessory prayer team; music team; video team; electronics team; publicity team; nursery team; children's team; set-up team; tear-down team; and hand-off team.

Those individuals who actually follow through, invite them to fulfill the same role at the next event. After several initial events, begin to discern which launch team members might fulfill each particular facet during your launch season.

- Outdoor sign hospitality.
  - At the major intersections leading to your event site, have temporary "sandwich" or "real estate" signs that direct people to your event.
  -At the parking lot entrance, have temporary "sandwich" or "real estate" signs that direct people to your event.

- Lots of cars in the parking lot are one way you witness and let the community know that something significant is happening. Don't hide cars in the back of the building. Instead, have your leadership park in front so neighbors can see.

- Parking lot hospitality. Give a couple of men orange vests to wear, and have them smile and wave as people pull into to the event location.

- Save the very best parking spaces for guests.

- Whatever facilities you are using, use the one main obvious entrance that visitors will naturally walk toward.

- Front door hospitality. As people approach the entrance, have two women standing outside, smiling, opening the door, and saying, *"Welcome. I am glad you are here."*

- When guests gets past the front door greeter, they should encounter a smiling faces, giving directions to worship and the nursery, offering coffee, sweet rolls or juice.

- At "elbow events" you may organize activities such as free kids carnivals or concerts. One effective way to gather contact information is to have a variety of door prizes that appeal to various ages and stages in life. You may have to spend $50 to $100 for each prize to make them attractive enough for the crowd to fill out the registration form.

- Establish a "first friends" team. Train a small pool of your launch team (from a variety of ages and stages of life) to watch for first time guests, to sit my them, to treat them to lunch, to telephone on Saturday, and to invite them to come back.

© 2018 Robert O. Crossman, www.UMNewChurch.org

No guest should enter the building alone. No guest should sit alone, No guest should eat lunch alone.

- Interior signs should direct guests toward the worship, nursery, and rest rooms.

- The nursery
  - The nursery should be close to the worship space. First-time guests do not feel comfortable if their infant is down a long maze of confusing hallways.
  - When a child is checked in, a name tag should be placed on the child's back, with duplicate tags on bottles and diaper bags.
  - The nursery space should be clean and bright. It should have new cribs, clean floors, soft clean floor covering and no diaper smell.
  - Toys should be sanitized weekly, and any with teeth marks removed.
  - The nursery should be staffed by a responsible adult. - You many also need some type of comforting security measures, with numbered tags, or pagers.

- The toddler children's spaces should also be clean, neat, lessons well prepared, and well staffed.

- Make the screen (or printed bulletins) visitor friendly. Use easy to read text, including the words to all songs, prayers or affirmations you may want everyone to recite. Words projected on the screen should be large enough to be easily read from the back of the room.

- The music should be well rehearsed, well performed, and of a style that appeals to your mission field. I wonder what style of music your worship guests were listening to in the car as they drove to your event?

- Be sure the sound system gives clear, sharp, and adequate volume to every seat in the room.

- Are the sermons, devotionals and meditations visitor friendly and well prepared? Are topics relevant to daily living and invitational? Worship guests, prodigals, and pre-Christians are usually not interested in Greek, Hebrew, Tilich or Kirkegard. Instead, they show up for worship looking for Jesus, for hope, help for their marriage, forgiveness for the past, healing for their brokenness or strength to make it through the week ahead. Doug Johnson reports that 90% of first-time guests are attending because they experienced some difficult event in the past thirty days.

- At your event, or worship, find a way to acknowledge and welcome guests, but not to single them out or embarrass them. Many first-time guest may prefer to be anonymous, and "sit in the balcony" and observe several times before they are comfortable introducing themselves publicly.

- Find a way to collect names and contact information of your worship guests. Be aware that they may want to visit a couple of times before they trust you with that personal contact information.

- At the event, or worship, have your launch team follow the rule to ten: they are to speak to everyone within ten feet of their seat. The message is simple, *"Good morning. I am glad you are here."* Notice that I do not recommend they say, *"Hello, my name is ___."* This puts pressure on the guest to give their name, and will make some guest uncomfortable. Have your team wait and see if the guest volunteers their name in that brief encounter.

- At the event, or worship, have your launch team follow the rule to three: at the close of the event, they are only to speak to people they do not know for the first three minutes. They are to resist the temptation to only talk to family and friends. Guests are normally headed straight for the exit, and will be in their cars within three minutes.

- At every event, or worship, have a "hand off." A hand off is an invitation (verbal, flyer, or both) to the next event.

Follow-up From Elbow Events, Pre-view Worship, or Soft Launch Worship

- Your mission field will quickly let you know the type of frequency of follow up that they prefer.

- Doug Anderson and Michael J. Coyner's, *"The Race to Reach Out: Connecting Newcomers to Christ in a New Century,"* is a great resource.

- Immediately add every contact to your weekly email network. This is your growing prospect list. A few might respond and attend your next event. Others may wait five years before they are ready. Do not remove them until the coroner notifies you.

- If they choose to give you a telephone number, do not neglect to call it! A simple 15 second telephone call within 24 hours, to say, *"Good evening. My name is Mark Normam, the pastor of Living Water UMC. Thank you for attending our community Gospel concert last night. I hope you will be able to attend our fall festival next month on the 15th."* If they respond, continue the conversation, otherwise end it quickly.

- After they have attended three events, or worship services, they may be ready for a home visit by the pastor. Adam Hamilton lays out the details of his process for these home visits in chapter six of *"Leading Beyond the Walls."* Adam reports that in all but one of the first 500 homes he visited, the household eventually joined The UM Church of the Resurrection.

© 2018 Robert O. Crossman, www.UMNewChurch.org

- If the guest chooses to give you a home address, consider making door step visits. Some communities respond very favorably to a 30 second door step visit by the pastor. Knock or ring, then step back five feet or so from the door. When they respond, quickly say, *"I don't want to come in. I just stopped by to thank you for coming to our event (worship) and to give you this gift. I look forward to seeing you next week (or next month at the ____)."* If they are not home, leave the gift and a hand written note. In my community, about thirty percent insisted that I come inside to visit more. Also, about eighty percent returned next week.

- If they have children, about five days later, your children's leader might call and ask to speak to the child to thank them for attending and invite them back.

- Many planters are finding that a short weekly e-newsletter is a winsome way to remain in contact with a growing list.

Respond to Absentees

- If one of your launch team members attends three or more consecutive events, and then misses unexpectedly, you will need to respond.
  - If they miss once, a hand written postcard from the pastor may be the most effective response.
  - If they miss two consecutive events, a fifteen second *"I've missed you"* phone call by the pastor and invitation to the next event, may be the most effective response.

- Great resources for additional follow-up strategies:
  Bob Farr's *Get Their Name: Grow Your Church by Building New Relationships,*

  Jim Ozier's *Clip In: Risking Hospitality In Your Church;*

  Doug Anderson and Michael J. Coyner's, The Race to Reach Out: Connecting Newcomers to Christ in a New Century,

  Lyle Schaller's 44 *Ways to Increase Worship Attendance.*

NOTE: This article reflects the personal opinions of its author and does not necessarily reflect an official position of Discipleship Ministries or Path 1.

 © 2018 Robert O. Crossman, www.UMNewChurch.org

X. What Is the Structure Within New Churches?

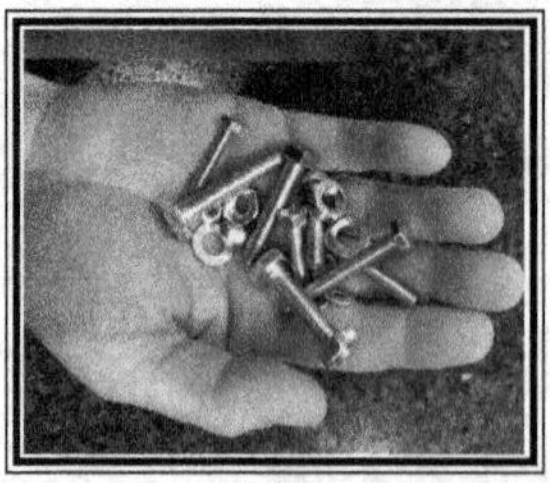

New Church Handbook
Nuts & Bolts for Planting New Churches In The Wesleyan Tradition

"What Does New Church Administrative Structure Look Like In The Early Years"

by Bob Crossman

Multi-site Strategy

In the multi-site strategy, typically the main campus will fulfill all the traditional functions of a church council, pastor parish relations committee, finance committee, and trustees.

All Other Strategies

In most all other strategies the district superintendent, conference minister of new church starts and the coach assigned to the new church pastor, will fulfill the traditional functions of a church council, pastor parish relations committee, finance committee, and trustees until the church has grown large enough to complete the 'charter' process and thereby elect these committees. These committees/councils do not exist in a new church prior to the constituting church conference outlined in ¶ 259.

How about a Financial System?

- Should you, the church planter, be a signatory on the new church's checking account? NO

- Should you, the church planter, be counting the money after launch team offerings are received? NO

- Should you, the church planter, be making the deposits? NO

- Should your new church have a credit card? Probably not. (In most annual conferences the planter is expected to make any approved purchases on their personal credit card and submit receipts for reimbursement.)

In most settings, you will be asking the financial secretary of a nearby healthy United Methodist Church or the district office administrative assistant to serve as your financial secretary. This person will make your deposits from your weekly launch team meetings, deposit grants received, and deposit all other income received. This person will also be reimbursing you for expenses that are within the limits of your approved budget for the year. In some conferences, this person will also be writing your monthly paycheck.

In many annual conferences, the non chartered new church start pastors have

 © 2018 Robert O. Crossman, www.UMNewChurch.org

authority to request reimbursement for items up to a set amount, typically $500, from their financial secretary. Each check beyond that amount, typically $500, must be approved by district superintendent or conference new church staff.)

NOTE: For more details on financial structure guidelines in new church starts, see the article, "Setting Up An Internal Financial System."

In most annual conferences, new church starts are not allowed to enter the 'charter' process (¶260.4 to ¶260.10) until they have at least 125 active adult members, are financially self sustaining, and have been holding public worship at least three years.

NOTE: Every annual conference has different chartering guidelines. Check with your annual conference New Church Director, and confirm that conversation with your district superintendent.

Structure of the Strategy Review Team in the Years Before Chartering

It is suggested that a strategy review session take place before moving day. Prior to the meeting time, the new church planting pastor would complete the document outlined in the article "*Pre-Moving Day Strategy Session and Quarterly Follow-up,*" responding to as many of the topics and questions as applicable.

The new church pastor would then forward the draft of the completed form in advance of the meeting time to the participants. Participants would probably include: the district superintendent, the new church development conference staff person, the new church coach, (and if there are sponsoring churches or a mother church' to the key laity involved - probably the lay leader and SPPR chair.)

To ensure clear lines of communication, a "Quarterly Connection" is held quarterly (or more frequently as needed) at the new church site involving the church planter and spouse (if married), the district superintendent, the conference minister of new church starts, and coach. NOTE: For more detail on the initial and quarterly strategy review sessions, see: "Pre-Moving Day Strategy Session and Quarterly Follow-up."

Additional Administrative Structure

A Launch Team

In the first few weeks and months the planter will be working to form a launch team. The launch team is very different from a typical church council. Until the new church has it's constituting conference and charters, those traditional role of finance, trustee and SPPR will be filled by the district superintendent, conference minister of new church starts.

What to Look For in Gathering Your Launch Team

One role of the launch team is to fill the gaps missing in the planter's spiritual gifts. Because of this, the process toward developing a healthy launch team begins with the planter. Self awareness by the planter is one of the keys for the formation of an initial launch team and eventual church council. As a potential planter, you have to know yourself, your gifts, your calling, your strengths and weaknesses, your personality.

You have to know about your self:

- Do you tend to be people oriented, or task oriented.
- Do you tend to be structured or unstructured.
- Honestly, how is your health?
- Honestly, how is your Spiritual life?
- Honestly, how is your Marriage?
- Honestly, how is your emotional life?
- Honestly, how is your physical stamina?

Knowing how your are wired and gifted, helps you do a better job in selecting your lay team. For example, if you are not a "people person" you need to be sure that you intentionally have several people on your team who are indeed "natural people persons." You get the idea...

In the New Church Leadership Institutes that Jim Griffith leads, you may have written a "Self-Reflective Essay." Your one page reflective essay should have included these topics:

- Pastor's Vision
- Pastor's Mission
- Pastor's Core Beliefs
- Pastor's Core Values
- A one paragraph summary of the pastor's affinity group
- What new church planting strategy suits your profile? Why?
- What would be your optimal new church planting scenario? Why?
- Concerning your possible appointment to plant a new church, what other conclusions have you made?
- Concerning your possible appointment to plant a new church, what questions remain for you? A review of the Self-Reflective Essay you wrote at NCLI might be helpful in this season of self-discernment too.

A more formal process for this season of self-discernment it taken from "Tent Makers" below:

Life Dimension Analysis

Where am I now?

A. In your walk with Christ...
   a. What are you thankful for in this area?
   b. What are the problems, frustrations, concerns or challenges in this area?

 © 2018 Robert O. Crossman, www.UMNewChurch.org

B. In your ministry...
   a. What are you thankful for in this area?
   b. What are the problems, frustrations, concerns or challenges in this area?
C. In your family...
   a. What are you thankful for in this area?
   b. What are the problems, frustrations, concerns or challenges in this area?
D. In your personal finances...
   a. What are you thankful for in this area?
   b. What are the problems, frustrations, concerns or challenges in this area?
E. In your personal health...
   a. What are you thankful for in this area?
   b. What are the problems, frustrations, concerns or challenges in this area?
F. In your community...
   a. What are you thankful for in this area?
   b. What are the problems, frustrations, concerns or challenges in this area?
G. In your career as a pastor...
   a. What are you thankful for in this area?
   b. What are the problems, frustrations, concerns or challenges in this area?
H. In your personal hobbies...
   a. What are you thankful for in this area?
   b. What are the problems, frustrations, concerns or challenges in this area?
I. In your personal development / education...
   a. What are you thankful for in this area?
   b. What are the problems, frustrations, concerns or challenges in this area?

Referring to the list above, choose five areas and list goals to achieve in the coming year:

- In your walk with Christ...
- In your ministry...
- In your family...
- In your personal finances...
- In your personal health...
- In your community...
- In your career as a pastor...
- In your personal hobbies...
- In your personal development / education...

For each of those five chosen from list above, develop a plan of action that includes the following:

- Goal (what, why and when).
- Assess resources.
- Brainstorm how.
- How is this to be done?
- Who needs to be involved? What will they do?
- Where?
- When (specific day or dates).
- Items to be done... a, b, c,
- Develop a way to monitor your progress in these goals.

Know Thy Vision

Be clear about:

Where are you going?
What is not negotiable?
What's negotiable?
What is needed?
What are you looking for in your launch team?
What characteristics do you need to fill the gaps in your personal gifts/graces?

In your launch team you will need:
(according to Bob Logan's, Church Plant Tool Kit)

- A shepherd - a caregiver.
- Financial - a business administrator (let a parent church or the district handle the money)
- Organizer - an implementer for the details
- Jesus - you are not doing this alone!
- Worship Leader -
- Recruiter - the evangelist to tell the story, inviting people
- Children's Ministry Leader - a recruiter
- A Recruiter - someone to involve the new people, a mobilizer

What to Look For in Gathering Your Launch Team

- Ministry partners to fill the gaps missing in your personal spiritual gifts
- You DON'T need warm bodies on your launch team. Rather people who...
  - are called as much as you are called.
  - are as committed as you are
  - share the vision and values
  - are proven multipliers {sales people, entrepreneurs, business people}
  - proven in community service
- You need people who are ...

 © 2018 Robert O. Crossman, www.UMNewChurch.org

- Capable
- Available
- Responsible
- Responsive
- Enthusiastic
- Teachable

Three Groups to Gather Into Your Launch Team

1. Christians - where do you find them?
- your personal friends
- your family
- from the Parent Church
- from Partner Churches
- from your personal core network
- short-term... 'will you give us six months'
- paid staff {you are likely to have to pay your musicians}
- {you may also get a GBGM to pay a Church and Community Worker}
- meal marketing... at dinner you make contacts with waitress, checker, etc.
- Facebook targeted ads, signs, advertising in classified ads, cable TV list of community events, free articles in newspaper, door hangers,
- web site information... put web address on door flyers for more information

Advantages of having Christians on your launch team

They will give more money.
They are more qualified workers.
Variety of mature christian personalities.

Disadvantages of having Christians on your launch team

Power plays. You may end up attracting some who didn't have power in their old church, so they want to take over your church.
Growth is largely transfer growth from other churches.

2. Conversions - brand new believers - Where do you find them?
- Neighborhood Bible Studies such as Alpha.
- Fishing Pool events with follow up - i.e. Halloween parties, concerts in the park, or carnivals {invite participants to a felt needs seminar}
- Felt Needs Seminars - i.e. toilet training, personal finance, parenting.
- Get 'into' the community - i.e. chamber of commerce.

Advantages of having new Converts on your launch team

- Yields the highest percentage of conversion growth.
- Provides the right mixture of people who are not too far ahead of each other spiritually.
- Builds credibility for you and the gospel. It also provides pace setting stories.
- The target is huge!

A new church as the best chance of growth through conversations if early members are...

- Highly committed to being evangelistically effective.
- Sent from a mother church that is effective in evangelism.
- United in their vision and strategy
- Willing to follow a faith-oriented planter with evangelistic gifts
- About to attract a large number of unchurched people quickly

Disadvantages of having new Converts on your launch team

- Give little financial support
- Can be lonely for the church planter & family, if you are the only mature believer in the new church
- Too much or too little work

3. **A Combination of Both Christians and New Converts**
   Most planters find that a combination of Christians and new converts on their launch teams.

How to Recruit a Launch Team

Don't formalize your launch team too soon. In the initial months, especially if you are working with new people with whom you have little history, invite them to do a small task. If they are faithful and effective, then invite them to do a larger task. If they are faithful and effective, then perhaps consider them for your launch team.

For example, don't 'recruit' someone saying, *"Will you serve on the launch team and be my director of nursery activities for the rest of your life."* Of course not. Instead, ask them to accomplish a specific task *(such as child care, refreshments, set-up, sound system, or parking lot greeters, etc).* for an upcoming event. *"We have a gathering on the 27th, would you recruit one or two people to assist you with It would be preferable to find people who have not yet been part of this church?"* If that goes well, invite them to do the same at another event.

Eventually, when you have discerned they have shown the right level of commitment, gifts and graces then consider asking them to be on the launch team for #___ months (not for five years!).

In general, how do you recruit a launch team?

- Briefly share your vision and strategy.
- Share the benefits.
- Be honest about the costs.
- Spell out your launch team requirements.
- Share your commitment to their personal leadership and spiritual development.
- Assign specific assignments.

 © 2018 Robert O. Crossman, www.UMNewChurch.org

- Ask them to pray about the decision to join your launch team.
- Orient and train new recruits.
- Assimilate them into the launch team.

How to Train Your Launch Team

- Teach your vision and strategy. help them buy into it.
- Show them examples of worship and small groups by visiting other churches together and evaluating the hospitality, music, preaching, facilities, etc.
- Teach 'gift-based' ministry, not committee based.
- Model and teach servant evangelism (Vineyard Church model).

Invite your Leadership Team to Personally Grow in Discipleship and Help Your New Congregation to Do The Same

Robert Schnase's book, *Five Practices of Fruitful Congregations,* might be helpful as a resource for you during your early launch team meetings. Begin to teach, train and invite your launch team to have:

- Radical Hospitality
- Passionate Worship
- Intentional Faith Development
- Risk Taking Mission Service
- Extravagant Generosity

Spiritual Life of the Launch Team

Central to the life of any congregation is its leadership. What happens in the launch team affects the life of the whole congregation. *"The congregation will look like your launch team."*

The launch team is made up of those leaders who are responsible for the spiritual life of others in your congregation. These include small group leaders, elected members of boards and committees, the staff, and the music ministry team.

1. What spiritual disciplines will your launch team be expected to practice?

__ Weekly worship
__ Daily Bible reading
__ Daily Prayer
__ Service to others: give examples ________
__ Fasting or abstinence
__ Family Prayer
__ Tithing, financial gifts growing to the
Biblical minimum of the 10% tithe
__ Witnessing, inviting (friends, relatives,

© 2018 Robert O. Crossman, www.UMNewChurch.org

recreational associates, work associates, neighbors) to worship
__ Receive the Lord's Supper
__weekly; __monthly ___Other: _______

2. Reflect on the degree to which you personally practice these spiritual disciplines (Holy Habits) that you expect your launch team to practice?

What spiritual disciplines will you expect of yourself, your launch team, and your congregation?

Structure Within the Launch Team

One church planter in North Alabama divided his launch team into several task groups, with the lead person of each team serving on the launch team.

Keep in mind that your future church will look like this team.
- Dick Freeman

Each of these initial groups is a task oriented group, yet at their heart they have Bible study, pray together, hold one another accountable for attendance and service every time they meet. Some of these initial groups also have a ministry beyond the local church as a mission such as singing in the nursing homes, visiting the hospital, etc. The planter is not expected to attend all of these gatherings and activities of every task group.

The nature and expectations of the launch team will have a direct influence on the DNA of the new church. These teams continue to be the basic structure of the new church until chartering. It's in part a DNA of an empowered laity, and as the body grows and strengthens the new church will have fully engaged laity.

While the pastor leads the Intercessory Prayer Team, the pastor begins to discern who has gifts and talents for leading these various other eleven small groups.

Look for leadership in the area of prayer, hospitality, electronics, advertising, set up, music, and drama. The exact name and function of the teams will vary, but you know the jobs that you need to fill.

Some of those you attract will not have these particular skills, so you many also be adding Small Groups *(often they look like adult Sunday School classes)* that meet in homes mid-week.

 © 2018 Robert O. Crossman, www.UMNewChurch.org

- **Intercessory Prayer Team** - they anoint and pray for the empty chairs, pray for the lost, pray for those the Lord wants to come to this church, they pray in each of the empty rooms on Sunday morning.

- **Worship Planning Team**, Worship Leader, and Pastor to plan 6 to 8 weeks in advance. On the first Sunday of regular weekly worship, you better have the next seven or eight Sundays already "in the can" with every song, drama, video, and sermon complete. This team has a representative/convener from most of the other teams. Usually have to pay worship leaders because they are so rare.

- **Music team** to implement the music program - plans the music. The performers don't have time to get all the charts together, etc. This team overlaps with the Praise Team below.

- **Praise Team** - the actual singers and musicians - three or four with voices and microphones - don't even think of starting worship if you don't have those key musicians in place. Sometimes you have to pay some of your musicians, sometimes you don't.

- **Drama Team** - a drama program if you have one

- **Video Team** - selects videos/editing

- **Electronics Team** to operate sound/video equipment - usually a large team

- **Logistics Team** to set up and take down every Sunday morning - about 20 people on this team

- **Publicity Team** to do advertising - including handouts

- **Hospitality Team** for food, name tag, greeters, usher people to the nursery

- **Special Events Team** to secure special guest, speakers, performers, testimony by star football players that will bring "butts in the seats." It's far easier to witness to people when they are in your seats.

- **Culture Surfers Team** - What is hot and what's not - meets at Star Bucks, reads the culture.

- **Small Home Groups Team -** Some of those you attract will not have any of these particular skills listed above, so you many also be adding Small Groups *(often they look like adult Sunday School classes)* that meet in homes mid-week.

As the New Church Matures

In most church planting strategies the district superintendent, conference minister of new church starts and the Coach assigned to the new church pastor, will fulfill the traditional functions of a church council, pastor parish relations committee, finance committee, and trustees.

As the months pass, and the church matures, and you sense it is time to begin moving toward chartering in a year or two, one of the ways to prepare for your future "Nominating Committee" type decisions, is to form teams that will eventually take on the formal roles of the church council, pastor parish relations committee, finance committee, and trustees. For example, a year before you anticipate chartering, you can form a Facilities Team, finance team, and HR Team.

Most new churches, upon chartering, for missional reasons intentionally have a VERY SMALL church council of nine people, and does not have separate finance, trustee, and SPPR committees. In this model, officially, the membership of the church council is identical to the membership of the finance committee, and the pastor parish relations committee, and trustees. When the church council meets (usually for an hour once a month), the chair calls the meeting to order.

• Then says, *"Becky, you are the chair of our SPPR. Is their anything you want to bring before us today."*

• Then after that, *"Fred, you are the chair of our finances. Is their anything you want to bring before us today."*

• Then after that, *"Sherry, you are the chair of our trustees. Is their anything you want to bring before us today."*

• This pattern could continue around the table including, perhaps, ministry areas of mission, children, youth, outreach, etc.

The Process of Moving from Launch Team to Chartering

In most annual conferences, new church starts are not allowed to enter the 'charter' process (¶260.4 to ¶260.10) until they:

- Have at least 125 active adult members.
- Are financially self sustaining for at least twelve months, and
- Have been holding public worship at least three years. {Every annual conference has different chartering guidelines. Check with your annual conference new church director, and confirm that conversation with your district superintendent.}

 © 2018 Robert O. Crossman, www.UMNewChurch.org

Of course, being United Methodist we have a formal required "method" for this process in the Book of Discipline, ¶259.5 thru ¶259.10 *(reprinted below in blue).*

¶259

5. When the number of people interested in being charter members of the new church reaches the number necessary as set by the conference to charter a new church, the district superintendent shall call the interested people to meet at an appointed time for the purpose of organizing them into a chartered (organized) local church, or may by written authorization designate an elder in the district to call such a meeting. The district superintendent or the designated elder shall preside and shall appoint a secretary to keep a record of the meeting. Following a time of worship, opportunity shall be given to those in attendance to present themselves for membership.
6. People desiring to become professing members by transfer or on profession of their faith in Christ shall also be given opportunity to present themselves for membership. Any who have not been baptized shall receive the sacrament of baptism, profess their faith and be received as members. Other baptized people are to be received as baptized members.
7. Those who will be members of the constituting church conference shall be those received into the professing membership.
8. The constituting church conference shall then be called to order by the district superintendent or by an elder whom the superintendent designates (see ¶ 246.5). A committee on nominations, elected on nominations from the floor as the conference may determine, shall nominate members of the proposed church council. The chairperson of the committee on nominations shall be the appointed pastor (see ¶ 258.1c). When the members have been chosen, the district superintendent or the designated elder shall declare the church properly constituted.
9. The district superintendent or an elder whom the superintendent designates shall then adjourn the constituting church conference and call to order the charge conference of the pastoral charge. The membership of the charge conference shall be those newly elected, and any others entitled to membership. The charge conference shall then elect such officers of the church as the Discipline requires, including trustees of church property, and shall organize its structure as provided in the Discipline. When such officers have been duly elected and such structure put in place, the church is duly organized, and from this point its work shall proceed as described in the Discipline, provided that when a newly organized church is attached to a circuit, the charge conference shall not be held until such time as representatives from all the churches of the charge can be properly assembled for that purpose.
10. The charge conference may take action, at its discretion, authorizing and directing the newly elected trustees to incorporate the newly organized church in accordance with local laws and the provisions of the Discipline.

Outside Your Launch Team, The Structure a New Church Pastor Needs

You are about to embark on a ministry that will require more than the strength of your hands and the sweat of your brow.

Church Planting will require
your mind to be a mind in harmony with the mind of Christ,
your mouth to be a mouth through whom Christ speaks, and
your hands to be hands through whom Christ touches your mission field.

You will need to be in touch with the one who said, "I am the vine and you are the branches." (John 15:5)

Your personal prayer life and spiritual disciplines will be an essential part in preparing you and sustaining your ministry as a new church planter.

Bob Crossman

On the difficult journey the planter will need several layers of support that might include:

- Supportive relatives {If married, a supportive spouse} who believe in you and support you in the dark of night. There will be dark nights, believe me. You need a spouse (or relatives) who will encourage you, and send you back out into the mission field in Jesus name. It is wonderful blessing if the planters parents and siblings are supportive and praying daily for the new ministry to be fruitful.
- An intercessory prayer team, made up of people outside the mission field. *See article on "Do I Need a Prayer Team?" in chapter four.*
- A coach.
- Someone to talk too in the dark of the night.
- A professional to call if you are in danger of crossing the line in relationships.
- A professional to call on for additional training, such as your conference new church starts staff person.

Implications of New Church Structure (or lack thereof) on the Church Planter's Family

Advantages to the planters family might include:

- The new church will have very few old style expectations on the spouse and family.
- The ability to set a new model for your private time with your family.
- In a society that is plagued with divorce, you can be a role model of healthy marriage.

© 2018 Robert O. Crossman, www.UMNewChurch.org

- New churches tend to be more supportive and loving of the pastor's family than traditional churches.
- If they want too, the spouse and family can be active and take many roles in the new church.

Stress and disadvantages for the family in planting a new church.

- The spouse can feel stress to assume too many of the empty spaces that will certainly exist in the new church.
- Loss of privacy - early meetings are always at your house.
- No place to escape - your office is at the house.
- No clearly assigned roles for the family.
- No support system built in for your children (nursery, sunday school, youth groups, etc.)
- No support system built in for the household (no welcoming church dinner, no SPRC committee to help unload your moving van, etc.)

†††

Addendum for Judicatories

Annual Conference Structure Within the for Making New Church Appointments

The initial 'idea' of exploring a particular community as a potential site for a new United Methodist Church may come from the discernment of a variety of sources:

- Bishop.
- District superintendent.
- Conference minister of new church starts.
- A nearby local UM church.
- District board of church building and location.
- Parish and community development.
- Board of global ministries.
- Hispanic ministries committee.
- Ethnic local church committee.
- Small membership church committee.
- Any UM pastor or laity (active or retired).

Any of the above sources can initiate a conversation with their district superintendent, and they may then be asked to file an *"Application for Approval to Launch a New United Methodist Church."*

- The application includes a survey to be conducted in the targeted population to determine the number of potential members, and the needs of the targeted community (actually physically walking the neighborhood, door to door contact with residents, and using all available information from county/city planning departments, chamber of commerce, civic organizations, and MissionInsite).

- If the targeted population is a language/cultural group, the Conference Commission on Ethnic Local Church Concerns or the Conference Committee on Hispanic Ministries and the leaders of that population need to be consulted and assistance sought in planning the new mission congregation.

- The bishop, the district superintendent, conference minister of new church starts, and cabinet will determine if a new church or mission church will be started in the area brought to their attention.

- Upon recommendation of the district superintendent and conference minister of new church starts, the bishop and the cabinet determines when a new congregation is to be launched to serve an unchurched population, and the MODEL or STRATEGY to be used in the new church start. *(For guidelines for starting Mission Congregations, see the following page.)*

- The bishop and cabinet (in consultation with the conference minister of new church starts) will determine the appointment of pastoral leadership to the new church start. See "How Will We Appoint Our New Pastors."

- In the appointive process, the bishop, conference minister of new church starts, and cabinet will determine the initial level of pastoral compensation compensation required. The district superintendent will prepare and submit an application for Key Charge pastoral compensation, if eligible, to the Commission on Equitable Compensation for action.

- The host district superintendent and conference minister of new church starts will determine the initial level of financial support support needed from all sources for the new church project.

- After the appointment is made, the district superintendent, conference minister of new church starts and the Coach assigned to the new church pastor, will work with the new church pastor to fulfill the traditional functions of a church council, pastor parish relations committee, finance committee, and trustees until the church has grown large enough to complete the 'charter' process and thereby elect these committees. These committees/councils do not exist in a new church prior to the Constituting Church Conference outlined in ¶ 259.

- In most annual conferences, new church starts are not allowed to enter the 'charter' process (¶259.4 to ¶259.10) until they have at least 125 active adult members, have been financially self sustaining for at least 12 months, and have been holding public worship at least three years.

 © 2018 Robert O. Crossman, www.UMNewChurch.org

Guidelines for Starting a Mission Church

1. Start them. Start all of them you can afford. Start them today in every place you can to reach every person you can.

2. When you are starting a mission congregation (and any new church start for that matter), be very clear what financial resources are available, for what period of time, and what measurable benchmarks must be met for funding to continue for that full time period.

3. When you are starting mission congregations and making 10 or 15 year financial commitments to them, be sure and run your "new church" conference budget out for that many years to be sure that you will have the funds to meet all the combined obligations. For example, if you start 2 new mission congregations each year, for ten years – will you have the funds to support all of that combined financial obligation?

4) In many mission settings, the people you are reaching are not completely devoid of financial resources. In many mission settings, because of the small number of people you are trying to reach in that mission field (like the new church pastor we just appointed to reach a Vietnamese population of only 2,400 in Fort Smith), or because of their limited financial resources (like an Anglo new church appointment we made two years ago in a very depressed financial part of Fort Smith) – you are not expecting them to meet the same financial benchmarks you would set for a new ministry reaching a financially wealthy segment of the population.

   So... in a mission setting, (and any new church start for that matter), be careful about loading them up with financial obligations (building or salary) they can never meet.

   For example, use the same financial common sense you use with your existing congregations. In hundreds of our old existing small Anglo congregations in Arkansas – we appoint pastoral leadership they can afford – whether it's a layspeaker (TBS) or a part-time local pastor – and we only approve building/remodeling expenses they can afford. Obviously, the cabinet does not appoint a full-time pastor with a heavy salary & benefits package to a setting that can only afford $50 a week for a part-time local pastor.

5) In some of your new church starts in mission settings, perhaps it is appropriate for them to be supported on a clearly defined 10 or 15 year declining basis, instead of a 3 year declining basis as you may do in other settings.

†††

NOTE: This article reflects the personal opinions of its author and does not necessarily reflect an official position of Discipleship Ministries or Path 1.

New Church Handbook
Nuts & Bolts for Planting New Churches In The Wesleyan Tradition

"How Do We Incorporate? Or, Should We?"

by Bob Crossman

Some annual conferences require every church to Incorporate.
In some annual conferences none of the churches are Incorporated.
Before incorporating your local church be sure and obtain written permission from your district superintendent and conference director of new church starts.
Also, be sure that you follow the policies and procedures of your annual conference.

The following 6 pages are from the UM GCFA Legal Manual, page 16-ff.

INCORPORATION OF A LOCAL CHURCH

Paragraph 2529.1a vests the charge conference with the authority to direct the local church BOT to incorporate the church. The incorporation must be accomplished in accordance with local law and the Discipline. Minimum standards for a local church corporation are found in ¶¶ 2506 and 2529.2b. Incorporation should protect and exempt the individual officers and members of the local church, jointly and severally, from legal liability for and on account of the debts and other obligations of every kind and description of the local church.[46]

The first step in the incorporation process should be the retention of qualified legal counsel. Legal counsel should be very familiar with the structure of the United Methodist denomination, the trust clause (¶ 2503), the local church structure, and the various roles of the district superintendent as to certain local church matters.

1. Advantages of Incorporation.

Under the law, a corporation is a separate legal entity from its officers, directors and incorporators, with the power to enter into contracts and agreements in its own name. The corporate form provides a continuous entity for the ownership and management of property and for the carrying out of the business and programs of the local church. If proven, assertions of liability for acts undertaken by the corporation may be satisfied only by corporate assets, not by the personal assets of the corporate directors, except in cases of fraud against the corporation by a director or when corporate formalities are not followed.

2. Powers.

A corporation derives its powers and existence from the state. The sources of its powers are its charter and the general statute under which the corporation was organized. The statutes grant numerous specific powers relating to organization, the use and conveyance of property, the election of officers, the amendment of articles of incorporation and by-laws, the right of dissolution, etc.

 © 2018 Robert O. Crossman, www.UMNewChurch.org

The "express powers" of a corporation are those related to the business activities in which the corporation is engaged and that are enumerated in its charter. "Implied powers" arise out of reasonable inferences about the scope and intent of the language of the charter powers as they relate to certain facts and circumstances. Great care should be taken by the local church corporation to ensure that its acts and transactions do not extend beyond its limits of authority. Such ultra vires acts should be expressly barred by the Articles of Incorporation.

3. Formation.

Procedures for forming and organizing corporations vary from state to state. However, general incorporation statutes in every jurisdiction provide for the issuance of a certificate of incorporation to certain persons by a designated state official (usually the Secretary of State). The typical statute requires:

1. The preparation and execution of the articles of incorporation by the incorporators, and the acknowledgment of their signatures before a notary public;
2. The delivery of the articles of incorporation to the Secretary of State, including any other required incorporation papers and payment of requisite organizational fees;
3. Filing of the articles by the Secretary of State, and subsequent issuance by him or her of the certificate of incorporation;
4. The recording of the Certificate and Articles of Incorporation with the Recorder of Deeds, or any other county officials as required in the county or parish where the corporation is located;
5. The convening of the first corporate organizational meeting at the call of the directors to adopt by-laws, elect officers, and transact other business.

The articles of incorporation generally include the following provisions:

1. The name and address of the corporation;
2. The address of its registered agent for the service of process, notice, or demand upon the corporation within the state;
3. The duration or tenure of the corporation, which may be perpetual or limited (church corporations are typically perpetual);
4. The names and addresses of the incorporators;
5. A statement of purpose for which the corporation is formed;
6. The names of the individuals constituting the initial board of directors and the names and addresses of those who are to serve as directors until the first called meeting;
7. Membership in the corporation, and, in the case of the local church, specific reference to the Discipline provisions on incorporation of the local church;
8. The powers of the corporation;
9. Procedures for the adoption of by-laws by the board of trustees;
10. Definition of the quorum of directors needed to transact corporate business;
11. Procedures for amending the articles of incorporation;

12. Provisions for the distribution of assets upon dissolution of the corporation.

Upon completion of the required charter application and the articles of incorporation, these documents must be submitted to the district superintendent for his or her written approval. The purpose of obtaining the superintendent's written approval is to insure conformity of the documents with the Discipline, including all of the requirements of ¶ 2529.2b. Particular attention should be devoted to the following:

1. The corporation's stated purpose and powers must support the doctrine of the United Methodist denomination, and all its property must be subject to the "laws, usages, and ministerial appointments" of the Church.
2. The board of trustees, which ordinarily will serve as the board of directors of the corporation, must be properly selected. Officers of the board of trustees are the officers of the board of directors of the corporation.
3. The powers and responsibilities of the corporation, and its board of directors, should include the powers and responsibilities about property specified for the charge conference by the Discipline.
4. The members of the corporation are to be the members of the charge conference.
5. Should the corporation cease to exist, the title to all its property is to be vested in another 501(c)(3) tax exempt organization. We suggest the title vest in the annual conference board of trustees, to be held in trust for benefit of the local church, if it should continue to exist, and, if not, for the benefit of the conference or successor entity.
6. The articles of incorporation and the by-laws of the corporation that are submitted to the state should include the provisions of the Discipline by reference.
7. After completion of the incorporation, care should be taken to deed all property to the new corporation. Real property can be deeded by use of a quitclaim deed. This transfer can present an excellent opportunity to review the title to property, to determine if there are any limitations on reversionary interests, and to ensure the inclusion of the trust clause (¶ 2503).

Many states now have special not-for-profit corporation statutes or religious corporation statutes that significantly decrease the reporting requirements and filing costs for such corporations. Local counsel should be instructed to incorporate under such statutes if possible.

It might be helpful as well to consult with other local churches that have recently incorporated in your state to obtain samples of their forms for review, assuming their incorporation forms have been prepared by a knowledgeable attorney with attention to the unique structure of the United Methodist denomination.

NOTE: ***Sample incorporation forms, including bylaws, are included at the end of***

 © 2018 Robert O. Crossman, www.UMNewChurch.org

this section. Each state has different incorporation requirements, so these samples should only be used as starting points for the creation of documents tailored to a respective state's requirements.

[46] ¶ 2529.1a.

SAMPLE ARTICLES OF INCORPORATION
[STATE]
SECRETARY OF STATE
ARTICLES OF INCORPORATION OF A [STATE] NONPROFIT CORPORATION

1. The name of this nonprofit corporation is
[CHURCH NAME, INCLUDING "INC." OR OTHER REQUIRED DESIGNATION]

2. The initial registered office and principal office of the nonprofit corporation is
[ADDRESS]
and the registered agent of the nonprofit corporation at that office is:
[TITLE]: _______

3. Purpose.

The nonprofit corporation is a religious corporation. It is organized as a local United Methodist Church exclusively for religious purposes, supports the doctrine of The United Methodist Church, and declares itself and all of its property subject to the law, usages and ministerial appointments of The United Methodist Church.

The Corporation is to be operated exclusively for charitable, religious, and educational purposes, including, for such purposes, the making of distributions to organizations that qualify as exempt organizations under Section 501(c)(3) of the Internal Revenue Code, or the corresponding section of any future federal tax code. No part of the net earnings of the corporation shall inure to the benefit of, or be distributable to its members, directors, trustees, officers, or other private persons, except that the corporation shall be authorized and empowered to pay reasonable compensation for services rendered and to make payments and distributions in furtherance of the purposes set forth above. No substantial part of the activities of the corporation shall be the carrying on of propaganda, or otherwise attempting to influence legislation, and the corporation shall not participate in, or intervene in (including the publishing or distribution of statements) any political campaign on behalf of or in opposition to any candidate for public office. Notwithstanding any other provision of its charter, the corporation shall not carry on any other activities not permitted to be carried on (a) by a corporation exempt from federal income tax under Section 501(c)(3) of the Internal Revenue Code, or the corresponding section of any future federal tax code, or (b) by a corporation, contributions to which are deductible under Section 170(c)(2) of the Internal Revenue Code, or the corresponding section of any future federal tax code.

4. Members.

The corporation will have members. Upon the filing of these Articles of

Incorporation, the members of the former unincorporated local United Methodist Church shall be members of such corporation. Only those members of the Corporation who are members of the Charge Conference, as defined in The Book of The United Methodist Church (hereafter "the Discipline"), are entitled to vote at a meeting of the members; provided, however if the district superintendent convenes a Charge Conference as a Church Conference, all members of the Corporation present shall be entitled to vote.

5. Powers.

The business of this corporation shall be conducted in conformity with the Discipline as the same now exists or as may hereafter be amended, changed, or modified, and the bylaws of the corporation shall include the Discipline and no bylaws shall be adopted inconsistent with the provisions of the Discipline.

In addition to the powers and duties granted to this corporation by the Discipline, the corporation assumes for itself all the rights, powers, and privileges and immunities which are now, and which may be during the existence thereof be conferred by law upon a corporation with a similar character, provided the same are not inconsistent with the Discipline. All amendments, bylaws, and regulations of this corporation shall at all times be in conformity with the Discipline and must be approved, in writing, by the pastor and the district superintendent.

But notwithstanding the above, however, at no time shall any of the amendments, bylaws, or regulations of the corporation be prohibited by or in conflict with the nonprofit corporate laws of the [STATE].

6. Term.

This corporation shall exist in perpetuity. If for any reason the corporation shall be abandoned, discontinued, or cease to exist as a legal entity and its charter shall expire or be terminated, the title to all its property both real and personal shall be vested in and be the property of the [ANNUAL CONFERENCE] of The United Methodist Church, pursuant to the Discipline, provided it is then an organization qualified under Section 501(c)(3) of the Internal Revenue Code of the United States; and if not, to any other organization, designated by such Annual Conference, which is then qualified under Section 501(c)(3) of the Internal Revenue Code of the United States. The Corporation cannot sever its connectional relationship to The United Methodist Church without the Annual Conference's consent.

7. The name, address (with zip code) and signature of each incorporator is as follows (only one required):

[LIST NAME, ADDRESS, AND SIGNATURE OF EACH INCORPORATOR]

 © 2018 Robert O. Crossman, www.UMNewChurch.org

SAMPLE CORPORATE BY-LAWS
BY-LAWS OF

[CHURCH NAME, INCLUDING "INC." OR OTHER REQUIRED DESIGNATION]
[CITY, COUNTY, STATE]

ARTICLE I
IDENTITY

These are the By-Laws of the above-named United Methodist Church, a nonprofit religious corporation organized and existing pursuant to the laws of [STATE], with its principal place of business at the above stated city and county in [STATE] (hereafter, "the Corporation").

ARTICLE II
PURPOSES AND POWERS

Section 1. The Corporation is organized as a local United Methodist Church exclusively for religious purposes, supports the doctrine of The United Methodist Church, and declares itself and all of its property subject to the law, usages and ministerial appointments of The United Methodist Church.

Section 2. All the powers authorized and permitted by The Book of Discipline of the United Methodist Church (as amended from time to time by its General Conference) (hereinafter, "the Discipline") for a local church corporation shall be the powers of this Corporation, together with such powers as granted to religious corporations in the [STATE NON-PROFIT OR RELIGIOUS CORPORATION ACT], as amended from time to time.

ARTICLE III
GOVERNANCE

Section 1. The Corporation shall look to these By-Laws, to the Discipline, and to the laws of [STATE] with reference to non-profit religious corporations for guidance in the operation of its affairs.

Section 2. Where these By-Laws conflict with the Discipline, the Discipline shall control.

Section 3. Where these By-Laws conflict with the laws of [STATE] with reference to non-profit religious corporations, [STATE] law shall control.

ARTICLE IV
MEMBERS

Section 1. The initial members of the Corporation shall be the members of the local church congregation immediately prior to incorporation. Persons subsequently becoming members of the local church congregation shall be members of the Corporation, and persons ceasing to be members of the local church congregation shall cease to be members of the Corporation.

Section 2. Only those members of the Corporation who are members of the Charge Conference, as defined in the Discipline, are entitled to vote at a meeting of the members; provided, however if the district superintendent convenes a Charge Conference as a Church Conference, all members of the Corporation present shall be entitled to vote.

Section 3. The annual meeting and any special meeting of the members (whether convened by the district superintendent as a Charge Conference or a Church Conference) shall be convened and held, with notice, quorum and voting rights, all as provided for in the Discipline.

ARTICLE V
BOARD OF TRUSTEES

Section 1. The number, qualifications, and constitution of the board of trustees, their term in office and their method of election, removal and replacement shall be in accordance with the provisions of the Discipline.

Section 2. An organizational meeting of the board of trustees shall be held in January. Section 3. Special meetings of the board of trustees may be called by the Chairperson or as otherwise provided by the Discipline.

Section 4. Notice of all regular and special meetings of the board of trustees shall be given to each trustee personally or by mail, church bulletin, telephone or fax machine, at least five (5) days prior to the date of the meeting. Notice may be waived as provided for in the [STATE NON-PROFIT OR RELIGIOUS CORPORATION ACT] and the Discipline. The notice shall include the date, hour and place of all such meetings.

Section 5. A quorum at any trustees' meeting shall consist of a majority of the board of trustees, as constituted at the time of such meeting. The acts approved by a majority of those present at any meeting, at which a quorum is present, shall constitute the acts of the board of trustees. Less than a quorum may adjourn a meeting, from time to time, until a quorum is present.

ARTICLE VI
OFFICERS

Section 1. The officers of the Corporation shall be a Chairperson, a Vice Chairperson, a Secretary and if need requires, a treasurer, or as provided in the Discipline. The office of Secretary and treasurer may be held by the same person. The Chairperson, Vice Chairperson, and Secretary shall be members of the board of trustees.

Section 2. The Chairperson, a Vice Chairperson, a Secretary and if need requires a treasurer shall be elected at the organizational meeting of the board of trustees, and all such officers shall hold office until the second annual meeting of the Board following their election and until such time as their successors are duly elected and qualified.

Section 3. Any officer may be removed from his or her office at any time by a

 © 2018 Robert O. Crossman, www.UMNewChurch.org

majority vote of the board of trustees, as then constituted, notwithstanding the fact that the term for which he or she may have been elected has not expired. No cause need be assigned for any removal under this section.

Section 4. Any vacancy in any office, regardless of the cause, may be filled by the board of trustees at any regular or special meeting.

Section 5. The Chairperson shall preside at all meetings of the board of trustees. The Chairperson shall execute all contracts authorized by the board of trustees and shall perform such other duties as are incident to the office or properly required of him or her by the board of trustees.

Section 6. The Vice Chairperson shall perform the duties of the Chairperson in the absence or disability of the Chairperson. In addition, the Vice Chairperson shall have such powers and discharge such duties as may be properly assigned to him or her, from time to time, by the board of trustees.

Section 7. The Secretary shall keep a record of all proceedings at the meetings of the board of trustees. He or she shall attend to the giving of notices, have custody of the corporate seal, attest when necessary the signature of the Chairperson, and affix the seal to all instruments required to be executed under seal and authorized by the board of trustees. He or she shall have such other powers and perform such other duties as are incident to the office or properly required of him or her by the board of trustees.

Section 8. If elected, the treasurer shall be in charge of all the monies and securities belonging to the Corporation. The treasurer shall cause the monies of the Corporation to be deposited in the name of the Corporation in such banks or other institutions as the board of trustees may designate; and shall cause the securities of the Corporation, together with other valuable documents of the Corporation to be deposited for safekeeping with such bank or institution as the board of trustees may designate. The Church treasurer who is elected by the Charge Conference may also serve as treasurer of the Corporation if the board of trustees and the Charge Conference so agree. The treasurer shall have such other powers and perform such other duties as are incident to the office or properly required of him or her by the board of trustees or the Charge Conference.

ARTICLE VII
FISCAL YEAR AND AUDIT

Section 1. The fiscal year of the Corporation shall commence on the 1st day of January and end on the 31st day of December.

Section 2. Audit requirements and procedures for the local church as set forth in the Discipline shall be complied with.

ARTICLE VIII
FIDELITY BONDS AND INSURANCE

The Corporation shall comply with the fidelity bond and insurance requirements for the local church as set forth in the Discipline.

ARTICLE IX
AMENDMENTS

Upon the written approval of the pastor and the district superintendent, these By-Laws may be amended by a two-thirds vote of the full board of trustees (as then constituted) at any meeting of the board of trustees, provided that the notice of such meeting clearly sets forth the proposed changes which are to be considered.

ARTICLE X
SEAL

The Corporation may have a seal of such design as the board of trustees may adopt setting forth the name of the Corporation.

ARTICLE XI
INDEMNITY OF TRUSTEES AND OFFICERS

The Corporation is authorized to indemnify its trustees and officers to the full extent permitted in the [STATE NON-PROFIT OR RELIGIOUS CORPORATION ACT], as amended from time to time.

Effective as of________________, 20____.

____________________________________ Secretary

NOTE: This article reflects the personal opinions of its author and does not necessarily reflect an official position of Discipleship Ministries or Path 1.

© 2018 Robert O. Crossman, www.UMNewChurch.org

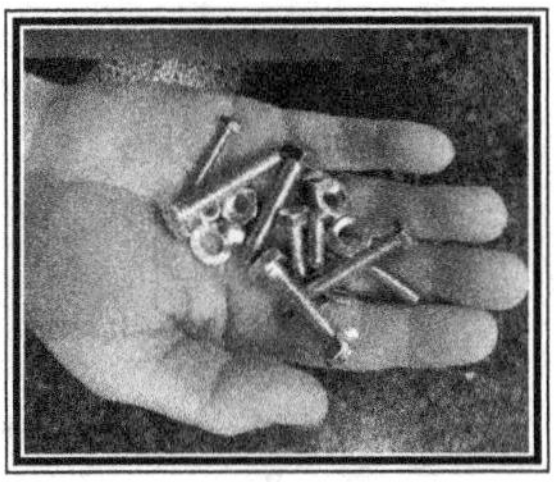

New Church Handbook
Nuts & Bolts for Planting New Churches In The Wesleyan Tradition

"We Don't Have a Building Yet, Do We Really Need Insurance?"

by Bob Crossman

Does My New Church Need Insurance?

YES! Yes, without exception your new church needs insurance coverage.

Check with your Annual Conference Office to see if they have minimum requirements, recommended levels of coverage, or a group policy.

If you are meeting in homes and have not launched worship yet, you still need liability insurance.

If you are sharing facilities with an established church, or meeting in an elementary school or strip center you still need what is called "renter's insurance" which would include liability coverage and property coverage for contents you own. Also, depending on your lease you may be responsible for some building coverage such as glass breakage, legal liability or property damage to the building that is caused by you, or improvements you may make to the building.

If you have a building of your own, you need what is called "building insurance."

So, whether you have renter's insurance or building insurance, you will need to be sure it includes liability coverage for accidents that may occur, and content coverage for your equipment.

Church Mutual Insurance Company prepared the following basic article to introduce points to consider.

Insuring Your Church: Points to Consider
Edited for use at the United Methodist
New Church Leadership Institute
October 2010

No matter what precautions you take to protect your property and congregation, some accidents will happen and some property may be damaged or destroyed. For these unavoidable situations, you need a well-tailored insurance program. A program that eliminates or reduces the financial consequences of a tragedy at your church.

At Church Mutual, we believe that a basic working knowledge of insurance can help you select and maintain the coverages that best meet your individual needs. So we prepared "Insuring Your Church Points to Consider" to provide important information in language a non-insurance person will understand.

We have attempted to provide an unbiased review of types of coverages, insurance terms and how to judge how much insurance is necessary. But even if you're a veteran insurance buyer, you might find sufficient details to gain new knowledge and understanding.

This booklet is not, however, intended to be a complete "do-it-yourself" insurance buying guide. Use it to supplement, not replace, the advice of a qualified insurance agent, broker or consultant.

Buying insurance: A major responsibility.

If you are entrusted with the responsibility of securing property and liability insurance for your church, you hold an extremely important position. Though religious organizations are special, they are not immune to the problems of our world and are generally not given any special consideration by our courts.

In today's legal system, religious not-for-profits are treated like businesses that are exposed to more opportunity for accidents and property damage than most.

Your potential for encountering lawsuits is high. You have dozens, hundreds or thousands of members and guests visit your facility each week. Each is capable of slipping on a loose step or wet floor.

The activities you sponsor — sports teams, socials, dinners, picnics, field trips, campouts, retreats, schools and so on — hold tremendous potential for injury. You probably use automobiles occasionally, and may own one or a fleet. You have volunteers doing a wide variety of tasks, sometimes with less than professional skill and equipment. You may also have full and part-time employees.

For your property exposures, consider the probable high value of the building and contents your congregation owns. Also keep in mind that your building is likely to be unoccupied for hours or days at a time, making it prone to vandalism, theft and arson.

Your steeple presents an attractive target for lightning. And the use of kitchen equipment, candles and other electrical apparatus increases your chance for fire.

A congregation with a well-organized safety committee and maintenance program can reduce the chances of an accident or property damage. It can't eliminate them.

It is your important responsibility to see that the financial risk associated with an accident or property damage is eliminated or greatly reduced by transferring it to an insurance company.

The decisions you make might, one day, prove to be among the most important operational choices ever made.

Selecting your insurance company and agent

An insurance policy is only as good as the company behind it and the agent who helps construct it. Select a company that is financially reliable, service-oriented

 © 2018 Robert O. Crossman, www.UMNewChurch.org

and familiar with the special needs of religious organizations.

The best indicator of the financial stability of an insurance company is the rating it has been assigned by A.M. Best Company. A.M. Best has been an independent analyst of insurance companies since 1899. Look for insurers with high ratings, preferably "A" or better, for your greatest security. And seek a nonassessable policy, so that your insurance company can't come to you for a special premium assessment when financial times get rough.

The A.M. Best rating addresses a company's ability to pay its claims, not its spirit of cooperation in so doing, or the competence and concern of its agents. So, it's important when selecting a company and agent to ask for and check references. Call three or four others who are insured by the company, and through the agent, you are considering.

Ask these questions:

- Are you pleased with the service you receive?
- Did the agent clearly explain the coverages?
- Is he or she responsive to your questions and concerns?
- Are phone calls returned promptly?
- Does the agent follow up on important matters in writing so that no misunderstandings develop?
- Does the agent meet periodically with your insurance committee?
- If you've had a claim, was it handled promptly, courteously and fairly?

In addition, judge the agent for yourself during his or her preliminary work for you and presentation to your decision-makers.

- Does the agent show genuine concern for the well-being of your ministry?
- Did the agent thoroughly analyze your needs and become familiar with your operation and activities?
- Does the agent have a good understanding of insurance and clearly express how it meets your needs?

Many clergy and board members feel more secure when dealing with companies that specialize in insurance for religious organizations. These companies have specifically-designed coverages and time-tested methods for determining the amount of insurance you should carry. Their agents spend a great deal of time in churches and are typically better at identifying and handling exposures unique to religious ministries. They might have specialized loss control, underwriting, legal and claims support staff to work on your behalf.

The group insurance option

Group coverage has never been as popular or commonplace for property and liability insurance as it is for life and health insurance. Nevertheless, some congregations do have the option to enroll in a local, state or national property and liability insurance program. This can be advantageous, but isn't always.

Your insurance is too important and complicated to purchase by mail and too individualized to accept a "canned" program. No two ministries are exactly alike in architecture, activities and budgets. Consider a group program if: 1. Participation does not eliminate or substantially reduce personal service, AND 2. Your insurance program can be tailored to your needs.

If you lose personal service and can't buy the protection you need, the potential savings of a group plan might not be worth the cost.

The Multi-peril Policy — your Insurance Foundation

The foundation of your insurance program is a multi-peril policy. It provides coverage for most of your property and general liability exposures. There's wide variation from company to company, so compare carefully.

Multi-peril property protection

Determining the right amount of insurance. The amount of insurance you carry on your building and contents affects how much you receive for a total loss.

It also can affect how much you receive for a partial loss.

To arrive at the proper amount of insurance, you must calculate the cost to replace your building and contents. Original purchase price and market value can usually be ignored.

You may hire a professional appraiser or, as many do, accept the value your agent recommends. This makes it critical that you select a company and agent familiar with the architecture and construction costs of churches.

Some policies stipulate that your insurance be not less than 80% of the value of the property at the time you suffer a partial loss. If you fail to have enough insurance to meet the requirement, you might incur a coinsurance penalty. This means you will share in the loss with your insurance company — beyond your deductible.

Through examples, the affect of a coinsurance penalty on your claim settlement becomes clear.

Example A: Failure to meet coinsurance requirement. Assume that the value of your property is $250,000, that the coinsurance requirement is 80% and that you are carrying only $100,000 of insurance. Also assume that you have a $500 deductible and incur a $40,000 loss.

Step 1: $250,000 (value) x 80% (coinsurance percentage) = $200,000. This is the minimum amount of insurance you must carry to meet the coinsurance requirement.

Step 2: $100,000 (what you carry) divided by $200,000 (what you are required to

© 2018 Robert O. Crossman, www.UMNewChurch.org

carry) = .50, or 50%. This represents the percentage of insurance you actually carry, in relation to the amount you were required to carry to avoid a penalty.

Step 3: $40,000 (the loss) x .50 = $20,000.

Step 4: $20,000 – $500 (deductible) = $19,500. $19,500 is the amount you receive from your insurance company. The remaining $20,500 is not covered. The coinsurance penalty cost you $20,000 and the deductible cost $500.

Example B: Adequate insurance to meet coinsurance requirement. Assume all of the same facts as in the above example, except that you carry $200,000 of insurance.

Step 1: $250,000 x 80% = $200,000.

Step 2: $200,000 (what you carry) divided by $200,000 (what you are required to carry) = 1.00, or 100%.

Step 3: $40,000 (the loss) x 1.00 = $40,000.

Step 4: $40,000 – $500 (deductible) = $39,500. $39,500 is the amount you receive from your insurance company. You recoup all of your loss except the deductible.

To avoid a coinsurance penalty, set your insurance amount accurately and keep it up-to-date with periodic reviews.

You may also ask your insurance company to attach an "agreed value" endorsement to your policy. This removes the coinsurance penalty from your policy.

In periods of moderate to high inflation, purchase "inflation guard" coverage to automatically adjust your limit between policy reviews.

Note that the concern with coinsurance is partial losses. You may have adequate insurance to avoid a coinsurance penalty on partial losses, but inadequate insurance to fully cover a total loss. Insurance to satisfy the coinsurance requirement should be your absolute minimum. You may purchase insurance equal to 90% or 100% of value in order to be better protected against a total loss.

Replacement cost vs. actual cash value. Some policies provide for settlement of claims on an actual cash value basis, while others do so on a replacement cost basis. Be aware of what you're buying. Most congregations want and need replacement cost coverage for their buildings and contents.

The distinction between the two can be technically complicated. But, simply defined, replacement cost is the amount it would cost to repair or replace an item with material of comparable kind and quality. Actual cash value is the replacement cost less an allowance for deterioration, depreciation and obsolescence.

Blanket insurance. Normally, a multi-peril policy will list a limit of insurance for each insured building and a limit for the contents of each building. ("Building" might include far more than the structure itself — items such as pews and organs, for example.) Consider having coverage written on a blanket basis instead. This means combining your building and its contents under one limit of insurance. And, if you have more than one building, it can mean combining all buildings (and their contents) under one limit.

If you own one building, there is an advantage only if your blanket limit is comfortably above the coinsurance requirement or if there is no coinsurance requirement. Blanketing then serves to better cover contents you acquire over time — additional contents that would make a separate content limit inadequate.

If you have more than one building, blanketing allows you to shift contents from building to building without concern that a specific contents limit at one building is inadequate. Camps find this advantage particularly attractive.

And, with blanket insurance, you can be insured for 100% of the value at each building without purchasing 100% of the combined value. For example, you have two buildings, each having a value of $100,000. With a blanket limit, you could purchase $180,000 of insurance (90% of the combined value is typically required for blanket insurance), meet the coinsurance requirement and still apply $100,000 to either building.

Because there are coverage advantages to blanket insurance, your insurance company may charge a higher premium for it. Consult with your agent and weigh the advantages against the disadvantages before making your decision.

Antique, rare and highly valuable items. Some items, because of their rarity, antiquity or unique design, are worth far more than ordinary items of comparable utility. Certain paintings, statues, Bibles, communion ware and intricate stained glass are examples. You and your insurance company should agree in advance on the value of these unusual items and specifically list them in your policy. This is generally referred to as "scheduling" an item or providing "inland marine" coverage for it.

Without this advance scheduling or inland marine coverage, you might have a difficult time proving the value of an item stolen or destroyed. And it might be so valuable that it makes your content limit inadequate — subjecting you to a coinsurance penalty.

Choosing your coverages. Once you've determined how much insurance you need, you may select the causes of loss for which you need and can afford protection.

Your building and contents may be insured on a "special" basis or on a "specified cause of loss" basis.

A "specified cause of loss" policy (sometimes referred to as a "named peril" policy) lists the causes of loss for which you are covered, such as fire, lightning, windstorm and hail. Generally, you do not choose on a cause-by-cause basis. Rather, your insurance company groups causes, providing you either a few basic causes or several causes (broad form).

Under a "specified cause of loss" policy, you must prove that your loss was

 © 2018 Robert O. Crossman, www.UMNewChurch.org

caused by a listed cause of loss before you can file a claim.

A "special" policy (sometimes referred to as "all risk" or "comprehensive") covers all direct causes of loss except those which are listed as exclusions — such as wear and tear, war, flood and earthquake. To file a claim, you need only prove that loss occurred — and not its cause. To deny your claim, your insurance company must prove that the cause of loss is specifically excluded.

With its more comprehensive coverage and shift of burden of proof to the insurance company, a "special" policy is preferable for most religious organizations. It does cost more than a "specified cause of loss" policy, but the greater security is well worth it.

Even with a "special" policy, there are some coverage concerns. The most common are the treatment of signs, glass, building ordinances, earthquakes and floods, and system and equipment breakdowns.

Signs: The sign on your lawn is probably covered by your multi-peril policy. Signs at locations other than your church might not automatically be covered or might be insured for an inadequate amount. Tell your agent where your signs are located, and their value, so they can be properly insured.

Glass: Some insurance policies have limitations on the amount you may collect for glass broken accidentally or by vandals. Typical limitations are $250 per pane, with $1,000 maximum for all panes. If the value of your windows — individually or collectively — exceeds your policy's limitations, purchase "full" glass coverage.

Building Ordinances: Many communities have ordinances restricting the repair of heavily damaged buildings, causing you to make costly modifications or to rebuild entirely. Watch out for them! Your policy can be endorsed to account for increased building costs or demolition costs resulting from compliance with such ordinances. Contact your local building inspector to learn which ordinances may affect you.

Earthquakes and Floods: Rarely are earthquakes and floods automatically covered under a multi-peril policy. If you are located in a flood plain or area subject to earthquakes, your insurance agent can assist you in obtaining coverage — either through his or her company or through government programs.

System and Equipment Breakdowns: In our modern world of complex mechanical and electronic equipment, System and Equipment Breakdowns coverage (SEB) has become so popular that some insurance companies automatically include it as part of their multi-peril policy. Others offer it as an optional coverage.

SEB includes mechanical breakdowns, artificially generated electrical currents, and steam boiler explosions as additional covered causes of loss.

Among the items that are within the scope of SEB coverage are:

- Computers, telephone systems, fax machines and copiers

- Sound, lighting and video equipment
- Air conditioning motors, compressors, systems and piping
- Electrical cable, wiring, panel boards, switch gear and transformers
- Engines, motors, compressors, turbines, pumps, fans, blowers and generators
- Steam boilers, steam piping, steam turbines, steam engines and gas turbines
- Alarm systems and elevators Typically, SEB even provides for boiler safety inspections, where required by law.

Theft and employee dishonesty. Theft coverage for your building and content items is usually included under a "special" policy and is available as an option under a "specified cause of loss" policy. It is therefore treated like any other covered cause of loss and subject to the policy limits.

Theft of money and securities is treated differently. You must generally purchase separate coverage for them — at a limit equal to your average weekly offerings. With some policies, the amount you purchase for normal offerings is automatically increased on special holidays — such as Christmas and Easter — when offerings are much greater than normal.

If you have fund-raising projects that generate more income than a normal offering, advise your insurance agent so that adequate coverage is provided.

For greatest security, purchase money and securities coverage that includes disappearance and destruction, as well as theft. This gives you coverage when money is missing but you can't prove it was stolen. It also covers money destroyed by fire or other means.

Another concern for religious organizations is the theft of money or of other property by employees and volunteers. In insurance jargon, this is considered employee dishonesty, not theft.

Usually, your best protection for employee/volunteer dishonesty is to purchase a blanket bond. Set your limit at the greatest amount someone could steal over time without getting caught or before leaving the position of responsibility. Include your weekly offerings and money from fund-raisers, building funds and other income and accounts.

Extensions or additions of coverage. Most multi-peril policies automatically include several coverage "extensions" or "additions." Some are very important. It is in this area that you will normally find coverage for contents taken off premises, extra expenses of operation following a loss, personal property of members, guests and others, and many other coverages that can save you money at the time a loss occurs.

Some companies rely heavily on these coverages to differentiate their policy from their competitors. Compare carefully, identifying those that are meaningful to your ministry.

 © 2018 Robert O. Crossman, www.UMNewChurch.org

Loss of income protection. If your ministry depends on rental property or tuition fees for operational income, consider purchasing special coverage to continue the income if it is interrupted by a fire or other cause of loss.

For example, you own an apartment house that generates $1,250 per month in net income. If it was destroyed by fire (or wind, etc.), your ministry would lose the income. Insurance is available to protect you from this kind of loss.

A similar coverage is available for loss of rental value. Assume you provide a parsonage for the pastor. It is heavily damaged by fire and you must rent another home for the pastor while repairs are made. The cost of renting this temporary home can be covered by insurance.

Insurance for buildings under construction. If you plan to construct a new building or add to an existing one, some important insurance concerns need to be addressed.

Builders' Risk Insurance: You can add builders' risk coverage to your current multi-peril policy or purchase a new policy for the building under construction. It makes little difference.

Set the limit of insurance equal to the estimated completed value of the building or addition. This value should be the amount a general contractor would charge to rebuild — even if you use volunteer labor for the actual construction. A damaged structure can be far more difficult to repair than it is to build the first time. Volunteers might lack the skill to make major repairs or the interest to repeat their task. You might incur penalties — like coinsurance — if you underinsure.

Certificates of Insurance: Obtain certificates of insurance from your general contractor, showing coverage for comprehensive general liability, XC&U (explosion, collapse and underground damage to property) liability, products and completed operations, umbrella liability, workers' compensation and automobile liability. Your insurance company might ask you for these certificates.

Construction Bonds: Several types of bond coverages are available, and it is best to seek an attorney's advice regarding bonds you should require from your contractor. The most common bonds you will want are performance bonds and labor and material payment bonds. The performance bond "guarantees" that the contractor will meet the terms and conditions of your contract or pay a penalty. Labor and material bonds are used to ensure that workers are paid and materials paid for, thereby keeping your ministry free of liens.

Deductibles. Deductibles are applicable to most property claims and typically range from $500 to $1,000 or more per occurrence. The higher your deductible, the lower your premium. Base your decision on your ability to pay and the premium savings you might enjoy.

Multi-peril liability protection. Insurance for when you're sued. Every church should obtain insurance that responds to lawsuits involving bodily injury, personal injury, property damage and sexual misconduct or molestation. The insurance should apply whether the injury or damage occurs at or away from your premises and is caused by the negligence of a member, employee or virtually anyone else acting on your behalf.

Most multi-peril policies protect against lawsuits alleging bodily injury and property damage, though there are some subtle but important variations from policy to policy.

Fewer policies provide coverage for personal injury and sexual misconduct/ molestation. Personal injury includes libel, slander, invasion of privacy and other infringements on the rights of an individual or organization.

In most churches, no one would intentionally cause personal injury. But it can, and does, happen unintentionally, and lawsuits are filed. Even lawsuits without merit can be expensive to defend.

Reports of sexual misconduct and molestation, especially child sexual abuse, occur with frightening frequency at churches, schools, camps and day care centers.

Some insurance companies, fearing excessive exposure from lawsuits, have chosen to exclude coverage for these acts. Some, recognizing the serious financial consequences to a ministry from this type of lawsuit, have chosen to specifically include coverage for the organization and individuals wrongly accused of an act.

Purchasing insurance for this exposure is a wise financial decision. It should not be viewed negatively — coverage does not apply to individuals who commit the offense, so you are in no way condoning the act. Instead, you are recognizing that the problem is real, and that despite all your precautions, it could happen. And you are protecting your ministry and innocent employees, volunteers and members.

Special activities require special protection. Depending on the activities of your congregation, you might need one or more special liability coverages. A few of the most common coverages are explained below.

Fire Legal Liability: If you use facilities you don't own, you might be legally responsible for damage to them — including fire. Some multi-peril policies automatically provide a limited amount of insurance for this, but very likely an inadequate amount. Advise your agent so that your policy can be endorsed to provide sufficient protection.

Schools and Day Care Centers: Liability protection for teachers is not always automatic. Make sure your teachers are covered. For greater protection, it is recommended that corporal punishment coverage also be purchased even if you have guidelines that prohibit corporal punishment. Educators' Liability coverage is available to schools. It provides liability protection for lawsuits alleging such issues as failure to educate, discrimination against a student and inappropriate financial aids or admissions policies.

 © 2018 Robert O. Crossman, www.UMNewChurch.org

Alcohol: Many policies exclude coverage for damages arising out of the use or sale of alcoholic beverages. If you serve these beverages, have your policy include "host liquor liability" coverage. If you are engaged in the sale of alcoholic beverages, consult with your attorney and agent. A separate "liquor liability" policy might be called for.

Broadcasting/Publishing: Your primary exposure from broadcasting and publishing is personal injury — libel and slander. If your policy provides personal injury coverage, it might include incidental activities like your weekly bulletin or Sunday morning radio service at a local station. But virtually no multi-peril policy protects you if you are in the business of publishing or broadcasting. A separate policy is needed for this.

Watercraft: Many policies provide automatic coverage for liability arising out of the use of small, nonowned watercraft. Separate coverage may be needed if you own a watercraft or use a large one.

Counseling: Most clergy appreciate this coverage and feel more comfortable handling delicate matters because of it. Counseling liability insurance is inexpensive protection for your ministry and clergy.

Products: For churches, "products" usually means food. Many multi-peril policies automatically protect you for products liability (food poisoning, for example) if the product is served at your facility. You may need a special endorsement to cover products distributed away from your premises.

Worldwide Travel: Rarely does a multi-peril policy provide liability protection for acts which occur outside of the United States or Canada. It is wise to purchase an international travel (liability and sickness) and assistance policy if you plan to travel outside the policy territory.

Insurance for vehicles you don't own. If you ever rent or borrow a vehicle, or ask someone to drive on behalf of your organization, you create a liability exposure for your church. If the vehicle is involved in an "at-fault" accident, you will probably be named in a lawsuit. You need not rely on the driver or vehicle owner to have adequate insurance to protect your ministry. Purchase "hired and nonowned" automobile liability insurance — it usually can be made part of your multi-peril policy.

Errors and omissions insurance. A good multi-peril policy will include your directors, officers and trustees as insureds for lawsuits involving bodily injury, property damage and personal injury. But almost no multi-peril policy automatically covers them for errors and omissions — "bad judgment" types of lawsuits.

Such coverage is available from some companies, either as an option in your multi-peril policy or as a separate professional liability policy. This coverage is correctly referred to as "directors and officers" or "directors, officers and trustees" insurance.

Having this insurance may help you get more capable people involved in your operations. It lets them make decisions freely and in your best interest, without undue fear of reprisal from those who might take legal issue with their decisions.

Discrimination, harassment and other actions. As an employer, you are exposed to "employment practices liability" risks from employee relations. Lawsuits alleging discrimination, sexual harassment and wrongful termination represent a growing concern for religious organizations. You may be able to add coverage to your multi-peril policy or purchase a separate policy.

Employee benefits liability. You are responsible for properly administering whatever employee benefit plans you offer. You can be sued for providing incorrect information, for negligently counseling employees about their benefits and for errors in administering your employee benefits program. You may be able to add coverage to your multi-peril policy or purchase a separate policy.

Setting adequate liability insurance limits. Imagine what a jury might award to a 30-year-old husband and father of three children who is permanently disabled. Medical bills, physical therapy, handicap modifications to home and vehicles, lost income and pain and suffering can reach seven figures.

There is no formula for determining the right amount of liability insurance. Consider $1,000,000 to be a minimum acceptable limit. You'll find that the additional cost of going from $300,000 or $500,000 to $1,000,000 is not great.

Medical expense insurance: goodwill protection. Liability insurance responds to certain lawsuits and pays if negligence is proven. "Medical expense" insurance is a goodwill-oriented coverage designed to cover expenses of less serious injuries without regard to negligence or fault. It's usually offered in conjunction with the liability section of a multi-peril policy.

Typical limits for medical expense insurance range from $5,000 to $15,000 for each injured person.

Medical expense insurance may be purchased so that it takes the place of an injured person's medical insurance or acts as a supplement to it. The first is called "primary," and the latter, "excess."

Make sure that your policy pays for injuries that occur both at and away from your premises and for those that are sports-related. All members, guests and volunteers should be covered.

Important additional coverages to consider.

Workers' compensation. In all but a few states, religious organizations, like any business, are required to carry workers' compensation insurance for their employees. Even where insurance is not required, the benefits must still be paid, and these can be extremely expensive. Failure to pay the benefits can lead to fines and other legal action.

Don't overlook your clergy. The federal government may classify some clergy

 © 2018 Robert O. Crossman, www.UMNewChurch.org

as "self-employed" for tax purposes, but most state industrial commissions consider them to be employees, and subject to the laws and benefits of the Workers' Compensation Act.

Workers' compensation benefits are prescribed by state law (not by your insurance company) and vary from state to state. They typically include compensation for lost wages, medical expenses, rehabilitation costs for severe disabilities and survivor benefits for family members.

Most health, accident, pension and other insurance programs contain exclusions regarding work-related illnesses and accidents. If this is the case with your insurance program, then a workers' compensation insurance policy is your only source of benefits.

In four states (North Dakota, Ohio, Washington and Wyoming), this insurance can be purchased only through a state fund. In all other states, it is available through private insurance companies.

Buses and cars. If you own or lease one car or a fleet of buses, it is imperative that you carry adequate automobile insurance.

Liability protection. Automobile liability insurance protects your organization and drivers against bodily injury and property damage lawsuits arising out of at-fault accidents involving your vehicles.

Limits of $1,000,000 are readily available and should be purchased. An automobile can cause tremendous damage to property and people — far more than contemplated by many congregations with low limits of insurance. Saving a few dollars on low limits can prove very costly if your vehicle is involved in an accident.

Uninsured motorists. Uninsured motorist coverage protects you for accidents caused by drivers who have no insurance or who carry inadequate insurance to pay for your injuries and damages. This coverage is important, since many drivers (even in states with compulsory insurance laws) carry no insurance or minimal limits.

Medical payments. "Medical payments" insurance pays for minor medical expenses of those injured in your vehicle, and for pedestrians struck by your vehicle, without the need for them to sue your ministry. Limits for this protection typically range from $1,000 to $15,000 per person. Some policies also carry a maximum aggregate limit.

In some states, "no-fault" or "personal injury protection" coverages take the place of medical payments insurance.

Damage to your vehicle. Your liability insurance is not designed to reimburse you for damage to your vehicle. For this protection, turn to collision and comprehensive coverages.

Collision: This coverage pays for damage to your vehicle that results from overturn or collision with another object (such as a car or tree).

Comprehensive: This covers your vehicle for most damages other than collision and overturn, such as fire, theft, glass breakage and vandalism.

No specific limits of insurance are set for collision and comprehensive coverages. The actual cash value of your vehicle, minus any deductible, determines the maximum amount you will be paid. Minor and moderate damage will probably be repaired. Extensive or total damage usually results in a cash settlement, but your insurance company has the option of providing you a vehicle similar in type, age and condition to your damaged vehicle.

There might come a time when the value of a vehicle, coupled with a deductible, is so low that collision coverage isn't worth the premium. You may or may not feel the same regarding comprehensive coverage. But there is never a time when you should be without liability insurance. Even the "old beater" can cause tremendous bodily injury and property damage.

Umbrella (or excess) liability protection. An umbrella (or excess) liability policy provides higher limits of insurance for your general liability, automobile and counseling liability exposures.

$1,000,000 is the standard umbrella limit, and higher limits — in multiples of $1,000,000 — are available from most insurance companies.

If you own or use a bus or van, an umbrella (or excess) liability policy is an important component of your insurance program. The potential for serious injury to several passengers makes your automobile and multi-peril policy limits inadequate.

Even without the use or ownership of a van or bus, an umbrella (or excess) liability policy is a smart precaution in today's world of seven-figure court judgments.

Look beyond cost in making your decisions. When operational funds are limited, as they are for most congregations, it is tempting to focus more on what you pay (premiums) than on what you get (services and coverages).

Insurance is not a generic product. Companies vary a great deal in financial stability, insurance expertise, service and claims philosophies, coverages and price. Base your decision on all of these factors and you will have handled your insurance buying responsibility admirably.

Take an inventory of your property. A thorough inventory, including the value of items and photographs, is important. Inventories help you and your insurance agent establish adequate insurance limits. After a loss, an inventory makes it much easier to settle your claim.

The best way to record property values is at the cost to replace it. For most items, you don't need a professional appraiser. Volunteers can record your property items and contact suppliers or check catalogs and stores for current cost

 © 2018 Robert O. Crossman, www.UMNewChurch.org

information. Photographs or videotapes are highly recommended, especially for property that is rare, highly valuable or can't be adequately described by words.

Store your inventory at a bank or other location away from your building. You may provide a copy to your insurance agent.

Provide continuity to your insurance program. Turnover of insurance committees, board members or individuals responsible for handling your insurance matters is natural. It's natural for any organization that relies on volunteers for administrative guidance. But it can create problems if simple measures aren't taken to maintain continuity in your insurance program.

If a committee handles your insurance, stagger the terms for members so that complete turnover cannot occur in less than three years. If one individual is responsible, have him or her describe the duties and current programs to the successor before leaving the position.

Keep your pastor informed about your insurance programs, if he or she isn't actively involved in the decision-making process. Often, it is the pastor who works most closely with the insurance company during settlement of claims.

Maintain a file of your insurance policies and correspondence — in a safe place away from your building. At least two people should know where the file is kept and have access to it. This will help prevent delays in reporting claims and determining what coverage applies.

If you lose your policies, or no longer understand what coverages you have, ask your insurance agent for new copies or explanations.

About Church Mutual

Church Mutual is the leading insurer of churches and church-related institutions in America. The company provides property and casualty coverages to more than 100,000 worship centers, schools, camps and senior living communities across the nation. Founded in 1897, Church Mutual is a mutual insurance company, meaning it is owned by its customers. It is not affiliated with any other organization. Church Mutual is rated "A (Excellent)" by A.M. Best and is listed as one of the nation's strongest business insurers by Weiss Ratings.

Church Mutual Insurance Company
3000 Schuster Lane
Merrill, Wisconsin 54452
Phone: 800 554-2642
Web: www.churchmutual.com
Email: marketing@churchmutual.com

Church Mutual insures more than 10,000 United Methodist churches!

NOTE: This article reflects the personal opinions of its author and does not necessarily reflect an official position of Discipleship Ministries or Path 1.

New Church Handbook
Nuts & Bolts for Planting New Churches In The Wesleyan Tradition

"Do We Need A Video & Audio License?"

From the Florida Annual Conference website

Here's what you should know about licensing and the limited use of music and videos in your church and ministries:

Each year your church will receive renewal notices and invoices for payment directly from Christian Video Licensing International (CVLI) and Christian Copyright Licensing International (CCLI). These licenses allow your church and ministries certain limited use of music, songs, lyrics, movies, DVDs and videos. Your license is for a period of one year. We encourage you to maintain your license and to follow the copyright laws as specified in the licensing agreements.

MUSIC, SONG and LYRICS:
Christian Copyright Licensing International (CCLI)

Licensing is offered to your church by Christian Copyright Licensing International (CCLI). Questions arise most often about the use of music and song lyrics in our churches and ministries. Licensing is a frequent area of confusion and misuse.

The licensing is for song lyrics and includes over 200,000 songs. The license does not cover the copying of musical arrangements (i.e., sheet music). The license allows you to reproduce and distribute lyrics in a church bulletin or on a screen, create songbooks, and record original performances of the music by the licensee's (i.e. your church) musicians.

Playing copyrighted religious music in worship services is covered without a license. U.S. Copyright Law Section 110 [c] provides an exemption for performance and display of "a work, in the course of services at a place of worship or other religious assembly;..."

Visit CCLI's website if you want more information and for terms of the agreement: http://www.ccli.com/.

Here's what you can do with a CCLI license

- Print songs, hymns and lyrics in bulletins, programs, liturgies and song sheets for use in congregational singing.
- Create your own customized song books or hymnals for use in congregational singing.
- Create overhead transparencies, slides or use any other format whereby song lyrics are visually projected (such as computer graphics and projection) for use in congregational singing.
- Arrange, print and copy your own arrangements (vocal and instrumental) of songs used for congregational singing, where no published version is available.
- Record your worship services (audio or video) provided you only record live music. Accompaniment tracks cannot be reproduced. You may charge up to $4 each for audiocassette tapes and CDs, and $12 each for videotapes and DVDs.

 © 2018 Robert O. Crossman, www.UMNewChurch.org

Here's what you can NOT do with a CCLI license

- Photocopy or duplicate octavos, cantatas, musicals, handbell music, keyboard arrangements, vocal scores, orchestrations or other instrumental works.
- Translate songs into another language. This can only be done with the approval of the respective publisher.
- Rent, sell or lend copies made under the license to groups outside the church or to other churches. (It is OK to distribute recordings to shut-ins, missionaries or others outside the church.)
- Assign or transfer the license to another church or group without CCLI's approval.

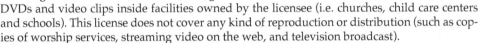

MOVIES, VIDEOS and DVDs:
Christian Video Licensing International (CVLI)

Christian Video Licensing International (CVLI) offers licensing to churches to cover the showing of videocassettes, DVDs and video clips inside facilities owned by the licensee (i.e. churches, child care centers and schools). This license does not cover any kind of reproduction or distribution (such as copies of worship services, streaming video on the web, and television broadcast).

The licensee – your church - may buy, rent, or borrow an original copy of the video clip for legal use. CVLI enables legal access to clips from thousands of movies. If you are not currently covered, you may obtain a license directly from CVLI.

The fee is determined by church membership size. (*Note: your annual conference may have negotiated an agreement with CVLI. If they have your church would be eligible for a discount.)*

For more information and for terms of the licensing agreement, I encourage you to go to CVLI's website at: http://www.cvli.com/.

Here's what you can do with a CVLI license

- Pastors can use selected movies to illustrate sermon points.
- Sunday schools and youth groups can view the latest videos.
- Educational classes can use videos for teaching and training.
- Churches can host special event movie nights.
- Show DVDs and videocassettes of motion pictures. Coverage includes playing just a clip up to showing the full-length movie.

Here's what you ca NOT do with a CVLI license

- This license does not cover materials that have been copied from another source or recorded from television. It also does not cover charging an admission fee for video showings or where specific titles have been advertised or publicized.
- This license covers manufactured DVD's, video cassettes and video discs purchased, rented or borrowed.

NOTE: This article reflects the personal opinions of its author and does not necessarily reflect an official position of Discipleship Ministries or Path 1.

New Church Handbook
Nuts & Bolts for Planting New Churches In The Wesleyan Tradition

"Are You Really Thinking About Purchasing a Bus or Van?"

by Bob Crossman

If you've decided that a Church Van is a strategic piece of reaching your mission field - think twice.

First, this is an old strategy that was effective in some mission fields back in the 1960's and 1970's. Are you sure it will be effective today in your mission field? If the answer is yes, before you invest funds in the purchase of a vehicle, consider this:

Companies that provide transportation services to school districts on school days might be willing to give discounted service to churches on weekends.

Also, some School Districts will rent a school bus and provide a driver to non-profits and churches. This would eliminate the "headaches" of owning a vehicle, including the initial expense, maintenance, and obtaining background checks and driving record reports on drivers.

Rental vehicles would also allow you to test the mission field before investing significant funds in the purchase of a vehicle.

†††

The Legal Manual of the United Methodist General Council on Finance and Administration

www.gcfa.org/ls_legalmanual.html

1. Federal Bus Regulations.

Churches that use buses or large vans to transport passengers across state lines may be subject to certain federal safety regulations. The regulations apply to any interstate transportation of "business private motor carriers of passengers" and "nonbusiness private motor carriers of passengers". A church that owns or leases a bus or van will be a "nonbusiness private motor carriers of passengers" if: (1) the bus or van has a gross vehicle weight of 10,001 or more pounds or is designed to transport more than 15 passengers (including the driver), and (2) the bus or van is "involved in interstate transportation of passengers," which basically means taking the bus or van outside of the state in which the church is located.

As nonbusiness private motor carriers, churches must comply with certain portions of the federal regulations in this area. Churches must mark all

© 2018 Robert O. Crossman, www.UMNewChurch.org

of their commercial motor vehicles ("CMV") with the church name and the USDOT number and ensure that the CMV is properly equipped with all required operational and safety devices and is properly inspected, maintained, and repaired.[61]

Additionally, drivers of church buses must meet certain criteria in order to drive the vehicle. The driver must:

1. Be able to read and speak English;
2. Have enough experience and/or training to safely operate the CMV and to determine that any cargo (including passenger baggage) has been properly located, distributed, and secured;
3. Be physically qualified to drive a CMV;[62]
4. Have a current and valid CMV operator's license from only one state;
5. Not be disqualified to drive a CMV;[63]
6. Pass a road test, or its equivalent;
7. Confirm that various parts of the CMV are in good working order;[64]
8. Not be ill or fatigued.[65]

Church buses may also be subject to certain state regulations, as well. Every local church that owns, or is considering the purchase of, a bus should inquire of the appropriate state authority regarding the existence of any such regulations.[66]

2. Van Safety Concerns.

It is important to be well advised on what type of vehicle is the safest. Many churches use large vans to transport children or adults because they cost less than buses. Buying a used or less expensive vehicle that does not have adequate safety standards should never happen. From the standpoint of protecting children, federal government studies have determined that vans of any size are not only less safe than school buses, but are also less safe than ordinary private passenger cars (which in recent years have had to meet certain design standards for safety).

[61] See 49 C.F.R. §§ 390-93, 96.

[62] See § 391.41 for the list of specific physical qualifications. Note that § 391.68 exempts church bus drivers from all medical examination and medical examiner's certificate requirements.

[63] See § 391.15.

[64] See § 392.7.

[65] See generally, §§ 391, 392, 396.

[66] See e.g., the Ohio Church Bus Inspection Manual.

†††

"Avoiding Transportation Accidents: *Understanding the safety and legal issues of using vans and buses"*

by Richard R. Hammar, at *www.churchlawandtax.com*

If your church owns one or more 15-passenger vans, there are a number of legal concerns that you should understand, including the following:

15-passenger vans are prone to roll over, and this risk increases dramatically when they are heavily loaded with passengers and luggage. In 2001 the National Highway Traffic Safety Administration (NHTSA) issued a "consumer advisory" that documents this risk. This advisory was reissued in 2002, in part because "the summer of 2001 saw several tragic rollover crashes involving religious groups on trips." It was reissued again in 2004 and 2005. It is important for church leaders to be familiar with these advisories, and with NHTSA recommendations to reduce the rollover risk (www.nhtsa.gov).

Churches that continue to use 15-passenger vans to transport people are assuming an increased risk of liability unless they take specific steps to reduce the risk. Ten specific recommendations made by the NHTSA are mentioned in the complete special report, "Reducing the Risk of Transportation Accidents," (Church Law & Tax Report, 2006), along with 15 additional precautions churches can take to reduce the risks associated with the use of 15-passenger vans. If a court concludes that a church's use of a 15-passenger van amounts to gross negligence, then the church may be assessed punitive damages (which are not covered under its general liability insurance policy) and the members of the church board may be personally liable.

Richard R. Hammar is the senior editor of Church Law & Tax Report, a bimonthly newsletter reviewing significant legal and tax developments for churches and clergy. He is the author of several books, including *Pastor, Church & Law*, the annual *Church & Clergy Tax Guide, Reducing the Risk*, the biannual *Compensation Handbook for Church Staff*, and the *Essential Guide to Copyright Law for Churches*. His web site is a tremendous resource: www.churchlawandtax.com

Copyright 2013 Christianity Today. Used with permission.
For additional information on keeping your church safe, legal, and financially sound visit ChurchLawAndTax.com.

†††

"Before You Buy a New Bus: *3 tips to remember when shopping for new ministry transportation"*

by Tyler Charles,*www.churchlawandtax.com*

"Parkway Southern Baptist in New Albany, Indiana, relies on church transportation to shuttle people to and from church, bring kids to Wednesday night programs, and travel for mission trips. When the church decided to replace its 15-passenger van, Pastor Henry Ford sought guidance from other churches. He learned about the construction of different buses, issues with specific parts, and other details that guided his church's search.

In a similar spirit to Ford's search, here are three tips to help your church before it buys a new bus:

1) Your transportation needs are unique

Many elderly people use ministry transportation at Parkway Southern Baptist, and getting in and out of the van was a struggle for them.

"You have to be a contortionist to get in and out of a 15-passenger van," Ford says. "We've actually had people fall getting out of the van. They've tripped on a seatbelt or something else and literally fallen to the ground."

Parkway chose a new 14-passenger bus (purchased from ChurchBus.com) with a high ceiling and center aisle that gets riders in and out with ease.

For other churches, a lift and wheelchair accessibility might be necessary. Others might not need the wheelchair lift, but they might choose to purchase a bus with a built-in ramp. Rear storage space might be a prerequisite for churches planning to use the bus for longer trips.

Jerry Remus, sales manager for Carpenter Bus Sales, says every church must consider its unique needs, but the unique nature of buses also may pose one significant challenge to churches: someone qualified to drive it.

"Any bus over 15 passengers requires a Class C with P endorsement driver's license," Remus says.

A church-owned bus—with its name on the side—also provides marketing. "It's a moving billboard," says Rob Zimmerman, president of BestChurchBus.com. "It's a great way to get people interested in the church."

Carpenter Bus Sales reports that 15- and 26-passenger buses account for 60 percent of sales in the ministry transportation market. Other common bus sizes are 26-passenger (with or without rear storage) and 33-, 40-, and 45-passenger.

If a church only needs a bus occasionally, or for special trips, it may make more sense to rent rather than purchase, Remus says. That eliminates the upfront expense, as well as ongoing maintenance and insurance costs.

2) Safety matters

Many churches still use 15-passenger vans, which can result in liability issues for church leaders, says Jacob McBurnie, national sales manager for ChurchBus.com.

"The National Transportation Safety Board first declared 15-passenger vans unsafe over a decade ago," McBurnie says. "They have released several warnings about their unsafe nature since. Most insurance companies are taking steps to clear their books of 15-passenger vans, and most church denominations have sent regular warnings to church leaders as well."

According to Carpenter Bus Sales, 15-passenger buses are the safe alternative to 15-passenger vans.

"Buses are built to safely carry passengers." Remus says. "They are designed with full steel cage construction, side impact beams, and a chassis designed for stability, thus reducing the possibility of rollover."

Buses also provide a low first step, hand rails, and wider, more accessible aisles, making entries and exits easier—and safer. McBurnie says other important safety features include an emergency rear door and side marking turn signals.

3) Know the company

When talking to various dealers, McBurnie recommends asking these questions:

- Will the dealer assist with service needs?
- How familiar is the company's representative with church needs?
- Does the company carry products designed specifically for church groups?
- How long has the company been in business?

"Choose to work with a company that has built a good reputation," McBurnie says. "Church groups often make the mistake of ruling out a particular company early in the process because they are located farther away. But most service needs will be handled at a local chassis manufacturer dealership regardless of where the bus was purchased."

New vs. used

Church leaders might assume that a used church bus is the best fit for their budget, but buying a used bus is not the same as buying a used car. Unlike automobiles, new bus prices are not regulated by a Manufacturer's Suggested Retail Price (MSRP). And Kelley Blue Book values don't cover buses.

"Since buses are a tool—and not a personal vehicle—there has never been a desirable used bus market," Remus says. "Churches should understand that a bus is not an investment as viewed purely from an economical perspective, but rather a liability and a depreciating expense that serves the ministry."

Copyright 2010 Christianity Today. Used with permission. For additional information on keeping your church safe, legal, and financially sound visit ChurchLawAndTax.com.

NOTE: This article reflects the personal opinions of its author and does not necessarily reflect an official position of Discipleship Ministries or Path 1.

 © 2018 Robert O. Crossman, www.UMNewChurch.org

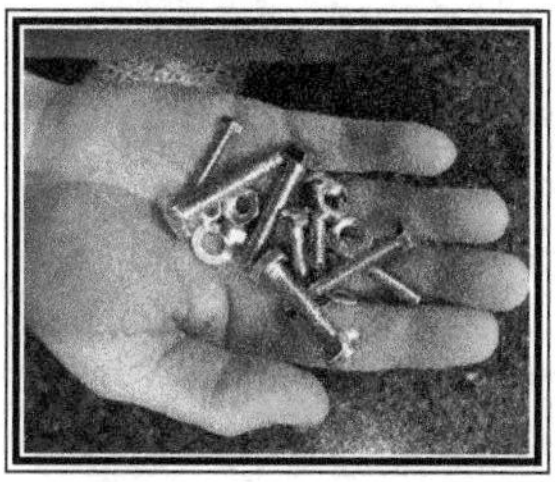

New Church Handbook
Nuts & Bolts for Planting New Churches In The Wesleyan Tradition

"What Does 'Chartering' Mean?"

by Bob Crossman

The Book of Discipline rarely uses the word 'charter.' What most people are actually referring to with this word is the "Constituting Conference" described in the 2016 Book of Discipline's ¶259.3 to 259.10.

I recommend that there should NOT be a rush to "charter." Rather, I believe a new church start hold its constituting Conference (charter) when the presence of formal committees (trustees, SPPR, finance, and church council) will enhance the effectiveness of the new church reach more people, more younger people, and more diverse people.

For more details about the administrative structure of new churches before and after the Constituting Conference, refer to my article on "What Does Local Church Structure Look Like In the Early Years" where I state, in part:

> **In the multi-site strategy**, the main campus will fulfill all the traditional functions of a church council, pastor parish relations committee, finance committee, and trustees.
>
> **In most all other strategies** the district superintendent, conference minister of new church starts and the Coach assigned to the new church pastor, will fulfill the traditional functions of a church council, pastor parish relations committee, finance committee, and trustees until the church has grown large enough to complete the 'charter' process and thereby elect these committees. These committees/councils do not exist in a new church prior to the Constituting Church Conference outlined in ¶ 259.
>
> As the months pass, and the church matures, and you sense it is time to begin moving toward chartering in a year or two... one of the ways to prepare for your future "Nominating Committee" type decisions, is to form teams that will eventually take on the formal roles of the church council, pastor parish relations committee, finance committee, and trustees.
>
> For example, a year before you anticipate chartering, you can form a facilities team, finance team, and HR Team.

© 2018 Robert O. Crossman, www.UMNewChurch.org

Most new churches, upon chartering, for missional reasons intentionally have a VERY SMALL church council of nine people, and does not have separate finance, Trustee, and SPPR committees. In this model, officially, the membership of the church council is identical to the membership of the finance committee, and the pastor parish relations committee, and trustees. When the church council meets (usually for an hour once a month), the chair calls the meeting to order.

- Then says, *"Becky, you are the chair of our Pastor Parish Relations. Is their anything you want to bring before us today."*
- Then after that, *"Fred, you are the chair of our finances. Is their anything you want to bring before us today."*
- Then after that, *"Sherry, you are the chair of our* trustees. *Is their anything you want to bring before us today."*
- This pattern could continue around the table including, perhaps, ministry areas of Mission, Children, Youth, Outreach, etc.

I believe that "chartering," when done well, empowers the laity to hold official roles of leadership, and frees the pastor from being the 'gatekeeper' and 'funnel' through which every decision must flow... **allowing the pastor to focus on what the pastor can uniquely do for the church and it's primary mission of making new disciples who make more new Disciples for the transformation of the world.**

There are serious financial implications of "Chartering" too. Once a new church start holds its constituting conference, it is then expected to share in the joy (and responsibility) of providing financial support for the shared ministries of the annual conference and district - that is to pay apportionments.

In ¶259.4, the annual conference is given the authority to set the minimum number of members and other criteria required before a new church start may hold a Constituting Conference and "charter."

Most annual conference guidelines include something like these three guidelines:

1) The new congregation must have an average worship attendance of 125 to 150. Some annual conferences require that this be adult attendance. Some annual conferences do not refer to worship attendance, but simply state, 'have at least 125 active adult members.'

2) are financially self sustaining for at least twelve months, and

© 2018 Robert O. Crossman, www.UMNewChurch.org

3) have been holding public worship at least three years.

Every annual conference has different chartering guidelines. Check with your annual conference new church director, and confirm that conversation with your district superintendent.

The 2016 Book of Disciple: ¶259.3 to 259.10

3. A pastor of The United Methodist Church, while serving as the pastor of a new church prior to the convening of a constituting conference (¶ 259.7), may receive a person into the membership of The United Methodist Church under the conditions of ¶ 217. When a person is received as either a baptized or a professing member, the pastor shall send the name, address, and related facts to the annual conference secretary for recording on a general membership roll. These names shall be transferred as soon as possible to the roll of the new church, when constituted, or to another church upon the member's request. If the new church is being sponsored by an existing church, membership may be recorded on the roll of that church.

4. Each annual conference or its equivalent may determine the minimum number of members and other criteria required for the organization of a local United Methodist church.

5. When the number of people interested in being charter members of the new church reaches the number necessary as set by the conference to charter a new church, the district superintendent shall call the interested people to meet at an appointed time for the purpose of organizing them into a chartered (organized) local church, or may by written authorization designate an elder in the district to call such a meeting. The district superintendent or the designated elder shall preside and shall appoint a secretary to keep a record of the meeting. Following a time of worship, opportunity shall be given to those in attendance to present themselves for membership.

6. People desiring to become professing members by transfer or on profession of their faith in Christ shall also be given opportunity to present themselves for membership. Any who have not been baptized shall receive the sacrament of baptism, profess their faith and be received as members. Other baptized people are to be received as baptized members.

7. Those who will be members of the constituting church conference shall be those received into the professing membership.

8. The constituting church conference shall then be called to order by the district superintendent or by an elder whom the superintendent designates (see ¶ 246.5). A committee on nominations, elected on nominations from the floor as the conference may determine, shall nominate members of the proposed church council. The chairperson of the committee on nominations shall be the appointed pastor (see ¶ 258.1c). When the members have been chosen, the district superintendent or the designated elder shall declare the church

properly constituted.

9. The district superintendent or an elder whom the superintendent designates shall then adjourn the constituting church conference and call to order the charge conference of the pastoral charge. The membership of the charge conference shall be those newly elected, and any others entitled to membership. The charge conference shall then elect such officers of the church as the Discipline requires, including trustees of church property, and shall organize its structure as provided in the Discipline. When such officers have been duly elected and such structure put in place, the church is duly organized, and from this point its work shall proceed as described in the Discipline, provided that when a newly organized church is attached to a circuit, the charge conference shall not be held until such time as representatives from all the churches of the charge can be properly assembled for that purpose.

10. The charge conference may take action, at its discretion, authorizing and directing the newly elected trustees to incorporate the newly organized church in accordance with local laws and the provisions of the Discipline.

NOTE: This article reflects the personal opinions of its author and does not necessarily reflect an official position of Discipleship Ministries or Path 1.

 © 2018 Robert O. Crossman, www.UMNewChurch.org

XI. What About Financial Systems Within New Churches?

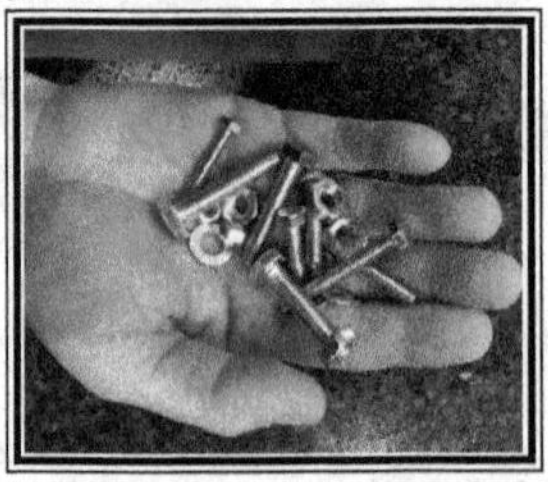

New Church Handbook
Nuts & Bolts for Planting New Churches In The Wesleyan Tradition

"Raising Virtue Capital Through Investors and Stewards"

by Bob Crossman
including material from Jim Griffith

{The good parts of this article are from Jim Griffith's Boot Camp. I take credit for any bad advice this article may contain.}

It takes money to carry out ministry, and to increase ministries it takes more money. As a new church start you need to have enough money to sustain you not only through the launch of weekly worship, but to sustain for several years as the ministry grows toward financial sustainability.

There is a difference between the financial stewardship of tithing members of your launch team and virtue capital investors. Investors are friends and family, outside of your launch team, who believe in you and your vision, and out of their relationship with you they are willing to invest in you financially.

What I am suggesting is this: following Jim Griffith's virtue capital process, with approval of your district superintendent and conference minister of new church starts begin to ask for "virtue capital" financial gifts from family, relatives, and personal friends. Many annual conferences expect the planter to raise $50,000 to $100,000 in three year pledges from this source.

Clarify this process and amount to be sought with your conference minister of new church starts BEFORE taking the advice of this article.

Action Plan

• Make a list of 20 to 30 households NOT on your launch team. Include your relatives, friends and colleagues. These people will give 90% to 95% of the virtue capital to start your new church.

This is NOT giving you permission to do a conference wide campaign. Rather, you are ONLY contacting your relatives, personal friends and colleagues. If you have an Uncle Art who loves you, if you ask he might make a gift of $250. Your Aunt Betty might pay your entire salary for the first year, if you ask. Your parents might give your new church $1,000, if you ask.

 © 2018 Robert O. Crossman, www.UMNewChurch.org

The Letter

- This is NOT a prayer letter, it is a fund-raising letter - so DON'T blend the two subjects.

- Limit this letter to ONE page - not typed - not an email - not photocopied each handwritten.

- Use decent paper and envelope, not cheap typing paper. Resist the temptation do do this by email. Write with a nice fine point sharpie pen.

- Send the letter in September so this process will be completed by November first, because charitable organizations ask for money in December.

There are ONLY 4 sentences, each beginning a new paragraph, in your fund-raising letter:

1: Dear_____, "As you know we are starting a new church…" *{complete the sentence with your BRIEF winsome vision for the new church.}*

2 "Please consider making a onetime gift to our project."

3: "Prayerfully consider the enclosed card and return it by _______. {set exact date about 4 weeks into the future}

4: "Thanks for your consideration."

Attached a card that gives them 5 "options":
I have enclosed:

___ $ 250
___ $ 500
___ $ 1,000
___ other amount $________________
___ No, I (we) cannot participate at this time but want to remain on your email update list.

{Note: These cards should be customized since each person should be challenged according to their ability and willingness to support you. Not all people will give equally, therefore each household should be challenged accordingly. You may ask a seminary classmate for $100; $300; $500 and 'other.' You may ask your Aunt Betty for $1,000; $5,000; $10,000 and 'other.' You may ask your best friend for $10,000; $25,000; $50,000 and 'other.'

The amounts should grow from the least to the greater amount.

Seventy percent of the people will check the second box, so design accordingly. The first box should be a MINIMUM of three figures.

You must include a self-addressed, stamped, reply envelope.
Handwritten address on the envelope. Do not use an address label.

Put a stamp on your letter, but also put a stamp on the enclosed reply envelope too.

Action Plan
Write a draft of your fund-raising letter... perfect the letter and handwrite to your relatives and friends.

When the Gift Arrives
Immediately write a Thank You Note on decent paper from a stationary store - not an email, and not typed, and not on cheap typing paper. Use a black sharpie pen, not a normal ballpoint. Send a thank you note EVERY TIME a financial response comes from your Virtue capital letter.

Action Plan
Write a first draft thank you note.

Dear ________,
Thanks so much for your generous gift - it means a lot to me and will make a difference for Christ and his Kingdom!
God's Best,
Bob

After 3 weeks, send a letter to ALL on your list, reporting the results to date. After 8 weeks, write a final letter, reporting the final results. Repeat the process every year.

Resources
Stewardship & Giving: How to Increase the Financial Support of Your Congregation by Rev. Kevin Martin. $9.95 plus $2.00 handling. dean@episcopalcathedral.org
Free email Template: EGivingSystems.org

†††

NOTE: This article reflects the personal opinions of its author and does not necessarily reflect an official position of Discipleship Ministries or Path 1.

© 2018 Robert O. Crossman, www.UMNewChurch.org

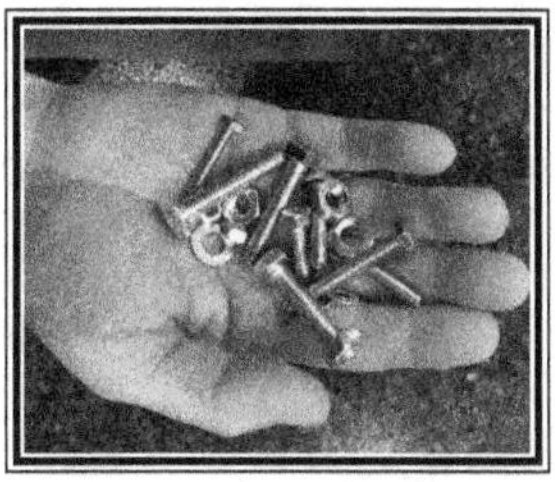

New Church Handbook
Nuts & Bolts for Planting New Churches In The Wesleyan Tradition

"Building a Budget For Your New Church"

by Bob Crossman

When you are approached by your district superintendent or bishop, and your church planting appointment is fixed - within a few weeks afterward you will need to sit down with your district superintendent or Conference staff person to clarify the level and term of financial support that will be available to you in this new church planting appointment. Typically, annual conference and District funding is for a 36 to 48 month period, declining annually until reaching zero in month 36 or 48. Mission Congregation plants may have funding over a declining 10 year time period instead of 36 or 48 months.

Also, in most annual conferences, your church planting ministry will need to reach certain benchmarks at month 6, 12, 18, 24, 30 and 36 for the full grant to be continued. Before "moving day" you will need to clarify exactly what those benchmarks will be.

Who Makes Deposits & Writes Checks for Your New Ministry?

You will also need clarify WHO will be handling the treasurer duties for you. Until a new church is three or four years old and has held its Constituting Conference, there are no official finance committee or trustees in the new church. In most annual conferences, the district superintendent and the conference minister of new church starts will function as the Council, trustees, finance committee, and pastor parish relations committee for the new church until the church is mature enough to charter. In most settings, a "Quarterly Connection" will take place between these parties for such decisions.

Typically, the new church pastor, in cooperation with the district superintendent and the conference minister of new church starts will select someone to function as financial secretary for the new church. In some annual conferences this will be either the District Office Administrative Assistant or the financial secretary of a strong UMChurch nearby.

Most annual conferences have adopted a working policy to protect the church planter from any question of financial impropriety. Typically, when the new church pastor is requesting a check to be cut, larger than a previously agreed upon amount (typically $500 or $1,000), that requisition along with a description of the suggested expenditure, is first sent to the district superintendent and the conference minister of new church starts. After comparing the request to the annual budget line items, a return email is sent approving the request. That email must be attached to the requisition before the Financial Secretary will cut any check over the agreed upon limit of $500 or $1,000.

When does a new church begin to participate in supporting the apportionment?

Each annual conference answers this question differently.

I usually propose a model to the pastors that communicates from the start that faithful stewardship and generosity is an essential facet of healthy new church DNA. I recommend that the offering basket be passed at every gathering of the initial launch team. At times that basket is passed with the knowledge that 10% of this week's offering is going to support our 'sister' new church in _______. At the next gathering it may be announced that 10% of the offering will support our Campus Minister at the University, or to provide a pension for our retired pastors, etc. Sending in these early gifts on the apportionment form to the conference treasurer.

New church pastors are also encouraged to contact the conference treasurer in the early months of worship and ask, *"If we were a chartered congregation, based on our current offering receipts and attendance, what would our apportionment amount be?"*

In the Arkansas Conference, they have recently developed to a simple apportionment formula for all congregations: 10% of the offering is to be turned in at the end of each month.

In a "Mission Congregation" (¶259.1.a), while they might not officially come into the apportionment formula, generosity is still an essential facet of a heathy congregation, and they are encouraged to generously support mission and ministries beyond themselves by sending gifts to the conference treasurer on the apportionment form.

What about a Budget?

In most annual conferences, you will also be asked to prepare a tentative working budget for your new church plant. Financial support from the annual conference will not be identical for every new start. Salaries of pastors and missioners are not all the same, cost of rental space will vary across the state, grants from the District and sister congregations vary, and the financial ability of the new members will vary. Some new Mission Congregations will be eligible for grants from the General Board of Global Ministries. However, in every case a maximum amount of potential funding support will be set for each new church early in the appointment process.

 © 2018 Robert O. Crossman, www.UMNewChurch.org

What Offering Plate Income (not including grants from district or conference) Should You Project?

Great question, but there is **NO** simple answer due to so many variables.

In a survey of new United Methodist Churches started between 2008 and 2015, and new churches from 17 different denominations, Lifeway Research found this information:

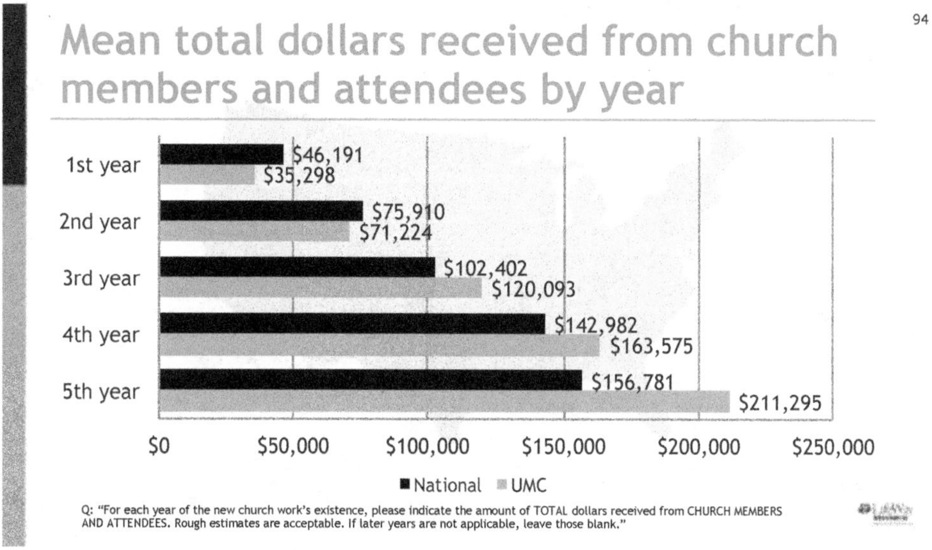

In the following two pages, you will find two templates that might help you make those projections of income and expenses. **Of course your budget will be different, but these samples may help you prepare for the variety of income sources and expenses to anticipate.** The first is for a full-time appointment, and the second is for a part-time mission appointment.

Traditional New Church Planting Model Financial Projections

What will actual income and expenses be in a new church? Difficult question since every new church is different!
The following might be a template to start to making budget projections for each new church start.

Assumptions: appointment in June, worship begins in 4 months, launch in Sept/Oct, & community has potential of 350 in worship within ten years. In the appointive process, the new church pastor will revise this chart and present a proposed budget, set benchmarks, and negotiate grant levels.

ROUGH PROJECTION OF EXPENSES	*1st 7 months* 2017	2018	2019	2020	2021	2022	2023	2024
Pastor's Compensation - *in most cases, at or above pastor's current salary of 30,000 to 45,000*								
Salary, Utility, Travel, Cont Ed., Pension	15 to 22,500	30 to 45,000	35 to 45,000	40 to 50,000	45 to 55,000	50 to 60,000	55 to 65,000	60 to 70,000
Furnished Apartment Allowance	5 to 6,000	10 to 12,000	10 to 12,000	11 to 13,000	11 to 13,000	12 to 15,000	12 to 15,000	15 to 17,000
Health Insurance	7,000	14,000	14 to 15,000	15 to 16,000	16 to 17,000	17 to 18,000	18 to 19,000	19 to 20,000
School of Cong. Development or Planter Tune-up Cont. Ed.	1,000	1,500	1,750	1,750	2.000	2.000	2,000	2,500
Office Space								
Office Space Rental	at mother church or parsonage	mother church or parsonage	at worship site or parsonage	at worship site or parsonage	at worship site or parsonage	at worship site or parsonage	at worship site or parsonage	at worship site or parsonage
Postage, Copier, Supplies	3,000	3,000	4,000	5,000	6,000	7,000	8,000	9,000
Equipment, Furniture, Computer	4,000	3,000	3,000	4,000	4,000	5,000	5,000	6,000
Apportionments (Missions/Pension) Conf/Dist	0	1,000	2,000	*est. 4,000*	*est 8,000*	*est 16,000*	*est 32,000*	*est 64,000*
Second Mile Local Missions	0	1,000	1,000	2,000	2,000	4,000	4,000	8,000
Worship	*3 months*	*12 months*			*or build?*	*or build?*	*or build?*	
Site Rental for worship	0 to 18,000	0 to 72,000	12 to 72,000	12 to 75,000	12 to 75,000	12 to 80,000	12 to 80,000	12 to 85,000
Utilities for worship site	0 to 2,000	0 to 6,000	0 to 6,000	0 to 8,000	0 to 8,000	0 to 8,000	0 to 8,000	0 to 8,000
Maintenance/Custodial for worship site	0 to 1,000	0 to 3,000	0 to 3,000	0 to 5,000	0 to 5,000	0 to 6,000	0 to 6,000	0 to 6,000
Renters/Building/Liability Insurance	2,000	2 to 3,000	2 to 3,000	2 to 3,000	2 to 3,000	2 to 3,000	2 to 3,000	2 to 3,000
Electronic Equipment for worship	10 to 15,000	10 to 15,000	5,000	5,000	5,000	5,000	5,000	5,000
Nursery Equipment	2 to 3,000	1,000	1,000	1,000	1,000	1,000	1,000	1,000
Discipleship: Sunday School / Small Group Literature	500	1,000	1,500	2,000	3,000	4,000	5,000	5,000
Part-time Staff as the church grows								
Music Minister *The need for staff will be*	0 to 4,000	0 to 8,000	0 to 8,000	8 to 16,000	16 to 24,000	20 to 30,000	25 to 35,000	30 to 35,000
Children's Minister *determined by growth in*	0 to 4,000	0 to 9,000	0 to 8,000	8 to 16,000	16 to 24,000	20 to 30,000	25 to 35,000	30 to 35,000
Youth Minister *worship attendance.*	0 to 4,000	0 to 8,000	0 to 8,000	8 to 16,000	16 to 24,000	20 to 30,000	25 to 35,000	30 to 35,000
New Comer Visitation Minister	0	0	0 to 4,000	0 to 8,000	4 to 8,000	6 to 10,000	8 to 12,000	10 to 14,000
Membership Care Minister	0	0	0	0 to 4,000	0 to 8,000	4 to 8,000	6 to 10,000	8 to 12,000
Advertising/Marketing								
Saturation Mailings or other marketing	3,000	1 to 3,000	1 to 3,000	1 to 3,000	1 to 4,000	1 to 4,000	1 to 5,000	1 to 5,000
Signs/Banners for Worship Site	1 to 2,000	500	1,000	1,000	1,000	1,000	1,000	1,000
Web site, Flyers, banners, radio, theaters, cable, etc.	1,000	2,000	2,000	2,000	3,000	3,000	3,000	4,000
TOTAL EXPENSES RANGE	**38 to 100,000**	**97 to 175,000**	**108 to 200,000**	**140 to 230,000**	**181 to 257,000**	**219 to 301,000**	**262to 344,000**	**329to 395,000**
ROUGH PROJECTION OF FINANCIAL RESOURCES/GIFTS	*1st 7 months* **2017**	**2018**	**2019**	**2020**	**2021**	**2022**	**2023**	**2024**
Mother/Sponsoring Church - minimum expectations								
- provide housing allowance	up to 6,000	up to 12,000	up to 12,000	0	0	0	0	0
- provide office supplies, copies, etc.	up to 3,000	up to 3,000	0	0	0	0	0	0
- provide gift of office computer & desk	up to 2,000	up to 1,000	0	0	0	0	0	0
- salary support, if possible	up to 23,000	up to 46,000	up to 23,000	0	0	0	0	0
-"Baby Showers" to provide in kind gifts	0	up to 10,000	5,000	0	0	0	0	0
District -								
- provide health insurance, if funds needed	7,000	14,000	15,000	7,000	0	0	0	0
- provide rent for worship site, if possible	0	0 to 12,000	0 to 24,000	0	0	0	0	0
- provide program support, if possible	0 to 4,000	0 to 12,000	0 to 24,000	0 to 12,000	0	0	0	0
- encourage special offering from District churches	*0*	*up to 10,000*	*up to 5,000*	*0*	*0*	*0*	*0*	*0*
Pastor's Fund Raising from FRAN, 3 yr pledges, goal	*33,000*	*33,000*	*33,000*	___	___	___	___	___
Parish and Community Development Funds	0	0	0	0	0	0	0	0
Hispanic Ministry Funds	0	0	0	0	0	0	0	0
Ethnic Local Church Funds	0	0	0	0	0	0	0	0
Equitable Comp/Key Charge - if available	up to 12,000	up to 22,000	up to 17,000	up to 12,000	up to 7,000	0	0	0
Conference New Church Funds -	up to 25,000	up to 45,000	up to 30,000	up to 10,000	0	0	0	0
Offering plate from the new church/leaders	up to 20,000	up to 50,000	up to 150,000	up to 200,000	up to 250,000	up to 300,000	up to 400,000	up to 500,000
TOTAL POSSIBLE gifts	**50 to 140,000**	**80 to 211,000**	**240 to 293,000**	**207 to 241,000**	**250 to 257,000**	**300,000**	**400,000**	**500,000**
Based on projected worship attendance of:	***100***	***100 to 150***	***150 to 200***	***200 to 250***	***250 to 300***	***300 to 350***	***350 to 400***	***400 to 450***
POSSIBLE GIFTS FOR LAND OR BUILDING CONSTRUCTION - there is NO guarantee that any construction or land funds will be available								
DISTRICT building construction grant???	0	0	0	0	0 to 50,000	0	0	0
Conf. Catch the Vision Funds - construction grants??	0	0	0	0	0 to 50,000	0 to 50,000	0	0

Parish and Community Development - grants up to $5,000 might be available for specific projects

©2017 Robert O Crossman

© 2018 Robert O. Crossman, www.UMNewChurch.org

MISSION New Congregation Model Financial Projections

A Mission Congregation exists when "membership opportunities and resources are limited and not likely to result in a chartered congregation for an extended period of time..."
Planting pastor is often a part-time Local Pastor or part-time Missioner.

	2017 (*1st 7 months*)	2018	2019	2020	2021	2022	2023	2024
ROUGH PROJECTION OF EXPENSES								
Part-Time Pastor's Compensation *(in most cases, at or above the pastors current compensation of 10,000 to 16,000)*								
Salary, Utility, Travel, Cont Ed	5 to 8,000	10 to 16,000	10 to 16,000	12 to 18,000	12 to 18,000	14 to 20,000	14 to 20,000	16 to 22,000
Furnished Apartment Allowance	0	0	0	0	0	0	0	0
Health Insurance	0	0	0	0	0	0	0	0
School of Cong. Development or Planter Tune-up Cont. Ed.	1,000	1,500	1,750	1,750	2.000	2.000	2,000	2,500
Office Space								
Office Space Rental	at pastor's home or woship site	at pastor's home or worship site	at pastor's home or worship site	at pastor's home or worship site	at pastor's home or worship site	at pastor's home or worship site	at pastor's home or worship site	at pastor's home or worship site
Postage, Copier, Supplies	1,000	1,000	2,000	2,000	2,000	3,000	3,000	3,000
Equipment, Furniture, Computer	2,000	1,000	1,000	1,000	1,000	1,000	1,000	1,000
Apportionments (Missions/Pension) Conf/Dist	0	1,000	1,000	*estimate* 2,000	*estimate* 2,000	*estimate* 3,000	*estimate* 3,000	*estimate* 4,000
Second Mile Local Missions	0	1,000	1,000	2,000	2,000	2,000	2,000	3,000
Worship	*6 months*	*12 months*		*or build?*	*or build?*	*or build?*	*or build?*	
Worship Site Rental and Utilities	0 to 4,000	0 to 8,000	0 to 8,000	0 to 8,000	0 to 9,000	0 to 9,000	0 to 9,000	0 to 9,000
Maintenance/Custodial for worship site	0	0 to 1,000	0 to 3,000	0 to 5,000	0 to 5,000	0 to 6,000	0 to 6,000	0 to 6,000
Renters/Building/Liability Insurance	1,000	1,000	1 to 2,000	1 to 2,000	1 to 2,000	1 to 2,000	1 to 2,000	1 to 2,000
Electronic Equipment for worship	3,000	1,000	1,000	1,000	0	0	0	0
Nursery Equipment	1,000	2,000	0	1,000	0	1,000	0	1,000
Sunday School / Small Group Literature	1,000	1,000	1,000	1,000	1,000	1,000	1,000	1,000
Part-time Staff as the church grows		*6 months*						
Music Minister	0 to 4,000	0 to 4,000	0 to 5,000	0 to 5,000	0 to 6,000	0 to 6,000	0 to 7,000	0 to 7,000
Children's Minister	0 to 4,000	0 to 4,000	0 to 5,000	0 to 5,000	0 to 6,000	0 to 6,000	0 to 7,000	0 to 7,000
Youth Minister	0	0	0 to 4,000	0 to 4,000	0 to 5,000	0 to 5,000	0 to 6,000	0 to 6,000
Advertising/Marketing								
Saturation Mailings	4,000	4,000	4,000	4,000	4,000	4,000	4,000	4,000
Signs/Banners for Worship Site	0,000	1 to 2,000	1 to 2,000	1,000	1,000	1,000	1,000	1,000
Flyers, banners, radio, theaters, cable, etc.	1,000	1,000	1,000	1,000	1,000	1,000	1,000	1,000
TOTAL EXPENSES RANGE	**19 to 34,000**	**25 to 49,000**	**24 to 57,000**	**29 to 63,000**	**27 to 65,000**	**32 to 71,000**	**31 to 73,000**	**36 to 78,000**

The need for staff will be determined by growth in worship attendance. Mission Congregations rarely reach the size to need staff, nor have the resources to hire staff.

ROUGH PROJECTION OF FINANCIAL RESOURCES/GIFTS	2017 (*1st 6 months*)	2018	2019	2020	2021	2022	2023	2024
Mother/Sponsoring Church - if available								
- provide office supplies, copies, etc.	1,000	1,000	1,000	0	0	0	0	0
- provide gift of office computer & desk	2,000	1,000	1,000	0	0	0	0	0
- salary support from sponsor, if possible	up to 8,000	up to 16,000	up to 16,000	up to 14,000	up to 14,000	up to 12,000	up to 12,000	up to 10,000
- *"Baby Showers" to provide in kind gifts*	*0*	*up to 10,000*	*5,000*	*0*	*0*	*0*	*0*	*0*
District - if funds available								
- provide health insurance	0	0	0	0	0	0	0	0
- provide rent for worship site, if possible	0 to 4,000	0 to 8,000	0 to 8,000	0 to 6,000	0 to 5,000	0 to 4,000	0 to 3,000	0 to 2,000
- provide program support, if possible	0 to 4,000	0 to 4,000	0 to 3,000	0 to 3,000	0 to 2,000	0 to 2,000	0 to 1,000	0
Pastor's Fund Raising from F.R.A.N.s 3 yr pledges, goal	*20,000*	*20,000*	*20,000*					
Parish and Community Development Funds	0	0	0	0	0	0	0	0
Hispanic Ministry Funds/Ethnic Local Church Funds	0	0	0	0	0	0	0	0
Grants from the General Board of Global Ministries	0	0	0	0	0	0	0	0
Equitable Comp/Key Charge	up to 7,000	up to 13,000	up to 10,000	up to 8,000	up to 6,000	0	0	0
Conference New Church Funds	up to 10,000	up to 20,000	up to 15,000	up to 5,000	0	0	0	0
Offering plate from the new church/leaders	5,000	7,000	10,000	14,000	20,000	26,000	32,000	38,000
TOTAL POSSIBLE gifts	***7 TO 38,000***	***12 TO 66,000***	***12 TO 56,000***	***8 TO 36,000***	***8 TO 25,000***	***6 TO 18,000***	***6 TO 16,000***	***4 TO 12,000***
Based on Worship Attendance projection of...	*15 to 20*	*20 to 30*	*30 to 40*	*40 to 50*	*50 to 60*	*60 to 70*	*70 to 80*	*80 to 90*

Financial support from the Annual Conference will not be identical for every new Mission Congregation start. Salaries of part-time pastors and missioners are not all the same, cost of rental space will vary across the state, grants from the District and sister congregations vary, and the financial ability of the new members will vary. Some new Mission Congregations will be eligible for grants from the General Board of Global Ministries. However, in every case a maximum amount of potential funding support will be set for each new church early in the appointment process.

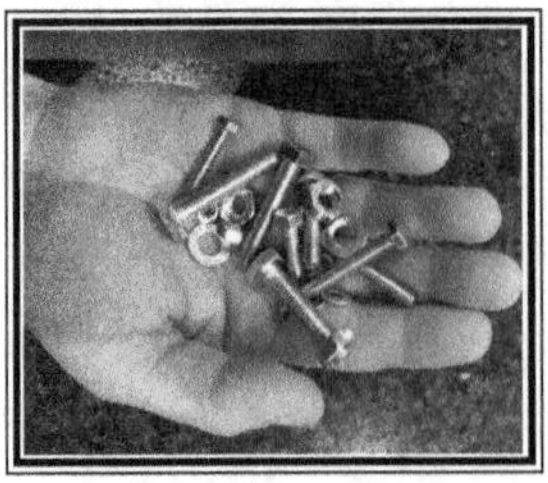

New Church Handbook
Nuts & Bolts for Planting New Churches In The Wesleyan Tradition

"E-Giving Guide For New Churches"

Including material from Richard Rogers

Richard Rogers, Ministry Strategist with Horizons Stewardship, is the wisest person I know when it comes to e-giving in the church. Last year, Abingdon Press published Richard's book, **"The E-Giving Guide for Every Church: Using Digital Tools To Grow Ministry."**

The remainder of this article is an introduction to his book. You may purchase a copy at www.cokesbury.com or any book retailer.

RRogers@horizonsstewardship.com
www.horizons.net

The E-Giving Guide for Every Church: Using Digital Tools To Grow Ministry (Abingdon Press) by Richard Rogers

Introduction

As I travel around the country talking to pastors, local church and denominational leaders, and other Christians, there is growing concern about the ability to resource vital ministry. I have yet to meet a pastor who enjoys raising money, but every single one of them understands that money equals ministry. Many churches have God-sized plans and dreams to have an impact in their neighborhood, city, state, and around the world. What most of them lack are sufficient resources to pursue those plans and dreams. Personally I'm not excited about raising more money for the sake of having more stuff. But when I meet Christians who want to meet a need someone has today, so they can build a caring relationship with them, so they can introduce them to Jesus, so the person's life can be changed forever… that stirs my soul! The desire to see the next one impacted by the love of God challenges me to look for solutions, inspires me to get personally involved, and pushes me beyond my natural inclination to resist change.

 © 2018 Robert O. Crossman, www.UMNewChurch.org

After decades of involvement in the local church and experiencing in my own family how the community of faith has shaped my marriage and the lives of my children, I've never been more excited about the opportunities facing local congregations. Today, fewer young people are connected in a vital relationship with Jesus through a local church than we have seen in our lifetime. What a fantastic opportunity we have to BE THE CHURCH! And because I understand that in our economic system, money is the tool that allows us to do more ministry and see more lives changes, then I absolutely have a ball working with leaders to grow the financial base of their church. My first goal throughout the writing of this book has been to develop a resource that will help you have the money needed to achieve God's vision for your ministry. Secondly I hope that your church will begin to look more and more like the Macedonian churches talked about by the Apostle Paul in chapters 8 and 9 of 2 Corinthians. I pray that your churches will be a people who are generous and enthusiastically prioritize the use of their resources to build God's Kingdom instead of their own.

One of the obvious ways in a digital society that a congregation can increase the number of families that are providing regular support for the ministry budget, and increase the level of support from those already participating, is through the use of electronic giving tools. The tools have become readily available and continue to improve, but I constantly hear questions and comments like these:

- How do we get started?
- What are the fees?
- Our young families don't give.
- What's the difference between an ACH, an EFT and an E-Check?
- When our members go on vacation, their summer giving goes with them.
- Do we have to take credit cards?
- It's too expensive!
- Will our members' information be secure?
- What does "optimized for mobile use" mean?
- We don't want an ATM in our church.
- What's our next step?
- Can we use PayPal?
- We don't think it's wise to give up 3% in fees.
- What is a kiosk?
- Whenever we lose a Sunday for snow and ice, we lose a week of income that we never get back.

- How can we get our members to give regularly?
- We have electronic giving on our website but nobody uses it.
- How do we increase participation?
- Are there any good service providers with whom we can partner?
- Will it integrate with our church management or bookkeeping software?
- I like to put my offering in the plate as part of my worship experience.
- What is PCI DSS?
- I gave $10 to the Red Cross in 10 seconds with a text message, but I can't give digitally to my church!

These are just some of the questions and comments I hear whenever the topic of electronic giving comes up with pastors, finance committee members, stewardship teams, church business administrators, administrative councils, church staff and board members. Questions and comments that come from a lack of good information, which, if it were available, could remove the doubt, and fear that paralyze them. In my search for information I discovered an educational void in this emerging industry. The facts assert that electronic giving will profoundly impact your church's ability to resource its' mission in the days and years ahead. I believe it already has.

The E-Giving Guide has been written to be a vital tool for ministry today and change the trajectory of resourcing for the future of your church. I want to demystify the tech and banking jargon that keeps us confused. I'll give you a resource to evaluate the costs associated with electronic giving, and teach you what you need to consider when you talk to the service providers who have the tools to help you succeed. Most importantly, I'll help you develop a plan to begin immediately, regardless of your situation, collecting more money for ministry and missions.

You may purchase a copy at
www.cokesbury.com
www.abingdonpress.com
or any book retailer.

†††

NOTE: This article reflects the personal opinions of its author and does not necessarily reflect an official position of Discipleship Ministries or Path 1.

© 2018 Robert O. Crossman, www.UMNewChurch.org

THE DENVER POST — Wednesday, September 18, 2002

More churches go electronic with "e-tithing"

Automatic draft provides them more steady income

By Brett Hoffman
Knight Ridder Newspapers

FORT WORTH, Texas — Gayla Oatman tithed once a year at University Christian Church in Fort Worth until the beginning of this year.

That's when the local church began offering members the option of tithing electronically — by credit card.

Donors submit credit card or bank account numbers to the church and indicate how much money is to be deducted and how frequently.

Some local houses of worship have been using e-tithing for at least five years, and more church financial officers are considering it.

The practice crosses faith boundaries. Among those that accept electronic giving are St. Michael Catholic Church in Bedford, Texas; Beth-El, a Jewish congregation in Fort Worth; and Dominion Church, an interdenominational congregation in Arlington, Texas.

Local church business executives say they are uncertain just how much e-tithing increases giving overall. But they attest to its advantage: It provides a steady stream of contributions on which to build budgets, and it spreads church contributions more evenly throughout the year.

For example, electronic giving can make it easier for busy parents who are scrambling to get children off to church or synagogue and may forget to take their checkbooks.

And church giving usually dips in the summer when many families take vacations, but a planned electronic deduction keeps the tithes coming while the parishioners are away, said Don Houk, business manager at University Christian.

"It's steady income, and that's very helpful to us," Houk said.

The idea takes some getting used to, but many people use electronic deductions in much of their secular lives.

"They're accustomed to making their house payment by an automatic withdrawal from their checking account. So, they can make another house payment, this one to their house of worship, by the same method, or by credit card," said Sid Johnston, financial director at First Methodist Church of Fort Worth, a congregation that has used credit-card giving for the past 1½ years.

Leighton Haselgrove, director of operations at Lakeside Baptist Church in Granbury, Texas, said that although the church has offered the option of giving through automatic bank drafts since 1998,

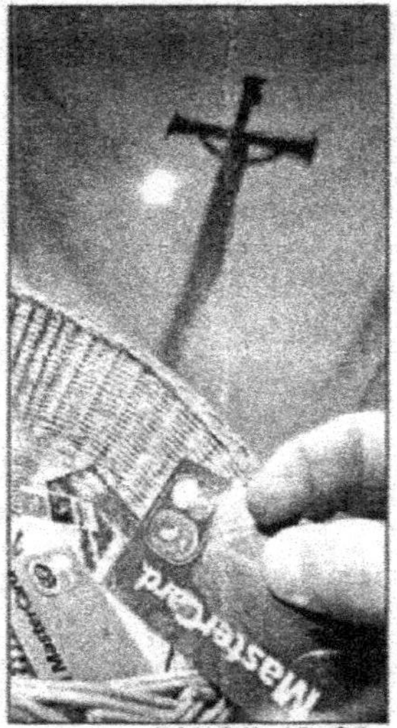

Knight Ridder / Jim Gehrz

While some houses of worship see the acceptance of credit cards as a convenience to members, other churches are loath to accept plastic.

only about 30 of the church's 600 families use the service.

"I think that it will change in the next six months or a year, with more emphasis," said Haselgrove, who practices electronic tithing. "The younger generation are more prone to do electronic transfers, and we will be putting our emphasis on that age group."

Lakeside's electronic banking is handled by Minnesota-based Vanco, a five-year-old company that contracts with more than 5,000 churches in 50 states and 18 denominations.

Vanco said it charges 25 cents per electronic transfer, which translates into $13 a year for the company from a worshipper who gives weekly.

About 67 percent of Vanco's clients give monthly, 13 percent semimonthly and 20 percent weekly, said Len Thiede, Vanco's senior account manager. Nationally, a monthly donor gives about $2,800 a year, a semimonthly donor about $3,200 and a weekly donor about $3,800.

Vanco helps churches collect by credit cards or by an electronic transaction from a bank account. More than 99 percent of Vanco's clients prefer electronic deductions from their bank accounts.

"Giving by credit card has not been terribly popular with churches," Thiede said. "The reality is that most people do not pay off their credit cards, so churches do not want to do anything that would help people get into debt."

Jim Hackney, minister of Midtown Church of Christ in the Fort Worth area, said the church is exploring the use of bank account debits but won't inquire about credit card use.

"With some people, having a credit card is like having alcohol, and they should never take a drink," Hackney said. "You have people who learn about the church and they want to tithe, but they can't because they are knee-deep in debt. What happens is that many young families don't pay off their credit cards."

Arlington's Dominion Church allows members to give by credit card, but church leaders discourage the practice if it causes a financial strain, said Darla McBride, the church's business administrator.

"It can go against common sense and Biblical principle," McBride said of tithing on a credit card. "The Bible says to be a lender and not a borrower."

But churches like giving parishioners the option. Larry Sweat, business manager at St. Michael in Bedford, said, "I don't expect the majority of people" to began giving electronically.

"Some people enjoy the physical aspects of dropping it into a plate," Sweat said, "particularly the older people."

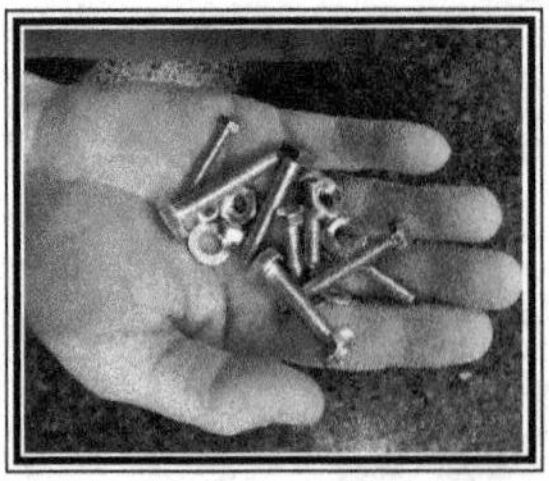

New Church Handbook
Nuts & Bolts for Planting New Churches In The Wesleyan Tradition

"Setting Up An Internal Financial System"

by Bob Crossman

Should you, the church planter, be a signatory on the new church's checking account? NO

Should you, the church planter, be counting the money after launch team offerings are received? NO

Should you, the church planter, be making the deposits? NO

Should your new church have a credit card? Probably not. *(In most annual conferences the planter is expected to make any approved purchases on their personal credit card and submit receipts for reimbursement.)*

Check with your annual conference director of new church starts
and/or your Conference Treasurer
to discover the system required by your particular annual conference.

In most settings, you will be asking the Financial Secretary of a nearby healthy United Methodist Church or the District Office Administrative Assistant to serve as your Financial Secretary. This person will make your deposits from your weekly launch team meetings, deposit grants received, and deposit all other income received. This person will also be reimbursing you for expenses that are within the limits of your approved budget for the year. In some conferences, this person will also be writing your monthly paycheck.

In the early months, your new church is not chartered and therefor can not have a duly elected finance committee or Treasurer - that is why you will probably be required to use the Financial Secretary of a nearby healthy United Methodist Church or the District Office Administrative Assistant to serve as your Financial Secretary.

You will probably also be asked to designate two persons, who are not related to you or to each other, to count any offering received. These two will count any offerings together, record the agreed upon total, and relay these funds to your Financial Secretary for depositing. This transfer of funds may be done through a locked bank bag and the night deposit of a nearby branch bank.

 © 2018 Robert O. Crossman, www.UMNewChurch.org

In most settings you will be asking the bank to send duplicate monthly statements to your Financial Secretary, to you, and to your conference minister of new church starts. This will continue until you charter.

A record of all gifts received will need to be kept so that your new church can send a "receipt" at the first of the year for tax purposes. In some cases this part of the record keeping will be made by "your" people, in others it will be made by your Financial Secretary.

In most annual conferences, you will have permission to make any purchases up to an agreed upon amount ($500 or $1,000 typically) and upon presentation of the receipt to be reimbursed by your Financial Secretary if the purchase has already been included in one of your approved budget line items. In most annual conferences, any upcoming purchase over this agreed upon amount ($500 or $1,000) will need to be approved in writing in advance. *(i.e. You will write to your conference director of new church starts with a cc to your district superintendent: "As we discussed last week, I have obtained and attached three bids for a projector. The one from Long's Electronics seems to be the best all around. I am requesting permission to purchase and be reimbursed for $1,287.53 for the purchase of this projector." They will reply and you will attach a print out of their email to the receipt so that your Financial Secretary can officially reimburse you for the purchase.)*

Your annual conference may ask you, after you have launched weekly worship and gained some level of stability, to appoint a local Financial Task Force that will begin to assume some of these financial duties on a growing basis as the months pass and you move toward your Constituting (Chartering) Conference.

The following pages are recommendations from the Arkansas Conference for all local churches.

Internal Controls in United Methodist Churches

Basic Goals and Recommendations for All Churches

*(prepared by Audit Committee
of Arkansas Conference of the United Methodist Church)*

The church has a judiciary responsibility to its donors to ensure that the resources made available to the church are used in a manner consistent with the church's mission and any donor restrictions. Therefore, every church, regardless of size, should have a system of internal controls. Objectives of internal controls are:

- prevent loss or theft of the church's assets
- minimize the opportunity for an employee or volunteer to steal or misuse the assets and/or records of the church
- provide timely and accurate information to management; and
- ensure compliance with laws and regulations

The goal of a sound system of internal control is to balance asset protection with efficient operation. Only those controls in which the benefits outweigh both the financial and emotional costs should be implemented. Often, internal controls are installed due to the fear of fraud or in response to fraud. May people may resent the discussion of controls. However, a system of internal controls benefits not only the church but also the employees and volunteers of the church. The employees and volunteers can be protected them from false accusations of fraud or misuse of assets.

Cash Receipts

The goals for internal controls over cash receipts are:

- to protect all revenue
- to record all receipts
- acknowledge contributions and any restrictions on contributions
- to comply with Internal Revenue Service requirements

Church offerings make up the majority of cash receipts. Some recommendations are:

- Always follow the principle of two - At least two people should always collect and count the offering. Offerings should never be left in the possession of only one person. Also, the collection/count teams should be rotated and the same individuals should not always be paired together.
- Count the offering as soon as possible. The shorter the length of time between the receipt of funds and counting it, the potential for mishandling the funds decreases.
- Count in a secure area - No one should be allowed in the count room other than those counting. Also, coats, purses, or briefcases should not be allowed to be brought into the count room.
- Deposit all offerings intact - All offering should always be counted and deposited intact. This means not allowing cash in the offering to be used to pay church expenses or exchanged for other cash or a check. An unidentified variance could occur if offerings are not deposited intact.
- Use a restrictive endorsement - Before or while counting, a restrictive endorsement should be stamped on the back of all checks.
- Verify amounts on offering envelopes - When the count team removes contents from offering envelopes, the amount written on the envelope should be compared to the contents. Any differences should be noted on the envelopes and initialed by the count team.
- Provide a secure location when offerings are stored on church property - Again, follow the principle of two. No one person should have access to the collections at anytime. This can be accomplished by placing the offerings in a locked bag before placing them in a lock box.
- Use count sheets
- Segregate duties - Someone separate from the count team should record in-

 © 2018 Robert O. Crossman, www.UMNewChurch.org

dividual gifts in donor records. Also, count sheets should be reconciled regularly to deposits by someone other than the person making the deposit.

Cash Disbursement

The goals for internal controls over cash disbursements are:

- to ensure disbursements are made only upon proper authorization.
- to ensure expenditures are for valid business purposes
- that they are properly recorded in church's records.

Again, segregation of duties is important. One person should not handle a transaction from beginning (authorization) to end (reconciliation). An individual should not have an opportunity to make an accounting error, whether intentional or unintentional, and also conceal it. Generally, the same person should not authorize, process, sign the check, record and reconcile a transaction.

Expenditures should be controlled by an approved budget, should be based on approved purchase orders or requisitions and receipt of goods and services should be verified before the payment of an invoice. Payments of customer statements should generally be avoided, however, periodic statements received from vendors should be reconciled to underlying invoices received from the vendor.

All disbursement checks should require two authorized signatures. Checks should be submitted for signatures with all properly approved original invoices or receipts attached to each individual check. Authorized signers should never sign any checks without reviewing the check and the attached supporting documentation information. The church financial secretary or bookkeeper should not be given the authority to sign checks.

Credit Card Charges

Absolutely, under no circumstances should church credit cards be used for personal reasons. Certain church staff members may be issued a church credit card. They will be personally responsible for all charges made on that card. Additional cards may be available for church members to use. These cards will need to be signed in/out in the financial secretary's office. Receipts should be given to the financial secretary in order to support the charges on the bill and, if required, a payment request form should also accompany the receipt.

Reconciliations

Sound decisions are difficult to make if the information in the financial reports cannot be relied upon. Therefore, adequate steps should be taken to confirm the accuracy of the balances shown in checking accounts, and all other financial accounts. Balances of these accounts should be compared to detailed reports of any subsidiary ledgers. Differences should be documented using reconciling items.

Reconciliations should be completed monthly. All accounts should be reconciled to a subsidiary ledger on a regular and timely basis.

The person responsible for reconciling the bank accounts should not also authorize transactions.

Other

Often, the most valuable property the church owns is its building and facilities. The church may also own other properties like a parsonage or youth center. The church often owns personal property like office equipment, organ, piano, audio-visual equipment, and vehicles. Controls protecting such assets should ensure that the property is catalogued, present, and adequately insured with up to date coverage. In addition, purchases or dispositions should be properly authorized. This can be accomplished by instituting a policy or policies regarding use of the facilities - wedding policy, building use policy, and van policy.

In many small churches, the most important component of internal control is the control environment which is influenced by the governing board and management. Often, it is the minister who is the driving force of the control environment. The minister's attitude with respect to internal controls has a significant impact on the church's control environment. Most church members want to believe that anyone connected with their church is trustworthy and in such arena of trust let their guard down, thus, making the church vulnerable. Even though no system is foolproof and it is difficult to put a value on internal controls, consider whether there is a benefit to the church to:

- remove temptation for misappropriation
- prevent clouds of suspicion from developing over heads of honest staff members
- improve likelihood of errors, both intentional and unintentional, being discovered
- reduce risk of having to confront a member or employee who has taken funds
- reduce chance of having to tell congregation that their contributions are lost.

Agreed Upon AUDIT Procedures

"We don't want anyone suspecting us of taking one penny of this money for ourselves. We're being as careful in our reputation with the public as in our reputation with God." (2 Cor. 8:20-21- The Message)

The Book of Discipline contains provision for the committee on finance at each local church to adopt written financial policies and internal controls. The committee on finance is also tasked with the responsibility of making provision for an annual audit of the financial statements of the local church. Complete provisions are included in the Book of Discipline 2008 section 258.4. The General Council on Finance & Administration (GCFA) also publishes "The Local Church Audit Guide" which is an excellent publication for local churches to utilize regarding auditing

 © 2018 Robert O. Crossman, www.UMNewChurch.org

and internal controls.

The GCFA defines an audit for the local church as:
"A local church audit is an independent evaluation of the financial reports and records and internal controls of the local church by a qualified person or persons for the purpose of reasonably verifying the reliability of financial reporting, determining whether the assets are being safeguarded, and whether the law, the Discipline, and policies and procedures are being complied with."

A professional audit can be costly and require a significant amount of time. A certified audit requires independent verification by the auditor to substantiate representations made by the local church financial staff or volunteers about the financial records of the church. An alternative process called a financial review is less costly and more simply requires the auditor to make inquiries of church financial staff or volunteers to corroborate the financial records of the church. In lay terminology, an audit provides a high degree of assurance the financial statements are free of material errors and fraud, whereas the financial review just tests whether the financial statements make sense without applying the testing undertaken in an audit.

A certified audit or financial review should be undertaken as appropriate to protect both the church and the persons handling and managing the financial operations of the church. It also provides certain assurances to the congregation that the funds are being managed wisely and used as designated when given. Finally, it provides a system of checks and balances to insure that the financial operations of the church are operating within the guidelines of generally accepted practices and principles.

Because of the importance of safeguarding donations provided to local churches, the Arkansas Conference Council on Finance & Administration (CFA) recommends that each local church subscribe to certain minimum financial, reporting, and internal control procedures.

For churches with total income of less than $500,000 annually:

1) Ensure that the monthly/quarterly/annual bank statements for each account maintained by the church are received unopened by an appropriate person designated by the church that is not related to or affiliated with the person(s) responsible for deposits and disbursements of the local church. If the church receives statements online, then provisions will need to be made for the designated person to have access as a read only viewer of the statements. The designated person should have sufficient skill and knowledge to read and understand a bank statement and should review said statement for any irregularities. Any questions should be brought to the attention of the appropriate church representative (i.e. Treasurer, finance committee chairperson, Pastor, district superintendent).

2) That each church within this category seek to establish the minimal practice of conducting and completing a financial review by a qualified person or firm within six months of the end of each fiscal year. This may be accomplished by utilizing the services of a person within the congregation with financial knowledge or expertise or possibly by utilizing the treasurer of a neighboring church by trading review services with said neighboring church. Further, the person or firm conducting the review should not be the pastor and should have no relationship or appearance of a relationship with the person or persons responsible for the church's financial management. The person(s) conducting the financial review is not required to be a Certified Public Accountant (CPA) but must have appropriate qualifications for conducting the work asked to be performed.

As part of the financial review the following should be minimally accomplished:

- Review the minutes of all Church/Charge Conference, finance committee, Board of trustees, and Administrative Board/Council meetings for the period being reviewed.
- Review the financial policies and practices of the local church.
- A list of all bank and investment accounts should be obtained including authorized signatories.
- Review all bank and investment account statements for the review period.
- Review all bank reconciliations for the review period.
- Review all monthly financial statements for the review period.
- Conduct a review of an appropriate random sampling of bank deposits, and payroll records for the review period. This should include 941s, year end W-2s, 1099s, transmittal documents, and proper reporting of withheld employee taxes.
- Test supporting documentation of a random sampling of paid invoices to ensure that said invoices were properly approved, sufficiently documented, included in the budget, and paid from the appropriate account.
- Conduct a fluctuation analysis on balance sheet and income statement accounts which have had a significant change versus the prior year in terms of total dollar change or percentage change.
- Verify the existence of current W-4s and I-9s for all staff.
- If the church participates in a Section 125 plan or retirement plan, ensure that executed documents are in place for plan provisions and that withholding is being done properly.
- Inspect insurance policies of the church for appropriate levels of coverage, ensure that policy premiums have been paid timely, and that policies have not expired.
- If the church utilizes business credit cards, ensure that the church has a written policy and that it is being followed by inspecting an appropriate random sampling of statements and expenses paid by the church. Under no conditions should personal purchases be allowed with business credit cards.

 © 2018 Robert O. Crossman, www.UMNewChurch.org

The ____________________ United Methodist Church of __________________, _________

Record of Giving for the Year 20___

PLEASE RETAIN FOR INCOME TAX PURPOSES

Name: ____

Address: ____

We acknowledge with appreciation your gift as recorded. Regular contributions enable us to meet our financial obligations promptly. Contact the financial officer if you have questions regarding this report. Pursuant to Internal Revenue Code requirements for substantiation of charitable contributions, no goods or services were provided in return for these contributions.

Regular Gifts • Budget Gifts • Gifts for Current Expenses

January	
First Sunday	$
Second Sunday	$
Third Sunday	$
Fourth Sunday	$
Fifth Sunday	$

February	
First Sunday	$
Second Sunday	$
Third Sunday	$
Fourth Sunday	$
Fifth Sunday	$

March	
First Sunday	$
Second Sunday	$
Third Sunday	$
Fourth Sunday	$
Fifth Sunday	$

TOTAL FIRST QUARTER $ ____________

July	
First Sunday	$
Second Sunday	$
Third Sunday	$
Fourth Sunday	$
Fifth Sunday	$

August	
First Sunday	$
Second Sunday	$
Third Sunday	$
Fourth Sunday	$
Fifth Sunday	$

September	
First Sunday	$
Second Sunday	$
Third Sunday	$
Fourth Sunday	$
Fifth Sunday	$

TOTAL THIRD QUARTER $ ____________

April	
First Sunday	$
Second Sunday	$
Third Sunday	$
Fourth Sunday	$
Fifth Sunday	$

May	
First Sunday	$
Second Sunday	$
Third Sunday	$
Fourth Sunday	$
Fifth Sunday	$

June	
First Sunday	$
Second Sunday	$
Third Sunday	$
Fourth Sunday	$
Fifth Sunday	$

TOTAL SECOND QUARTER $ ____________

October	
First Sunday	$
Second Sunday	$
Third Sunday	$
Fourth Sunday	$
Fifth Sunday	$

November	
First Sunday	$
Second Sunday	$
Third Sunday	$
Fourth Sunday	$
Fifth Sunday	$

December	
First Sunday	$
Second Sunday	$
Third Sunday	$
Fourth Sunday	$
Fifth Sunday	$

TOTAL FOURTH QUARTER $ ____________

Did you have an annual pledge campaign? Record of pledges or commitments, if any:	
Pledge for current expenses:	**$**
Pledge for benevolences:	**$**
Pledge for building fund:	**$**

Designated Gifts • Special Gifts • Memorial Gifts

Date	Purpose	Amount

Total Designated/Special for the Year $

END OF YEAR SUMMARY OF GIFTS	
Total regular offerings:	**$**
Total special gifts:	**$**
Grand Total for Year:	**$**

© 2017 by Robert O. Crossman

Sunday Counter's Tally Sheet

Date: ____________________, 20___

FOR GENERAL FUND/CURRENT EXPENSES/BUDGET:

From identified donors:

Total # of checks: ______, totaling **$ ___________** *You should be able to fit 6 to 8 checks on each copy.* (make photo copy of checks before placing in bank bag

Cash from envelopes, totaling **$ ___________** (keep envelopes, and place totals on each one) *You will need these copies and empty envelopes to transfer information to the Giving Record for each household.*

From unknown donors: **(loose plate or blank envelopes)**

Cash (currency and change) **$ ___________**

ANY SPECIAL GIFTS DESIGNATED GIFTS OR MEMORIALS:

List each gift:

From:	Purpose	Amount

TOTAL OF SPECIAL GIFTS: **$ _________**

GRAND TOTAL **$ _________** (this should equal deposit amount)

Notes:

We have counted the offering twice, and we agree on the above amounts.

Signed ____

Signed ____

The Book of Discipline requires that the offering be counted by two people unrelated to each other.

Make three copies of this sheet:
1) place one copy inside the locked bank bag
2) save the second copy to give to the pastor later in the week
3) keep the third copy in 3 ring notebook (keep for 3 years).

© 2018 Robert O. Crossman, www.UMNewChurch.org

FORM B - PURCHASE REQUISITION FORM

Date Requested ______________________________

Date Needed By ______________________________

Person Making the
Requisition ______________________________

Amount Requested ______________________________

Account Charged ______________________________

Check to be issued to:
Name ______________________________

Address ____

____

Description of purchase or service ____

____

____

____

Signature ______________________________
Requester

Signature ______________________________
Financial Secretary

Signature ______________________________
Pastor or Authorized Member

FORM D - PETTY CASH CHARGES

PLEASE TYPE OR PRINT ALL INFORMATION
RECEIPTS FOR ALL EXPENSES MUST BE ATTACHED

Date Received ______________________

Person Receiving ______________________

Amount Received ______________________

Account Number ______________________

Explanation ______________________________________

____

____

____

____

Each request must be accompanied by a separate form. Receipts must be attached. If unavailable for a phone purchase a detailed description of the purchase must be provided. For internet purchases please print out any type of receipt that the site provides. The form should be signed by the Financial Secretary before purchases are made to verify the availability of funds.

Signature ______________________ Signature ______________________
Requester *Financial Secretary*

Signature ______________________
Pastor or Authorized Member

© 2018 Robert O. Crossman, www.UMNewChurch.org

SafeChurch®

Key Components to a Financial Safeguard Program

Developing a Financial Policy

The first step to putting financial safeguards into place is to develop a policy that identifies how money is handled, counted, deposited, reported, and audited. The policy should address procedures for handling funds from the time collections are taken until money is disbursed. Instituting a policy that includes this information will help prevent the misappropriation of funds and ensure that both staff members and volunteers are protected if an accusation is ever made against them. In addition, a financial policy is more likely to deter individuals from embezzling funds because they know that the cash management system is being carefully observed.

Taking the Collection

In most churches, ushers play a key role in the collection process. It is important that ushers are trained in more than handing out bulletins and seating congregation members. Safeguarding funds begins with them. Ushers should be trained on what to do to safeguard the collection during and after it is taken. They should watch for anyone who seems out of place or suspicious and should use visual and verbal communication between them. Once the collection is taken, it should be secured, instead of remaining unattended in front of the church. Two ushers should take the collection and lock it up in a safe or other secure location until the money is counted.

Safekeeping and Depositing of Collection

From the time it is collected to the time it is deposited, the two unrelated person rule should apply to the handling of funds. Once the collection is secured, several options are available. Some churches choose to count the collection immediately following the services, where others count the funds the following day.

For those who count after church, this should be conducted in a locked room. At least two people should be present when the collection is moved from the safe to the counting area. For those who count the following day, the collection should remain in a safe (or double locked area) or safely taken to the bank by two adults. The bank bags should be placed in another nondescript bag when taken to the bank. Varying routes to the bank are suggested. Look around the bank area for suspicious cars or individuals. Only place the collection in the night deposit once the area is safe.

Counting of Collection

It is important that a team of people count the collection. Again, this should be done in a secure room. Counting teams should be rotated weekly or monthly. Envelopes, cash, and checks should be kept visible at all times. Double checking figures and balancing the funds is important. A signed and dated form that lists all currency, coins, and checks should be listed. A deposit slip should be completed. Collections should never be taken home.

GuideOne® Insurance

Internal Controls

It is important to have separation of duties between the counting team, the treasurer, and the financial secretary. For example, the person who prepares the checks should not have authority to sign the checks. Likewise, blank checks should not be available to those with check signing authority; and those signing checks should never sign a blank check or a check made out to "cash." Dual signatures should be required for all checks over a specified dollar amount. The bank statement should be first opened and reviewed by someone who is not involved in writing the checks. Not only do these safeguards offer financial integrity, but they can reduce the appearance of impropriety.

Screening Workers

Volunteers and employees who handle funds need to be screened by running criminal background checks and/or checking financial references. Some churches have chosen to conduct credit checks on those handling money. At a minimum, people with high integrity should be selected. They should have the ability to be discreet with sensitive financial information. Rotating people in these positions is helpful to ensure safeguarding of funds.

Purchases

To ensure accountability, all purchases should be made through a voucher system in which check requests are accompanied by appropriate paperwork supporting the expense. Purchases over a specified amount should require the approval of a church or ministry leader. If anything is purchased with personal funds, a receipt and form for reimbursement should be used.

Petty Cash Funds

The purpose of a petty cash fund is to cover small, unanticipated expenses that are needed immediately, such as postage due and COD deliveries. Funding larger expenditures should be planned and handled through the church's regular purchasing process discussed above. For petty cash funds, establish a small cash limit that is kept in the custody of designated office personnel. Guidelines concerning appropriate uses of the fund should be communicated to those personnel. The fund should be stored in a locked location. Distributions from the fund should be documented. When the fund balance falls below a predetermined limit, documentation of the expenditures should be submitted in order for the fund to be replenished. The fund should be subject to periodic, unannounced audits.

Pastor's Discretionary/Benevolent Fund

Many churches utilize a pastor's discretionary or benevolent fund for the minister to address cases of special financial need within the congregation. Churches should be very careful in establishing such funds because there can be income tax implications to the pastor if they are not set up correctly. Consultation with the church's tax advisor is recommended. Other controls for such funds include a monetary account limit, documentation of all expenditures, prohibition on cash gifts, bank account reconciliation, and periodic audits of the fund.

 © 2018 Robert O. Crossman, www.UMNewChurch.org

Special Funds

Often there are special funds and accounts held by groups in the church. In addition to these, one time or ongoing collections of money (bazaars, craft fairs, dances, and dinners) also can leave the funds vulnerable. Every effort should be taken to safeguard these funds and accounts as well. Again, the two-person rule should apply. Monies should never be taken directly from a collection and given to an individual or ministry group. They should be counted, deposited, and disbursed according to the church's regular financial procedures. These special accounts should be audited periodically on an unannounced basis.

Reporting

To preserve integrity in a sensitive area, financial reporting is necessary. The donors in the congregation have a right to know their funds are being used. Some churches offer a monthly financial statement, while others do it quarterly. Regardless, some method of accountability and reporting should be a part of every financial program.

Audit of Financial Records

To continue a program of safeguarding finances, regular audits should be conducted. Someone other than the financial secretary or treasurer should conduct these audits. A congregation member who is a CPA or has a strong financial background might be a good candidate. While these audits should be done annually, some churches elect to have an outside firm do a complete audit every two or three years. In the intervening years, a financial review by someone uninvolved in the church's finances is recommended. It is especially important to complete an audit before a new person steps into the role of church treasurer or financial secretary. In connection with the audit, it is important that the church address any recommendations provided by the auditor(s) in their "management letter."

Bonding

Churches may reduce the financial impact of embezzlement losses by securing a fidelity or employee dishonesty bond on those people who handle funds. It also is possible to purchase insurance coverage that blankets all officers and employees.

Responding to Incidents

If an accusation or suspicion is reported, it is important to act promptly and with care. The suspected embezzler or thief should be confronted and asked to provide a full accounting of the situation. If not already completed, an audit should be performed. If sufficient information or a confession points to guilt, church leaders then need to decide whether to turn the matter over to the police. Church leaders also must remember that they owe a responsibility to the members and donors to be good stewards of the church's resources.

Reduce the Chances of Robbery or Embezzlement

By ensuring that the above components are in place, the chances of robbery or embezzlement can be reduced. It is important to remember that we are called to take care of those people and resources God has entrusted to our care. This includes the finances that keep ministry alive in our churches.

(05.01.07)

© 2010 GuideOne Center for Risk Management, LLC. All rights reserved.

This material is for information only and is not intended to provide legal or professional advice.
You are encouraged to consult with your own attorney or other expert consultants for a professional opinion specific to your situation.

New Church Handbook
Nuts & Bolts for Planting New Churches In The Wesleyan Tradition

"Obtaining a GCFA Number"

by Bob Crossman

Every United Methodist Church has an official number assigned by the General Council on Finance and Administration of the United Methodist Church. This official number is obtained by filling out the form on the following page and sending the completed form to dataservices@gcfa.org

Several years ago a GCFA number was only assigned after the Chartering Constituting Conference. **Now, however, GCFA will issue a number immediately after the appointment is made, even before the first worship service is held.**

Each church with a GCFA number is asked to complete Tables I, II, III, and IV at the end of each year to officially report baptisms, professions of faith, attendance, and finances.

NOTE: Please check with your District Superintendent and Conference New Church Developer before sending in this form. In some annual conferences, this form can only be submitted by the Conference Treasurer, or district superintendent.

See the following page for the form to request a GCFA number.

NOTE: This article reflects the personal opinions of its author and does not necessarily reflect an official position of Discipleship Ministries or Path 1.

© 2018 Robert O. Crossman, www.UMNewChurch.org

Please report all New Church Starts and Chartered/Organized churches to GCFA as soon as possible. Send copies to: dataservices@gcfa.org

Note	Field	Entry
	Today's date:	____
GCFA will assign #	Church Number:	____
	Annual Conference Name:	____
	District Name:	____
	Name of Church	____
(only if charge name is different from church name)	Name of Charge:	____
(only if church is in a parish)	Name of Parish:	____
0= White, 1=Asian, 2=Black/Afr Am, 3=Hispanic, 4=Native Am, 5=Pacific Islander, 6=Multi Racial, 7=Other	Ethnic Code of Church:	____
	Preffered Mailing Address:	____

Organized/Chartered Information:

Note	Field	Entry
Chartered, New Church Start, Satellite, Mission	Church Type:	____
Required for all Satellite Churches	Parent Church:	____
(GCFA needs this for New Church starts)	FOUNDED Effective Date:	____
	Organized/Chartered Effective Date	____
(optional)	Church Phone:	____
(optional)	Church Fax:	____
(optional)	Church Email:	____
01=English, 02=Spanish, 03=Russian, 04=French, 05=Kiswahili,06=Korean, 07=Portuguese, 08=German, 09=ASL	Church Spoken Language (s):	
	Name of Pastor:	____
	Effective Date of Appointment:	____
(such as FE for Full Elder)	Clergy Status:	____
0= White, 1=Asian, 2=Black/Afr Am, 3=Hispanic, 4=Native Am, 5=Pacific Islander, 6=Multi Racial, 7=Other	Ethnic Code of Pastor	____

Data Services Department, GCFA, dataservices@gcfa.org or PO BOX 340029, Nashville TN 37203-0029

© 2018 Robert O. Crossman, www.UMNewChurch.org

New Church Handbook
Nuts & Bolts for Planting New Churches In The Wesleyan Tradition

"Obtaining an EIN Number from the IRS and Tax Exempt Status Letter from GCFA"

by Bob Crossman

When the first checking account is established for the new church, in most cases the bank will ask for your EIN number (Federal employer identification number) and also request proof that your church is exempt from Federal taxes. How do you obtain these two items?

Some Conferences require that these two items be secured by the District, conference minister of new church starts, or Conference Treasurer instead of by the church planting pastor.
Before initiating this process clarify your Conference's policy.

- **Some annual conferences require that the EIN numbers are to be secured by the District, or Conference Treasurer instead of by the church planting pastor. Before initiating this process clarify your Conference's policy.**

  It is a simple process to obtain a EIN for your new church over the telephone. Simply call (800) 829-4933.

  They will ask for the church name, mailing address, and for your name as the contact person. A number will be assigned and given to you on the phone. They will mail you a letter of confirmation for your files.

- Once you have obtained the EIN number over the phone, you can then secure a Group Ruling 501(c)(3) letter for your church, and a copy of the 1974 IRS ruling from GCFA. You can apply by completing the form on the next page, and sending the completed form to legal@gcfa.org

  You can also apply on line at **umgroupruling.org**. When you complete the Group Ruling Request form, on the line asking for your "charter" date, simply write in *"This is a new church, that will begin worship in about six months. We have not chartered yet."*

- This Group Ruling letter does not necessarily exempt you from any local or state sales taxes. In Arkansas, for example, churches pay sales tax. In some states, churches are exempt from sales tax but the state may also require the church to apply for that exemption directly with the state. Check with your Conference for clarification.

- See sample of the response letter on the following page:

 © 2018 Robert O. Crossman, www.UMNewChurch.org

GCFA
GENERAL COUNCIL ON FINANCE AND ADMINISTRATION
THE UNITED METHODIST CHURCH

PO Box 340029
Nashville TN 372030029

March 8, 2010

RIVER OF LIFE UNITED METHODIST CHURCH
c/o Reverend Gary Tobar
2303 East Barton Avenue
West Memphis, AR 72301

Re: Certification of Inclusion in The United Methodist Church Group Tax Exemption Ruling
Affiliated Organization: River of Life United Methodist Church
Affiliated Organization's Employer Identification Number (EIN): 30-0608954
Date of Inclusion: October 1, 2009

Dear Reverend Tobar:

This letter will certify that the affiliated organization named above has been and continues to be included in The United Methodist Church Group Tax Exemption Ruling ("UMC Group Ruling"). In particular, as stated in the group ruling determination letter issued to The United Methodist Church by the Internal Revenue Service ("IRS"), this affiliated organization is exempt from federal income tax under Section 501(c)(3) of the Internal Revenue Code.

This certification letter is issued by the General Council on Finance and Administration of The United Methodist Church ("GCFA"). As the central organization for the UMC Group Ruling, GCFA has been granted the authority by the IRS to determine which organizations are included in the UMC Group Ruling. Thus, this certification letter, together with the enclosed copy of the IRS group ruling determination letter, serves to verify the tax-exempt status of this affiliated organization.

If you have any further questions, please feel free to contact the GCFA Legal Department at (866) 367-4232 or legal@gcfa.org.

Sincerely,

GENERAL COUNCIL ON FINANCE AND ADMINISTRATION OF THE UNITED METHODIST CHURCH

Dan Gary

J. Daniel Gary
Administrative Counsel

Enclosures

General Council on Finance and Administration

REQUEST FOR INCLUSION IN THE UNITED METHODIST CHURCH GROUP TAX EXEMPTION RULING

(PLEASE PRINT OR TYPE)

DATE: ______________________

CHURCH / ORGANIZATION NAME: ______________________
(Local Church, District, Annual Conference, or General Agency)

ADDRESS: ______________________

____

____

PHONE NUMBER: ______________________ **FAX NUMBER:** ______________________

E-MAIL ADDRESS: ______________________

EMPLOYER IDENTIFICATION NUMBER (EIN): ______________________
(This is a nine digit number issued to your organization by the IRS. Your request cannot be processed without this number.)

CHARTER / INCORPORATION DATE: ______________________

CONTACT PERSON: ______________________

PHONE NUMBER: ______________________

E-MAIL ADDRESS: ______________________

COMMENTS: ______________________

____

____

BY MY SIGNATURE BELOW, I CERTIFY THAT TO THE BEST OF MY KNOWLEDGE AND BELIEF, THE ABOVE INFORMATION IS TRUE, CORRECT, AND COMPLETE; THAT I AM A DULY AUTHORIZED OFFICER OF THE ORGANIZATION NAMED ABOVE; AND THAT THE ORGANIZATION NAMED ABOVE HEREBY AUTHORIZES THE GENERAL COUNCIL ON FINANCE AND ADMINISTRATION TO INCLUDE THE ORGANIZATION IN THE UNITED METHODIST CHURCH GROUP TAX EXEMPTION RULING.

____
[SIGNATURE]

____
[PRINTED NAME]

____
[TITLE]

[Note: If the requesting organization is a local church, a pastor of that local church is authorized to sign this form.]

Fax your completed request to GCFA's Legal Department – 866-246-2516 or
E-mail to legal@gcfa.org

© 2018 Robert O. Crossman, www.UMNewChurch.org

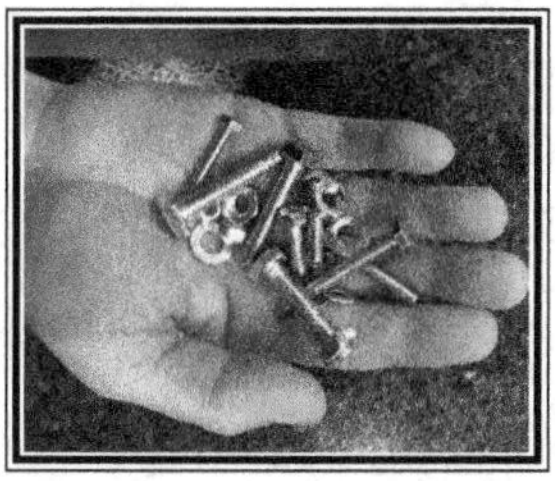

New Church Handbook
Nuts & Bolts for Planting New Churches In The Wesleyan Tradition

"Stewardship: If I Could Start From Scratch"

by Bob Crossman

In established church settings it is very difficult to change the stewardship DNA of the congregation. I wish to repent of the low expectations I presented to new members early in my ministry. As a young pastor in my twenties, I was so excited when the local bank president, college president, or state senator wanted to join the church. I am afraid I communicated to these new members something like this: *"We are so honored that you have chosen First Church. We know you are busy, but anytime you can attend worship, or volunteer, or give – that would be great."*

These new members met my low expectations. They attended a little bit. They volunteered a little bit. They gave a little bit.

Today, twenty years later, I am confident that their new pastor is struggling to invite these same parishioners to discover the joy of a deeper walk with Christ, a more holistic stewardship, and a higher level of discipleship. I pray that these parishioners will accept the invitation to journey toward becoming deeply devoted disciples of Christ.

Set High Expectations

Hilbert Berger's teachings, later reinforced by Mike Slaughter and Adam Hamilton, helped me to understand the importance of helping new believers journey toward the high expectations that Christ has of all who seek to be disciples. No more invitations to lukewarm Christianity, fence sitting, or pew warming.

In new church settings, the pastor has the opportunity to plant a high-expectation church that has a healthier stewardship DNA. The new church's stewardship can be driven by ministry and changed lives, rather than by constant concern of meeting the budget. New church pastors can set up a discipleship system with a broad level of expectations for new parishioners. These expectations usually include personal devotional time, reading the Scriptures, attendance at worship, lifestyles at home, heartfelt commitment, and a healthy view of money – all the while communicating clearly what Jesus Christ expects of those who desire to be faithful followers.

Some churches that are setting higher expectations for membership say up front that members are expected to tithe 10 percent. There is no pressure to make the commitment of membership, but for those who want to go beyond simple attendance, the bar is set for not just their prayers and participation, but their giving as well.

Adapt Your Methods

Setting high expectations doesn't mean being rigid with your methods of ministry, including with the ways people can give. For example, many 25- and 30-year-olds tend not to carry cash or checkbooks. There is a new generation of young adults who conduct all their financial transactions electronically.

Some denominational headquarters, such as that of The United Methodist Church, have provided simple resources to help churches take advantage of the electronic transfer of funds from parishioners' bank accounts directly to the church account on a steady, uninterrupted basis. Ken Sloan reports that the church he attends places a QR Code in the worship bulletin, so parishioners can scan the code on their smart phones, which takes them immediately to the church's online giving page.

Kim Griffith, of Griffith Coaching, encourages people to set up the church as a payee on the bill-pay list with their online banking. She suggests, "If people are not comfortable having the money automatically taken out, they can still give electronically when they pay their bills. We received a lot of payments that way every month at my church."

Kim also suggests that when people view or download sermons online at the church Web site, they be given a link to the giving page. There are people who may be coming to the site every week to listen to the sermon who may never have attended church. Consider providing a link saying something like this: "We hope you enjoy the sermons from First Church! If you would like to contribute to the ongoing ministries of this church, please click here." People who are moved by what they have heard will contribute.

Congregations that are reaching younger parishioners have found ways to allow online giving with credit cards, recognizing those who prefer this method and the reward points they accumulate. While some complain that allowing credit card giving enables people prone to accumulating debt, some of these same churches are offering programs to deal with the issue of credit card abuse and crushing debt, raising the bar on responsible finances and discipleship rather than avoiding the issue altogether.

NOTE: This article reflects the personal opinions of its author and does not necessarily reflect an official position of Discipleship Ministries or Path 1.

© 2018 Robert O. Crossman, www.UMNewChurch.org

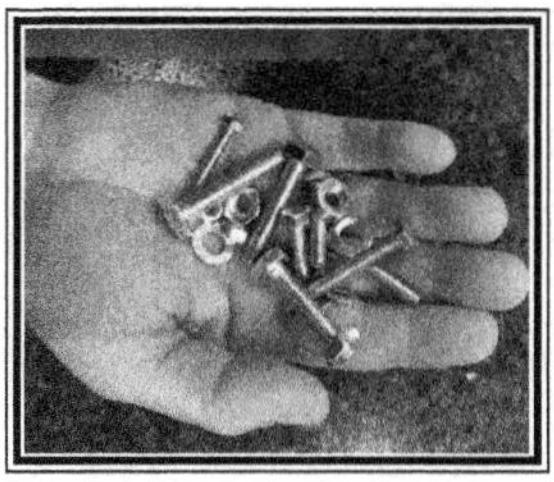

New Church Handbook
Nuts & Bolts for Planting New Churches In The Wesleyan Tradition

"Stewardship: Generosity Is Not Budget Driven"

by Bob Crossman

In far too many of our churches the pastor and finance committee are focused on developing the budget, perfecting the budget, and meeting the budget so that bills and payroll can be paid.

A fair amount of energy in August and September is spent reviewing the current budget, tweaking a few line items, adding a new line or two to support new ministries – all designed to have the new year's budget ready in October or November. This process is often driven by a desire to present to the congregation a budget with only a 2 or 3 percent increase – in the belief that the congregation would accept that as a reasonable increase. The line-item shifting process is also driven by a desire to inform the congregation of fixed increases the finance committee is facing in insurance and utility cost, to move some dollars out of ministry areas that have fallen out of favor, and to reward the pastor and staff with at least a cost of living increase.

As soon as the new year's budget is perfected, the energy shifts to exploring ways to distribute copies of the line item budget to as many congregational households as possible.

The pastor and congregational leadership are committed to spending a hundred days on this budget perfecting process in the belief that when the average parishioner sees the perfection of the new budget, and the ministries contained within, they will proportionally increase their giving to cover the 3 percent increase needed to pay the church's bills in the new year.

It's time for this paradigm to change.

Bill Easum has been calling for this change for some time. In Unfreezing Moves: Following Jesus Into The Mission Field, he writes, "Do your stewardship of money drive first, and then draw up a budget. Encourage people to give because they want to, rather than because the church needs money."

Herb Miller in his New Consecration Sunday, Revised Edition, also recommends conducting the campaign before building the annual operating budget. He writes, "Setting the budget first, then raising the money, holds giving down.

Church members, remembering the 'fair share' motto of many secular organizations, make minor increased in their giving when they see that the new budget is only 4 percent higher than last year. Building the budget after the campaign takes the lid off potential increases by eliminating the fair-share, dues-paying syndrome and by eliminating the inevitable negative reaction everyone has to one or two items in the printed budget proposal."

Church finance committees are finding it hard to leave the old methodology behind. There are tremendous forces shouting, "We've always prepared our annual budget before the stewardship campaign." There are three or four people on your finance committee who have always relied on first discovering if the proposed budget contains a 2 percent or a 3 percent increase before deciding what percentage to increase their personal annual giving. There are also three or four people on your finance committee who believe that the proposed budget itself is a powerful tool for encouraging every parishioner to give. For years the theme of your finance committee has been, "Your church needs money to accomplish the ministries described in our budget. Please give generously so that these ministries can be accomplished."

Imagine a new paradigm where you build your stewardship program, not on the church's need for money, but rather on each parishioner's need to give. Imagine the primary theme of your stewardship program, year after year, to be "What percentage of your income do you feel God is calling you to give?" Imagine discovering the amount of financial support the Lord is going to provide through your parishioners, and then deciding the best way to use those resources to serve the Lord. Imagine using the total of these commitment cards, subtracting anticipated shortfall and adding anticipated loose-plate offerings, in preparing your budget for the new year.

It is indeed time for this new paradigm to become your church's paradigm.

In an earlier "Nuts & Bolts: Common Pitfalls" article I shared research that supports the fruitfulness of this "percentage-giving" model. There are their practical reasons to make this shift.

More compelling for me, however, is the fact that faithful stewardship is a vital part of each individual's journey toward becoming a deeply devoted disciple of Jesus Christ. As a church, we should be inviting our parishioners to stop being luke-warm, to stop 'sitting on the fence,' and to reengage in the journey toward faithfully following the Lord in every facet of our lives, hearts, hands, and homes. With equal energy we should be inviting our parishioners to grow in their prayers life, worship life, love of the scriptures, financial giving growing to the biblical minimum standard of the 10 percent tithe, giving our time to serve the Lord by the strength of our hands and the sweat of our brow, and inviting others in a winsome

 © 2018 Robert O. Crossman, www.UMNewChurch.org

way to join us in this journey to the cross.

Imagine a finance committee that discovers the amount of financial resources the Lord is going to provide in the coming year, and then deciding the best way to use those resources to serve and honor the Lord. It's time for all of us to focus – not on simply paying the church's bill – but rather to discover "What percentage of my income do you feel God is calling me to give?"

†††

NOTE: This article reflects the personal opinions of its author and does not necessarily reflect an official position of Discipleship Ministries or Path 1

Committed to Christ: Six Steps to a Generous Life
by Bob Crossman

Boxed Kit• Program Guide w/ CD
Adult Reading and Study Book • DVD
Small Group Leader's Guide • 40 Devotions Booklet

Order at: cokesbury.com or from your favorite bookstore.

New Church Handbook
Nuts & Bolts for Planting New Churches In The Wesleyan Tradition

"Stewardship: Common Pitfalls to Avoid"

by Bob Crossman

If you want to strengthen your congregations' financial stewardship, there are several pitfalls to avoid.

1. Focusing on Shortfall

In the vast majority of Christian Churches, in particular the small congregations, the only financial stewardship emphasis occurs when the church treasurer announces in the one adult Sunday School class that there is not enough in the church's checking account to fill the propane tank (or pay the preacher) this week. This may be the most common stewardship pitfall, but it is certainly not the only one.

2. Rattling the Cup

The second most common stewardship pitfall is to rely entirely on the physical presence of an offering plate or basket, as a non-verbal invitation to be faithful financial stewards. In the landmark book Money Matters: Personal Giving in American Churches, Dean R. Hoge and his colleagues report that churches fall into three general categories regarding how they ask parishioners to contribute money.

The first category is called an offerings church. These churches do not hold an annual financial stewardship campaign. The parishioners are simply invited to respond to the offering plate each week. In these churches, parishioners on average give 1.5% of their income to the church.

A second category is called a pledging church. In these churches, the leadership prepares an annual budget. Parishioners are then asked to give financial resources to support the budget. The message is: Your church needs money to accomplish the ministries described in our budget. Please give generously so that these ministries can be accomplished. In pledging churches, parishioners on average give 2.9% of their income to their church—about twice as much as in churches that do not ask their parishioners to pledge. In other words, research has shown that when a church asks parishioners to write their financial intentions on a pledge card and turn it into the church office, on average the parishioners will give twice as much as churches who no not ask their parishioners to pledge.

 © 2018 Robert O. Crossman, www.UMNewChurch.org

There is a third, and more fruitful way to ask parishioners to contribute money. This method is called the percentage-giving church. In these churches, instead of preparing an annual budget first and asking parishioners to support it, the church first conducts an annual stewardship campaign that asks parishioners: What percentage of your income do you feel God is calling you to give? Parishioners decide the percentage, translate it into a dollar amount, and write the dollar amount on a commitment card. The church then uses the total of these commitment cards, subtracting anticipated shortfall and adding anticipated loose-plate offerings, in preparing its budget.

In The New Consecration Sunday, Herb Miller says that in percentage-giving churches, parishioners are not asked to pay the bills or support the budget—rather, they are asked to grow spiritually, giving a percentage of their income to the work of the Lord through their congregation. In these percentage-giving churches, parishioners on average give 4.6% of their income to their church—about three times more per year than in churches that only rely on passing the offering plate. In other words, research has shown that when churches annually ask, "What percentage of your income do you feel God is calling you to give?," parishioners on average give three times more dollars per year than in churches that only rely on passing the offering plate.

3. Taking the Top-Down Approach

There is a third common pitfall in both the pledging and percentage giving congregations: For any stewardship campaign to succeed, it must truly be a congregational effort, with many people involved at several different levels. Bad Idea: The entire program will be "run" by the pastor and office assistant, with a lay figurehead willing to have letters sent over their signature. Good Idea: The program will involve 10% to 20% of the active congregation to play some level of leadership. Instead of looking for ways to simplify and fast-track the campaign, the stewardship campaign will be far more effective and fruitful if ways are explored to involve more people in the process.

Lovett Weems, in *"50 Ways to Improve Your Annual Stewardship Program"* suggests several ways to increase the lay participation in the annual financial emphasis.

- Be strategic in building a leadership team. Involve a large group of people to build their sense of ownership in the outcome.
- Include persons from different age groups and different ministry areas.
- Be sure that the generous givers of the congregation are well represented on the stewardship team and other groups related to the church's funding just as you would be sure to include those most active in other ministry areas as you plan for those ministries.

4. Communicating Poorly

A fourth common pitfall is poor communication. Fruitful stewardship campaigns have a comprehensive communication strategy using sermons, personal testimonies in worship and small groups, worship bulletins, bulletin boards, direct mail, e-newsletter articles, banners, web site, blogs, Twitter, Facebook, and other social media. Tailor messages for the likely audience of each medium, but be consistent in your design and overall vision.

5. Failing to Cast a Vision

A fifth common pitfall relates to the content of our communication. In the past, churches have assumed that parishioners will increase their financial support of the church if we simply give them more information about the churches budget. In Not Your Parents' Offering Plate, Clif Christopher helps pastors understand that the primary reason people give their financial resources is to be a part of the church's mission to change lives. He suggests that "most of our worship services would be greatly improved if five minutes of anything was replaced with five minutes of testimony, either video or live, each week. Our newsletters and websites would finally become effective if we would get all the announcements out and substitute one person's testimony of how Christ, through the church, changed his or her life."

NOTE: This article reflects the personal opinions of its author and does not necessarily reflect an official position of Discipleship Ministries or Path 1

Committed to Christ: Six Steps to a Generous Life
by Bob Crossman
Boxed Kit• Program Guide w/ CD
Adult Reading and Study Book • DVD
Small Group Leader's Guide • 40 Devotions Booklet
Order at: cokesbury.com or from your favorite bookstore.

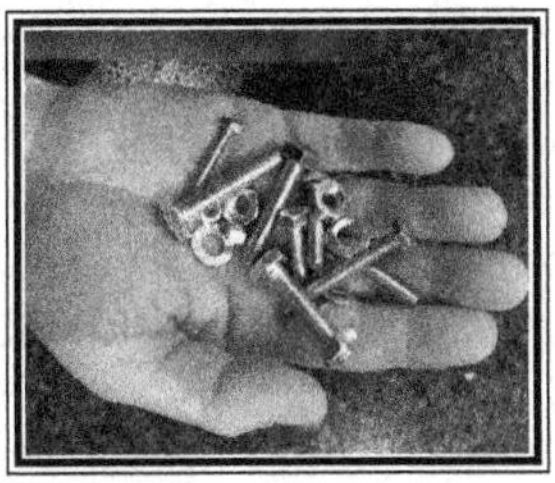

New Church Handbook
Nuts & Bolts for Planting New Churches In The Wesleyan Tradition

"Stewardship & Vitality Go Hand in Hand"

by Bob Crossman

Has your offering plate been emptier this year? If your church is typical, the offering this year was smaller than in the previous year. Adjusted for inflation, giving to religious organizations has been declining annually for decades.

Why?

It's not simply due to a downturn in the national economy. The Giving USA 2012 Report by Bill Enright points to several larger issues. He suggests the five issues that have affected local church giving include:

- A decline in both church attendance and formal institutional membership.
- Generational shifts in religious practice, participation and styles of giving.
- Dominance of large congregations as the church of choice of attendees (the larger the congregation, the greater the number of "free riders"—people who attend but do not give).
- Silence of religious leaders and congregations in talking and teaching about the faithful use of possessions apart from the annual obligatory stewardship or giving sermon.
- Failure to adapt best fund raising practices to congregational life, leaving congregations dependent on an outmoded, one-dimensional approach to giving.

Local church leaders may be tempted to shrug their shoulders and hope that giving will increase someday as the local economy rebounds. I want to suggest that a different response may bear more fruit.

First of all, be proactive about increasing weekly worship attendance. There are a few deeply devoted disciples who give by automatic draft, or who will double their gift if they were absent last Sunday. However, a great number of church attenders only give to the church on the Sundays they attend worship. You may have noticed that your offering was often larger on large attendance Sundays this summer. On the Lewis Center web site (www.churchleadership.com), I've listed 50 ways church leadership can be proactive about increasing worship attendance.

Second, be proactive about helping your congregation to get control of their personal financial lives. Church attenders who are being crushed by credit card debt find it very difficult to increase their giving on Sunday. Churches that repeatedly offer *"Financial Peace University"* by Dave Ramsay, or *"Crown Financial Ministries"* are discovering that marriages are strengthened, home environments are improved, and participants are inspired and empowered to financially support the church they love and attend.

Third, be proactive about electronic ways to give to your church. There is an increasing number of people who do not carry cash and do not have a checkbook. Instead, they do all their financial transactions electronically. If the only way to give to your church is to place cash or a check in the offering plate, you are making it very difficult for an increasing number of your attendees to make financial gifts.

Fourth, be proactive about inviting new attendees or new members to journey toward becoming deeply devoted disciples. Consider an intentional move toward becoming a high expectation church that clearly expresses the expectations through sermon, website, blogs, Twitter, and most importantly through a four to six week class that all newcomers are directed to attend.

Finally, be proactive about finding an annual way to invite your congregation to grow, step by step, across a broad range of discipleship areas that include financial giving. Committed to Christ: Six Steps to A Generous Life by Abingdon Press is a powerful invitation for every person in your congregation to enter into, or re-engage, in a journey toward becoming a deeply devoted disciple of Jesus Christ. It carries the potential to transform every household and the church itself. The "generous life" engendered by the program involves having the people of your church live and serve in the saving grace of the Lord, not as an obligation but as a joyous response. The program's holistic, six-step invitation is closer to the broad range of the Lord's high expectations for those who seek to follow faithfully: prayer, Bible reading, worship attendance, service, financial giving, and witness. These six primary comments are worthy of giving one's life to.

A recent study in one faith tradition has shown some of the benefits of having lay leadership exhibit such signs of vital personal faith. A church with leadership exhibiting these signs is 48% more likely to be a high attendance church; 54% more likely to be a high growth church; 30% more likely to be a high engagement church; and 84% more likely to be a high "vital" church.

Churches with a high level of vitality are rare. In the typical congregation, it

 © 2018 Robert O. Crossman, www.UMNewChurch.org

seems that only a small portion of the congregation is actively engaged and striving to become faithful disciples of Jesus Christ; in contrast, the vast majority of the typical congregation seems to be more passive or lukewarm in their response. The same study cited above found that only 15% of its churches in the United States were high vitality; 49% were medium vitality; and 36% were found to have low vitality.

"Committed to Christ: Six Steps to A Generous Life" invites every household in the congregation to take at least one step in six different areas, beginning with a growing commitment to Jesus Christ. Through these six invitations, you can lay the foundation for the vitality of your church to surge forward as commitments are made and kept.

†††

NOTE: This article reflects the personal opinions of its author and does not necessarily reflect an official position of Discipleship Ministries or Path 1

"Committed to Christ: Six Steps to a Generous Life"
by Bob Crossman
Boxed Kit• Program Guide w/ CD
Adult Reading and Study Book • DVD
Small Group Leader's Guide • 40 Devotions Booklet

Order at: cokesbury.com or from your favorite bookstore.

New Church Handbook
Nuts & Bolts for Planting New Churches In The Wesleyan Tradition

"Stewardship: 26 Ways to Improve Your Annual Stewardship Program"

by Bob Crossman

Year Round

A. Teach, preach and practice holistic stewardship. Stewardship is about our relationship with God, it is NOT about paying the church bills, NOR simply something we slipped into the membership vows. Financial giving is a part of what it means to be a deeply devoted disciple – right alongside of prayer, bible study, faithful worship attendance, hands on service, and witnessing. These are the fruits that follow a commitment to Christ. Stewardship is about Sanctification, it is about Holy Living, it is about following Jesus.

B. Teach, preach that stewardship is a joyful response to God's generosity. The tithe is not a tax, nor a clever way to pay the church's bills.

C. While the ushers are coming to the front, use that 45 seconds to share a story of a changed life in the church. People give to change lives, not to pay the bills.

"On Wednesday, Jennifer asked me to read a Bible story during our after school program. Little kindergartner Blake Grayson, sat right next to me. While I held the Bible in my lap, waiting for the other children to gather, Blake reached over and gently touched the Bible. He whispered to me –Preacher, I love the Bible. His simple words touched me, and it took me a moment to gain my composure before I could read to the children. Thank you! Thank you for supporting this church with your generous gifts. Your gifts are making a difference right here with our children – and in missions we support in a 100 countries around this world. Thank you."

Tell stories of how lives have been changed because of their giving. People need to know their giving makes a difference.

D. The offering should be a high and holy moment within every worship service. It is not a necessary evil. It is not fund raising. It is an act of worship, responding to free gift of God's grace.

 © 2018 Robert O. Crossman, www.UMNewChurch.org

E. Set a good example – the offering plate should be seen passing through the band, choir, instrumentalist, and pastors on stage. The congregation needs to see the pastor placing a gift in the offering plate in every worship service.

The Annual Program Itself

F. Choose a time of year when there is a high probability of connecting with the most people. Often this is October/November. It could also be mid-January/February.

G. Set a realistic time line. In a large church, planning and implementation can take six months or more.

H. Avoid the temptation to rush this through. If you are asking your current givers to consider increasing their gift – they need time for those discussions at home. If you are asking people to consider giving for the first time in their lives – they need time for those discussions at home. Preachers, I know your sermons are the best in the country – however your congregation will not make this important of a discussion, and stick to it, on the spur of the moment in the closing moments of your sermon.

I. Avoid the temptation to have your annual program stand alone. It should be part of a year-round approach to stewardship and stewardship education.

J. Be realistic about your expectations from the annual program. Increases in giving are typically incremental – not astronomical.

K. The goal is NOT equal gifts. NEVER divide the budget by the number of households and say, "If everyone would give $5,000…" Such comments are counter productive – it does not inspire the non-giver to start, and it may give permission for your most generous givers to cut back on their giving because you have just asked them to! Remember that in Jesus' math, the goal IS equal sacrifice. The widow's $30 may represent a 10% tithe of her resources that week. The profession couples $30 may represent less than 1% of their resources that week.

L. Put together a team to lead each annual campaign. For any stewardship campaign to succeed, it must truly be a congregational effort, with many people involved at several different levels. The program will involve 10% to 20% of the active congregation to play some level of leadership. Instead of looking for ways to simplify and fast-track the campaign, the stewardship campaign will be far more effective and fruitful if ways are explored to involve more people in the process. It would be a **bad idea** for the entire program to be "run" by the pastor and office assistant, with a lay figurehead willing to have letters sent over their signature.

M. The team leader should be a faithful giver, preferably someone who tithes at least 10% of their income.

N. The team should include every age level, and the different active ministry areas of your church all designed to help build a sense of ownership in the outcome.

O. The team should include the generous givers of your church.

P. Ask the team members to make their pledges first. As leaders, ask them to lead in this way as a sign of their commitment and to encourage the balance of the congregation.

Q. Ask the team to be a part of your comprehensive communication strategy. Use every available method: sermons, music, testimony in worship, bulletins, newsletters, web site, twitter, facebook, blogs, bulletin boards, banners, and their testimony in each small group they are a part of.

R. Remember to actually ASK people to give, across all your communication mediums, including the sermon. Many never give because they have never been asked.

S. Remember the 90 / 10 rule. In almost every church 90% of the funds come from 10% of the congregation. Most of your new funds this year will also come from your current generous givers. They need your personal attention and relationship. Don't neglect the 90% - they need invitations to begin to grow toward the tithe, but it will be a 6 to 8 year process.

T. Make giving my automatic withdrawal from checking accounts simple for persons to choose when making their pledges. Understand the financial patterns in your community. If very few people carry cash, an impulse offering will not work. Remember that older women are more likely to carry a checkbook than older men,. Younger generations do not carry checkbooks, or even have one, since they are more inclined to pay electronically. A 25 year old is not likely to make a gift of stock, while an older member might be interested in an estate gift.

U. Be positive in everything you communicate. People respond to positive language. Few people will give generously to a church in financial distress that communicates that it is about to close.

© 2018 Robert O. Crossman, www.UMNewChurch.org

Follow Through

V. Send a personalized thank you letter immediately after the program. Do not send a "Dear member" form letter. Send a personal typed or better yet, a hand written note.

W. Through the year, find multiple occasions to say "thank you" and report on changed lives because of their giving - in the sermons, newsletters, blogs, website and bulletins.

X. Prepare the budget AFTER your stewardship program. The Lord has just revealed your anticipated income, so set the budget accordingly. Use the total of the commitment cards, subtract anticipated shortfall and add anticipated loose-plate offerings, in preparing the budget.

Y. Once the detailed budget is prepared, make it available to all who ask, but do NOT mail it to everyone. Instead, prepare a Missional Budget, that in narrative form indicates that $80,000 provides meaningful, life-changing worship each week; $37,000 nurtures persons in their faith journey; and $83,000 to witness to our faith in service beyond ourselves; totaling $200,000 to fulfill our mission of "Changing Lives for Christ."

Z. With the quarterly statements, have it look more like a thank you letter than a bill from VISA.

†††

NOTE: This article reflects the personal opinions of its author and does not necessarily reflect an official position of Discipleship Ministries or Path 1

Committed to Christ: Six Steps to a Generous Life, by Bob Crossman
Boxed Kit• Program Guide w/ CD
Adult Reading and Study Book • DVD
Small Group Leader's Guide • 40 Devotions Booklet
Order at: cokesbury.com or from your favorite bookstore.

© 2018 Robert O. Crossman, www.UMNewChurch.org

XII. Appendix For Judicatories

The articles that follow are written with District Superintendents and Conference Staff in mind.

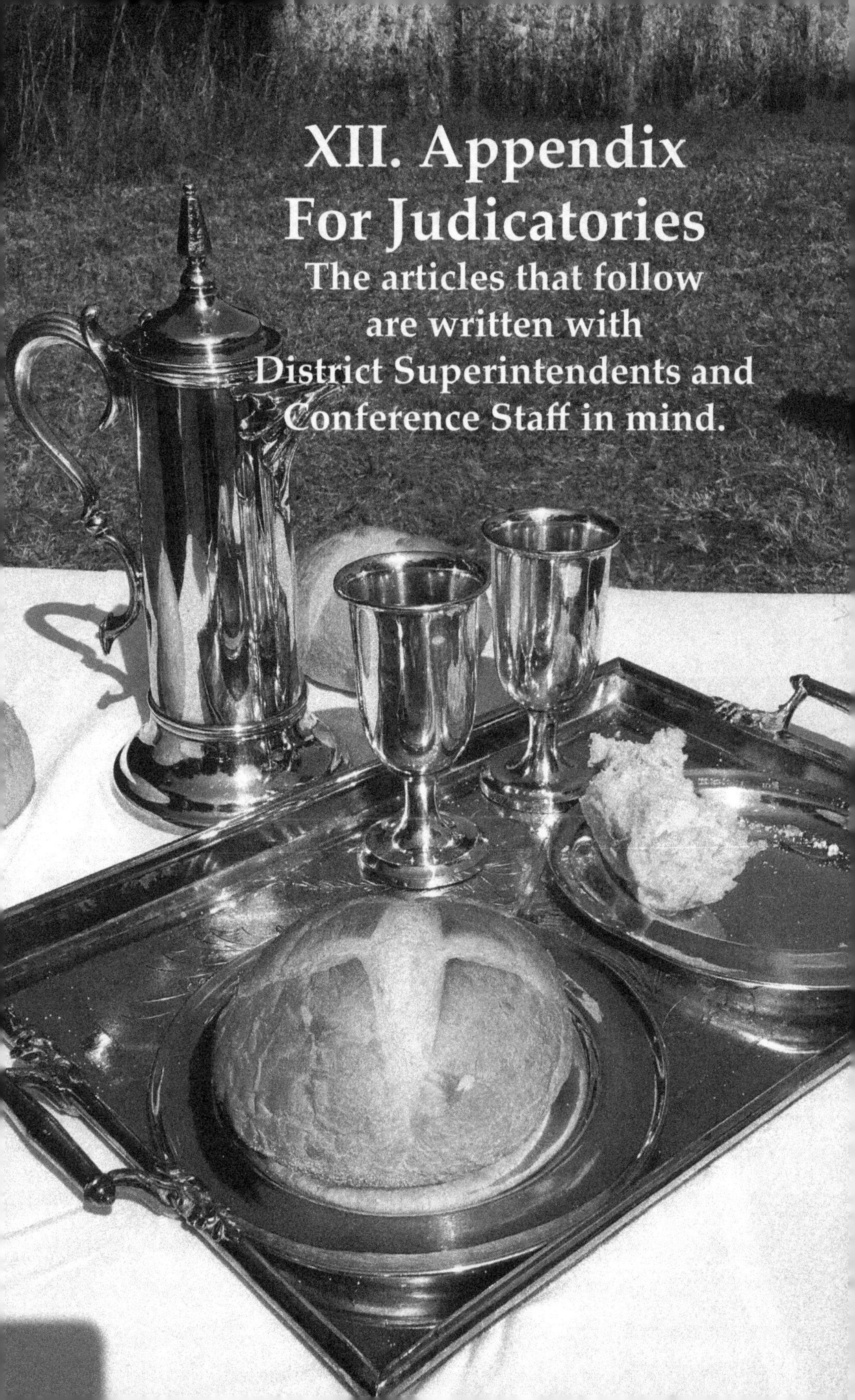

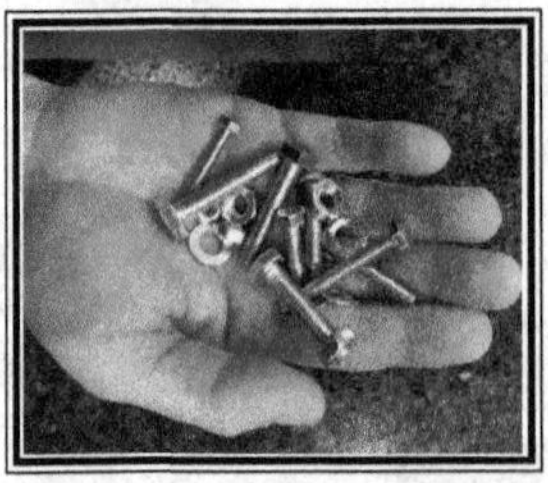

New Church Handbook
Nuts & Bolts for Planting New Churches In The Wesleyan Tradition

"21 Ways to Create A Church Planting Culture in Your Conference"

by Bob Crossman

- You may have heard about the Council of Bishops' desire to focus the resources of the entire church on our mission of making disciples of Jesus Christ, designating their #1 Vision Pathway to be "developing new congregations." (November, 2005)

- You may have heard about the Connectional Table's Four Provocative Proposals, including "create a strategy to develop new congregations." (November, 2006)

- You may have heard about the General Conference's Four Foci, including starting new churches.

- You may have heard about the Connectional Table's desire to move toward starting "one new church a day" (365 per year).

What would a positive church-planting culture look like?

A Few of the Bishops of the United Methodist Church

- I dream of the day when all United Methodist new church planters are supported prayerfully, relationally, and financially by their bishop, district superintendent, conference staff, every clergy in the annual conference, and every local church council and lay leader in their district.

 © 2018 Robert O. Crossman, www.UMNewChurch.org

I dream of the day when no United Methodist church planter feels alone or unsupported on the day appointments are read at annual conference (or two years into the new church start appointment).

I dream of the day when the term "parachute drop" is accurately and truthfully replaced with the term "connectional" church start - because we are truly connectional.

I dream of the day when it may truthfully be said, *"No denomination stands behind its planters as well as the United Methodist Church does."*

I dream of the day when pastors are calling their district superintendent, asking, *"May I be trained to be a church planter?"*

I dream of the day when local churches are calling their district superintendent requesting, *"Please start a new church in our town so we can work together to reach more people, more diverse people, and more younger people for Jesus Christ."*

I dream of the day when we are more "connectional" when it comes to starting and supporting new churches in every annual conference, even sharing planters and resources across conference lines.

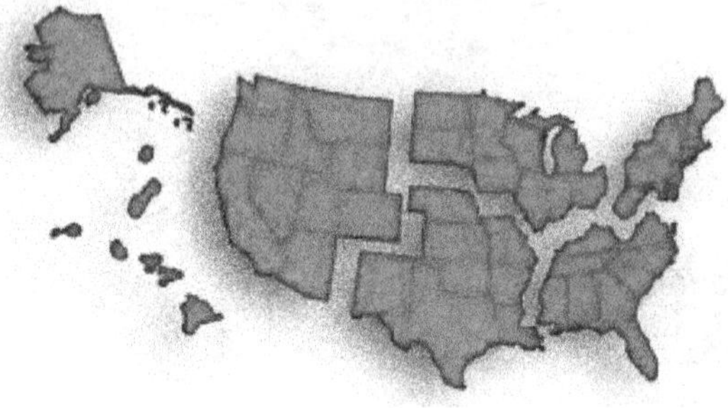

GREAT DREAM!

Let's start new churches! Lots of churches!

Let's increase our pace from 120 per year to 365 per year!

How do we decide which path to take to reach that goal?

...when all the possible roads seem a bit confusing?

 © 2018 Robert O. Crossman, www.UMNewChurch.org

...with so many different signs calling for our attention?

... feels like attempting to nail Jello to a tree...

or, trying to teach an elephant to play chess with a mouse...
or like trying to heard cats.

One place you might begin is to move toward changing:

- The way your conference thinks about idea of starting new churches.
- To change the conference culture.
- The level of emotional support.
- The very DNA of your annual conference.

A Few of the Bishops of the United Methodist Church

I do not know how to change the new-church-planting culture of your conference. However, many annual conferences have successfully changed their new-church-planting culture. Perhaps in hearing pieces of these stories, you will discern key elements that will need to be in place to change the new-church-planting culture of your conference.

In almost every case, THE ROLE OF THE BISHOP was central to this transformation. Often the story I hear goes something like this:

#1 When our newly elected bishop looked at the LONG LIST of their duties and responsibilities, they decided that New Church Planting would be one of their top personal priorities for their tenure as bishop.

They communicate that personal decision in many different ways...

#2 The bishop decided to communicate THAT personal priority through their Episcopal Address at the annual conference Sessions - the single time they have the most contact with pastors and lay members.

#3 The bishop decided to communicate that personal priority through WEEKLY COLUMNS in the conference newspaper, and e-news.

An Occasional Word
from the Bishop

Charles Crutchfield

Dear Friends,

As I write, it is the week following Easter. "Low Sunday" approaches. So called, I suppose because the attendance is down, the offering is down, and spirits are exhausted following the spiritual high of the Resurrection Sunday. I think of Elijah every year during this week. He experienced such a great triumph on Mount Carmel in the contests with the priests of Baal. He had once again stuck his finger in the eye of Jezebel. He was victorious by every account, and yet the scriptures record he went into a "blue funk" (my words not the Bible's), laid down to die under a juniper bush or a broom tree (check your translation!), and then off to hide in a cave. He was convinced that he was all alone in his loyalty and faithfulness to God. God told him to there were a bunch more where he came from and to get off his pity-pot and get to work.

It is a great story about the depression that can follow great victories. It is a reminder to us that the work of the Kingdom is not all Palm Sundays, Christmas Eves and Easters. The work of the Kingdom of God is with God's everyday people in the valleys of life, not just God's holiday triumphs on the mountain tops. In the end the lesson Elijah learned is that the difference is made in whom you trust. Can you trust God to see you through "low Sunday" or "low Monday" or "low Friday"?

Just as Jesus was born in the muck and mud of a stable, so the Risen Christ returns not to the palaces or courts of kings but to individuals blinded by fear and grief, or to friends who having run from him in the hour of his need now run away to go fishing. The Risen Christ comes to the commonplace in human experience. Do we trust the Savior who offers his hand to walk with us through lonesome valleys and deserts of heartbreak? After "the tumult and the shouting dies, the captains and the kings depart" who do you trust?

Elijah found his answer in the "still small voice."

Thomas found his answer in the wounds of Christ.

Peter found his answer in the one who asked "do you love me?"

Who do you trust?

Faithfully,

 © 2018 Robert O. Crossman, www.UMNewChurch.org

#4 The bishop made it clear to the **appointive cabinet** that new church planting was one of their top priorities.

#5 In their relationships with the **conference lay leader, CFA, key laity, and key clergy leadership** - the bishop makes it clear that new church planting was one of their top priorities.

#6 The bishop also solicited official and formal support from the Conference Council (Leadership Team), and the Conference Council on Finance and Administration.

#7 The bishop used their other points of influence - sermons, clergy clusters, seminary visits, major donors, etc. to communicate that starting new churches was one of their top priorities.

Appointments

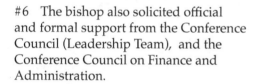

#8 The bishop decided that the new church appointments would be among the very first appointments made every February. You might describe this as,

"first fruit appointments or missional appoints and not leftover appointments for new church settings."

The stories I hear also involve THE VITAL ROLE THE DISTRICT SUPERINTENDENTS played...

#9 It's not uncommon to hear, *"Several of our district superintendents decided that new church planting was one of their top personal priorities during their tenure."*

#10 And, *"Several of our district superintendents established a District Apportionment to start new churches* (ranging from about $1/member to $4/member in existing churches)."

#11 And, "Every October, our cabinet discerned a list of potential new church pastors for a possible new church appointment for each of the next four years...

#12 And *"Every December the extended cabinet reviewed and perfected a list of potential new church communities looking five years into the future."*

#13 And, *"Our cabinet agreed with the bishop that the New Church Appointments would be among the very first made each year."*

The stories I hear also involve the vital role the LAY LEADERSHIP played...

 © 2018 Robert O. Crossman, www.UMNewChurch.org

#14 For the culture of the conference to change, the conference council and the conference council on finance and administration (CFA) played a vital role. The conference council officially set 'new church starts' as one of their top strategic initiatives. The CFA established a new apportionment line item for new church starts, and approved an annual special offering among the congregations.

The stories of conference culture change are also vitally connected to decisions and actions of the DIRECTOR OF CONNECTIONAL MINISTRIES (DCM) and the NEW CHURCH CONFERENCE STAFF person.

#15 The DCM decided that new church planting was one of their personal priorities for their tenure of service.

#16 The DCM kept in constant contact with the cabinet and bishop - *(the only ones with the Disciplinary authority to start a new church.)*

#17 The DCM designated a staff person to be responsible for new church starts.

#18 The conference new church staff person proposed to the DCM and cabinet a comprehensive plan for discerning potential sites and the training, assessing, appointing, and supporting of new church pastors.

#19 The conference new church staff person held annual "Fishing expeditions" in each District.

#20 At the annual conference session, the New Church staff person sponsored new church luncheons, displays, recognition of new churches, and a new church report was printed in the conference journal.

#21 The New Church staff person also utilized the conference newspaper and enews with major articles and blogs in several of the spring editions before annual conference met.

#22 Following Steve Compton's model, the conference researched the history of church planting in their conference.

For example, the Arkansas conference research revealed:

- Between 1968 - 2003 Arkansas had attempted 41 new church starts, including 7 in non-anglo contexts.
- They discovered 83% of these attempts survived.
- They discovered that 74% grew beyond 100 on Sunday, averaging 250 in attendance.
- They also discovered that among these new churches, they paid their apportionments at 99.3%, totaling about 1 million a year.

All of these facts were a great surprise. Before this research, no one knew these numbers and everyone believed that Arkansas had a horrible history of starting new churches, because they only remembered the starts that had failed.

It was said,
"The smoke from our failed new church attempts lingered in the air a long time."

So the invitation is this:

THINK THROUGH YOUR PLAN OF ACTION

- ***Is the starting of new churches one of the greatest opportunities for spiritual and numerical growth for your annual conference?***

- ***Is new church planting a vital part of your "clear vision" for the next quadrennium?***

- ***What is the biggest obstacle that keeps you from taking advantage of this opportunity?***

- ***As you think about the "new-church-start future," where do you hope your Conference will be three to five years from now?***

- ***To achieve this, what are the five most important things you need to do that will move your Conference towards becoming a New-Church-Start-Disciple-Making Community?***

1. ______________________________

2. ______________________________

3. ______________________________

4. ______________________________

5. ______________________________

What do you need to change about YOURSELF in order to help make these happen?

NOTE: This article reflects the personal opinions of its author and does not necessarily reflect an official position of Discipleship Ministries or Path 1

© 2018 Robert O. Crossman, www.UMNewChurch.org

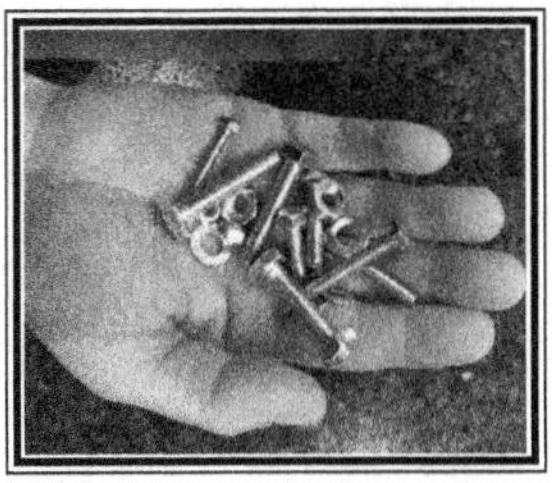

New Church Handbook
Nuts & Bolts for Planting New Churches In The Wesleyan Tradition

"Creating a Conference System For Planting New Churches"

by Bob Crossman

For United Methodist Conferences, the 2016 Book of Discipline gives the basic structure for a church planting system. (¶259, 247.22, 2520, 604.10, 633.5e, 642.4b)

Conferences that are successfully, fruitfully, and economically starting vital new churches have taken the basic structure provided by the discipline and have developed policies that clarify the process for planting in their particular mission field. These conference policies, while each are unique, address four basic questions.

1) What is a new church?

A clear answer to this question is valuable in deciding which projects to fund with new church apportion money. Many worthy new missions, ministries, and projects will request funds. A clear definition of a new church will help to determine which of these request are more appropriately funded by conference revitalization or transformation funds.

Most conferences have adapted the Path 1 definition of a new church to fit their particular mission field. The Path 1 definition includes these characteristics:

- Follow the theology of John Wesley.
- Gather frequently to worship.
- Celebrate the sacraments of baptism and Holy Communion.
- Make disciples through small-group covenant, spiritual formation, and mission.
- Teach and practice biblical stewardship of money and time.
- Engage in mission and works of peace and justice aimed toward community transformation.
- Welcome and encourage new disciples.
- Celebrate lay and clergy involvement.
- Foster a culture of ministry multiplication and commit to planting other new congregations within three to five years.
- Remain connected and accountable to The United Methodist Church.

Most conferences have expanded their understanding of what a new church is to include strategies such as: the typical suburban parachute drop, multi-sites of vital churches, launching a new church within closed church buildings, vital

© 2018 Robert O. Crossman, www.UMNewChurch.org

mergers; and a wide variety of micro communities to reach particular a niches within the mission field.

2) How will we discern, train, assess, appoint, and support new church pastors?

Most conferences have discovered that the typical appointive cabinet process for deploying pastors to local churches, is **inadequate** for the deployment of pastors to the specialized field of starting new faith communities.

Beginning with the district board of ordained ministry, be sensitive to the entrepreneurial and high energy characteristics of fruitful new church planters. Develop a clarity how those characteristics contrast with the characteristics of successful turn-around pastors, pastors of fast growing congregations, and hospice pastors.

Successful planting conferences also host several systems for discovering potential church planters that include:

- Introductory events at the annual conference session.
- District level introductory events.
- Use of Path 1's Lay Missionary Planting Network nine month training/discernment process.
- Personal contact by district superintendents.
- Seminary visits.

All of these facets are seeking to discover who the Prevenient Grace of God is already preparing to start new United Methodist churches.

Fruitful conferences have also discovered the advantage of offering pre-appointment training to potential planters. These training events, cohorts, incubators, academies are often modeled after the New Church Leadership Institute (NCLI) that I designed. These pre-appointment trainings have the following purpose:

- Help potential planters to discern if they are gifted and called to this unique ministry.
- Help the conference congregational developer to begin assessing the potential planters.
- Reduces the number of planters who make "fatal" mistakes in the first month.
- Enables the planter to fruitfully "hit-the-ground-running" instead of spending the first year trying to decide how to proceed.

After attending these pre-appointment trainings each participant should be required to submit a self-reflective essay to their district superintendent and conference congregational developer.

 © 2018 Robert O. Crossman, www.UMNewChurch.org

Vital planting conferences have also found that a formal de-briefing assessment interview with each potential planter after attending the discernment event helps to clarify the planters gifts, and the particular affinity group in which this planter might fruitfully launch a new church.

Years ago conferences believed that location was primary, and that ANY pastor could plant a new church if the right property were purchased. From Clay Jacobs in the North Georgia Conference, we have learned that it is not location, but instead that new church pastoral leadership is THE critical factor.

"We have discovered in North Georgia
that the most important piece in church planting is leadership.
If the pastor is called by God to this new work,
has a passion for reaching unchurched people,
has a commitment to unconditional excellence,
and possesses the unique set of church planting gifts and graces -
this pastor will draw people to Christ,
even in the desert."

Clay Jacobs

A new facet within most conference church planting policies includes a post-appointment pre-moving day strategy session with the planter and the stakeholders of the project. This session helps to clarify in writing the plan, grants, and benchmarks for the project.

As a follow-up to this strategy session, for the first year or two, quarterly on-site strategy review sessions are held with the planter, the planters launch team, and the stakeholders of the project.

3) Where will we start new churches?

Most conferences are developing systems and policies to discern where the Prevenient Grace of God is already preparing a community to receiving a new church. These systems might include:

- The district superintendent as district mission strategist considering repurposing empty or near empty church buildings.
- District boards of church location and building (¶259.2, 247.21) formal recommendation of "areas" approved for planting.
- The District Lay Leaders.
- Local church charge conferences that express a desire to plant multi-sites or sponsor a new start.
- Demographic studies to determine population growth mission fields, under-served mission fields, and testing those demographic reports by physically walking and driving through the potential new church communities.

Path 1 has a system called "Church Planting Zone" where a local team meets to discern and recommend the planting of a cluster of new faith communities within a particular district, county, or metropolitan area. All of these systems are designed to listen for the movement of the Holy Spirit, and not just to the "squeaky wheel" when deciding where to plant a new church.

4) How will we support our new church planters in the field?

Conferences have discovered that the typical support systems for pastors in traditional appointments are inadequate for the highly stressful appointment of planting a new church.

Planter support systems typically include:

- A two to five year relationship with a trained coach at least until the new plant is viable and stable. A list of potential new church coaches are available from Path 1.
- Weekly prayer team from outside the new congregation.
- Quarterly strategy review sessions mentioned above.
- Peer groups of other church planters.
- Attending the School of Congregational Development annually.
- If the agreed upon benchmarks are met, the financial support from the conference, district and sponsoring congregations declines over a scheduled 3 to 8 year period.
- Planter completes Tables I, II, III, and IV at the end of each year so that the conference can account for the baptisms, new members, and financial progress of the new church.
- Most importantly, appointive cabinets actually follow the new church policies and procedures they have developed.

A PDF version of the following flow chart is available from Bob Crossman at bcrossman@arumc.org

This blog previously appeared in:
"5 ways you can better equip Vital Congregations from GBOD (August 2014)" and at ***www.bcrossman.org***

†††

NOTE: This article reflects the personal opinions of its author and does not necessarily reflect an official position of Discipleship Ministries or Path 1

 © 2018 Robert O. Crossman, www.UMNewChurch.org

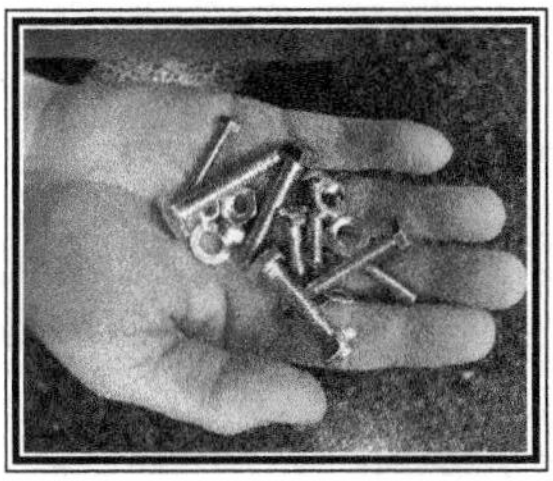

New Church Handbook
Nuts & Bolts for Planting New Churches In The Wesleyan Tradition

"Flow Chart for Conference Systems"

by Bob Crossman

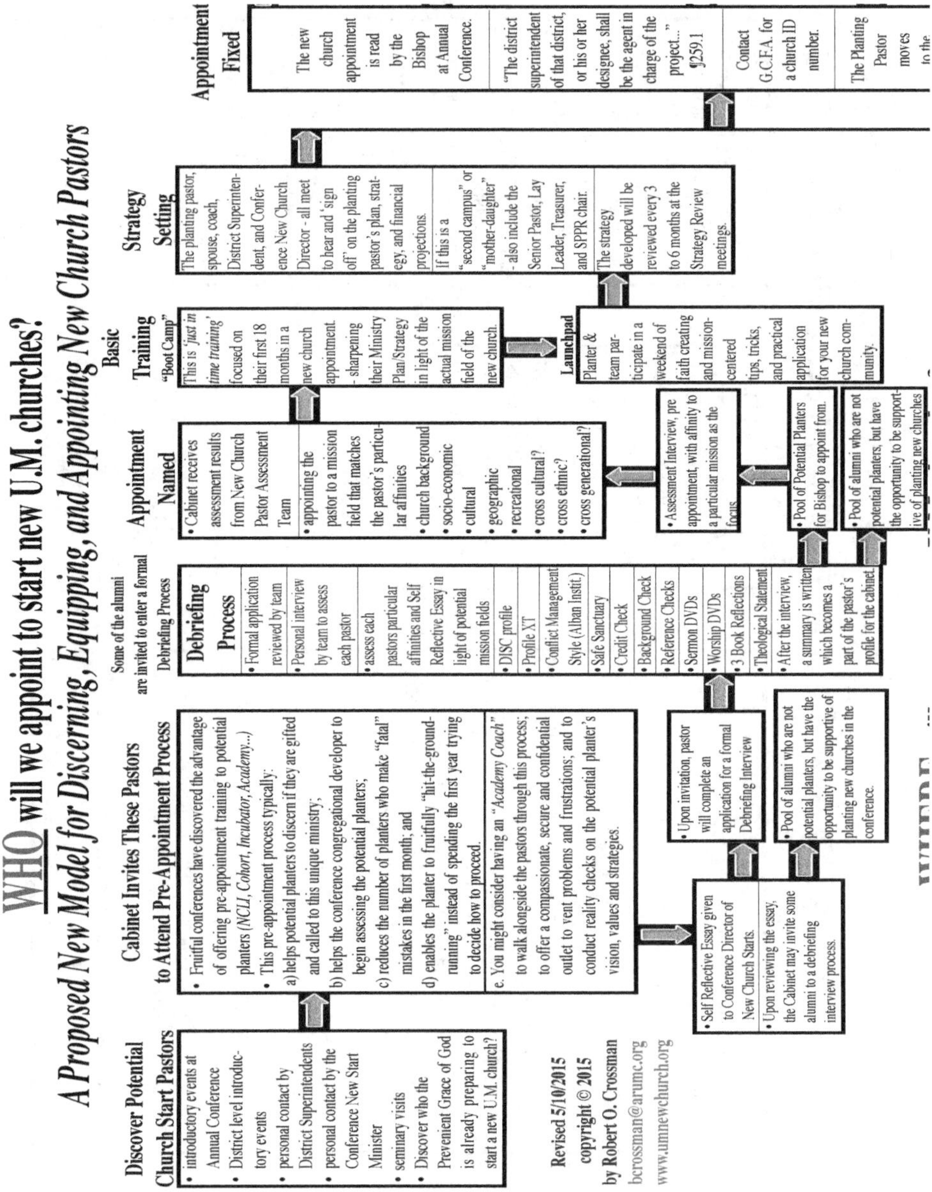

WHO will we appoint to start new U.M. churches?
A Proposed New Model for Discerning, Equipping, and Appointing New Church Pastors
Discover Potential Church Start Pastors
• introductory events at Annual Conference
• District level introductory events
• personal contact by District Superintendents
• personal contact by the Conference New Start Minister
• seminary visits
• Discover who the Prevenient Grace of God is already preparing to start a new U.M. church?
Cabinet Invites These Pastors to Attend Pre-Appointment Process
• Fruitful conferences have discovered the advantage of offering pre-appointment training to potential planters (NCLI, Cohort, Incubator, Academy...)
• This pre-appointment process typically:
a) helps potential planters to discern if they are gifted and called to this unique ministry;
b) helps the conference congregational developer to begin assessing the potential planters;
c) reduces the number of planters who make "fatal" mistakes in the first month; and
d) enables the planter to fruitfully "hit-the-ground-running" instead of spending the first year trying to decide how to proceed.
e. You might consider having an "Academy Coach" to walk alongside the pastors through this process; to offer a compassionate, secure and confidential outlet to vent problems and frustrations; and to conduct reality checks on the potential planter's vision, values and strategies.
• Self Reflective Essay given to Conference Director of New Church Starts.
• Upon reviewing the essay, the Cabinet may invite some alumni to a debriefing interview process.
• Upon invitation, pastor will complete an application for a formal Debriefing Interview
• Pool of alumni who are not potential planters, but have the opportunity to be supportive of planting new churches in the conference.
Some of the alumni are invited to enter a formal Debriefing Process
Debriefing Process
• Formal application reviewed by team
• Personal interview by team to assess each pastor
• assess each pastors particular affinities and Self Reflective Essay in light of potential mission fields
• DISC profile
• Profile XT
• Conflict Management Style (Alban Instit.)
• Safe Sanctuary
• Credit Check
• Background Check
• Reference Checks
• Sermon DVDs
• Worship DVDs
• 3 Book Reflections
• Theological Statement
• After the interview, a summary is written which becomes a part of the pastor's profile for the cabinet.
• Pool of Potential Planters for Bishop to appoint from.
• Pool of alumni who are not potential planters, but have the opportunity to be supportive of planting new churches
• Assessment Interview, pre appointment, with affinity to a particular mission as the focus.
Appointment Named
• Cabinet receives assessment results from New Church Pastor Assessment Team
• appointing the pastor to a mission field that matches the pastor's particular affinities
• church background
• socio-economic
• cultural
• geographic
• recreational
• cross cultural?
• cross ethnic?
• cross generational?
Basic Training "Boot Camp"
This is 'just in time training' focused on their first 18 months in a new church appointment. - sharpening their Ministry Plan/Strategy in light of the actual mission field of the new church.
Launchpad
Planter & team participate in a weekend of faith creating and mission-centered tips, tricks, and practical application for your new church community.
Strategy Setting
The planting pastor, spouse, coach, District Superintendent, and Conference New Church Director - all meet to hear and 'sign off' on the planting pastor's plan, strategy, and financial projections.
If this is a "second campus" or "mother-daughter" - also include the Senior Pastor, Lay Leader, Treasurer, and SPPR chair.
The strategy developed will be reviewed every 3 to 6 months at the Strategy Review meetings.
Appointment Fixed
The new church appointment is read by the Bishop at Annual Conference.
"The district superintendent of that district, or his or her designee, shall be the agent in charge of the project..." ¶259.1
Contact G.C.F.A. for a church ID number.
The Planting Pastor moves to the
Revised 5/10/2015
copyright © 2015
by Robert O. Crossman
bcrossman@arumc.org
www.umnewchurch.org

WHERE will we start new U.M. churches?

A Proposed New Model for Discerning, Selecting & Prioritizing Potential Starts

Ongoing

- Pray to discern where the Prevenient Grace of God already preparing the soil of a mission field for the planting of a new UM church.
- Listen to the formal recommendation of "areas" from the District Board of Church Location and Building. (¶ 259.2 and ¶247.21)
- Listening to our District Leadership Teams & District Lay Leader for potential new church mission fields.
- Listening to local church Charge Conferences for signs of potential multi-site/mother/sponsoring churches.
- Demographic studies to determine potential mission fields:
  - *Where are our current UM churches located?*
  - *Are they growing in proportion to the population growth?*
  - *Any near empty buildings,size appropriate,where we might plant?*
  - *What counties have grown in the past 5 years?*
  - *What counties are projected to grow in the next 5 years?*
  - *What zip codes have grown in the past 5 years?*
  - *What zip codes are projected to grow in the next 5 years.*
  - *What zip codes do not currently have a UMC?*
    Are they being adequately served by nearby UMC?
    - *smaller populations where we might send a part-time pastor?*
    - *larger populations where we might send a full-time pastor?*
  - *What mission fields have we successfully saturated and we should avoid planting another faith community?*
- Test demographics by physically walking & driving through potential new church communities.
- Listen for the movement of the Holy Spirit, not just the "squeaky wheel."

→

Late Summer (Aug. /Sept.)

EXTENDED CABINET
(OR in some conferences, the New Church Dev. Team)

Where will we work to start new UMChurches during the next 2 to 5 years?

- prayer
- Prioritize these potential starts
- identifying specific locations
- identifying potential mother or sister churches in that community
- begin to identify potential planting pastor(s) for each site
- need factors
- readiness factors
- availability of financial resources *conference/district/ mother church*

Lord, do you want to start any new churches in this Conference? Help us to see where your Prevenient Grace is already at work preparing new missions fields to receive new church planting pastors. Are there any underserved communities where a small church of 100 might be started? Are there any ethnic populations that are underserved by the UMC? Lord, as you look 5 years into the future, where can you use to to begin the new church appointive process? Speak Lord, your servants are listening. Amen.

→

During following 12 months:

DS & Conference Minister of New Church Starts prepare the soil to receive the future new church planter.

- *called meetings with UM pastors in each potential community*
- *called meetings with pastors & lay leaders in each potential community*

Strategy for Each Site Is Determined

- parent-daughter / sister church
- multi-site
- connectional start/parachute
- "friendly" takeover
- micro community, ...

Main Campus or Sister Church?

- *Recommend use of "Readiness to Plant 360"* ***www. readiness360.info***
- *called meetings with leadership of potential mother/sister churches to invite and clarify levels of support they will provide the new church or new campus*

Obtain formal approval of the "area" from the District Board of Church Location and Building. (¶ 259.2 and ¶247.22)

→

Every November

Appointive Cabinet & Conference Minister of New Church Starts

- prioritize starts for this appointment cycle *(in some conferences, the New Church Dev. Committee makes recommendations)*
- receive results from New Church Pastor Assessment Team
- Develop profile for preferred pastoral leadership in each top rated site -giving attention to desired affinities *(economic, cultural, church background, geographical, and recreational.)*

→

© 2018 Robert O. Crossman, www.UMNewChurch.org

How Will We SUPPORT our New Church Pastors?

Appointment Fixed

The new church appointment is read by the Bishop at Annual Conference.

"The district superintendent of that district, or his or her designee, shall be the agent in charge of the project..." ¶259.1

Contact G.C.F.A. for a church ID number.

The Planting Pastor moves to the new mission field.

Prayer

Prayers for the new church pastor and their mission by the Bishop, District Superintendents, Conference Staff, fellow new church planting pastors.
Within the Sub-District: in the every Sunday pastoral prayers.
Within Mother/Sister Churches: in every Council, SPPR, Finance and Trustee meeting.

Strategy Review Meetings

(Every 2 to 4 months the first year.)
The Church Planter & Spouse (if married)
The District Superintendent
Conference Minister of New Church Starts,
Coach, 2 or 3 key laity from the new church.
This group meets to hear a report, and function as the PPR, Trustees, & Finance Committee during the first 2 to 5 years before the Constituting Charge Conference and the election of officers in the new church.

Boot Camp - Alumni

For a reduced fee, planters can return to Boot Camp with several key laity to retool & strengthen their launch team.

School of Cong. Development

Each year the August SCD that offers a Post Launch Ministry Track.

Boot Camp 2.0 Tune-up

A three day retreat that focuses on year three to six of the new church start.

Financial Support
from District & Conference

(Declining over a three to seven year period.)
Pastor's compensation, rental of initial worship site, marketing / advertising, etc.

The District Treasurer or treasurer of a healthy UMC nearby shall serve as the bookkeeper during the first months. Each check over a set amount must be approved by Judicatory before bookkeeper will cut the check. As the project matures, bookkeeping is moved to lay leadership in the new church. Duplicate bank statements shall be mailed to the Conference Director and/or District Superintendent..

NCLI / Launchpad

New church pastors are encouraged to attend additional NCLI or Launchpads each year to help train the new group of potential planting pastors, meet with their Coach, and to revisit/tune-up and sharpen their own new church ministry plan.

Encourage your planters to form an informal peer support network with other planters in your juris-

Tables I, II & III

Every January, new churches complete GCFA's table I, II, and III to officially report baptisms, professions of faith, and financial stewardship.

COACH - *a two to five year relationship until the new church is viable and stable*

We no longer send the new pastor out and then hope they don't drown - instead we provide on going support through a coach.

- to hold the pastor accountable to the Ministry Plan / Strategy they developed
- to point out what the pastor can't, won't, or doesn't see
- to have a compassionate, secure and confidential outlet to vent problems and frustrations
- to provide a clear line of communication between the pastor and District/Conference
- to conduct reality checks on the planter's vision, values, and strategies
- to walk with the new church pastor through conflict when it arises
- to implement the Ministry Plan / Strategy in the proper sequence
- to ask the questions no one else is asking
- to develop strategies for recruiting, launching and fund-raising
- to help the new church pastor balance the demands and stress of a new church start while maintaining a healthy family life

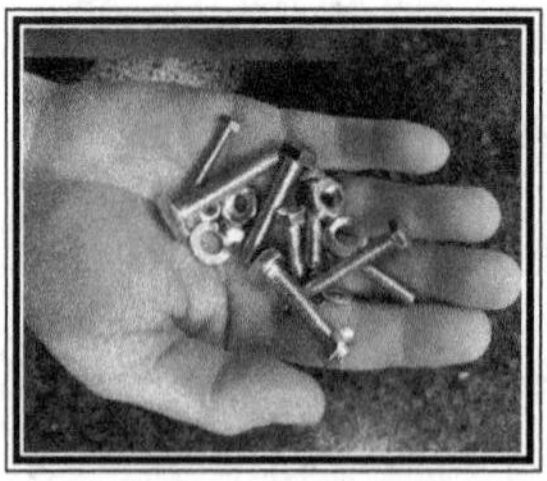

New Church Handbook
Nuts & Bolts for Planting New Churches In The Wesleyan Tradition

"Audit of Conference Planting Systems"

Reprinted here by permission of Bener Agtarap granted on January 26, 2018.
Source: www.Path1.org

CONFERENCE PLANTING AUDIT — PATH1 NEW CHURCH STARTS AT GBOD

Creating an Effective System for Planting New Churches and New Faith Communities

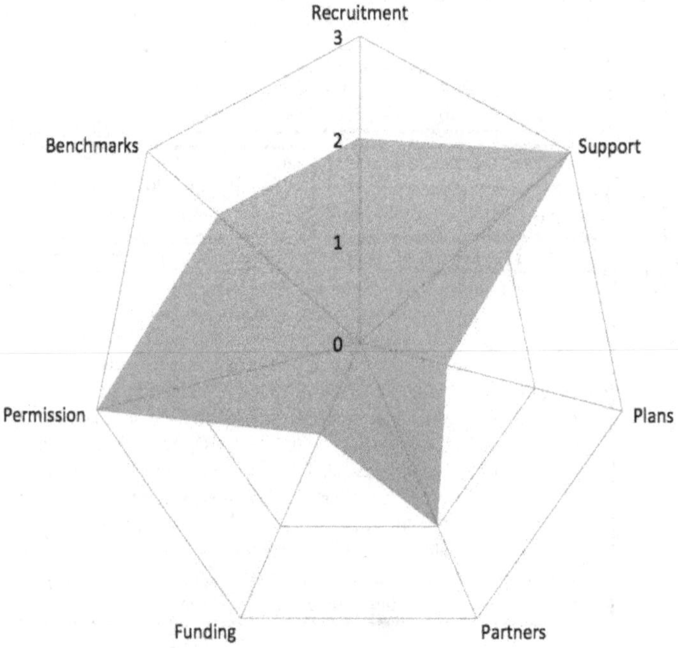

© 2018 Robert O. Crossman, www.UMNewChurch.org

Welcome

This self-assessment is designed to help conference new church leadership teams gain a fuller self-understanding of their resources and challenges in creating an effective system for starting new churches. Through looking at recently started new churches and current practices, a leadership team will assess their conference new church systems and practices. Path 1 staff will help coach the process and review the results, but the decisions and assessments are entirely owned by the conference team and leaders.

Instructions

With the coaching of a Path1 New Church Strategist, this self-assessment is best used by a team of leaders tasked with strategizing about the development of new churches and new faith communities. This is a working team of 3-5 people and should include:

- Area bishop or bishop's designated representative
- Member of the conference appointive cabinet (may also be bishop's designee)
- Conference staff person responsible for resourcing new church planting
- Conference staff persons responsible for ethnic and/or Hispanic/Latino ministries
- Leader of Conference board or committee responsible for new church planting

The team may need to request assistance from additional people for gathering information and completing the self-assessment, but many questions are designed to help gauge the response of senior, decision-making leadership.

Goals for Self Assessment Process

- understand and appreciate conference assets for starting new churches an faith communities
- identify possible challenges and obstacles for starting new churches and faith communities
- prepare conference new church leadership team for development of a new or updated plan for starting new churches and faith communities
- inform conference of new church starting goals and aims

Assessment Approach

Your team will analyze recent practices in starting new churches and new faith communities within your Conference. Your practices will be compared against best practice standards developed by United Methodist church planting practitioners within the United States. This comparison will yield a grade of:

- Needs Work – most responses in this area were lower than accepted best practice standards, and Conference could make improvements to increase effectiveness

- Good – most responses in this area were within accepted best practice standards, but Conference still could make improvements to increase effectiveness
- Excellent – most responses in this area exceeded accepted best practice standards, and Conference can build on these strengths to increase effectiveness

Contact Information

Annual Conference: ______________________

Congregational Developer or Contact for New Church Starts: ____________

Contact Phone or Cell: ______________________

Email: ________________@______________________

Mailing Address 1: ______________________

Mailing Address 2: ______________________

City: ______________ State: _______ Zip: ______________

Contact Person's Assistant: ______________________

Assistant Phone: ______________________

Assistant Email: ______________________

New Church Starts Team:

1. Area/Conference bishop: ______________________
   Bishop's Phone: ____________ Email: ______________
   Bishop's Admin Assistant: ______________________
   Admin"s Phone: ____________ Email: ______________

2. Appointive cabinet member or bishop's Designee: ____________
   Phone: ________________ Email: ______________

3. Conference Staff for New Church Starts: ______________
   Phone: ________________ Email: ______________

4. Conference Staff for Ethnic Ministries:
   Phone: ________________ Email: ______________

5. Conference Staff for Hispanic/Latino Ministries:
   Phone: ________________ Email: ______________

6. Leader of Conference Committee or Board for New Church Starts:
   Phone: ________________ Email: ______________

7. Other New Church Team Member (if needed):
   Phone: ________________ Email: ______________

 © 2018 Robert O. Crossman, www.UMNewChurch.org

8. Other New Church Team Member (if needed):
Phone: ____________________ Email: ________________________

Finding Great Planters

What percentage of recent planters have been:

- _____% Women
- _____% People of color
- _____% Laity
- _____% Under the age of 30

What percentage of recent planters were assessed before appointment or assignment to a new planting project? • _____%

How many trained assessors are on your Conference Planter Assessment Team?

- o 5 or more
- o 3-4
- o 3 or less
- o none

How many hours of training has your Conference Planter Assessment Team received?

- o More than 8 hours
- o 4-8 hours
- o 1-4 hours
- o none

How many people are in your identified pool or pipeline of potential planters?

- _____ people

How many potential future planters have you identified compared to how many new planting projects you want to start in the next two years?

- o 6 potential planters for each (1) planting projects
- o 4 planters for 1 project
- o 2 planters for 1 project
- o 1 planter for 2 or more projects

Does the Appointive Cabinet review Conference Planter Assessment Team reports before appointment?

- o Every time
- o Frequently
- o Sometimes
- o Irregularly

Does the bishop personally review Conference Planter Assessment Team reports before appointment?

- o Every time
- o Frequently

- o Sometimes
- o Irregularly

Supporting Planters

What percentage of recent planters have a coach?

- _____%

What is the quality of coaching?

- o Excellent
- o Adequate
- o Mostly OK, with some problems
- o Problematic

What percentage of coaches are certified:

- _____% by International Coaching Federation
- _____% by Path1
- _____% by other certifying group

How much of the coaching cost is paid by the Conference?

- _____%

How often are coaching relationships evaluated?

- o Rarely
- o Occasionally
- o Annually
- o Semi-annually
- o Constantly

What percentage of coaches are on site annually?

- _____%

What percentage of coaches participate in annual stakeholders meetings?

- o _____%

How much money is budgeted annually for each planter's continued training?

- o $3000 or more
- o $1000-$3000
- o $1000 or less
- o none

How many days of training do planters receive each year?

- o 10 or more
- o 5-10 days
- o 1-5 days
- o none

 © 2018 Robert O. Crossman, www.UMNewChurch.org

What percentage of planters participated in a LaunchPad and/or Planter Boot-camp experience?

- _____%

What percentage of planters report that they receive adequate training? (You'll probably have to ask them.)

- _____%

How often do your Conference leaders pray for specific planters and new faith communities in public gatherings?

- o Every time
- o Frequently
- o Sometimes
- o Irregularly

How often do your Conference leaders pray for specific planters and new faith communities in private prayers?

- o Every time
- o Frequently
- o Sometimes
- o Irregularly

How many people participate in your intercessory Conference prayer team for new church starts?

- _________ people

Planning for Success

What percentage of new planting projects had an approved launch plan in place at the beginning of the project?

- _____%

How often do the approved launch plans have adequate funding plan to meet their start-up goals?

- o Every time
- o Frequently
- o Sometimes
- o Irregularly

How often are launch plans revised and updated?

- o Every few years
- o Annually
- o Quarterly
- o Constantly
- o Never

What percentage of launch plans have measurable goals and date-specific targets to meet these goals?

- _____%

What percent of recent new church and new faith community planting projects have met their goals for the last year?

- _____%

Growing Planting Partners

What percentage of recent new church and new faith community planting projects have:

- _____% 3 or more partner churches or groups
- _____% 2 partner churches or groups
- _____% 1 partner church or group
- _____% no partners

What percentage of largest 10% of Conference churches have recently partnered or are actively planning to start a new church or faith community?

- _____%

What percentage of the most vital and strategic Conference churches have recently partnered or are actively planning to start a new church or faith community?

- _____%

What percentage of largest 10% of Conference churches' senior pastors are supportive of multiplying new churches and new faith communities?

- _____% very supportive
- _____% interested and open
- _____% unsure
- _____% opposed to the idea

How often is training offered for leaders of established churches in which planting new churches and faith communities is encouraged?

- o Every few years
- o Annually
- o Quarterly
- o Constantly
- o Never

What percentage of active leaders in the Conference have received training that encourages planting new churches and faith communities?

- _____% lay leaders
- _____% clergy leaders

 © 2018 Robert O. Crossman, www.UMNewChurch.org

How often are Conference churches personally invited by bishop or district superintendent to partner in starting a new church or new faith community?

- o Every few years
- o Annually
- o Quarterly
- o Constantly
- o Never

Funding Planting Vision

How much money has been budgeted for each recent new church or new faith community plant?

- $__________ per plant

What percentage of of expenses for recent new plants have come from:

- _____% Conference or District funds
- _____% other partner funds
- _____% participant giving
- _____% planter fund raising from other donors

How often do planters have to demonstrate fund raising capability before they are appointed or assigned to a new plant project?

- o Every time
- o Frequently
- o Sometimes
- o Irregularly
- o Never

How many days of fundraising training have recent planter received?

- o 10 or more
- o 5-10 days
- o 1-5 days
- o none

What percentage of potential planters have received new start fundraising training?

- _____%

Is adequate funding available to meet the Conference new church and faith community planting goals for the next ten years?

- o Yes
- o Probably
- o Maybe
- o No

© 2018 Robert O. Crossman, www.UMNewChurch.org

Is adequate funding available to provide adequate Conference staffing to support new church and new faith community goals for the next ten years?

- o Yes
- o Probably
- o Maybe
- o No

Does your Conference have a specific policy approved by annual conference to designate most of the assets from discontinued congregations toward starting new churches and faith communities?

- o Yes
- o Sort of
- o We're working on it
- o No

Where does Conference support for new churches and faith communities come from?

- _____% annually apportioned funds
- _____% accrued funds (such as endowments or previous fundraising)
- _____% special giving requests and campaigns
- _____% funds from assets of discontinued congregations

Granting Permission for Innovation

Which groups or individuals have to give permission before a new church or faith community project can begin?

- o Congregational Development staff
- o Bishop
- o District superintendent
- o Appointive cabinet
- o District Church Planting Committee
- o District Church Location & Building
- o District Lay Leader
- o Partner Church pastor
- o Partner Church board
- o Neighboring churches' pastors
- o Neighboring churches' boards
- o Other Conference groups: ____
- o Other District groups: ____
- o Other groups: ____

What percentage of new church and faith community projects made it from initial suggestion to fully approved projects?

- _____%

 © 2018 Robert O. Crossman, www.UMNewChurch.org

What percentage of new church and faith community plants are discontinued each year?

- _____%

How often has bishop been on-site at recent new church and faith community plants?

- o Every few years
- o Annually
- o Quarterly
- o Irregularly
- o Never

How often has district superintendent been on-site at recent new church and faith community plants?

- o Every few years
- o Annually
- o Quarterly
- o Irregularly
- o Never

What staffing does the Conference provide to coordinate new church and faith community planting?

- o No Conference staff
- o A Conference staff person has this as part of their broad portfolio
- o A less-than full-time Conference staff person in Congregational Development
- o A full-time Conference Congregational Development staff person
- o A full-time staff person dedicated specifically for new churches and new faith communities
- o More than one full-time Conference staff person in this area

How does Conference staff assigned to new church and faith community planting relate to the appointive cabinet?

- o Does not relate to appointive cabinet
- o Prepares information, but is rarely present in appointive cabinet
- o Occasionally present in appointive cabinet to present specific reports
- o Regularly present in appointive cabinet on broad range of topics
- o Non-voting member of appointive cabinet
- o Voting member of appointive cabinet
- o Other relationship: ______________________________

Benchmarking for Growth

What percentage of new church and faith community plants in the Conference provide regular benchmarking reports that include specific metrics for growth?

- _____%

What percentage of new church and faith community plants are regularly meeting their benchmarks? • _____%

Who approves benchmarks for each new church and faith community?

- o Planter
- o Planter & Coach
- o Planter, Coach & Conference Staff
- o Planter, Coach, Conference Staff, & district superintendent
- o Others: ______________________________________

How often are benchmarking reports submitted?

- o Weekly
- o Monthly
- o Quarterly
- o Yearly

How often does Conference staff review benchmarking reports:

- o As often as submitted
- o Quarterly
- o A couple of times a year
- o Yearly
- o Rarely

How often does Conference new church board review benchmarking reports:

- o As often as submitted
- o Quarterly
- o A couple of times a year
- o Yearly
- o Rarely

How often does appointive cabinet review benchmarking reports:

- o As often as submitted
- o Quarterly
- o A couple of times a year
- o Yearly
- o Rarely

Reprinted here by permission of Bener Agtarap granted on January 26, 2018.
Source: www.Path1.org

†††

 © 2018 Robert O. Crossman, www.UMNewChurch.org

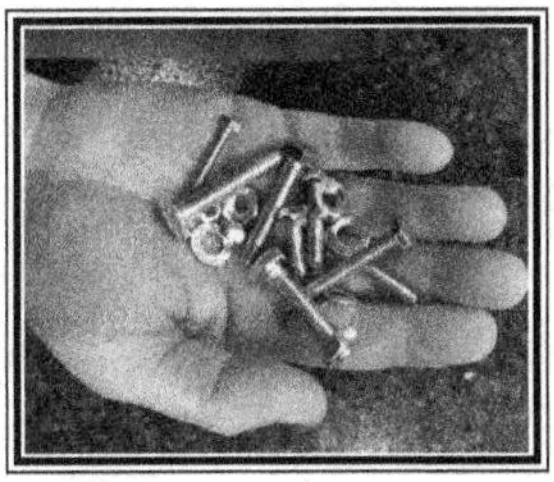

New Church Handbook
Nuts & Bolts for Planting New Churches In The Wesleyan Tradition

"What Are Some of The Best Practices In Healthy Conference Planting Systems"

by Path 1

PATH1

In any healthy church multiplication system, certain "best practices" seem to produce more fruit, as we find leaders, equip for effectiveness, plant and multiply. We offer some key recommendations here. **Path 1 New Church Strategists are available to help you develop these practices within your ministry territory.**

Find

1. Invite and challenge a broader base of people to hear a personal call to plant new congregations—including clergy, laity, young people and more diverse people.
2. Develop a reliable planter assessment and discernment process, aligned with the particular planting strategies being pursued…
   - To determine gifts and calling of potential church planters.
   - To help match potential planters with strategies and teams that fit with their gifts and affinities.
3. Create a pool of prospective planters, both clergy and lay…
   - Who have participated in an assessment and discernment process.
   - Who have received some basic training in new church development and multiplication (such as a Launchpad event, Exponential, Boot Camp, or regional New Church Leadership Institute).
   - With customized plans for all prospective planters to develop their skills and to monitor their ministry fruitfulness.
4. Support and challenge local churches to lead in planting new churches and multiplying their healthy congregations. Utilize resources to assess and increase readiness for effective planting.

Equip

5. Where possible, deploy or connect these high-potential leaders to serve on a successful planting team or within the leadership team of a vibrant, growing congregation before beginning their work as lead planter for a new church.
6. Provide training for all planters once they have been assigned to specific planting projects, making use of Basic Training for Church Planters or the Path 1 Launchpad events.
7. Assign a qualified new church development coach to the project for at least three years to work with the planter, the local partners and the district superintendent. Consider working with a Path 1 recommended coach for this critical role.

8. Develop appropriate benchmarks before the planting project starts, in conversation with the coach, planter(s), connectional partners, district superintendent and conference staff person for new church starts. Plan to review and possibly adjust the benchmarks about six months in.

Plant

9. In project planning, think first in terms of the people we seek to reach with the Good News of Jesus Christ, taking into consideration the generational, cultural and theological contexts. This site selection task is much more important than putting a point on the map.
10. When planting racial-ethnic and multi-ethnic faith communities consider specific recommendations for effective partnering that may differ from common assumptions or Anglo-majority planting experiences. Contact New Church Strategists for Path1 resources for specific racial/ethnic planting constituencies.
11. Always seek to plant with a well-developed connectional partnership – a partnering congregation, a partnering group of congregations or some other dependable resources (people and seed funding) to help begin an effective launch team quickly. If you need to delay a year or assign the pastor to the staff of the partnering church until a local launch team has been cultivated, please wait.
12. Develop a plan tailored to each community context, with these considerations: financial streams, stewardship development, connectional giving and sustainability. Financial streams include funds from launch team and planter tithing and may also include individuals, connectional partners, district and annual conference. Build into the budget the congregation's giving back to the conference. Consider creating a Path 1 Missional Planting Zone in areas where conventional strategies are not feasible or likely to succeed.
13. Establish benchmarks that support an exit strategy. Allow benchmarks to guide decisions related to continued funding, ministry strategy, fruitfulness, leadership effectiveness, and planting appointment transitions (see also 19 below). An exit strategy relates specifically to discontinuing external financial investment in an emerging faith community that fails to develop to a certain level within a certain time window. This strategy may involve reassignment of the planter. It must always involve a good pastoral plan for continuing to disciple the persons involved and to grow ministry in a more sustainable manner. Occasionally, you may adjust benchmarks but please don't ignore or discard them.
14. Be sure the planter appropriately matches the needs and challenges of the community. If the planter is new to the area, look for ways s/he might live and serve in the community before the planting appointment formally begins.
15. Only assign planters to projects after they have completed assessment and discernment processes, where their gifts, affinities, and previous experiences appropriately match their particular planting challenges. Upon assignment to

 © 2018 Robert O. Crossman, www.UMNewChurch.org

planting projects, ensure that planters receive ongoing support and appropriate training, such as prayer partners, formal and informal peer support groups, coaching and accountability. Consider funding training opportunities for the planter and key leaders for a specified length of time.

16. Provide a clear line of communication from the planter to the district superintendent and others involved with conference congregational development and offer a safe, confidential environment in which the planter can share concerns, frustrations, and ministry successes.
17. Build an infrastructure of small groups, mission teams and ministry teams within the planting team before launching weekly public worship. Small group multiplication and discipleship systems lay the foundation for success and sustainability of a new church.
18. Resist the temptation to launch weekly public worship prematurely or to wait too long. Right timing depends on the leadership of the Holy Spirit, critical mass, momentum and cultural context. Churches that launch weekly public worship too soon often get stuck as very small, cash-dependent fellowships with reduced chances of growth and financial self-sustainability.
19. When, eventually, a succeeding pastoral assignment occurs (either the assignment of a new lay pastor, the assignment of a new campus pastor within a multi-site church staff or the appointment of a new pastor by the bishop), those in oversight pay extremely close attention to gifts, affinities, and calling of the second pastor, as well as the unique culture and growth (or lack thereof) of the new faith community. When a clergy appointment is involved, the cabinet works collaboratively with the church and founding planter in the appointive process.

Multiply

20. Think "multiplication" from the start. Create a culture for multiplication of leaders, ministries and congregations in existing churches and new church starts. Include a focus on leaders and team members constantly mentoring new leaders and team members.
21. Protect the planter's time by releasing her/him from annual conference committee work and other connectional leadership demands that steal focus from the church plant. Specifically, planters serving in their first three years at a new church should not serve on conference board overseeing church planting. This type of distraction sometimes involves conflicts of interest.
22. Leave the planter long enough in the new church appointment to stabilize the new church. If the new church has good potential to grow into a high-attendance congregation and to multiply, plan for the planter to remain long-term with the church.
23. In reaching new people for Christ, keep existing congregations from blocking or undermining the efforts to plant a new church. In many communities, the diversity and sheer quantity of people require more and varied congregations to increase the share of the population connected to The United Methodist Church. New approaches and creative, missional faith communities will ap-

peal to different people groups and serve new populations.

24. When existing churches close, designate a significant portion of the assets toward new church development in the annual conference. Annual conferences that employ such a policy typically keep a good reservoir of funding for new church start projects.

For additional information or support exploring or implementing these best practice recommendations, please contact any of the New Church Strategists on the Path1 staff.

Reprinted here by permission of Bener Agtarap granted on January 26, 2018. Source: www.Path1.org

PATH1

 © 2018 Robert O. Crossman, www.UMNewChurch.org

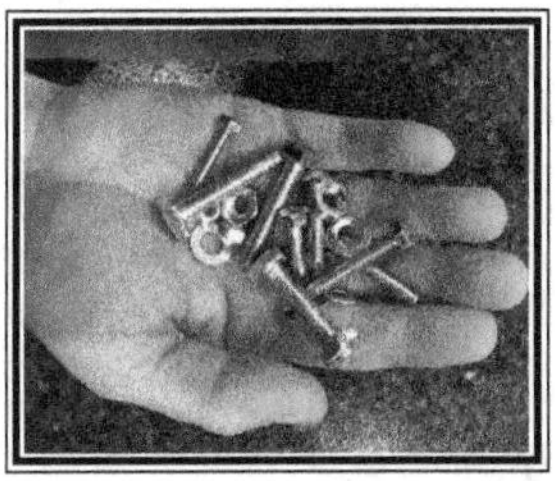

New Church Handbook
Nuts & Bolts for Planting New Churches In The Wesleyan Tradition

"Implementing These Best Practices"

PATH1

by Path 1

This document accompanies the Church Planting Best Practices document. Whereas the other document lists key best practices around the themes of Find, Equip, Plant and Multiply, this document invites us to think at a higher altitude, in terms of key moves that can enable conferences to implement excellent church planting practice.

Build and Align your Conference Team

1. **A good conference team will include...**
   - A congregational development director in the annual conference (the conferences that bear the most fruit in new church development work to retain this position).
   - A member of the cabinet focused on issues of congregational development (more than a cabinet representative, this person helps the cabinet and conference team communicate, stay on the same page, and work together).
   - Laity and clergy.
   - People who have planting experience (you can borrow from other denominational tribes, other conferences and from the national Path 1 staff if needed).
   - People under the age of 35.
   - Racial and cultural diversity, reflecting the mission field.
   - If there is an endowment or independent fund for church planting, someone who can represent the group that manages the fund.
   - A clear sense of purpose regarding the team's role in sustaining vital congregations; specifically, how to plant new churches while supporting established congregations that seek to improve their vitality (and, perhaps, sub-teams that remain focused on these very different – yet complementary – functions).

2. **Take the time necessary to build this team.**
   - The teams that function best spend formative time together early and reg-

ularly. Two or three day face-to-face retreats may be worth two years of monthly meetings.
- Consider resourcing this team-building time with a facilitator from the Path 1 national team (pick who you want!) or a seasoned congregational development director from another annual conference.
- Maintain regular communication to stay focused on agreed-upon goals and progress toward them. If the team contains task forces or sub-teams to oversee specific responsibilities, provide opportunities for sharing updates and offering feedback among the sub-teams.

3. **Create multiple teams if needed.**
You may choose to build teams at the district level or focused on a particular population or region of your conference. If you decide upon this strategy, consider starting with one or two teams, rather than building a team in every district. Think strategically. Think about places where you can start, and get some early wins, creating momentum that will help in building other regional teams later.

Cultivate the Climate for Planting

4. **Connect vital congregations – new and existing churches.**
Be very clear about the connection between the initiative for vital churches and the challenge of planting. In many conferences, people readily understand the need for vital congregations, and significant initiatives may already be underway to cultivate more vital congregations.

Preparation

- Assess where the Prevenient Grace of God may already be preparing a community to give birth to a new United Methodist church. Obtain district feedback regarding potential partner congregations, leaders and locations. Pay attention to demographic trends and prayerfully examine neighborhoods to identify underserved populations in unexpected places. Listen for the movement of the Holy Spirit and not just to the loudest local voices.

Places

- Working with the conference team, identify and prioritize specific locations for starting new churches during the next two to five years. Consider availability of financial and other resources at both the conference and district level. Clarify in advance the roles partners will play in determining planting strategy, support for new churches/new campuses, and selection of planters.

- Engage district superintendents and conference congregational development team members in preparing communities to receive planters. Frequently reinforce

© 2018 Robert O. Crossman, www.UMNewChurch.org

the message that successful new churches can raise the United Methodist brand value in a community – and that helps all affiliated congregations.

Partners

- We plant best through a strong connection of vital, existing congregations! Vital churches succeed in planting new churches and in creating new ministry sites, while less vital churches more often fail. Use Readiness 360 (www.readiness360.org) to assess prospective partner churches and their potential strengths before determining planting strategies (see Church Development Strategies document for details).
- A new United Methodist church planted near an existing United Methodist church may stimulate the older church to innovate and take long-needed action to update and improve its ministry. New churches more readily attempt new methods and often prove the value of those methods to older churches and their leaders.
- In many cases, the road to church transformation and recovery of a vital ministry in a local church will include birthing a new thing within the established congregation. This new thing will often involve intentional outreach to a new people group, including a new worship service and involving an associate pastor whose training and methodology will borrow heavily from the playbook of a good church planter.

Planters

- Develop profiles for preferred planter leadership in each prioritized location, giving attention to desired affinities. Prioritize the new starts for each appointment cycle and work closely with the cabinet and boards of ordained ministry to assess the best "fit" and timing of planter assignments.

5. **Tell stories at every level!**
   We need to hear stories of lives blessed and new ministry methods that are working, with a balance between stories of new churches and stories of new initiatives in long-established churches. Invite pastors of extraordinary ministries to speak at conference events. Especially invite them to bring along folks who met Christ through the churches they lead! Be sure that churches regularly share their "Snapshots of Hope" through www.path1.org and other communication channels.

6. **Teach people about church planting.**
   Training events help to change the conference climate, in addition to training individuals the skills they need to plant effectively. Sponsor year-long academies, offer short-term workshops, partner with the New Church Leadership Institute, and send folks to planter training "boot camps," national planter events like Exponential, Path 1's regional Launchpad training, and the School of Congregational Development. The more folks in a conference that experience the training, the bigger the difference you will see in the overall conference climate.

Build systems that will outlast your current bishop and leaders

7. **Create self-sustaining momentum.**
   In all cases, think beyond the present generation of leadership: mentor others, create autonomous systems, and cultivate a planting community shared among vital churches and vital church pastors. In most cases, building a sustainable, long-term movement of church multiplication will require multiple leaders' tenures.

8. **Address all major system components.**
   Think in terms of Find, Equip, Plant and Multiply when building your systems (see related Church Planting Best Practices document). Building systems that don't have these key elements is like finding perfectly good cars with no spark plugs. We can do much with excellence and then we wonder why we can't plant well or sustain our movement. By focusing on all four major areas of a planting system, we see better results.

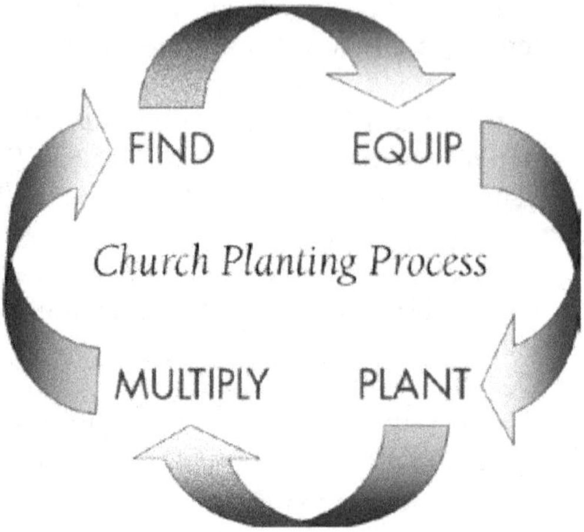

9. **Encourage independent funding.**
   The less future planting depends upon the annual conference, the better! Within a few years, if most funding, initiative, and volunteers come from vital churches and networks within the conference, the movement will be poised for continued growth. Find ways to plant without high dependency on conference funding. Conference funding will not sustain the level of new ministry development needed in the United States. Depending too much on conference funding can lead us to take fewer risks to reach new people groups and may cause planting movements to jolt to a sudden halt because of changes in conference leadership or diminishing funds.

   Try diverse approaches: don't put all your eggs in one basket.

10. **Explore new strategies.**
    Committing to a few highly-funded ventures does not stop you from cultivating a dozen or more very low-cost ventures. When you assess planting priori-

 © 2018 Robert O. Crossman, www.UMNewChurch.org

ties carefully consider planting strategies, too (see Church Development Strategies document for cost, benefits, and challenges of various planting options). The Northern Illinois Conference, during a major church planting expansion in 2009-2012, mixed projects that required high conference capital with those that found significant funding from other sources, along with others that were very low-cost, at least at the start. In this way, they leveraged their resources to create a wave of new plants and to jump start a planting movement not seen for decades in the Chicago area.

11. **Multiply healthy DNA through multi-site planting.**
Multi-site networks should be a key component of most conference plans. A multi-site network can begin with a very vital congregation growing and expanding its ministry, or it can begin with a church plant that is designed to multiply quickly from the start. One church often can leverage its good DNA more easily than it can align a district or conference around that DNA. Thus it is wise and realistic to think that at least half of new ministry sites that United Methodists will plant in the next decade will be multi-site expansions of very healthy evangelistic churches.

12. **Equip and assign lay planters.**
Remember that laity can make highly effective, evangelistic and passionate leaders for new church starts. Most new churches in recent history have been started by clergy, but these approaches have not always effectively reached unchurched people. The Lay Missionary Planting Network (LMPN) allows for laity to find their calling in church planting. The LMPN curriculum adapts to a wide range of uses in preparing laity to lead in church planting – from being assigned as a lead planter, to being part of a team, to training other laity for planting. The key: a conference plan to assign training participants to planting projects, partner congregations, and mentors even before the training begins!!

For additional information or support exploring or implementing these best practice recommendations, please contact any of the New Church Strategists on the Path1 staff.

Reprinted here by permission of Bener Agtarap granted on January 26, 2018.
Source: www.Path1.org

†††

PATH1

New Church Handbook
Nuts & Bolts for Planting New Churches In The Wesleyan Tradition

"What Are Some Best Practices For Recruiting Planters From Other Denominations"

PATH1

Editor's Note:

While this was originally written in the context of recruiting Hispanic/Latino Planters from other denominations, these recommendations may be helpful for receiving ALL planters from other denominations.

In many areas across the United States, the largest and/or fastest-growing segment of the population is Hispanic/Latino. In some of these areas there is no Hispanic/Latino United Methodist faith community present. annual conferences that are serious about reaching their mission fields have an urgent need to find pastors who can start and/or grow these new faith communities. This urgency, along with our desire to find persons who possess the marks of successful church planters, compels some to consider recruiting planters from outside our United Methodist system.

Even non-United Methodist pastors with the recommendation of a United Methodist pastor will need to go through a process of annual conference education and assessment. We need to very clearly communicate our expectations about the culture in which we want them to work and whether the prospect has the experience, education and capacity to function in a new ecclesiastical culture. We recommend that you do a thorough and frank interview with all prospects to explore their ecclesiology and doctrinal understandings to assess their ability to adjust to the United Methodist culture.

If the candidate cannot adjust, problems will emerge that may lead to conflict, disappointment, or even the loss of a congregation and/or a pastor after the conference has made a significant investment. The severity of these problems may lead to the discouragement of the district or conference leadership. They may have invested both emotionally and financially in Hispanic/Latino ministry or new church starts and may have a sense of failure that prevents them from trying again.

Step 1: Interview

In preparation for the interview the prospect should be asked to bring a written résumé of life experience (and academic degrees, if available). The potential planter should receive a set of simple questions detailing the topics for prior to the interview to all her/him to prepare and not be surprised.

 © 2018 Robert O. Crossman, www.UMNewChurch.org

Topics to be addressed in the interview (Prepare questions in advance):

1. Understanding the Sacraments as Means of Grace
   a. Baptism
   In particular, ask their views on infant Baptism. If the person is not comfortable with the United Methodist practice of infant baptism s/he will not perform this ritual with children.
   b. Holy Communion
   Many non-United Methodist pastors cannot accept the open table and place conditions or requirements that are not consistent with UMC beliefs to exclude persons from the Communion Table.

2. Understanding the Priesthood of all Believers
   In other traditions the pastoral leader makes most of the decisions for the congregation. This style of leadership may lead to conflict with our system of representative democracy and our understanding of the polity of the church.

3. Itineracy, the appointment system and Episcopal authority
   This is particularly important for pastors who join our church with a congregation that they have organized, for whom itineracy is a foreign concept.

4. The connectional system, the importance of apportionments and accountability to the annual conference for their ministry.

5. The ability to work with persons who have different perspectives on homosexuality and abortion.

6. The reasons why he or she is seeking to change his or her denominational affiliation by joining The United Methodist Church.

7. Expectations and options for certification or licensing, the requirements needed for a Local Pastor's License and the ordination process

Step 2: Verify

Verification comes through letters of recommendation and background checks. Secure at least three letters of recommendation from the former denomination or an organization that knows his or her history and effectiveness in ministry. If all else checks out, conduct a background check before hiring. Some annual conferences have been able to secure background checks for persons coming from other Latin American nations.

Step 3: Decide To Assign/Appoint

The bishop and cabinet, in consultation with conference Hispanic/Latino ministry leaders, fix an appointment or assign a planter. All stakeholders in the process agree to establish benchmarks, measures, and evaluation processes in advance, ensuring that all parties understand the expectations.

© 2018 Robert O. Crossman, www.UMNewChurch.org

Step 4: Sign a Covenant

A written agreement helps clarify the relationship and expectations for both the conference and the pastor. It will also help to guide the pastor in self-evaluation, along with a more formal evaluation by the district superintendent or annual conference at the end of an agreed-upon time period.

Step 5: Assign a Mentor

The district superintendent assigns an elder in good standing to serve as a mentor to the new pastor. The expectation is that there shall be regular meetings with the mentor/coach and visits with the congregation to provide guidance on local church structure and polity in areas such as:

1. Continuing Education requirements
2. Sexual misconduct guidelines of our church
3. Supervisory role of district superintendent
4. Accountability to The Book of Discipline of The United Methodist Church
5. Ability to deal with diversity: cultural and linguistic

A Probationary Period

If a pastor is approved as a United Methodist probationer there needs to be a probationary period of one to two years with a follow up interview mid-way through the probationary period and a final interview at the end of the time. The purpose of the probationary period is to provide the pastor the opportunity to see if she or he is able to function within the United Methodist system, and the conference will have the time to assess both his or her effectiveness as well as her or his ability to participate in the United Methodist culture. During the probationary period either the pastor or the conference could discontinue the relationship.

Additional Resources

Several other Path 1 resources may prove useful as you begin cultivating Hispanic/Latino church planting ministries in your annual conference. Please contact the New Church Starts Division/Path 1 at GBOD for these and other resources:

- High-Potential Planter Traits (English and Spanish language versions available)
- Church Planting Best Practices in an Hispanic/Latino Context
- Project Partnerships and Ministries in an Hispanic/Latino Context
- Information about the Lay Missionary Planting Network (English and Spanish language versions available)
- Recommendations Regarding Shared Facilities Path 1 gratefully acknowledges MARCHA West for its foundational work and collaboration on the recommendations in this document.

Reprinted here by permission of Bener Agtarap granted on January 26, 2018.
Source: www.Path1.org

†††

PATH1

 © 2018 Robert O. Crossman, www.UMNewChurch.org

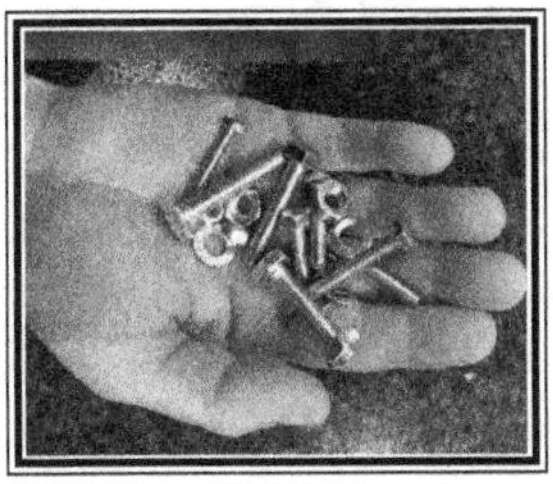

New Church Handbook
Nuts & Bolts for Planting New Churches In The Wesleyan Tradition

"Best Practices for Funding Planting in the Annual Conference"

by Path 1

PATH1

Top Ten Effective Funding Strategies for New Church Development in Annual Conferences

1. **Expect and Train New Church Pastors to Raise Funds**
Set an expectation that planters will immediately begin to tithe to their churches. Also, establish a percentage of the new church's budget to be raised by the planter. Train planters how to raise these funds for their ministries. Encourage launch team members to raise "virtue capital" by inviting friends and family to support the church's ministries. Launch teams may develop a brochure or flyer that explains the vision, mission and core values of their new church and whenever possible ask friends and family, in person, to consider making a financial commitment to their project.

2. **Allocate a Percentage of the Conference Budget**
Adjust the budget of the annual conference so that a percentage could be set aside and used to start new churches. Set a five-year goal of reaching a tithe. Begin at 2% in year one and increase to 4% in year two and so on until a tithe is allocated to new church development.

3. **Use Funds Gained from the Sale of Properties**
Consider using the funds gained from the sale of property to support new church starts. Many annual conferences have found this to be a helpful strategy when churches are moving toward closure. In addition to funding new churches the leaders of these closing congregations may see the use of the resources as their legacy to advance the kingdom.

4. **Receive an Offering Each Year for New Church Starts**
Encourage congregations to receive an offering for new church development on a specific Sunday each year. Churches might receive their "love" offering on the Sunday nearest to Valentine's Day, or Pentecost when we celebrate the birth of the church. In rural communities the offering might be received on Rogation or Harvest Sunday.

5. **Designate an Offering at Annual Conference Session**
Encourage each church in the annual conference to invite every member to contribute $10 per year for church planting. This gift could be received prior

to annual conference session and offered when a collection is taken at opening worship and designated for new church development.

6. **Encourage Support from Local Church Funding Campaigns**
Invite congregations that are conducting (or considering) capital stewardship programs to designate a percentage of what they raise to new church starts. Inviting congregations to do this enables them to become church-planting partners with other churches in the conference.

7. **Create an Endowment through Major Donors**
Ask the lead pastors of your larger congregations to suggest persons who have the heart and the financial means to create an endowment for new church starts. Develop a strategy to visit these individuals and invite their response.

8. **Plan a Capital Stewardship Campaign**
Consider a conference-wide stewardship campaign to create funds for new church development. Often conference-wide campaigns seek to raise funding support for more than one ministry (e.g. new church development, camping, revitalization programs for existing churches, etc.) Check out Path 1's "Best Practices for Interviewing and Selecting a Capital Stewardship Company" white paper at www.path1.org.

9. **Share Resources Among Annual Conferences**
Encourage annual conferences to share resources with other conferences to help them plant new churches. Some annual conferences in the country, like those devastated by natural disasters, may not have the funds to build new churches to replace displaced or newly emerging congregations. For example, the Florida Conference gave $90,000 to the Mississippi annual conference to support their efforts to develop new congregations in hurricane-devastated areas.

10. **Consider Ecumenical Partnerships**
Consider partnerships with other denominations in a target area to pool resources together to plant a new church. This strategy may not be popular because of the difficulty it presents in the appointive process but is nonetheless a proven strategy worth considering. For example, Hot Metal Bridge, in Pittsburgh, PA, is a partnership between the United Methodist and Presbyterian Church (USA) denominations. The Village @ Northwest Ohio is a planting partnership of The United Methodist Church and United Church of Christ.

Reprinted here by permission of Bener Agtarap granted on January 26, 2018.
Source: www.Path1.org

†††

PATH1

 © 2018 Robert O. Crossman, www.UMNewChurch.org

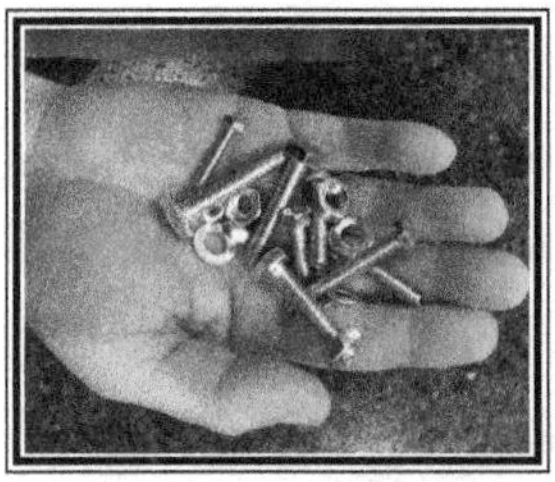

New Church Handbook
Nuts & Bolts for Planting New Churches In The Wesleyan Tradition

"What Is The Lay Missionary Planting Network (LMPN)?"

by Path 1

PATH1

We believe gifted, called lay people will effectively lead new congregations.

Having been called to find even better ways to reach all people for Jesus Christ by planting new congregations, and recognizing that our current approaches will limit our ability to reach our goals, we embark on a new thing—the Lay Missionary Planting Network (LMPN).

Find

We seek lay people who have:

- A Passion for the Gospel
- Compassion for God's people
- Demonstrated potential for reaching the targeted population(s) in the region, and
- A job or other source of income to support their families

We also seek mentors and partner churches for these lay persons and their possible church plants.

Equip

Practical, experiential, mentor-supported discernment and training enable these lay persons to lead new church starts. Retreat settings offer open dialogue, growing theological competence and accountable, spiritual community. Training includes:

- Sessions drawn from the most effective practices to equip planters for new church ministry
- Mentors assigned to provide potential lay missionaries with needed support, encouragement and, in some cases, opportunities for internship
- Opportunities to experience the United Methodist connection in action and learn from some of the best and brightest denominational thought-leaders and practitioners in church planting
- Assessment of best fit: some will continue as high-potential planters, others as launch team members and still others as prospective Lay Missionary Planting Network coordinators

Plant

We seek to enter into covenant relationship with at least five annual conferences per year to train at least fifty lay people and at least twelve qualified lay missionaries per network to start new congregations, for a total of sixty new church starts per year.

Multiply

As these new churches prepare leaders for new church starts and plant other congregations we see the multiplication of God's reign – as 60 becomes 120 becomes 240 and so on. Additionally, high-potential coordinators will help seed other Lay Missionary Planting Networks from the pilot to multiply the reach.

Partnerships with Annual Conferences and National Plans

The Lay Missionary Planting Network exists to find, equip and deploy lay people to start new faith communities in partnership with clergy and in populations and contexts in which traditional approaches have not proven fruitful.
The first Lay Missionary Planting Networks are located in the Baltimore-Washington/Virginia, Desert Southwest, East Ohio, Greater New Jersey, and Rio Grande annual conferences (yellow stars on map below).

We expect to double the number of LMPN sites in 2010 and 2011, within the following annual conferences/sites (gray stars on map):

- Austin, TX
- Boise, Idaho
- Florida
- New England
- New York
- Oklahoma Indian Missionary
- Eastern Pennsylvania
- Rocky Mountain
- Salem, Oregon
- Yellowstone

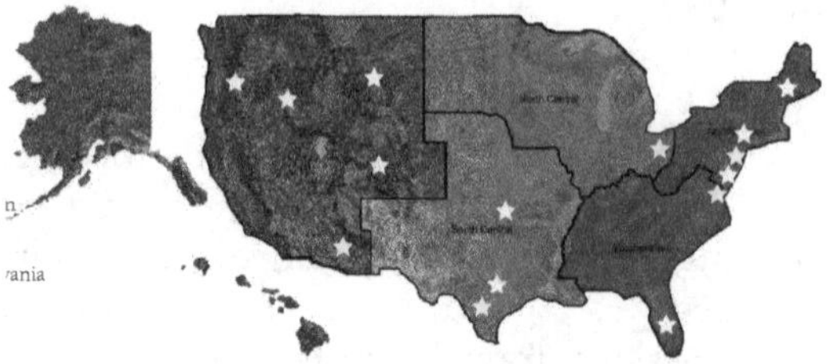

These partner conferences all possess:

- Large existing populations, continuing to increase (growth corridor)
- Capacity for additional United Methodist congregations
- Leaders who are passionate about and committed to starting new churches
- Presence of strong, healthy partner congregations
- Commitment to promote and support racial ethnic new faith communities

 © 2018 Robert O. Crossman, www.UMNewChurch.org

We also celebrate strong partnerships and mutual support between Path 1 and the National Plan for Hispanic/Latino Ministries (NPHLM) and the Native American Comprehensive Plan (NACP) through this effort. Most of the LMPN sites are located and in around the annual conferences that the leaders of NPHLM will intentionally develop this quadrennium. The NACP leadership is currently identifying five strategic sites for the LMPN, along United States growth corridors and exploring partnerships with annual conferences within the targeted areas.

Reprinted here by permission of Bener Agtarap granted on January 26, 2018.
Source: www.Path1.org

†††

PATH1

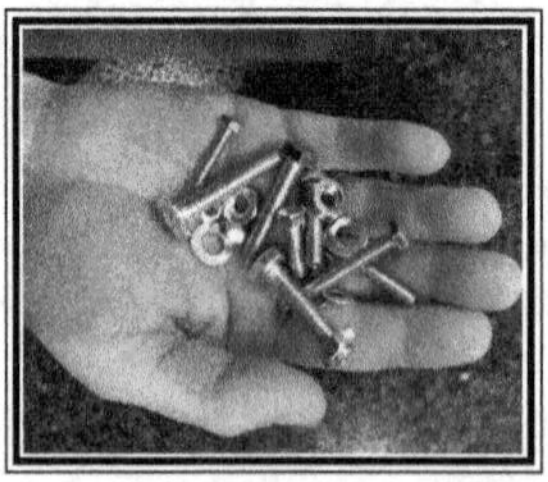

New Church Handbook
Nuts & Bolts for Planting New Churches In The Wesleyan Tradition

"What Does the LMPN Workbook Look Like?"

PATH1

On this and the following page you will find the first two pages of the sixteen page chapter for the morning of the first session of LMPN, "Church Planting 101."

Welcome to the first session of the Lay Missionary Planting Network, a training opportunity offered in partnership between your local United Methodist church, district or annual conference and Path 1, the United Methodist church planting movement within the U.S. Today's topic, "Church Planting 101," is the first of ten sessions for training lay church planters.

Church Planting 101 - Agenda

1. Welcome, Opening Prayer and Introductions
2. Introduction to "Church Planting 101"
3. Studying the Scriptures #1: Acts 2
4. "A New Thing"

Break

5. Lay Missionary Planting Network Overview
6. Studying the Scriptures #2: Acts 8

Break

7. Why New Churches Effectively Reach New People
8. How the Lay Missionary Planting Network Will Start New Churches
9. Affinity Activity

Lunch Break

10. 7 Seasons of Church Planting

Break

11. Studying the Scriptures #3: Seasons (your choice)
12. Top 10 Tips from Church Planters
13. Closing Covenant Ceremony

 © 2018 Robert O. Crossman, www.UMNewChurch.org

Opening Video: "To Galilee"

(Please watch the video according to the directions from the facilitator and prepare to ***share your responses to the following questions*** *when instructed)*

What words made an impression on you?

What images caught your eye?

What other questions do you have for today or for later in the training process?
(Please write them in the space provided here.)

What is Path 1 and how does it relate to the Lay Missionary Planting Network?

Path 1 is a team of mission-driven, passionate and diverse leaders drawn from national, regional and local levels of The United Methodist Church, providing collaborative leadership to **evangelize the United States through new congregations**. The Path 1 Team leads a denominational movement to **reach more people – more young people, more diverse people –** as disciples of Jesus Christ for the transformation of the world, by creating new places for new people. Ultimately, Path 1 seeks to create the leaders, cultures and processes needed to regain our healthy denominational habit of starting at least **one new church each day.** By influencing the conversation, the agenda and the vision for church planting at many tables, Path 1 encourages investment in relationships, lay and clergy leadership, best practices and healthy partner churches, so that multiplication of world-transforming disciples happens in more places for more people. Visit www.path1.org to learn more about the ministry of Path 1.

PATH1
NEW CHURCH STARTS AT GBOD

As participants in the Lay Missionary Planting Network, you will receive ongoing support from Path 1, in the form of this curriculum and in relationships with the network design team, facilitators, and mentors. As you join this movement, you will learn from the best practices of planters in other parts of the country, as well as provide insights that benefit others.

Lay Missionary Planting Network

Reprinted here by permission of Bener Agtarap granted on January 26, 2018.

New Church Handbook
Nuts & Bolts for Planting New Churches In The Wesleyan Tradition

"What is The High Impact Residency?"

PATH1

The Church's hope rests in the hands of young people who will carry on the mission to plant new churches.

- **Are you . . . entrepreneurial and future-focused with a desire to share the gospel in relevant, contextual new ways?**

- **Are you . . . interested in a one-year hands-on learning experience in a vital, high impact church setting?**

- **Would you like to be considered for a one year, paid residency in church planting?**

If you answered yes to the above three questions, we would like to speak with you!!!

Residency Overview and Partners

Path 1, the church planting movement of The United Methodist Church, is committed to encouraging and supporting the next generation of church planters. We believe young people are critical to our mission to reach the growing number of unchurched people in the world and to stay relevant to the changing trends and needs of the world. In accordance with that commitment we are providing Residencies for young adults who feel called to plant new churches.

We are creating partnerships with annual conferences to fund these Residencies. Our Residency program helps address the denomination's need to increase the number of young and diverse clergy under 35 years of age. These Residencies are designed to help our UMC plant vital, new large impact churches with a relevant, contextual, outward focus on ministries and mission.

The partners involved in this program are the planter resident, the host church, the annual conference, and Path 1. The host church will act as the temporary employer of the resident while the annual conference and Path 1 will serve as co-sponsors of the program. Each sponsor will contribute money, time, and resources to the program and evaluate the effectiveness of the planter, the Residency program, and the fund development process.

 © 2018 Robert O. Crossman, www.UMNewChurch.org

What You Will Gain from a Church Planting Residency?

- First-hand experience working at a High Impact Church for one year
- A salary, housing and benefits
- Wisdom and insight from experienced planters and conference staff, who will help you prepare for the journey ahead
- The opportunity to attend national planter training events (New Church Leadership Institute, Church Planting Boot Camp, Launchpad, etc.)
- Hands-on experience planning worship, leading small groups, organizing community outreach, and raising money for projects
- Possible field education if you are attending seminary
- An assignment to plant a high impact church upon successful completion of the program
- A greater vision of your calling and a greater readiness for the ministry that awaits you!

Residency Expectations - Highlights

- All Residents will attend an orientation meeting with Path 1 and with the congregational development staff and committee of their annual conference.
- The Residents will be assigned to a recognized high impact vital congregation in (or, in some cases, outside) their annual conference to serve for one year, working regular, full-time hours.
- The resident will work carrying out duties as the church directs him/her, while also fulfilling the requirements laid out in his/her covenant with Residency sponsors.
- The resident will be paired with a mentor who is a member of the church's pastoral staff.

What is a High Impact Church?

- High volume of professions of faith
- High scores on the "UMC Vital Congregations" signs of a healthy church
- Inviting and Inspiring Worship
- Engaged Disciples in mission and outreach
- Gifted, Empowered and Equipped Lay Leadership
- Effective, Equipped and Inspired Clergy Leadership
- Small Group Ministries
- Strong Children's and Youth Ministry
- Strong Discipleship system
- May not be in your annual conference but reflect the kind of church you desire to plant.
- Other traits determined by the annual conference

What's Next?

- Prayerfully consider whether you are called to be a planter and to pursue this Residency opportunity.
- Talk to your pastor, district superintendent, or seminary professor about your desire to become a church planter.
- Ask your annual conference to provide or recommend a planter assessment process to determine whether you have the qualities of a high-potential planter. Your Congregational Developer will find assessment tools for you.

- **Contact Path 1 for more information about the Residency program.**

Reprinted here by permission of Bener Agtarap granted on January 26, 2018.
Source: www.Path1.org

†††

PATH1

 © 2018 Robert O. Crossman, www.UMNewChurch.org

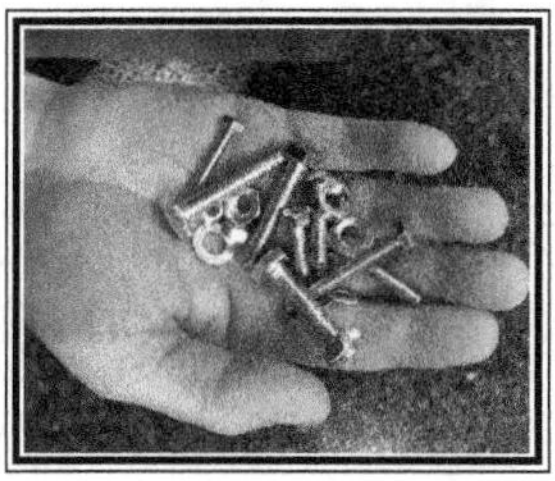

New Church Handbook
Nuts & Bolts for Planting New Churches In The Wesleyan Tradition

"What is The Covenant for The High Impact Residency?"

by Path 1

Name of Initiative -
High Impact Church Planting Residency

Mission

Path 1 partners with annual conferences in creating a residency experience that forms leaders capable of planting, leading and growing a high impact church.

Goal

A high impact church planted in every annual conference of The United Methodist Church in the United States.

Key Participants

1. Annual Conference
2. Host High Impact Church
3. Church Planting Resident
4. Path 1
5. In some circumstances, Seminaries with a vision/excitement for equipping planters

What is a 'High Impact Church'?

1. High volume of professions of faith
2. High scores on the "UMC Vital Congregations" signs of a healthy church
   a. Inviting and Inspiring Worship
   b. Engaged Disciples in mission and outreach
   c. Gifted, Empowered and Equipped Lay Leadership
   d. Effective, Equipped and Inspired Clergy Leadership
   e. Small Group Ministries
   f. Strong Children's and Youth Ministry
3. Strong Discipleship system
4. Other traits determined by the annual conference

© 2018 Robert O. Crossman, www.UMNewChurch.org

Important considerations in the selection of the Resident

1. Resident must NOT be in college during the Residency period. Must be willing to take a year off from studies.
   i. Exception: When a Residency is created for "bi-vocational" ministry
2. Must be an active member of a United Methodist conference, congregation or fellowship.
3. Must have experience working in a faith community or Christian organization (as volunteer, resident, or staff).
4. Must have completed or be willing to complete a formal assessment to determine planter characteristics and be recognized by one's annual conference as a high-potential planter.
5. Must meet any additional requirements set by sponsoring annual conference (e.g., certifications, board of ordained ministry criteria, etc.).
6. Applicants are not required, but encouraged to have undergone additional pastoral or theological training beyond what is required by the annual conference.

Key traits desired in a Resident Church Planter

1. Sincere desire to plant new churches and make disciples
2. Commitment to reaching the unchurched
3. Experience in at least one vibrant, growing church
4. Experience growing ministries from small to large (e.g. Youth Group grew from 10 to 100 or a Bible Study grew under his/her leadership).
5. Spiritual maturity and vitality
6. Strong leadership and team-building skills
7. Receptive to the needs of others and committed to building relationships
8. Creative mind and flexible work habits
9. Willingness to be held accountable to goals
10. Engaged in regular spiritual practices of prayer, Bible reading, accountability, and reflection
11. Willing to be mentored - coachable

Expectations of Residents

1. All Residents will attend two "Cohort" gatherings with Path 1:
   - An orientation for mentors and residents. (All travel costs to be covered by Path 1)
   - A Spring gathering – location TBD
2. The Residents will be assigned to a recognized large impact vital congregation in (or, in some cases, outside) their annual conference to serve for one year, working regular, full-time hours.

 © 2018 Robert O. Crossman, www.UMNewChurch.org

3. The Resident will work according to the plan negotiated with the Host Church, carrying out duties as the church directs him/her, while also fulfilling the requirements laid out in his/her covenant with the annual conference and Path 1.
4. The Resident will raise $7500 toward his or her salary package.
5. The Resident will work with a mentor who is a member of the church's pastoral staff.
6. The Resident will read books on the Path 1 Reading List. This list may be edited according to the context of Residency and in communication with Path1.
7. The Resident will journal his/her experiences and observations twice a month and discuss his/her entries with the mentor. The Resident will also incorporate the reading materials into his/her journal entries.
8 The Resident will prepare a demographic study of his/her assigned area and submit findings to the annual conference with recommendations on how to reach people in that area.
9 The Resident will become familiar with the following Path 1 materials:
   a. Church Development Strategies
   b. High-Potential Planter Traits
   c. Best Practices
   d. Implementing Best Practices
   e. 7 Seasons of Church Planting
   f. Multiplication Dynamics
   g. Church Planting Foundations
10. The Resident will attend at least one of the following planter training events during the year of the Residency:
   a. NCLI
   b. Boot Camp
   c. Church Planting 101
   d. Launchpad
   e. Exponential
   f. Catalyst
   g. Multi-ethnic or Multicultural church planting
11. The Resident will work on "Core Competencies" of Church Planting:
   a. Preaching and Worship Leadership
      - The Resident will participate in weekly worship in whatever capacity the mentor or the senior pastor sees fit.
      - The Resident will plan and lead a worship service at least six times during the residency period.
   b. Community Network and Relationship Building
      - The Resident will explore the community and get to know the people.

- The Resident will discuss ways to reach the unchurched in the area as part of weekly meetings with the mentor.
- The Resident will plan and execute one community event or "taster" during the residency.
- The Resident will coordinate two mission opportunities geared to meeting the needs of the surrounding community.
- The Resident will suggest additional mission opportunities based on his/her assessment of community needs.

c. Teaching and Leading Others (Discipling)
- The Resident will lead at least one small group during his/her residency.
- The Resident will apprentice members of the group to lead their own small groups.
- The Resident will form a "Launch Team" to work on a plan of action for the new church plant (if planting out of the residency location),

d. Administrative Duties
- The Resident will learn about making and keeping budgets.
- The Resident will learning how to enlist volunteers and staff.
- The Resident will learn about dismissing those who cannot perform effectively.
- The Resident will learn how to delegate tasks so that he or she doesn't have to carry the burden of administration.
- The Resident will learn how to evaluate ministry utilizing metrics to determine if a ministry is done well or not.

e. Fund Development
- The Resident will demonstrate the ability to raise funds to support his/her future planting ministry by participating in ongoing funding projects of the host church and raising $7500 toward salary package.
- The Resident will secure an agreed-upon amount of funding and funding partners for his/her planting project before the residency ends.

The Next Steps

1. The Resident will begin meeting with annual conference congregational developer (or annual conference equivalent) at least four times during the second half of the residency to begin discussing his/her assignment after the program.
2. The Resident will complete tasks assigned by the annual conference developer to prepare for the new planting assignment.
3. Resident will commit to begin the assignment as soon as the residency program ends.

 © 2018 Robert O. Crossman, www.UMNewChurch.org

Expectations for Resident Initiative Partners

The partners involved in this initiative are the Resident Planter, the Host Church, the annual conference, and Path1. The Host Church or the annual conference will act as the employer of the Resident and the annual conference and Path1 will serve as co-sponsors of the initiative. Each sponsor will contribute money, time, and resources to the initiative and evaluate the effectiveness of the Resident Planter, the program, and the fund development process.

In addition to the Resident Expectations outlined above, the other parties to this initiative also have responsibilities:

Host Church

George Mason writes, "A successful residency program enriches the life of a church and strengthens the broader Church at the same time" (Preparing The Pastors We Need: Reclaiming the Congregation's Role in Training Clergy, Alban, 2012, p.17).

1. The key element for a Host Church is to embrace the teaching role a residency program provides. It should see itself as the learning community that offers a safe environment where a Resident learns core competencies of ministry prior to launching out on his or her own.
2. Provide the Resident with a place to work and responsibilities that match the requirements laid out by the sponsors.
3. Provide a mentor who will meet with the Resident weekly to provide instruction, constructive criticism, prayer, and pastoral care. This mentor must be a member of the church's pastoral staff. If the mentor is not the senior pastor, the resident will also meet with the senior pastor regularly.
4. Introduce the Resident to the community and help him/her build relationships.
5. Provide periodic reports to the annual conference and Path 1 on the Resident's progress to confirm that he/she meets the basic requirements of the program according to the established time line.
6. Allow the Resident to attend national conferences or planter training events during residency period.
7. Recommend additional training, resources, or assistance for the Resident as needed.

Annual Conference

1. Select a Resident for the program that meets the qualifications laid out by Path 1.
2. Partner in funding the residency program to include (salary, benefits and housing).
3. Establish qualifications as needed in addition to Path 1requirements (provided they do not conflict with those established by Path 1).

4. Provide and/or administer assessment process for Resident.
5. Review Path 1's program requirements, making any additions without removing any of Path 1's requirements.
6. Match Resident with appropriate high impact church.
7. Once requirements of both sponsors are understood, the annual conference will sign the covenant with Resident and Host Church and Path 1 at a "Stakeholder's Meeting." Electronic versions of the Covenant, including the signature page, will be sent to all Stakeholders.
8. Provide appropriate orientation with the annual conference new church development staff prior to the start of the Residency.
9. Collect periodic reports from the Host Church on the Resident's progress.
10. Provide staff person from the annual conference new church development office to receive assignments from Resident and meet with him/her regularly during the second half of the residency.
11. Assign the Resident tasks to complete in order to prepare him/her for subsequent planting assignment.
12. Determine location of assignment following the residency and insure that the Resident is prepared and properly supported upon assignment.

Path 1

1. Establish minimal qualifications and program requirements for all annual conferences and Residents participating in the program.
2. Sign covenant agreement with annual conference, Resident, and Host Church and keep copy for records.
3. Host an orientation of all current year residents and mentors.
4. Receive periodic reports on the Resident from Host Church (frequency determined by annual conference).
5. Provide Resident with necessary Path 1 materials required as part of the program.
6. Make other Path 1 resources available to resident based upon requests.
7. Encourage Resident or Host Church to contact Path 1 directly for questions, concerns, or the sharing of good news from the residency experience.

Covenant Agreement

Purpose: To identify the roles of participants to the "High Impact Church Planting Residency" (HIR).

Objective: To establish a successful strategic partnership to facilitate the planting of a healthy, multiplying church with a passion for making disciples of Jesus Christ for the transformation of the world, incorporating mutual participation, trust, and ownership through the "High Impact Church Planting Residency" (HIR).

The general objectives that we will mutually agree and strive to accomplish are:

 © 2018 Robert O. Crossman, www.UMNewChurch.org

1. Establish acceptable guidelines to which all participating entities will agree.
2. Commit to working relationships as outlined in this Covenant.
3. Participate in periodic (frequency of which to be agreed upon by the participants) meetings for prayer, encouragement, and evaluation of progress on strategy and accomplishment of goals.

In alignment with the expectations outlined in this document, the undersigned parties enter into a covenant relationship, under the guidance of the Holy Spirit, to plant a new church through the "High Impact Church Planting Residency" initiative. All agree that the final authority and responsibility for the actions and activities of this new church plant rests primarily with the sponsoring annual conference, Path1 and the Host Church Congregation.

The Resident will be mentored by ________________________________ ______ of the Host Church and they will meet weekly during the Residency period.

The covenant agreement is a commitment of all the undersigned participants to provide support to the HIR from ______________________ through ______________________.

The signatures below represent a commitment of all participants to this Covenant Agreement and guidelines for the above outlined High Impact Church Planting Residency.

Resident ______________ Date _______

Mentor _______________ Date _______

Host Church Lay Representative ________________ Date _______

Path1 Staff Representative ________________ Date _______

District Superintendent where Host Church is located ___________ Date ______

Annual Conference Staff where Host Church is located ________ Date ______

© 2018 Robert O. Crossman, www.UMNewChurch.org

Appendix: Residency Reading List

Introductory Resources

Arment, Ben. Church in the Making: What Makes or Breaks a New Church Before it Starts.

Bird, Warren and Ed Stetzer. Viral Churches.

Cole, Neil. Church 3.0.

Easum, Bill and Jim Griffith. Ten Most Common Mistakes Made By New Church Starts.

Kawasaki, Guy. The Art of the Start.

Mason, George. Preparing The Pastors We Need: Reclaiming the Congregation's Role in Training Clergy.

Nebel, Tom and Gary Rohrmayer. Church Planting Landmines: Mistakes to Avoid in Years 2 through 10.

Shockley, Gary. The Meandering Way: Leading by Following the Spirit.

Models

Bird, Warren, Greg Ligon, and Geoff Surratt. A Multi-Site Church Road Trip: Exploring the New Normal.

Steve Nerger. Bivocational Church Planters: Uniquely Wired for Kingdom Growth.

Aubrey Malphurs. A New Kind of Church: Understanding Models of Ministry for the 21st Century.

Nebel, Tom. Big Dreams in Small Places Church Planting in Smaller Communities.

Nixon, Paul. Finding Jesus on the Metro.

Searcy, Nelson and Kerrick Thomas. Launch: Starting a New Church from Scratch.

Discipleship

Putman, David and Ed Stetzer. Breaking the Discipleship Code.

Ferguson, Dave and John. Exponential.

Hunter, George G. The Apostolic Congregation.

Breen, Mike. Building a Discipling Culture.

Missional Outreach

Breen, Mike. Launching Missional Communities.

Heath, Elaine, and Larry Duggins. Missional. Monastic. Mainline: A Guide to Starting Missional Micro-Communities in Historically Mainline Traditions (2014).

McNeal, Reggie. Missional Renaissance: Changing the Scorecard for the

 © 2018 Robert O. Crossman, www.UMNewChurch.org

Church (Joessey-Bass Leandership Network Series, 2009).

Nelson, Gary V. Borderland Churches: A Congregation's Introduction to Missional Living.

Putman, David and Ed Stetzer. Breaking the Missional Code: Your Church Can Become a Missionary in Your Community.

Stetzer, Ed. Planting Missional Churches.

Reaching Young People

Kinnaman, David. You lost me.

Kinnaman, David. Un Christian.

Merritt, Carol Howard. Tribal Church: Ministering to the Missing Generation.

Rainer, Sam S., III and Thom S. Rainer. Essential Church?: Reclaiming a Generation of Dropouts.

Stetzer, Ed. Lost and Found: The younger Unchurched and the Churches that Reach Them.

Fundraising

Christopher, J. Cliff. Not Your Parents' Offering Plate.

Henri J. M. Nouwen. A Spirituality of Fundraising.

Reeves, Michael. Extravagant Generosity: Program Guide with CD: The Heart of Giving.

Reprinted here by permission of Bener Agtarap granted on January 26, 2018.
Source: www.Path1.org

†††

PATH1

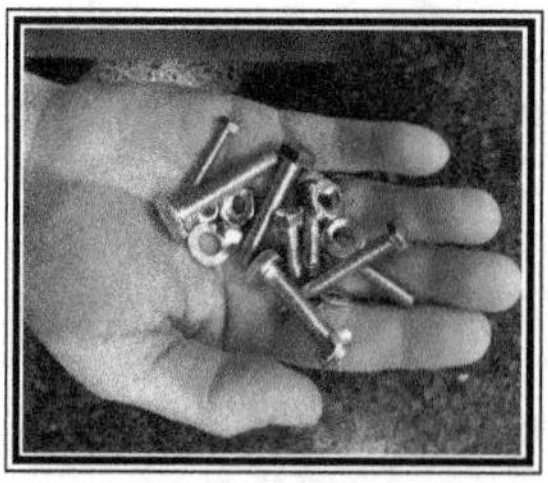

New Church Handbook
Nuts & Bolts for Planting New Churches In The Wesleyan Tradition

"What is First Twelve?"

by Path 1

First 12 Participant Workbook

gathering and growing
the First Twelve core team members
and leaders
for a new ministry, new faith community, or new congregation

What is First 12?

The first twelve people to join you in starting a new ministry, new church, or new faith community will set the tone and shape for the future, set the pattern for replicating leadership, and begin a cascade of invitation. Finding those first twelve people who are invested and committed as leaders with you in helping start a new ministry is a key initial step in growing into something larger without your vision burning out or stalling out before a successful ministry launch.

First 12 is a two-day training event designed to help you gather and grow the first twelve committed, core people. Combined with a year of practical coaching follow-up, you will learn the skills, habits, and lifestyle practices that will give your new vision the best chance of launching with a team of twelve committed leaders. Although designed the team at Path1 New Church Starts from principles of new faith community planting, this training is equally valuable for existing church leaders who want to start new small groups, new fellowships, new mission outreaches, new worship services, or new gatherings

 © 2018 Robert O. Crossman, www.UMNewChurch.org

What Will Happen During First 12?
Day 1 – Gathering (6 hours)

- Discovering yourself
- Identifying your affinities
- What is your leadership style?
- Patterns of cross-cultural communication
- Going where the people are
- Researching people in your community
- Getting invited to someone else's party: Events, Clubs, Sports
- Becoming a "regular" or "the art of strategically hanging out"
- 10 marbles practice
- Make friends, contacts, interested leads
- How to meet new people
- Making small talk that matters
- Communication your vision quickly (like during an elevator ride)
- How to get contact information for follow-up
- Deepen leads: follow, build, [track], repeat
- Building a relationship tracking system
- Conducting 1-on-1 meetings
- Developing a habit of constant invitation
- Invite others to help start new thing
- Connecting their interest in your vision
- Making the ask
- Building a launching team of 12 people
- Create missional community
- 5 practices of missional community
- Avoiding terminal small-group syndrome

Day 2 – Growing (4 hours)

- Deepen discipleship
- Beginning a journey with Jesus
- 6 practices of effective discipleship coaching
- uninviting some people
- Deepen investment: heart, time, money
- Planter passion, investment, tithe, and commitment
- Getting to "Yes!" with vision and mission
- Asking for money: Fund Raising and Spiritual Care
- Deepen leadership
- From followers to leaders, the apprenticeship cycle
- Discovering strengths, gifts, and skills
- Building multiplication culture
- Deepen invitation: lifestyle, habits, practices
- Your marketing is your life
- Teaching and practicing invitation
- Working with your First 12 coach & cohort
- Meeting your cohort
- Drafting your First 12 plan

PATH1

Reprinted here by permission of Bener Agtarap granted on January 26, 2018.

New Church Handbook
Nuts & Bolts for Planting New Churches In The Wesleyan Tradition

"What Are The Characteristics of Multiplying and Non-Multiplying Churches?"

There are no pure multiplication cultures in church life – every regional and denominational culture has aspects of both columns below. To the degree that the culture aligns more with the characteristics in the left column, we can say that there exists a "culture of multiplication" within that system. Here are 30 points of comparison.

Multiplication	Non-Multiplication
1. Extremely simple local church organization and focus (often worship, small group and outreach).	1. Lots of committees and complicated decision making. Church involved in major issues and projects beyond the minimum core of focus.
2. Minimum of centralized activity. Groups lead, initiate new things.	2. Most ministry is staff-led or planned by a central committee.
3. Trust of leaders at every level; Sacraments are given to the people.	3. High value for uniformity, managing down and central control.
4. No one seems harried or rushed.	4. Staff are over-worked and exhausted, at capacity.
5. Theology is indigenous to the culture so that unattached laity can easily jump onboard.	5. Theology: a priestly task with seminary education required for any perceived competency.
6. There is a high view of Bible and it is used easily and freely in every type of gathering. Laity trusted.	6. The Bible is problematic and tricky. Most are illiterate – with many hostile, others protective.
7. Within the shared theological Context, pastor's major role is to teach Bible in large venue worship times and to pastor the leaders.	7. Pastor: CEO, theologian in residence, shepherd for as many people as s/he can manage. Doing too much.
8. Pastors are gifted as strong communicators and visionaries.	8. Pastors responsible for a wide array of concerns. They may be weak in the most critical areas.
9. Anyone can lead a small group, and the group works well enough to nurture a dozen other folks. Groups regularly recognize when a group member is ready to be leading out on their own.	9. Training is required. Possibly uniform curriculum. Anxiety about theology being propagated in the group. Few are deemed trustworthy to lead.
10. To belong is to serve. Everyone pitches in.	10. Church is service that we pay others to do for us.

 © 2018 Robert O. Crossman, www.UMNewChurch.org

Multiplication	Non-Multiplication
11. Pastors come together to lead. Prayer/ deliberation lead to consensus. No one ever votes.	11. Democratic process surrounds many decisions at multiple levels of church.
12. Church may often choose to avoid position statements on sticky issues, leave it to conscience of diverse membership. Pastors will still teach a position, but social statements are downplayed.	12. Social principles. Denomination position papers, politically charged environment.
13. No creed, no membership.	13. Confirmation, learning information, affirming creed.
14. Theological agreement on a short list of principles by pastors and staff, but a very simple process of pastoral certification.	14. Cumbersome, lengthy process of theological formation with prospective pastors.
15. Plain, functional (often leased) meeting space. Not expensive.	15. Elaborate facilities. High overhead costs.
16. Evangelization is about finding the next leaders, the people who have the gifts and or passion. It is everyone's concern.	16. Evangelization is about finding paying customers. Management's problem.
17. They pray about everything. Prayer is the main strategy. Prayer is central.	17. Prayer is perfunctory, often a ritual performed only by a "professional."
18. Widespread consensus on the relationship between the gospel and God's plan for human beings. Common, simple theological language and framework.	18. Soteriological confusion. Disconnect about what difference the gospel makes for the world.
19. Sometimes a franchise framework for like groups who wish to hop on board the network.	19. Distrust of anything our management team did not initiate.
20. Sweet spot between grace and order. A lot of leaders fit here because there is grace to give them a chance here (without seminary, after divorce, after jail, etc.).	20. Though we may pride ourselves on grace, there is a culture of works and control operative on many levels. Snob factor.
21. Small groups can feel like a marriage improvement cult. Groups will definitely form around the agendas of average people.	21. Small groups are not given freedom to become marriage cults (or other kinds of special interest groups). Staff picks the agenda.
22. You pastor those entrusted to you, be it a group or a group of leaders. Very rare meetings for administration or fellowship.	22. Lots of leader meetings.

Multiplication	Non-Multiplication
23. Church on "the cheap." The value of "Good Enough."	23. Expensive church. The value of "Excellence in all things."
24. Innovation at the local level. Pastor held accountable for fruit.	24. Uniformity anxiety by the area management. Conference-wide initiatives mandated for all.
25. Pastors have no tenure. They hold each other accountable. They are terminated from within their ranks.	25. Strong clergy union with no easy exit strategy when effectiveness ceases.
26. New initiatives originate locally – churches plant churches.	26. Planting is centralized.
27. Everybody, every group every church is expected to reproduce. Multiplication at all levels.	27. We add new members, classes, and churches, one by one.
28. All shapes and sizes of church affirmed, the simpler the better.	28. Churches should be big enough to have "critical mass" and pay full-time pastor plus denominational dues.
29. Reproduction is rapid and possible within weeks or months.	29. Reproduction takes years.
30. Church health rooted in spiritual depth and outward focus.	30. Church health measured in people in pews and dollars in plates.

As you work to cultivate a culture of multiplication, discuss these indicators with key leaders. You may identify additional points of contrast that reflect your congregational or conference culture. These discussions may offer ideas for strategic planning that address specific concerns.

Reprinted here by permission of Bener Agtarap granted on January 26, 2018.
Source: www.Path1.org

PATH1

 © 2018 Robert O. Crossman, www.UMNewChurch.org

New Church Handbook
Nuts & Bolts for Planting New Churches In The Wesleyan Tradition

"Any Research on African-American New Church Starts?"

by Path 1

PATH1

For a copy of the full 82 page report, contact either:
wchaney@umcdiscipleship.org OR bcrossman@arumc.org

Executive Summary

This brief summary contains key findings from a study of Protestant African-American church plants nationwide. The study was conducted by LifeWay Research. Lists of church plants were provided by 6 denominations and a list of African-American churches was rented to include additional groups and non-denominational churches. Data was collected through an online survey during February – May 2012. This executive summary highlights key findings from the total sample of the study. The sample size was 290 church plants.

Worship Service

- Average worship attendance for the first year of African-American church plants is 37.
- By year four, the average worship attendance has doubled (80).

New Commitments to Jesus Christ

- The average number of new commitments to Jesus Christ is 16 for the first year of the church plant.
- The average number of new commitments to Jesus Christ per year peaks in year 3 (20) and remains at 12 or higher for all years measured.

Characteristics With a Positive Impact on Attendance and New Commitments

- 32 characteristics have a positive impact on worship attendance including three items present in more than two-thirds of the churches:
  - Delegation of leadership roles to volunteers
  - Leadership training for new church members
  - Plan for spiritual formation for the church planter
- 23 characteristics have a positive impact on new commitments to Jesus Christ including two practices present in more than two-thirds of the churches:
  – Door-to-door evangelism
  – Conducing a new member class
- Six characteristics were shown to impact both worship attendance and new commitments to Jesus Christ. They are:
  - Church building of their own used as facility during first 5 years
  - Church planter compensated for their work

- Church planter worked 60 hours a week or more on the church plant during the first two years of the church plant
- Sponsor or mother church permitted the church plant to meet in the sponsoring church building
- Week long Boot Camp or Basic Training provided
- Contemporary worship style

Churches Represented

- Church plants from more than 20 denominations participated plus non-denominational churches.
- 23% have been part of or resourced by a national church planting network.
- 43% were started since 2007

Community

- 41% of churches estimate the community where the church started contained more than 20% Bible believing Christians.
- On average, the ethnic make-up of the community where the African-American churches were planted were:
  - 42% African-American
  - 35% White
  - 13% Hispanic
  - % African or Caribbean decent
  - 3% Asian
  - 3% Other
- In 42% of the churches, there has been a major shift in the demographics of the community since the church began. This includes 23% who saw a major shift but stayed in the community and 19% who saw a major shift and moved to a new community.

Congregation

- During the first two years of the church plant, an average of 75% of the congregation was African-American.
- 80% of the church plants stated that their congregation was at least 50% African-American during the first two years.
- 68% indicated that they sought to target African-Americans as they tried to reach their community.
- More than 80% of the church planters intentionally sought to reach a cross-cultural or multi-ethnic group of people.
- Over 60% intentionally encouraged an African-American culture within the church.
- Nearly 70% emphasized racial reconciliation as a primary part of the church's vision and practices.
- 36% of the attendees during the first 5 years were estimated to be previously unchurched.

Facilities

- The most common facilities used by church plants in the first year were a church building shared with another congregation (22%), a business establish-

 © 2018 Robert O. Crossman, www.UMNewChurch.org

ment (19%), homes (15%), a church building of their own (14%), and schools (13%).

- The most common facilities used any time during the first five years are a church building shared with another congregation (34%), a church building of their own (30%), a business establishment (28%), homes (25%), and schools (24%).

Worship Style

- The most common worship styles used are blended (45%), contemporary Gospel (14%), contemporary (13%), and urban contemporary (12%).

Church Planting Models

- Church planters could select from a series of models which ones most strongly influenced the approach used in planting the church.
- Two models were selected by over 40% of the church planters: ministry based (47%) and attractional (41%).

Funding

- Average funding in year one is $49,800 growing steadily through year 4 ($97,726) then falling off until resuming growth in year 7.
- Average dollars received from outside sources averages $21,818 in the first year. Over the first 7 years average outside funding declines 44% while dollars received from members or attendees grows 211%.

Sponsoring Church

- 48% of the church plants had a sponsoring or mother church. 36% of church plants received funding from one or more sponsoring churches.

Church Planter

- About two-thirds (66%) of the church planters have at least a Bachelor's degree. For theological education, 45% have at least a Master's degree.
- 55% of church planters received specific training for church planting prior to planting the church. The most common types were conferences on church planting (51%) and week-long boot camps (42%).
- Only 16% of church planters received specific training on the dynamics of the African-American context prior to planting. 69% believe they would benefit from that specific training today.
- Only 6% of the church plants had a paid, staffed team of more than one person to start the church.
- In the first two years of the church plant's existence, over 60% of the church planters worked 40 hours a week or more at the church plant.
- 52% of the church planters received some financial compensation for their work as a church planter.
- 69% of church planters had an outside job in addition to their work as a church planter during the first two years of the church plant's existence.

Reprinted here by permission of Bener Agtarap granted on January 26, 2018.
Source: www.Path1.org

†††

New Church Handbook
Nuts & Bolts for Planting New Churches In The Wesleyan Tradition

"What Is the Role of The Bishop in New Church Planting?"

by Bishop William W. Dew

The Role of the Episcopal Office in Starting New Churches

by Bishop William W. Dew

The establishment of new faith communities with the goal of becoming chartered churches and the vitalization of existing congregations are two effective means whereby annual conferences fulfill the vision of making disciples for Jesus Christ in the 21st century. Bishops have gleaned and experienced many strategies for implementing visions of new future churches throughout their ministry prior to becoming bishops. As episcopal leaders they are in unique positions to join with the leadership of an annual conference in establishing a vision, a strategic plan, and financial undergirding of resources to accomplish significant development within their area. All bishops share some skills and ideas in common in this arena, but they also have different thoughts about which is the best leadership method for an annual conference.

The following are some thoughts about leadership and some key steps that each episcopal leader should consider.

Attempt to develop a leadership style that maximizes participation of as many people as appropriate so that the ownership of a new vision is wide-spread and understood by as many people as possible.

The best administrators seldom "tell" their staff what to do, but rather provide a creative climate and utilize processes that enable people to discover for themselves the most effective ways to accomplish their goals and priorities. Decentralization, freedom and participative democratic procedures allow for the maximum involvement of people who provide leadership in an annual conference.

A first step in an annual conference is to hold gatherings of laity and clergy to address the questions of what should be done to fulfill our gospel mandate and to address the human needs of people who are moving into our communities. The use of demographic data is vital to this enterprise of gathering data. Above all, the episcopal leader must demonstrate that he/she is committed to listening to the people at these gatherings.

Another step is to recruit highly effective motivated clergy and laity, the "best"

 © 2018 Robert O. Crossman, www.UMNewChurch.org

pastors and the" "best" laity, to serve on a leadership team that accepts the challenge of shaping the vision that will be placed before the annual conference.

Once the vision is agreed upon by the leadership team, then all of the constituencies of the annual conference must be given opportunities to gain ownership of the vision and the priorities that flow from the vision.

When this is accomplished the episcopal leader makes clear that moving toward the vision and being guided by the priorities are two important responsibilities he or she has in the conference. This is accomplished by including these commitments in preaching, teaching and administration throughout the conference.

The episcopal leader, along with the extended cabinet (district superintendents and other connectional ministry personnel), work together as a team to demonstrate the power of the collaborative approach to leadership. The extended cabinet understands that it exists to serve the congregations and the mission of the conference and not vice versa.

A designated staff position giving leadership to congregational development and new congregation location and support is vital. The episcopal leader must have 100% confidence in the person who fills this position.

It is necessary for the district superintendents and the congregational development person to identify, train, equip, support and strategically place persons who are being asked to start new faith communities.

Annual conference budgets usually do not have sufficient resources within their parameters on an annual basis to support the work of starting new faith communities and the vitalizing of existing congregations. A financial plan needs to be developed and presented to the annual conference for the completion of the vision for the future. Finally, and most importantly, the episcopal leader should be willing to be the key leader of the financial campaign and be willing to make it a top priority for the first year of the campaign. I believe that the episcopal leader should be willing to attempt to raise at least 50% of the financial goal of a campaign by requesting lead gifts and major gifts of individuals and foundations.

In summary, the office of the episcopal leader is the key component that provides leadership for the success of establishing new faith communities and the vitalization of existing congregations within the annual conference in making Disciples for Jesus Christ in the 21st century.

This article first appeared in The United Methodist Manual for New Church Development, editors Rev. Scott Ray and Rev. Clay Jacobs

Bishop Dew died at age 74, July 14, 2010, at his home in Elk Grove, CA

†††

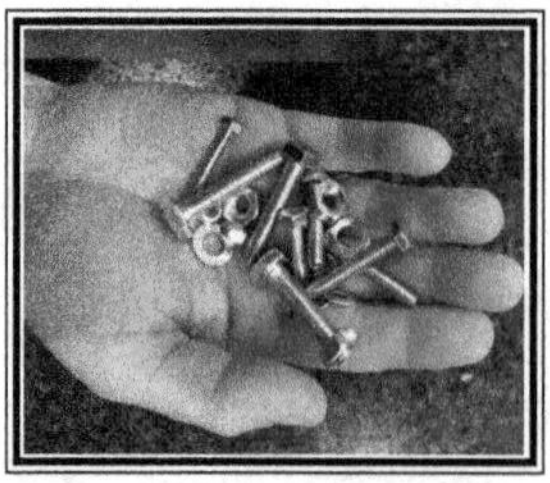

New Church Handbook
Nuts & Bolts for Planting New Churches In The Wesleyan Tradition

"What Is the Role of The D.S. in New Church Planting?"

by Tom Butcher

This article first appeared in The United Methodist Manual for New Church Development, editors Rev. Scott Ray and Rev. Clay Jacobs

The Role of the District Superintendent in Starting New Churches

by Rev. Tom Butcher

The establishment of new churches, with the goal of becoming chartered, is one of the most effective means of evangelization in the 21st century. This has been true in United Methodism since the time of John Wesley. The role of the district superintendent is vital in fulfilling the mandate to make Disciples of Jesus Christ.

The district superintendents' responsibility for starting new churches is made clear in the Book of Discipline. ¶259.1, The Method of Organizing a new local church states the following:

> A new local church or mission congregation shall be established only with the consent of the bishop in charge and the cabinet and with due consideration of the conference entity assigned the responsibility for congregational development. The bishop shall designate the district within whose bounds the church or mission congregation shall be organized. The district superintendent of that district, or his or her designee, shall be the agent in charge of the project and shall recommend to the district board of church location and building (¶ 2519) the method of organization, and whether a specific site shall be selected or an area of organization be designated. The district superintendent shall avail him/herself of existing demographic, lifestyle and ethnographic information in the process of establishing a new congregation and its location, or shall recommend to the board of trustees of a selected local church that they share their facility with the proposed congregation. If there is a city or district missionary organization, or if funds for the project are anticipated from a conference organization, those bodies shall also be asked to approve the method of organization and location for a new congregation.

Therefore, the district superintendent is the main supervisory person for any new church start and the pastor that is appointed.

© 2018 Robert O. Crossman, www.UMNewChurch.org

More and more annual conferences are designating a staff person to provide leadership to congregational development and new church starts. It is necessary for the district superintendents and the new church start staff person to work together to identify, train, equip, support and strategically place persons who are being asked to start new faith communities. However, the Discipline is clear that the district superintendent is responsible for supervising the new church start pastor. The new church starts staff person can be very helpful in the mentoring process.

An important aspect in helping district superintendents to start new churches is the development of a strategic plan for the entire annual conference. An intentional and coordinated effort involving all the districts will both focus and maximize the resources that are needed. If the annual conference does not have a strategic plan for beginning new faith communities, the district superintendent, with the support of the bishop, can be a catalyst for the development of such a plan.

It is also imperative that the district superintendent take the initiative in developing a district strategic plan for starting new churches. This means there is a vital need to have a "passion" for beginning new faith communities. Clay Jacobs, Director for the Office of Church Development of the North Georgia Conference, has put it this way, "If you don't have a passion for starting new churches, you need to get it!" The understanding here is that beginning new faith communities is the most effective method today of making new disciples for Jesus Christ. Also, the district superintendent knows where the need is. Nobody knows the district better than the D.S.; where the growth is taking place and where the emerging ethnic, language, generational and cultural groups are located that need to be reached in fresh, new, creative and exciting ways. Develop a keen eye when looking at these areas to see just where a new faith community might be planted. Then study those areas with your District Board of Church Location and Building Committee and together form a plan!

As a district superintendent, it is crucial in providing leadership and inspiration for the entire district to support the new church start. To be sure, there will be those pastors and churches within your district that feel "no new churches are needed in their area." However, it is most difficult for new churches to survive without the total support of every church in the district. District support for a new church start can come in a variety of ways. Cash is always helpful and usually the most needed. The new fellowships need dollars to rent facilities; advertise; hire staff; and develop missions. Laity serving as "missionaries" can be very helpful in the launch of a new church start. Usually these folks are sent out for six months to a year from other existing churches from within the district. A new video projector with a computer, screen and new sound system can make all the difference in the world. Making the new church start a District Advance and Mission special greatly improves the new church start's success.

The most important factor in the success of a new church start is leadership

It has been stated that the most important factor in the success of a new church start is leadership. As a district superintendent, realization that it is critical to give your very best pastors to these appointments is imperative. Starting a new church is about the hardest task we ask our pastors are asked to do. Therefore, an invitation to the ministry must be given to the most talented pastors. Perhaps only 10% of the pastors in any given district are able to grow a new church through their gifts, graces and passions. Even though a number of churches in the district would benefit from such leadership; the mission field, however, now surrounds us and for the sake of the Kingdom identification of these pastors, training them and using them to plant new churches must be the first priority.

The district superintendent needs to understand that there are several models available for starting new churches. Some persons may indicate that there is only one way to do this successfully. This is not true. Additional new successful models are being discovered every day and there is a high learning curve when it comes to talking about how we start new faith communities and how to develop them into chartered churches.

Finally, the district superintendent must be willing to energetically encourage new church start pastors. While the Book of Discipline states that the district superintendent is the primary supervisor of this pastor, he/she also needs to be his/her biggest cheerleader! Giving birth to a new faith community is one of the loneliest tasks in all of ministry. Keep in close contact with each new church pastor and make sure they take care of themselves and their families. Make sure also that the new church pastor remains United Methodist, and that they have a mentor and/or a coach.

It is very gratifying to watch each district grow and become stronger because the district superintendent is willing to start new churches with their best leadership in areas where the Good News of Jesus Christ is most needed.

This article first appeared in The United Methodist Manual for New Church Development, editors Rev. Scott Ray and Rev. Clay Jacobs

†††

Originally from Corunna, MI, Pastor of Sun City, Arizona's Lakeview UMC, Tom Butcher attended Adrian College in southern Michigan and has a Master's degree from Pacific School of Religion in Berkley, CA. Tom joined the Lakeview UMC staff in July of 2013 after having spent three years as Executive Officer for Path 1, the United Methodist national strategy team for starting new churches. He has been a member of the Desert Southwest Annual Conference since 1979 and has served at Los Arcos UMC, Scottsdale, AZ; Velda Rose UMC in Mesa, AZ; First UMC of Gilbert, Gilbert, AZ; and St. Matthew UMC, Mesa, AZ. Tom has also served as Council Director, district superintendent, and Director of New Faith Communities for the Desert Southwest Conference.

 © 2018 Robert O. Crossman, www.UMNewChurch.org

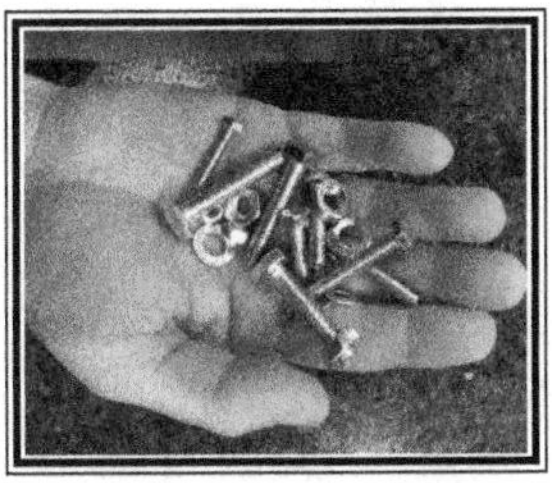

New Church Handbook
Nuts & Bolts for Planting New Churches In The Wesleyan Tradition

"What Is the Role of The D.S. as Chief Missional Strategist?"

by Path 1, Douglas Ruffle

The District Superintendent as "Chief Missional Strategist" by Douglas Ruffle

The 2012 Book of Discipline of The United Methodist Church added a new expectation to the office of district superintendent: to he "chief missional strategist." Other than mentioning lt as an expectation of the Church in ¶419, the Discipline does not spell out explicitly the work of a chief missional strategist. Yet, Implicitly, through other directives regarding superintending and with the help of District Boards and/or Strategy Committees, one can put the pieces together lor how this can be done.

The following is Path 1's attempt at doing just that.

The Purpose of Superintending

According to ¶401 of The Book of Discipline 2012, "The purpose of superintending is to equip the Church in its disciple-making ministry. Those who superintend carry primary responsibility for ordering the life of the Church. It is their task to enable the gathered Church to worship and to evangelize faithfully." **Superintending** refers to bishops and district superintendents. The latter whom serve as an extension of the office of bishop. The same paragraph goes on to say, "It is also their task to facilitate the initiation of structures and strategies for the equipping of Christian people for service in the Church and in the world in the name of Jesus Christ and to help extend the service in mission... " (*The Book of Discipline* 2012, ¶401).

As we look at the district superintendent (DS) as chief missional strategist it is Important to be clear about the overall purpose of the position. Everything flows out of the mission of the Church, which is to make disciples of Jesus Christ for the transformation of the world. Superintending equips the church for disciple-making.

Missional Mindset

The term "missional" also picks up on a movement that seeks to help the church transition from an attractional mode of being to a more outward-focused

© 2018 Robert O. Crossman, www.UMNewChurch.org

missional mode of being. Much has been written recently to help the Church embrace this shift. Many of us grew up under the old paradigm that is often characterized by the phrase, "We go to church." The church was something we went to; to be nourished in the faith; to hear the word of God preached; to be inspired by good music; to ensure that our children were instructed in the ways of God. There is nothing wrong with any of these reasons for going to church. However, the mind set of this outlook places the Church as one more object of a consumeristic society. The church is construed as a provider of religious goods and services, and thus we go "shopping" for a church and if the preaching is not to our liking and the music doesn't move us, we go to another place of worship that meets our needs better.

The challenge for all of us is to help the Church move toward the phrase, "We are the church.'" The church in this sense is the body of people who are sent on a mission by God. We still gather for worship to hear good preaching, music. and instruction. However, the mind set becomes "both/and" where in addition to having our own souls fed, we become the living hands and feet of Jesus engaged in the community to make a difference in peoples' lives and thus to be instruments or God for the transformation or the world.

An Opportunity to be Strategic

The conversation of the district superintendent as Missional Strategist provides an opportunity to be strategic. Under the section of the Discipline that outlines the ''Specific Responsibilities of district superintendents" (Section VI of Chapter Three, "The Superintendency'"), ¶419 says:

> *"The Church expects . .. That the superintendent will he the chief missional strategist of the district and be committed to living out the values or the Church, including a mandate or inclusiveness ... And working with persons across the Church to develop programs of ministry and mission that extend the witness of Christ into the world."*

Moreover, this section or the Discipline continues, "The superintendent, in consultation with the bishop and cabinet, shall work to develop the best strategic deployment of clergy possible in the district, including realignment of pastoral charges when needed and the exploration or larger parishes, cooperative parishes. multiple staff configurations, new faith communities, and ecumenical shared communities." (*The Book of Discipline* 2012, ¶419).

The Church expects ... *a strategy*. It expects its leaders to come up with a plan to be about the business or making disciples of Jesus Christ for the transformation of the world. With all the demands on a Superintendents time, how is she or he to develop such a strategy?

 © 2018 Robert O. Crossman, www.UMNewChurch.org

The Discipline provides ways to go about building a strategic plan. The DS can put together a District Strategy Committee or direct the District Board of Church Location and Building to fulfill the functions of a strategic committee. In either case the DS gives leadership to the formulation of a strategy.

Purpose of District Boards of Church Location and Building

District Boards of Church Location and Building serve to help churches avoid mistakes when they engage in building projects. A church brings their project plans to the Board and they review it, ask questions, and help assure that the church's plan makes sense economically, structurally, and missionally. In this role, the Board is reactive to plans made by churches. It is an important role.

The essential tasks of the District Board of Church Location and Building include:

- Investigate all proposed local church building sites
- Approve plans for construction' purchase, or remodeling or local churches
- Make sure local churches analyze needs of church and community
- Project potential membership with average worship attendance
- Have a written plan of the church's program of ministry
- Work with district superintendent on a District Strategy in the absence of a District Strategy Committee

This latter point allows for the District Board of Church Location and Building to serve a proactive role. Unless a District Strategy Committee exists, the Board can fulfill the role of strategy team along with the DS.

¶2520.2 of *Thc Discipline* 2012 states:

> *If there is a district strategy committee for parish development or a metropolitan commission in the district, the [District Board of Church Location and Building] shall consider its recommendations in planning a strategy for continuing the service or The United Methodist Church in changing neighborhoods. If no parish development committee or commission is operative, the board shall study the duties assigned to each and seek ways to provide continuity or service in parishes where there is a change in the racial, ethnic, or cultural character of the residents ...*

District Strategy Committee?

The Book of Discipline does not outline the responsibilities or a District Strategy Committee. Yet by acknowledging that they may be operative, a district superintendent, in order to fulfill his or her task as "Chief Missional Strategist" could form such a committee to help gel the work done. The bottom line is: come up with a plan! Either form a District Strategy Committee or ask the District Board of Church Location and Building to serve a strategy function and help you, the DS. to formulate the plan.

What should be included in District Strategy?

A District Strategy should include:

- Plans for starting new churches
- Strategies for revitalizing existing congregations
- Identifying which churches should be encouraged to relocate
- Inviting churches to come together for a 'Vital Merger" (where assets are surrendered to start a new church from the merging congregations)
- Encourage churches to form cooperative parishes
- Which churches, if any, should be assessed for their potential according to the guidelines of ¶213 of the *Discipline?*

A District plan will prioritize the elements listed above. It will formulate a budget and identify income sources to carry out the plan. It will put the plan into a time frame with clear goals and objectives. By prioritizing and focusing resources, Districts can employ good stewardship principles as they plan for the expansion and vitalization of mission opportunities.

Steps of the Process

1. The DS through appropriate nominating process of the annual conference, forms a District Strategy Committee or convenes the District Board of Church Location and Building for the purpose of strategizing (Hereafter referred to as "District Team")
2. The District Team engages in a strategy development process in order to produce a District Strategic Plan.
3. The Strategic Plan will:
    - Thoroughly review the demographics of the District to identify churches in areas of transition
        I. In areas where demographic changes have resulted in church decline, plan for the continuity of United Methodist presence through planting new churches or revitalizing existing churches
        II. Seek ways to fortify existing churches through appropriate training so that they can better reach the changing demographics of the community.
    - Prioritize the areas, costs, and time lines for starting new Churches
    - Identify churches for revitalization, relocations, mergers, cooperatives, and "vital mergers"
    - Provide time lines, money needed, and sources of finances necessary to implement the Plan, and recommend a method and process for approving, updating and monitoring the Plan

Phases of the Process

1. Forming the District Team
2. Using Data for Planning

© 2018 Robert O. Crossman, www.UMNewChurch.org

3. Make assignments for visitation of each church in the District
4. Identify target areas for new church starts
5. Identify churches that could benefit from a revitalization process
6. Identify targets for mergers, relocations, cooperatives, and "vital mergers"

Data Evaluation and Creating a Preliminary Plan

Once sub-teams have scheduled visits to the churches of the district, have each report back to the entire District Team to present findings. Gather a picture of the entire district from the findings from the visits and demographic analysis. Draft a preliminary plan that aligns the District for maximum leverage of human, financial, and property resources to fulfill the mission of making disciples.

Invite input from others In the District about the preliminary plan. Revise the draft plan and finalize priorities based on available assets. Present the plan to the appropriate district or conference committees and then to the entire Districl Conference for a vole.

Be sure to organize "monitoring teams" who will assist with the implementation or the plan. Some churches will need guidance or coaching to fulfill the strategic vision. The district superintendent, as 'chief missional strategist,' supervises the entire process.

Appointment making is a crucial part of the overall strategy. Reverend Sky Lowe-McCracken, a district superintendent in the Memphis Annual Conference, underscored this importance in a blog he wrote entitled, "Missional Strategy and Mindset" (January 29. 2013). McCracken wrote:

> Bishops and cabinets will have to be less tied to "salary sheets" and tenure when making pastoral appointments and see ALL appointments as MISSIONAL- putting gifts and abilities above tenure. As Gil Rendle has warned us, our "clients" are no longer churches and pastors- the MISSION FIELD is our client. If we're truly going to be missional. our clergy can no longer expect to be served by our congregations and our laity can no longer expect their clergy to simply keep them happy. Indeed, if clergy and laity are to lead together, both will find that we will be meddling in each others' lives and the lives or others. Being disciples
> means living a higher standard and expecting greater things. It also means that we adopt the shift toward making disciples rather than making "members." Membership in the Church doesn't have its privileges; it has responsibilities.
>
> EVERYTHING we do must be geared toward mission, and should be- not just for Institutional survival and relevance, but to fulfill our Great Commission, which is missional and not institutional: Make disciples

of Jesus Christ for the transformation or the world. The institution on is a TOOL, but it's not the end-all.[1]

The DS as "chief missional strategist'. may be new to the Discipline but the practice of thinking strategically for the overall mission of the church goes back to the days of Francis Asbury and John Wesley.

The DS does not have to do this work alone. He or she can organize a "District Strategy Committee" or empower a District Board of Church Location and Building to help with the task. The important outcome is to put into place a plan that leads the Church to make disciples of Jesus Christ.

The Path I Team includes strategists who can help district superintendents fulfill the role or "chief missional strategist." Contact us to help you put the process together for developing a District Strategic Plan. Call us at 1-800-899-2780 extension 7130 or email us at druffle@umcdiscipleship.org

---

[1] From the blog, '"Missional Strategy and Mindset," dated January 29. 2013 in Kyrie Ellison: Pastoral thoughts from a United Methodist in Western Kentucky (USA), by Rev. Sky Lowe-McCracken., http :/lrevdsky.blogspot.com/. The Rev. Sky Lowe-McCracken serves as district superintendent of the Paducah (Kentucky) District of the Memphis Annual Conference.

Reprinted here by permission of Bener Agtarap granted on January 26, 2018.
Source: www.Path1.org

†††

Rev. Dr. Douglas Ruffle
Associate Executive Director
Editor for Wesleyan Resources
druffle@umcdiscipleship.org
Blessed husband of Tammie, Path1 team member, writer, baseball fan, Jesus follower
Dr. Ruffle, Ph.d. is the author of *Roadmap to Renewal: Rediscovering the Church's Mission-Revised Edition with Study Guide,* and *A Missionary Mindset: What Church Leaders Need to Know to Reach Their Community - Lessons from E. Stanley Jones*

PATH1

© 2018 Robert O. Crossman, www.UMNewChurch.org

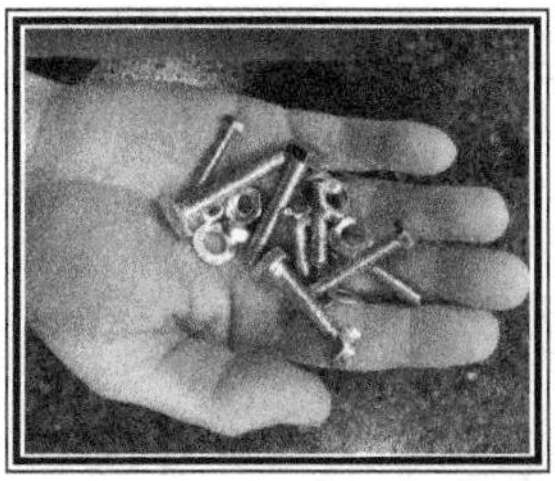

New Church Handbook
Nuts & Bolts for Planting New Churches In The Wesleyan Tradition

"What Is the Role of The Congregational Developer in New Church Planting?"

by Dick Freeman

This article first appeared in The United Methodist Manual for New Church Development, editors Rev. Scott Ray and Rev. Clay Jacobs

The Discipline of the United Methodist Church clearly recognizes a conference level position to direct conference efforts in new church development and congregational development. Section 259.1 reads, *"A new local church or mission congregation shall be established only with the consent of the bishop in charge and the cabinet and with due consideration of the conference entity assigned the responsibility for congregational development."*

To be effective, new church development or congregational development must be a full time position in the annual conference. It is helpful for the position to be cabinet level or part of the extended cabinet as much of the long range planning for new church development involves leadership development and clergy appointments.

The director of congregational development is the major conference advocate for new church development with the bishop and cabinet. The position may have an additional portfolio in revitalization of existing congregations. The dual portfolio gives the director of congregational development access to every church in the annual conference. Directly connecting the congregational development function with every church in the annual conference allows the director to establish widespread support for new church development. Furthermore, strong established churches often serve as the launching pad for new churches.

In addition to being the major conference advocate for new church development, the director of congregational development is the primary fund-raiser for new church development. In this capacity, the director of congregational development may direct the efforts of a New Church Builders team or perhaps a "Team 1000" composed of 100-200 members who each give at least $1000 per year to support new church development. The office of congregational development will mail one or two call letters per year to each member of the New Church Builders team, or" "Team 1000," and provide a newsletter to keep the team participants informed on conference issues impacting new church development as well as reporting how the money is used. The director of congregational development must strive to have new church development become an apportionment priority in the annual conference. Apportioned giving is the most reliable source of continuing financial support for new church development in the United Methodist connectional system. If new church development is not a direct apportionment it may be a conference special asking or, at a minimum, an advance special.

New church development must become endowed as soon as possible and the director of congregational development must raise endowment funds and manage the funds through a conference foundation or some other non-taxable entity. In the early stages of an endowment, the capital fund should be allowed to grow with only the interest available to support the office of congregational development. As the capital fund increases, low interest loans to new church plants may be made directly from the capital fund.

In some annual conferences, local church properties may, from time to time, be abandoned or discontinued. Directors of congregational development must work with the bishop and district superintendents to ensure that proceeds from the sale of the property of abandoned or discontinued churches are used to plant new churches, even when the new church is not in the same district as the abandoned or discontinued church. Directors of congregational development must encourage districts to enter into joint venture arrangements in which funds from two or more districts may be pooled to help finance new church plants.

New church development is clearly a conference level activity. The director must have access to knowledge of the entire conference including detailed demographic data on the conference. The congregational development office must establish relationships with public utilities and state, county and municipal governmental agencies as well as local school systems. Such agencies are helpful in projecting residential and commercial growth. The information provided is essential in determining fertile areas for new church planting. Congregational development staff must have access to the latest demographic data regarding the annual conference. Up-to-date demographic data and two to five year demographic projections are essential in new church planting, as well as in assisting established congregations identify the indigenous populations in their service areas. Current data and projections are particularly helpful in geographic areas of significant cultural and economic transition.

Congregational development staff must establish and maintain relationships with banks, real estate agents and brokers, architects, construction companies and lawyers. Parsonages must be acquired for new church pastors, or where housing allowances are the practice, new church pastors need assistance in finding affordable housing in the area of the new church plant. In situations where existing housing

 © 2018 Robert O. Crossman, www.UMNewChurch.org

is not available, houses must be built. Many pastors have never bought or built a house and, therefore need assistance in home acquisition or construction. In some cases, rental houses may be appropriate. Renting should always be temporary and used only until adequate housing can be purchased or constructed. As the new congregation develops, space for worship and educational activities must be rented. Storefronts, schools and shopping centers are alternatives worthy of consideration. Later, when the congregation is ready, large tracts of land for the new church must be acquired and buildings planned, financed and constructed.

Leadership in the area of Congregational Development is critical to the success of both new church development and renewal of existing congregations. Congregational development staff must provide training opportunities for new church pastors and lay leaders. Some opportunities may be provided by the conference while others may be provided by general church agencies or other agencies providing training. There are many "teaching churches" around the country that offer a great variety of training in areas such as worship planning and discipleship processes, staff development, and mission and ministry outside the walls of the church. The General Board of Discipleship School of Congregational Development is an excellent training opportunity. Many conferences are offering Academies for Congregational Development that may be tailored to the specific needs of the particular conference and its personnel. Such academies demonstrate commitment by the conference in the area of Congregational Development. Furthermore, there are many for-profit entities and professional trainers available to present training for an annual conference. It is the responsibility of the conference office of congregational development to stay abreast of training opportunities for those who are starting new churches, as well as those who desire to find the next steps for existing churches.

The position of Director of Congregational Development requires a variety of skills and spiritual gifts. It requires a clear vision for reaching people for the Lord Jesus Christ. Anyone who aspires to fill the position must be willing to stay in the position long enough to establish a variety of networks. Through networking, the director of congregational development can greatly expand, not only the influence of the annual conference, but also the effectiveness of the office of congregational development. The greatness of the United Methodist connectional system resides in a willingness to make the connection work and produce positive results for the annual conference. Effective ministry in the postmodern Age is relational and experiential. The effective director of congregational development must have a deep spiritual desire to reach postmodern generations. The future of United Methodism depends on our ability to reach those people who will lead the Church in the Twenty-first Century.

This article first appeared in The United Methodist Manual for New Church Development, editors Rev. Scott Ray and Rev. Clay Jacobs

†††

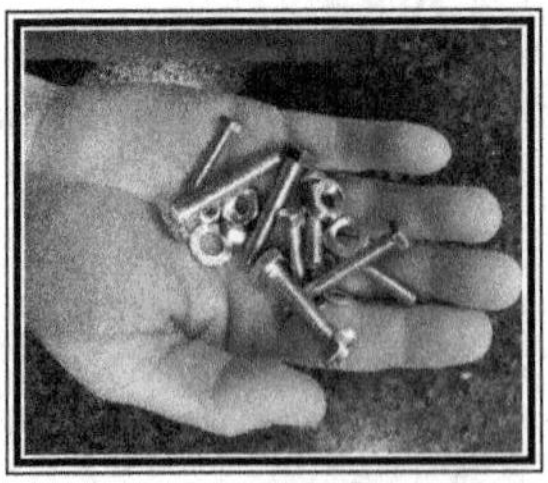

New Church Handbook
Nuts & Bolts for Planting New Churches In The Wesleyan Tradition

"Where Should We Start New Churches?"

Has the success of church planting priorities in other conferences or has the invitation from The Connectional Table and Path 1 caught your attention?

Are you exploring the possibility of starting new United Methodist Churches in your conference?

Are wondering how to select the communities to send planting pastors to?

†††

When I first began as a conference new church developer, I entered the staff position thinking that the process for determining WHERE to start a new church was a simple demographic decision. *For example, I wrongly assumed that when the total population of a mission field reached a particular number, and the growth % reached a tipping point, that is where we would start a new church.* **I quickly discovered that my initial assumptions were WRONG.**

I wish to propose that answering the question,
"Where should we start a new church in this district?"
is a spiritual process of discerning
where the Prevenient Spirit of God
is already preparing the "soil"
to receive a new United Methodist Church.

Bob Crossman

While the process for determining the particular area to start a new church is not a simple demographic decision, the population growth studies of Mission Insite can help determine those areas where it might be fruitful to "sow seeds" and explore the possibility of starting a new church in that area.

In addition to areas with significant new population growth, it may be fruitful to "sow seeds" in areas that are not growing but are instead 'underserved' by the United Methodist Church.

Remember that while location was once perceived as THE determining factor of success, Clay Jacobs in the North Georgia Conference has discovered ***"that THE most important piece in church planting is pastoral leadership. If the planting-***

© 2018 Robert O. Crossman, www.UMNewChurch.org

pastor is called by God to this new work, has a passion for reaching unchurched people, has a commitment to unconditional excellence, and possesses the unique set of church planting gifts and graces - this pastor will draw people to Christ, even in the desert."

†††

Here are a few steps that might inform your decision on where to plant new churches:

Step One

A great place to begin discerning WHERE to send planting pastors to start new churches in the next ten years is to begin with prayer.

"Lord, do you want to start any new churches in this Conference? If you do, help us to discern WHO your Prevenient Grace is already preparing to be the pastor of those new churches. Help us discern WHERE each pastor might be sent:

- *where your Prevenient Grace is already at work preparing a new mission field to receive a new church planting pastor;*
- *any underserved communities where a small church of 100 might be started;*
- *any large communities where a church of 1,000 might be started;*
- *any ethnic populations that are currently underserved by our church?*

Lord, as you look five and ten years into the future, where can you use each of us to begin the new church appointive and planting process? Speak Lord, your servants are listening. Amen"

Who to invite to pray?

The Book of Disciple makes it clear that whatever particular system you design for your conference or district, it must involve a collaboration of the bishop, cabinet, district superintendent, the conference 'entity' assigned the responsibility for congregational development, and the district board of church location and building. This would be a good group to invite to join in prayer.

Step Two

Each district superintendent can have conversations with the district lay leader and district leadership team about their impressions of potential new church areas in the district. The district board of church location and building can also be helpful in this discernment process. In face, the Book of Discipline ¶ 259.2 and ¶247.21 requires that district board to approve the "areas" for new churches and for multi-sites.

Step Three

One of your first steps might be to discern where is the Prevenient Grace of God already at work preparing a new mission field to receive a new church planting pastor.

- What large, heathy, vital existing congregations are asking you for permission to start a second campus?

- What pastors are asking you for permission to re-start a new church in a community nine miles down the road in an abandoned UMChurch building?

- In the charge conference season, did you discover churches:
  - That may be in the final months/year of life.
  - The mission field is one we know how to reach.
  - The building is appropriate size.
  - The building is still in good repair.

These are often the best places to begin!

Step Four

If you are planning to start two churches each year, you just need two potential mission fields each year. Right? NO!

Your team needs to keep pool of 6 to 8 potential new church start sites *(and planters)* in process, if you hope to start two. WHY? Because each year, a whole variety of situations may arise for any one potential site:

- The biggest barrier is this one - THE "right" planting or campus pastor may not be available for a particular site, and if you don't have THE right pastor, you don't want to start.
- The mother, sponsoring, or host church may have a change of Senior pastors, and decide to wait a year.
- The financial situation in the district or sponsoring church may falter.

Step Five

Demographic studies from MissionInsite can help you determine where it might be fruitful to "sow seeds" and explore the possibility of starting a new church in that area.

If your annual conference is planning to start thirty new churches in the next ten years:

You might consider starting them in the counties, cities, or zip codes with the greatest population growth the past five or ten years.

 © 2018 Robert O. Crossman, www.UMNewChurch.org

You might consider starting them in the counties, cities, or zip codes that are PROJECTED to have the greatest population growth in the next five to ten years. Growth is usually very localized. You may have zip codes that are projected to grow, within counties that are projected to decline.

You might consider starting churches in communities where you currently have NO existing churches. On a conference map, locate every one of your churches, and highlight the population centers where you currently have no churches. Determine the size population you typically need to have a self-sustaining congregation (20,000 people, for example) and highlight those communities. You might also have smaller communities where it might be reasonable to have a congregation of 50 to 75 on Sunday.

Where are your existing UM churches located?

Which of them are increasing in attendance, and which of them are declining?

Any large communities where a church of 1,000 might be started?

Any towns of 1,000 without a UM church yet?

Any smaller communities (5,000 people, perhaps) that might support a part-time / tent maker planting pastor?

You might consider starting new churches in communities that are UNDERSERVED by your existing churches. For example, you might want to discover communities where there few UM Churches (perhaps only one UMC for every 30,000 in population)

Where are too few UM churches located?

Any communities where existing UM Churches are not keeping pace with the population growth?

Any inner city without any UM Churches?

You might consider AVOIDING communities where you may have already successfully saturated the mission field. For example, you might want to avoid communities where you already have one UM church for each 10,000 in population.

If you are going to start new churches designed to reach a particular ETHNIC group, you might consider locating them where that ethnic group CURRENTLY

LIVES and where that population is projected to grow in the next five to ten years. Produce a separate zip code population map for each specific ethnic group you are attempting to target: such as Anglo, African American, Hispanic/Latino, Asian, Korean, Native American.

Where are ethnic populations currently living? Where are ethnic populations projected to increase?

In addition to areas with significant new population growth, it may be fruitful to "sow seeds" in areas that are not growing but are instead 'under served' by the church.

Any growing communities where your existing UM churches are not growing proportionately?

Any under served communities where a small church of 100 might be started?

Any city of 50,000 with only one UM church?

Any ethnic populations that are under served by the UM church?

Where have you been effective in saturating the mission field with UM churches, and there is no immediate need to start an additional new church?

Step Five: After the Demographics Studies?

After you have prayed and carefully reviewed these demographic maps, reflect on insights from district superintendents, district lay leaders, district leadership teams, and district boards of church location. With all this information, then select which areas are your priorities for years one to three, years four to six, and years seven to ten.

Beginning with the first priority mission fields, confirm the demographics by actually walking the mission field. Observe and talk to community leaders, city planners, pastors, and people on the streets. Make an appointment and visit with the strongest churches of other denominations. Are any of the existing churches, of any denomination, effectively reaching the unchurched?

 © 2018 Robert O. Crossman, www.UMNewChurch.org

Does this "feet-on-the-ground" experience confirm your earlier prioritization? These on-the-ground experiences will help you to determine the best strategy for each area (parachute drop, parent-daughter, multi-site, house church, etc.) These experiences will also help you to determine the unique affinities you need to be looking for as you determine which pastor has the best natural affinity match to each mission field.

The Book of Discipline ¶ 2520, 259.1, and 2544.2 also requires the district board of church location and building to approve the areas for new churches and for multi-sites.

After obtaining the district board approval, you might have called meetings with your pastors in each of these priority areas – not to ask their permission, but to inform them of your future plans and to ask for their support of this new faith community that may begin in the next few years.

At a second gathering, invite your pastors to bring their key lay leadership – again, not to ask their permission, but to inform them of your future plans and to ask for their support of this new faith community that may begin in the next few years.

Step Six

These conversations will help you to determine the best strategy for each site. One site might be best suited for a multi-site, while others would work best as a Lazarus start, connectional (parachute drop), "Weird Church", or any of a dozen different possibilities. (See the article: *"What Are Some of The Strategies or Models For Starting a New Church?"*)

Summary

These six steps are just a brief overview of a process that might help your conference be more proactive in seeking the best soil for planting new churches in the next ten years.

The initial 'idea' of exploring a particular community as a potential site for a new United Methodist Church may come from the discernment of a variety of sources:

- Bishop
- District superintendent
- Conference minister of new church starts
- A nearby local UM church
- District Committee on Church Building and Location
- Committee on Parish & Community Development
- Board of Global Ministries
- Hispanic Ministries Committee
- Ethnic Local Church Committee

- Small Membership Church Committee; or
- any UM pastor or laity (active or retired)

Suggested Process For Seeking Approval to Start A New Church

1. Any of the above sources can initiate a conversation with their district superintendent, and they may then be asked to file an *"Application for Approval to Launch a New United Methodist Church."* (See the article: *"Application to Start a New Church"*)

   a. The application includes a survey to be conducted in the targeted population to determine the number of potential members, and the needs of the targeted community *(actually physically walking the neighborhood, door to door contact with residents, and using all available information from county/city planning departments, chamber of commerce, civic organizations, and the MissionInsite reports).*

   b. If the targeted population is a language/cultural group, the conference commission on ethnic local church concerns or the conference committee on Hispanic ministries and the leaders of that population need to be consulted and assistance sought in planning the new mission congregation.

2. The bishop, the district superintendent, conference minister of new church starts, and cabinet will determine **IF** a new church or mission church will be started in the area brought to their attention.

3. Upon recommendation of the district superintendent and conference minister of new church starts, the bishop and the cabinet determines **WHEN** a new congregation is to be launched to serve an unchurched population, and the **MODEL** or **STRATEGY** to be used in the new church start.

4. The bishop and cabinet *(in consultation with the conference minister of new church starts)* will determine the **APPOINTMENT** of pastoral leadership to the new church start. See *"How Will We Appoint Our New Pastors."*

5. In the appointive process, the bishop, conference minister of new church starts, and cabinet will determine the initial level of pastoral **COMPENSATION** required. The district superintendent will prepare and submit an application for key charge pastoral compensation, if eligible, to the commission on equitable compensation for action.

6. The host district superintendent and conference minister of new church starts will determine the initial level of **FINANCIAL SUPPORT** needed from all sources for the new church project.

© 2018 Robert O. Crossman, www.UMNewChurch.org

7. After the appointment is made, the district superintendent, conference minister of new church starts and the coach assigned to the new church pastor, will work with the new church pastor to fulfill the traditional functions of a church council, pastor parish relations committee, finance committee, and trustees until the church has grown large enough to complete the 'charter' process and thereby elect these committees. These committees/councils do not exist in a new church prior to the constituting church conference outlined in ¶ 259.
8. In most annual conferences, new church starts are not allowed to enter the 'charter' process (¶259.4 to ¶259.10) until they have at least 125 active adult members, and have been holding public worship at least three years.
9. See the article: *"A Word About Starting a Mission Church"* for the unique nature of that ministry.

On the following pages you will find the process I have led several appointive cabinets through.

The example on the following pages was designed for the Arkansas extended cabinet.

The process outlined on the following pages is an attempt to:

- To begin to pray together,
  "Lord, do You want to start any new churches in this Conference? Help me to where where your Prevenient Grace is already at work preparing a new mission field to receive a new church planting pastor. Are there any underserved communities where a small church of 100 might be started? Are there any large communities where a church of 1,000 might be started? Are there any ethnic populations that are underserved by the UMC? Lord, as you look 5 years into the future, where can You use me to begin the new church appointive process? Speak Lord, your servant is listening. Amen."
- To take advantage of the collective wisdom in the room inviting a collaborative process among the team.
- Gain ownership of the entire district leadership team & district board of church location and building in the site selection process.
- To encourage hesitant pastors and laity to start new churches in their towns.
- Help the cabinet to begin 'nominating' a pool of pastors that might match any site with a unique 'affinity.'
- Help the cabinet to begin 'penciling' in where potential planters might be appointed.
- To begin to establish an accountability system. The bishop can now say to the cabinet, *"At our last meeting we selected _______, ______, and _____ as sites for new churches next June. What progress has been made preparing that community to receive a pastor?"*

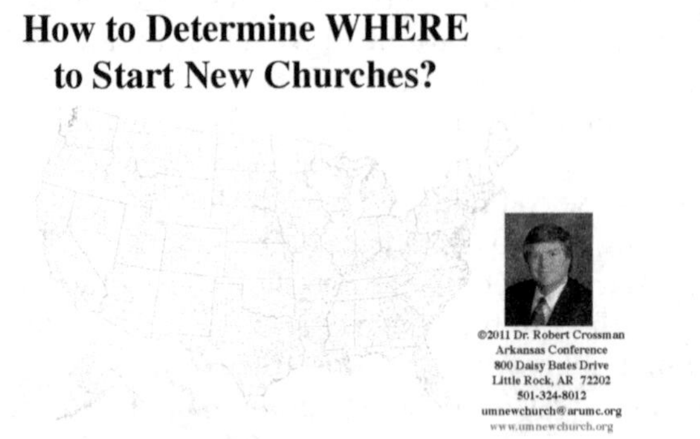

How To Determine
Where To Start New Churches?

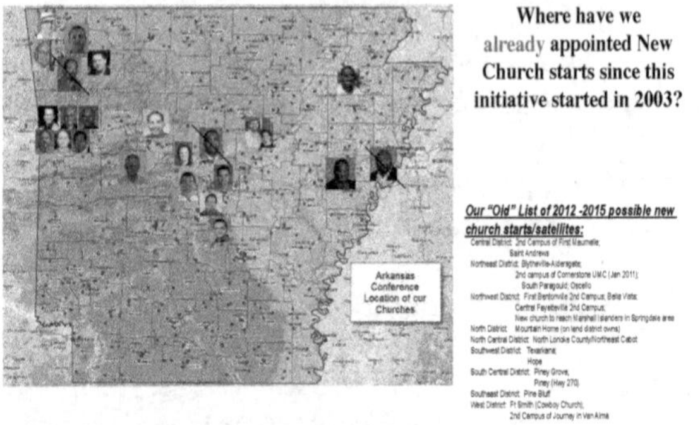

Where have we already appointed new church starts in the past ten to twenty years?

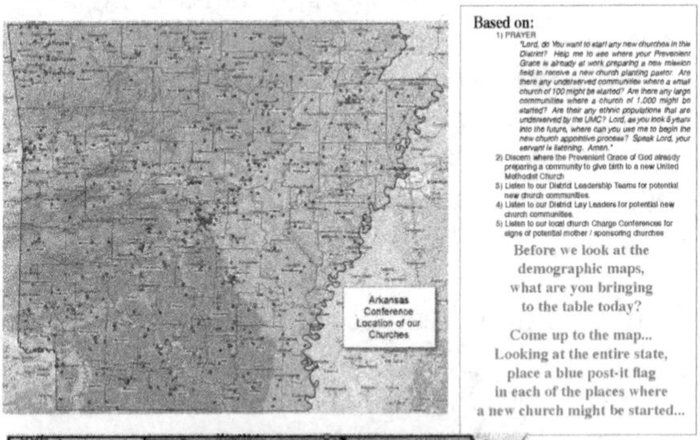

Before we look at the demographic maps, what are you bringing to the table today?

Come up to this map. Looking at the entire state, place a blue post-it flag in each of the places where a new church might be started.

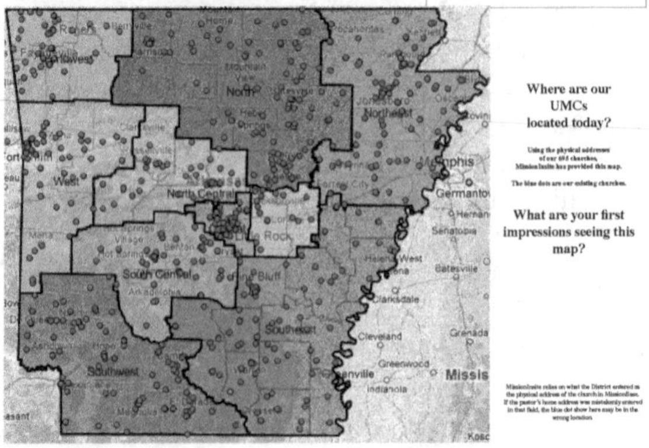

Where are our UMCs located today?
Each blue dot represents one of our churches.

What are your first impressions seeing this map?

© 2018 Robert O. Crossman, www.UMNewChurch.org

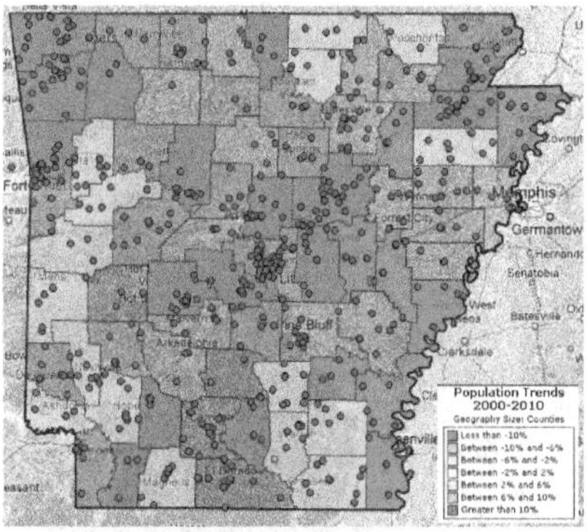

WHERE?
If we are going to start new churches in the next five years, we might consider locating them in the counties that have grown in the past ten years.

Population Growth by County - 2000 to 2010?

(sorted, descending from from highest percentage)

County	2000 Pop	2010 Pop	% Change
Benton	153,406	226,277	47.50
Faulkner	86,014	111,540	29.70
Washington	157,715	203,648	29.10
Lonoke	52,828	68,055	28.80
Saline	83,529	101,597	21.60
Craighead	82,148	95,517	16.30
White	67,165	77,114	14.80
Garland	88,068	99,847	13.40
Crawford	53,247	60,064	12.80
Madison	14,243	16,058	12.70
Greene	37,331	41,618	11.50
Baxter	38,386	41,657	11.10
Pope	54,469	60,165	10.50
Carroll	25,357	27,891	10
Boone	33,948	37,178	9.50
Grant	16,464	17,947	9
Johnson	22,781	24,817	8.90
Miller	40,443	44,010	8.80
Stone	11,499	12,459	8.30
Yell	21,139	22,876	8.20
Pulaski	361,474	387,109	7.10
Sevier	15,757	16,856	7
Sebastian	115,071	122,964	6.90
Cleburne	24,046	25,715	6.90
Conway	20,336	21,704	6.70
Crittenden	50,866	53,798	5.80
Hot Spring	30,353	32,088	5.70
Newton	8,608	9,064	5.30
Sharp	17,119	17,799	4
Pike	11,303	11,751	4
Marion	16,140	16,660	3.20
Independence	34,233	35,007	2.30
Clark	23,546	24,030	2.10
Van Buren	16,193	16,526	2.10
Perry	10,209	10,419	2.10
Polk	20,229	20,508	1.40
Randolph	18,195	18,439	1.30
Franklin	17,771	17,972	1.10
Cleveland	8,571	8,669	1.10
Little River	13,628	13,771	1
Howard	14,300	14,399	0.70
Drew	18,723	18,757	0.20

ALL OTHER COUNTIES HAD A DECREASE IN POPULATION

Where?

If we are going to start new churches in the next five years, we might consider locating them in the COUNTIES that have grown in the past ten years.

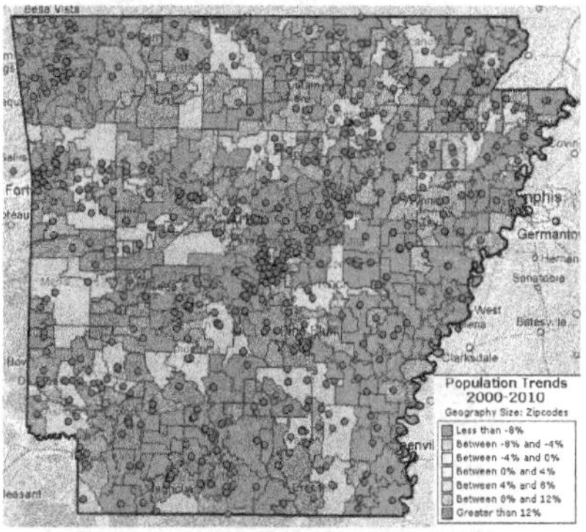

WHERE?
If we are going to start new churches in the next five years, we might consider locating them in the zip codes that have grown in the past ten years.

Population Growth by Zip Code - 2000 to 2010?

(sorted below from highest % to lowest %)

Zip	City	2000 Pop	2010 Pop	% Change
72719	Centerton, Benton Co.	2,419	8,363	245.70
72718	Cave Springs, Benton Co.	322	831	158.10
72739	Hiwasse, Benton, Co	228	450	97.40
72758	Rogers, Benton Co.	20,138	35,973	78.60
72714	Bella Vista, Benton Co.	6,092	10,586	73.80
72712	Bentonville, Benton Co.	25,666	44,140	72
72113	Maumelle, Pulaski Co.	12,863	21,489	67.10
71828	Cale, Nevada Co.	156	254	62.80
72176	Ward, Lonoke Co.	5,095	7,919	55.40
72223	Little Rock, Pulaski Co.	12,385	19,046	53.80
72704	Fayetteville, Washington Co.	14,648	21,883	49.40
72764	Springdale, Washington Co.	32,848	48,919	48.90
72715	Bella Vista, Benton Co.	9,932	14,617	47.20
72007	Austin, Lonoke Co.	4,562	6,659	46
72745	Lowell, Benton Co.	8,113	11,758	44.90
72852	Oark, Johnson Co.	262	370	41.20
72023	Cabot, Lonoke Co.	25,166	35,199	39.90
72404	Jonesboro, Craighead Co.	16,679	23,328	39.90
72022	Bryant, Saline Co.	10,155	14,191	39.70
72751	Pea Ridge, Benton Co.	4,088	5,668	38.60
72916	Bonanza, Sebastian Co.	5,719	7,860	37.40
72034	Conway, Faulkner Co.	32,320	44,296	37.10
72631	Eureka Springs, Carroll Co.	3,293	4,408	33.90
72854	Ozone, Johnson Co.	464	621	33.80
72058	Greenbrier, Faulkner Co.	12,314	16,411	33.30
72012	Beebe, White Co.	9,140	12,126	32.70
72762	Springdale, Washington Co.	26,875	35,447	31.90
72173	Vilonia, Faulkner Co.	6,547	8,583	31.10
72210	Little Rock, Pulaski Co.	10,392	13,526	30.20
72761	Siloam Springs, Benton Co.	16,108	20,777	29
72662	Omaha, Boone Co.	2,420	3,115	28.70
72730	Farmington, Washington Co.	5,795	7,437	28.30
72136	Romance, White Co.	1,324	1,683	27.10
72839	Hagarville, Johnson Co.	479	609	27.10
72364	Marion, Crittenden Co.	12,770	16,147	26.40
72417	Brookland, Craighead Co.	2,738	3,433	26.10
72845	Knoxville, Johnson Co.	1,066	1,340	25.70
72087	Lonsdale, Garland Co.	1,572	1,973	25.50
72122	Paron, Saline Co.	1,061	1,326	25
72905	Fort Smith, Sebastian Co.	152	189	24.30
72663	Onia, Stone Co.	708	878	24
72032	Conway, Faulkner Co.	25,094	31,071	23.80

If we are going to start new churches in the next five years, we might consider locating them in the ZIP CODES that have grown in the past ten years.

(It is possible to have a county that is declining, but a zip code within it that has significant growth.)

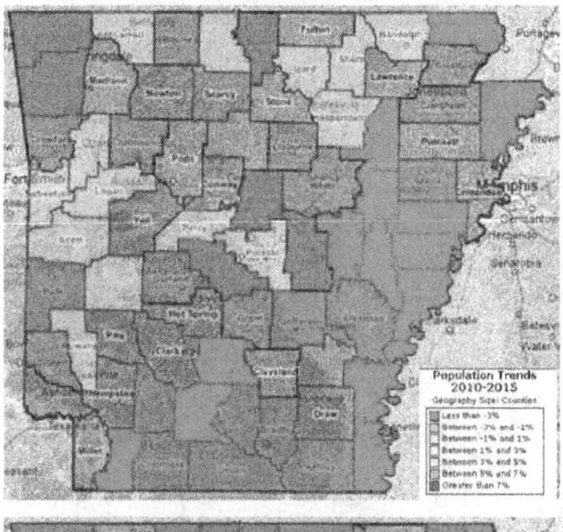

WHERE?
If we are going to start new churches in the next five years, we might consider locating them in the counties that are projected to have the greatest growth in the next five years.

Projected Growth by County - 2010 to 2015?

(sorted below from highest % to lowest %)

County	2010 Pop	2015 Projection	% Change
Benton	226,277	263,764	16.60
Lonoke	68,055	76,925	13.00
Faulkner	111,540	124,181	11.30
Washington	203,648	225,628	10.80
Baxter	42,657	46,008	7.90
Saline	101,597	109,551	7.80
Crawford	60,064	64,069	6.70
Craighead	95,517	101,750	6.50
Grant	17,947	19,022	6.00
Boone	37,178	39,383	5.90
Greene	41,618	43,938	5.60
Sevier	16,856	17,776	5.50
Cleburne	25,715	27,095	5.40
Garland	99,847	104,895	5.10
White	77,114	81,044	5.10
Johnson	24,817	26,067	5.00
Fulton	11,618	12,186	4.90
Madison	16,058	16,843	4.90
Miller	44,010	45,901	4.30
Pope	60,165	62,623	4.10
Cleveland	8,669	9,012	4.00
Van Buren	16,526	17,133	3.70
Stone	12,458	12,842	3.10
Sebastian	122,964	126,481	2.90
Independence	35,007	35,911	2.60
Marion	16,660	17,098	2.60
Logan	22,460	23,029	2.50
Montgomery	9,039	9,266	2.50
Carroll	27,891	28,516	2.20
Franklin	17,972	18,372	2.20
Perry	10,419	10,619	1.90
Randolph	18,439	18,791	1.90
Scott	10,963	11,172	1.90
Sharp	17,799	18,121	1.80
Izard	13,139	13,369	1.70
Howard	14,399	14,596	1.40
Pulaski	387,109	391,517	1.40
Hot Spring	32,088	32,184	0.30
Newton	9,064	9,071	0.10
Clark	24,030	24,036	0.00

ALL OTHER COUNTIES HAD NO GROWTH OR DECLINE

If we are going to start new churches in the next five years, we might consider locating them in the COUNTIES that are PROJECTED to have the greatest growth in the next FIVE years.

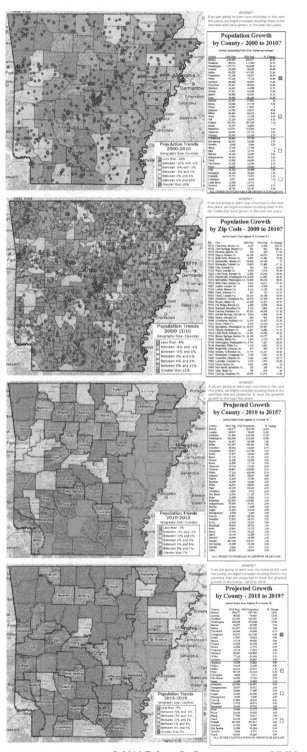

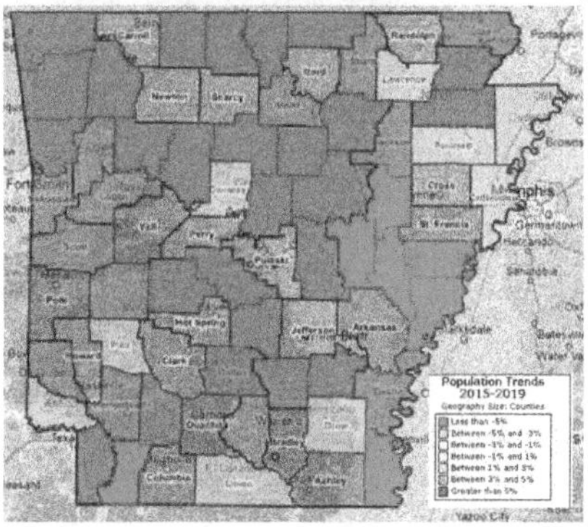

WHERE?
If we are going to start new churches in the next five years, we might consider locating them in the counties that are projected to have the greatest growth in the future... 2015 to 2019.

Projected Growth by County - 2015 to 2019?

(sorted below from highest % to lowest %)

County	2015 Proj.	2019 Projection	% Change
Benton	226,277	263,764	16.60
Lonoke	68,055	76,925	13.00
Faulkner	111,540	124,181	11.30
Washington	203,648	225,628	10.80
Baxter	42,657	46,008	7.90
Saline	101,597	109,551	7.80
Crawford	60,064	64,069	6.70
Craighead	95,517	101,750	6.50
Grant	17,947	19,022	6.00
Boone	37,178	39,383	5.90
Greene	41,618	43,938	5.60
Sevier	16,856	17,776	5.50
Cleburne	25,715	27,093	5.40
Garland	99,847	104,895	5.10
White	77,114	81,044	5.10
Johnson	24,817	26,067	5.00
Madison	16,058	16,843	4.90
Fulton	11,618	12,186	4.90
Miller	44,010	45,901	4.30
Pope	60,165	62,623	4.10
Cleveland	8,669	9,012	4.00
Van Buren	16,526	17,133	3.70
Stone	12,459	12,842	3.10
Sebastian	122,964	126,481	2.90
Independence	35,007	35,911	2.60
Marion	16,660	17,098	2.60
Logan	22,460	23,029	2.50
Montgomery	9,036	9,266	2.50
Carroll	27,891	28,516	2.20
Franklin	17,972	18,371	2.20
Randolph	18,439	18,791	1.90
Scott	10,963	11,172	1.90
Perry	10,419	10,619	1.90
Sharp	17,799	18,121	1.80
Izard	13,139	13,368	1.70
Pulaski	387,109	391,517	1.40
Howard	14,399	14,596	1.40
Hot Spring	32,088	32,194	0.30
Newton	9,064	9,071	0.10
Clark	24,030	24,036	0.00

ALL OTHER COUNTIES WERE NO GROWTH OR DECLINE

If we are going to start new churches in the next five years, we might consider locating them in the COUNTIES that are PROJECTED to have the greatest growth in years FIVE TO TEN.

© 2018 Robert O. Crossman, www.UMNewChurch.org

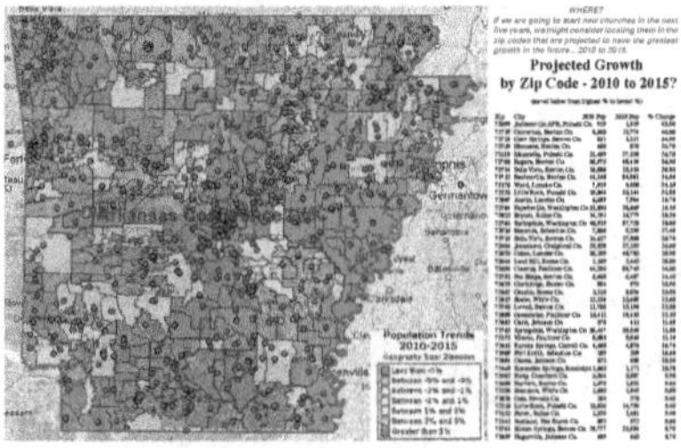

If we are going to start new churches in the next five years, we might consider locating them in the ZIP CODES that are projected to have the greatest growth five to ten years from now.

Are there any LARGE UNDERSERVED population clusters? Not an easy question to answer.

- You may have many communities where a existing UMC has decided to be a "family chapel" and not a church with open doors to the entire community around their building ...failing to reach across economic or racial lines. Each District will have to individually discern where this might be happening in.
- You may have many churches that have NOT received a single Profession of Faith in years - failing to make new disciples.

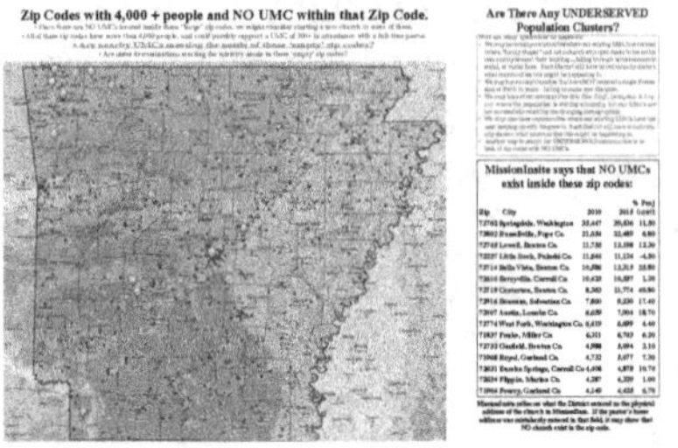

- You may have other communities where the population is shifting ethnically or economically, but our UMCs are not successfully reaching the changing demographics.
- You may also have communities where our existing UMCs have not been keeping up with the growth.

Another way to search for UNDERSERVED communities is to look at population clusters with NO UMCs.

After identifying these towns, then ask:

- Are nearby UMCs meeting the needs of these 'empty' population clusters?
- Are sister denominations meeting the ministry needs in these clusters?

Are there any zip codes with 2,000 to 4,000 people with NO UMC within that Zip Code?

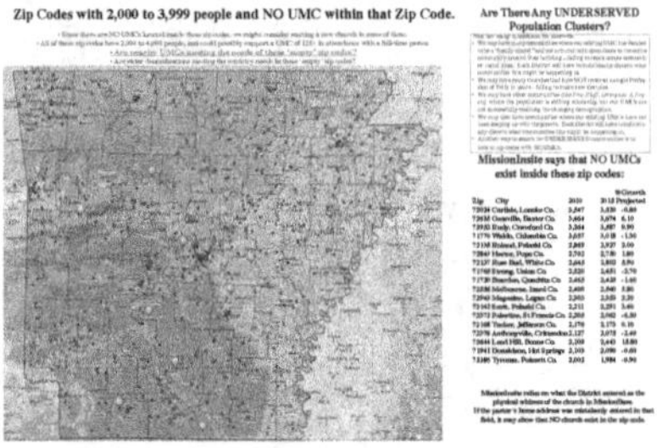

Are there any zip codes with 1,000 to 2,000 people with NO UMC within that Zip Code?

These are smaller population centers or smaller towns where you might start a new church with an attendance potential of 50 or 100 on Sunday.

Perhaps you might train a nearby pastor to start the new church and end up with a two-point circuit. Or, you might deploy a layperson or a part-time local pastor.

Where do we have FEW UMC when compared to the population?

In Arkansas, for example, they average one UMC per 4,000 people statewide.

They identified about two dozen communities that less than 1 UMC per 6,000 people.

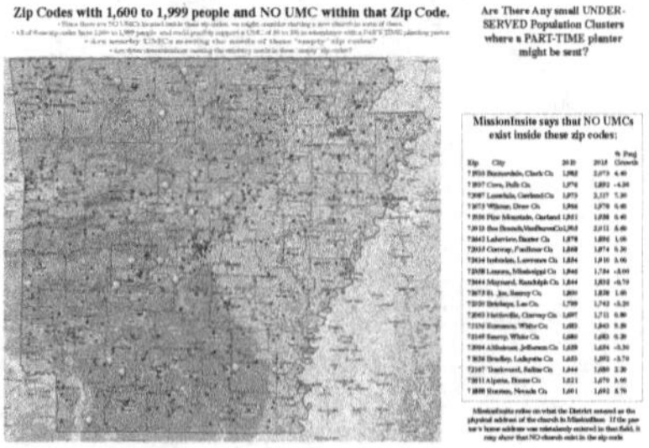

Questions to ask:

Is there actually room for another UMC in any of these towns?

Are these circles actually underserved populations?

Are the existing churches in these circles keeping pace with the growth?

Are existing churches NOT reaching across economic lines?

Are existing churches NOT reaching across ethnic

 © 2018 Robert O. Crossman, www.UMNewChurch.org

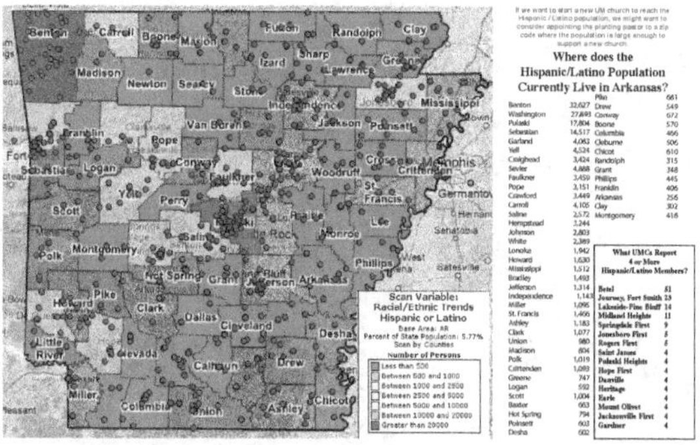

If we want to start a new UMC church designed to reach a particular ethnic population, we might want to consider appointing a planter pastor to the zip codes where that ethnic population is large enough to support a new church.

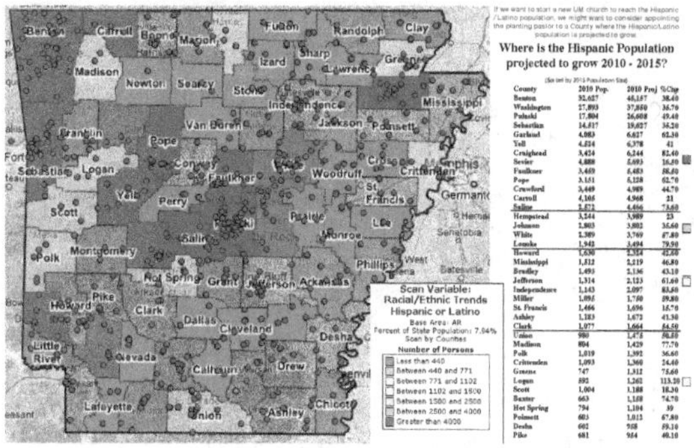

If we want to start a new UMC church designed to reach a particular ethnic population, we might want to consider appointing a planter pastor to a COUNTY where that particular ethnic population is PROJECTED to grow.

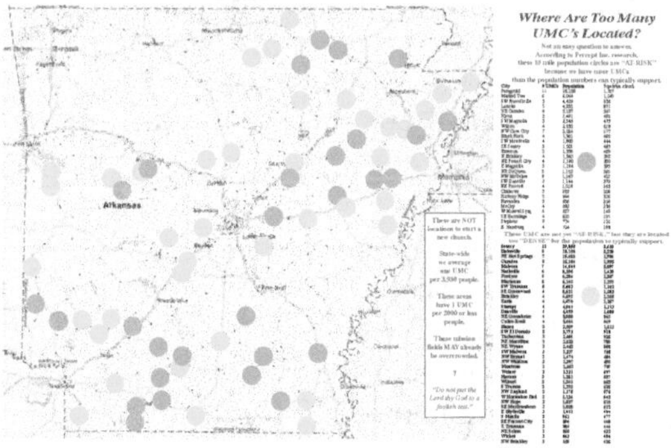

Where have we successfully "saturated" the mission field? Most likely, we should NOT start a new church in any of these location.

Arkansas, for example averages 1 UMC, per 3,930 people.

These areas already have 1 UMC per 2000 or less people, AND MAY BE AT RISK.

Hamburg, for example has 4 UM churches, but only has a population of 724.

Marked Tree has 6 UM churches, but only has population of 6,064

These mission fields MAY already be overcrowded,

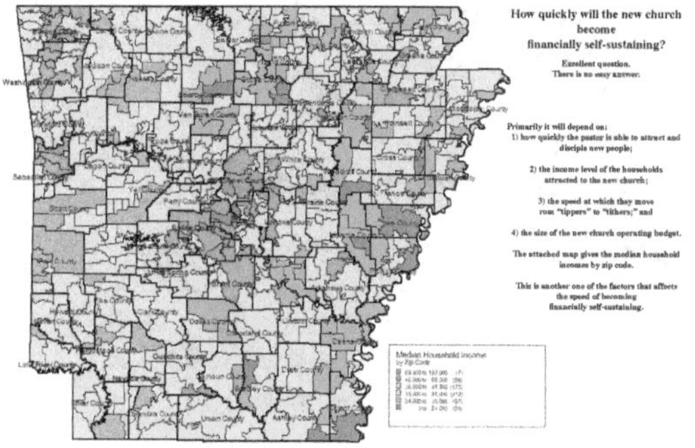

Look at the median household income by county or zip code.

This might give you a glimpse of giving potential and how quickly a new church might be able to become financially self-sustaining.

In every mission field, set the new church up to succeed - pastoral compensation and facility rent that they can afford, etc.

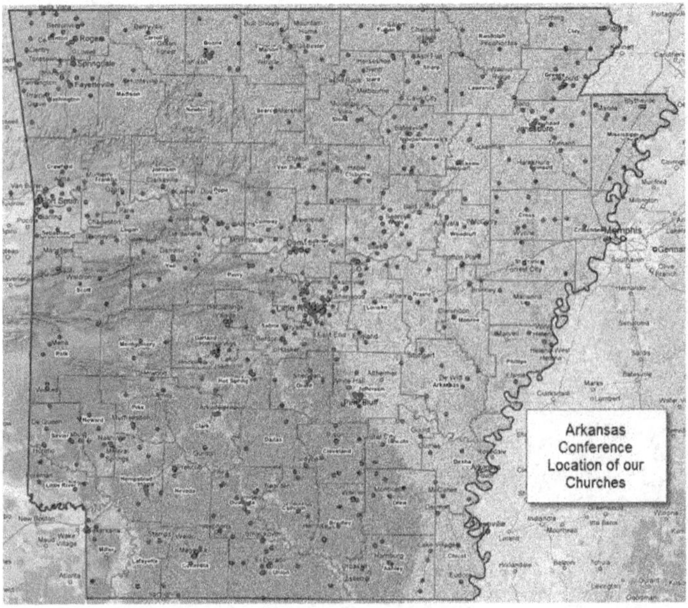

Now, based on all that we have brought with us and learned today, each of you are invited to place up to 30 "flags" where you discern the next 30 new church planting pastors should be appointed?

- RED - a hot spot for a new church next year
- YELLOW - a warm spot for a new church in two to three years.
- GREEN - a spot that may be ready to "go" in four to six years.

Now, looking at the map with hundreds of colored flags...
Has the Lord lead us to a consensus?
Where should the next 30 new churches be located?
"The largest grouping is here… with 12 red flags here…
would someone who flagged this mission field tell us why?"

Now, complete a 3x5 card for each of the heavy clusters, beginning with the red flags…
Name of mission field _____
Any unique characteristics ___________
Any potential planters come to mind already with those affinities ______

†††

NOTE: This article reflects the personal opinions of its author and does not necessarily reflect an official position of Discipleship Ministries or Path 1

© 2018 Robert O. Crossman, www.UMNewChurch.org

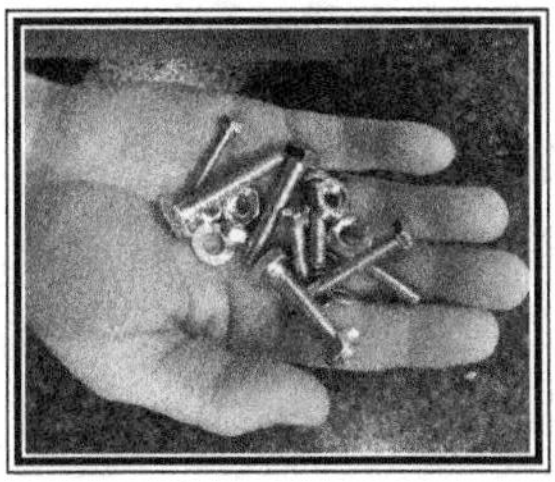

New Church Handbook
Nuts & Bolts for Planting New Churches In The Wesleyan Tradition

"Assessment Interview of Potential Planters"

by Bob Crossman

Including Jim Griffith's Behavioral Interview Process

I want to propose that the process of making an appointment, or deployment, of people to start a new church should be different than typical church appointments.

Currently around the appointive tables, every pastor is "assessed" as appointments are made. However, I am suggesting something far more than a 15 minute conversation, moments before the appointment is fixed, about whether "Bob" should be deployed to plant a church.

I am proposing that,
for potential new church planters,
every appointive cabinet needs to
design an indigenous assessment system they believe in
and will use in EVERY situation with out exception.

One reason for this is that in a new church setting, pastoral leadership is far more critical than in a typical pastoral setting. An established congregation will most likely survive poor pastoral leadership for a year or two. However, in the launching of a new church, the wrong pastoral leadership will never gather the first 100 people to hold the first worship service.

Years ago conferences believed that location was primary, and that any pastor could plant a new church if the right property were purchased.

Clay Jacobs was instrumental in helping the United Methodist appointive cabinets understand this when he began saying fifteen years ago:

"We have discovered in North Georgia that the most important piece
in church planting is LEADERSHIP.
If the pastor is called by God to this new work,
has a passion for reaching unchurched people,
has a commitment to unconditional excellence, and
possesses the unique set of church planting gifts and graces
- this pastor will draw people to Christ,
even in the desert."

Fruitful conferences have discovered the advantage of offering a 9 to 24 month pre-appointment season of training for potential planters. This becomes a season of discernment for the potential church planting pastor (and spouse). This also gives your cabinet time to discern each pastors' behaviors, and unique affinities.

By contrast, in the "old days" Bishop Richard Wilkie gave me 48 hours to accept an appointment to be a new church planter.

During this 9 to 24 month training season, some of these pastors will discern they are NOT called to be a planter, perhaps saving their careers, and saving your conference $300,000 in precious apportionment funds. However, they will still become more effective pastors in existing churches because of this training.

These training events, cohorts, incubators, academies or new church leadership institutes (NCLI), have the following purpose:

- Help potential planters to discern if they are gifted and called to this unique ministry.
- Help the conference congregational developer to begin assessing the potential planters. and to make more accurate recommendations to the appointive cabinet.
- Reduce the number of planters who make "fatal" mistakes in the first month.
- Enable the planter to fruitfully "hit-the-ground-running" instead of spending the first year trying to decide how to proceed.

After attending these pre-appointment trainings, each participant should be required to submit a self-reflective essay to their district superintendent and conference congregational developer.

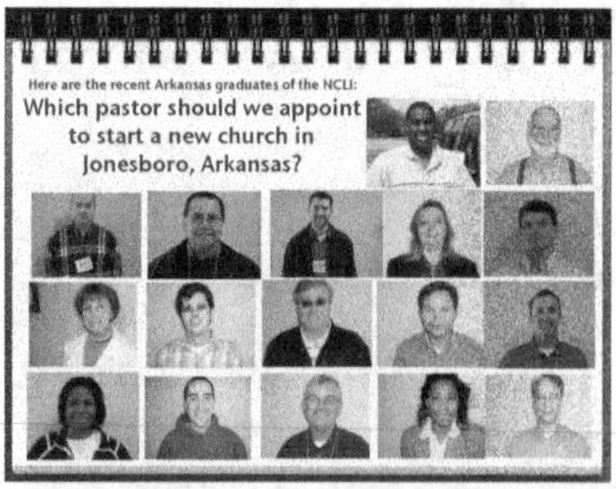

Here are the recent Arkansas graduates of the NCLI:
Which pastor should we appoint to start a new church in Jonesboro, Arkansas?

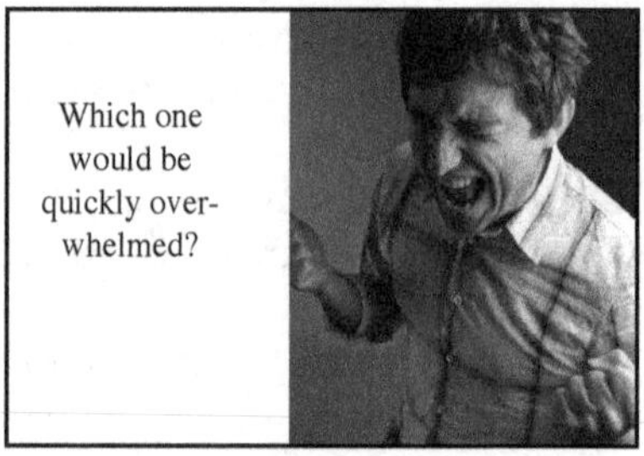

Which one would be quickly overwhelmed?

Which one would "hit the ground running"?

Which one would rather spend time alone on a private spiritual journey?

 © 2018 Robert O. Crossman, www.UMNewChurch.org

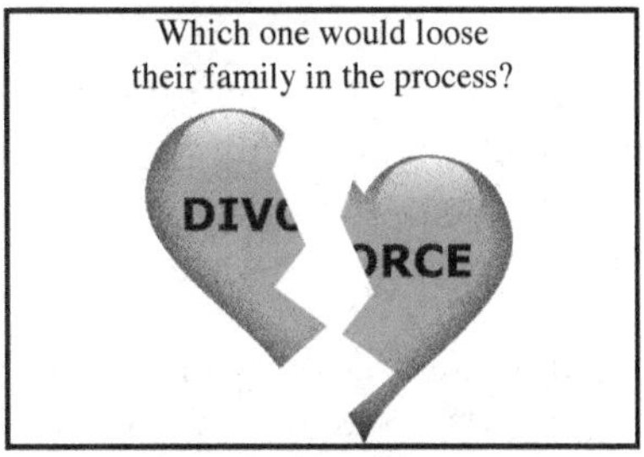

Which one would loose
their family in the process?

Which one would quickly build
a stable church?

Which one would be unable
to put people in the seats?

Which one would make all heaven rejoice?

Now that you have a pool of potential planters...

Vital planting conferences have also found that a formal de-briefing / assessment interview with each potential planter after attending the discernment event helps to clarify the planters gifts, and the particular affinity group in which this planter might fruitfully launch a new church.

In a traditional job interview, the candidate is asked a collection of straightforward questions such as, *"Tell me about yourself"* or *"What are your strengths and weaknesses?"* or *"What major challenges and problems did you face? How did you handle them?"* or *"Describe a typical work week."*

I am proposing a different kind of interview. A **behavioral interview** is designed to get an idea if the candidate has the skills and competencies needed for the job. The rationale behind behavioral interviews is that discovering how a candidate performed in previous specific employment-related situations in the past, will help give a sense of how the candidate might do in the future in similar situations.

Behavioral interviewing, in fact, is said to be 55 percent predictive of future on the job behavior, while traditional interviewing is only 10 percent predictive. *(Behavioral Interviewing Strategies for Job-Seekers, by Katharine Hansen, Ph.D.)*

In a behavioral interview, an employer has decided what skills are needed in the person they hire and will ask questions to find out if the candidate has those skills.

Instead of asking, *"What would you do if... ?* you instead ask *"Tell me about a time when...?* You are seeking to find out **how** the candidate actually handled a situation in the past, instead of asking them to fantasize what they **might** do in the future.

The behavioral interview is much more probing than the traditional interview. In a traditional job interview, a candidate can often get away with telling the interviewer what he or she wants to hear, even if they have to fudge a bit on the truth. Even if asked, *"What would you do if....?"* the candidate has minimal accountability. How does the interviewer know, after all, if the candidate would really react in a given situation the way they say they would?

In a behavioral interview, it is more difficult for the candidate to give responses that are untrue to their character. When the candidate starts to tell a behavioral story, the behavioral interviewer typically will pick it apart to try to get at the specific behavior(s). The interviewer probes further for more depth or detail asking, "What were you thinking at that point?" or "Tell me more about your meeting with that person," or "Lead me through your decision process." If the candidate has told a story that's anything but totally honest, the candidates response will not hold up through a barrage of probing questions.

It's best to make a deployment decision based on fact rather than fantasy.

When it comes to behavioral interviews of potential new church planters, the best person in the business is Jim Griffith.

Jim proposes that a telephone call be made to the prospective planter to invite them to the interview and answer any concerns they may have about the invitation. That telephone conversation is followed up by a detailed letter that INCLUDES the interview questions, and details about who will

 © 2018 Robert O. Crossman, www.UMNewChurch.org

be interviewing, and what is expected.

By the way, if married, the interview can not take place unless the spouse attends the full interview. In new church planting, we have discovered that if married, spousal support is a critical factor.

I am not suggesting that the spouse is to be a free associate pastor, coordinator of the set-up team, director of children's ministries, or leader of the music ministry. I am suggesting that, if married, spousal support is critical.

The spouse may be a pastor at a different church and never attend the new church - but that would not keep the spouse from being supportive.

The kind of support I am talking about takes place during the dark nights of the soul. And believe me, in church planting there are dark nights of the soul:- when the planter has spent the last three days networking, talking to strangers, knocking on doors, telling the new church story, and comes home to say: *"This week I have only encountered six potential people, and they are all dysfunctional. I have actually prayed that all six of them loose my contact information and never show up."*

That planter needs a spouse who says, *"I believe in you. I believe God wants to start this new church through you. Why don't you follow up on that family you met last week. I bet if you called them, they would let you come to their house tomorrow evening. This is going to work. I believe in you."*

That planter does NOT need a spouse who says instead, *"I knew this wasn't going to work. I don't know why you ever brought us to this awful town. Our kids don't have a Sunday School class anymore. We used to go to worship together as a family. Here, we don't even have a church. I knew this was a crazy idea from the start!"*

The assessment interview team needs to include the conference staff person, a district superintendent, a lay member of the conference new church committee, and at least one church planter. The team should include men and women, and a person of the same ethnicity of the candidate. Be sure the spouse is sitting next to someone of the same gender.

Following the interview, after the candidate has left the room, a brief summary is written by the interview team. A copy should be sent to the candidate by email a day or two later, giving them time to suggest changes or even offer a rebuttal.

The revised summary is then passed on to the conference new church development staff, the bishop, and appointive cabinet.

NOTE: **See articles:**
***"Are There Any On-Line Assessments I Can Take?"* and**
"The Use of Profile XT to Assist Your Assessment Interview, Supervision and Coaching"

Below you will find:
a sample letter,
a sample "Self Reflective Essay," and
several sample Assessment Team summaries for the appointive cabinet.

Sample Letter

Dear ________,

This letter is a follow-up of our telephone conversation this morning. Your assessment interview will be November ____, __:__ am, at the conference office. As we discussed on the phone, your spouse is expected to attend with you. If he can not attend on this date, we will need to reschedule.

The members of the assessment team include: Mark Norman, conference new church developer; John Barker, lay leader of the Southside District; Mary Yarbarough, new church planter in the Robinsdale District; and Sheila Cape, new church planter in the Louisville District.

Please complete the following and return them to me at least ten days prior to your assessment interview appointment.

1. Prepare a brief "reflective essay" based on your participation in the New Church Leadership Institute, including:
   a. What questions were answered for you in the institute?
   b. What questions remain unanswered?
   c. A one paragraph summary of your Affinity Group
   d. DiSC profile summary
   e. Your optimal church planting scenario, and
   f. Any conclusions you have made
2. **Brief (one or two sentence) written responses to the attached questions.**
3. Mail (or email) these to me before __________, ___, 2018.

This interview will focus on "past behavior' focusing on the areas that relate to the skills needed for your ministry. There are no "right or wrong" answers. Questions will be along the lines of "tell me about a time when" instead of "what would you do if"…"

The Assessment Team may begin the time by saying:

1. We'll cover all the issues listed on the worksheet, but not all questions will be asked. Remember, the goal is not to answer all the questions, but get a healthy overview of your "story."
2. This is not a psychological or character evaluation. Any reference

 © 2018 Robert O. Crossman, www.UMNewChurch.org

to character or theological issues is unintentional unless previously noted.

3. The interviewer(s) will be taking notes as the interview proceeds. Their notes will help with the written profile.
4. Think of the interview as an opportunity to:
   - Debrief your experience in the New Church Institute
   - Tell your story
   - Paint a Picture
5. In your answers, please be:
   - As descriptive and specific as possible, try to avoid opinions.
   - Be concise: take your time, but if you've answered enough to help the interviewer get what they need, they will prompt you on the next question.
6. This interview is confidential. If there is anything in the interview questions that makes you uncomfortable, please let the interviewer know ahead of time.
7. If you need a break at any time during the interview, let your interviewer know, and a break will be called.
8. Expect the interview to last 90 minutes. If you finish early, its because the interview team's questions have been sufficiently answered.
9. To begin, tell us where you grew up? What is your background?

I am looking forward to seeing you and your spouse at assessment interview, November ____, __:__ am, at the conference office.

†††

Sample Self Reflective Essay

a. **What questions were answered for you in the institute?**

I went to the first training with many questions, but I have known all along that starting a new church was what I wanted to do.

The questions I came with were logistical in nature.

b. **What questions remain unanswered?**

Most of the questions have been answered through my time at the NCLI. Presently, I look forward to an opportunity to attend the 'Nuts and Bolts" seminar of starting a new congregation. My desire is to be a part of both the challenge and excitement of a new church. I want to minister in an environment where the congregation is excited about seeing lives transformed by Jesus Christ.

c. **A one paragraph summary of your Affinity Group**

My affinity group is white, upper-middle class, suburbanite minded folk. My father was a successful business owner and my mother was a homemaker. My wife's parents were both educators. Both my parents and my wife's parents currently live in St. Paul, Minnesota. Our friends generally come from similar backgrounds and look very similar to us: young, educated, white collar, with children. I do not come from a church background, my wife does. We both, however, relate to people both within and outside of the church.

d. **DiSC profile summarized**

My DiSC profile shows that I have what is termed a "creative pattern." I have a high D and a high C with a lower I and S. The results show that I have opposing forces in my behavior. I have a drive for tangible results counterbalanced by an equally strong drive for perfection, and my aggressiveness is tempered by sensitivity. I wish to explore all possible solutions before making a decision. My pattern generally exhibits foresight when focusing on projects and I am a change agent. The profile of my pattern says that in my drive for perfection and results that I may not be concerned about social poise. As a result, I may be cool, aloof, or blunt.

I have felt called to a new church for about four years. I can imagine doing little else than this. I hold myself to a high standard in word and deed. I want to be called one thing by God on my last day – faithful. I want it to be said of me that I was faithful to the church, faithful to my family and faithful to my Lord. I am organized, thorough, persistent, and have a heart for evangelism.

e. **Your optimal church planting scenario**

I can see myself in a parachute drop, Mother-Daughter plant, or as a second pastor (if the church is less than 7 years old). In years to come I will definitely help sponsor / mother new churches. I cannot, however, see myself working in a 'church within a church' model.

f. **Conclusions made**

I have always been 'gifted' at starting new ventures. My father started and ran several successful corporations while I was growing up. I worked with him and learned from him for a number of years. I also started my own company which I intended to run full-time before being called into ministry. The company was a financial blessing to me as it paid for seminary and allowed my wife and me to live without worry while I was a student pastor.

Through the leading of the Holy Spirit, discernment, prayer and confirmation through the NCLI, I feel called and ready to begin a "new community of faith."

†††

To begin the interview, say...

"______ & _______ I want to begin by thanking you for both being here today. I know it was an inconvenience to find childcare and for you (spouse) take the afternoon off of work to be here.

Those of us around the table are the annual conference Assessment Team for potential new church planters. Let me introduce each member. My name is Fred Merkle and I am the district superintendent of the Southside District. John Barker is the Lay Leader of the Southside District; Mary Yarbarough, new is a church planter in the Robinsdale District; and Sheila Cape is new church planter in the Louisville District.

 © 2018 Robert O. Crossman, www.UMNewChurch.org

This today interview will focus on "past behavior' focusing on the areas that relate to the skills needed for your ministry.

- There are no "right or wrong" answers.
- Questions will be along the lines of "tell me about a time when" instead of "what would you do if"..."
- We will cover all the issues in the list of questions, but not all questions will be asked.
- Remember, the goal is not to answer all the questions, but get a healthy overview of your "story."
- This is not a psychological or character evaluation.
- Any reference to character or theological issues is unintentional unless previously noted.
- We will be taking notes as the interview proceeds to help with the written profile.
- Think of the interview as an opportunity to:
  - Debrief your experience in the New Church Institute
  - Tell your story
  - Paint a Picture
- In your answers, please be:
  - As descriptive and specific as possible
  - Try to avoid opinions.
  - Be concise: take your time
  - If you've answered enough to help us get what they need, I will prompt you on the next question.
- This interview is confidential.
- If there is anything in the questions that makes you uncomfortable, please let me know and we will move on..
- If you need a break at any time during the interview, let your interviewer know, and a break will be called.
- Expect the interview to last 90 minutes.
- If we finish early, its because our questions have been sufficiently answered.

So, are we ready to begin?
Great.

- To begin, tell us where you grew up? What is your background?"

†††

Include the Following Interview Questions In the Letter Mentioned Above

Prepare brief written response (one or two sentences) to each of the following questions. If you need clarification about any of the questions contained in this assessment, contact your supervisor.

1. **Opening Questions**
   - As a result of your discernment process, (perhaps attending New Church Leadership Institute, Incubator, Cohort, Boot Camp, Exponential, or your personal reading of church planting resources) what questions have been answered for you?
   - What has become clearer?
   - Where do you need more clarity?
   - What conclusions have you drawn?

2. **Your Call**
   - Give your "life verse" from the Scripture, and the reason it has shaped you?
   - What do you believe the Spirit is calling you to do?
   - What are your top two core values? Give two examples of how you've lived them out in the past six months.
   - Describe your "affinity group " profile.
   - What pre-Christian experiences have equipped you for ministry, especially in church planting?

3. **Leadership**
   - Give three examples of when you were asked or elected to be a leader in a group. What did you do? What were the results?
   - How does your DISC profile fit church planting ministry?

4. **Catalytic Capacity**
   - Give examples of ventures you started as a child, teen or adult.
   - Describe the most successful venture you ever started.
   - What was the last venture, in the church or outside that you started?

5. **Faith**
   - Give an example of a time when God gave you direction that seemed to lack rational underpinnings, but you obeyed Him anyway? What happened?
   - Describe a time when others said "it can't be done" but you went ahead anyway and proved them wrong?

6. **Visioning Capacity**
   - Tell about a time when you were asked to head a project. What did you do to gather people, get them organized and headed in the right direction, and finish the project? What did the outcome look like?

 © 2018 Robert O. Crossman, www.UMNewChurch.org

- Give two examples of a vision you came up with, made a plan for, and brought others together to pull it off.

7. **Evangelism/Reaching Others**
    - Give three examples of people you've helped enter a faith relationship with Jesus? How did you reach them?
    - Tell about the most recent times you've been with a Pre-Christian in your home … their home …done something together.
    - Tell about a time when you spearheaded an effort to help Pre-Christians come to a better understanding of Jesus.

8. **Equipping/Developing Others**
    - Give three examples of people in your ministry who you've helped move from nominal faith to a fuller relationship with Jesus.
    - Give two examples of people you've helped discover their gifts and begin to use in ministry.
    - Describe a time when someone you placed in ministry failed. What did you learn from the experience? What did you do?

9. **Conflict Resolution Skills**
    - Describe a time when someone wrongfully accused you. What did you do to attempt to resolve it?
    - Give examples of conflict you've had in relationship, including the most recent. How did you handle them?

10. **Spousal Cooperation (to be answered by the spouse):**
    - What are the main reasons you believe your spouse will be successful in church planting ministry?
    - What energizes your spouse? What drains them?
    - Describe your current participation in your spouses' church?
    - What are the ways you support your spouses' ministry?
    - To what extent have you and your spouse discussed the implications of starting a new church?
    - To what extent have and your spouse discussed the increased time demands of the typical work week in starting a new church? *(Typical planter time demands: 65+ hour work week)*
    - To what extent have you and your spouse discussed the emotional impact of the rigors of planting a new church?
    - To what extent have you and your spouse discussed the losses due to the changes in routine? (For example, not having traditional church activities for the children and regular worship in the early months.)
    - As you may or may not be aware, church planting is a higher stress appointment, is there anything going on in your family right now that church planting would exacerbate?
    - If you are working outside the home, what extra curricular activities does your job

require?

- If you are working outside the home, and your clergy spouse had to relocate to start the new church, would there be consequences in your current employment? What are the consequences?
- What challenges have you and your clergy spouse discussed that you will face in starting of a new church?

11. Family (to be answered with spouse)

- Describe any recent changes in the home, or family system, that we need to know about?
- If you have children, do any of them have special needs?
- If you have children in the home, what has their response been to this new opportunity?

12. Approach to Money:

- Describe the process you went through to start tithing as an individual, and as a family?
- What is the current level of debt that you are now caring?
- What is your process for paying down your debt?
- What annual salary level (excluding housing and health insurance) would you require to be a church planter at this point in your life?

13. Personal Health and Wellness

- Describe your personal health and any conditions, episodes, and addictions?
- Describe the health challenges you face, and how you manage them?

14. Perseverance

- Tell about a time when you faced a distasteful assignment. How did you face and complete it?
- Tell about a time when you thought you couldn't finish a project, but you pressed on and finished it.

15. Adaptability/Indigenous Worship

- What are some of the most common mistakes churches make in relating to people outside the Christian faith?
- Give an example of a service or ministry that you designed that became a "safe place: to hear the Gospel?

16. Church Planting Models

- What planting strategy best suits your "profile?" Why?
- What models of church planting pose a difficult match for you? Why?

17. Coachability / Teachability

- Tell me about a time you took advice from someone.

© 2018 Robert O. Crossman, www.UMNewChurch.org

- Tell me about a recent time you ran into a problem and called a colleague for help.
- What is the last learning event you went to, and what did you learn?
- Name five people you've called in the past six months to ask advice?

18. Your "Place" in Organizations

- What types of organizations have you worked in?
- What was your role in their "life cycle?"
- Knowing what you know now, what ministry scenario suits you best?
- Had I known you better, what questions would I have asked that I haven't so far?
- If money was no object and you couldn't fail, describe your dream job.

†††

SAMPLE #1
ASSESSMENT TEAM REPORT TO THE CABINET

Jane Doe
New Church Start Pastor Interview

On February 24, the New Church Start Assessment Interview Team met with Jane Doe to explore Jane's interests in starting a new church and gathered the following information:

- Jane is extremely aware of the issues involved to start a new church, and she is fully aware of her gifts and limitations.
- She has gifts and a desire to start a new church, particularly in Austin where she knows the community and the context where the church might be started.
- Her training, as a part of the New Church Leadership Institute, has given her more knowledge than most in the Institute on what is required, as well as having heard and observed the failure stories.
- Her personality (high C) and gifts don't emphasize her being the front person for a new church venture, however her passion for winning people to Christ overcomes what she lacks in natural gifts.
- She understands the events involved in reaching the unchurched and pre-Christian and she is good at seeing that details are taken care of in planning. She is willing to take the necessary risks when she can visualize the hoped for outcome.
- She understands the time line of starting a new church and can see herself in a mother/daughter relationship because of the support and structure it offers.
- Her spouse is not only supportive but completely partnered with her in wanting to start a new church.
- Her background in the public schools lends itself to identify her affinity group as semi-professionals and highly qualified blue collar workers, particularly in suburb not city or rural.
- She and her husband relate to being outside the Church, as they were not in the church for 17 years and then became part of a small church and became immersed in ministry leading to her call to ministry.
- **The Assessment Team believes that she is capable of doing a new church start.**

SAMPLE #2
ASSESSMENT TEAM REPORT TO THE CABINET

John Doe
New Church Start Pastor Interview

On February 24, the New Church Start Discernment Interview Team met with John and Jane Doe to explore John's interests in starting a new church and gathered the following information:

- The Discernment Team affirms John's ministry thus far and his heart and passion for God's people.
- The Team sees John as being well suited in an appointment with an existing structure and potential for growth, perhaps in a turn-around setting where there can be new life.
- John is teachable and the Discernment Team commends him for the ways in which he has learned new ideas and skills at the New Church Leadership Institute and implemented them in his current ministry setting.
- The Team appreciates John's willingness to share the Gospel with others but would like to see John intentionally have more experience in relating to pre-Christians and inviting them into a relationship with Christ.
- The Discernment Team recognizes John's concerns for his family, expressed desire for structure and expressed reluctance to embrace conflict. The Team would reemphasize that conflict is not absent from a new church start, although it may manifest differently than in an established church setting.
- John indicated that he remains unclear as to whether he is called to start a new church. Without a discerned passion for reaching people for Christ through a new church start, **the Assessment Team is reluctant to recommend John for an appointment to a new church start.**

SAMPLE #3
ASSESSMENT TEAM REPORT TO THE CABINET

John & Jane Doe
New Church Start Pastor Interview

John: DiSC Profile: High D, I "Entrepreneur"; Organizational Preference: Designer/ Developer; Team Preference: Presidential Captain

Jane: DiSC Profile: High D, S :Investigator"; Organizational Preference: Developer/ Stabilizer; Team Preference: Middle Captain7 **Sample Interview**

<u>Observations</u>

1. John & Jane have warm hearts for God and care deeply for people. Together they make a compassionate, gifted ministry team. John's wife, Jane, is a tremendous complement to John and his calling. She meets people extremely well and will be a great support to John and his ministry. Due to Jane's charm, the Doe home will be a place where many will

© 2018 Robert O. Crossman, www.UMNewChurch.org

find love, warmth and acceptance. Jane's organizational skills will serve their ministry quite well.

2. John displays the fruits and competencies to launch new projects and build them: While a law student, he began a Bible study, and doing primary relational evangelism among Episcopal students. Six months later, he was hired to start and build a youth program at an Episcopal church. Within three years, he had built the program, in the 13th largest church in the diocese, into the largest program in the diocese.
3. The DISC Profile characterizes John as an entrepreneur: perseverant, aggressive, ambitious, competitive, self confident, and decisive; Jane's profile indicates she is positive, sociable, flexible, and thorough, as well as cautious and conservative.
4. John demonstrates good time management skills, simultaneously able to manage a wide range of tasks and projects. He operates in a highly organized and efficient manner, using systematic methods to keep himself on track.
5. John's very direct and knows exactly what he wants, leaving no hidden agendas. Truly "what you see is what you get."
6. John's primary ministry experience came through a Bible church, Young Life, and campus Bible studies. Therefore he's more suited to know what ministry avenues to take in a church planting setting.
7. John's early childhood experiences will serve him well in starting a new work and adapting to all the curve balls: Moving over 20 times during his life, John learned how to adapt to new environments and how to make friends quickly. Moreover, his family was involved in two church plants when he was a teenager.
8. John's decisiveness and impulsiveness may lead him to move ahead without consulting others, leaving his launch team feeling left out and frustrated.
9. If not seen as his own man and given a great deal of latitude, John will appear unteachable and difficult to manage. To interpret this as resistant to authority would be a grave error, resulting in frustration, both by the organization and the Doe's.

***Affinity Group*:** A son of divorced and remarried parents, John grew up in a middle and upper middle class home in a bi-cultural community. Jane grew up in South Georgia and is also bi-cultural. John and Jane will most successfully connect with urban or suburban middle to upper-middle class, among professional and university-educated South Georgia with some religious background. While accepting of people of all strata, they do not have an affinity for a rural, hispanic, or lower middle income community. These mission fields would be a cross-cultural situation and the Doe's do not appear to possess gifts consistent with this type of calling.

Ministry Recommendations

1. The Doe's have a strong sense of God's call on their lives to launch new projects to advance the Kingdom, and the Lord appears to have provided a "window" at this time to explore the possibilities.
2. **John demonstrates the calling, spiritual gifts, attributes, and personal skills necessary to be a fruitful church planter. He is better suited to plant and pastor that church, rather than plant and move on to plant another one.**
3. John & Jane will require a coach whom they can respect, who is competent in the task, who will minister to them, and earn proper trust in order to ask the hard questions.

†††

NOTE: This article reflects the personal opinions of its author and does not necessarily reflect an official position of Discipleship Ministries or Path 1

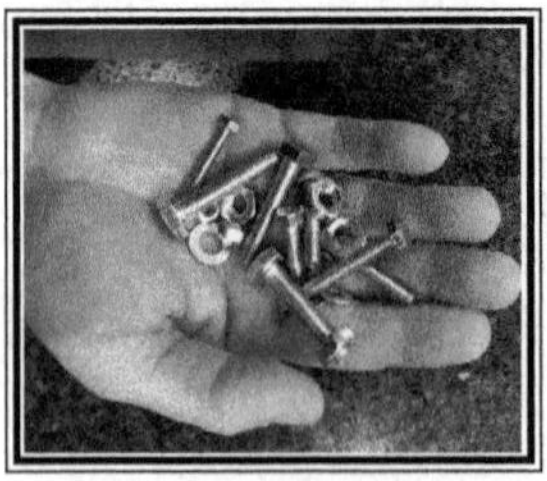

New Church Handbook
Nuts & Bolts for Planting New Churches In The Wesleyan Tradition

"The Use of Profile XT to Assist Your Assessment Interview, Supervision and Coaching"

by Bob Crossman

In many annual conferences the assessment process is primarily based on the behavioral assessment interview process of Jim Griffith. The questions designed by Jim Griffith for discovering past behavior are excellent.

Those questions, while excellent, are generic. One way to take the behavioral interview and assessment to the next level is by using a profile provided by a professional assessment company.

I recommend the ProfileXT®, designed by Profiles International Inc. of Waco, Texas. Profiles International services over 120 countries in over 30 languages, with over 40,000 clients including most of the Fortune 500 Companies.

The ProfileXT® helps you screen potential new church planters and choose the best candidates to deploy to your mission fields. ProfileXT® helps you identify if a person CAN do a job, if they WILL do a job, and if they WILL BE HAPPY doing so.

The cost for this service is approximately $250 for each prospective planter (typically paid for by the conference office), and available by sending the candidate names and email addresses to: bcrossman@arumc.org

Bob Crossman will send an email invitation (in English or Spanish) and a link to each candidate, and send you an invoice for the ProfileXT.

When each candidate completes the ProfileXT, Bob Crossman will send you four reports:

Interview Guide

Performance Model Comparison

Summary Graph

Individual Profile

The potential church planter takes a 60 minute inventory on the internet. Profiles International Inc. then generates reports for us.

The *Profile XT* provides a report for the assessment team - **Interview Guide for _______, Church Planter"** cover page reads:

"The interview is an important part of the selection process; however, studies show that most interviews are poorly done. Using a stock list of interview questions to ask every

 © 2018 Robert O. Crossman, www.UMNewChurch.org

candidate will not lead the interviewer to the important areas necessary for the effective placement of each individual.

This Interview Guide, coupled with the ProfileXT Performance Model Comparison, will help make each interview a valuable tool.

The scientifically developed Performance Model for this position reflects a solid understanding of what the job requires. The Total Person information related to this model allows us to create interview questions that will allow you to get the information you need to make the best possible decision about each candidate.

This report reflects the responses provided by ______ when he completed the ProfileXT assessment.

A Summary Graph is included that shows his scores and how he fits to the Performance Model for this position. It gives a quick overview of where he is in or out of the model and also shows his overall percentage match. The result for each characteristic is illustrated on a scale from 1 to 10. The darker area on each scale represents the best Job Match for the position. The enlarged segment of the scale shows where _____ scored. If the enlarged segment is dark, ___ is in the Job Match model. If it is lighter, he is not.

The interview questions provided are based on how well ____ fits the Performance Model. Where he is outside the model the questions will take the interviewer into areas where potentially important information will be addressed. The questions provided where he is in the model provide you with confirmation that he is right for the job. Each question should be considered for use in his placement interview. A space is provided to record the interviewer's thoughts when the response to a question provides important information regarding placement in the position for which _____ is being considered.

Please consult the User's Guide for additional information on using these results when working with _____.

As discussed in the User's Guide for this product, the results from this or any assessment should never make up more than a third of the final decision in placements."

†††

I recommend that no written reports be given to the candidate with results of their Profile XT. If the potential church planter asks or insists, only give the candidate the **"Individual Profile."**

The first page of the **Individual Profile** reads:

"Message to ____ ______

Behavioral science has proven that the most successful people are those who know themselves, both their strengths and weaknesses. This knowledge is important to them as they develop the strategies necessary to meet the demands and challenges of achieving success.

The purpose of this report is to help you to identify and make full use of your strengths, and to help you develop an awareness of any areas that could be limiting your effectiveness. The goal of this report is to help you to achieve greater success for yourself.

The report gives you a Profile of the Total Person

- ***Thinking Style*** *- Learning Index, Verbal Skill, Verbal Reasoning, Numerical Ability, and Numeric Reasoning.*
- ***Behavioral Traits*** *- Energy Level, Assertiveness, Sociability, Manageability, Attitude, Decisiveness, Accommodating, Independence, and Objective Judgment.*
- ***Interests*** *- Enterprising, Financial/Administrative, People Service, Technical, Mechanical, and Creative.*

The information in your report can be useful in planning a self improvement program for your professional development and personal growth."

To use the Profile XT as part of your assessment process, contact Bob Crossman, 501-908-8177, bcrossman@arumc.org

Sample of the Summary Graph

© 2018 Robert O. Crossman, www.UMNewChurch.org

The **Summary Graph** on the previous page reflects the responses provided by a potential church planter when he completed the ProfileXT assessment.

The result for each characteristic is illustrated on a scale from 1 to 10.
The darker area on each scale represents the best Performance Model for the position.
The enlarged YELLOW or BLUE segment of the scale shows where this particular person scored.
If the enlarged segment is YELLOW then this particular potential planter is NOT within the Performance Model.
I also suggest playing attention when the score is blue, but on one of the extremes of the scale.

Below is a summary of some of the information that the Interview Guide provided for this candidate.

OVERALL JOB MATCH
The ProfileXT scores an overall job match percentage. Any percentage under 80% might be a yellow or red caution flag.

PERFORMANCE MODEL
The ProfileXT also scores 1 to 10 in thirteen different areas:
THINKING STYLE

Learning Index
An index of expected learning, reasoning, and problem solving potential.

Verbal Skill
A measure of verbal skill through vocabulary

Verbal Reasoning
Using words as a basis in reasoning and problem solving.

***Numerical Ability**
A measure of numeric calculation ability.
we have not found this to be indicators of future performance as a new church planter.

***Numeric Reasoning**
Using numbers as a basis in reasoning and problem solving.
we have not found this to be indicators of future performance as a new church planter.

BEHAVIORAL TRAITS

Energy Level
Tendency to display endurance and capacity for a fast pace.

Assertiveness
Tendency to take charge of people and situations.
Leads more than follows.

Sociability

© 2018 Robert O. Crossman, www.UMNewChurch.org

Tendency to be outgoing, people-oriented, and participate with others.

Manageability

Tendency to follow policies, accept external controls and supervision, and work within the rules.

Attitude

Tendency to have a positive attitude regarding people and outcomes.

Decisiveness

Uses available information to make decisions quickly.

Accommodating

Tendency to be friendly, cooperative, agreeable. To be a team person.

Independence

Tendency to be self-reliant, self-directed, to take independent action, and make own decisions.

Objective Judgement

The ability to think clearly and be objective in decision-making.

INTERVIEW QUESTIONS

Interview questions are provided to facilitate an effective interview process. When the scores is within the Performance Model, one interview question is provided. When the score falls outside of the model, additional questions are provided.

Learning Index

Describe a situation in the past when you were asked to learn a new skill. Did you get the idea best by listening to instructions or by practicing over and over?

In the past, what means of training or instruction were most effective for you? Do you prefer clearly laid out steps, generalized information or some other style of training?

When people ask you to do something new, do you prefer they show you or tell you how to do it?

What do you find most frustrating about the way some people train others to do things?

Verbal Skill*

When scores are outside Performance Model in this area, it would be wise to drop in to a couple of worship services to observe their worship language and sermon.

How often do you read instructions or memos and have difficulty understanding what they mean? Give some examples.

Some people read well but don't always remember what they have read. Do

© 2018 Robert O. Crossman, www.UMNewChurch.org

you ever experience this type of situation? How do you deal with it? Have you ever had someone become upset because you needed instructions repeated? How have you dealt with such a situation?

Describe a past situation in which a ~~co-worker~~ *(substitute 'church member')* didn't seem able to get the point across to you. What did you do and how did you handle it?

Would you say you are a speed reader, or do you prefer to carefully study written information? Or are you somewhere in between?

When receiving instructions from a ~~co-worker~~ *(substitute 'district superintendent')* how do you prefer they explain themselves and what they want?

If they score above the model, they may experience frustration in trying to communicate. Explore this by asking:
- *Have you found yourself feeling impatient with how slow others are in understanding simple ideas?*
- *What are the advantages of a diverse and comprehensive vocabulary? The disadvantages?*
- *Do people have to ask you what the meaning is of some words? Describe a time this has happened.*

Verbal Reasoning*

When scores are outside Performance Model in this area, it would be wise to drop in on a couple of worship services to hear a sermon or two.

How often do people misunderstand what you have said?

Describe a time when you dealt with a miscommunication and tell me how you discovered that an error in understanding had been made.

Did you ever work with someone who liked to use unnecessarily complex language, when "plain English" would have worked even better? What did you do about it?

How do you know people have understood what you are trying to communicate?

When discussing things with people and you "get lost" and lose the train of thought, how do you get back on track? How do you know you understand what they mean?

Numerical Ability*

we have not found this to be indicators of future performance as a new church planter.

Some people understand numbers better in a graph or picture, others can solve equations when the information is given in straight numbers. Which are you? What do you do when the information is given in the other form?

If they score above the model:
Does it take the other people you work with longer to figure results or understand the numerical information than it does for you? How do you handle this?

When expressing numerical data to others, what method has been most successful for you, even when some of them are not numerically inclined?

Numeric Reasoning*

we have not found this to be indicators of future performance as a new church planter.

In the past, have you developed a budget? Tell me about that experience.

What resources have you used in the past to obtain help with mathematical tasks that you found difficult for you?

Tell me about the last time that you reviewed the figures from a chart, spreadsheet, or graph, drew a conclusion and were incorrect. How did you resolve the situation and how often does this kind of mistake happen for you?

Tell me about a time when you had to get someone else to finish a portion of a mathematical task in which the difficulty and/or time available prevented you from finishing it on your own.

Energy Level

Tell me about a time when you had to cope with strict deadlines or time demands. Give me an example.

What kind of experiences have you had involving multiple projects? How do you typically cope with such a situation?

How do you handle the stress when work demands are high and deadlines press you to work long hours?

We all have to make decisions on the job about the delicate balance between personal and work objectives. When have you felt you had to make personal sacrifices in order to get the job done?

© 2018 Robert O. Crossman, www.UMNewChurch.org

In what ways have you made sacrifices of your time to motivate others to accomplish more work for a deadline?

Tell me about a time when you had to work very hard to reach your goals and how you achieved the best results, despite sacrifices of your time.

Tell me about a time when you had to choose between personal priorities and unusual work demands.

Assertiveness

Describe a time when you communicated something unpleasant or difficult to say to a friend or family member. How did you assert yourself?

If score is above model:

- *Tell me about a time when you had to suppress your thoughts and be quiet about a problem even though you believed you had a better solution.*
- *Has there ever been a time when speaking up about your ideas has gotten you into trouble? What happened and how did it make you feel?*
- *Tell me about a situation when you had to "stand up" for a decision you made even though it made you unpopular.*

Sociability

Tell me about an experience you have had in which you were required to make "small talk" to promote relations with a ~~client or co-worker.~~ *(substitute 'church member').*

Have you ever been in a situation where you had to initiate a conversation in a group of people you did not know? How did you handle it?

What is your preference for how to make productive use of your time when things are quiet in the office?

If one person had to remain in the office while the rest went to a meeting, would you volunteer to stay? How would you make the best use of that time?

How do you typically create a network of contacts?

Manageability

In what manner do you typically resolve conflicts at work?

In your own words, what is the role of ~~management~~? *(substitute 'district superintendent')*

Tell me about a situation when you had to follow a rule or policy even though it kept you from getting the job done.

How do you react when a supervisor requires you to do something that is not in line with your personal goals and objectives?

Describe the results of a past conflict with a supervisor. How did it happen, whose fault was it, and how was it resolved?

Describe your efforts in the past to bring an argumentative group together. How successful were you?

When is it better to do things in the conventional manner? Explain.

Attitude

Give a real-world example of the effect of your attitude on a ~~customer or client.~~ (substitute 'church member').

Tell me about a specific time when your ability to encourage others created a positive attitude.

Pick any event from the last five years in which you were an example of a positive attitude for other people to follow. Being specific, tell me about the event.

Tell me about a time when you were skeptical about the outcome of a project and how you shared that feeling with ~~coworkers~~ *(substitute 'church or Board members').*

What role have you played in the recent past in which your ~~team~~ *(substitute 'church')* was unmotivated and how did you resolve the problem?

Describe the last time you experienced a big change in the workplace, like a new set of regulations, for example. How did you feel about those changes?

Decisiveness

Describe a situation in which you had to draw a conclusion quickly and take speedy action.

Describe a situation in which you had to take immediate action in a crisis involving human life or severe financial consequences.

Describe daily decision making situations for which you have been responsible.

Tell me about a decision you made that you regret. How long did you deliberate before you made that decision?

 © 2018 Robert O. Crossman, www.UMNewChurch.org

Many situations at ~~work~~ *(substitute 'as a pastor')* will require fast thinking and speed in making decisions. Give me an example of a situation in which you were especially skillful in making a decision quickly.

Accommodating

Give me an example of a time when another person really tried your patience. Specifically, talk about a time when you were angry or frustrated.

What is your viewpoint about co-workers that never speak their mind?

If score is above model:

- *When, if ever, is conflict a positive factor in the ~~workplace~~ (substitute 'church')?*
- *When a co-worker is wrong about a work issue, what is the best way to confront him or her?*
- *Describe a time when you were able to be personally supportive and reassuring to a person who needed a friend.*
- *What is more productive for the team: communication, group unity, or something else? Explain.*
- *Give an example of a time when you acted as a mediator between two sides in your team of coworkers.*
- *How do you handle frustration when dealing with an argumentative co-worker?*

Independence

Describe your preferences concerning supervision of your work and explain the ideal situation that produces the best work you can do.

How have you dealt with a co-worker *(add 'or church member)* who wanted to try some new approach rather than stick with what is known to work?

Would you describe yourself as more inclined to follow established procedures or go with an innovative approach? Why?

Describe a situation you have experienced in which established procedures were NOT helpful in defining the best course of action.

Creative persons seem to offer fresh insights. Give me an example of a time when one of your insights was particularly well received by others.

Objective Judgement

Describe the process involved when you have to make a decision under pressure.

What sources of information do you typically use in reaching a decision ~~at work~~?

Describe a high-pressure situation you had to handle at ~~work~~ *(substitute 'church').* Tell me what happened, who was involved and what you did in terms of problem solving.

Have you ever had to take decisive action based on your gut feelings alone? How did that make you feel?

If they score above the model this suggests that their decision-making process involves less of a perspective for the "big picture" than the position typically requires. Explore the possibility that the position could be somewhat frustrating for him, asking:

- *Explain when a decision is best made with subjective information, like opinions from relevant sources or intuitive hunches.*
- *Good judgment is needed to complement logic in choosing a practical solution. Describe an event when you used good judgment in solving a problem.*
- *Describe a situation you have experienced when an immediate decision had to be made, even if most of the relevant data was not available.*

†††

The ***Profile XT*** also provides a report for the conference minister of new church starts and coach: **"Performance Model Comparison for _______, Church Planter."** The cover page reads:

"Every employable person will match some positions better than other positions. This report provides information about ______ presented in a manner to help you understand how he matches with this selected position within your organization.

This report reflects the responses provided by ________ when he completed the Profile XT assessment. The result for each characteristic is illustrated on a scale from 1 to 10. The darker area on each scale represents the best Performance Model for the position. The enlarged segment of the scale shows where _____ scored. If the enlarged segment is dark, ____ is in the Performance model. If it is lighter, he is not.

Information about ____ is reported in these four categories:

- ***Profile for Thinking Style*** *- Learning Index, Verbal Skill, Verbal Reasoning, Numerical Ability, and Numeric Reasoning.*
- ***Profile for Behavioral Traits*** *– Energy Level, Assertiveness, Sociability, Manageability, Attitude, Decisiveness, Accommodating, Independence, and Objective Judgment.*
- ***Profile for Interests*** *- Enterprising, Financial/Administrative, People Service, Technical, Mechanical, and Creative.*
- ***The Total Person & Management Considerations*** *- Description of Mark as a person and how to most effectively maximize his potential.*

Note: Additional considerations are displayed when ____falls outside your Performance Model.

© 2018 Robert O. Crossman, www.UMNewChurch.org

If ____ is being considered for this position and his results fall outside the Performance Model, you should print the companion Interview Guide for _____. This Guide provides appropriate interview questions for each instance where Mark is outside the model. These interview questions will guide the interviewer in exploring important areas where information from the interview will effectively assist the interviewer in making an informed decision about his placement.

Please consult the User's Guide for additional information on using these results when working with _____.

As discussed in the User's Guide for this product, the results from this or any assessment should never make up more than a third of the final decision in placements.

The Performance Model Comparison gives detailed suggestions for each of the thirteen areas on how best to supervise or coach this particular individual.

†††

SAMPLE OF ONE PAGE OF THE 20 PAGE REPORT
for Supervisors and Coaches of Fred Smith.

Energy Level
Tendency to display endurance and capacity for a fast pace.

1 2 3 4 5 **6** 7 8 9 10

Behavioral Considerations
- Mr. Smith generally focuses on timely results.
- He is moderately energetic; his work pace will show few peaks and valleys.
- Mr. Smith is capable of taking action in a timely manner.
- Fred typically acts with a sense of urgency under routine conditions.

Management Considerations
- Fred demonstrates somewhat low motivational intensity. Provide a structured environment in which to work and maintain short-term goals. Help him monitor his effectiveness during long term projects.
- When the workload reaches extremes, you may notice an increase in his stress. Coach him on effective stress management techniques and provide occasional rewards for efficient and timely results.
- Mr. Smith may occasionally appear less motivated when the hours of work increase due to deadlines and the demands of production. Keep open communication and listen to his needs, providing opportunities, when possible, for him to gather his reserves. Congratulate his efforts to stay focused.
- Reward his extra efforts often at first, eventually increasing the time between pats on the back. If his motivation or productivity drops, maintain rewards at a constant rate until he is back on track.

Additional Considerations
Mr. Smith achieved an Energy Level score that is outside the designated profile for this Performance Model. This suggests that his work pace is not at the level the position typically requires. Discussions with him should explore the pos-

sibility that for Mr. Smith, the position may be too challenging and could lead to frustration and a reduction in her level of performance.

Objective Judgment
The ability to think clearly and be objective in decision-making.

1 2 3 4 5 6 7 8 9 10

Behavioral Considerations

- Fred has a tendency to take an objective view and to adjust judgment as needed to reach accurate conclusions.
- Mr. Smith typically shows sound judgment under pressure.
- His judgment and decisions usually indicate consistent and thoughtful consideration of the information available.
- He is highly inclined to make considered judgments, applying experience to current problems and situations.

Management Considerations

- Coach him on how to gather information of a subjective nature, like the opinions of team members and subordinates, in order to make decisions that require more intuition on his part.
- Coach Mr. Smith on techniques of gathering useful information from others, assimilating this information holistically and making a decision based on his overall impressions.
- Mr. Smith has a tendency to rely heavily on objective data when making decisions. He needs practice and guidance in using a more intuitive approach. If needed, focus training on looking at information in a holistic and general way, emphasizing a more personal approach to decision making.
- Fred may benefit from opportunities to make decisions based more on intuition. Begin with low risk decisions and allow time for him to gain more confidence in a holistic approach to decision making.

Additional Considerations

On the Judgment scale Mr. Smith is above the designated Performance Model for this position. This suggests that his decision-making process involves less of a perspective for the "big picture" than the position typically requires. Discussions with him should explore the possibility that the position could be somewhat frustrating for him.

To use the Profile XT
as part of your assessment process,
contact Bob Crossman, 501-908-8177,
bcrossman@arumc.org

NOTE: This article reflects the personal opinions of its author and does not necessarily reflect an official position of Discipleship Ministries or Path 1

© 2018 Robert O. Crossman, www.UMNewChurch.org

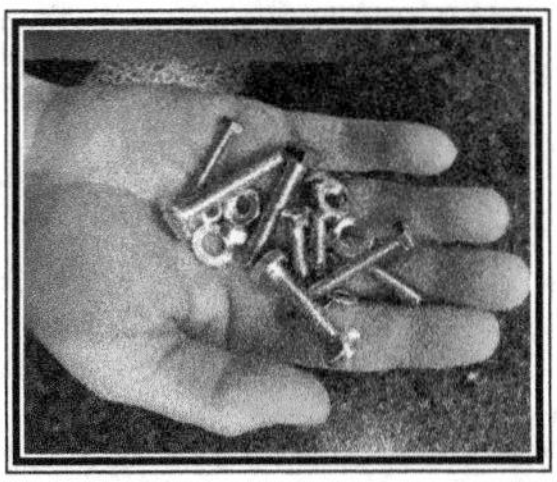

New Church Handbook
Nuts & Bolts for Planting New Churches In The Wesleyan Tradition

"How To Appoint New Church Planters"

by Bob Crossman

A stereotype of the "Old" model of new church starts might go something like this:

- The #1 priority was location, location, location!
  - First, buy expensive land.
  - Or, buy an empty building.

- The #2 priority: Who will be the pastor?
  - What pastor is available?
  - Can we afford the compensation package?
  - Does it "feel like" this pastor will do a good job?
  - Is this pastor friendly and outgoing?
  - Does this pastor really need this appointment?

- The appointment is fixed.
- Wait and see what happens.

What were the results of this "old" method?

On far too many occasions, an elder was appointed to a fast growing community, along with $200,000 to $500,000 in salary, and ministry support - and perhaps $1,000,000 in land.

The "old" goal was simple. All we asked was for the new church to have 250 in worship within 5 years, be financially self supporting, to hold their constituting (charter) conference, and to begin paying their fair share of conference apportionments.

The typical results however, were heartbreaking to the planting pastor, to the new church, and to the conference: 50 adults and 15 children in worship, and requests for more funds.

Precious new church apportionment funds were invested, and the conference watched the new church start and end far too quickly.

For example, in Arkansas, between 1968 - 2003 we attempted 46 starts, including 7 in non-anglo context. However, using the "old" method of starting new churches, 17% of our attempts had closed, and 26% never grew beyond 100 on Sunday.

We knew that there had to be a better way!

In 2003-2005, the College of Bishops in the South Central Jurisdiction began to place new emphasis on the planting of new churches.

However, we had to find better way to start new churches!
- New strategy & financial decisions had to be made.
- How much is it going to cost?
- What new apportionment line do we request at the next annual conference sessions?
- Do we spend the money on land & buildings?
- What are the other conferences doing across the general church?

For Arkansas' research, Bishop Janice Riggle Huie sent me on a field trip to discover a better way to use our limited new church funds. Searching for a better way, together the churches of the South Central Jurisdiction experienced seven different paradigm shifts in thinking about new church starts:

#1 It's not about location, it's about leadership.
- From Clay Jacobs in the North Georgia Conference we learned that New Church pastoral leadership is THE critical factor.
  "We have discovered in North Georgia that the most important piece in church planting is leadership. If the pastor is called by God to this new work, has a passion for reaching unchurched people, has a commitment to unconditional excellence, and possesses the unique set of church planting gifts and graces - this pastor will draw people to Christ, even in the desert."

#2 The Kit Carson method of "Shooting the Slowest Buffalo before they stampede away" may not the most effective appointment method.
- From George Howard in West Ohio *(George is now with GBGM)* and Dirk Elliott in the East Ohio Conference *(Dirk is now with the Detroit Conference)* we learned that we could increase the 'fruitfulness' of our new church starts by training a pool of pastors for the cabinet to appoint from:
  - Take the pastors 'nominated' by the cabinet and involve them in a New Church Leadership Institute.
  - Equip them with knowledge and skills for church planting.
  - Connect them with successful church planters.
  - Give these pastors time to discern if they are called to this ministry.
  - Give the cabinet time to assess if they have the characteristics of a successful church planter.

 © 2018 Robert O. Crossman, www.UMNewChurch.org

- From Craig Miller *(Craig is with the General Board of Discipleship)* we learned that if you want to change the DNA of the annual conference *(the atmosphere, level of emotional and financial support)* do not invite only 3 pastors to the New Church Leadership Institute, instead involve 20 pastors. Over time, a few of these will actually be appointed to start new churches, but others graduates will:
- Become district superintendents who take the initiative to start new churches in their districts.
- Chairs of the board of ordained ministry who can recognize potential church planting pastors entering the system.
- Chairs of CFA, who will support new church funding requests.
- Pastors of large churches who will be more supportive of sponsoring a new church on the edge of town.
- So, that in ten years, most of the newer pastors (local and elders) in the Conference will be graduates of the Institute & more likely to be supportive of this new church initiative.

#3 The 'parachute' drop may not be the most effective method.

- From Jim Griffith, consultant to 35 annual conferences and trainer of more than 6,000 new church pastors, we learned that the multi-site and re-purposing models are working best right now.

#4 Assessment prior to appointment is critical.

- We also learned from Jim Griffith that, *"The process through which new church pastors are recruited, assessed, trained, deployed, and supported by a coach after appointment determines the success or failure of any church planting system."*
- The goal of an effective church planting system is to:
  - Attract high quality candidates.
  - Clearly identify their strengths and patterns of behavior.
  - Develop their skill sets and assign them to a context in which they have an affinity for the target population. Taken together, these are the components for the foundation for starting strong, vital faith communities.

#5 A coach for new church pastors is critical.

#6 Be VERY clear about benchmarks before moving day.

- From Don Smith and the North Texas Conference, we learned that after the appointment is fixed, but before moving day, hold a formal Strategy session.
  - Who should attend?
    The church planter (and spouse - if married), district superintendent, and Conference director of new church starts. If this is a mother daughter plant, then include the Senior Pastor, Lay Leader finance chair, and SPPR Chair of the mother church.

- The church planter distributes her response to about 20 questions, and walks the group their her plan - including benchmarks that must be met for funding to continue.
- Everyone around the table, literally, signs off on the plan.
(See article: Nuts & Bolts: Pre-Moving Day Strategy Session & Quarterly Follow-ups)

#7 Don't surprise your neighbors.

- When the cabinet is preparing to appoint a new church pastor, don't ask permission of nearby UMCs, but don't surprise them either.
The fruitfulness of the new church start can be improved with a support base provided from a 'mother church' or a cluster of 'sister' churches. So, invite neighboring churches to:
  - Pray for the new church.
  - Provide 'baby showers,' office space, and copier access.
  - Provide volunteers for the parking lot, nursery, refreshments, meals, making phone calls, office work, worship greeters, distributing door hangers, etc.
  - Encouraging up to 10% of the faithful worshipping congregation to be missionaries in the new church.
  - Provide financial grants (housing, health insurance, salary, etc.).
  (See article: Nuts & Bolts - Finding Support From Neighboring Congregations)

With this information, we now had a plan for the quadrennium:

1. Establish a South Central Jurisdiction 'New Church Leadership Institute' at Mount Sequoyah to train a pool of potential new church pastors to appoint from.
2. Discern and develop a pool of healthy, growing UMC's who desire to be sponsoring 'Mother Churches' or start a multi-site.
3. Raise 'serious money.'
Note that "buy expensive land" is not in the list.

How do you discover a pool of POTENTIAL new church pastors? How do you discover who the Prevenient Grace of God is already preparing to start a new U.M. Church?

There are several possibilities, including:

- Introductory events at annual conference.
- District level introductory events.
- Personal contact by district superintendents.
- Personal contact by the Conference New Start Minister.
- Seminary visits.
- Path 1 has an on-line inventory that an exploring pastor might take early in the process. www.path1.org

Jim Griffith suggested several other places to find potential planters...

- Local Pastor "tent-maker" planters.

 © 2018 Robert O. Crossman, www.UMNewChurch.org

- Youth Pastors with the fruit of growing their youth ministry by reaching the unchurched.
- Pastoral staff who may not yet be United Methodist.
- Laity invited to be local pastors.
- Pastors transferring from other Wesleyan denominations.

Characteristics of Successful Church Planters

(See articles: Nuts & Bolts - Am I a Church Planter?)

When George Howard was on the staff of the West Ohio Conference, he looked for the following characteristics as indicators of potential to be a successful new church planter:

- Demonstrated ability to develop and implement a plan.
- Demonstrated record of growth in worship attendance and receiving professions of faith.
- Demonstrated commitment to continued education and retraining.
- Demonstrated strong faith in Christ.
- Passion for reaching the unchurched.
- Good communicator with a willingness to talk about Jesus.
- Evangelical, with the ability to articulate the Gospel in relevant ways.
- Able to move comfortably in the cultural setting of the new church start.
- Highly energetic and confident.
- Entrepreneur - innovative and self starter in ministry.
- Commitment to small group ministry.
- Adapts well in situations which require constant change.
- Visionary - can envision the direction and goals for their church.
- Spousal cooperation and support (if married).
- Primary friends and family support the unique challenges related to starting a church.
- Appearance and style appropriate to the church start's local setting.
- Spiritually centered and perceived as a person with integrity.
- Ability to think in business terms: organization, architecture, banking.
- Strategic thinker.
- Good communication skills.
- Good preacher, able to stand up and deliver the Word.
- Friendly, outgoing and a sense of humor.
- Optimistic and persistent.
- Committed to team ministry.
- Personal self esteem.
- Effectively builds relationships.
- Committed to spiritual growth in self and others.
- Bounces back from disappointments with renewed energy.
- Committed to the mission and ministry of the United Methodist Church.

Once you have identified a pool of POTENTIAL new church pastors, what's next?

- Church planting is very different than a traditional local church appointment...
- So, I recommend that you offer each potential church planting pastor (and spouse) a season of discernment. (And give your cabinet time to discern each pastors' behaviors, and unique affinities.)
  By contrast, in the "old days" Bishop Wilkie gave me 48 hours to accept an appointment to be a new church planter.
- Offer your potential planting pastors advance training to equip them with the knowledge and skills for a successful church start.
- Some of these pastors will discern they are NOT called to be a planter - perhaps saving their careers. (And, saving your conference $300,000 in precious apportionment funds.) However, they will still become more effective pastors in existing churches because of this training.

Which planter should we deploy
to start a new church in Jonesboro?

Which one would rather spend time alone
on a private spiritual journey?

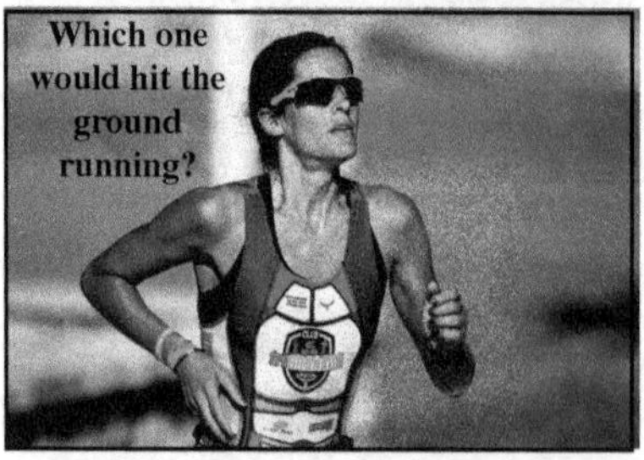

Which one would hit the ground running?

Which one would be super organized?

Which one would be quickly overwhelmed?

Which one would loose their love life in the process?

© 2018 Robert O. Crossman, www.UMNewChurch.org

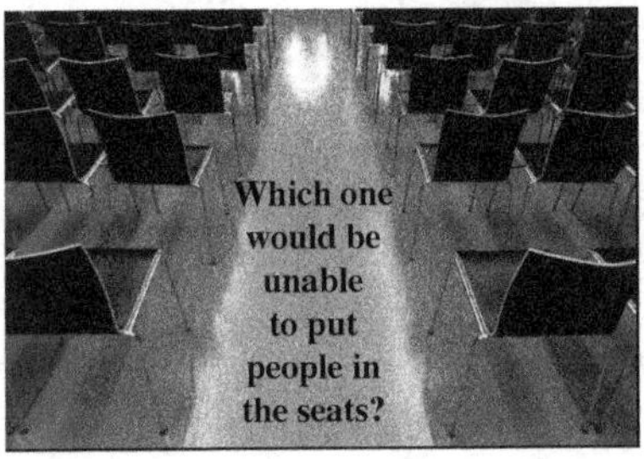
Which one would be unable to put people in the seats?

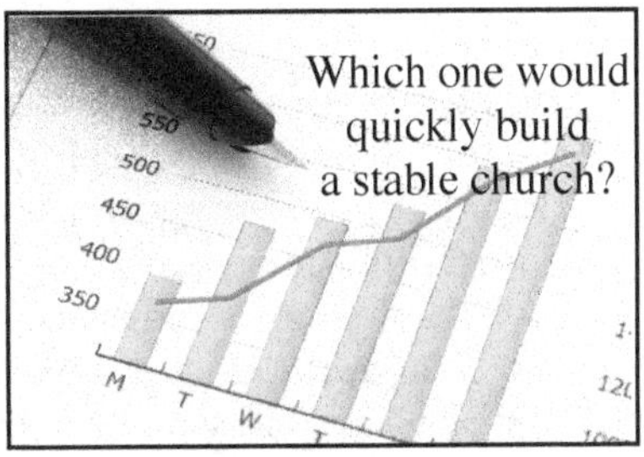
Which one would quickly build a stable church?
550
500
450
400
350
M
T
W

Which one would fail to gain sustainability?
CLOSED
KEEP OUT

Which one would make all of heaven rejoice?

Once you have a pool of potential planters TRAINED, what's next?

The next step is to design a "Pre-Appointment Assessment Process" to help decide who to deploy, and where to deploy them so that they might be the most fruitful for the kingdom. The process would help you decide:

I recommend that after completing training *(New Church Institute, or Cohort, or Incubator process)*, and IF the pastor still seeks appointment as a new church planter, then require the potential planting pastor to enter a formal assessment process.

Develop a formal assessment process designed to:

- to determine if this pastor has the gifts & graces,
- competencies,
- characteristics,
- behavior patterns, and
- the particular set of affinities you are looking to match the mission field (community) where you are looking to start a new church.
- The process might include asking the pastor to first write a self-reflective essay for the assessment team.
- **Hold a formal 90 minute assessment interview with planter (& spouse).** The assessment team will want to ask the planter to pre-submit responses to a set of interview questions, and may wish to also include objective profiles (DISC profile, Team Management Profile, and / or Profile XT) The team might consist of 1 district superintendent, 2 successful church planters, and the Conference New Church Staff person.
  - Set the date for the interview
  - Send invitation letter to planter & spouse; with questions to answer, DISC contact, Profile XT

- Team meets first to review questions, and select lead interviewer.
- 90 minute interview, asking same questions from letter above
- Profile XT may suggest questions to probe further
- Post Interview
    - Team reviews interview, listing strengths/weaknesses.
    - In about 10 days, planter gets copy to review & respond.
    - Revised Assessment Summary sent to New Church Start Staff, and appointive cabinet.

- In the weeks after the interview, the potential planter is asked to write a summary essay, which is attached to the assessment team's comments, and become a part of the pastor's profile for the appointive cabinet.
  (See the following articles:
  "What is a Self-Reflective Essay?"
  "Application for a Formal Interview", and
  "Assessment Interview of Potential New Church Planters")

WHAT IS ALL THE FUSS ABOUT 'AFFINITY'?

When deploying new church pastors to various mission fields, it is always wise to appoint each planter to a context in which they have an affinity for the target population.

Each planter may wish to reach everyone in their mission field, however each planter will tend to have a natural affinity to reach people who are like themselves.

For example, if they grew up in a "country club crowd" they may have a natural affinity to reach that slice of the population. Or, for example, if they have "oil" in their veins, and love to ride their Harley to the office every day, then they may have a natural affinity to reach that slice of the population.

In part the question isn't "who does the planter love" but rather "who has a natural attraction / affinity with the planter" and after interacting with them wants that planter to be their pastor.

There are many different affinities that might come into play:

- economic affinity
- church background
- recreational affinity
- cultural affinity
- geographic affinity

What slice of the community does each planter have a natural affinity to reach?

- cowboys
- chamber of commerce
- government housing residents
- young families
- bikers
- young professionals
- country club crowd
- empty nesters

 © 2018 Robert O. Crossman, www.UMNewChurch.org

Do any of the planters in question have the rare gift of cross-ethnic affinity or cross-generational affinity?

See article on *"What's All The Talk About Affinity?"*

WHAT ABOUT THE APPOINTMENT PROCESS?

In the appointment process, more so than in a traditional setting, the planter will be most effective in a mission field (community) that uniquely matches the planters' affinities. (economic, cultural, church background, geographic, recreational, etc.)

After the appointment is named, send the pastor (and spouse) to "Basic Training Boot Camp: everything you need to survive... and succeed in your first year" training that focuses on exactly what they need to do their first 12 months in the new appointment.

Before moving day, hold a formal strategy benchmark setting session. *(See the article: Pre-Moving Day Strategy Session & Quarterly Follow-ups)*

SUPPORT SYSTEMS AFTER APPOINTMENT?

More so than in a traditional appointment setting, the assignment to launch a new church is more stressful and fragile too.

I recommend:

- "Basic Training Boot Camp: everything you need to success in planting a new church" offered by Jim Giffith.
- Formal quarterly connection.
  (See the article: "Pre-Moving Day Strategy Session & Quarterly Follow-up")
- Financial support from district & conference.
- New church coach phone contact twice a month for the first 3 to 4 months, then monthly for the next 12 to 18 months.
  The coach's primary responsibly is to provide mentoring, support and encouragement to help the church planter remain on task. With few exceptions, all coaching e-mails and conversations will include the following people: Church Planter, Church Planter's spouse, Coach, district superintendent, conference minister of new church starts, and Senior Pastor if using a multi-site model.
- Tune-Up (formal & informal).
- Attend the annual School of Congregational Development.
- Peer support clusters among fellow new church planters.

For a flow chart of how these pieces might fit together, see the articles:
"Creating a Conference System for Planting New Churches"
and *"Flow Chart for Conference Systems"*.

†††

NOTE: This article reflects the personal opinions of its author and does not necessarily reflect an official position of Discipleship Ministries or Path 1

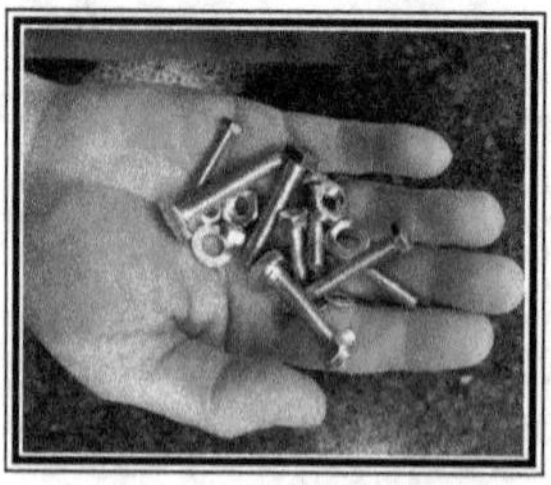

New Church Handbook
Nuts & Bolts for Planting New Churches In The Wesleyan Tradition

"A Word About Financial Support for New Churches"

by Bob Crossman

We have learned several things about finances and new church starts:

- Be cautious not to 'over promise' financial support to the new church or to the new church pastor.
- It is interesting to note in Jim Griffith's article, *"Ten Reasons Why Church Plants Fail"* inadequate conference funding is not among the reasons.
- At the 2004 annual meeting of the United Methodist New Church Developers, in a discussion about failures and having to "pull the plug," the fifty two participates could not identify a single occasion when the conference funding level was the reason for a new to church fail.
- Ed Stetzer, when he was on staff with Lifeway Research (Southern Baptist Church) did a study of the effects of financial grants. They compared new church plants who received a milion dollar grant with those who received no financial support. Counterintuitively they discovered that by the fifth year there was no statistical difference between the two new church's strength.
- One of the characteristics of a successful new church plant is that it will become financially self-supporting in less than 36 months.

How Much Does It Cost to Start a New Church?

The amount and sources of funding for our new churches will be different for each new church depending on several factors:

- Different strategies or models used to start the new church or new faith community have differing financial needs.
  - Modest or No Conference or District funding
    - Multi-site
    - Restart Model
    - Lazarus (Elijah/Elisha) Model
    - Church-Within-a-Church
    - Vital Merger
    - Surprise Birth
  - Modest Conference or District funding
    - Repurposing Empty church Buildings
    - Most "Weird Church" strategies
    - House Church
    - Mission Congregation
    - Peer Church
    - Multiple Partner

 © 2018 Robert O. Crossman, www.UMNewChurch.org

Shared Facility
Extensive Conference or District funding
Connectional or Parachute Drop
Mother-Daughter (typically)

- **Mission Congregations** typically require less initial financial support because it often begins with part-time pastoral leadership. However, long-term financial support is normally required because of sparse population or lower economic means of the congregation.

- **District Funding**
The financial support available from the districts will vary greatly. Some annual conferences will ask each district to provide the housing allowance for the new pastor, and hopefully a portion of the health insurance as well. Some districts will not be able to do this, other districts will be able to cover ALL the financial needs without any conference funds.

- **Multi-Site, Mother-Daughter or Church-Within-a-Church**
The financial ability of the sponsoring or parent church will vary greatly. In some cases the parent church will decide to cover all the financial needs without requiring any conference for district funds.

- **Compensation Package**
Each new pastor's compensation package will vary. Most conferences make an attempt to have the new pastor begin at about the same support as their previous appointment. The compensation package for the pastor is negotiated between the district superintendent and the potential new church pastor before the appointment is made.

- **Worship Space Cost**
The repurposing of empty, or near empty church buildings does not require purchase of land and construction, but the cost of remodeling or updating facilities varies greatly.
The cost to use public school spaces on Sunday mornings is modest in many communities.

  Shared Facilities with a sister congregation can not involve rent (according to Book of Discipline restrictions), but usually there is some utility and custodian reimbursement negotiated.

  The cost of renting commercial space will vary greatly from community to community, although occasionally planters have been able to negotiate modest or free situations. (i.e. *"Your cafe typically closes at 7 on Mondays. Would you be willing to stay open an hour longer, allowing us to have worship here? We will attempt to bring 40 to 75 people every Monday, and I am sure many of them will order something to eat, and all will want to order something to drink."*)

- **Financially Self Supporting**

  Some new church starts will be financial self-supporting within twenty-four months because of the generosity of the new members. Others will need support for three or four years on a declining basis. A mission congregation may be on a ten year declining funding plan from the conference.

- All this is to simply say that financial support can not be identical for every church start.

What About Land and Construction Cost?

Most annual conferences do not have enough funds for any purchase of land, bricks or mortar. In most new church starts, the new congregation itself will need to purchase the land and make the down payment on the phase one construction. Some annual conferences are able to make small grants toward land or construction usually in the $25,000 to $100,000 range.

In the last few years, many conferences are taking a closer look at empty or near empty buildings as potential sites for repurposing. Criteria typically involves: is the building is the right size (not too small or too large); is the building is still in good repair; is it is located in a mission field that we know how to reach; and is clergy / lay leadership is available to plant a new church? An additional criteria often includes: is a healthy. vital large church with multiplication DNA located within a reasonable distance to place a multi-site in this facility?

Okay, But Just How Much Money Will Each New Church Get? What's The Bottom Line?

Each annual conference handles the funding of new church starts differently.

Financial support can not be identical for every church start. Typically a maximum amount of funding support will be set for each new church in the appointment process, and no further grants are available. **Some new church starts happen without the use of any Conference or District Funds. Other starts receive anywhere from $10,000 to $300,000 total *(given on a declining bases over the first 36 to 48 months)*.**

In the spring of 2007, the Path 1 Team of the General Board of Discipleship completed a survey of 48 annual conferences in the USA. Thirty-two of those conferences reported that between 2001 and 2006 they attempted to start 561 new UMChurches. (including parachute drop, parenting, and multi-site strategies) (47% or 262 of these starts are in a non-anglo contexts) **On average nationwide, the total Conference & District funds spent in the first 4 years: $230,000 for each of these 561 new church starts.**

Where did this $230,000 go?

48% salaries of the new church pastors;
4% to train the new church pastors;
2% to provide coaches for new church pastors;

© 2018 Robert O. Crossman, www.UMNewChurch.org

2% obtaining demographic research;
25% to purchase land;
9% building construction grants; and
9% other -
Totaling 100%

In 2015, Lifeway Research did an extensive survey attempting to reach 12,000 new churches in 17 different denominations (including UMC). One of the questions was: *"For each year of the new church work's existence, please indicate the amount of TOTAL dollars received from OUTSIDE SOURCES. This does not include funds given by church's members. Rough estimates are acceptable. If later years are not applicable, leave those blank."*

What they discovered was that the typical United Methodist new church received grants totaling $226,289 in the first 5 years from Conference, District, and other sources.

Among all 17 denominations in the national survey, the typical new church received grants totalling $136,901 in the first 5 years from outside sources. The differences here reflect that a great number of UMC starts in the study were full-time appointments with a compensation package to match. In contrast many of the non-UMC starts were part-time, and some of the non-UMC start-up funds were entirely funded out of the planter's life savings.

Mean total dollars received from outside sources by year

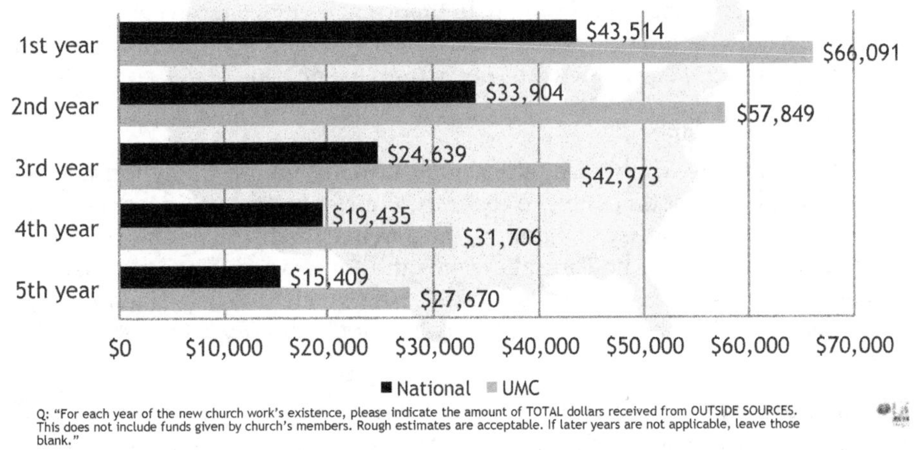
1st year
$43,514
$66,091
2nd year
$33,904
$57,849
3rd year
$24,639
$42,973
4th year
$19,435
$31,706
5th year
$15,409
$27,670
$0
$10,000
$20,000
$30,000
$40,000
$50,000
$60,000
$70,000
National
UMC
Q: "For each year of the new church work's existence, please indicate the amount of TOTAL dollars received from OUTSIDE SOURCES. This does not include funds given by church's members. Rough estimates are acceptable. If later years are not applicable, leave those blank."

The typical United Methodist new church start received grants totaling $226,289 in the first 5 years from conference, district, and other outside sources. Among all 17 denominations in the national survey, the typical new church received grants totalling $136,901 in the first 5 years from all outside sources.

Offering Plate Receipts

The Lifeway Research mentioned above also asked, *"For each year of the new church work's existence, please indicate the amount of TOTAL dollars received from CHURCH MEMBERS AND ATTENDEES. Rough estimates are acceptable. If later years are not applicable, leave those blank."*

Mean total dollars received from church members and attendees by year

Q: "For each year of the new church work's existence, please indicate the amount of TOTAL dollars received from CHURCH MEMBERS AND ATTENDEES. Rough estimates are acceptable. If later years are not applicable, leave those blank."

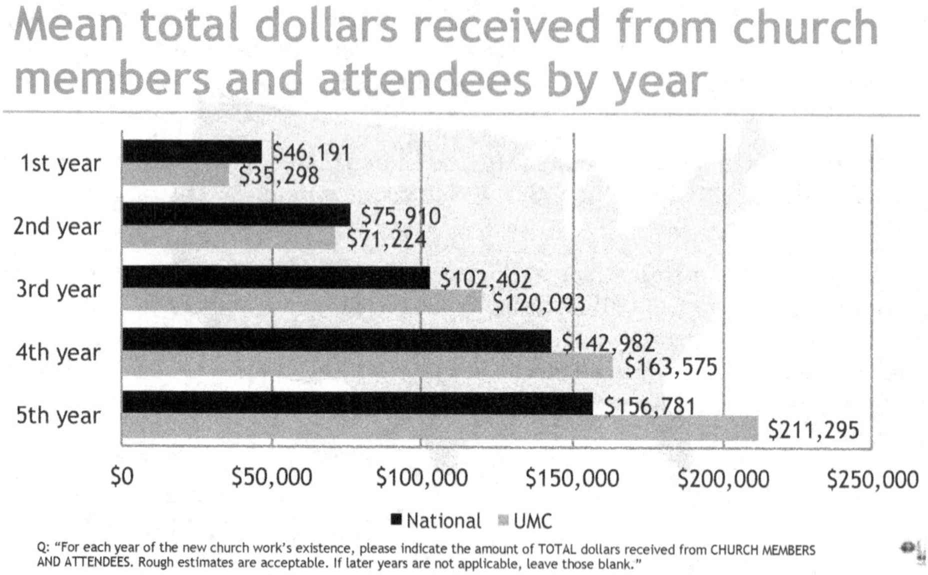

They found that the typical United Methodist new church received $601,485 in the first 5 years from the offering plate. The national average among all 17 denomination new starts was $ 524,266 in the first 5 years from the offering plate.

Sponsoring Church Support

In the Multi-site, Mother-Daughter, and Church-Within-a-Church strategies, the parent church is sometimes able to cover the entire cost of starting the new church. Typically with the strategy of planting, the parent church will be able to contribute toward the new pastor's housing allowance and/or salary package, supplementing conference or district grants. *(In one conference, the parent church typically pays 25% of the salary/benefits package in the first year, 50% in the second year, and 0% in the third year.)*

There are also 'in kind' gifts the parent church might be able to give too. They might offer free use of a parsonage, free access to the church copier, office space, or volunteers *(phone callers, distribution of door hangers, worship greeters, nursery workers, providing refreshments, etc)*. They might also offer 'baby showers' to provide many physical items the new church will need in preparation for the first worship services *(portable nursery equipment, coffee pots, chairs, sound or video components, signage, Bible study materials, etc.)*

© 2018 Robert O. Crossman, www.UMNewChurch.org

District Funding

Most districts will be able to provide some level of assistance, but the financial resources differ greatly between districts. In many annual conferences, they anticipate that the district will be able to provide the housing allowance and perhaps funds for the new pastor's health insurance.

Some annual conferences allow for district apportionments *(perhaps each church in the district to give the equivalent of $1 to $4 per member)* to provide a housing allowance, health insurance, and to supplement salary funds, land purchase, or construction assistance for new churches in that district.

It is recommended to each district, and required in some annual conferences, that when old land or empty buildings are sold, that money be used exclusively for new church plants, even transferring funds to another district where a church plant is needed.

Multi-site Funding

Each annual conference handles the funding of Multi-site, Extension Campus, Second Campus and Satellites differently.

In many conferences, request for financial support from multi-site models will be considered only if they qualify for funding by following the same conditions as other new church models:

- If the area to be served is approved by the bishop, district superintendent, cabinet, conference minister of new church starts, and the district committee on church building and location.
- If the multi-site campus pastor is a graduate of the same training process (New Church Leadership Institute, Cohort, or Incubator) as all the other planters.
- If the campus pastor successfully completes the assessment process the conference uses for all other potential new church planters.
- If the funds requested are to be used almost exclusively for campus pastor compensation.
- To be successful in the launch of a second campus ministry, like all new church starts, the new campus pastor must spend an enormous amount of actual time exclusively on this task. In harmony with the grants given to the other models of new church starts, many conferences require that the campus pastor shall be appointed to spend at least 85% of their time exclusively on the new multi-site campus. If the time involved is less than 85%, then funding grants will be denied or proportionally reduced in size.

At the New Church, Who Approves Expenditures and Who Writes the Checks?

The policy on this varies by annual conference.

I typically recommend the following:

- Until a new church is three or four years old and has held a constituting conference, there are no official trustees or finance committees in the new church. Therefore the district superintendent and the conference minister of new church starts fulfill the functions of the council, trustees, finance committee, and pastor parish relations committee for the new church. In most settings, an on-site "Quarterly Connection" will take place between these parties for such decisions.
- The new church pastor, in cooperation with the district superintendent and the conference minister of new church starts will prepare an annual operating budget.
- The new church pastor, in cooperation with the district superintendent and the conference minister of new church starts will select someone to function as financial secretary for the new church - this needs to be either the district office administrative assistant or the financial secretary of a strong United Methodist church nearby.
- When the new church pastor is requesting a check to be cut, larger than a previously agreed upon amount ($500 or $1,000), that requisition along with a description of the suggested expenditure, is first sent to the district superintendent and the conference minister of new church starts. After comparing the request to the annual budget line items, a return email is sent approving the request. That email must be attached to the requisition before the financial secretary will cut any check over the agreed upon limit of $500 or $1,000.

What about apportionments?
When does a new church begin to participate in supporting apportionments?

Each annual conference has its own unique answer to this question.

I typically proposes to the planters that faithful stewardship and generosity is an essential facet of healthy new church DNA.

- Therefore, I anticipate that the new church will already be in the holy habit of generously supporting missions and ministries through the conference apportionment process even before they are "required" to do so.
- I recommend that the offering basket be passed at every gathering of the initial launch team. At times that basket is passed with the knowledge that this week the offering is going to support our 'sister' new church in Cabot, or support our campus minister at the university, or to provide a pension for

 © 2018 Robert O. Crossman, www.UMNewChurch.org

our retired pastors, etc. Sending in these early gifts on the apportionment form to the conference treasurer.

- I also encourage new church pastors to contact the conference treasurer in the early months of worship and ask, *"If we were a chartered congregation, based on our current offering receipts and attendance, what would our apportionment amount be?"*

  In many annual conferences, officially the conference treasurer is not able to accurately determine the apportionment until two years of statistics have been turned in at the end of the year.

- A reasonable expectation is for the new church to send in 10% of it's receipts toward apportionment line items.
- In a "Mission Congregation" (¶259.1.a), while they might not officially come under the apportionment formula, generosity is still an essential facet of a heathy congregation. They are encouraged to generously support mission and ministries beyond themselves by sending gifts to the conference treasurer on the apportionment form.

Should the Conference Provide Grant Funds Until The Maximum Is Reached?

No.

Bench marks will be established so that the new start pastor and local launch team clearly understand the expectations of the conference.

In many annual conferences, before moving to their new appointment, the new pastor will work with the conference minister of new church starts and the district superintendent (and parent church) to revise their ministry plan in a *"Pre-Moving Day Strategy Session and Quarterly Follow-ups"* process. The new pastor will be held accountable to that plan, with the agreed on benchmarks written in it. (*See article "Pre-Moving Day Strategy Session and Quarterly Follow-ups" in chapter three.)*

This process helps make it clear to the pastor, the launch team, the district superintendent, the parent church, the coach and the minister of new church starts if the benchmarks are not being met, and that the appointment needs to end. In many annual conferences, during the formal consultation process in January (month 6 and month 18 of the appointment) between the new church pastor and the district superintendent, in consultation with the parent church and conference minister of new church starts - a decision will be made if the appointment should continue past June.

Although formal consultation occurs every January, there are a number of benchmarks that would cause funding to stop and the "plug to be pulled" at any point.

In many annual conferences, the funds will be released in pieces through the year. At the January consultations, if the benchmarks are not met, the next piece of funding will not be released to the new church start. These are precious funds entrusted to us from the offering plates in churches across the conference. We must be careful to use these holy funds as efficiently as possible for making Disciples for Jesus Christ.

Criteria for "Pulling the Plug"

Criteria for ending the new church start might include any of a number of factors.

- The pastor's inability to build on the initial group of people. *For example, if a new start pastor begins an appointment in July with a launch team of twenty people - a reasonable benchmark might be for that group to reach 60 by Thanksgiving, and reach 100 by Easter.*
- Loss of morale.
- Loss of hope.
- Limited financial ownership creating a 'welfare culture.'
- Little or no stewardship program.
- Lack of an accounting system.
- Inability to put essential ministries in place.
- Permanently stalled - loss of momentum.
- Loss of trust in pastor.
- Pervasive sin.

Accountability?

I typically recommend that the oversight of the new church start pastor (church planter) will be seen as a team effort, including the district superintendent, conference minister of new church starts, senior pastor and SPRC chair of the local church (if using a birthing, mother church or multi-site model) and a coach. (*See article "Pre-Moving Day Strategy Session and Quarterly Follow-ups" in chapter three.)*

What About Mission Congregations?

Start them. Start all of them you can afford. Start them today in every place you can to reach every person you can.

When you are starting a mission congregation (and any new church start for that matter), be very clear what financial resources are available, for what period of time. Also be very clear what measurable benchmarks must be met for funding to continue for that full time period.

When you are starting mission congregations and making 10 or 15 year financial commitments to them, be sure and run your "new church" conference budget out

 © 2018 Robert O. Crossman, www.UMNewChurch.org

for that many years to be sure that you will have the funds to meet all the combined obligations. For example, if you start 2 new mission congregations each year, for ten years – will you have the funds to support all of that combined financial obligation?

In many mission settings, the people you are reaching are not completely devoid of financial resources. In many mission settings, because of the small number of people you are trying to reach in that mission field *(like the new church pastor appointed to reach a Vietnamese population of only 2,400 in Fort Smith)*, or because of their limited financial resources *(like Anglo new church appointments in a very depressed financial part of Fort Smith)* – you are not expecting them to meet the same financial benchmarks you would set for a new ministry reaching a financially wealthy segment of the population.

Therefore, in a mission setting (and any new church start for that matter), be careful about loading them up with financial obligations (building expenes or salary) they can never meet.

For example, use the same financial common sense you use with your existing congregations. In hundreds of our old existing small Anglo congregations in Arkansas, we appoint pastoral leadership they can afford. We might deploy a lay-speaker (TBS) or a part-time local pastor. Also, the district board of church location and building only approves building or remodeling expenses they can afford. The cabinet does not appoint a full-time pastor with a heavy salary and benefits package to a setting that can only afford $50 a week for a part-time local pastor.

In some of your new church starts in mission settings perhaps it is appropriate for them to be supported on a clearly defined 10 or 15 year declining basis, instead of a 3 year declining basis as you may do in other settings.

Sample Conference Mission Congregation Policy

As an example, one conference set the following policy.

> We will charter mission congregations according to the following rules:
>
> A mission congregation shall serve marginalized and or low-income people.
>
> A mission congregation shall be formed only when the full structure of a chartered local church is not feasible and or would be a hindrance to disciple making work of the new congregation.
>
> Specific administrative and financial responsibilities of the mission churches may be assigned to a partner organization. Partner organizations may include another chartered local church, an agency or judica-

tory body of the United Methodist Church, a not for profit corporation that is affiliated with the United Methodist Church, or some other body approved by the district board of church location and building and then ratified by the district superintendent and conference appointive cabinet.

A Mission Congregation shall meet all of the following four criteria.

- Conduct weekly worship services.
- Develop and implement an effective plan for making disciples of Jesus Christ.
- Celebrate the sacraments and receive persons into membership according to the procedures set forth in The Book of Discipline.
- Develop and implement a comprehensive stewardship plan that sustains the mission congregation. This plan may be developed in cooperation with any partner organizations.

The responsibilities and functions that may be delegated to a partner organization include the functions of the following committees in a chartered Local Church:

- Trustees
- Finance
- Staff parish relations
- Church council *(administration, staffing and finances)*

The organizational plan for the mission congregation including the role of each partner organization shall be approved by the district strategy committee. This plan shall be ratified by the appointive cabinet.

Every mission congregation shall function as a missional outpost of the United Methodist connection. As such a mission congregation shall be exempt from paying apportionments for a period not to exceed eight years.

The chartered status of a mission congregation shall be reviewed every four years by the district strategy committee, district board of church location and building, and by the appointive cabinet. At that time the charter may be renewed, amended, or discontinued.

NOTE: This article reflects the personal opinions of its author and does not necessarily reflect an official position of Discipleship Ministries or Path 1

© 2018 Robert O. Crossman, www.UMNewChurch.org

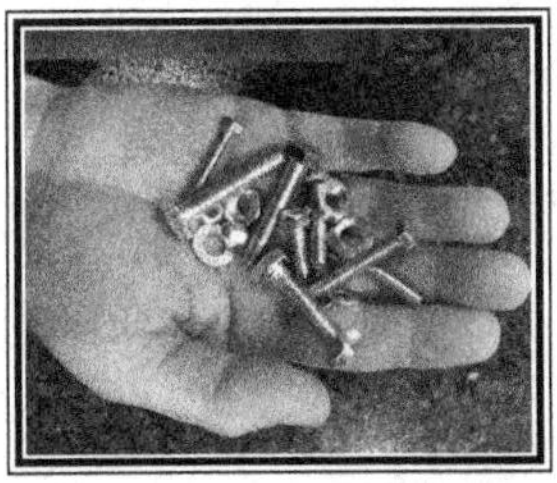

New Church Handbook
Nuts & Bolts for Planting New Churches In The Wesleyan Tradition

"A Word About Mission Congregations"

by Bob Crossman

The Mission Congregation

The 2016 Book of Discipline (259.1.a) allows a new church start to be designated as a "Mission Congregation" when any of the following conditions exist:

- Membership opportunities and resources are limited and not likely to result in a chartered congregation for an extended period of time.
- A strategic demographic, cultural or language opportunity for serving a limited population is present.
- It is expected that long-term sustaining funding from sources outside the Congregation will be necessary to enable the congregation to exist, and the assumption of full connectional support items by the congregation is unlikely.
- It is probable that the annual conference will need to provide long-term administrative guidance, including attention to the distinctive property needs of the Congregation.

When any of these conditions exist, the cabinet, in consultation with the congregational development staff of the annual conference, may designate an entity a "Mission Congregation." The mission congregation may be organized in the same manner and have the same rights and powers as any local church.

Advantages of the Mission Congregation

- Designed to reach a mission field with a sparse population and or a population with limited financial resources.
- Requires less initial financial support from all sources because it often begins with part-time pastoral leadership (lay missioner or part-time local pastor).

Disadvantages of the Mission Congregation

- Long-term financial support is normally required because of sparse population or lower economic means of the congregation.
- Because the financial resources and size of the congregation are limited, they often share facilities with a stronger UMC. Through the years conflicts can arise over sharing limited space.

© 2018 Robert O. Crossman, www.UMNewChurch.org

Summary Thoughts About Starting Mission Congregations

Start them. Start all of them you can afford. Start them today in every place you can to reach every person you can.

When you are starting a mission congregation (and any new church start for that matter), be very clear what financial resources are available, for what period of time, and what measurable benchmarks must be met for funding to continue for that full time period.

When you are starting mission congregations and making 5, 10, or 15 year declining financial commitments to them, be sure and run your "new church" conference budget out for that many years to be sure that you will have the funds to meet all the combined obligations. For example, if you start 2 new mission congregations each year, for ten years will you have the funds to support all of that combined financial obligation?

In many mission settings, the people you are reaching are not completely devoid of financial resources. In many mission settings, because of the small number of people you are trying to reach in that mission field you are not expecting them to meet the same financial benchmarks you would set for a new ministry reaching a large or financially wealthy segment of the population.

So in a planting a new mission congregation *(and every new church start for that matter)* be careful not to load them up with financial obligations (building expenses or salary) they can never meet.

Use the same financial common sense you use with your existing congregations. In hundreds of our old existing small congregations of every ethnicity across the country we appoint pastoral leadership they can afford. We typically deploy a layspeaker or a appoint a part-time local pastor to such a small congregation. Also, the district board of church location and building only approves building or remodeling projects they can afford. Of course the cabinet does not appoint a full-time pastor with a heavy salary and benefits package to a setting that can only afford $50 a week for a part-time local pastor.

In some of your new church starts in mission settings, perhaps it is appropriate for them to be supported on a clearly defined 5, 10, or 15 year declining basis, instead of a 3 or 4 year declining basis as you may do in other settings.

NOTE: These articles reflect the personal opinions of the author and do not necessarily reflect an official position of Discipleship Ministries or Path 1

© 2018 Robert O. Crossman, www.UMNewChurch.org

XIII. Are there any written resources about church planting?

New Church Handbook
Nuts & Bolts for Planting New Churches In The Wesleyan Tradition

"Are There Any Written Resources About Church Planting?"

Path 1's Growing List of Wesleyan Church Planting Resources:

Descubriendo Tus Dones Espirituales: Una guía teorética y práctica, by César Durán (Scheduled for publication, 2018)
Don't Look Down (working title), by Rosario Picardo, (Scheduled for publication, 2018)
Failing Boldly: How Falling Down in Ministry Can be the start of Rising Up, by Christian Coon, Foreword by Bishop Robert Schnase (2017)
Flipping Church: How Successful Church Planters Are Turning Conventional Wisdom Upside-Down, by Michael Baughman, editor (2016)
A Missionary Mindset: What Church Leaders Need to Know to Reach Their Community - Lessons from E. Stanley Jones, by Douglas Ruffle (2016)
New Church Handbook: Nuts & Bolts for Planting New Churches In The Wesleyan Tradition, by Bob Crossman (2018)
Small Church Checkup, by Kay Kotan and Phil Schroeder, (2018)
Viral Multiplication in Hispanic Churches: How to Plant and Multiply Disciple-Making Churches in the Twenty-first Century America, by Iosmar A'lvarez (2016)
Vital Merger: A New Church Start Approach That Joins Church Families Together, by Dirk Elliott, published by Fun and Done Press (2013)

Additional Print Resources - Church Planting, Discipleship Systems, and Stewardship:

10 Prescriptions for a Healthy Church, by Bob Farr
A Multi-Site Church Road Trip: Exploring the New Normal, by Warren Bird, Greg Ligon, and Geoff Surratt.
Big Dreams in Small Places Church Planting in Smaller Communities, by Tom Nebel
Bivocational Church Planters: Uniquely Wired for Kingdom Growth, by Steve Nerger
The Changeover Zone: Successful Pastoral Transitions, by Jim Ozier
Church in the Making: What Makes or Breaks a New Church Before it Starts, by Ben Arment
Church Planting Landmines: Mistakes to Avoid in Years 2 through 10, by Tom Nebel and Gary Rohrmayer.
Clip In: Risking Hospitality in Your Church, by Jim Ozier and Fiona Haworth
Committed to Christ: Six Steps to a Generous Life (Boxed Kit: Program Guide, Adult Readings and Study Guide, Small Group Leader Guide, 40 Devotions, and DVD), by Bob Crossman
Discipler: An Interactive Guide to Intentional, Relational, Accountable Discipleship, by Phil Maynard and Eddie Pipkin
E-Giving Guide for Every Church: Using Digital Tools To Grow Ministry, by Richard Rogers
Finding Jesus on the Metro, by Paul Nixon
Fling Open the Doors: Giving the Church Away to the Community, by Paul Nixon

 © 2018 Robert O. Crossman, www.UMNewChurch.org

Fresh Expressions: A New Kind of Methodist Church For People Not In Church, by Audrey Warren and Kenneth H. Jr. Carter
Get Their Name: Grow Your Church by Building New Relationships, by Bob Farr
High Yield: Seven Disciplines of the Fruitful Leader, by Lovett Weems
I Refuse to Lead a Dying Church,! by Paul Nixon
Launch: Starting a New Church from Scratch, by Nelson Searcy, and Kerrick Thomas.
Membership to Discipleship: Growing Mature Disciples Who Make Disciples, by Philip Maynard
Multiply Your Impact: Making the Leap from Church Maintenance to Gospel Movement, by Paul Nixon and Christie Latona
The Necessary Nine: Things Effective Pastors Do Differently, by Bob Farr
A New Kind of Church: Understanding Models of Ministry for the 21st Century, by Aubrey Malphurs
The Nomadic Church: Growing Your Congregation Without Owning the Building, by Bill Easum, Peter C. Theodore
Not Your Parents' Offering Plate: A New Vision for Financial Stewardship, by J. Clif Christopher and Mike Slaughter
Overflow: Increase Worship Attendance & Bear More Fruit, by Lovett Weems
Roadmap to Renewal: Rediscovering the Church's Mission, Revised Edition with Study Guide, by Douglas Ruffle
Rich Church / Poor Church, Keys to Effective Financial Ministry, by Clif Christopher
Shift: Helping Congregations Back Into the Game of Effective Ministry, by Phil Maynard
Six Steps to a Generous Life: Living Your Commitment to Christ, by Bob Crossman
The Surprise Factor: Gospel Strategies for Changing the Game at Your Church, by Paul Nixon and Kim Shockley
Ten Most Common Mistakes Made By New Church Starts, by Jim Griffith and Bill Easum
The Art of the Start, by Guy Kawasaki
The Church Money Manual, by Clif Christopher
Viral Churches, by Ed Stetzer and Warren Bird
We Refused to Lead a Dying Church!: Churches That Came Back Against All Odds, by Paul Nixon
Weird Church: Welcome to the Twenty-First Century, by Paul Nixon and Beth Estock
Whose Offering Plate Is It? New Strategies for Financial Stewardship, by Clif Christopher
Zero to 80: Innovative Ideas for Planting and Accelerating Church Growth, by Olu Brown

Additional Titles Published by Discipleship Resources

7 Myths of the United Methodist Church, by Craig Kennet Miller
Growing New Churches, by Stephen C. Compton and G. Steven Sallee
Next Church.Now: Creating New Faith Communities, by Craig Kennet Miller,
Encounters With Jesus: A Group Study in Baby Boomer Spirituality, by Craig K. Miller
Celebrating the Offering, by Melvin Amerson and James Amerson
Extraordinary Money: Understanding the Church Capital Campaign, by Michael Reeves
Holy Smoke!: Whatever Happened to Tithing? by J. Clif Christopher and Herbert Mather
Stewardship in African-American Churches: A New Paradigm, by Melvin Amerson
That's What My Mother Taught Me and Other Ways Generous Givers Develop, by Herb Mather

Jim Ozier

"Over the years church planting has learned a lot. In clear, concise, and comprehensive ways Bob Crossman has captured what we've learned and why it works. 'New Church Handbook' is a necessary resource not only for new church planters, but for those involved in the system of church planting regarding the who, what, when, where, why, and how."

Jim Ozier – Ozier Coaching, LLC., author of *"The Changeover Zone: Successful Pastoral Transitions"* and *"Clip In: Risking Hospitality in Your Church."*

Olu Brown

"Bob Crossman's longevity in the ministry demonstrates his faithfulness to sharing Christ with the world, and his new book is a prime example. New Church Handbook is a tool to guide new church plants (and existing churches) to be the hands the feet of Christ. It is a resource that you will read, highlight and read again. It is an essential read for new church planters and denominational leaders who desire to plant vital and healthy new churches."

Olu Brown – planter and founding pastor of Atlanta's Impact Church
author of *"Zero to 80: Innovative Ideas for Planting and Accelerating Church Growth," "Flipping Church"* and *"Leadership Directions from Moses"*

Emily Reece

"Bob Crossman's 'New Church Handbook' offers a comprehensive approach to supporting those who start new congregations, at every level of The United Methodist Church. A 'must-have' resource, this new edition contains the best of previous versions and adds fresh reflections and guidance for the ways in which churches come into being today. You will refer to this volume all the time!"

Emily Reece – Associate Director of Church Development, Indiana Conference

Doug Ruffle

"The 'New Church Handbook' is a treasure trove of information. It is like an encyclopedia of knowledge wrapped into one volume. It should be a standard reference resource for church planters."

Doug Ruffle – Associate Executive Director and General Editor of Wesleyan Church Planting Resources for Path 1 (New Church Starts at Discipleship Ministries) and author of *"A Missionary Mindset: What Church Leaders Need to Know to Reach Their Community - Lessons of E. Stanley Jones"*

Lovett H. Weems

"Handbook is the perfect name for this information-rich resource. Church planters and those who work with them will return to this book regularly for just-in-time guidance about pivotal aspects of new church starts."

Lovett H. Weems, Jr. – Senior Consultant, Lewis Center for Church Leadership, Wesley Theological Seminary, author of *"High Yield: Seven Disciplines of the Fruitful Leader," "Overflow: Increase Worship Attendance & Bear More Fruit," "Focus: The Real Challenges Facing The United Methodist Church," and many others.*

Bob Farr

"I highly recommend Bob Crossman's 'New Church Handbook: Nuts & Bolts for Planting New Churches' to any new church plant pastor, judicatory leader, district superintendent or bishop as a comprehensive resource tool kit on how and why to start new churches. Bob has spent a lifetime in the new church plant field and shares all his learning in this book. Plus, he is great at gleaning and sharing learning from others with the same passion of starting new churches. This is a library that should be on every leader's shelf."

Bishop Robert Farr – Missouri Conference of The United Methodist Church, author of *"The Necessary Nine: Things Effective Pastors Do Differently," "Get Their Name: Grow Your Church by Building New Relationships," "10 Prescriptions for a Healthy Church, "and "Renovate or Die."*

Gary E. Mueller

"Bob Crossman has been there and done it, and he has now brought it all together in a single comprehensive volume. New Church Handbook: Nuts & Bolts For Planting New Churches in the Wesleyan Tradition provides exactly the sort of overview and detailed expertise that is essential for all church planters and those who work with church planters."

Bishop Gary E. Mueller – Arkansas Conference of The United Methodist Church

Rodney Smothers

"Bob has captured a deep well of accumulated wisdom that reflects shared experience from practitioners. This resource unpacks the do' and don'ts of church planting in proven and practical ways."

Rodney Thomas Smothers – Director of Leadership and Congregational Development for the Baltimore-Washington Conference

© 2018 Robert O. Crossman, www.UMNewChurch.org

CPSIA information can be obtained
at www.ICGtesting.com
Printed in the USA
FSHW04n2344140318
45438FS

9 780999 657805